Rützel/Wegen/Wilske

Commercial Dispute Resolution in Germany

Commercial Dispute Resolution in Germany

– Litigation Arbitration Mediation –

Stefan Rützel

Gerhard Wegen

Stephan Wilske

2nd edition
2016

C.H.BECK

Authors

Rechtsanwalt **Dr. Stefan Rützel**, born 1962, studied law at the Universities of Frankfurt am Main, Speyer and University of Georgia School of Law/USA (LL. M. 1994). He is a partner in the Frankfurt office of Gleiss Lutz specializing in corporate, financial institutions and general commercial litigation. He also has a considerable arbitration practice. Stefan Rützel chairs the firm's dispute resolution practice group.

Rechtsanwalt and Attorney-at-law (New York) **Prof. Dr. Gerhard Wegen**, born 1950, studied law at the Universities of Hamburg, Geneva/Switzerland, Tübingen and Harvard Law School/USA (LL. M. 1981). He is a partner in the Stuttgart office of Gleiss Lutz specializing in M&A, corporate, securities regulation, capital markets and international commercial litigation and arbitration in this context. Gerhard Wegen also has considerable practice as mediator for business disputes. Since 1997 he is also a professor at the Law Faculty of the University of Tübingen where he teaches international business transactions.

Rechtsanwalt and Attorney-at-law (New York) **Dr. Stephan Wilske**, FCIArb, born 1962, studied law at the Universities of Tübingen, Aix-en-Provence/France (Maîtrise en Droit 1987) and Chicago Law School/USA (LL. M. 1996). He is a partner in the Stuttgart office of Gleiss Lutz specializing in international arbitration and litigation and cross-border transactions. Stephan Wilske currently heads the firm's arbitration working group. Since 2011 he is a member of the American Law Institute (ALI). He is also a lecturer at the universities of Hannover and Heidelberg.

www.beck.de

ISBN 978 3 406 68225 4

© 2016 Verlag C.H.Beck oHG
Wilhelmstraße 9, 80801 München
Druck: Beltz Bad Langensalza GmbH
Neustädter Straße 1–4, 99947 Bad Langensalza
Satz: Fotosatz Buck
Zweikirchener Str. 7, 84036 Kumhausen
Umschlaggestaltung: Bütefisch Marketing und Kommunikation,
Schlaitdorf

Gedruckt auf säurefreiem, alterungsbeständigem Papier
(hergestellt aus chlorfrei gebleichtem Zellstoff)

Preface

While globalization has an increasing impact on the harmonization of many national laws it is, at least, these authors' opinion that dispute resolution is still to a large extent characterized by national idiosyncrasies. This is particularly true with respect to litigation in state courts, where fundamental traits of one judicial system might be viewed as defiance of the basic notions of justice and fairness of another judicial system. In particular, the German law and practice relating to litigation still surprises businesses and practitioners on the other side of the Atlantic, as does – *vice versa* – the U. S. litigation practice.

With the first edition, the authors provided a non-German business person or lawyer who is involved or interested in dispute resolution practices in Germany with a quick and, most importantly, practice-related overview.

The second edition covers essential developments in the legal framework as well as case law in Germany since 2005 and offers more content (and slightly less annexes), which will provide a foreign lawyer with up-to-date knowledge of commercial dispute resolution in Germany. For practical purposes we have decided to include the 10th and 11th book of the German Code of Civil Procedure only. The second edition contains new EU regulations and international treaties, the German Mediation Act of 2012, updated lists of bilateral and multilateral treaties relevant to international procedural and arbitration law in Germany, as well as updated lists of arbitration and mediation institutions in Germany. We have also attached updated sample calculations of attorney fees in German proceedings, a German-English glossary with descriptions of some of the most important legal terms and a bibliography for further insight into German dispute resolution.

While this book still cannot realistically aim to make a German lawyer representing a foreign party in German court proceedings superfluous, this book should at least guide a foreign reader through the various stages of such proceedings. A non-German reader will quickly recognize that in contrast to court proceedings, arbitration and mediation proceedings in Germany reflect the general standards an international practitioner is already familiar with.

We are very thankful to Andreea Condurache, Anna Lechermann, Dr. Matthias Müller, Laura Riedner, Sabrina Schäfer, Dorothea Schrimpf, and Jan Ulrich for their contributions to the form and contents of this book. We also express our gratitude to Hildegard Rosenzweig and Elaine Ikizer for their indispensable support as regards the translation of major parts of German statutes into English and Sarah Kimberly Hughes for linguistic revision and a critical review of German dispute resolution procedures through the eyes of a common law practitioner. We would also like to thank the responsible persons at C. H. Beck for their cooperation and patience.

August 2015 *The authors*

Dr. Stefan Rützel
Gleiss Lutz Rechtsanwälte
Taunusanlage 11
D-60329 Frankfurt am Main
Germany
stefan.ruetzel@gleisslutz.com

Prof. Dr. Gerhard Wegen
Gleiss Lutz Rechtsanwälte
Lautenschlagerstraße 21
D-70173 Stuttgart
Germany
gerhard.wegen@gleisslutz.com

Dr. Stephan Wilske
Gleiss Lutz Rechtsanwälte
Lautenschlagerstraße 21
D-70173 Stuttgart
Germany
stephan.wilske@gleisslutz.com

Summary Table of Contents

Preface V
Table of Important Abbreviations XXIII

Part 1: Introduction to Commercial Dispute Resolution in Germany

Chapter 1: Commercial Litigation 1
A. Some Distinct Features of Litigation in German Courts 1
B. Basic Elements of the German Civil Justice System 2
C. The Court System 12
D. Jurisdiction 15
E. Pleading in German Litigation 22
F. Fact-Finding prior to Commencing Action 26
G. Preparing and Securing Evidence 35
H. Strategy Considerations 38
I. Commencing the Action 51
J. Court Order and Service of Process 54
K. Possible Responses by Defendant 59
L. Third-Party Intervention 62
M. Further Actions by Plaintiff 63
N. Joint Actions by the Parties 65
O. Additional Court Orders 67
P. Interruption of Proceedings 69
Q. The Oral Hearing 69
R. Evidentiary Proceedings 72
S. Establishing the Law 87
T. Judgments 89
U. Appellate Remedies 93
V. Enforcement and Execution of German Judgments 103
W. Provisional Relief 111
X. Legal Assistance in Aid of Foreign Proceedings 118

Chapter 2: Arbitration ... 125
  A. Introduction ... 125
  B. The Arbitration Agreement ... 128
  C. Constitution and Composition of the Arbitral Tribunal ... 136
  D. The Arbitrator's Contract ... 143
  E. Jurisdiction of Arbitral Tribunal ... 148
  F. The Arbitral Proceedings ... 149
  G. Making of Award and Termination of Proceedings ... 164
  H. Recourse against Award ... 179
  I. Recognition and Enforcement of Arbitral Awards ... 187

Chapter 3: Mediation ... 191
  A. Introduction to Mediation in German Commercial Disputes ... 191
  B. International Regulatory Developments ... 193
  C. Statutory Framework of Mediation in Germany ... 194
  D. Mediation Clauses and Agreements ... 198
  E. Mediation and Court Proceedings ... 199
  F. Mediation Procedure ... 200
  G. Conclusion of Mediation Proceedings ... 206

Part 2: Relevant Statutory and Regulatory Materials

  A. German Statutory Instruments ... 211
  B. EC Regulations ... 318
  C. Bilateral and Multilateral Treaties ... 395
  D. German Institutions and Rules for Arbitration ... 426
  E. German Institutions and Rules for Mediation ... 446

  Appendix 1 Selected Sample Calculations of Fees in German Proceedings ... 453

  Appendix 2 Bibliography ... 461

  Appendix 3 German-English Glossary ... 467

Table of Contents

Preface V

Table of Important Abbreviations XXIII

Part 1: Introduction to Commercial Dispute Resolution in Germany

Chapter 1: Commercial Litigation 1

A. Some Distinct Features of Litigation in German Courts 1

B. Basic Elements of the German Civil Justice System 2
    I. The German Civil Law System 2
    II. Sources of Civil Procedure Law 3
        1. Constitutional Law 3
        2. Statutes 3
            a) Core Statutes 3
            b) Major Reforms 4
        3. European Legislation and International Treaties 4
    III. General Principles of Civil Procedure Law 6
    IV. The Actors in German Litigation 6
        1. The Parties 6
        2. The Lawyers 7
            a) Education and Training 7
            b) Judges 7
            c) German Attorneys 8
            d) Foreign Attorneys 8
        3. Court Officers 8
    V. Efficiency of the System 9
        1. Duration of Proceedings 9
        2. Litigation Costs 9
            a) Court Costs 9
            b) Attorney Fees 10
                aa) Statutory Fees 10
                bb) Negotiated Fees 10
            c) Reimbursement of Costs 11
            d) Examples 11

C. The Court System 12
    I. Jurisdictional Branches 12
    II. The Civil Courts 12
        1. Entry-Level Courts 12
            a) Local Courts 12
            b) Regional Courts 12
        2. First Appellate Level (*Berufung*) 13
            a) Regional Courts 13

		b) Higher Regional Courts	13
	3. Second Appellate Level (*Revision*)		13
	III. Extraordinary Appeals		14
		1. Federal Constitutional Court	14
		2. European Court of Justice	14
		3. European Court of Human Rights	14

D. Jurisdiction 15

    I. Overview: Jurisdiction, Applicable Law, Sovereign Immunity 15
        1. Jurisdiction 15
        2. Applicable Procedural Law 15
        3. Sovereign Immunity 15
    II. Proper Jurisdictional Branch 16
    III. Exclusive Jurisdiction 16
    IV. Agreement on Jurisdiction 17
    V. Jurisdiction by Failure to Raise an Objection 17
    VI. General and/or Special Jurisdiction 18
        1. General Jurisdiction 18
        2. Special Jurisdiction 18
        3. In Particular: Long-Arm Jurisdiction 18
    VII. Multiple Jurisdiction and Lack of Jurisdiction 19
    VIII. Jurisdiction Determined by a Superior Court 19
    IX. Forum Shopping and *Lis Pendens* 20
    X. Challenges to Jurisdiction 21
        1. Forum Non Conveniens 21
        2. Anti-Suit Injunctions 21
    XI. Reference to a Valid Arbitration Agreement 22

E. Pleading in German Litigation 22

    I. The Method of "Comparative Analysis" 22
    II. Submissions and Pleading 23
        1. Principle of Oral Procedure and the Differing Practice 23
        2. Number and Timeliness of Submissions 24
        3. Contents of Submissions 24
            a) Statement of Facts 24
            b) Specifying Evidence 25
            c) Pleading the Law 25
        4. Length and Style of Submissions 25

F. Fact-Finding prior to Commencing Action 26

    I. General 26
    II. Exploring the Information Available to the Party 26
        1. Review of Documents, Physical Inspections and Interviews ... 26
        2. Use of Commercial Information Providers 27
        3. Use of Outside Experts 27
        4. Public Registers 27
            a) Registers to Determine Domicile 27
            b) Company Registers 28
            c) Debtors' Register 28
            d) Land, Ship, Aircraft and Matrimonial Property Registers .. 29
    III. Using Inspection Rights for Files kept at Public Authorities 29
        1. Files at Regulatory Authorities 29

a)	Information Rights under Federal and State Freedom of Information Acts	29
b)	Information Rights under General Administrative Law	30

    2. Files in the Criminal Justice System 30
       a) Inspection Rights 30
       b) Reporting Alleged Crimes 31
    3. Files at the Civil Courts 31
    4. Files at Other Courts 32
    5. Requests for Information and for Forwarding of Files 32
    6. Blocking Inspection Rights 33
  IV. (Expedited) Court Procedures for Obtaining Information 33
    1. Court Proceedings for Information 33
    2. Expedited Court Procedures for Information in Company Law 33
  V. Disclosure Proceedings Abroad 34

G. Preparing and Securing Evidence 35
  I. Preparing Evidence 35
    1. Means of Evidence 35
    2. Preparing Documents and Objects for Inspection 35
    3. Preparing Expert Testimony 36
    4. Preparing Witness Testimony 36
       a) Securing Potential Witnesses 36
       b) Preparing Witnesses 37
  II. Independent Procedure for the Taking of Evidence 37

H. Strategy Considerations 38
  I. Selection of Forum 38
  II. Selecting the Right Parties 39
    1. Plaintiff 39
       a) Assignment of Claim 39
       b) Joinder of Multiple Plaintiffs 39
    2. Multiple Defendants 40
       a) Joinder 40
       b) Increased Cost Risk 41
    3. Third-Party Notice 41
    4. Class or Group Actions 42
       a) Registered Interest Group Acting as Plaintiffs 42
       b) Common Representative Acting as Plaintiff 42
       c) Capital Markets Model Case Act 42
  III. Timing Issues 44
    1. General 44
    2. Limitation Period 44
  IV. Choice of Procedure 45
    1. Collection Proceedings 45
       a) Collection Proceedings under German Law 45
       b) European Collection Proceedings for Uncontested Claims.. 46
       c) Collection proceedings by an European Order for Payment 46
       d) European Proceedings for Small Claims 47
    2. Summary Proceedings Based on Documentary Evidence or a Bill of Exchange 47
    3. Action by Stages 48

4. Ancillary Procedures	48
V. Reducing Cost Risks	49
1. Action for a Partial Claim Only	49
2. Legal Aid	50
3. Legal Cost Insurance	50
4. D&O and other Business-Related Types of Insurance	51
5. Litigation Financing	51

I. Commencing the Action ... 51
I. Filing the Statement of Claim ... 51
    1. Contents of the Statement of Claim ... 52
        a) Specifying the Court and the Parties ... 52
        b) Specifying the Relief Sought ... 52
            aa) Types of Relief Available ... 52
            bb) Motion for Relief ... 52
        c) Statement of Value of the Matter and Signature ... 53
    2. Exhibits to the Statement of Claim ... 53
        a) Interdependencies between the Statement of Claim and its Exhibits ... 53
        b) Foreign-Language Exhibits ... 53
II. Prepayment of Court Costs ... 53

J. Court Order and Service of Process ... 54
I. The Role of the Court ... 54
    1. Structuring the Proceedings by Court Orders ... 54
    2. Duty to Give Indications and Feedback ... 54
II. Initial Court Order on Further Proceedings ... 55
III. Service of Process ... 55
    1. Initial Service of Statement of Claim ... 55
        a) Domestic Service ... 56
        b) Service Abroad ... 56
        c) Service by Public Notice ... 57
        d) Defects of Service ... 58
        e) Effects of Service ... 58
    2. Subsequent Service ... 58

K. Possible Responses by Defendant ... 59
I. Defending Against the Action ... 59
    1. Statement of Defense ... 59
    2. Grounds for Defense ... 59
        a) Defense on the Merits ... 59
        b) Defense by Set-Off ... 59
        c) Defense and Counteraction ... 60
    3. Motion for Security for the Costs of the Proceedings ... 60
II. Termination of the Action by Default ... 60
III. Termination of the Action by Acknowledgement of Claim ... 61

L. Third-Party Intervention ... 62
I. Main Third-Party Intervention ... 62
II. Auxiliary Third-Party Intervention ... 62

M. Further Actions by Plaintiff ... 63
I. Further Substantiation of Claim ... 63

II. Amendments and Extension of Claim	63
III. Termination by Withdrawal of Action	64
IV. Termination of Action by Waiver of Claim	64
V. Termination of Action by Declaring the Proceedings Moot	64

N. Joint Actions by the Parties 65
    I. Suspension of Proceedings 65
    II. Termination of Action by Settlement 65
        1. Settlement in Court 65
        2. Out-of-Court Settlement 66

O. Additional Court Orders 67
    I. Court Orders Designed to Expedite the Proceedings 67
    II. Court Orders for Joinder of Actions and for Severance 67
    III. Court Order for Stay of Proceedings 67
    IV. Disclosure Orders by the Court 68
        1. Disclosure Orders for Production of Evidence 68
        2. General Disclosure Orders 68

P. Interruption of Proceedings 69

Q. The Oral Hearing 69
    I. General 69
        1. Function 69
        2. Record of Hearing 70
        3. Publicity 70
    II. Conduct of the Oral Hearing 71
        1. Opening of the Hearing 71
        2. Conciliation Hearing 71
            a) Introduction by the Presiding Judge 71
            b) Pleading and Discussion 71
            c) Settlement Attempt 71
        3. Main Oral Hearing 72
            a) Asserting the Motions 72
            b) Pleading and Discussion 72
            c) Taking of Evidence 72
            d) Conclusion of the Hearing 72

R. Evidentiary Proceedings 72
    I. General 72
        1. Scope of Taking Evidence 72
        2. Evidentiary Means 73
        3. Order to Take Evidence 73
    II. Taking Evidence 73
        1. Proof by Documentary Evidence 73
        2. Proof by Inspection by the Court 74
        3. Proof by Third-Party Witness Testimony 75
            a) Duties of a Witness 75
            b) Hearing of the Witness 75
            c) Recording of the Witness Testimony 76
            d) Remuneration of Witnesses 76
            e) Probative Value of Witness Testimony 76
        4. Proof by Expert Testimony 76

		a) Appointment of an Expert	76
		b) Duties of an Expert	77
		c) Opinion of the Expert	77
		d) Challenges to the Opinion by the Expert	77
		e) Remuneration of Experts	78
		f) Probative Value of Expert Testimony	78
		g) Expert Witnesses	78
	5. Proof by Party Testimony		78
		a) Informal Hearing of a Party	78
		b) Formal Party Testimony	79
	6. Frustration of Taking Evidence		79
III. Privileges			79
	1. Party Privilege		80
		a) Privileges as to Informal Hearings and as to Serving as a Party Witness	80
		b) Privilege and Disclosure Orders	80
	2. Privileges for Third-Party Witnesses		80
		a) Professional Privilege	80
		aa) (Former) Corporate Officers	80
		bb) Bank Secrecy Rules	80
		cc) Professional Advisors	81
		dd) In-house Counsel	81
		ee) Clergy and Media	81
		b) Personal Privilege	82
		aa) Familial Privilege	82
		bb) Privilege to Avoid Financial Harm, Disgrace, or Self-Incrimination	82
		cc) Privilege to Protect Trade Secrets Owned by Third Parties	82
		c) Public Servants Privilege	82
		d) Invoking Privilege	83
	3. Privilege for Experts		83
	4. Third-Party Privileges Relating to Orders for Document Production and for Inspection		83
IV. Evidence Located Abroad			83
	1. Statutory Sources		83
	2. Procurement of Evidence by the Court		84
	3. Requests for Legal Assistance		84
		a) Brussels Evidence Regulation	84
		b) Hague Evidence Convention	85
	4. Direct Taking of Evidence		86
	5. Foreign Privileges		86
V. Evaluation of Evidence and Standard of Proof			87

S. Establishing the Law 87
   I. German Law and German Private International Law 87
   II. Establishing Foreign Law 88

T. Judgments 89
   I. Uncontested Judgments 89
   II. Contested Judgments 89

	1. Types of Judgments	89
	2. Form and Contents of a Judgment	90
	3. Corrections of Judgments	90
	a) Apparent Mistakes	90
	b) Amendments and Supplements	91
	c) Practical Relevance	91
	4. Service of Judgment	91
III.	Effects of a Judgment	91
	1. Binding Effect on the Court	91
	2. Binding Effect on the Parties	91
	3. Procedures for Setting Aside a Final and Binding Judgment	92
	a) Motion for a New Trial	92
	b) Action for Damages	92

U. Appellate Remedies ... 93

I.	General	93
	1. Overview: Appellate Remedies	93
	2. General Features of Appellate Remedies	94
II.	First Appeals	94
	1. Competent Appellate Court	94
	2. Admissibility of Appeal	94
	a) Decisions Subject to Appeal	94
	b) Aggrievement of Appellant	95
	3. Waiver of Appeal	95
	4. Appellate Written Pleadings	95
	a) Statement of Appeal	95
	b) Statement of Grounds for Appeal	95
	c) Statement of Defense	95
	d) Withdrawal of Appeal	96
	5. Court Orders	96
	a) Procedural Orders by the Court	96
	b) Dismissal of Appeal by Court Order	96
	6. Scope of Appellate Review	96
	7. Judgment	97
III.	Second Appeal	97
	1. Competent Appellate Court	97
	2. Admissibility of Appeal	98
	a) General	98
	b) Admission of Appeal and Miscellaneous Appeal against Refusal to Grant Leave to Second Appeal *(Nichtzulassungsbeschwerde)*	98
	c) Waiver	98
	3. Submissions	99
	a) Statement of Second Appeal	99
	b) Statement of Grounds for Second Appeal	99
	c) Statement of Defense	99
	4. Court Orders	99
	a) General	99
	b) Court Order for Dismissal	100
	5. Scope of Appellate Review	100
	6. Judgment	100

IV. Miscellaneous Appeals *(Beschwerde)* ... 101
1. General ... 101
2. Immediate Miscellaneous Appeal ... 101
a) Competent Court ... 101
b) Admissibility of Appeal ... 101
c) Submissions ... 101
d) Court Decision ... 102
3. Miscellaneous Appeal on Points of Law *(Rechtsbeschwerde)* ... 102
a) Competent Appellate Court ... 102
b) Admissibility ... 102
c) Submissions ... 102
d) Court Decision ... 103

V. Enforcement and Execution of German Judgments ... 103
I. Enforcement and Execution in Germany ... 103
1. General ... 103
2. Execution of Monetary Claims ... 104
a) Execution by Garnishment of Monetary Claims and Other Proprietary Interests ... 104
b) Execution against Tangible Personal Property ... 105
c) Execution against Real Property ... 105
aa) Options for a Creditor ... 105
bb) Procedure ... 105
d) Forced Disclosure Proceedings ... 106
3. Execution of Non-Monetary Claims ... 107
a) Delivery or Recovery of Movables ... 107
b) Surrendering Possession of Real Property ... 107
c) Performance of an Act ... 107
d) Refraining from or Acquiescence to an Act ... 107
e) Declarations of Intent ... 108
4. Remedies in Execution Proceedings ... 108
II. Enforcement Abroad ... 108
1. Enforcement within the European Union ... 109
a) Brussels Regulation 2012 ... 109
b) Other European Enforcement Regimes ... 109
2. Lugano Convention 2007 ... 110
3. Others ... 110

W. Provisional Relief ... 111
I. General ... 111
1. Provisional Remedies Available ... 111
2. Practical Aspects ... 111
II. Attachments ... 112
1. Application for an Attachment ... 112
a) Jurisdiction ... 112
b) Motions ... 112
c) Attachment Claim ... 113
d) Grounds for Attachment ... 113
2. Protective Writ ... 114
3. Attachment Judgment or Order ... 114
4. Execution ... 114

		5. Remedies	115
	III.	Preliminary Injunction	115
		1. Application for a Preliminary Injunction	115
		a) Jurisdiction	116
		b) Motions	116
		c) Injunction Claim	116
		d) Grounds for Injunction	116
		2. Protective Writs	117
		3. Injunction Judgment or Order	117
		4. Execution	117
		5. Remedies	117
	IV.	No-Fault Liability	117
	V.	Enforcement of German Provisional Decisions Abroad	118
X.	Legal Assistance in Aid of Foreign Proceedings		118
	I.	Service of Process	118
		1. Brussels Service Regulation 2007	118
		2. Hague Service Convention	119
		3. Other Requests	120
	II.	Taking of Evidence in Germany in Aid of Foreign Proceedings	120
		1. Brussels Evidence Regulation	120
		2. Hague Evidence Convention	120
		3. Other International Instruments	121
	III.	Information on German Law	121
	IV.	Enforcement of Foreign Judgments	121
		1. Judgments of Courts in the European Union	121
		2. Other Foreign Judgments	122
	V.	Provisional Remedies in Aid of Foreign Proceedings	123
		1. European Union	123
		2. Decisions by Courts Outside the European Union	123

Chapter 2: Arbitration 125

A. Introduction 125
    I. Brief History 125
       1. German Arbitration Law 125
       2. Legislative Intent behind New German Arbitration Law 125
       3. Arbitration in Germany Today 126
    II. Statutory Landscape of German Law on Arbitration 126
       1. International Treaties 126
       2. Scope of New Legal Regime 127
          a) Place of Arbitration in Germany 127
          b) Applicability to Arbitral Proceedings without German Seat ... 127

B. The Arbitration Agreement 128
    I. Arbitrability 128
       1. Subjective Arbitrability 128
       2. Objective Arbitrability 129
          a) Disputes Involving an Economic Interest 129
          b) Disputes Not Subject to Arbitration 129
    II. Content Requirement of an Arbitration Agreement 130
    III. Form Requirements 131

1. "In Writing" and Signature Requirement under German Arbitration Law 131
   a) Non-Consumers 132
      aa) "In Writing" and Signature Requirements for Non-Consumers. 132
      bb) Arbitration Agreement by Incorporation. 132
      cc) Unilateral Arbitration Agreement. 132
   b) Consumers 133
   c) Remedying Form Defects in Arbitration Agreement 133
2. "In Writing" and Signature Requirement of the New York Convention 134
IV. Effect on Third Parties 135
V. Termination and Breach 136

C. Constitution and Composition of the Arbitral Tribunal 136
I. Party Autonomy 136
II. Number of Arbitrators 137
III. Appointment of Arbitrators and Chairperson 137
   1. Qualifications of Arbitrators. 137
   2. Party Autonomy in Appointment of Arbitrators 138
   3. Default Rules for Appointing Arbitrators 138
      a) Default Rule for Proceedings with Sole Arbitrator 138
      b) Default Rule for Proceedings with Three Arbitrators 139
   4. Court Intervention in Appointment of Arbitrators 139
      a) Court Appointment of Arbitrators When Nomination Procedures Fail 139
      b) Court Appointment of Arbitrators when Nomination Procedures are Unconscionable 139
      c) Petition to the Court 140
IV. Multi-Party Arbitration 140
V. Challenge, Removal and Replacement of Arbitrators 141
   1. Challenge of an Arbitrator 141
      a) Grounds upon which Arbitrators can be Challenged 141
      b) Procedure for Challenging an Arbitrator 142
   2. Removal of an Arbitrator 142
   3. Replacement of an Arbitrator 143

D. The Arbitrator's Contract 143
I. Arbitrator Contract under German Law 143
II. Remuneration of Arbitrator 144
   1. Duty to Compensate Arbitrator 144
   2. Amount of Fees 145
   3. Accrual and Expiration of Claim for Compensation 146
III. Liability of Arbitrator – Duties of the Arbitrator(s) 147
   1. Liability for Negligence 147
   2. Liability for Specific Performance 147
   3. No Liability for Decision in Award 147

E. Jurisdiction of Arbitral Tribunal 148
I. Competence of Arbitral Tribunal to Rule on its Jurisdiction 148
II. Interim Measures of Protection 148

F. The Arbitral Proceedings 149
  I. General Rules of Procedure 149
  II. Place of Arbitration 150
  III. Language of Arbitral Proceedings 151
  IV. Exchange of Submissions and Notifications 152
    1. Initiation of Proceedings 152
    2. Statements of Claim and Defense 152
    3. Notification for Insolvency 153
  V. Oral Hearings and Written Proceedings 153
  VI. Default of a Party 153
  VII. Establishing the Facts of the Case 154
    1. General Approach to Fact Finding and Gathering Evidence ... 154
    2. Documents 155
      a) Production of Documents in the Possession of a Party 155
      b) Production of Documents in the Possession of Third Parties 156
      c) Confidentiality of Documents and Privilege 156
    3. Witnesses 156
      a) Written Statements and Testimony 156
      b) Preparation of Witnesses 157
      c) Transcript or Summary of Witness Testimony 158
      d) Parties as Witnesses 158
      e) Reimbursement of Witnesses 158
    4. Experts 159
      a) Party-Appointed Experts in Common Law and Court-Appointed Experts in Civil Law 159
      b) Impartiality and Independence of Tribunal-Appointed Expert 159
      c) Appointing a Tribunal-Appointed Expert 159
      d) Duties of a Tribunal-Appointed Expert 160
      e) Party-Appointed Experts 161
    5. Court Assistance in Taking Evidence 161
      a) Possible Assistance Measures 161
      b) International Character of ZPO § 1050 161
      c) Sanctions Available to German Courts 162
      d) Competent Court 162
      e) Requirements for the Application 162
      f) Admissibility of a Request 163
    6. Privileges 163

G. Making of Award and Termination of Proceedings 164
  I. Rules Applicable to Substance of Dispute 164
    1. Determination by the Parties 164
    2. Determination by the Arbitral Tribunal 164
  II. Making of the Award 165
    1. Majority Voting 165
    2. Recalcitrant Arbitrator 166
    3. Separate, Concurring, and Dissenting Opinions 166
    4. Decisions on Procedure by Chairperson Alone 167
  III. Form and Contents of Award 168
    1. Required Contents 168
    2. Termination of Proceedings by Award 169

IV. Settlement 170
　1. Types of Settlement 170
　2. Form and Contents of Award on Agreed Terms 171
V. Termination of Proceedings 171
　1. Types of Awards 171
　　a) Final Award 172
　　b) Partial Award 172
　　c) Interim or Interlocutory Award 172
　2. Order Terminating the Proceedings 173
VI. Decision on Costs 173
　1. Discretion of the Arbitral Tribunal 173
　2. Costs of the Arbitration 174
　3. Costs of a Procedural Award 176
　4. Enforceability of Decision on Costs 176
VII. Correction and Interpretation of Award; Additional Award . 177
　1. Formal Requirements 177
　2. Correction and Interpretation 178
　3. Additional Award 178

H. Recourse against Award 179
I. Reasons for Setting Aside an Award 179
　1. Invalid Arbitration Agreement 179
　2. Due Process 180
　3. Excess of Competence or Authority 181
　4. Improper Composition of the Arbitral Tribunal and Violation of the Procedural Rules Applicable to Arbitration 182
　5. Public Policy 183
　6. International Public Policy 184
II. Procedure and Time Limits 185
　1. Relationship between Setting Aside Proceedings and Enforcement Proceedings 185
　2. Time Limits and Formal Requirements 186
　3. Content of Decision Setting Aside the Award 186

I. Recognition and Enforcement of Arbitral Awards 187
I. Procedure for Enforcement Proceedings 187
II. Decision on Enforcement 188
III. Foreign Arbitral Awards 189

Chapter 3: Mediation 191

A. Introduction to Mediation in German Commercial Disputes .. 191
I. Brief History and Development of Mediation in Germany 191
II. Introduction to Mediation in Germany and the European Union Today 192

B. International Regulatory Developments 193

C. Statutory Framework of Mediation in Germany 194
I. Brief Legislative History of the Mediation Advancement Act .. 195
II. In-Court Mediation: *Güterichter* Model 195
III. Out-of-Court Mediation During Ongoing Proceedings 196
IV. Mandatory Court-Annexed Mediation 196

V. Further Mandatory Mediation	197
VI. The Mediation Act	197

D. Mediation Clauses and Agreements ... 198
    I. Content of a Mediation Clause ... 198
    II. General Terms and Conditions ... 198

E. Mediation and Court Proceedings ... 199
    I. Defense of Mediation ... 199
    II. Suspension of the Limitation Period ... 199

F. Mediation Procedure ... 200
    I. Mediator ... 201
        1. Selection of the Mediator ... 201
        2. Independence and Impartiality – Disclosure Obligations of the Mediator ... 202
        3. Mediator's Duty to Guarantee each Party's Integration into the Mediation ... 202
        4. Mediator's Duty of Confidentiality ... 202
        5. Mediator Contract ... 203
            a) Remuneration of Mediator ... 203
            b) Liability of Mediator ... 204
            c) Termination ... 204
    II. Agreement on Procedures ... 205
    III. Reference to Rules of a Mediation Institution ... 205

G. Conclusion of Mediation Proceedings ... 206
    I. Termination of Mediation and its Consequences ... 206
        1. Mediation after Initiation of Court Proceedings ... 206
        2. Mediation without Initiation of Court Proceedings ... 206
    II. Conclusion of a Settlement Agreement ... 207
    III. Enforcement of the Settlement Agreement ... 207
        1. Final and Binding Judgments ... 208
        2. Court Settlements ... 208
        3. Settlements before a State-Approved Conciliatory Entity ... 208
        4. Notarial Deeds ... 209
        5. Enforceable Lawyers' Settlements ... 209
        6. Award on Agreed Terms ... 209

Part 2: Relevant Statutory and Regulatory Materials

A. German Statutory Instruments ... 211
    I. Code of Civil Procedure (Excerpts) ... 211
    II. German Judicature Act (Excerpts) ... 261
    III. Recognition and Enforcement Implementation Act (AVAG) (Excerpts) ... 284
    IV. Act on the Implementation of the Hague Convention ... 306
    V. German Mediation Act ... 311

B. EC Regulations ... 318
    I. Regulation (EU) No 1215/2012 of the European Parliament and of the Council of 12 December 2012 on jurisdiction and

	the recognition and enforcement of judgments in civil and commercial matters (recast)..................................	318
	II. Regulation (EC) No 1393/2007 of the European Parliament and of the Council of 13 November 2007 on the service in the Member States of judicial and extrajudicial documents in civil or commercial matters (service of documents), and repealing Council Regulation (EC) No 1348/2000	348
	III. Council regulation (EC) No. 1206/2001 of 28 May 2001 on Cooperation between the Courts of the Member States in the Taking of Evidence in Civil or Commercial Matters	359
	IV. Regulation (EC) No 1896/2006 of the European Parliament and of the Council of 12 December 2006 creating a European order for payment procedure.......................................	369
	V. Regulation (EC) No 805/2004 of the European Parliament and of the Council of 21 April 2004 creating a European Enforcement Order for uncontested claims	382
C. Bilateral and Multilateral Treaties		395
	I. List of Treaties Relevant to International Procedural and Arbitration Law in Germany..................................	395
	II. Hague Convention on the Service Abroad of Judicial and Extrajudicial Documents in Civil or Commercial Matters	398
	III. Hague Convention on the Taking of Evidence Abroad in Civil or Commercial Matters..	405
	IV. CONVENTION ON CHOICE OF COURT AGREEMENTS	414
D. German Institutions and Rules for Arbitration		426
	I. List of Arbitration Institutions in Germany	426
	II. Arbitration Rules of the German Institution of Arbitration (Deutsche Institution für Schiedsgerichtsbarkeit e.V. (DIS)) in force as of 1 July 1998 (Schedule of Costs in force as of 1 April 2014)..	430
E. German Institutions and Rules for Mediation		446
	I. List of Mediation Institutions in Germany	446
	II. Mediation Rules of the German Institution of Arbitration (Deutsche Institution für Schiedsgerichtsbarkeit (DIS)) in force as of 1 January 2002, amended in 2010 (Schedule of Costs in force as of 1 October 2004)	448
Appendix 1 Selected Sample Calculations of Fees in German Proceedings		453
Appendix 2 Bibliography		461
	I. Commentaries and Books in the German Language	461
	II. Commentaries, Books, and Articles in the English Language.....	462
Appendix 3 German-English Glossary		467

Table of Important Abbreviations

AktG	Stock Corporation Act (*Aktiengesetz*)
ArbGG	Labour Courts Act (*Arbeitsgerichtsgesetz*)
AVAG	German Act for the Implementation of International Treaties and for the Implementation of European Community Regulations in the Area of Recognition and Enforcement in Civil and Commercial Matters (*Anerkennungs- und Vollstreckungsausführungsgesetz*)
BayObLG	Bavarian Highest Regional Court (*Bayerisches Oberstes Landesgericht*)
BGB	Civil Code (*Bürgerliches Gesetzbuch*)
BGH	Federal Court of Justice (*Bundesgerichtshof*)
BNotO	Federal Regulation on Notaries (*Bundesnotarordnung*)
BORA	Professional Code for Attorneys (*Berufsordnung für Rechtsanwälte*)
BörsG	Stock Exchange Act (*Börsengesetz*)
BRAGO	Federal Attorney's Fees Act (*Bundesrechtsanwaltsgebührenordnung*)
BRAO	Federal Attorney's Code (*Bundesrechtsanwaltsordnung*)
Brussels Convention	Brussels Convention on jurisdiction and the enforcement of judgments in civil and commercial matters of 27 September 1968
Brussels Evidence Regulation	Council Regulation (EC) No. 1206/2001 of 28 May 2001 on cooperation between the courts of the Member States in the taking of evidence in civil or commercial matters
Brussels Regulation 2001	Council Regulation (EC) No. 44/2001 of 22 December 2000 on jurisdiction and the recognition and enforcement of judgments in civil and commercial matters
Brussels Regulation 2012	Regulation (EU) No 1215/2012 of the European Parliament and of the Council of 12 December 2012 on jurisdiction and the recognition and enforcement of judgments in civil and commercial matters (replaces the Council Regulation (EC) No. 44/2001 of 22 December 2000)
Brussels Service Regulation 2000	Council Regulation (EC) No. 1348/2000 of 29 May 2000 on the service in the Member States of judicial and extrajudicial documents in civil or commercial matters
Brussels Service Regulation 2007	Regulation (EC) No 1393/2007 of the European Parliament and of the Council of 13 November 2007 on the service in the Member States of judici-

	al and extrajudicial documents in civil or commercial matters (service of documents), and repealing Council Regulation (EC) No 1348/2000
BVerfGG	Federal Constitutional Court Act (*Bundesverfassungsgerichtsgesetz*)
CISG	United Nations Convention on Contracts for the International Sale of Goods of 11 April 1980
DIS	German Institution of Arbitration (*Deutsche Institution für Schiedsgerichtsbarkeit e.V.*)
DIS Rules	Arbitration Rules of the German Institution of Arbitration (DIS) of 1 July 1998
EGBGB	Introductory Law of the German Civil Code (*Einführungsgesetz zum Bürgerlichen Gesetzbuch*)
EGGVG	Introductory Law of the Judicature Act (*Einführungsgesetz zum Gerichtsverfassungsgesetz*)
EGZPO	Introductory Law of the Code of Civil Procedure (*Einführungsgesetz zur Zivilprozessordnung*)
EStGB	Introductory Law of the German Penal Code (*Einführungsgesetz zum Strafgesetzbuch*)
FGG	Act on Non-Contentious Jurisdiction (*Gesetz über die Angelegenheiten der freiwilligen Gerichtsbarkeit*)
FGO	Fiscal Courts Act (*Finanzgerichtsordnung*)
Geneva Protocol	Protocol on Arbitration Clauses of 24 September 1923
GG	Basic Law (*Grundgesetz*)
GKG	Court Fees Act (*Gerichtskostengesetz*)
GmbHG	Law on Limited Liability Companies (*Gesetz betreffend die Gesellschaften mit beschränkter Haftung*)
GVG	Judicature Act (*Gerichtsverfassungsgesetz*)
Hague Civil Procedure Convention	Hague Convention on Civil Procedure of 1 March 1954
Hague Evidence Convention	Hague Convention on the Taking of Evidence Abroad in Civil or Commercial Matters of 18 March 1970
Hague Service Convention	Hague Convention on the Service Abroad of Judicial and Extrajudicial Documents in Civil or Commercial Matters of 15 November 1965
HGB	Commercial Code (*Handelsgesetzbuch*)
IBA	International Bar Association
IBA Rules on Evidence	IBA Rules on the Taking of Evidence in International Arbitration
ICC	International Chamber of Commerce (*Internationale Handelskammer*)
ICC Rules	Rules of Arbitration of the International Chamber of Commerce
ICSID	International Centre for Settlement of Investment Disputes
ICSID Convention	Convention on the Settlement of Investment Disputes between States and Nationals of Other States of 18 March 1965
InsO	Insolvency Code (*Insolvenzordnung*)
LG	Regional Court (*Landgericht*)
LuftVG	Federal Air Traffic Act (*Luftverkehrsgesetz*)

Lugano Convention 1988	Lugano Convention on jurisdiction and the enforcement of judgments in civil and commercial matters of 16 September 1988
Lugano Convention 2007	Lugano Convention on jurisdiction and the enforcement of judgments in civil and commercial matters of 30 October 2007
New York Convention	United Nations Convention on the Recognition and Enforcement of Foreign Arbitral Awards of 10 June 1958
OLG	Higher Regional Court (*Oberlandesgericht*)
ÖRA	Public Legal Advice and Settlement Center (*Öffentliche Rechtsauskunft und Vergleichsstelle*)
RVG	Federal Attorney Remuneration Act (*Rechtsanwaltsvergütungsgesetz*)
StGB	German Penal Code (*Strafgesetzbuch*)
UNCITRAL	United Nations Commission on International Trade Law
UNIDROIT	International Institute for the Unification of Private Law
UNIDROIT Principles	UNIDROIT Principles of International Commercial Contracts 2004
UWG	Unfair Competition Act (*Gesetz gegen den unlauteren Wettbewerb*)
VwGO	Administrative Courts Act (*Verwaltungsgerichtsordnung*)
ZPO	Code of Civil Procedure (*Zivilprozessordnung*)
ZRHO	Regulation on Judicial Assistance in Civil Matters (*Rechtshilfeordnung für Zivilsachen*)
ZVG	Law on Involuntary Sale and Administration (*Gesetz über die Zwangsversteigerung und Zwangsverwaltung*)

Part 1
Introduction to Commercial Dispute Resolution in Germany*

Chapter 1: Commercial Litigation

A. Some Distinct Features of Litigation in German Courts

German civil litigation differs in many respects from what a lawyer with foreign background may expect. There are a number of features of German civil litigation which in particular U.S. parties usually find surprising:

(i) *No Pre-trial Discovery:* In the United States as well as in Germany, a judgment will be based on the facts pleaded by the parties. In the U.S., the parties gather much of this information through extensive pre-trial discovery. The concept of pre-trial discovery, however, is alien to German law. German law does not even permit German courts to honor requests for legal assistance if the requests involve assisting in pre-trial discovery. Instead, the German system relies on an elaborate system of allocating the burden to submit and to prove the facts. It grants the parties only limited rights to request information from the opponent, and protects confidential information quite extensively. The parties to a litigation are, therefore, neither required to produce vast quantities of internal corporate documents, as is the case in U.S. style pre-trial discovery of documents, nor are corporate officers and key employees subject to potentially hostile questioning by opposing counsel in the context of depositions.

(ii) *Specific Pleading Only:* In U.S. litigation, a statement of claim may be based on a very vague notion of the facts surrounding the claim, and may be phrased in the most conclusory terms. The relevant facts and the relief sought are established later through the pre-trial discovery process. In contrast, a plaintiff bringing an action before a German court must exactly specify the relief sought by him. Further, the statement of claim already must provide a complete and concise narration of the relevant facts. In addition, the statement of claim will usually also state the evidence on which the plaintiff intends to rely, and describe the legal rules upon which his claim is based. If the court finds the statement of claim insufficient, the case may be dismissed even before the opponent has submitted his statement of defense. In German litigation, therefore, a plaintiff must have largely established his case before initiating court proceedings.

(iii) *No Excessive Damage Awards:* Plaintiffs in U.S. proceedings often claim to be entitled to recover more than their actual damages, i.e. treble or punitive

---

* For ease of reference, the authors have used the pronoun "he" to refer to "he or she" and the pronoun "his" to refer to "his or her".

damages. Excessive damage awards granted by a jury of laymen, who are sometimes subject to sophisticated manipulation by plaintiff attorneys, are not – at least from a non-U.S. perspective – uncommon. This is not the case in German commercial litigation. The lay element is restricted to "honorary judges" chosen from the business community who are guided by a professional judge. Further, a party may only be awarded its actual damages, and there is a strict standard of proof for damages to be met by the plaintiff.

(iv) *Cost Rules:* Court fees in the USA are comparatively moderate. Even a successful party is normally not entitled to recover its attorney fees from the opponent ("American cost rule"). Attorneys in the U.S. are allowed to enter into contingency arrangements which tie their remuneration to the success of the case. Therefore, there is usually only a very limited cost risk for a plaintiff who brings a multi-million dollar lawsuit in United States courts. An opponent faced with a claim having no merit may nevertheless be compelled to settle just to avoid the defense cost. Quite differently, contingency arrangements of any kind are prohibited by the German rules of professional conduct and are legally void.[1] The court fees and the statutory attorney fees in Germany are tied to the value of the matter, the cost may add up to very sizeable amounts and are to be borne by the unsuccessful party ("English cost rule"). The statutory attorney fees to be reimbursed by the opponent quite often cover all legal expenses incurred by the prevailing party.

B. Basic Elements of the German Civil Justice System

I. The German Civil Law System

The Federal Republic of Germany is a federation consisting of 16 federal states (*Länder*). The basic structure is set out in the federal constitution (Basic Law, *Grundgesetz, GG*)[2] and in the constitutions of the federal states. Germany is a representative democracy under the rule of law with separate legislative, judicial and executive branches. The original authority for enacting legislation lies with the federal states insofar as it is not expressly allocated to the federal government. However, almost all areas of private procedural and substantive law are governed by federal law.

Germany is a civil law country in the Roman law tradition. In the German legal system, statutes are the most prevalent source of law. The basic legislation in the field of civil and commercial law are the German Civil Code (*Bürgerliches Gesetzbuch, BGB*)[3] and the Commercial Code (*Handelsgesetzbuch, HGB*)[4] both of which were first enacted prior to 1900. Both codes have been revised and amended several times over the last hundred years, not the least as a result of European legislation. The last major revision of the BGB took place with effect as of 1 January 2002, revising and modernizing the code in part and incorporating a number of

---

[1] But see *infra*, at pp. 10 et seq.
[2] An English translation is available at www.gesetze-im-internet.de.
[3] An English translation is available at www.gesetze-im-internet.de.
[4] A translation into English of the first four books is provided in: *Rittler*, Handelsgesetzbuch (HGB) – German Commercial Code, 2012; an English translation of the fifth book is available at www.gesetze-im-internet.de.

provisions which were formerly contained in separate legal codes. The BGB and the HGB are surrounded and complemented by a large number of additional statutes. This legislation forms the basis for the abstract and deductive method of the German legal tradition, as opposed to the inductive thinking of the common law lawyer.

Different from common law countries where the legal system is essentially based on the doctrine of binding precedent (*stare decisis*), judicial precedents are not legally binding upon the German courts.[5] Not even the courts of first instance are under a legal obligation to follow the precedents set by their appellate courts. However, in practice it is rare for German courts to deviate from a consistent line of precedents established by the higher courts. Therefore, judicial precedents in particular of the higher regional courts (*Oberlandesgerichte, OLG*) and the Federal Court of Justice (*Bundesgerichtshof, BGH*) will be widely followed by the lower courts when applying the relevant statutes.

The practice of law is considered to be one of the learned professions in Germany. German lawyers see themselves as academics. Therefore, the opinions of academic writers profoundly influence the daily practice of law. In particular, handbooks and commentaries are available on basically every statute.[6] They are consistently consulted and cited not only in submissions to the courts, but also in judgments and other court decisions.

II. Sources of Civil Procedure Law

Provisions governing German civil procedure law are to be found in the *Grundgesetz*, in the federal state constitutions, in several statutes, and in a number of European regulations and international treaties:

1. Constitutional Law

The federal constitution (*Grundgesetz, GG*), contains some fundamental procedural guarantees, i.e.
(i)   the right to be heard by the court (GG Art. 103 (1));
(ii)   the right to legal recourse;
(iii)   the right to be heard by the lawful judge (GG Artt. 101 (1) section 2, 20 (3) and Art. 19);
(iv)   the right to a fair trial according to the rule of law;
(v)   the right to be treated equally by the court (GG Art. 3 (1)); and
(vi)   the duty of the courts to follow the law (GG Art. 20 (1)).

Most federal state constitutions contain similar provisions. In case of conflict, the GG prevails.

2. Statutes

a) Core Statutes

Different from the U.S., which has numerous state and federal jurisdictions with corresponding civil procedure laws, basically all relevant areas of civil procedure law in Germany are governed by federal statutes. Many of these statutes date back

---

[5] The exception being decisions of the Federal Constitutional Court, see Federal Constitutional Court Act (*Bundesverfassungsgerichtsgesetz, BVerfGG*) §31.
[6] Appendix 3 lists the most widely used handbooks and commentaries on civil procedure law.

to the 19th century and have been revised and re-enacted several times. The most important ones are

(i) the Judicature Act of 1877 (*Gerichtsverfassungsgesetz, GVG*),[7] setting out the structure and the internal organization of the administration of justice as well as some fundamental principles on court proceedings,

(ii) the Judicial Officers' Act of 1969 (*Rechtspflegergesetz, RPflG*),[8] relating to the distribution of powers between judges and judicial officers (*Rechtspfleger*) in the administration of justice,

(iii) the Code of Civil Procedure of 1877 (*Zivilprozessordnung, ZPO*),[9] containing the rules governing civil and commercial court proceedings, the general rules on the execution of judgments, and the rules governing arbitral proceedings,

(iv) the Law on Involuntary Sale and Administration of 1898 (*Gesetz über die Zwangsversteigerung und die Zwangsverwaltung, ZVG*), relating to the execution of judgments in real property, in maritime vessels, and in aircraft,

(v) the Court Fees Act of 1975 (*Gerichtskostengesetz, GKG*) on court fees,

(vi) the Federal Attorney Remuneration Act of 2004 (*Rechtsanwaltsvergütungsgesetz, RVG*), governing the fees of attorneys,[10] and

(vii) the Judicial Remuneration and Compensation Act of 2004 (*Justizvergütungs- und –entschädigungsgesetz, JVEG*) on the remuneration of witnesses and expert witnesses.

b) Major Reforms

A major reform of German civil procedure law was effected in 2002. The reform aimed at making access to justice easier and was intended to streamline the proceedings. It focused mainly on the law on appeals, which was changed in large part. In addition, the law on service of process was modernized.

The provisions concerning the enforcement of monetary claims were fundamentally revised, effective 1 January 2013. Whereas the earlier provisions focused on liens against movable property, the new provisions focus more on the garnishment of monetary claims and other proprietary interests, also taking into account the creditor's need for information and modern technologies.

New provisions relating to judicial cooperation within the European Union and that implement European provisions into German domestic law are added to the ZPO on a continuous basis.[11]

The German legislator also announced its goal to foster electronic communication between attorneys and the courts in order to streamline proceedings. While electronic communication with the courts currently has no significant relevance, the legislator has set out to make it gradually compulsory in civil proceedings at the latest from 2022.

3. European Legislation and International Treaties

Germany is a Member State of the European Union. Particularly since the beginning of the new century, the European Union has rendered several legislative acts

---

[7] An English translation is available at www.gesetze-im-internet.de.
[8] An English translation is available at www.gesetze-im-internet.de.
[9] An English translation is available at www.gesetze-im-internet.de.
[10] An English translation is available at www.gesetze-im-internet.de.
[11] ZPO §§ 1067 *et seq.*

B. Basic Elements of the German Civil Justice System

relating to civil procedure law. A number of European Union directives were implemented into German domestic law. Several directly applicable European Union regulations supersede or may be applicable alternatively to German domestic civil procedure law. More recently, some of these European regulations have already been replaced by newer ones.[12]

In addition, Germany is a signatory to a number of multilateral and bilateral treaties dealing with, *inter alia*, issues of international civil procedure.[13] The federal government has enacted implementation statutes (*Ausführungsgesetze*) relating mostly to organizational issues such as determining the competent authorities under these treaties.[14]

With regard to civil and commercial matters, the following European Union regulations and international treaties are the most relevant in practice:[15]

(i) The Regulation (EU) No 1215/2012 of the European Parliament and of the Council of 12 December 2012 on jurisdiction and the recognition and enforcement of judgments in civil and commercial matters ("Brussels Regulation 2012"),[16] which as of 10 January 2015 replaces the Council Regulation (EC) No. 44/2001 of 22 December 2000 on jurisdiction and the recognition and enforcement of judgments in civil and commercial matters ("Brussels Regulation 2001"),

(ii) the Lugano Convention on jurisdiction and the recognition and enforcement of judgments in civil and commercial matters of 30 October 2007 ("Lugano Convention 2007"),[17] which replaces the Lugano Convention on jurisdiction and the enforcement of judgments in civil and commercial matters of 16 September 1988 ("Lugano Convention 1988"),

(iii) the Hague Convention on Civil Procedure of 1 March 1954 ("Hague Civil Procedure Convention"),[18]

(iv) the Regulation (EC) No 1393/2007 of the European Parliament and of the Council of 13 November 2007 on the service in the Member States of judicial and extrajudicial documents in civil or commercial matters, which repeals the Council Regulation (EC) No 1348/2000 ("Brussels Service Regulation 2007")[19] and replaces the Council Regulation (EC) No. 1348/2000 of 29 May 2000 on the service in the Member States of judicial and extrajudicial documents in civil or commercial matters ("Brussels Service Regulation 2000"),

(v) the Hague Convention on the Service Abroad of Judicial and Extrajudicial Documents in Civil or Commercial Matters of 15 November 1965 ("Hague Service Convention"),[20]

---

[12] See http://europa.eu/legislation_summaries/justice_freedom_security/judicial_cooperation_in_civil_matters/index_en.htm.
[13] See the list of relevant treaties in Part 2. C. I.
[14] English translations of the most relevant parts are available in Part 2. A. III. and IV.
[15] The English text of all regulations is available at http://eur-lex.europa.eu/homepage.html.
[16] The Regulation also indirectly applies to Denmark. The English text of the Convention is available at http://eur-lex.europa.eu/homepage.html.
[17] The Lugano Convention of 2007 is also applicable to Switzerland, Norway and Iceland. The English text of the Convention can be found at http://ec.europa.eu/world/agreements/default.home.do.
[18] The English text of the Convention and a list of its member states can be found at http://www.hcch.net/upload/conventions/txt02en.pdf.
[19] The Regulation also applies to Denmark. The English Text of the Convention is available at http://eur-lex.europa.eu/homepage.html.
[20] The English text of the Convention can be found at http://www.hcch.net/upload/conventions/txt14en.pdf.

(vi) the Council Regulation (EC) No. 1206/2001 of 28 May 2001 on cooperation between the courts of the Member States in the taking of evidence in civil or commercial matters ("Brussels Evidence Regulation"),[21]
(vii) the Hague Convention on the Taking of Evidence Abroad in Civil or Commercial Matters of 18 March 1970 ("Hague Evidence Convention"),[22] and
(viii) the Regulation (EC) No. 1896/2006 of the European Parliament and of the Council of 12 December 2006 creating a European order for payment procedure.[23]

III. General Principles of Civil Procedure Law

The main statute governing German civil litigation is the ZPO, which sets out in detail all aspects of civil procedure in a German court. Its provisions are based on a number of abstract principles that are useful for understanding and interpreting the ZPO. These principles include
(i) the principle of party control of the subject matter of the lawsuit (*Dispositionsmaxime*),
(ii) the principle of party control of factual pleadings and proof (*Verhandlungs- und Beibringungsgrundsatz*),
(iii) the principle of oral procedure, i.e. that the court decision may be based only on statements by the parties made or reiterated orally (*Mündlichkeitsgrundsatz*),
(iv) the principle of publicity (*Öffentlichkeitsprinzip*),
(v) the principle of immediacy (*Unmittelbarkeitsgrundsatz*), i.e. conducting the proceedings in front of the court,
(vi) the principle of expediting the proceedings (*Beschleunigungsgrundsatz*), and
(vii) the right to be heard by the court (*Anspruch auf rechtliches Gehör*).

IV. The Actors in German Litigation

1. The Parties

Each person, as well as any legal entity, may become a party to litigation in Germany.[24] Except for the duty of foreign plaintiffs from a number of countries to provide security for the costs of the proceedings, the nationality of a litigant is irrelevant. Foreign parties to a litigation in the German courts are not treated any differently than German nationals.

Naturally, a certain language-related burden arises for foreign litigants with respect to their communications with the court. The language in court is German, and German courts do not accept written pleadings in foreign languages.[25] This burden, however, is somewhat eased by the fact that under German cost rules, the cost for all necessary translations are part of the cost of the proceedings, which are

---

[21] The Regulation does not apply to Denmark. The English Text of the Convention is available at http://eur-lex.europa.eu/homepage.html.
[22] The English text of the Convention can be found at http://www.hcch.net/upload/conventions/txt20en.pdf.
[23] The Regulation does not apply to Denmark. The English Text of the Convention is available at http://eur-lex.europa.eu/homepage.html.
[24] ZPO §§ 50 *et seq.*
[25] GVG § 184.

B. Basic Elements of the German Civil Justice System

to be reimbursed by the non-prevailing party regardless of whether or not such party has caused the translation cost by being an alien. Furthermore, the court is required to engage an interpreter if a person involved in the proceedings does not have sufficient command of the German language.[26]

2. The Lawyers

a) Education and Training

Regardless of their future professional goals, lawyers in Germany follow one uniform course of legal education. It consists of four to five years of law studies at a university, followed by a two-year mandatory practical training period with rotations in the courts, in private practice settings, and in public administration. Top graduates often obtain additional education by either studying for a foreign law degree or a doctorate (comparable to a Ph.D. in the U.S.) in law or both. After passing the final state exam, a lawyer may choose to be admitted to the bar or may pursue a different career choice in business, public administration, or in the judiciary.

b) Judges

German judges are not appointed by public election, as is the case in some courts *e.g.* in the U.S. Instead, the German judiciary is comprised of career judges. Entry level judges are selected by an independent commission (*Richterwahlausschuss*) mainly on the basis of their academic qualifications. The successful candidates are formally appointed by the governments of the respective German federal states.

A young judge is supervised for at least the first three years of his service so that his qualities as a judge can be assessed. After successfully passing this probationary period, he will be employed for life as one of approximately 20,000[27] judges. The career of a civil judge may include serving as a judge sitting alone at a local court (*Amtsgericht*), as a judge in a chamber at a regional court (*Landgericht*), sometimes with a mandatory period at the public prosecutor's office trying criminal cases, serving as a presiding judge at a regional court, or as a judge at a higher regional court (*Oberlandesgericht*). Being appointed as a presiding judge at a higher regional court or as one of the approximately 130[28] judges at the Federal Court of Justice (*Bundesgerichtshof*) is very rare and requires, in addition to outstanding legal skills, often a certain degree of political patronage.

The standards of the German judiciary, both on a professional and an ethical level, are very high. Corruption in the administration of justice is unheard of. However, becoming a professional judge is a career choice that is usually made before the age of 35, and it is accordingly quite uncommon that a judge has had any previous work experience outside the judiciary.

---

[26] GVG § 185.
[27] According to the statistics for 2012 provided by the Federal Ministry of Justice at http://www.bmjv.de/.
[28] According to the statistics for 2013 provided by the Federal Ministry of Justice at http://www.bmjv.de/.

c) German Attorneys

The majority of the approximately 160,000[29] attorneys (*Rechtsanwälte*) admitted in Germany are either sole practitioners or practice in law firms with less than ten lawyers. After a large influx of foreign law firms in the 1990s that set up offices or merged with established German firms, law firms comprising several hundred attorneys have evolved and become more common.

German attorneys are members of the local bar associations (*Rechtsanwaltskammern*). Their rights and duties are set out in the Federal Attorney's Code of 1959 (*Bundesrechtsanwaltsordnung, BRAO*) and ancillary regulations such as the Professional Code (*Berufsordnung*). The bar associations have the authority to enforce compliance with these professional rules of conduct.

Each German attorney is admitted to practice before all local courts, all regional courts and all higher regional courts. Only 44[30] attorneys, however, are admitted to the Federal Court of Justice. They are prohibited from acting before any local, regional or higher regional court, they may only form a law firm with one other attorney also admitted to the Federal Court of Justice, and they need to maintain their offices at the seat of the court in Karlsruhe. Being one of these chosen few is prestigious, but drastically reduces the scope of professional activities of an attorney.

Generally, most German attorneys consider themselves competent trial lawyers, although most are actually general practitioners with limited or no specialization whatsoever. For some time now, however, many of the large law firms have formed separate dispute resolution departments specializing in complex commercial matters and in international or multi-jurisdictional disputes. A relatively recent phenomenon is boutique firms concentrating on contentious work only.

d) Foreign Attorneys

An attorney from a European Union Member State may in certain cases act before German courts as an agent and in cooperation with a German attorney. He may also be admitted to a German bar association, which gives him the same rights as a German attorney. Lawyers from countries which are not Member States of the European Union are not admitted to practice before the German courts.

Although the number of foreign lawyers practicing in Germany is increasing, the representation of a party before a German court by a non-German attorney is exceptionally rare.

3. Court Officers

In addition to the judges, the German courts employ a variety of other court officers in the administration of justice. With regard to commercial litigation, the judicial officers (*Rechtspfleger*) are, *inter alia*, in charge of the execution of judgments in real property and the garnishment of monetary claims and other proprietary interests. The bailiffs (*Gerichtsvollzieher*) are entrusted with the enforcement of judgments by executing payment claims in movable property, causing the return of property and serving, on request by the parties, all notices and documents

---

[29] According to the statistics for 2014 provided by the Federal Bar Association (*Bundesrechtsanwaltskammer*) at http://www.brak.de/.

[30] See the homepage of the bar association of the attorneys at the Federal Court of Justice (BGH): http://www.rak-bgh.de/.

which are not performed by the court *ex officio*. Other court officers are in charge of all issues relating to court and attorney costs (*Kostenbeamte*).

V. Efficiency of the System

In terms of length of proceedings and cost, the German system of civil justice is quite efficient, at least when compared to many other countries.[31]

1. Duration of Proceedings

The average period of time between commencement and conclusion of an action is between 4.7 to 8.7 months at the trial level, and between 6.3 to 8.7 months at the first appellate level.[32] Of course, complex commercial cases may take substantially longer, in particular when involving time-consuming elements such as the taking of evidence abroad. Nevertheless, even in more complex cases, it is realistic to obtain a judgment from a court of first instance within one to two years as of commencing an action.

The reasons are manifold. The strict requirement of specific pleading and the absence of extensive discovery procedures tend to focus and limit the amount of facts presented to the court.[33] Further, German civil procedure law is designed to streamline the process and generally does not allow for delays by dwelling on technicalities. German judges are highly trained and are usually capable professionally. They are under an obligation to expedite the proceedings and play an active role in the proceedings. Court hearings are very limited in number and usually last not more than one to two hours, quite often even less. Without a substantial lay element, there are neither time-consuming jury selection procedures, nor lengthy attempts by attorneys in the hearings to impress the jurors. Finally, compared to other legal systems, the German civil law system allows the judge to find and apply the relevant law in a relatively efficient manner. This, however, is not to say that German court proceedings cannot be lengthy and tedious.

The general efficiency of the German courts in civil and commercial matters and their obligation to aim at an amicable settlement of the dispute between the parties are the main reasons why alternative dispute resolution techniques which are so common in Anglo-Saxon jurisdictions have not gained as much ground in Germany.[34]

2. Litigation Costs

a) Court Costs

The Court Fees Act (*Gerichtskostengesetz, GKG*) governs the fees and expenses charged by a German court.

The court fees are calculated on the basis of the value in dispute (*Streitwert*). The value in dispute is determined by evaluating the financial interest which the plaintiff is pursuing through the action. There are special statutory provisions

---

[31] There are new provisions for remedies, including remuneration, in case of excessively long proceedings, GVG §§ 198 *et seq.*

[32] *Cf.* the detailed statistics for 2013 provided by the Federal Statistical Office at https://www.destatis.de (https://www.destatis.de/DE/Publikationen/Thematisch/Rechtspflege/GerichteP-ersonal/Zivilgerichte2100210137004.pdf?__blob=publicationFile).

[33] ZPO § 253.

[34] See *infra*, at pp. 71 et seq.

and an extensive body of judicial precedents. With regard to monetary claims, the value of the matter usually equals the amount sought by the action. The value of a matter has, for the purpose of calculating the court fees, been capped at EUR 30 million. The plaintiff has to indicate the value in dispute when filing the action if he does not sue for a certain sum of money.[35]

The court fees for the proceedings in general are due with the filing of the action. The court will not serve the defendant with the statement of claim until these fees are paid[36] and will therefore demand prepayment by the plaintiff.[37] For this purpose, the court fixes the value in dispute preliminarily. The court then will determine the amount of one fee-unit (*eine Gebühr*) from a schedule annexed to the Court Fees Act. This amount is multiplied by the number of fee-units prescribed by law for the court's specific activities. Normal proceedings including a written judgment usually amount to three fee-units. When rendering its final decision, the court ultimately will determine the value in dispute for calculating the court fees.[38]

In addition, the court also charges for the expenses relating to the proceedings, such as the remuneration of witnesses or of court-appointed expert witnesses, or the cost for service of process made by the court. In case of a foreign defendant, the cost for translating the statement of claim is also included.

b) Attorney Fees

aa) Statutory Fees. Statutory attorney fees are based on the Federal Attorney Remuneration Act (*Rechtsanwaltsvergütungsgesetz, RVG*). As regards representation in court, the attorney fees are calculated in a manner similar to the court fees. The attorney will determine the value in dispute, which usually equals the value fixed by the court. The maximum value in dispute is capped also at EUR 30 million. If an attorney represents multiple parties, the respective value in dispute for each of these parties will be added up to a maximum of EUR 100 million.

Based on the value in dispute, the attorney will determine the amount of one fee-unit from a schedule annexed to the RVG.[39] The amount of one fee-unit is then multiplied by the number of fee-units the attorney is entitled to. For conducting the court proceedings, he receives 1.3 fee-units (*Verfahrensgebühr*). The fee for the court hearings and any meetings with the attorneys for the opponent is set at 1.2 fee-units (*Terminsgebühr*). If the parties reach a settlement after proceedings have been initiated, the settlement fee (*Einigungsgebühr*) is 1.0 fee-units.

Statutory fees charged by the attorney for extrajudicial advice relating to a matter can range from 0.5 to 2.5 fee-units (*Geschäftsgebühr*). More than 1.3 fee-units are justified if the matter is difficult and complex. If the same matter is litigated later, 50 % of these fees (up to a total amount of 0.75 fee-units) will be deducted from the fees accruing for the representation in the litigation.

In addition, an attorney may charge his client reasonable expenses.

bb) Negotiated Fees. It is common practice in litigation matters to negotiate attorney fees. However, fee arrangements tying the attorney's remuneration to

---

[35] GKG § 61.
[36] GKG § 12.
[37] See *infra*, at p. 53.
[38] GKG § 63 (2).
[39] The respective schedules to the Court Fees Act and to the Federal Attorney Remuneration Act differ slightly.

the success of the case are generally not allowed and are void under German law. However, after the Federal Constitutional Court declared in a decision in 2006 that such fee arrangements are unconstitutional,[40] German law now provides for an exception.[41] Fee arrangements tying remuneration to the success of the case are now allowed if the client would otherwise be deterred from proceedings because of his financial situation. The related statutory provisions set out in detail what such fee arrangements should contain. German law also explicitly allows for the payment of no fees or fees lower than the applicable statutory fees where a case has been unsuccessful.

Apart from that, an attorney may not charge negotiated fees for the representation of a client in court which are lower than the applicable statutory fees. However, negotiated fees which exceed the statutory fees are permissible. Engagement letters with German attorneys for litigation matters therefore often include a provision that even if negotiated fees are agreed upon, the attorney may need to charge the statutory fees as a minimum.

In complex civil and commercial matters, time-based fees are frequently agreed upon, which are sometimes capped. Time-based fees are sometimes agreed as "blended" rates (*i.e.* one single rate applies regardless of the qualification of the attorney who performs the work), or with a volume discount when the total amount of fees exceeds certain thresholds. Hourly rates in Germany generally are in the range between EUR 200.00 to EUR 770.00, depending on the reputation of the law firm and of the attorney handling the case.

While these rates may seem steep at first glance, it may be noted that litigation in Germany is generally much less costly than, for example, in the U.S. Even complex matters can usually be handled by a small team of attorneys, mostly due to the absence of extensive discovery proceedings and lengthy court hearings.

c) Reimbursement of Costs

In Germany, the unsuccessful party must pay the court cost. It must further reimburse its opponent's statutory attorney fees, but not any negotiated fees that exceed the statutory fees. Expenses incurred by the parties such as translation costs necessary to conduct the proceedings are to be reimbursed as well.

The amount of costs to be reimbursed is fixed by the court of first instance upon motion by one of the parties.[42] If a party is only successful in part, the court divides the cost *pro rata*. If a litigating party prevails in the proceedings, it can thus recover a substantial part, if not all, of its attorney fees.

d) Examples

Appendix 1 includes some examples of the court fees and statutory attorney fees for a model proceeding with regard to different values in dispute.

---

[40] Federal Constitutional Court (*Bundesverfassungsgericht*), Decision of 12 December 2006 (Docket No. 1 BvR 2576/04), Bundesverfassungsgerichtsentscheidungen, Vol. 117, p. 163-202.
[41] BRAO §49b (2), RVG §4a.
[42] ZPO §§ 103 *et seq.*

C. The Court System

I. Jurisdictional Branches

The German court system is divided into five distinct jurisdictional branches (*Gerichtsbarkeiten*):[43]
(i) the so-called "ordinary" courts (*ordentliche Gerichtsbarkeit*), which deal with civil and commercial matters (including insolvency matters) (*Zivilgerichtsbarkeit*) and with criminal matters (*Strafgerichtsbarkeit*);
(ii) the labor courts (*Arbeitsgerichtsbarkeit*);
(iii) the administrative courts (*Verwaltungsgerichtsbarkeit*);
(iv) the fiscal courts (*Finanzgerichtsbarkeit*); and
(v) the social courts (*Sozialgerichtsbarkeit*).

The courts in each of these jurisdictional branches have exclusive jurisdiction for disputes falling within their jurisdiction. Therefore, the civil courts as part of the "ordinary" jurisdictional branch exclusively deal with commercial and civil matters. However, a civil court also has supplemental jurisdiction to decide on issues arising in a civil lawsuit which, as a separate matter, would fall within the jurisdiction of a different jurisdictional branch.

II. The Civil Courts

Civil and commercial matters are dealt with by the civil courts. Different from the U.S., where parallel court systems exist on the federal and on the state levels, only one uniform court system is in place in Germany. The civil courts are organized as follows:

1. Entry-Level Courts

At the trial level, either the local court (*Amtsgericht*) or the regional court (*Landgericht*) has subject matter jurisdiction as the court of first instance.

a) Local Courts

The 650[44] local courts have jurisdiction for disputes involving claims of up to EUR 5,000.00, for landlord-tenant disputes, and for a number of other civil matters, in particular those relating to family law. Disputes at the local court level are heard and decided by a single professional judge.

b) Regional Courts

With some exceptions, the 116 regional courts have jurisdiction over all other entry-level matters. The regional courts are organized in chambers (*Kammern*) usually consisting of three professional judges. It however is the rule that also at the regional court level, a single professional judge hears and decides the case.

---

[43] Sometimes, the courts competent to hear patent disputes (*Patentgerichtsbarkeit*), disciplinary actions in the public sector (*Disziplinargerichtsbarkeit*), military criminal courts (*Wehrstrafgerichtsbarkeit*) and the constitutional courts (*Verfassungsgerichtsbarkeit*) are considered as separate jurisdictional branches.

[44] According to the statistics for 2014 provided by the Federal Ministry of Justice at http://www.bmjv.de/.

However, certain commercial matters *e.g.* in the areas of banking and finance, insurance, or corporate law are to be heard by the chamber.[45] Cases relating to other areas deemed to be complex may also be referred by the judge to the chamber.[46]

At the larger regional courts, there are chambers for commercial matters (*Kammern für Handelssachen*) consisting of one professional judge who sits together with two lay judges appointed from the business community. These chambers for commercial matters have jurisdiction over most commercial disputes. However, a new case falling within their general jurisdiction is referred to the competent chamber for commercial matters only upon motion by one party.[47] By refraining from a motion, the parties therefore may jointly decide to bring a matter to a regular chamber even if a chamber for commercial matters exists at the respective regional court.

Some of the larger regional courts have formed specialized chambers for certain kinds of disputes, such as intellectual property or banking and securities matters. These chambers are either organized as ordinary civil chambers or as chambers for commercial matters. The judges sitting at these specialized chambers often have an in-depth understanding of the legal as well as the business issues arising in disputes in their respective field of expertise.

2. First Appellate Level *(Berufung)*

Judgments of courts of the entry level may be appealed on issues of fact or law either to the competent regional court, or the respective higher regional court:

a) Regional Courts

As a general rule, decisions of the local courts may be appealed to a specialized chamber of the respective regional court (*Berufungskammer*). Appellate cases on this level will be heard and decided by three professional judges.

b) Higher Regional Courts

Jurisdiction for appeals against entry-level regional court decisions lies with the 24[48] higher regional courts (*Oberlandesgerichte*). Cases before the higher regional courts are usually heard and decided by a panel (*Senat*) consisting of three professional judges.

The higher regional courts also have entry-level jurisdiction for certain special matters, *e.g.* the recognition and enforcement of domestic and foreign arbitral awards.[49]

3. Second Appellate Level (*Revision*)

Judgments delivered on first appeal may be further appealed to the Federal Court of Justice (*Bundesgerichtshof, BGH*). The Federal Court of Justice is organized in panels (*Senate*) consisting of five professional judges.

---

[45] ZPO §§ 348, 348a.
[46] ZPO §§ 348 (3), 348a (2).
[47] GVG §§ 96 (1), 98 (1).
[48] According to the statistics for 2014 provided by the Federal Ministry for Justice at http://www.bmjv.de/.
[49] ZPO § 1062 (1). Higher regional courts also have jurisdiction for certain appeals involving international aspects, GVG § 119 (1) No. 1 lit. b, c.

III. Extraordinary Appeals

1. Federal Constitutional Court

The Federal Constitutional Court (*Bundesverfassungsgericht*) has jurisdiction over all matters related to the federal constitution, the GG. The fundamental principles of the organization, the structure and the competence of the Federal Constitutional Court are set out in the GG. The proceedings at the court are governed, *inter alia*, by a separate statute, the Code of the Federal Constitutional Court (*Bundesverfassungsgerichtsgesetz, BVerfGG*).[50]

The Federal Constitutional Court does not have the function of a general super-appellate court. However, a judgment may be appealed to the Federal Constitutional Court on the grounds of a violation of the fundamental guarantees on civil procedure contained in the GG.[51] In principle, a constitutional appeal (*Verfassungsbeschwerde*) may be lodged only after all other judicial remedies have been exhausted. An appeal is subject to acceptance proceedings designed to dismiss cases of little importance or with little hope of success. Less than 3 % of all constitutional appeals brought are accepted by the Federal Constitutional Court.

Judgments by the Federal Constitutional Court are legally binding, *inter alia*, on all other courts. If the Federal Constitutional Court finds a law to be unconstitutional or void, its decision acquires the force of law.

2. European Court of Justice

With regard to European Union legislation and certain European treaties such as the Lugano Convention 2007, the European Court of Justice has the ultimate jurisdiction regarding all disputes arising as to their implementation into German law, as well as to their interpretation by the German courts.[52]

In civil litigation, any German court may request an authoritative resolution by the European Court of Justice with regard to an unresolved question of European Union law which is material to the outcome of a pending case. The highest national appellate court to which an appeal may be brought must do so. The decisions of the European Court of Justice are binding on the German courts.

3. European Court of Human Rights

Germany is a signatory to the European Convention on Human Rights.[53] The European Court of Human Rights exercises jurisdiction over matters involving human rights guaranteed by the Convention. A party must first exhaust all available judicial appeals in Germany before a complaint may be brought to the European Court of Human Rights. The basis of a complaint would be that a party asserts a violation of a basic human right guaranteed by the European Convention on Human Rights by, *inter alia*, a German court. In principle, a decision by the European Court of Human Rights is binding on German parties and German courts.[54] However, this appeal only serves as a last resort and is rarely used in practice.

---

[50] An English translation is available at www.iuscomp.org/gla.
[51] See *supra*, at p. 3.
[52] See *Nagel/Gottwald*, Internationales Zivilprozessrecht, 7th ed., 2013, § 3 nos. 13 *et seq.*, also for the rather complex situation regarding the Lugano Convention 2007.
[53] Available in English at www.hri.org/docs/ECHR50.html.
[54] However, see Federal Constitutional Court (BVerfG), Decision of 14 October 2004 (Docket No. 2 BvR 1481/04), Neue Juristische Wochenschrift, 2004, p. 3407. The court ruled on 14 October

D. Jurisdiction

I. Overview: Jurisdiction, Applicable Law, Sovereign Immunity

1. Jurisdiction

When an action is filed with a German court, the court first determines the international jurisdiction (*internationale Zuständigkeit*) of the German courts. Further, the court decides whether the matter at hand falls within its jurisdictional branch (*Rechtswegzuständigkeit*). The court then determines whether the court itself or a different court has subject matter jurisdiction (*sachliche Zuständigkeit*), i.e. is competent to hear the case as the entry-level court, and whether or not it has local jurisdiction (*örtliche Zuständigkeit*). Finally, the court decides which judge or chamber is competent to hear the case according to the internal organization of the respective court (functional jurisdiction, *funktionelle Zuständigkeit*).

A court determines its jurisdiction on the basis of the facts and the law as pleaded at the time the matter becomes legally pending. If the relevant facts or the law change subsequently, this will not affect the jurisdiction of the court (*perpetuatio fori*).

2. Applicable Procedural Law

The applicable rules on jurisdiction in domestic disputes are mainly contained in the ZPO.[55]

If a case has an international element, the Brussels Regulation 2012 or the Lugano Convention 2007 may apply.[56] These rules are exclusive and do not allow the application of domestic German law concerning jurisdiction.

To the extent these international rules do not apply, it is well established in German law that the international jurisdiction of the German courts follows the domestic rules on local jurisdiction.[57]

3. Sovereign Immunity

German courts will not assume jurisdiction on certain disputes based on the principle of sovereign immunity.

The Federal Constitutional Court has explicitly acknowledged that Germany adheres to the international principles relating to the immunity of foreign states

---

2004, that a decision of the European Court of Human Rights has to be "taken into consideration" and to be weighed with the rights under the German constitution. The schematic "execution" of the European Court of Justice decision may be a violation of the German constitution.

[55] ZPO §§ 12 *et seq.*

[56] The European Union has ratified the Hague Convention on Choice of Court Agreements on 11 June 2015. The Convention entered into force on 1 October 2015, and applies to all member states of the European Union (except Denmark) and Mexico. Other signatories are Singapore and notably the United States, which however both have not ratified the Convention yet. In addition, Germany is a signatory to a number of international treaties which govern jurisdiction for specific areas such as transport law, *e.g.* the Warsaw Convention for the Unification of Certain Rules Relating to International Carriage by Air of 12 October 1929 or the Convention on the Contract for the International Carriage of Goods by Road (CMR) of 19 May 1956. In case of conflict, domestic German law is superseded by applicable international treaties.

[57] Federal Court of Justice (BGH), Decision of 17 December 1998 (Docket No. IX ZR 196/97), Neue Juristische Wochenschrift, 1999, p. 1395. German rules on local jurisdiction, therefore, have a "double function".

and their representatives from German jurisdiction.[58] Moreover, Germany is a signatory to a number of international treaties establishing immunity of foreign states and international organizations and their personnel.[59] A court would, therefore, dismiss an action brought against a foreign state or an international organization on these grounds.

However, commercial activities of foreign states or of international organizations and their respective personnel are not covered by immunity. Moreover, German courts are reluctant to grant immunity to subdivisions of a foreign state, and in particular to separate legal entities engaged in commercial activities such as state banks or wholly state-owned enterprises.[60]

II. Proper Jurisdictional Branch

A civil court needs to determine whether the matter at hand falls within its jurisdictional branch (*Rechtswegzuständigkeit*). Certain disputes, *e.g.* disputes relating to state liability or to competition law, are referred to the civil courts by specific legal rules. For all other disputes, the civil court must determine whether the matter is a "civil dispute" within the scope of GVG § 13. Usually, this is obvious. In case of doubt, the court relies on the vast body of precedents from other courts and the Federal Court of Justice on this issue.

If a court finds that it has no jurisdiction, it will determine *ex officio* which court in which jurisdictional branch is competent to hear the case, and will then transfer the case to that court. The court to which the case is transferred is bound by the decision of the transferring court as to what is the proper jurisdictional branch.

III. Exclusive Jurisdiction

The civil court will further determine whether the court itself or another court has exclusive international, subject matter and local jurisdiction for the matter at hand. Exclusive jurisdiction pre-empts all other jurisdiction. In particular, it is not possible for the parties to deviate from such jurisdiction by waiver or by agreement.

Exclusive jurisdiction under the Brussels Regulation 2012, the Lugano Convention 2007 and under German domestic law is established for disputes relating to real property, to land-lease agreements and for certain corporate matters.[61] Furthermore, the Brussels Regulation 2012 and the Lugano Convention 2007 confer exclusive jurisdiction on certain courts regarding public register matters and the enforcement of court judgments. Under German domestic law, main examples

---

[58] GVG § 20; Federal Constitutional Court (*Bundesverfassungsgericht*), Decision of 30 April 1963 (Docket No. 2 BvM 1/62), Bundesverfassungsgerichtsentscheidungen, Vol. 16, 1964, p. 27.

[59] GVG §§ 18 *et seq.*; Vienna Convention on Consular Relations of 24 April 1963, available at www.un.org/law/ilc/texts/consul.htm.; European Convention on State Immunity of 16 May 1972, available at http://conventions.coe.int/treaty/en/treaties/html/074.htm.

[60] See for example Regional Court (LG) Frankfurt, Decision of 2 December 1975 (Docket No. 3/8 O 186/75), Neue Juristische Wochenschrift, 1976, p. 1044; Federal Court of Justice (BGH), Decision of 7 June 1955 (Docket No. I ZR 64/53), Neue Juristische Wochenschrift, 1955, p. 1435; Higher Regional Court (OLG) Frankfurt, Decision of 4 May 1982 (Docket No. 5 U 202/81), Praxis des Internationalen Privat- und Verfahrensrechts, 1983, p. 68.

[61] Brussels Regulation 2012 Art. 24; Lugano Convention 2007 Art. 22; ZPO §§ 24, 29a; Law on Limited Liability Companies (*Gesetz betreffend die Gesellschaften mit beschränkter Haftung, GmbHG*) § 61(3); Stock Corporation Act (*Aktiengesetz, AktG*) § 246 (3).

for exclusive jurisdiction are disputes relating to environmental damage,[62] unfair competition[63] and insolvency matters.[64]

IV. Agreement on Jurisdiction

Unless there is exclusive jurisdiction, the Brussels Regulation 2012, the Lugano Convention 2007, the Convention on Choice of Court Agreements and German domestic law acknowledge agreements on jurisdiction (choice-of-forum agreements) between the parties as to international and local jurisdiction.[65] Provided the court which is agreed upon has entry-level jurisdiction for disputes of this kind, the agreement may also include subject-matter jurisdiction, *e.g.* agreeing on that the regional court has jurisdiction instead of the local court. The agreement on jurisdiction must relate to disputes arising from a particular legal relationship.

In cases where the Brussels Regulation 2012 or the Lugano Convention 2007 applies, an agreement on jurisdiction must be in writing or must be evidenced in writing. Alternatively, it must be in a form which accords with practices which the parties have established between themselves. In international trade or commerce, it is also sufficient if the form of the agreement accords with the common usage in the respective international trade or commerce of which the parties are, or ought to be, aware of. An agreement on jurisdiction governed by the Brussels Regulation 2012 or the Lugano Convention 2007 is presumed to confer exclusive jurisdiction.

Under domestic German law, no requirements as to form apply to an agreement on jurisdiction if the parties qualify as "merchants" (*Kaufleute*), *i.e.* either have a certain minimum commercial organization and structure or are registered in the German commercial register (*Handelsregister*).[66] If they are not, the agreement must be explicit and in writing and must have been entered into after the dispute arose. There is no presumption under German law that an agreement on jurisdiction is exclusive.

V. Jurisdiction by Failure to Raise an Objection

Under the Brussels Regulation 2012, the Lugano Convention 2007 and German domestic law,[67] a defendant's appearance in court without objecting to the court's jurisdiction will generally give that court international and local jurisdiction over him by way of (deemed) submission.

German civil courts regularly order preliminary written proceedings in preparation for the first oral hearing.[68] Under German domestic law, an objection to a court's jurisdiction is not deemed to have been waived by a failure to raise such an objection in these written proceedings.[69] Even a defendant who explicitly states in his written pleading that he does not intend to object to jurisdiction is not bound by this declaration and may nevertheless raise a jurisdictional objection in the

---

[62] ZPO §32a.
[63] UWG §14.
[64] Insolvency Code (*Insolvenzordnung, InsO*) §180 (1).
[65] Brussels Regulation 2012 Art. 25; Lugano Convention 2007 Art. 23; Convention on Choice of Courts Agreements, Art. 1 *et seq.*; ZPO §§38, 40.
[66] *Cf.* HGB §§1 *et seq.*
[67] Brussels Regulation 2012 Art. 26; Lugano Convention 2007 Art. 24; ZPO §§39, 40.
[68] See *infra*, at p. 55.
[69] *Vollkommer* in: Zöller, Zivilprozessordnung, 30th ed., 2014, §39 no. 8.

oral hearing.[70] When objecting to jurisdiction at the hearing, however, the party must clarify that its appearance is only made for the purpose of objecting to the court's jurisdiction.

VI. General and/or Special Jurisdiction

1. General Jurisdiction

Under the Brussels Regulation 2012, the Lugano Convention 2007 and German domestic law, general jurisdiction over a dispute is determined by the defendant's domicile.[71] The courts at the place of the defendant's domicile have international, subject matter and local jurisdiction.

2. Special Jurisdiction

Special jurisdiction relates to particular circumstances which provide an alternative forum. There are numerous provisions under the Brussels Regulation 2012, the Lugano Convention 2007 and German domestic law which confer international and local jurisdiction on certain courts. The most important ones are:
(i) for disputes arising out of contracts, the court of the place of performance of the obligation in dispute, the place of performance to be determined in accordance with the applicable substantive law,[72]
(ii) with respect to torts, the courts both at the place in which the tort was committed and at the place where the damage occurred,[73] and
(iii) with regard to all activities directly conducted from the establishment or branch of a business and regardless of whether the branch is a separate legal entity, the court where the establishment or branch is located.[74]

3. In Particular: Long-Arm Jurisdiction

Lawsuits concerning monetary claims against a person with no domicile in Germany come within the jurisdiction of the German court in whose district the non-domiciliary's property is located.[75] This jurisdiction conferred upon the court does not only relate to local jurisdiction, but also to international jurisdiction.[76]

According to its literal wording, ZPO § 23 contains no minimum requirements as to the value of the prospective defendant's property or any other connection of the dispute to Germany. However, the Federal Court of Justice has repeatedly held that for a German court to assume jurisdiction based on this provision, the subject matter of the dispute must have a "sufficient domestic link" (*hinreichender Inlandsbezug*) to Germany,[77] thereby limiting the otherwise wide wording of ZPO

---

[70] Federal Court of Justice (BGH), Decision of 19 February 2013 (Docket No. X ARZ 507/12), Neue Juristische Wochenschrift Rechtsprechungsreport (NJW-RR) 2013, pp. 764 *et seq.*
[71] Brussels Regulation 2012 Art. 4; Lugano Convention 2007 Art. 2; ZPO § 13.
[72] Brussels Regulation 2012 Art. 7 No. 1; Lugano Convention 2007 Art. 5 No. 1; ZPO § 29.
[73] Brussels Regulation 2012 Art. 7 No. 2; Lugano Convention 2007 Art. 5 No. 3; ZPO § 32.
[74] Brussels Regulation 2012 Art. 7 No. 5; Lugano Convention 2007 Art. 5 No. 5; ZPO § 21.
[75] ZPO § 23.
[76] Federal Court of Justice (BGH), Decision of 28 October 1996 (Docket No. X ARZ 1071/96), Neue Juristische Wochenschrift, 1997, p. 325; *Vollkommer* in: Zöller, Zivilprozessordnung, 30th ed., 2014, § 23 no. 1.
[77] Federal Court of Justice (BGH), Decision of 24 April 1996 (Docket No. IV ZR 263/95), Neue Juristische Wochenschrift, 1996, p. 2096.

§ 23. German courts have found that a sufficient domestic link exists, for example, where the plaintiff was a German resident, where contract negotiations took place in Germany, or where contractual obligations of one of the parties were to be performed in Germany.

ZPO § 23 allows jurisdiction to be exercised over foreign defendants in Germany in many cases. It has to be noted, however, that many countries do not recognize judgments based on such "exorbitant" jurisdiction. The Lugano Convention 2007 explicitly stipulates that ZPO § 23 is not applicable to disputes between nationals of European Union Member States in main proceedings (*Hauptsacheverfahren*).[78] ZPO § 23 is also excluded under the Brussels Regulation 2012.[79] However, jurisdiction in attachment or injunctive relief proceedings may be based on this provision.[80]

VII. Multiple Jurisdiction and Lack of Jurisdiction

If the German courts do not have international jurisdiction, the court to which the action was addressed will render a judgment dismissing the case on these grounds. If the court finds the German courts competent to hear the case, and provided no foreign court has been seized earlier, it will assume jurisdiction even if the courts of another country may also have jurisdiction.

As regards subject matter jurisdiction, only one specific German court can be the competent court of first instance. If the court seized of the matter concludes that it lacks subject matter jurisdiction, it will notify the parties accordingly. Upon motion by the plaintiff, the court will transfer the case to the court competent to hear the case.[81]

If more than one court has local jurisdiction *e.g.* because of general or special jurisdiction or multiple domiciles of a defendant, the plaintiff may choose the court in which he would prefer to commence the action.[82] The right to choose is irrevocably exercised when an action brought by the plaintiff to one of the competent courts becomes legally pending, or upon motion by a plaintiff to a court not having local jurisdiction to transfer the case to a different court having local jurisdiction, as specified by the plaintiff.

If a statement of claim is addressed to the proper court, but to one of its judges or its chambers, who is not competent to hear the case according to the internal organization of the court (functional jurisdiction), the judge or chamber so addressed will transfer the complaint to the competent judge or chamber *ex officio*.

VIII. Jurisdiction Determined by a Superior Court

In certain circumstances, the court competent to hear the case is determined by the superior court upon motion by one of the parties.[83] A frequent example is

---

[78] Lugano Convention 2007 3 (2), Annex I.
[79] According to the notification by Germany under Brussels Regulation 2012 Art. 76; see the European e-justice Portal at https://e-justice.europa.eu/content_brussels_i_regulation_recast-350-de-en.do?init=true&member=1.
[80] Brussels Regulation 2012 Art. 35; Lugano Convention 2007 Art. 31.
[81] ZPO § 281.
[82] ZPO § 35.
[83] ZPO §§ 36, 37.

when a lawsuit is directed against multiple defendants for which there is no joint subject matter or local jurisdiction.

IX. Forum Shopping and *Lis Pendens*

Under German domestic law, a German court must dismiss an action as inadmissible if another lawsuit with identical parties and identical subject matter (*gleicher Streitgegenstand*) is pending in another German or foreign court (*lis pendens, anderweitige Rechtshängigkeit*).[84]

Under the Brussels Regulation 2012 as well as under the Lugano Convention 2007, a court must stay its proceedings if a lawsuit between the same parties concerning the same subject matter is pending in a court of another member state. Once the court first seized has established its jurisdiction the court later seized has to decline its own.[85]

According to German domestic law, a matter is "pending" only after the statement of claim has been served on the defendant by the court.[86] However, under the laws of many countries such as, *e.g.*, the U.S., a matter is pending upon filing the claim with the court.[87] This discrepancy as to the point in time a court action is deemed to be "pending" allows for so-called "torpedoes" when a defendant whose opponent has already filed a statement of claim with a German court could file a "negative" action involving the same parties and the same subject matter with a competent court in another jurisdiction to avoid the jurisdiction of the German courts.

While such "torpedo" actions may be possible in some countries, they are limited in the EU under the Brussels Regulation 2012 and the Lugano Convention 2007, which provide that for an action to become "pending", it is sufficient that the statement of claim has been filed, so long as service upon the defendant(s) follows in a timely manner.[88] In addition, with regard to jurisdiction based on an agreement conferring exclusive jurisdiction on a court, the Brussels Regulation 2012 establishes an exemption to the basic *lis pendens* rule in order to further limit such "torpedo" tactics. If not only the court designated in the agreement to have exclusive jurisdiction is seized by a party but also another court, the latter court is required to stay its proceedings until the court designated in the agreement has ruled on its jurisdiction, no matter which court was seized first. If the court designated in the agreement establishes its jurisdiction, the other court must decline jurisdiction.[89] Otherwise, the other court may proceed. There are certain restrictions to this rule, however. Agreements on jurisdiction are void in insurance, consumer and employment matters.[90] Overall, the Brussels Regulation 2012 and the Lugano Convention 2007 have reduced the number of "torpedoes" significantly.

However, it is often still possible for a party expecting litigation in Germany as a defendant to commence an action in a court within a jurisdiction where the duration of court proceedings is extremely long. The favorites in Europe are Italy and, to a lesser degree, Belgium. Even if the action filed by the party in the foreign

---

[84] ZPO § 261 (§) No. 1.
[85] Brussels Regulation 2012 Art. 29; Lugano Convention 2007 Art. 27.
[86] ZPO § 261 (1).
[87] The same was true under the Lugano Convention 1988 and the Brussels Convention.
[88] Brussels Regulation 2012 Art. 32; Lugano Convention 2007 Art. 30.
[89] Brussels Regulation 2012 Art. 31 (2), (3).
[90] Brussels Regulation 2012 Art. 31 (4).

court is ultimately dismissed by that foreign court for lack of jurisdiction or for other reasons, the process may take many years, and may induce the opponent to settle the case on terms it would otherwise not agree to.[91]

X. Challenges to Jurisdiction

1. Forum Non Conveniens

Different from the U.S., the concept of *forum non conveniens* is not accepted in Germany. From a German perspective, it seems not to be in line with fundamental principles on jurisdiction to grant a court discretion whether to accept or to deny jurisdiction in cases where statutory law provides for jurisdiction of the German courts. Therefore, if a German court has jurisdiction, it must hear the case.

Furthermore, the consolidation of two lawsuits by court order is admissible only if they are pending at the same court.[92] Accordingly, German courts will not apply Art. 30 (2) of the Brussels Regulation 2012 or Art. 28 (2) of the Lugano Convention 2007, which, on motion of one of the parties, gives a court discretion whether or not to assume jurisdiction on a matter connected to a lawsuit already pending at another court if that other court is a German court.[93]

2. Anti-Suit Injunctions

German courts also do not give effect to anti-suit injunctions rendered by foreign courts.[94] German courts view foreign anti-suit injunctions as a violation of German sovereignty. Accordingly, preliminary injunctions aiming to prevent anti-suit injunctions ("counter-injunctions") are also not admissible in German courts.

Likewise, the European Court of Justice has acknowledged (for the Brussels Convention) that courts must not order anti-suit injunctions against proceedings in other states which are contracting parties.[95] The same reasoning must also apply to the Brussels Regulation 2012 and the Lugano Convention 2007.[96]

Although European and German law is clear on that point, things may be different in practice. Even if anti-suit injunctions do not take effect in Germany, a party violating a foreign injunction may be subject to coercive measures and to liability in the country where the anti-suit injunction was rendered. This will often force a party to comply with the foreign injunction.

---

[91] *Cf. Watt*, Avoiding an Unfavorable Forum: A Civilian Perspective, International Litigation News, 2004, p. 10 *et seq*. The European Court of Justice has upheld this practice for the Brussels Convention and found in favor of the *lis pendens* rule even if the parties had exclusively agreed upon another forum, *Erich Gasser GmbH ./. MISAT Srl.*, Decision of 9 December 2003, (Docket No. C-116/02), ECR 2003 I-14693, the decision is available at www.curia.europa.eu; *cf. Hibbert/Hardy*, Jurisdiction: the ECJ Tightens the Grip, International Litigation News, 2004, p. 51.

[92] ZPO § 147.

[93] *Cf. Geimer* in: Zöller, Zivilprozessordnung, 30th ed., 2014, Annex I EuGVVO Art. 28 no. 8.

[94] Higher Regional Court (OLG) Düsseldorf, Decision of 10 January 1996 (Docket No. 3 VA 11/95), Praxis des Internationalen Privat- und Verfahrensrechts 1997, p. 260.

[95] *Turner v. Grovit*, Decision of 27 April 2004 (Docket No. C-159/02), ECR 2004 I-03565; the decision is available at http://curia.europa.eu/, *cf. Hibbert/Hardy*, Jurisdiction: the ECJ Tightens the Grip, International Litigation News, 2004, p. 51.

[96] *Cf.*, for the Brussels Regulation 2001, ECJ [*Allianz SpA and Generali Assicurazioni Generali SpA v West Tankers Inc. ("West Tankers")*], Decision of 10 February 2009 (Docket No. C-185/07), ECR 2009 I-00663; the decision is available at http://curia.europa.eu/.

XI. Reference to a Valid Arbitration Agreement

Each of the parties may challenge the court's jurisdiction by reference to a valid arbitration agreement binding both parties (*Einwand der Schiedsabrede*). Such reference has to be submitted to the court before the first oral hearing. Otherwise the party's willingness to appear in the oral hearing will be deemed an acknowledgment of the court's jurisdiction.[97] If the defense of an existing arbitration agreement is raised in a timely manner, the court will have to examine the arbitration agreement in detail and decide on its validity. If the arbitration agreement is binding on both parties, the court is under the obligation to dismiss the action as not admissible in the state courts. This is explicitly confirmed by the Brussels Regulation 2012.[98]

E. Pleading in German Litigation

Pleading in German civil litigation, and in particular the style, length and contents of the pleading, is very different *e.g.* from U.S. style "notice pleading":

I. The Method of "Comparative Analysis"

The key to understanding German civil litigation are the concepts of "conclusiveness" (*Schlüssigkeit*) and "relevance" (*Erheblichkeit*). These are parts of a three-step technique used by the courts and known as the "comparative analysis" (*Relationstechnik*) to identify those disputed facts "at issue" of a case that are critical to its outcome. By using this method, the court limits the issues on which evidence will be taken.

The judge first accepts (for analytical purposes only) the truth of the plaintiff's factual allegations and analyzes whether those facts, in combination with the uncontested facts, make out a *prima facie* case. A plaintiff will base his claim and the relief sought on the relevant legal provisions. These legal provisions implicitly contain certain factual prerequisites. For example, a plaintiff requesting payment of the purchase price out of a sales contract relies on BGB § 433 (2). This provision stipulates that the buyer shall pay the purchase price agreed upon by the parties in the sales contract. The factual prerequisites are, therefore, that the parties entered into a sales contract by a manner of conduct constituting an offer and acceptance,[99] and that they agreed on a certain purchase price. The plaintiff must state these factual elements in his statement of claim. A judge will analyze the submissions of the plaintiff and determine whether they are "conclusive" (*schlüssig*). This means that, assuming the facts stated are proven, all elements of a claim under BGB § 433 (2) are met.

In a second step, the judge then assumes the truth of the defendant's factual allegations and assesses whether those facts, again in combination with all uncontested facts, rebut any or all of the claims made by the plaintiff, or constitute a valid defense. Apart from accepting or contesting the facts brought forward by

---

[97] ZPO § 1032 (1).
[98] Brussels Regulation 2012, recital 12.
[99] Validly entering into a contract under German law requires only offer and assent, but not consideration.

the plaintiff, the defendant may also introduce new facts. If the defendant raises, for example, the defense that he has already paid the purchase price, he must state the facts as to when and how such payment was made. A judge will apply a test similar to that in regard to the plaintiff's submissions also to the statements of the defendant in order to determine whether they are "relevant" (*erheblich*) for deciding the case. This means, assuming the facts relied upon by the defendant are proven, the defendant would be successful under the law, either because the factual prerequisites of the plaintiff's claim are not met, or the defendant states facts that fulfill all prerequisites of a valid defense.

If the plaintiff's submission is found to be inconclusive, and if upon request by the court he fails to provide the additional facts necessary to remedy his submission, the court will decide the case without further discussion. In the worst case, a plaintiff's complaint may be dismissed as "inconclusive" even before the defendant has submitted a statement of defense. Similarly, defenses of the defendant are not further considered if they are "irrelevant".

In a third step, the judge derives from these first two steps those contested facts that the outcome of the case depends on, *i.e.* which facts at issue are "relevant" for the resolution of the case. The court will determine which party has the burden of proof for the respective facts at issue, and which means of evidence have been offered by such party (as well as any counter-evidence offered by the opponent). As to documentary evidence, the court will assess the documents submitted as evidence and form an opinion thereon. As to witness testimony or expert opinions, the court will list the respective facts at issue in a procedural order, will order the witnesses to appear in court, and/or will select and instruct a suitable expert to provide a written expert opinion and subsequently to appear in court for questioning.

II. Submissions and Pleading

1. Principle of Oral Procedure and the Differing Practice

The test of "conclusiveness" and "relevance", as well as the method of "comparative analysis" in general, is a highly sophisticated procedure designed to streamline the proceedings and to avoid unnecessary submissions of fact or unnecessary taking of evidence. The basis on which this procedure is applied is mainly the written pleadings by the parties. Therefore, the contents of the submissions prepared and submitted to the court by the parties are of crucial importance.

According to the principle of oral procedure underlying the ZPO, the only purpose of the parties' submissions contained in their written pleadings is to prepare the court and the opponent for the oral hearing. Theoretically, the attorneys will plead the contents of their submissions as well as further arguments orally in open court, even if all these components have already been submitted in writing.[100] In practice, the contents of the submissions made in their written pleadings are deemed to be pleaded in the oral hearing by way of reference even if they are not mentioned at all. Although there is, in fact, some discussion in the oral hearing, the contents of the submissions made in the written pleadings will, therefore, be determinative for the outcome of the lawsuit.

---

[100] ZPO §§ 128 (1), 129.

In practice, this means that many cases have already been decided when the attorneys appear for the first oral hearing. Frequently, the judges have a draft judgment in hand when entering the court room.

2. Number and Timeliness of Submissions

In addition to the statement of claim (*Klageschrift*) and the defendant's statement of defense (*Klageerwiderung*), the parties may submit further written pleadings. There is no strict limitation to the number of written pleadings that each party may prepare. In practice, the plaintiff usually comments on the statement of defense, and the defendant will sometimes reply to these comments.

The parties are, however, required to submit their written pleadings to the court in a timely manner prior to the oral hearing.[101] The court will also set time limits for the submission of written pleadings.[102] The court usually will set a time limit of two weeks for the defendant to declare whether he intends to defend himself against the action. If the statement of claim has to be served abroad, the court will set an appropriate time limit. Furthermore, the court will set a time limit of at least two further weeks for filing the statement of defense, usually more. The court may also set a time limit of at least two weeks for the plaintiff to respond to the statement of defense and may set further time limits as appropriate. Failure to observe these time limits may result in the contents of the written pleadings filed in an untimely manner being rejected by the court.[103]

3. Contents of Submissions

a) Statement of Facts

In principle,[104] a German civil court does not investigate the facts relevant to the case. The production of the facts is left to the parties (*Beibringungsgrundsatz*). The parties are required to state all the facts on which their claim or defense is based in their submissions in a concise and clear manner.[105]

With regard to pleading the facts, the statements made by the parties must be truthful and complete (*Wahrheitspflicht*).[106] This obligation to make a complete and truthful pleading, however, only prohibits intentionally false statements and intentional omissions of relevant facts. Violations of this obligation may be a criminal offence under German law.

The burden of submitting the facts (*Darlegungslast*) generally is on the party which bases its claim or defense on these facts. As there are only limited obligations to disclose information under German law, a party must rely mainly on its own sources and on publicly available information in order to state its case.

The law, however, allows the pleading of certain facts as true, even if the respective party has little evidence to support its assertion. It may, for example, be sufficient to state only general observations indicating certain facts or to provide reasonable assumptions. If the opponent typically has better knowledge of particular facts, the opponent's response must then be more precise and must rebut

---

[101] ZPO § 132.
[102] ZPO §§ 276 *et seq.*
[103] ZPO § 296 (1).
[104] See, also for exceptions, *Hartmann* in: Baumbach/Lauterbach/Albers/Hartmann, Zivilprozessordnung, 73rd ed., 2015, Foundations before § 128 no. 20 *et seq.*
[105] ZPO §§ 130, 131, 138.
[106] ZPO § 138 (1).

the factual allegations in a more detailed way (*sekundäre Darlegungslast*). In certain cases where specific information relevant to the litigation is typically not available to one party but is available to its opponent, the burden of providing the facts may shift (*Umkehr der Darlegungslast*).

In practice, pleading the relevant facts, and pleading them in sufficient detail, is quite a complex exercise.

b) Specifying Evidence

The party which has the burden of submitting the relevant facts for its case usually also has the burden of proof (*Beweislast*). If a factual allegation is disputed, the party having the burden of proof needs to explicitly set out in a submission by way of which evidence it intends to prove the respective fact (motion to take specific evidence, *Beweisantrag*).[107]

In practice, the parties specify in their written pleadings the evidence they intend to rely on. The opponent's opportunity to assess the evidence offered and to decide whether it is worthwhile to dispute certain facts is meant to avoid unnecessary disputing of facts and thus streamlines the proceedings. Since many factual allegations will not be disputed by the opponent and since the court will use the method of "comparative analysis", very little of the evidence specified by the parties in their submissions will be actually taken by the court.

If a disputed statement of fact is relevant to the outcome of the case, *i.e.* is "at issue", the judge is bound to admit and to order the taking of the evidence offered in a submission.

c) Pleading the Law

The German system of civil justice is based on the assumption that the court knows the law. Therefore, the parties have to provide only the facts. At least in theory, legal reasoning by the parties is not necessary.

However, a party is well advised to set out at least briefly the legal concepts it relies on in the litigation. As outlined above,[108] the legal concept underlying a claim or defense determines what facts a party needs to plead, and ultimately, what evidence needs to be taken. Very often it may be sufficient for a party to just point out the respective statutory provisions. In complex cases involving rarely used concepts of law, in matters where the law may not be easy to find, or where the law is not sufficiently clear, a detailed argument on issues of law citing precedents and legal authors is advisable and common. In high stakes litigation, legal opinions by leading law professors setting out the applicable law are frequently used.

4. Length and Style of Submissions

The length and style of submissions vary, according to personal preference and sometimes to local practice.

Courts generally do not favor submissions which are very aggressive in style. Personal attacks on opposing counsel are frowned upon, in particular in proceedings at the higher regional courts. However, litigation by its nature is adversarial, and a certain aggressiveness in substance and in tone is common.

---

[107] ZPO §§ 130 No. 5, 371, 373, 420, 445.
[108] See *supra*, at p. 22 et seq.

Written pleadings may vary in length from a few pages to several hundred pages, accompanied by sometimes large amounts of exhibits.[109] There is quite some debate among lawyers in Germany as to the proper length of written pleadings. On the one hand, the concept of "conclusiveness" and the method of "comparative analysis" only require that the essential facts be stated. On the other hand, it is quite often not clear before the judgment is rendered what will be deemed by the court to be relevant. Furthermore, it may require some elaboration to properly establish the essential facts and to put them into context. There is no provision that allows a German court to set a maximum length for written proceedings.[110]

F. Fact-Finding prior to Commencing Action

I. General

In the U.S., a party may commence litigation with only a vague idea of the facts of the case. The pleadings submitted by the parties describe the subject matter of the case only in very vague notions. The facts are then established during extensive pre-trial discovery.

In contrast, a plaintiff in German courts needs to submit a conclusive written pleading setting out the relevant facts and stating the evidence which the party intends to rely on. A party, therefore, needs to gather most of the facts relevant for making its case prior to commencing a court action.

This is somewhat mitigated by the fact that it is admissible to plead certain facts as true even if the party has little evidence that they are. A party may, therefore, try to substantiate such allegations in more detail and to prove them in the course of the proceedings. However, the basic principle remains that a party needs to gather the relevant facts to the greatest possible extent prior to commencing an action. The ways and means to this end are set out in the following sections.

II. Exploring the Information Available to the Party

1. Review of Documents, Physical Inspections and Interviews

The preparation of a case will start with a review of all documents and electronically stored data available to the party. The preparation will further include searching the internet, using publicly available databases such as newspaper archives etc., and obtaining information from trade associations or professional organizations active in the respective field.

Sometimes, a physical inspection *e.g.* of a particular site will be helpful. Interviews of employees and of third parties concerned with the matter will be conducted.

---

[109] ZPO § 131.
[110] *Cf.* Higher Regional Court (OLG) Frankfurt, Decision of 20 September 2007 (Docket No. 22 W 41/07), Neue Juristische Wochenschrift Rechtsprechungsreport 2008, p. 1080.

2. Use of Commercial Information Providers

Additional information, in particular relating to the financial situation of a commercial entity, may be obtained by accessing private databases compiled by business information providers such as Dun & Bradstreet,[111] Creditreform[112] or Bürgel.[113] These databases usually contain information on the legal structure, the corporate officers and main shareholders, and the financial situation of commercial entities. Information on the major assets as well as data regarding the key information from the annual accounts are usually also available. These databases are generally quite comprehensive but often not entirely up to date.

Where appropriate, private investigators may be used for specialized research and assistance, *e.g.* with regard to asset search and recovery.

3. Use of Outside Experts

A party may commission outside experts to give their opinion on certain factual issues and to help clarify technical or business issues relevant to the dispute.

Commissioning forensic accountants in complex corporate and commercial matters is quite common. The German operations of the large accounting firms have set up separate forensic services departments. There is also a number of smaller auditing firms specializing in litigation-related work. Large law firms in Germany usually have either in-house capability in this area or established working contacts with outside experts.

The German Chambers of Commerce (*Industrie- und Handelskammern*) compile lists of certified experts for basically every conceivable area of expertise.[114] Other experts can be found via the respective trade associations.

4. Public Registers

A German peculiarity is the various public registers containing a host of potentially useful information for a prospective litigant.

a) Registers to Determine Domicile

Different from *e.g.* the U.S., the domicile of a person resident in Germany can in many cases be located via the reporting register or the postal service:

The German municipalities keep a reporting register (*Melderegister*) of all citizens domiciled in their city or within their township limits at their reporting office (*Meldestelle*). Since it is an administrative offense under German law not to register, most people do. A person is under a legal obligation to report his new address to the reporting office whenever he moves house. The information registered with the reporting office is open to the public. Anybody has the right to request the address of a third person without the need to show a justifiable interest to get that address. If information on an earlier domicile is available, it may therefore be possible to locate the current domicile of a person.

In addition, the German postal service provides the current postal address of any person or legal entity upon request.

---

[111] http://www.dnb.com.
[112] http://www.creditreform.de.
[113] http://buergel.de.
[114] To be found at http://svv.ihk.de.

b) Company Registers

Company registers kept at the local courts at the seats of commercial entities are useful for obtaining legal and financial information.

The most important source is the commercial register (*Handelsregister*). It provides up-to-date information on most commercial entities. It contains information on the legal form of an entity (*e.g.* sole proprietorship, corporation or partnership), on structural changes (*e.g.* mergers), on past and present corporate officers, on shareholders and on whether the entity is in liquidation.

In addition, companies have to submit corporate information, such as their articles of association, lists of shareholders, agreements on mergers and, in particular, their annual accounts, to the commercial register. If certain information on a commercial entity such as annual accounts are not available at the register, anybody may request that the local court enforces submission of such information to the register by coercive penalties.

Most of this information can be researched electronically either via the common register portal of the German federal states at www.handelsregister.de or via commercial databases.

Any person has the right to inspect these documents and to request copies. For certain additional information contained in the files kept at the local court, a party requesting inspection needs to show a justifiable interest (*berechtigtes Interesse*) in the contents, *e.g.* an economic or scientific interest.

Similar public registers exist for cooperatives (register of cooperatives, *Genossenschaftsregister*), for registered associations (register of associations, *Vereinsregister*) and for certain partnerships (register of partnerships, *Partnerschaftsregister*). The inspection rights are similar to those concerning the commercial register. These registers are also part of the above mentioned common register portal of the German federal states.

Searching these registers and analyzing the information obtained quite often result in an accurate picture of the corporate structure and the legal and financial situation of a commercial entity.

c) Debtors' Register

In addition, financial information may be obtained by inspecting the debtors' register (*Schuldnerverzeichnis*). The provisions concerning the debtors' register have been subject to a major reform effective 1 January 2013.[115]

The register now lists, among others, debtors who did not comply with their duty to provide information of their assets to the bailiff,[116] debtors who, according to the information provided, do not have sufficient assets to pay the debt owed, debtors who did not indicate within one month after providing information on their assets that they paid their debt to the creditor, and debtors whose insolvency proceedings were dismissed because of insufficient assets.[117]

This information is available to everybody who needs it for, *inter alia*, execution purposes or simply to avoid economic disadvantages which may occur if the debtor is not complying with his obligations to pay.[118] The information may only be used for the purpose for which it was provided.

---

[115] See *supra*, at p. 4.
[116] See *infra*, at pp. 106 et seq.
[117] ZPO §§ 882b, 882c.
[118] ZPO §§ 882 *et seq.*

There is one debtors' register in every federal state at a specified local court. All registers can be accessed via a common electronic portal of the German federal states at www.vollstreckungsportal.de.

d) Land, Ship, Aircraft and Matrimonial Property Registers

All real property in Germany is listed in the land register (*Grundbuch*) kept at the local courts. The owner of a specified plot of real property can be determined by investigating the land register. Further, the land register lists all public and private charges on real property and is thus helpful for estimating the value of real property. However, the right of inspection is subject to the applicant demonstrating a justifiable interest (*berechtigtes Interesse*) in obtaining the information sought. The land registers in every federal state can also be accessed electronically via a common internet portal at www.grundbuch-portal.de. However, there are special prerequisites for participating in these so-called automatic proceedings.[119]

Similar information concerning ships can be found in the ship register (*Schiffsregister*), and concerning aircraft, in the aircraft register (*Luftfahrzeugrolle*) and the register for liens on aircraft (*Register für Pfandrechte an Luftfahrzeugen*). Various restrictions apply with regard to access to these registers.[120]

As regards the matrimonial property relation, information may be obtained from the marriage property register (*Güterrechtsregister*) kept at the local courts. This register is open to the public. An inspection may be useful for assessing the financial situation of a prospective opponent in litigation.

III. Using Inspection Rights for Files kept at Public Authorities

1. Files at Regulatory Authorities

There is a vast number of regulatory and administrative authorities in Germany. Their files may also contain information which is useful for a party preparing for civil litigation.

a) Information Rights under Federal and State Freedom of Information Acts

As of January 1, 2006, the federal Freedom of Information Act (*Informationsfreiheitsgesetz, IFG*)[121] was enacted. The IFG establishes a general right to obtain information from federal public authorities. Most of the German federal states, but not all of them, have in the meantime enacted similar statutes applying to the respective state's public authorities. The IFG as well as the state statutes may be used to gain information about private third parties.

Under the IFG, everyone is entitled to make a request for information kept at all federal public authorities. There is no requirement to have a specific interest. However, the right to request information is limited by certain exemptions which mainly aim to protect the public interest. These include an exemption for information subject to secrecy obligations under statutory provisions or administrative

---

[119] *Grundbuchordnung (GBO)* §133.
[120] Federal Air Traffic Act (*Luftverkehrsgesetz, LuftVG*) §64 (8).
[121] Freedom of Information Act (*Informationsfreiheitsgesetz des Bundes, IFG*) §1; an English translation of the act is available at www.gesetze-im-internet.de.

regulations.[122] Furthermore, there are exemptions to protect the decision-making process of the public authorities, to protect personal data as well as data on intellectual property rights and on trade secrets. In practice, requests for information held by the German Federal Financial Supervisory Authority (*Bundesanstalt für Finanzdienstleistungsaufsicht, BaFin*) have proven to be of special interest.

The public authority at which the information is kept will decide on whether or not the requested information, in full or in part, will be disclosed. The decision of the respective public authority can be challenged in the administrative courts.

b) Information Rights under General Administrative Law

Insofar as the freedom of information legislation does not apply, only the parties to the administrative proceedings to which the files relate generally have the right to inspect such files. However, certain administrative proceedings may affect, even if only remotely, the legal rights of a plaintiff or defendant in a civil case. In such a case a non-party may, upon its own motion or by order of the respective authority, formally become a party to the administrative proceedings.

However, the right even of a party to inspect the files has limitations. It does not extend to information the disclosure of which is contrary to the reasonable interest of one or all of the parties to the administrative proceedings or of third parties. In particular, the right to inspect the files does not extend to trade secrets.

It is up to the respective public authority to decide which parts of the files, if any, will be available for inspection. Such decision can be challenged in the administrative courts as well.

2. Files in the Criminal Justice System

a) Inspection Rights

Quite often the facts underlying a civil lawsuit may also constitute a criminal offense, such as fraud or other business crimes.

The German public prosecutor's office (*Staatsanwaltschaft*) is under a legal obligation to start investigations when notified of reasonable suspicions of a crime having been committed. In the course of these investigations and due to his special powers, the public prosecutor will collect a host of information relating to the matter. The files containing this information will be kept at the public prosecutor's office. Once the public prosecutor indicts the person charged with the crime, the court of criminal justice will take over the files.

A person planning, or a party engaged in, civil litigation may make a request for inspection of the files either to the public prosecutor or to the presiding judge of the court of criminal justice.[123] In order to be successful, the party needs to state a justified interest (*berechtigtes Interesse*) to inspect the files. If the request is made via an attorney, it is often sufficient for the attorney to truthfully state that his client intends to prepare, or is engaged in, a civil action against the person accused in the criminal proceedings, and that the information contained in the files may be relevant for this purpose.

---

[122] *Cf.* a recent decision by the ECJ [*Annett Altmann and Others v. Bundesanstalt für Finanzdienstleistungsaufsicht*], Decision of 12 November 2014 (Docket-No. C 140/13), the decision is available at www.curia.europa.eu.

[123] German Code of Criminal Procedure (*Strafprozessordnung, StPO*) §406e; the party itself may not make such a request.

The public prosecutor or the presiding judge will make a decision on whether or not to grant access to the files. The interests of the accused person as well as of any third parties involved in the case will be balanced against the interest of the party requesting inspection. Access to the file may be limited to certain documents only. In practice, however, quite often extensive inspection rights are granted.

The inspection generally takes place at the public prosecutor's offices or at the court. The attorney inspecting the files may take copies there. Upon request, an attorney is often allowed to exercise the inspection rights in his own offices. In this case, the criminal law files are then forwarded to the attorney for a few days for his review and for copying. The information received may only be used for the purposes the inspection was allowed for.[124]

b) Reporting Alleged Crimes

Against this background, prospective civil litigants sometimes notify the public prosecutor of facts which relate to their dispute and which allegedly constitute a criminal offense. The goal is to induce the public prosecutor to initiate investigations and to inspect the files at a later stage in order to obtain information potentially useful in the civil litigation.

The legal risk to a party taking this approach is limited. Under German law, everyone has the right to notify the public prosecutor of facts possibly constituting a criminal offense. German law assumes that the German Code of Criminal Procedure (*Strafprozessordnung, StPO*)[125] sufficiently protects the legitimate interests of the accused. Therefore, criminal or civil law liability will only arise for a person making allegations which prove to be unfounded, if the notice was made intentionally and in bad faith in order to damage the accused.

Choosing this approach, however, may cause ethical problems. It may also have tactical disadvantages. The criminal investigations will be directed personally against natural persons such as corporate officers of the potential opponent in the civil litigation. Initiating such investigations will very likely result in emotionalizing a dispute on the personal level, and thus reduce chances for an amicable settlement.

3. Files at the Civil Courts

A party to civil litigation in the German courts has the right to inspect the contents of all the court files. Since a third-party intervener is considered a party for this purpose, a prospective litigant may intervene in a pending court action solely for the purpose of obtaining information from this action if the prerequisites for a third-party intervention are met.[126] With limited exceptions,[127] the party may further demand copies of all or part of the files.[128]

Furthermore, a prospective litigant may want to access court files relating to disputes between third parties which may be relevant for his prospective litigation. There is no register on a state or federal level setting out pending or past

---

[124] German Code of Criminal Procedure (*Strafprozessordnung, StPO*) §406e (6) in conjunction with §477 (5).
[125] An English translation is available at www.gesetze-im-internet.de
[126] See *infra*, at pp. 62 et seq.
[127] ZPO §299 (4).
[128] ZPO §§299 (1), (3), 299a.

lawsuits. Therefore, it is not possible to find out whether (and where) there are other civil lawsuits. Sometimes, however, this can be investigated via publicly available information such as *e.g.* press reports.

If the third parties to such lawsuit agree, such request will be granted.[129] Alternatively, the person seeking inspection may demonstrate a legally acknowledged interest (*rechtlich geschütztes Interesse*) to inspect all or part of the court files of a particular case. Generally, it is sufficient to credibly substantiate (*glaubhaft machen*)[130] the intent to enforce a legal claim which bears a legal relation to the claim being pursued in the case to which the court files relate.

The decision on inspection rights will be made by the president of the respective court. The decision is in the president's discretion, and he may restrict the scope of the inspection rights to parts of the contents of the files. Any decision may be appealed by a special remedy (*Anfechtung*).[131]

The right to inspect civil court files is often exercised. It may prove very helpful, for example if a potential defendant is already engaged in similar or related lawsuits.

4. Files at Other Courts

The rights and limitations to inspect files kept at the labor[132] and administrative[133] courts are similar to the ones applying to the inspection of civil court files. Due to the confidential nature of fiscal cases, third parties have no inspection rights with regard to files kept at the fiscal courts.[134]

5. Requests for Information and for Forwarding of Files

A civil court may find in the course of preparation for an oral hearing that information from or documents stored at another public authority might be relevant. If one of the parties has at least implicitly mentioned in its submissions that such information may be relevant, the civil court may request information (*Auskunft*) or the forwarding of parts or all of the files from that authority.[135].

Furthermore, a party to civil litigation may offer documentary evidence by asking the civil court to request the forwarding of specified documents contained in the files of a public authority (*Antrag auf Aktenbeiziehung*).[136] The requests by the civil court for information or for the forwarding of documents may be directed to public authorities of any kind, including regulatory authorities, public prosecutor's offices and all courts of all jurisdictional branches.

The public authority that receives such request may refuse to provide the information or documents in whole or in part on the grounds of confidentiality

---

[129] ZPO § 299 (2).
[130] ZPO § 294.
[131] Introductory Law of the Judicature Act (*Einführungsgesetz zum Gerichtsverfassungsgesetz, EGGVG*) § 23.
[132] Labour Courts Act (*Arbeitsgerichtsgesetz, ArbGG*) § 46 (2) in conjunction with ZPO § 299.
[133] Administrative Courts Act (*Verwaltungsgerichtsordnung, VwGO*) §§ 100, 173 in conjunction with ZPO § 299. There is some dispute whether third parties may have inspection rights at all, *cf.* Kopp/ Schenke, Verwaltungsgerichtsordnung, 20th ed., 2014, § 100 no. 2.
[134] Fiscal Courts Act (*Finanzgerichtsordnung, FGO*) § 78. An exception may apply in extraordinary cases, *cf.* Koch in: Gräber, Finanzgerichtsordnung, 7th ed., 2010, § 78 no. 7.
[135] ZPO § 273 (2) No. 2.
[136] ZPO § 432.

or privilege. In practice, however, public authorities very often fully comply. The forwarded information will become part of the file of the civil court.

As mentioned, parties to civil litigation have the right to inspect the complete civil court files. By combining a motion for request of information or the forwarding of files with its right to inspect the civil court files, a party may gain access to information which it would otherwise not have.

6. Blocking Inspection Rights

Given the extensive possibilities to access files kept at public authorities, including the courts, a (prospective) party to a civil lawsuit in Germany is well advised to block its opponent's access to all files which may be relevant.

An initial step would be to identify the public authorities that have information which might be relevant to the litigation. In a second step, a party should then discuss with its attorneys on what grounds this information could be withheld. The attorneys will then make an application to the authorities stating in detail the factual and legal reasons why certain information should not be disclosed. In practice, contacting the person in charge at the respective public authority and explaining the reasons why access should be denied is often an effective way to block inspection rights.

IV. (Expedited) Court Procedures for Obtaining Information

1. Court Proceedings for Information

A potential litigant may have a contractual or statutory claim for information against a future defendant or against a third party.[137] Prior to commencing an action,[138] these claims need to be enforced in a separate, full-fledged civil lawsuit. These lawsuits are quite rare.[139]

2. Expedited Court Procedures for Information in Company Law

German substantive law grants shareholders extensive rights to information from the company's management. For example, the shareholder of a German stock corporation (*Aktiengesellschaft, AG*) has the right to ask questions regarding the business of the corporation in the shareholders' meeting (*Hauptversammlung*).[140] The shareholder of a limited liability company (*Gesellschaft mit beschränkter Haftung, GmbH*) may request information from the management at any time and has the right to inspect the business records of the company.[141] Similar rights are available to partners in a limited partnership (*Kommanditgesellschaft, KG*),[142] a general com-

---

[137] See, *e.g.*, BGB § 810, HGB § 118.
[138] In a pending lawsuit, the court may order production of information based on a substantive law claim, see *infra*, at p. 68.
[139] In certain cases, an action by stages (*Stufenklage*) could be considered, see *infra*, at p. 48.
[140] AktG § 131.
[141] GmbHG § 51a.
[142] HGB § 161 (2) in conjunction with § 118, HGB § 166; the information rights of a limited partner are limited, but the court may upon application by a limited partner order the partnership to disclose more extensive information.

mercial partnership (*offene Handelsgesellschaft, OHG*)[143] or a general partnership (*Gesellschaft bürgerlichen Rechts, GbR*) [144].

If the management does not answer the questions or does not provide the information requested, German corporate law provides for expedited proceedings to enforce these information rights of shareholders of stock corporations and of limited liability companies.[145] The regional court at the seat of the company may order the management to grant the information requested upon application by a shareholder. Different from normal civil proceedings, the court will investigate the relevant facts to expedite the proceedings.[146] The decision is made by court order.

A limited partner in a limited partnership may enforce his right to inspect the business records of the partnership for good cause[147] in similar proceedings.[148] However, there are no expedited proceedings available to the partner of either a general commercial partnership or a limited partnership.

V. Disclosure Proceedings Abroad

A party planning to commence or already engaged in litigation in a German court might consider initiating legal proceedings for disclosure of information in a foreign court.

A noteworthy example is the U.S. According to 28 USC Section 1782 (a), an "interested" foreign party may petition a United States federal district court to order a person who resides or who may be found in the U.S. to give his testimony or statement or to produce a document or other thing for potential use in proceedings in a foreign tribunal.

The U.S. Supreme Court has held that it is not a prerequisite for a petition that the foreign proceedings have already started, that these proceedings are proceedings in a court of law, or that the law applicable to the dispute before the foreign court contains provisions with regard to disclosure of information comparable in scope to those of the United States.[149] A petition pursuant to 28 USC Section 1782 (a) may be directly made to the United States district court by a foreign party. A formal request for legal assistance through the respective foreign court is not necessary. The prerequisites for a petition are, therefore, not very strict.

However, the decision whether to order discovery in the U.S. is within the discretion of the U.S. district court. The U.S. Supreme Court held in 2004 that a petition should be denied when the person from whom information is requested is a party to the foreign proceedings, when the petition is made to circumvent restrictions under foreign law as regards collecting evidence, or when the foreign court already dismissed a similar motion by a party. The U.S. district court must further take into account whether the person being requested to disclose information may be unreasonably burdened by the discovery order. The U.S. district

---

[143] HGB § 118.
[144] BGB § 716.
[145] AktG §§ 99, 132; GmbHG § 51b.
[146] FamFG § 26.
[147] HGB § 166 (3).
[148] GVG § 23a (2) No. 4 in conjunction with FamFG § 375 No. 1.
[149] Intel Corp. vs. Advanced Microsoft Devices, 293 F.3d 664 (9th Cir. 2004); *cf. Fellas*, Supreme Court Permits Foreign Litigants to Engage in Broad Evidence Gathering in the United States, International Litigation News, 2004, p. 72; *Shore/Smith*, The U.S. Supreme Court Broadens Evidence-Gathering Assistance to Foreign Tribunals, DAJV-Newsletter, 2004, p. 117.

court may dismiss a petition on these grounds or may grant it only in part or under certain restrictions.

In the meantime, quite a few litigants in Germany have successfully relied on 28 USC Section 1782 (a).[150] In one of the pertinent decisions of the U.S. courts, the U.S. Court of Appeals for the Seventh Circuit in 2011 took a broad view.[151] The court mainly focused on potential abuses of Section 1782 (a) and on the defendant's failure to obtain a ruling by the German court to bar or to limit U.S. discovery. It remains to be seen how German courts will react and whether they will try to prevent U.S. discovery on their own initiative. Further issues remain open in applying Section 1782 (a) such as *e.g.* whether discovery can be sought in regard to documents located outside the U.S.[152] Nevertheless, Section 1782 (a) is potentially a powerful tool for obtaining information located in the U.S., and there is a notable increase in attempts by parties to litigation in Germany to use this provision.

G. Preparing and Securing Evidence

I. Preparing Evidence

In German litigation, the initial written pleadings of the parties need to contain detailed statements of fact and need to specify the evidence upon which the respective party intends to rely. For this reason, the parties will prepare evidence at a very early stage.

1. Means of Evidence

German civil procedure law acknowledges five different forms of evidence (*Beweismittel*), *i.e.* (i) proof by documentary evidence,[153] (ii) proof by inspection by the court,[154] (iii) proof by witness testimony,[155] (iv) proof by expert testimony,[156] and (v) proof by party testimony.[157]

Naturally, there are different ways to prepare these forms of evidence for use in the proceedings.

2. Preparing Documents and Objects for Inspection

According to German civil procedure law, only a written communication is deemed to be a "document".[158] Documents are by far the most important evidentiary means in German litigation. Technically, the party needs to present the original of the document to the court for inspection. In practice, photocopies are

---

[150] See *Schaner/Scarbbrough*, Obtaining Discovery in the USA for Use in German Legal Proceedings – A Powerful Tool: 28 U.S.C. § 1782, Anwaltsblatt 2012, p. 325.
[151] U.S. Court of Appeals for the Seventh Circuit, Decision of 24 January 2011, Heraeus Kulzer v. Biomet, Gewerblicher Rechtsschutz und Urheberrecht – Internationaler Teil 2011, p. 361.
[152] See *Schaner/Scarborough*, Obtaining Discovery in the USA for Use in German Legal Proceedings – A Powerful Tool: 28 U.S.C. § 1782, Anwaltsblatt 2012, p. 324.
[153] ZPO §§ 415 *et seq.*
[154] ZPO §§ 371 *et seq.*
[155] ZPO §§ 373 *et seq.*
[156] ZPO §§ 402 *et seq.*
[157] ZPO §§ 445 *et seq.*
[158] Federal Court of Justice (BGH), Decision of 28 November 1975 (Docket No. V ZR 127/74), Neue Juristische Wochenschrift, 1976, p. 294.

enclosed with written pleadings. Usually, the opponent does not dispute that the photocopy accurately reflects the original. The content of the document is then deemed to be uncontested, and no formal taking of evidence is required.

Pictures, photos, drawings, plans, and in particular electronically stored information including printouts are not considered "documents".[159] For information of this kind, the proper evidentiary means is proof by inspection by the court (*Augenscheinseinnahme*). The way to introduce these objects into the proceedings for inspection is similar to the production of documents, *i.e.* the parties usually attach copies to their written pleadings.

With regard to all other objects proposed to be inspected by the court, the parties will offer in their written pleadings to present the respective object in the oral hearing. If this is not possible, *e.g.* with regard to buildings or heavy machinery, the party will offer in its written pleadings that the court may inspect the object where it is located. Very often parties attach photos or drawings of these objects to their written pleadings for illustration purposes.

3. Preparing Expert Testimony

Different from *e.g.* the U.S., experts are not presented by the parties, but appointed by the court.[160] Nevertheless, parties frequently submit expert opinions with their written pleadings. Such opinions relate mostly to technical or accounting issues. Technically they are not deemed to be evidence, but part of the statement of facts submitted by the respective party.

An expert opinion by an acknowledged expert supporting the case of a party may carry considerable weight with the court. However, very often a substantial amount of time and effort is required to prepare an opinion that a court can easily understand.

In certain technical areas, there is only a very limited number of experts available. Therefore, a party may choose to commission all or at least the leading experts in order to block them for the opponent or to prevent them from being appointed by the court as independent experts.

The content of foreign law is treated like a factual allegation for purposes of evidence under German civil procedure law. The court is under an obligation to investigate the relevant foreign law *ex officio*. However, in particular in cases where there is easy access by a party to such law, the court may request such party to submit the contents of the applicable foreign law. A party relying on foreign law is, therefore, well advised to prepare and submit an opinion by leading law professors or attorneys from the respective jurisdiction together with its written pleadings.[161]

4. Preparing Witness Testimony

a) Securing Potential Witnesses

The parties need to name in their written pleadings the witnesses who are to be called by the court to prove a statement of fact. Accordingly, the distinction between witnesses and party witnesses is relevant.

---

[159] This is, at least, partly disputed, *Geimer* in: Zöller, Zivilprozessordnung, 30th ed., 2014, before §415 no. 2.
[160] For a detailed discussion, see *infra*, at pp. 76 et seq.
[161] For a detailed discussion, see *infra*, at pp. 88 et seq.

Under German law, neither the plaintiff nor the defendant nor members of the board of management of either may serve as a witness, but only as a party witness. For the purpose of determining whether a person is deemed to be a witness or a party witness, the German courts apply strictly formal standards.[162]

Party witnesses may only be heard in limited circumstances in German court proceedings. If the testimony of a person qualifying as a party witness is crucial to a plaintiff, it is quite common that the potential plaintiff assigns his claim to a third party. Thereafter, the party witness formally no longer qualifies as such, but as a regular witness. In cases where the testimony of members of the management board is concerned, the respective board member sometimes resigns from office for the duration of the litigation in order to be able to testify as a witness.

b) Preparing Witnesses

German law in general does not prohibit the preparing of witnesses. Until recently, witness preparation played, however, only a relatively minor role in practice.

Different from other jurisdictions such as the U.S., the German system of civil justice does not require extensive preparation of witnesses. The examination of a witness is mainly conducted by the court, and although the attorneys of both parties may pose questions to the witness, the courts take great care to avoid U.S. style hostile questioning in court. Therefore, week-long training sessions and mock trials to prepare a witness for his appearance in court are unheard of.

In general, a German attorney will have a discussion with the potential witness at the outset of a case to determine whether he has any knowledge of the facts on which he is supposed to testify. Sometimes a potential witness will be asked by a party to prepare a written internal statement on these facts. A German attorney, however, will avoid anything which could look like influencing a witness to testify in a certain way.

However, even such limited steps for preparing a witness are regarded by many in Germany as somehow unethical. Recently, the preparation of witnesses in civil proceedings by, *inter alia*, mock trials not only caused a critical public debate but even criminal investigations based on suspicions of fraud. Against this background, there is always the risk that a court will not give a witness statement its full weight if the court learns that the witness has been prepared by a party. This risk has to be carefully balanced with the benefits of a witness having been prepared in a given case.

II. Independent Procedure for the Taking of Evidence

Even before a lawsuit is pending, the plaintiff may file a motion for an independent procedure for the taking of evidence (*selbständiges Beweisverfahren*)[163] with the court which would have jurisdiction over the taking of evidence.[164]

The party filing the motion needs to demonstrate a legally acknowledged interest in the independent procedure for the taking of evidence. Such an interest is deemed to exist for example if the procedure may serve to avoid a lawsuit or if there is the actual danger that the evidence which is at the moment easily available may soon be destroyed or changed. In particular, the plaintiff may request that a

---

[162] See *Greger* in: Zöller, Zivilprozessordnung, 30th ed., 2014, § 373 nos. 4 *et seq.*
[163] ZPO §§ 485 *et seq.*
[164] ZPO § 486.

court-appointed expert renders an opinion about the condition of an object or the object's value, the cause of damages or defect and/or the expenses to be incurred to repair such property or to cure the damage or defect.[165]

Independent procedures for the taking of evidence are frequently used in civil or commercial disputes relating to defective buildings, plants or products. Quite often, a plaintiff lacking sufficient knowledge of the respective facts may acquire them from the testimony of a witness heard in the proceedings or from the opinion rendered by the court-appointed expert. Since the testimony or the expert opinion will be introduced into the subsequent court proceedings as evidence,[166] and since the courts tend, in particular, to follow the opinions of court-appointed experts, the parties very often settle on the basis of the expert's opinion prior to commencing a lawsuit.

Independent procedures for the taking of evidence may, therefore, serve as a means to investigate the facts prior to commencing full-scale litigation and may be used as a means to reach an early settlement.

H. Strategy Considerations

I. Selection of Forum

When preparing an action or preparing a defense against a potential action, more than one forum may be available.

If the courts of countries other than Germany have international jurisdiction as well, a party will have to thoroughly weigh the arguments speaking for and against each of these forums. In particular, a potential defendant may consider the *lis pendens* doctrine by seizing a court in a jurisdiction which is known for its slow proceedings.

Even if the German courts have exclusive international jurisdiction, a potential plaintiff may have the choice between different German courts having local jurisdiction. The advantages and disadvantages of each of the forums available need to be carefully assessed.

One consideration may be not to bring a lawsuit in the courts of the place where the defendant is domiciled. German judges are usually fair and objective irrespective of whether a plaintiff hails from outside the local community, or even from abroad. Nevertheless, it cannot be ruled out entirely that a judge may be more favorably inclined to a defendant who is well known and respected at the seat of the court.

A more important consideration is the court's experience with international matters. A judge with previous exposure to international disputes usually has a better understanding, in particular, of "soft" factors such as language barriers or cultural habits. Further, although the language of the court is German, a judge may decide to accept foreign-language exhibits to the written pleadings of the parties if he feels to be sufficiently competent in the respective language. This will sometimes not only reduce translation costs dramatically, but has the additional benefit of the judge reading and understanding the entire documents submitted to the court, and not only translated parts thereof. Usually the younger the

---

[165] ZPO §485.
[166] ZPO §493.

judges and the larger the city, the more exposure to foreign cultures and foreign languages one can expect.

Certain courts in Germany are known to be more effective than others. A plaintiff may, therefore, choose the court where more expedient proceedings can be reasonably expected.

Many judgments rendered in particular by the higher regional courts are published. Sometimes, the legal opinions of different courts vary on certain issues of law. Usually, the judgments by the regional courts are in line with the legal views of the higher regional court which serves as their appellate court. Therefore, a plaintiff may choose a particular court on the assumption that it will most likely have a certain (favorable) view on a legal issue underlying the dispute.

II. Selecting the Right Parties

1. Plaintiff

A party intending to commence litigation in Germany has some leeway in determining who will be the plaintiff(s) in the civil action:

a) Assignment of Claim

A plaintiff must generally be the owner of the claim which he seeks to enforce in court. However, German courts look at this issue in a purely formalistic way, and it is acknowledged by the courts that it is admissible to assign claims in order for the assignee to act as the plaintiff in court proceedings. Therefore, claims are often assigned to allow members of the management board of a commercial entity to testify as third-party witnesses, and not as party witnesses, in the proceedings.[167] Sometimes, claims are assigned from foreign companies to a German company to avoid the burden of providing security for the costs of the proceedings.[168] A claim may in certain circumstances be also assigned in order to avoid a set-off by the opponent with regard to existing counterclaims, or for a variety of other reasons such as balance sheet considerations.

b) Joinder of Multiple Plaintiffs

German law allows several plaintiffs to join in one civil action.[169]

If a court's decision with regard to each plaintiff has to be identical, the joinder is a so-called "mandatory joinder" (*"notwendige Streitgenossenschaft"*).[170] This means that the principle that every litigant is acting only on his own behalf is restricted.[171] There are two kinds of mandatory joinder that should be distinguished.[172]

The first kind of mandatory joinder is not "mandatory" in the ordinary meaning of the word. A lawsuit can be brought by one plaintiff alone, where the decision would have binding effect on a party or parties that did not join the action (*Rechtskrafterstreckung*). Examples in commercial law of this kind of mandatory

---

[167] See *supra*, at pp. 36 et seq.
[168] See *infra*, at p. 60.
[169] ZPO §§ 59 *et seq.*
[170] ZPO § 62.
[171] *Cf. Vollkommer* in: Zöller, Zivilprozessordnung, 30th ed., 2014, § 62 no. 1.
[172] *Cf. Vollkommer* in: Zöller, Zivilprozessordnung, 30th ed., 2014, § 62 no. 1 *et seq.*

joinder include actions by several shareholders of a stock corporation or of a limited liability company for a declaration that a shareholders' resolution, or the formation of a stock corporation or limited liability company as such, is void.[173] A judgment in such proceedings is not only binding on the parties to the civil action, but also on all shareholders, board members and managing directors of the respective stock corporation or limited liability company. In the absence of such "mandatory" joinder, there would be confusion as regards the legal effects of possibly contradictory judgments in parallel proceedings.

The second kind of "mandatory" joinder includes lawsuits that are brought by, or against, all of the concerned parties, *i.e.* the joinder is "mandatory" in the ordinary meaning of the word. An example is an action brought by the partners of a general commercial partnership (*offene Handelsgesellschaft, OHG*) for expelling another partner[174] or for declaring his power to represent the partnership void. Since the judgment would only have binding effect on those who are parties to the lawsuit, to avoid contradictory judgments, such actions are only permissible if all partners are either plaintiffs or defendants in the civil action by way of joinder.[175]

Even if there is no mandatory joinder, potential plaintiffs may join an action if they assert claims which are legally or factually related (voluntary joinder, *einfache Streitgenossenschaft*).[176] If the court finds that the claims are not sufficiently related, it may sever the action, but will not dismiss the claims.

2. Multiple Defendants

a) Joinder

A plaintiff may choose to join multiple defendants in one action. While a mandatory joinder of defendants is rare, it is quite common to direct one civil action against more than one defendant by way of voluntary joinder.[177]

A voluntary joinder of defendants may have legal reasons. For example, with regard to claims against a general partnership, the partnership itself as well as all of its partners are jointly and severally liable.[178] A legal action is, therefore, usually brought against the partnership and all partners personally. The same applies to limited partnerships such as the commonly used GmbH & Co. KG, where civil actions are usually directed against both the limited partnership and the general partner. By joining these defendants, the resulting judgment will be enforceable against all joined defendants at the discretion of the plaintiff.

Bringing a civil action against multiple defendants may also have tactical reasons. It is frequently used to exclude key witnesses and to put pressure on the decision-makers of a legal entity. For example, in cases where a plaintiff feels defrauded by corporate officers acting for a legal entity, the plaintiff may decide to bring the action both against the legal entity and the officers personally. Since a defendant cannot be heard as a witness but only in exceptional cases as a party witness, this may result in blocking possible key witnesses for the defense from giving evidence. In addition, the respective corporate officers face a personal

---

[173] See, *e.g.*, AktG §§ 248, 249, 275 (4); GmbHG § 75 (2).
[174] HGB §§ 133, 140, 117, 127.
[175] *Vollkommer* in: Zöller, Zivilprozessordnung, 30th ed., 2014, § 62 no. 19.
[176] ZPO §§ 59 and 60.
[177] ZPO §§ 59, 60.
[178] HGB § 128.

risk in the litigation, which may increase the chance of settlement of the case as a whole.

b) Increased Cost Risk

Directing the action against multiple defendants, however, increases the cost risk of a plaintiff, should he be unsuccessful in the litigation. Normally, each of the defendants is allowed to retain its own attorney of record in the proceedings. In accordance with the general principle in German litigation that the unsuccessful party has to reimburse the opponent for the statutory attorney fees,[179] the plaintiff will in this case face the risk that the amounts to be reimbursed to the opponents in legal cost may multiply.

In practice, this effect is sometimes used by defendants as a strategy to deter a plaintiff from bringing an action at all, or to build up bargaining power for a possible settlement. Parties who become defendants by way of voluntary joinder are liable only for their own attorney fees when unsuccessful but have a claim for full reimbursement of their statutory attorney fees if their side is successful in the lawsuit.

3. Third-Party Notice

A party to a German lawsuit may, in case it does not prevail in the litigation, have a warranty claim or a claim for indemnification against a third party. A typical situation is the purchase of a product by a wholesaler who, after selling it to a customer, is sued by the customer based on alleged defects of the product. The wholesaler may in this case have a claim for reimbursement against the manufacturer if the wholesaler is unsuccessful in defending against the action brought by the customer.

In the ensuing litigation *e.g.* between the wholesaler and the customer, a party to the litigation – the wholesaler – may give the third party – the manufacturer – third-party notice (*Streitverkündung*).[180] The third party may then join the proceedings either on the side of the plaintiff or on the side of the defendant, or may refuse to join the proceedings at all.

If the party giving the third-party notice does not prevail in the litigation and, therefore, initiates further litigation against the third party for warranty or indemnification, the third party is, with some exceptions, precluded from asserting that the judgment rendered against the party giving the notice is incorrect. A third-party notice has this effect regardless of whether the third party chose to join the proceedings or not.[181]

A third-party notice, therefore, allows a party to prepare for and to conduct a possibly necessary second lawsuit for warranty or indemnification more effectively. In addition, a third-party notice may also have tactical benefits. Quite often third parties are hesitant to be drawn into litigation. Giving third-party notices may, therefore, encourage the parties to the litigation as well as the third party to resolve the dispute amicably.

---

[179] See *supra*, at p. 11.
[180] ZPO §§ 72 *et seq.*
[181] ZPO § 74 (3) in conjunction with ZPO § 68.

4. Class or Group Actions

It is a fundamental principle of German civil procedure law that only the parties to civil proceedings are bound by the result of such proceedings.[182] Therefore, a concept comparable to the U.S. "class action" or "group action" does not exist in Germany.

However, certain forms of collective actions are possible under German procedural law. Further, there is a vivid discussion in Germany on whether to introduce certain other forms of collective redress, which was triggered by *inter alia* the European Commission requesting its Member States in 2013 to introduce collective proceedings, in particular in the areas of consumer rights and competition law.[183]

a) Registered Interest Group Acting as Plaintiffs

The main existing form of collective proceedings is the right of certain registered interest groups (*Verbände*) to bring an action on behalf of their members and on behalf of the common interest.[184]

b) Common Representative Acting as Plaintiff

Another established form of collective redress is the power of the court in corporate litigation to appoint a common representative (*besonderer Vertreter*) to protect the rights of non-participating shareholders in proceedings for the fair evaluation of the amount of compensation for minority shareholders in connection with the transformation of companies pursuant to the Transformation Act (*Umwandlungsgesetz*),[185] the conclusion of control and profit transfer agreements or a squeeze-out under the Stock Corporation Act (*Aktiengesetz*).[186]

c) Capital Markets Model Case Act

Triggered by the more than 17,000 individual actions which were brought in the German courts as of 2001 against Deutsche Telekom for allegedly misrepresenting capital markets information, the German Capital Markets Model Case Act (*Kapitalanleger-Musterverfahrensgesetz, KapMuG*) was enacted in 2005. Following massive criticism in particular as to the duration of the proceedings, it was replaced in 2012 by the revised Capital Markets Model Case Act 2012.

The Capital Markets Model Case Act 2012 only applies to civil disputes concerning claims for damages based on false, misleading or omitted public capital markets information and/or its use, to claims based on failure to offer clarification, and to claims for performance of contract based on an offer under the Securities Acquisition and Takeover Act (*Wertpapiererwerbs- und Übernahmegesetz, WpÜG*).[187] The basic concept of the Capital Markets Model Case Act 2012 is to have certain legal or factual issues, which are relevant for a multitude of pending civil proceedings, decided in model case proceedings with binding effect on all of them.

---

[182] There are however exceptions to that rule, which are explained in the following.
[183] *Cf. Vollkommer* in: Zöller, Zivilprozessordnung, 30th ed., 2014, Annex to §77 no. 1.
[184] See, *e.g.*, Act against Unfair Competition (*Gesetz gegen den unlauteren Wettbewerb, UWG*) §8 (3); Act Authorizing Suits for Injunctive Relief in Consumer Protection and other Matters (*Gesetz über Unterlassungsklagen bei Verbraucherrechts- und anderen Verstößen, UklaG*) §§1-3.
[185] An English Translation is available at www.gesetze-im-internet.de.
[186] Act on Determination of Compensation for Minority Shareholders (*Spruchverfahrensgesetz, SpruchG*) §6.
[187] KapMuG §1.

H. Strategy Considerations

An individual plaintiff still has to initiate regular civil proceedings. Generally, a specific regional court has exclusive jurisdiction for the relevant matters.[188] Within such individual proceedings, either party thereto may apply to the court for model case proceedings, specifying the issue(s) to be established in such model case proceedings and their relevance to parallel cases.

The respective regional court reviews the application for model case proceedings and publishes *inter alia* the names of the defendant(s) and their attorneys, the name of the relevant issuer of securities or offeror of other investments, the issue(s) to be established in the model case proceedings as well as a summary of the relevant facts in a specific part of the Federal Gazette (*Bundesanzeiger*).[189] The respective proceedings before the regional court are thereby suspended.

If within six months at least nine further applications with the same issue(s) to be established in model case proceedings are published in the register, the regional court that made the first publication will refer the case to the competent higher regional court. Otherwise, the application for model case proceedings will be dismissed, and the regular court proceedings will continue.[190]

The higher regional court to which the case is referred will issue an order initiating model case proceedings, which is published in the register as well. All regional courts, regardless of whether a party thereto applied for model proceedings or not, will stay all pending proceedings which depend on the issue(s) to be established in model case proceedings.[191] A plaintiff however may revoke his court action in order to avoid a subsequent model decision binding on him within one month after publication in the register.[192]

The higher regional court chooses a lead plaintiff (*Musterkläger*). All other plaintiffs will be interested parties summoned (*Beigeladene*), and all defendants will also be defendants in the model case proceedings (*Musterbeklagte*).[193] The general rules of civil procedure apply. However, the court file is accessible for the parties in a special electronic data room,[194] and service of certain procedural measures as well as service of a model case decision is made by publication in the register.[195] The interested parties summoned to the model case proceedings are entitled to any procedural means as long as they do not contradict the lead plaintiff.[196] The lead plaintiff may be replaced,[197] and the issues to be established in the model case proceedings may be expanded during the proceedings.[198]

The model case proceedings are either terminated by a model case decision (*Musterentscheid*) or by court-approved settlement. The model case decision can be appealed by a miscellaneous appeal on points of law to the BGH.[199] Following the rendering of a final model case decision, the respective regional court(s) will resume their proceedings. The issues established in the model case decision are binding on the parties, including the interested parties summoned.[200] However,

---

[188] ZPO § 32b
[189] KapMuG § 3. The Litigation Register (*Klageregister*) can be found at *www.bundesanzeiger.de*.
[190] KapMuG § 6.
[191] KapMuG § 8.
[192] See KapMuG § 8 (2) in conjunction with § 22 (1) sentence 2.
[193] KapMuG § 9.
[194] KapMuG § 12 (2).
[195] KapMuG § 11 (2).
[196] KapMuG § 14.
[197] KapMuG § 9 (4).
[198] KapMuG § 15.
[199] KapMuG § 20.
[200] KapMuG § 22.

as to all other aspects of the respective cases such as *e.g.* contributory negligence or amount of damages, the regional court will have to decide.

If the lead plaintiff and the defendant(s) reach a settlement, they may forward a settlement proposal to the higher regional court. If the court finds the proposal appropriate, it may approve it.[201] The proposal then is published in the register, and it comes into force if within one month after publication less than 30 % of the interested parties summoned disagree.[202] If the proposal becomes effective, the higher regional court then confirms this fact by court order, whereupon the regional court(s) will terminate the pending proceedings.

A potential plaintiff becoming aware of already pending model case proceedings may, instead of initiating regular proceedings in the regional court, just register his claims with the higher regional court within a certain period of time.[203] Insofar as the registered claim is based on the issue(s) to be established in the model case proceedings, such registration suspends the lapse of any statute of limitations until three months after the final termination of the model case proceedings.[204] However, neither the model case decision nor a settlement is binding upon such potential plaintiff.[205]

III. Timing Issues

1. General

Filing a statement of claim at a particular point in time may have tactical benefits for a plaintiff. Delaying the commencement of the lawsuit, *e.g.* until a new management has taken over at the opponent, may enhance chances for a settlement. Chances to succeed in the litigation may improve if a statement of claim is filed after key employees who were dealing with the subject matter have left the opponent's organization. Timing the commencement of an action prior to the end of the financial year of the opponent may, in light of possible duties to make accruals for the lawsuit in the upcoming financial statements, expedite an amicable settlement. Depending on the situation at hand, a variety of other aspects may be relevant.

2. Limitation Period

The applicable limitation period is of course crucial in deciding when a claim should or must be brought into the courts.

Different from *e.g.* U.S. law, limitation periods are considered a substantive law issue under German law. In several areas of substantive German law, the applicable limitation periods are quite short.[206] The lapse of a limitation period is suspended when a statement of claim is filed. However, the potential plaintiff may not have fully completed his preparations for a lawsuit yet. Possibly, the potential plaintiff is still examining whether he has a case or not.

---

[201] KapMuG § 18.
[202] KapMuG § 17.
[203] KapMuG § 10 (2).
[204] BGB § 204 (1) No. 6a.
[205] See *Wardenbach*, KapMuG 2012 versus KapMuG 2005: Die wichtigsten Änderungen aus Sicht der Praxis, Gesellschafts- und Wirtschaftsrecht 2013, p. 35, 36.
[206] The regular limitation period is 3 years, BGB § 195. It applies to contractual claims for delivery or payment, claims for damages arising out of contractual relations or tortious conduct, unjust enrichment etc. Maximum periods range from 10 to 30 years.

It is a standard means in this situation to request the potential opponent to waive his defense of lapse of statute of limitations (*Verjährungsverzicht*). If the opponent refuses, a potential plaintiff having payment claims may initiate collection proceedings (*Mahnverfahren*).[207] With regard to other claims, or as an alternative to collection proceedings, the potential plaintiff may initiate proceedings at one of the registered conciliation institutions (*Gütestellen*).[208] Both collection and conciliation proceedings toll the statute of limitations.

In appropriate circumstances, filing a motion for an independent procedure for the taking of evidence[209] or filing a third-party notice[210] will toll the limitation period as well.

Sometimes, German substantive law provides for terms of exclusion ("*Ausschlußfristen*").[211] Whereas reliance on a statute of limitations requires a declaration by the respective party, this is not necessary when a term of exclusion applies. The measures described above will toll certain terms of exclusion, but not all of them.

IV. Choice of Procedure

In addition to or as an alternative to initiating regular court proceedings, a potential plaintiff may want to consider whether one of the following procedures may be advantageous:

1. Collection Proceedings

a) Collection Proceedings under German Law

German law provides for an accelerated procedure by which the applicant may obtain an enforceable collection order without a trial (collection proceedings, *Mahnverfahren*).[212]

The applicant must file a motion for a collection order (*Mahnantrag*) for payment of a specific amount of money with the competent local court.[213] The application must be filed on a specific form. The local court examines whether the formal requirements for collection proceedings are met. The court then issues a collection order (*Mahnbescheid*) without a hearing. The collection order is served on the opposing party, who may file a written protest within two weeks after service.

If no protest is filed, the applicant may request the court to issue an enforceable collection order (*Vollstreckungsbescheid*). The opponent may file an objection against the enforceable collection order. If no objection is raised, the enforceable collection order may be enforced against the assets of the opponent. Following an objection, the court refers the matter to the court having jurisdiction with regard to the dispute.

---

[207] ZPO §§ 688 *et seq.*, see *infra*, at pp. 45 et seq.
[208] The most widely used being the Public Legal Advice and Settlement Center (*Öffentliche Rechtsauskunft- und Vergleichsstelle, ÖRA*) in Hamburg (http://www.oera.hamburg.de).
[209] See *supra*, at pp. 37 et seq.
[210] See *supra*, at p. 41.
[211] *E.g.* AktG, § 246 (1).
[212] ZPO §§ 688 *et seq.*
[213] This is usually the local court at the applicant's domicile, unless there is a specific other local court designated by statute. If the applicant is not domiciled in Germany, the local court that would have special jurisdiction is competent to issue a collection order, ZPO § 703d.

Collection proceedings under German domestic law may be chosen even if the collection order has to be served abroad.[214] Furthermore, this possibility is not excluded in relation to the member states of the European Union by the respective European collection proceedings.[215]

Collection proceedings are only advisable if no protests or objections by the opponent are expected. They enable an applicant to obtain an enforceable instrument without having to pay the court costs for contentious proceedings and within a very short timeframe. They are also often used to avoid the lapse of a limitation period.

b) European Collection Proceedings for Uncontested Claims

Regulation (EC) No 805/2004 of the European Parliament and of the Council of 21 April 2004 creating a European Enforcement Order for Uncontested Claims applies to, *inter alia*, enforceable collection orders under German law. The Regulation was implemented into German law[216] and allows *inter alia* the enforcement of enforceable collection orders within all Member States of the European Union without previously having had them declared enforceable by the competent authorities of the applicable Member State.[217]

c) Collection proceedings by an European Order for Payment

Regulation (EC) No 1896/2006 of the European Parliament and of the Council of 12 December 2006 establishes cross-border collection proceedings via a European order for payment.[218]

An application has to be made by using the standard form[219] with the competent court, which in Germany is the local court in Berlin-Wedding.[220] In consumer cases, however, jurisdiction for proceedings against the consumer lies exclusively with the courts of the state where the consumer is domiciled.[221] The application must be for a monetary claim in a specific amount; certain kinds of claims are excluded from the scope of the Regulation.[222]

The court examines whether the requirements in regard to the scope, jurisdiction and content and formalities of the application are met and whether the claim seems to be founded.[223] If so, the court issues a European order for payment using the standard form,[224] which is served on the defendant.[225]

If the defendant does not file an opposition with the court that issued the order within 30 days, such court declares the order enforceable.[226] The order is

---

[214] ZPO § 688 (3) in conjunction with AVAG §§ 1, 32; *cf. Vollkommer* in: Zöller, Zivilprozessordnung, 30th ed., 2014, § 688 no. 10.
[215] Regulation (EC) No. 1896/2006 Recital 10; for the European collection proceedings under the mentioned Regulation see *infra*, at pp. 46 et seq.
[216] ZPO §§ 1079 *et. seq.*
[217] For the enforcement of German judgments under this Regulation in general see *infra*, at p. 110.
[218] ZPO §§ 1087 *et. seq.*
[219] Art. 7, Annex I.
[220] ZPO § 1087.
[221] Art. 6.
[222] Art. 2.
[223] Art. 8.
[224] Art. 12, Annex V.
[225] Artt. 13 *et. seq.*
[226] Art. 18, Annex V.

H. Strategy Considerations

enforceable in all Member States without any declaration of enforceability and in accordance with the applicable domestic law on enforcement.[227] In exceptional cases, the competent court in the Member State where the title is to be executed may refuse enforcement.[228]

Generally, there is no appeal against the European order for payment. Exceptions apply if the defendant was prevented without fault from defending himself or if the order was issued evidently contrary to the provisions of the Regulation.[229]

d) European Proceedings for Small Claims

Regulation (EC) No. 861/2007 of the European Parliament and of the Council of 11 July 2007 establishing a European Small Claims Procedure creates simplified proceedings for claims in cross-border cases whose value does not exceed EUR 2,000.[230]

A creditor may opt either for regular court proceedings in Germany or for proceedings under the Regulation. The latter are brought before the German court having jurisdiction pursuant to the Brussels Regulation 2012. While generally all claims in civil and commercial matters fall within the scope of the Regulation, a number of matters are excluded.[231] The proceedings are generally conducted in writing by using standard forms. There are also relaxed standards concerning the taking of evidence as the court may *e.g.* accept written statements of witnesses, experts or even the parties.[232] Upon application, the court rendering the decision will also provide a standard certification.[233] A first and second appeal may be admissible according to the applicable provisions of the ZPO.[234]

A judgment in European small claims proceedings is enforceable in other Member States without any further declaration of enforceability.[235]

2. Summary Proceedings Based on Documentary Evidence or a Bill of Exchange

In order to expedite the proceedings, a plaintiff may consider bringing summary proceedings based on documentary evidence or on a bill of exchange (*Urkunden-, Scheck-, Wechselprozess*).[236]

The typical feature of these summary proceedings is that the parties are allowed only to rely on documents and party testimony for evidence. All other means of evidence are excluded.[237] To ensure a speedy trial, counteractions are not admissible. A judgment subject to a reservation (*Vorbehaltsurteil*) will be rendered against the defendant.[238]

However, even after a judgment subject to a reservation has been rendered, the proceedings remain pending. A defendant who was not able to prove his factual

---

[227] Art. 19, 21 *et seq.*
[228] Artt. 22 *et seq.*
[229] Art. 20.
[230] ZPO §§ 1097 *et seq.*
[231] Art. 2.
[232] Art. 9.
[233] Artt. 20 *et seq.*; ZPO § 1106.
[234] Art. 17.
[235] *Cf.* Art. 22 for a refusal to enforce the decision.
[236] ZPO §§ 592 *et seq.*
[237] ZPO §§ 592, 595 (2), 602, 605a.
[238] ZPO § 599; a judgment subject to a reservation may be appealed separately, see *infra*, at p. 95.

statements by either documents or party testimony may in a later stage (*Nachverfahren*) raise objections and submit evidence without the restrictions as to these evidentiary means.[239]

Summary proceedings are usually advantageous for a plaintiff and are frequently used in commercial disputes. Even if the court finds that summary proceedings are not admissible, this will have no negative effects for the plaintiff. The plaintiff may abandon the summary proceedings based on documentary evidence or on a bill of exchange at any time during the proceedings. The action will then remain pending as regular proceedings.[240] Summary proceedings, however, allow a plaintiff to obtain a quick judgment with a reservation and to enforce this judgment. The mere fact that a judgment was rendered against him and, in particular, the ensuing enforcement proceedings may induce the opponent to seek an amicable solution to the dispute. At least obtaining and enforcing the judgment with a reservation will leave the plaintiff in a secured position.

Summary proceedings do, however, carry the risk for the plaintiff that the judgment with a reservation will be annulled at the later stage. If the plaintiff has enforced the judgment with a reservation, he will be liable to the defendant for all damages resulting from such enforcement on a no-fault basis.[241] Furthermore, the overall costs of these summary proceedings are generally higher because there are in effect two proceedings, *i.e.* proceedings leading to a judgment with a reservation and the regular proceedings.

3. Action by Stages

In certain circumstances, an action by stages (*Stufenklage*) may be available to a potential plaintiff.[242]

If a plaintiff has a claim for payment or for delivery or recovery of goods or objects but cannot determine what exactly is owed by the defendant, and if such plaintiff in addition has a claim for information relating to what is owed, he may bring an action for disclosure of specific information jointly with an action for payment or delivery or recovery of what is owed, to be determined in accordance with such information. The first stage, therefore, is an action for performance of disclosure obligations, and the second stage is an action for payment or delivery or recovery based on this information.

4. Ancillary Procedures

In addition to commencing the main civil proceedings, a plaintiff may opt for a number of ancillary procedures. A plaintiff may commence independent procedures for the taking of evidence in order to secure evidence during or outside pending court proceedings.[243] The plaintiff may try to secure his rights by filing for a preliminary injunction or by applying for an attachment order.[244] He may also choose to bring a separate civil action for disclosing certain information,[245] to

---

[239] ZPO § 600.
[240] ZPO § 596.
[241] ZPO § 302 (4) 3.
[242] ZPO § 254.
[243] See *supra*, at pp. 37 et seq.
[244] See *infra*, at pp. 111 et seq.
[245] See *supra*, at pp. 33 et seq.

initiate disclosure proceedings in a foreign court[246] or to initiate criminal law proceedings and to combine it with a request for inspection of criminal law files.[247]

V. Reducing Cost Risks

Under German law, the party that is unsuccessful in a lawsuit bears the full court costs and must reimburse the statutory attorney fees incurred by the opponent. These amounts may be substantial.[248] There are a number of ways to reduce that risk:

1. Action for a Partial Claim Only

A potential plaintiff wishing to reduce his cost risk or being in doubt as to the merits of his case may choose to bring an action for a partial claim only (*Teilklage*).

The advantages are obvious. Potential claims of the opponent for reimbursement of court and attorney costs are based on the value in dispute.[249] Bringing an action for only part of the claim reduces the value in dispute and thus the cost risk. Based on how the proceedings develop, the plaintiff may decide whether to extend the subject matter of the proceedings to the full amount of his claim. Even if the plaintiff does not extend the subject matter of the action, the resulting judgment may induce the opponent to either pay the residual amount of the claim on a voluntary basis or at least to settle the dispute also with regard to the remaining amounts.

In order to take advantage of this strategy, the plaintiff must design his action for a partial claim in such a way that the court will decide on all relevant aspects of the full claim. In case the plaintiff expects a set-off by the defendant or the defense of mitigation of damages (*Mitverschulden*), the amount of damages arising from the partial claim must exceed the amount recoverable by the set-off or defense for the court to be able to decide on the basis of the claim. Likewise, if the full claim of the plaintiff is based on a number of separate positions such as, *e.g.*, damages caused by the defendant to several objects, the action needs to include the damages for all objects on a *pro rata* basis.

Choosing an action for a partial claim also has some disadvantages. Only the amount of the partial claim becomes the subject matter of such action. The filing of the action only suspends the expiration of any applicable limitation periods as regards the partial claim. Therefore, a plaintiff needs to ensure that the remainder of the claim does not expire. In addition, bringing an action for a part of the full claim only may be viewed by the opponent, and also by the court, as a sign that the plaintiff does not believe in the merits of his claim.

The advantages of an action for a partial claim may be obstructed by a counteraction filed by the defendant for a declaratory judgment that the defendant does not owe the remainder of the claim. In this case, the full claim becomes the subject matter of the litigation. In practice, however, such counteractions are rare.

---

[246] See *supra*, at pp. 34 et seq.
[247] See *supra*, at pp. 34 et seq.
[248] See the examples in Appendix 1.
[249] GKG §3; RVG §2.

2. Legal Aid

Legal aid (*Prozesskostenhilfe*) is available for civil court actions both to natural persons and to business associations.[250] The European Council has adopted a directive to improve access to justice in cross-border disputes by establishing minimum common rules relating to legal aid for such disputes.[251] Germany has implemented this directive.[252] Accordingly, parties from a Member State of the European Union may receive legal aid in Germany when planning to litigate in the German courts. Therefore, the loss of material rights due to a lack of funds for litigation is not an issue in Germany.

In order to apply for legal aid the applicant must file his case in the court along with a detailed description of his financial situation.[253] The court will grant legal aid if the party is financially eligible according to the statutory income or property test and if the claim or defense has a reasonable prospect of success (*hinreichende Aussicht auf Erfolg*).[254] Legal aid covers all legal costs associated with litigation including court costs and reimbursement of attorney fees of a prevailing opposing party should the applicant ultimately be unsuccessful in the litigation.[255] Depending on the applicant's financial situation, legal aid might be granted for only part of the legal cost.

Legal aid is granted for one level of proceedings only.[256] Even if legal aid was granted by the court of first instance, a new application for legal aid covering the costs of an appeal has to be filed with the appellate court, which will be re-evaluated by the court with regard to the then current financial situation of the party and the reasonable prospect of success of the appeal. For purposes of legal aid, even proceedings in execution of judgment are considered separate proceedings which require a separate application.[257] The court's denial of legal aid may be appealed by filing a miscellaneous appeal.[258]

3. Legal Cost Insurance

In Germany, legal cost insurance (*Rechtsschutzversicherung*) is quite common. However, this kind of insurance usually covers only everyday disputes such as traffic accidents etc., but – with the notable exception of disputes arising from private investments such as *e.g.* mis-selling – generally not commercial disputes.

The insurance company will ask the policy holder to submit a detailed description of the claim to assess whether there is a reasonable prospect of success. If the insurer agrees to cover litigation costs, it will reimburse the policy holder all costs incurred including the reimbursement of costs of the prevailing opposing party should the policy holder not be successful in the litigation. Insurance companies, however, often reserve the right to be consulted before proceedings are terminated by the policy holder or prior to any amicable settlement between the parties.

---

[250] ZPO §§ 114 *et seq.*
[251] Council Directive 2002/8/EC. The directive is available at http://europa.eu.int.
[252] *Cf.* ZPO §§ 114, 116, 1075 *et seq.*
[253] ZPO § 117.
[254] ZPO §§ 114, 115.
[255] ZPO §§ 122, 123.
[256] ZPO § 119 (1).
[257] ZPO § 119 (2).
[258] ZPO § 127 (2); see *infra*, at pp. 101 *et seq.*

4. D&O and other Business-Related Types of Insurance

Directors & Officers (D & O) insurance has, due to an increased number of claims brought by German companies, their liquidators or by third parties such as shareholders, become quite relevant in practice. Such insurance typically covers legal costs incurred by a director or corporate officer in defending against claims of neglect of duties asserted by the company or by third parties. Different from other countries, the standard German D & O policies mostly do not provide for a right of the insurer to select legal counsel, but only to object to an obviously unreasonable choice by the respective director. Nevertheless, the defense of a claim covered by D & O insurance will have to be conducted in close cooperation with the insurer. Depending on the terms of the respective insurance policy, which vary greatly in practice, D & O insurance usually covers reasonable negotiated attorney fees instead of (only) the statutory fees.

There are a number of other business-related types of insurance which cover legal costs incurred by the respective company or by directors or employees insured under such policy. Notable examples are product liability insurance, fidelity insurance (*Vertrauensschadensversicherung*), or insurance for capital markets prospectuses (*Prospektversicherung*).

5. Litigation Financing

For many years now, litigation financing (*Prozessfinanzierung*)[259] has been available in Germany. Commercial firms offer funding for litigation proceedings they determine have a reasonable prospect of success. In return, such litigation financing firms reserve for themselves a certain percentage of the claim in case of a successful outcome, usually between 30 % and 50 %. As with legal cost insurance, the litigation financing firms will require the funded party to obtain their consent before the funded party terminates or settles the funded proceedings.

Litigation financing is in its effect quite close to the U.S. style contingency arrangements. It offers the same benefits and disadvantages. Although it is an interesting option for a party willing to offer the litigation financing firm a substantial share of the claim in return for bearing the full cost risk, this kind of arrangement is usually not available for high-volume litigation in Germany.

I. Commencing the Action

I. Filing the Statement of Claim

Court proceedings are initiated by filing a statement of claim (*Klageschrift*)[260] with the court. The statement of claim must be in the German language[261] and may be submitted either by letter or by facsimile.[262]

---

[259] See, e. g., Foris AG (www.foris.de); Acivo Prozessfinanzierungs AG (www.acivo.com); Legial AG (www.legial.de).
[260] ZPO § 253.
[261] GVG § 184.
[262] *Cf.* ZPO § 130 No. 6.

In some of the federal states as well as partly on the federal level, it is possible or even prescribed to use electronic documents in court proceedings.[263] However, insofar as not being prescribed, this is rarely done in practice (yet). As of 2018, the federal legislator will be competent to issue uniform rules for all civil and commercial proceedings.[264] As of 1 January 2022, attorneys will have to submit their submissions, including statements of claim, electronically.[265]

1. Contents of the Statement of Claim

a) Specifying the Court and the Parties

The statement of claim must designate the court to which the action is directed, the plaintiff(s), the defendant(s), third parties to which third-party notice of a pending lawsuit is given,[266] and the relief sought.[267]

b) Specifying the Relief Sought

aa) Types of Relief Available. German law distinguishes between three different types of relief: Actions for affirmative relief are directed at the performance of obligations by the defendant, including claims for payment and for damages (*Leistungsklage*). An action for a declaratory judgment (*Feststellungsklage*)[268] seeks a declaration of the existence or non-existence of a legal relationship or legal obligation. Finally, an action for the alteration of a legal relationship (*Gestaltungsklage*) is directed at changing an existing legal relationship by way of judgment. Examples for the latter in commercial litigation include actions for annulment of a shareholders' resolution in company law (*Anfechtungsklage*) or for the dissolution of a partnership (*Auflösungsklage*).

bb) Motion for Relief. The motion for relief (*Klageantrag*) is, together with the underlying facts, essential for defining the subject matter of the lawsuit (*Streitgegenstand*). The subject matter in turn determines to what extent an action is pending (*lis pendens*), when an action is modified, and the scope of the binding effect of a judgment (*res judicata*).

Further, the content of the motion for relief is binding on the court in that the court may not go beyond it in its judgment. Motions for relief which are too narrowly worded, therefore, limit the court's ability to grant relief otherwise justified by the facts and the legal situation.

And finally, a court may dismiss an action on the grounds that the motion for relief is not sufficiently clear or specific.[269] Even worse, courts tend to just copy the motion for relief into the operative provisions of the judgment (*Tenor*). If a court does so and if the judgment can, therefore, not be executed because the motion for relief was not specific enough or is unclear, the judgment may be not enforceable at all and thus useless to a plaintiff.

---

[263] *Cf.* http://www.justiz.de/elektronischer_rechtsverkehr/index.php.
[264] See ZPO § 130a as from 1 January 2018.
[265] *Cf.* ZPO § 130d as from 1 January 2022.
[266] See *supra*, at p. 41.
[267] ZPO § 253 (2) and (3), § 130.
[268] ZPO § 256.
[269] An exception is the action by stages (*Stufenklage*) where only for the action for information on the first stage, a specific motion for relief is required, whereas the second step for payment may be unspecific until the defendant has provided the information, see *supra*, at p. 48.

c) Statement of Value of the Matter and Signature

The statement of claim should state the plaintiff's estimate as to the value of the matter in dispute. This may be helpful for the court to determine whether the local court or the regional court has subject matter jurisdiction. It further shows the basis on which the plaintiff has calculated the prepayment of court fees.

The statement of claim needs to be signed by an attorney admitted to the court if the plaintiff has to be represented by an attorney in that court.[270]

2. Exhibits to the Statement of Claim

a) Interdependencies between the Statement of Claim and its Exhibits

All relevant facts of the case must be stated in the statement of claim itself. Documents to which reference is made shall be attached to the statement of claim.[271] In addition, it is common practice to submit additional exhibits with the statement of claim in order to further substantiate the relevant facts. For example, in a dispute over a contract, the plaintiff must summarize in its statement of claim the main contents of the contract and the contract clauses in dispute, and may in addition enclose the contract both to substantiate these statements of fact and as a form of evidence.

b) Foreign-Language Exhibits

In international cases, exhibits accompanying the statement of claim are very often in languages other than German. It is within the court's discretion to allow exhibits in a foreign language, provided the court has a sufficient command of the respective language. If the other party needs a translation, such party must initially obtain one at its own cost, which, however, may be recoverable if the party is successful in the proceedings.[272]

If a court does not allow foreign-language exhibits, the party relying thereon must on request by the court provide translations in full or at least of the relevant parts.[273] The court may either order a translation *ex officio* or request that a translation by a publicly certified translator be provided by the respective party.[274] This translation is considered to be correct and complete if certified so by the translator. However, a party may prove that it is not.[275]

II. Prepayment of Court Costs

A plaintiff is required to make a prepayment of the full court costs. The payment may be made when the statement of claim is filed with the competent court. Alternatively, a plaintiff may wait until he receives an order by the court requesting payment. Since the statement of claim generally will not be served by the court on the defendant until the prepayment has been received, waiting for a payment request by the court usually results in a substantial delay in the proceedings.

---

[270] ZPO §78; representation by an attorney is required in all courts except for local courts.
[271] ZPO §131 (1).
[272] *Greger* in: Zöller, Zivilprozessordnung, 30th ed., 2014, §142 no. 17.
[273] *Cf.* ZPO §131 (2).
[274] *Greger* in: Zöller, Zivilprozessordnung, 30th ed., 2014, §142 no. 17.
[275] ZPO §142 (3).

J. Court Order and Service of Process

I. The Role of the Court

A German court is under the duty to conduct the case in a manner conducive to reaching a prompt,[276] efficient and just resolution of the dispute. Although the parties, by their submissions and actions, govern the course of the proceedings according to the principle of party autonomy, the judge plays an active role in German litigation.

1. Structuring the Proceedings by Court Orders

The court will structure the proceedings mainly by court orders. After an action has been filed, the court will decide whether there will be preliminary written proceedings or an early first session for an oral hearing.[277] The court will also set dates and times for hearings and time limits for the submission of the statement of defense and subsequent written pleadings and other documents by the parties. The court will usually order the personal appearance of the parties at the hearings, and may request the production of documents and other objects.[278] Finally, the court is under a duty to initiate settlement discussions which may be conducted under the guidance of the court.[279]

2. Duty to Give Indications and Feedback

In addition, a German court is under the obligation to discuss the case with the parties and to provide indications and feedback to the parties already at an early stage as regards the relevance of factual or legal issues.[280] This does not mean that the court has inquisitorial rights. By their motions and the contents of their submissions, the parties frame the subject matter of the litigation by which the judge is bound. Rather, German law requires the judge to assist the parties on the proper way to resolve their dispute according to procedural and substantive law. Indications and feedback of the court have to be recorded in the court files of the proceedings. Often, the court will issue a formal order of indication (*Hinweisbeschluss*).

The obligation to provide indications and feedback to the parties puts the judge in a delicate situation. A judge over-exercising this obligation may appear to be partial to one of the parties. Foreign parties coming from jurisdictions where the role of the judge is more passive are sometimes taken aback by the active involvement of a German judge in the case and his stating (albeit "preliminary") views on the outcome. On the other hand, a judge not providing sufficient indications and feedback may fail to comply with his legal obligations, which may constitute grounds for an appeal.[281] Since the extent of the indications and the feedback required is largely a matter of the individual case, appeals are in practice very often based on alleged violations of this obligation.

---

[276] Duty to expedite proceedings, see *supra*, at p. 9.
[277] See *infra*, at p. 55.
[278] See *infra*, at p. 68.
[279] See *infra*, at pp. 71 et seq.
[280] ZPO § 139.
[281] See *infra*, at p. 97.

II. Initial Court Order on Further Proceedings

Once a statement of claim is filed with the court and the prepayment of court costs has been received, the court will analyse whether it has jurisdiction.

The competent court will then decide whether to order an early first session for an oral hearing (*früher erster Termin*), or whether to conduct written preliminary proceedings (*schriftliches Vorverfahren*).[282] In commercial cases, ordering written preliminary proceedings is far more common than ordering an early first session for an oral hearing.

In practice, the differences between the two ways of proceedings are minor. By ordering an early first session for an oral hearing, a court may attempt to discuss the case with the parties at an early stage. Then the court may decide on the further proceedings based on these discussions. Nevertheless, the defendant will have the opportunity to submit a statement of defense responding to the statement of claim, and the plaintiff will usually have an opportunity to comment on the statement of defense prior to the early first hearing.

This is not very different from proceedings where a court orders written preliminary proceedings. In that case, the defendant has to declare within a short time limit – usually two to four weeks – whether he intends to defend himself against the claim. If so, he needs to submit a statement of defense within a time limit set by the court. The plaintiff will then have the opportunity to comment on the statement of defense, and the defendant may reply to these comments. At least in more complex civil or commercial cases, the practical effects of the decision by the court how to proceed do not vary considerably.

The initial court order on how to proceed may contain additional directions for the further proceedings. In particular, the court will usually order the appearance of the parties in person in the upcoming oral hearing.[283] In routine litigation involving large enterprises such as banks, however, board members are neither acquainted with the facts nor do they have the time to appear in court. Therefore, parties frequently use the option to only send a representative to court who is able to clarify the facts and empowered to make all necessary declarations.[284]

Finally, the initial court order already may contain preliminary comments by the court as to possible deficiencies of the statement of claim, such as lack of jurisdiction of the court, inconclusiveness of the statement of claim, etc. The court may also request the plaintiff to clarify certain aspects of the statement of claim.[285]

III. Service of Process

1. Initial Service of Statement of Claim

The statement of claim, including its exhibits, must be served on the defendant together with the initial court order. Service will be made by the court *ex officio*[286] through the court clerk's office (*Geschäftsstelle*).[287]

---

[282] ZPO § 272 (2).
[283] ZPO §§ 273 (2) No. 3; 278 (3).
[284] ZPO § 141 (3).
[285] ZPO § 273 (2) No. 1.
[286] ZPO § 166 (2).
[287] ZPO § 168.

a) Domestic Service

The most common method of service at the request of the court is by registered mail with return receipt (*Einschreiben mit Rückschein*). Service is completed upon return of the return receipt. Alternatively, the court may commission the postal service or a bailiff to deliver the documents to the defendant and complete a form on return of service (*Zustellungsurkunde*). Service of process by handing-over the documents to the designated recipient at the court clerk's office is also possible, but rarely used.[288]

The statement of claim must be served on the defendant(s). If the defendant is a legal entity, service will be made on the legal representative(s).[289] Service of process is also valid on an employee present at the business premises of the defendant[290] or on the defendant's attorney if the attorney has been authorized by its client to accept such service.

If the defendant refuses to accept service, or if the defendant cannot be reached at his domicile or business premises, the statement of claim may be left at such premises[291] or may be deposited at the post office or at the competent local court with a notice given to the defendant.[292] Valid service of process is thereby deemed to be effected.

b) Service Abroad

In case of a foreign defendant on whom no domestic service can be effected, the court must institute proceedings to serve the statement of claim in the jurisdiction where the defendant is domiciled or has his residence.[293]

Service of process within the European Union is governed by the Brussels Service Regulation 2007.[294] With regard to service in other countries, the Hague Civil Procedure Convention,[295] the Hague Service Convention or one of the bilateral treaties to which Germany is a party may apply.[296] In the absence of a treaty, service of process will be made in accordance with the international principles relating to reciprocity in granting judicial assistance.[297] The ZPO contains some implementation provisions regarding the Brussels Service Regulation 2007.[298]

With regard to the technical details of how to conduct service of process abroad, the German courts follow the Regulation on Judicial Assistance in Civil Matters (*Rechtshilfeordnung für Zivilsachen, ZRHO*).[299] The ZRHO consists of a general part and a country-related part and sets out the specifics for service of process based on any of the legal rules mentioned above with regard to nearly all countries in the world.

---

[288] ZPO §§ 168, 173.
[289] ZPO §§ 170, 171.
[290] ZPO § 178 (1) No. 2.
[291] ZPO §§ 179, 180.
[292] ZPO § 181.
[293] ZPO § 183.
[294] *Cf.* ZPO § 183 (5); the Brussels Service Regulation 2007 replaces the Brussels Service Regulation 2000; the Regulation also indirectly applies to Denmark.
[295] *E.g.* with regard to Morocco.
[296] *Cf.* ZPO § 183 (1) and (2). Bilateral treaties covering service of process exist with regard to Morocco, Tunisia, Turkey and the United Kingdom. All treaties are available in German at http://www.justiz.nrw.de/Bibliothek/ir_online_db/ir_htm/index_zivilsachen.htm.
[297] ZRHO § 3 (1) No. 3.
[298] ZPO §§ 1067 *et seq.*
[299] The German version can be found at http://www.ir-online.nrw.de/index2.jsp.

J. Court Order and Service of Process

In practice, the Brussels Service Regulation 2007 and the Hague Service Convention are the most important sources governing service of process:

Under the Brussels Service Regulation 2007, each Member State designates transmitting agencies and receiving agencies responsible respectively for the transmission and receipt of the documents in question. In Germany, the court initiating service abroad is the "transmitting agency".[300] It will send the documents accompanied by a standard form to the receiving agency of the foreign Member State, which will check whether all formalities are met and if the mode of transmission is within the scope of the Regulation. Each Member State also designates a central body responsible for supplying information and resolving problems connected with the transmission of documents.[301]

Under the Hague Service Convention, the signatories also designate a central authority.[302] The German court will address the request for service to a German examining agency, usually the president of the respective regional court for such court and for the local courts located within its district, or the president of the higher regional court for the regional courts within its district.[303] Such authority will examine the request and will send it to the designated central authority of the foreign state.

Under both the Brussels Service Regulation 2007 and the Hague Service Convention, the foreign receiving agency or the foreign central authority, respectively, will then serve, or have the documents served, in accordance with its domestic law or – upon request – by a special form requested by the German court unless this is incompatible with the respective foreign law.[304] The completed service is evidenced by a standardized certificate of service.[305]

With regard to service to countries to which neither the Brussels Service Regulation 2007 nor the Hague Service Convention nor a treaty on service applies, the German court will follow the guidelines set out in the ZRHO. The usual way to effect service would be that the German court sends a request for service to the designated German authority, which will examine the request and will then transmit it to the foreign authority as specified in the ZRHO.[306] The foreign authority will effect service according to its domestic law if the respective country grants legal assistance.

c) Service by Public Notice

If no valid domestic service can be made, or if service of process on a foreign party abroad is not possible or not likely to succeed, the court may order service by public notice (*öffentliche Zustellung*).[307] The standards for service by public notice are exceptionally high. If an order is rendered, a summary of the statement of claim and a notice as to where the statement of claim can be examined will be

---

[300] ZPO §1069 (1) No. 1. With regard to extra-judicial documents, this is the local court where the person requesting service of process is domiciled or has his residence.
[301] The central bodies in the different German federal states can be found at http://ec.europa.eu/justice_home/judicialatlascivil/html/ds_centralbody_de_en.htm?countrySession=1&.
[302] See the list at http://www.hcch.net/upload/auth14_de.pdf.
[303] *Cf.* the information on the forwarding authorities in Germany at http://www.hcch.net/index_de.php?act=authorities.details&aid=257; see also ZHRO §9 (1) and (2).
[304] Brussels Service Regulation 2007 Art. 7 (1) and Hague Service Convention Art. 5 (1).
[305] Brussels Service Regulation 2007 Art. 10 and Hague Service Convention Art. 6.
[306] ZHRO §§ 11 *et seq.*
[307] ZPO §§ 185 *et seq.*

put on the respective court's notice board.[308] In addition, it will be published in the German federal gazette (*Bundesanzeiger*) and possibly also in daily journals.[309] Service of process generally is deemed to be made one month after the date of the last of these publications.[310]

d) Defects of Service

Without proper service of process, a defendant may not be in a position to protect his legal rights. In Germany, however, service of process is effected by the court and not by the plaintiff. German law, therefore, takes a pragmatic attitude towards defects in service. If the defendant received the documents to be served, or if a defendant argues on the merits of the case, a defect in service of process is deemed to be cured.[311] This applies regardless of whether the defective service of process is made under the Brussels Service Regulation 2007, the Hague Service Convention, other international treaties, or German domestic law.[312]

However, proper service of process usually is a prerequisite for the recognition and enforcement of a judgment abroad. Courts in other jurisdictions in which a German judgment needs to be enforced may take a different view on whether a defect in service was cured or not.

e) Effects of Service

Under German law, a case becomes legally pending (*rechtshängig*) not upon filing of the statement of claim, but only after the statement of claim has been served upon the defendant.[313] The service, therefore, has important consequences. While a case is legally pending in a court, the subject matter of the case cannot be raised by a statement of claim or otherwise in any other court (*lis pendens*).[314] Further, once a case is legally pending with a specific court, a change in circumstances relating to the basis of jurisdiction such as *e.g.* a change of domicile of the defendant etc. will not affect the jurisdiction of the court seized (*perpetuatio fori*).

2. Subsequent Service

The principles set out above for service of the statement of claim apply also to the service of the statement of defense (*Klageerwiderung*), any subsequent written pleadings in the proceedings, and to the service of court documents such as court orders or judgments. Once the litigation is pending, service is made on the attorney of record of each of the parties.[315]

With regard to service abroad, however, only the statement of claim and the initial court order are to be formally served on a foreign defendant. The court order will include a request by the court that the defendant nominate a service agent or attorney of record in Germany within a set time limit. All subsequent documents in the course of the proceedings will then be served on such service

---

[308] ZPO § 186 (2).
[309] ZPO § 187.
[310] ZPO § 188.
[311] ZPO § 189.
[312] *Hartmann* in: Baumbach/Lauterbach/Albers/Hartmann, Zivilprozessordnung, 73rd ed., 2015, § 189 no. 3.
[313] ZPO § 261 (1) in conjunction with ZPO § 253 (1).
[314] Except when used for set-off purposes in other proceedings, see *supra*, at pp. 20 et seq.
[315] ZPO §§ 172, 174.

agent or attorney, respectively. If the defendant fails to name a service agent or attorney, service of process is deemed to be effected by sending all documents to the defendant's foreign address by regular mail, irrespective of whether the defendant receives the mail or not.[316]

K. Possible Responses by Defendant

I. Defending Against the Action

1. Statement of Defense

Usually, a defendant will aim at having the action dismissed by the court. Therefore, the defendant will have to retain an attorney admitted to the respective court, declare his intent to defend against the action, and submit a statement of defense within the time limits set by the court. In proceedings where the representation of a party by an attorney is not mandatory, a foreign defendant needs to nominate a service agent for all future service of process if he wants to prevent service being effected by regular mail.[317]

Like the statement of claim, the statement of defense must name the court where the action is pending and the parties involved. It must also contain a specific motion, usually to dismiss the action in full or in part.[318]

2. Grounds for Defense

a) Defense on the Merits

A defense on the merits may be based on a (partial) denial of facts, on submitting additional facts which show that the claim is not founded, or on legal arguments disputing that there is a legal basis for the claim or for the relief sought by the plaintiff.

b) Defense by Set-Off

A defendant in an action for payment may have claims for payment against the plaintiff as well. The defendant may defend himself by setting off these payment claims in the lawsuit against the payment claims the plaintiff alleges to have (*Prozessaufrechnung*).

Quite often a defendant combines a defense on the merits with a provisional set-off made under the condition precedent that the defense on the merits will not be successful (*Hilfsaufrechnung*). A defendant that has claims against the plaintiff thereby minimizes his risk to be unsuccessful in the lawsuit and thus also the risk of having to bear the court costs and to reimburse the plaintiff for his attorney costs.[319]

---

[316] ZPO § 184.
[317] ZPO § 78.
[318] ZPO § 277.
[319] See *supra*, at p. 11.

c) Defense and Counteraction

Where appropriate, the defendant may defend against the claim on the merits and may at the same time file a counteraction (*Widerklage*) against the plaintiff. The court where the original action is pending also has jurisdiction for the counteraction if the subject matter of the counteraction is sufficiently connected with the subject matter of the original action.[320] Therefore, by way of a counteraction, a court which would otherwise not have international or local jurisdiction may become competent to decide a matter. In cases where the parties have a number of related disputes, counteractions are frequently used to bring all issues before one court for a comprehensive resolution of the overall dispute.

3. Motion for Security for the Costs of the Proceedings

Plaintiffs domiciled in a number of countries in which a German court decision on the reimbursement of attorney costs may not be enforceable need to provide security for the attorney costs the defendant is likely to incur in the German proceedings.[321] Upon motion by the defendant, the court has discretion in determining the amount of this security by court order.[322] Normally, the courts set an amount equal to the expected statutory attorney fees of the defendant on the entry level and on the first appellate level, and the court costs for a potential first appeal. In its order, the court may also determine the type of security the plaintiff is allowed to provide. In the absence of a decision by the court, the security may be posted by depositing money or securities with the court or by submitting a bank guarantee.[323] When ordering security for the costs of the proceedings, the court will set the plaintiff a time limit for providing the security. If the plaintiff fails to observe the time limit, the court will treat the action, upon motion by the defendant, as withdrawn.[324]

In cases with a high value in dispute, the required security may be substantial. In addition, a plaintiff needs to make a prepayment of the full court costs for the entry-level proceedings.[325] A successful motion for security for the costs of proceedings, therefore, forces the plaintiff to make a substantial up-front payment and at the same time secures the defendant's claim for reimbursement of attorney costs if the latter is successful in the litigation.

II. Termination of the Action by Default

An action may be terminated by default judgment (*Versäumnisurteil*) at an early stage. Although a default judgment may also be rendered against a plaintiff,[326] this is very rarely the case. Usually, a default judgment is issued against a defendant.[327]

If the court orders written preliminary proceedings and the defendant fails to respond to the statement of claim by giving notice that he intends to defend against the claim within the time limit set by the court, a default judgment may

---

[320] ZPO §33.
[321] See ZPO §110 for details. A list of the countries where this provision applies can be found at Zöller, Zivilprozessordnung, 30th ed., 2014, Appendix IV.
[322] ZPO §112 (1) and (2).
[323] ZPO §108.
[324] ZPO §113.
[325] See *supra*, at pp. 9 et seq, p. 53; GKG §12.
[326] ZPO §330.
[327] ZPO §331.

be rendered prior to the oral hearing. It is standard practice that a plaintiff, where appropriate, makes a motion to this effect already in the statement of claim.[328]

Upon motion by the plaintiff, a default judgment is also issued when the defendant "fails to appear" in the oral hearing.[329] Even if the defendant is physically present in the hearing, he is deemed to "fail to appear" in the legal sense if he either chooses not to plead before the court or if he is not represented by an attorney admitted to the court when representation by an attorney is mandatory.

If the court has rendered a default judgment, the respective party may lodge an objection (*Einspruch*) within two weeks after having been served with the judgment.[330] The litigation shall in this case be restored to the state in which it was before the default occurred.[331]

Another possibility for one of the parties to react to the other party's "failure to appear" in the oral hearing is to request the court to arrive at a decision on the merits of the case solely on the basis of the legal submissions presented by the parties up to this point (*Entscheidung nach Lage der Akten*).[332] Such decision, however, may only be rendered if there has been at least one oral hearing with both parties present prior to the hearing in which the plaintiff or the defendant "fails to appear" and if the party "having failed to appear" fails to explain its "failure to appear" until seven days before the scheduled decision.[333] A judgment delivered under these circumstances cannot be appealed by an objection, but has to be challenged by an ordinary first appeal.[334]

III. Termination of the Action by Acknowledgement of Claim

The defendant may acknowledge the claim (*Anerkenntnis*) in the written preliminary proceedings or in the oral hearing. If the court has ordered written preliminary proceedings, and if the defendant acknowledges the claim within the time limit set by the court for the statement of defense, a judgment by acceptance (*Anerkenntnisurteil*) will be rendered without an oral hearing.[335] Regardless of whether the court ordered preliminary written proceedings or a first oral hearing, upon an acknowledgement of claim in the oral hearing, a judgment by acknowledgment will be rendered in the oral hearing.[336]

If the defendant immediately acknowledges the claim in the proceedings, and if he did not induce the filing of the action by his conduct, the court will order the plaintiff to bear the cost of the proceedings, regardless of the fact that the plaintiff is successful on the merits.[337]

---

[328] ZPO § 331 (3).
[329] ZPO § 331 (1) and (2).
[330] ZPO §§ 338 *et seq.*
[331] ZPO § 342.
[332] ZPO § 331a.
[333] ZPO § 251a (2).
[334] See *infra*, at pp. 94 et seq.
[335] ZPO §§ 307, 276 (1).
[336] ZPO § 307.
[337] ZPO § 93.

L. Third-Party Intervention

A person who is not a party to the original action may intervene in the litigation in two ways:

I. Main Third-Party Intervention

The main third-party intervention (*Hauptintervention*) is relatively rare. It requires that a lawsuit be pending. A party who is not a party to that lawsuit who raises a claim concerning an object or a right in relation to which the lawsuit is pending may assert its claim in a civil action against both parties.[338] This situation typically arises when the parties to the original lawsuit are in a dispute about who is the owner of a right or an object, and the third party now asserts its own ownership against both of them.

The court that has jurisdiction over the lawsuit between the initial parties also has jurisdiction over the main third-party intervention.[339] The written pleading containing the main third-party intervention has to be served upon the attorneys of the parties in the original lawsuit.[340] Where appropriate, this enables a third-party intervener to obtain international and local jurisdiction at a certain court in Germany and to easily effect proper service of process.

II. Auxiliary Third-Party Intervention

A quite common form of intervention is the auxiliary third-party intervention (*Nebenintervention*).[341] A person who is not a party to a lawsuit thereby intervenes to support the position of one of the parties whose success or defeat will legally affect the interests of the intervener.[342] The intervener does not assert claims of his own in the action, but only assists one of the parties to the original action.

An auxiliary third-party intervention is made by filing a written pleading in the lawsuit, setting out the legal interest of the intervener in assisting one of the parties. The written pleading may be filed at any stage of the lawsuit prior to the judgment becoming final and binding.[343] An intervener does not become a formal party to the proceedings, but is only allowed to act in the interest of the party whom he assists. To this effect, the intervener may make assertions of fact and law, may nominate witnesses, and may participate in the oral hearings. However, any actions by the intervener inconsistent with actions by the party the intervener is assisting are void, and an intervener may not appeal a judgment if the party whom the intervener assisted does not.[344]

An auxiliary third-party intervener is not legally bound by the judgment. Nevertheless, in a subsequent lawsuit between the intervener and the party whom the intervener assisted in the lawsuit, the intervener is largely barred from arguing

---

[338] ZPO §64.
[339] *Cf.* ZPO §64, last sentence.
[340] ZPO §82; *Vollkommer* in: Zöller, Zivilprozessordnung, 30th ed., 2014, §82 no. 1.
[341] For a third-party motion leading to an auxiliary third-party intervention, see *supra*, at p. 41.
[342] ZPO §66 (1).
[343] ZPO §66 (2).
[344] ZPO §67.

that the judgment is incorrect,[345] the reason being that the intervener could have influenced the outcome of the lawsuit.

An auxiliary third-party intervention may be appropriate where a third party has an interest in gaining full information on a lawsuit between other parties. In addition, the third-party intervener has the opportunity to influence the outcome. Even if the party whom the intervener assists is unsuccessful in the litigation, an auxiliary third-party intervener is not liable for the court costs or the attorney costs of the opponent. However, in case of success of the party the intervener assists, the intervener has a claim against the opponent for reimbursement of his attorney costs.[346] An intervention is, therefore, comparatively risk-free from a cost perspective. However, these advantages have to be carefully balanced against the possible drawback of being to a large degree bound by the contents of the judgment in potential subsequent proceedings against the party whom the intervener had assisted in the initial lawsuit.

M. Further Actions by Plaintiff

I. Further Substantiation of Claim

The parties need to plead the facts in sufficient detail (*Substantiierungspflicht*).[347] In the course of the proceedings, the plaintiff may need to state additional facts in order to make his action conclusive. More commonly, providing additional facts may be necessary to clarify the original statements of fact submitted by the plaintiff in light of the factual assertions by the defendant. Generally, the more detailed a party is in rebutting relevant factual allegations of an opponent, the more detailed the response must be. Furthermore, if a party has better knowledge in relation to certain facts, *e.g.* because the relevant facts are within the sphere of observation of such party, this party must comment on these facts more precisely and in more detail, even if the party does not have the burden of proof (*gesteigerte Substantiierungslast*).

In addition to the statements of claim and of defense, it is common for both the plaintiff and the defendant to each submit at least one more substantial written pleading to the court in order to substantiate earlier statements of fact and to comment on the opponent's submission(s). There is no prescribed limit to the number of written pleadings the parties are allowed to file.

II. Amendments and Extension of Claim

A plaintiff may want to amend the subject matter of his claim during the proceedings (*Klageänderung*). He may want to change his motions for relief or may want to change or amend his statements of fact. Altering the subject matter of the lawsuit in the course of the proceedings, however, puts an additional burden on the defendant. The efforts of the defendant invested in defending against the initial claim will have been made in vain if the defendant is subsequently confronted with a different claim. Therefore, an amendment in a pending matter requires

---

[345] See in detail ZPO §68.
[346] See *supra*, at p. 11 and ZPO §101 (1).
[347] See *supra*, at pp. 24 et seq.

either the consent of the defendant, or that the court deems such amendment to be appropriate (*sachdienlich*).[348] However, extending or restricting[349] the original motions for relief or supplementing or correcting the original statements of fact are not deemed to be an amendment of claim.[350]

Further, the plaintiff may at any time extend the proceedings by adding additional claims to the action (*Klageerweiterung*).[351] The prerequisites in this respect are that the court has jurisdiction and that the proceedings are the same. As the extension is regarded as an amendment of claim, the defendant must either consent, or the extension must be deemed appropriate by the court.

III. Termination by Withdrawal of Action

The plaintiff may withdraw his action at any time prior to the first oral hearing. Thereafter, the action may only be withdrawn with the consent of the defendant. If the defendant does not object within a time limit of two weeks after having been served with a written pleading by the plaintiff declaring the withdrawal, the consent is deemed to be granted.[352]

In case of a valid withdrawal of claim, the lawsuit is deemed as not having become pending.[353] The court will decide on the allocation of the costs of the proceedings. Usually, the plaintiff is required to bear the court costs and to reimburse the defendant for his attorney costs.[354]

Withdrawing an action does not bar the plaintiff from filing an action with the same subject matter again at a later stage. However, the defendant may refuse to plead in that later lawsuit until the plaintiff has reimbursed the defendant the attorney costs resulting from the withdrawal of the earlier action.[355]

IV. Termination of Action by Waiver of Claim

A plaintiff may waive the claim (*Verzicht*) asserted in the lawsuit at any time during the proceedings. Upon motion by the defendant, the court will then render a judgment by waiver of claim (*Verzichtsurteil*) against the plaintiff.[356] By such judgment, the plaintiff will lose his claim. In practice, waivers are extremely rare.

V. Termination of Action by Declaring the Proceedings Moot

During the proceedings, the subject matter of the dispute may become moot (*erledigt*). Examples are when *e.g.* the defendant makes payment on the monetary claim the plaintiff pursues in the litigation, or he hands over objects the plaintiff seeks to recover.

---

[348] ZPO § 263.
[349] Regularly, the restriction of the claim will be a partial withdrawal of action which requires after the first oral hearing consent of the defendant, *cf.* Greger in: Zöller, Zivilprozessordnung, 30th ed., 2014, § 264 no 4a.
[350] ZPO §§ 260, 264.
[351] ZPO § 260.
[352] ZPO § 269 (1) and (2).
[353] ZPO § 269 (3).
[354] ZPO § 269 (3).
[355] ZPO § 269 (6).
[356] ZPO § 306.

The plaintiff may then declare the proceedings moot (*Erledigungserklärung*). If the defendant consents or fails to respond to the declaration by the plaintiff within two weeks,[357] the court is bound by the declaration that the proceedings are moot. The court will render a decision on the allocation of the cost of the proceedings only.[358] If, however, the defendant does disputes that the proceedings are moot, the court must decide by judgment whether the original action of the plaintiff would have been successful and have now become moot during the proceedings.[359] If the court finds in favor of the plaintiff, it will render a judgment that the proceedings have become moot,[360] and the defendant will have to bear the costs.

N. Joint Actions by the Parties

I. Suspension of Proceedings

When the parties are in settlement negotiations, they frequently make a motion to the court for suspension of the proceedings (*Ruhen des Verfahrens*).[361] Such motions are usually granted although it is in the discretion of the court to grant or deny such motion. If proceedings are suspended, the court will order to continue the proceedings upon motion by one of the parties.

II. Termination of Action by Settlement

1. Settlement in Court

German civil procedure law is based on the assumption that amicable settlements serve the interests of the parties best. Therefore, the court is under a legal obligation to promote a settlement at any stage of the proceedings.[362] Furthermore, settlements are very much favored by German judges in their own interest. When the parties settle, the judge does not have to render a judgment and, in particular, does not have to prepare detailed written reasons for his decision. This not only saves the judge time and effort and thus reduces his workload, but it also excludes that the judgment may be reversed on appeal. A judge's career generally benefits from being known to have the skills to get the parties to settle and having a low percentage of judgments that were reversed.

For these reasons, German judges actively promote settlements where feasible. The parties meet face to face in the courtroom at the oral hearing. When structuring their introduction to the case, judges tend to point out the weaknesses of their respective position to both parties. In the extreme, the presiding judge first explains to the plaintiff why he may lose the litigation and then points out to the defendant why his chances for success are also shaky. The judge may then propose a detailed settlement indicating to both parties that, at the end of the day, the judgment may look quite similar.

---

[357] See ZPO §91a (1), the defendant has to be informed about this possible effect.
[358] ZPO §91a.
[359] *Vollkommer* in: Zöller, Zivilprozessordnung, 30th ed., 2014, §91a no. 34 *et seq.*, esp. no. 44.
[360] *Vollkommer* in: Zöller, Zivilprozessordnung, 30th ed., 2014, §91a no. 45.
[361] ZPO §251.
[362] ZPO §278 (1).

Depending on the situation at hand, this may sometimes be perceived by a party as undue pressure. It is, however, the attorney's role to stand firm if the settlement proposal does not serve the best interests of his client. Very often, judges know the strength and weaknesses of the legal position of each party quite well and are open to a focused oral pleading by the attorney. If that does not help, an indication by the attorney that the appellate court may view certain aspects differently may. This kind of judicial participation frequently enables the parties (and sometimes their attorneys) to view the matter from another perspective. In particular, the clarifications offered by the judge regarding the strengths and weaknesses of the case often assist the parties in reaching, at least by objective standards, a fair and adequate settlement.

A settlement in court may be documented in the record of the hearing (*Prozessvergleich*). A settlement made of record is an execution title (*Vollstreckungstitel*) and may be enforced the same way as a final judgment.[363]

Parties quite often enter into a court-proposed settlement under the condition precedent that the settlement becomes final unless one of the parties formally objects to it in writing to the court within an agreed period of time (*Vergleich unter Widerrufsvorbehalt*). A conditional settlement of this kind is, for example, advisable when a party needs the consent of internal corporate bodies or of third parties with an interest in the litigation such as an insurer. A conditional settlement may also be used if a party does not want to object straight out to a settlement proposed by the court in the oral hearing.

2. Out-of-Court Settlement

The parties may also reach a settlement out of court (*aussergerichtlicher Vergleich*). Depending on the stage of the civil proceedings, this may save court costs and attorney fees. These settlement agreements are, however, not legally enforceable on their own. A party claiming the violation of an out-of-court settlement generally must bring a new civil action to enforce the settlement agreement.

Depending on the subject matter of the dispute, however, an out-of-court settlement agreement may be drafted in a way making an action for its enforcement unnecessary. For example, the parties may agree in the settlement agreement on the payment of a certain sum of money within a certain time limit. They may further agree not to terminate the civil proceedings, but just to jointly suspend them and to make the settlement conditional upon payment within the time limit. Then, if no timely payment is made, the lawsuit will just continue.[364]

Sometimes, however, obtaining an execution title will be necessary or at least advisable. There are two ways to convert an out-of-court settlement agreement into an execution title:

First, if the action is still pending, the parties may submit their out-of-court settlement agreement to the court. The court will render an order, thereby converting it into an execution title,[365] which normally does not require more than a few days.

Second, if the settlement agreement is signed by the attorneys of record for the parties and if the respective debtor expressly submits to immediate execution (*Unterwerfung unter die sofortige Zwangsvollstreckung*), the document may be converted

---

[363] ZPO §794 (1) No.1; Brussels Regulation 2012 Art. 59.
[364] See *supra*, at p. 65.
[365] ZPO §278 (6).

into an execution title as well (*Anwaltsvergleich*).³⁶⁶ The settlement agreement has to be filed with the local court where one of the parties is domiciled, or with a notary public. Upon application by the respective creditor, either the court having jurisdiction over the dispute which was settled, or the notary public with whom the document was filed, will convert the settlement into an execution title.

O. Additional Court Orders

I. Court Orders Designed to Expedite the Proceedings

The court has the duty to expedite the proceedings.³⁶⁷ In order to prepare for the oral hearing, the court may, therefore, render orders requesting the parties to amend or to elaborate on certain aspects of their written pleadings.³⁶⁸ The court may further order the production of documents or of objects to be inspected.³⁶⁹ It is the rule that the parties and their representatives³⁷⁰ are ordered to appear in person at the oral hearing. In rare circumstances, a court may even render an order to take evidence before the oral hearing has taken place, and will then order the expert or a third-party witness to appear and to testify at the first oral hearing.³⁷¹

II. Court Orders for Joinder of Actions and for Severance

If there are several separate lawsuits pending in one court, the court may join these actions if the subject matter of the claims is either legally connected or could have been asserted in one legal action (joinder of actions, *Prozessverbindung*).³⁷² It is not necessary that the parties to the lawsuits concerned are identical.

Likewise, the court may order that several claims raised in one lawsuit be severed and dealt with in separate proceedings (severance of actions, *Prozesstrennung*).³⁷³ This may be the case if the subject matter of the claims is not connected, or if a severance seems for other reasons more appropriate. The same applies when a counteraction is not legally connected with the subject matter of the lawsuit.³⁷⁴

Both the decision on joinder and on severance of actions are within the court's discretion. The court may set aside its order at any time.³⁷⁵

III. Court Order for Stay of Proceedings

The court may at its discretion stay the proceedings in certain cases (*Aussetzung*).³⁷⁶ If the outcome of the civil proceedings depends *e.g.* on questions of fact or

---

[366] ZPO §§ 796a *et seq.*
[367] ZPO § 273 (1).
[368] ZPO § 273 (2) No. 1.
[369] ZPO § 273 (2) No. 2; ZPO § 273 (2) No. 5 in conjunction with ZPO §§ 142, 144.
[370] ZPO § 273 (2) No. 3; ZPO § 141.
[371] ZPO § 273 (2) No. 4, (3).
[372] ZPO § 147.
[373] ZPO § 145 (1).
[374] ZPO § 145 (2).
[375] ZPO § 150.
[376] ZPO §§ 148 *et seq.*

of law which are the subject matter of administrative or criminal law proceedings, the courts very often order a stay until these issues are clarified.

When lawsuits with the same or a closely connected subject matter are brought into the courts of several Member States of the European Union, the Brussels Regulation 2012 requires[377] or allows that[378] the courts seized later stay the proceedings.[379]

IV. Disclosure Orders by the Court

1. Disclosure Orders for Production of Evidence

In a pending lawsuit where a document or an object for inspection is in the possession of the opponent, a party may specify such document or object as evidence for its own statements of fact by making a motion that the opponent produce the document or object, respectively.

If such party has a substantive claim to this effect, the court may order the opponent to produce the document or object.[380] The court may, however, refuse to issue an order if the opponent shows that there are compelling interests not to disclose the document or the object.[381] Compelling interests may include *e.g.* economic or other disadvantages likely or possibly resulting from producing the information, the threat of criminal prosecution or fear of disclosing trade secrets.

The court may also order the opponent, upon motion by the party, to produce the document or object if the opponent referred thereto in his submissions as a means of evidence.[382] The opponent is then deemed to have waived all privileges by such reference.

A court order to produce information is not enforceable. The court may, however, draw negative inferences from a refusal by the opponent to comply.[383]

2. General Disclosure Orders

The court also may order a party, or a third party, to produce documents which are in its possession and to which one of the parties in the proceedings has referred.[384] The court can render an order to the effect that a party or a third party shall present an object which is in its possession for inspection by the court or to allow such inspection by the court on the relevant party's premises. Likewise, the court may order an expert to examine an issue of fact.[385]

The provisions from which the court derives this power are broadly worded. They are designed to allow the court to educate itself on the subject matter of the dispute in order to understand and to assess the submissions of the parties properly. However, the court may only issue a disclosure order to clarify a question of fact which was already pleaded in sufficient detail by one of the parties. Further,

---

[377] Brussels Regulation 2012 Art. 29.
[378] Brussels Regulation 2012 Art. 30; German courts will, however, not apply Brussels Regulation 2012 Art. 30 (2).
[379] See *supra*, at p. 20.
[380] ZPO §§ 422 *et seq.*; ZPO § 371 (2).
[381] See *Geimer* in: Zöller, Zivilprozessordnung, 30th ed., 2014, § 422 no. 4; see *infra*, at p. 79.
[382] ZPO §§ 421, 423.
[383] ZPO §§ 427; ZPO 371 (3).
[384] ZPO §§ 144, 142.
[385] ZPO § 144.

it is in the court's discretion whether to issue a disclosure order. When exercising its discretion, the court must balance the interests of the requested party in not disclosing the information, *e.g.* considering reasons of protection of privacy and trade secrets, against the interest of verifying questions of fact and thus ascertaining the truth. In particular, the legitimate interests of a third party who is not a party to the lawsuit, and who will normally not be indemnified for expenditures incurred in producing the documents, must be given weight by the court.

Since the right of the court to issue general disclosure orders is not fully compatible with the general principle of party control on the proceedings, the courts are reluctant to issue disclosure orders.[386]

If a party does not comply with a general disclosure order directed against it, such party only bears the risk that the court will draw negative inferences from this conduct. The order is not otherwise enforceable against an uncooperative party. Further, the respective document or object may be precluded from the proceedings at a later stage, even if the initially uncooperative party then would like to present it. Uncooperative third parties, however, risk much more. The court may order coercive penalty payments and even detention to enforce cooperation.[387]

P. Interruption of Proceedings

There are a number of events which lead to an interruption of proceedings (*Unterbrechung*).[388] The most frequent example in commercial cases is the formal commencement of insolvency proceedings with regard to one of the parties to the lawsuit. The interruption will end either when the insolvency proceedings are terminated or when the liquidator formally makes a declaration to the court that he resumes the litigation.[389]

Q. The Oral Hearing

I. General

1. Function

The oral hearing is the core of German litigation proceedings.[390] The court, the parties and their attorneys address the factual and legal issues of the case in an oral argument. Part of the oral hearing is the evidentiary proceedings.[391]

Technically, there is only one oral hearing. In practice, however, this hearing may be adjourned, so the litigants and the court meet more than once for the oral hearing. The court and the parties are under an obligation to conduct the proceed-

---

[386] However, see Regional Court (LG) Ingolstadt, Decision of 22 March 2002, (Docket No. 4 O 1729/01), Neue Zeitschrift für Insolvenzrecht, 2002, p. 390. The court granted an order requesting disclosure of a complete folder.
[387] ZPO §§ 142 (2), 144 (2) in conjunction with ZPO § 390.
[388] ZPO §§ 239 *et seq.*
[389] ZPO § 240.
[390] See ZPO § 128 (1).
[391] See *infra*, at pp. 72 et seq.

ings as expediently as possible and to limit the number of hearings to a minimum. Therefore, the court has the power to set time limits for the submission of written pleadings,[392] to render court orders to prepare for the oral hearing,[393] and to reject submissions by the parties which are not made within the time limits or which could have been made at an earlier stage in the proceedings.[394]

2. Record of Hearing

The formalities and the essential proceedings during the oral hearing are recorded in writing in the record of the oral hearing (*Protokoll über die mündliche Verhandlung*).[395] The record includes formal matters such as the caption of the case, the name of the judges, the attorneys and the parties present, the time and place of the hearing, and the substantive contents of the proceedings which took place. Applications, claims or motions made at the hearing, party admissions, statements and testimony by witnesses, the results of inspecting evidence, any orders by the courts, matters such as withdrawals of claim or waivers of appeal, and the result of the efforts to promote a settlement must be reflected in the record.[396]

The record is usually dictated by the presiding judge in the presence of the parties. It is not a verbatim transcript or a record of all and everything that was said, but just a summary of the key elements of the oral hearing. Documents may be attached to and thus technically included in the record.[397]

The record is the official documentation of a hearing. The observance or omission of any required formal or procedural step may only be proven by the record.[398] The parties and their attorneys, therefore, have the right to request that certain events or statements be included in the record.[399] Further, the attorneys to the parties receive a copy of the record and have the right to make a motion to the court to correct the record.[400]

3. Publicity

Oral hearings as well as the taking of evidence are open to the public. Radio or TV transmissions of oral hearings are, however, prohibited.[401]

In exceptional cases the court may, upon a motion by one of the parties, order that the public be excluded.[402] In commercial matters, the discussion of business or trade secrets in the hearing may constitute grounds for such exclusion order.[403] The court may further formally order all persons allowed to participate in the hearing to maintain strict confidentiality.[404]

---

[392] ZPO § 132.
[393] See *supra*, at p. 54.
[394] ZPO §§ 282, 296, 296a.
[395] ZPO § 159.
[396] *Cf.* ZPO § 160.
[397] ZPO § 160 (5).
[398] ZPO § 165.
[399] ZPO § 163 (4).
[400] ZPO § 164.
[401] GVG §§ 169 *et seq.*
[402] GVG §§ 171b *et seq.*
[403] GVG § 172 No. 2.
[404] GVG § 174 (3). A violation of this order is a criminal offence (Penal Code, StGB § 353 c Nos. 1, 2).

II. Conduct of the Oral Hearing

The sole judge[405] or the presiding judge (if the court is composed of more than one judge) will direct the proceedings.[406] The normal course of an oral hearing will be as follows:[407]

1. Opening of the Hearing

The presiding judge will open the proceedings at the set date by calling the parties and their attorneys and recording their presence in the record.

2. Conciliation Hearing

The court is legally obliged to facilitate an amicable settlement. For this purpose, the main oral hearing will be preceded by a conciliation hearing (*Güteverhandlung*).[408]

a) Introduction by the Presiding Judge

The presiding judge will introduce the matter. Usually, the judge will summarize the view of the court regarding the factual and legal issues of the case, pointing out the strengths and weaknesses of both parties' arguments.[409]

b) Pleading and Discussion

This introduction is followed by a discussion with the parties and their attorneys. However, since the parties have already filed extensive written pleadings, new aspects which may change the initial assessment of the case by the court are the exception. Rather, the discussion will focus on points raised by the court, on clarifications and on summaries of the respective arguments. If no relevant facts are in dispute, courts frequently have prepared a draft of the judgment from which they read when summarizing the case.

This practice sometimes disconcerts foreign parties attending the hearing. They have the impression that the judge is partial to one of the parties, and they are under the impression that the attorney to such party does not sufficiently argue the case in the hearing. The attorneys, however, have already extensively presented their arguments in their written pleadings. After a thorough preparation of the case and carefully prepared written pleadings, there is often little left which needs to be raised in the hearing.

c) Settlement Attempt

Based on the introduction to the case and the discussion with the parties and their attorneys, the court will attempt to settle the case.[410] Quite often, the court may even suggest the contents of a potential settlement.[411] Where appropriate, the court

---

[405] Who is adressed as „presiding judge" as well.
[406] ZPO § 136.
[407] *Cf.* ZPO §§ 136 *et seq.*
[408] ZPO § 278.
[409] See ZPO § 139 (1).
[410] ZPO § 278.
[411] See *supra*, at pp. 65 et seq.

may also suggest that the parties attempt out-of-court mediation proceedings.[412] The parties are, however, not under a duty to follow the suggestion.

3. Main Oral Hearing

If, in the reasonable opinion of the court, it appears that a conciliation hearing will not be successful,[413] the court may proceed to the main hearing immediately after the opening of the hearing.[414]

a) Asserting the Motions

The court will then request the attorneys to the parties to formally assert their motions (*Stellen der Anträge*).[415]

b) Pleading and Discussion

The court will then give an introduction to the case, and the parties and their attorneys will discuss the legal and factual issues.[416] If a conciliation hearing took place already, another introduction and discussion may be skipped. If not, the introduction and discussion is basically identical to the one in the conciliation hearing described above.

c) Taking of Evidence

Thereafter evidence will be taken, if necessary, and the parties will have the opportunity to comment on the results of the taking of evidence.[417]

d) Conclusion of the Hearing

At the conclusion of the hearing, the court will set a date on which the judgment will be rendered (*Verkündungstermin*), which has to be within three weeks' time unless special reasons like size or complexity of matters request more time. Sometimes, the judgment is rendered immediately after the main oral hearing (*Stuhlurteil*).[418]

R. Evidentiary Proceedings

I. General

1. Scope of Taking Evidence

In order to streamline the proceedings, the court will only take that evidence which is relevant for deciding the case. By applying the method of "comparative

---

[412] ZPO § 278 (5).
[413] *Cf.* ZPO § 278 (2).
[414] ZPO § 279 (1).
[415] ZPO § 137 (1).
[416] It is assumed that the parties implicitly plead the full contents of their written pleadings in the hearing , ZPO § 137 (2) and (3).
[417] ZPO § 279 (2) and (3), ZPO § 284 and see *infra*, at pp. 73 et seq.
[418] ZPO § 310 (1).

analysis",[419] the court will determine the relevant factual issues which are disputed.

The court will further determine whether the taking of evidence regarding disputed facts is necessary. This is not the case if the fact is publicly known or if the relevant facts are known by the court *ex officio*, *e.g.* from taking evidence in parallel proceedings.[420] For facts which need to be proven, the court will look to whether the party bearing the burden of proof has offered evidence.

2. Evidentiary Means

There are five forms of evidence available, *i.e.*
(i)   proof by documentary evidence (*Beweis durch Urkunden*),
(ii) proof by inspection by the court (*Beweis durch Augenschein*),
(iii) proof by third-party witness testimony (*Zeugenbeweis*),
(iv) proof by expert testimony (*Beweis durch Sachverständige*), and
(v)   proof by party testimony (*Beweis durch Parteivernehmung*).

3. Order to Take Evidence

If facts need to be proven, the court will render an order to take evidence (*Beweisbeschluss*) setting out the time and date of the hearing in which the evidence shall be taken, the factual issue on which evidence is taken, the evidentiary means including the names of the witnesses to be heard or the object to be inspected, and which of the parties has referred to the respective means of evidence, usually indicating which party has the burden of proof for the disputed fact.[421] The order will usually make the summoning of a witness or of an expert subject to the party bearing the burden of proof advancing the likely costs of hearing the witness or expert.

II. Taking Evidence

The taking of evidence usually[422] takes place in front of the court and in the presence of the parties and their attorneys.[423] If the taking of evidence involves a person who does not have sufficient command of the German language, the court will provide for a sworn interpreter.[424]

1. Proof by Documentary Evidence

Documentary evidence[425] is by far the most important evidentiary means in German litigation. German law distinguishes between two kinds of documents. An official document (*öffentliche Urkunde*) has been created by a German or foreign public official in the course of public duty.[426] The most important category of official documents in practice are documents created by German public notaries (*Notare*), *e.g.* wills, real estate deeds, or certain corporate documents. A German

---

[419] See *supra*, at pp. 22 et seq.
[420] ZPO § 291.
[421] ZPO §§ 358 *et seq.*
[422] ZPO § 355 (1); for exceptions see ZPO §§ 362 *et seq.*
[423] ZPO § 357.
[424] See *supra*, at pp. 7.
[425] For a definition, see *supra*, at pp. 35 et seq.
[426] ZPO §§ 415, 438.

or foreign official document is sufficient to prove the facts recorded in the document.[427] Therefore, *e.g.* a contract concluded before a notary public constitutes sufficient proof that the parties signed the contract and that the declarations in the contract originate from them. However, a party may prove that the official document does not accurately reflect the recorded facts.[428]

All other documents are considered private documents (*Privaturkunden*). They (only) prove that the statements made in such documents are those of their author(s),[429] provided that it has been proved that the document is authentic, *i.e.* originated from the author(s). The court may then draw whatever conclusions are justified by the statements in the document. A court will normally assume that facts happened as stated in the document, unless there is evidence to the contrary.

Documentary evidence usually is introduced to the proceedings by one of the parties submitting copies of the relevant documents together with a written pleading. In case of official documents, a party may make a motion that the respective official or public authority shall be requested to forward the documents to the court.[430] The court also may order one or both of the parties or third parties to submit documents.[431]

The authenticity of a document is generally deemed to be admitted by the parties, unless it is explicitly contested by a party.[432] There is a presumption under German law as to the authenticity of domestic official documents. The same applies to legalized foreign official documents.[433] In case of doubt, the court may investigate the authenticity of a domestic or foreign official document.[434]

If a party disputes the authenticity of a private document, the party relying on the document has the burden of demonstrating its authenticity.[435] This may be done by any evidentiary means available. If the document is signed, the authenticity of the signature may be established by comparison of the signature with a specimen of known origin. If the signature is found to be genuine, the authenticity of the document and its contents preceding (but not following) the signature may be inferred. Comparison of the signatures may be made by the court or by an expert appointed by the court. In practice, disputes regarding the authenticity of public or private documents are quite rare.

2. Proof by Inspection by the Court

Proof by inspection[436] encompasses all forms of sensory perception of persons, places and things by the court. This may include the physical condition of products or of business premises, pictures, photos, construction plans or electronically stored data.[437]

Usually, all members of the court take part in the inspection. However, they may delegate the inspection to a single member of the court or even to another

---

[427] See ZPO §§ 415, 417, 418 for details.
[428] ZPO §§ 415 (2), 418 (2).
[429] ZPO § 416.
[430] ZPO § 432.
[431] ZPO §§ 421 *et seq.*, see *supra*, at pp. 68 et seq.
[432] ZPO § 439.
[433] ZPO § 438; concerning the translation of documents written in a foreign language see *supra*, at pp. 6 et seq, p. 53.
[434] ZPO §§ 437, 438.
[435] ZPO § 440.
[436] ZPO §§ 371 *et seq.*
[437] See *supra*, at p. 36.

court.[438] The court may inspect objects presented in the oral hearing or objects in the public domain or objects within the control of either of the parties, such as *e.g.* business premises. Further, the court may order third parties to make such objects available to the court for inspection.[439] The relevant facts observed during the inspection will be documented in the record of the hearing.

3. Proof by Third-Party Witness Testimony

a) Duties of a Witness

The court may order almost any natural person as a third-party witness.[440] Witnesses domiciled or residing within the jurisdiction of the German courts have the duty to appear when summoned,[441] to prepare for their testimony,[442] to truthfully testify,[443] and to give testimony under oath when ordered by the court.[444]

b) Hearing of the Witness

Almost always, witnesses testify in open court in the presence of the parties and their attorneys.[445] Each witness is examined individually and without the presence of witnesses to be heard later.[446] Witnesses whose statements are contradictory, however, may be confronted with one another by the court.[447]

The witness is expected to testify in a matter-of-fact and non-conclusory form. He is supposed to consult relevant documents to refresh his recollection in advance and to bring such documents with him to assist him in giving his testimony, if appropriate.[448] However, a witness is not required by law to extensively prepare for the testimony.[449]

The presiding judge will ask the witness for his name, age, address, and profession or trade and will admonish him to speak the truth.[450] The witness then will be asked to state his personal knowledge on the relevant facts at the beginning of the witness hearing.[451] The presiding judge may pose questions to the witness to clarify and expand the testimony. Only thereafter, the parties and their attorneys may ask questions.[452] Different from witness examinations *e.g.* in the U.S., this will usually not be done in an aggressive or inquisitorial way or in the form of a cross-examination. Presiding judges usually take great care to protect witnesses from intimidation by attorneys or by parties. In addition, a witness is entitled to the assistance of his own legal counsel in preparation for and in the course of giving testimony.[453]

---

[438] ZPO § 372 (2).
[439] Exceptions apply to ZPO § 371 (2).
[440] Limitations exist for public officials, judges etc; ZPO § 376.
[441] ZPO §§ 377, 380, 381.
[442] ZPO § 378.
[443] *Cf.* ZPO § 395 (1).
[444] ZPO § 391.
[445] *Cf.* ZPO § 397.
[446] ZPO § 394 (1).
[447] ZPO § 394 (2).
[448] ZPO § 378.
[449] But see ZPO § 378.
[450] ZPO § 395.
[451] ZPO § 396.
[452] ZPO § 397.
[453] Federal Constitutional Court (BVerfG), Decision of 8 October 1974 (Docket No. BvR 747/73), Neue Juristische Wochenschrift, 1975, p. 103.

The court may administer the oath if this seems advisable, *e.g.* the oath is likely to lead to a truthful statement.[454] However, in practice the oath is seldom administered, unless one of the parties insists. A witness who intentionally provides untruthful testimony – or in the case of testimony administered under oath, negligently or intentionally provides untruthful testimony – has committed a criminal offense and is subject to up to 15 years imprisonment.[455] Since the court decides only at the end of the testimony whether the witness shall confirm his previous statements under oath, a witness is well advised to stick to the truth.

c) Recording of the Witness Testimony

Witness testimony is not recorded verbatim. Instead, the presiding judge usually dictates summaries of the witness's statements and the questions posed for the record of the hearing. Sometimes the court record, therefore, only reflects what the presiding judge has understood to be the essence of the witness's statements rather than what has been really said. Since the contents of the record of the witness testimony form the factual basis for the judgment and for any subsequent appeal,[456] the attorneys for the parties have to make sure that relevant statements of the witness are properly documented in the record.

d) Remuneration of Witnesses

A witness is compensated for the loss of time and earnings according to the German Judicial Remuneration and Compensation Act (*Justizvergütungs- und -entschädigungsgesetz, JVEG*). The court will request an advance for the likely cost of hearing the witness from the party offering the witness testimony.[457]

e) Probative Value of Witness Testimony

In practice, courts tend to believe in the truthfulness of a witness statement.[458] Possibly in view of the stiff criminal law sentences for untruthful witness testimony, courts frequently tend to treat a witness's statement appearing to be untruthful as not being relevant, or interpret it in a way consistent with the true facts as apparent from other sources.

4. Proof by Expert Testimony

a) Appointment of an Expert

If the determination or the proper assessment of specific facts requires special expertise, the court may appoint an expert.[459] It is in the discretion of the court to decide whether it has the ability and expertise to assess the issue itself, or whether to retain an expert. However, failure to appoint an expert may give grounds for an appeal.

Quite often, the parties to a litigation submit written expert opinions (*Parteigutachten*). These opinions are technically treated as part of the respective party's

---

[454] ZPO § 391.
[455] German Penal Code (*Strafgesetzbuch, StGB*) §§ 153 *et seq.*
[456] See *infra*, at p. 97, p. 100.
[457] ZPO § 379.
[458] *Cf. Hartmann* in: Baumbach/Lauterbach/Albers/Hartmann, Zivilprozessordnung, 73rd ed., 2015, Overview § 373 no. 6.
[459] ZPO § 404 (1) and (2).

pleadings.[460] Therefore, to prove the allegation of fact made in such an expert opinion, the respective party must make a motion to the court to appoint an independent expert to confirm the allegation. Only the evidence given by a court-appointed expert constitutes proof by expert testimony.

If the court intends to appoint an expert, it usually asks the parties to suggest suitable experts.[461] If the parties agree on a specific expert, the court is at least in practice bound by their proposal.[462] If the parties cannot agree, and the court then appoints an expert, each of the parties may challenge the expert on the same grounds that a judge would be subject to a challenge.[463]

b) Duties of an Expert

In German litigation, the expert serves as an assistant to the court rather than as a witness for or against one of the parties. An expert accepting an appointment by the court has a number of duties.[464] Besides his duty to be impartial, the expert has to consider the assignment and to make sure that he is qualified and has the time to render the expert opinion requested. Once the appointment has been accepted, the expert may only withdraw or resign for good cause and only with the consent of the court.[465]

c) Opinion of the Expert

The expert will receive a description of the factual issue on which he is to testify and any specific instructions by the court through a court order.[466] Usually, the court submits the entire court file to the expert as well.

The expert will normally render his opinion in writing.[467] The court will send copies to the parties who have the opportunity to comment on the findings by the expert. The parties may request that additional questions be posed to the expert and be addressed by him.[468] They may further ask the court to summon the expert to an oral hearing to be questioned on his testimony.[469] Although permissible under German law,[470] experts are rarely sworn in.

d) Challenges to the Opinion by the Expert

The parties may argue that the expert testimony should not be taken into account by the court for a particular reason. In practice, parties not satisfied with the findings of the court-appointed expert often submit opinions of party experts commissioned by them to substantiate such argument. If the court is in doubt as to the accuracy of the expert opinion, it may appoint a second expert to address the issues again.[471] If the testimonies of these court-appointed experts differ on an

---

[460] See *supra*, at p. 36.
[461] ZPO § 404 (3).
[462] ZPO § 404 (4).
[463] ZPO § 406 (1) in conjunction with ZPO §§ 41 *et seq.*
[464] ZPO §§ 407 *et seq.*
[465] *Cf.* ZPO §§ 408 (1), 409.
[466] ZPO § 405.
[467] ZPO § 411 (1).
[468] ZPO § 411 (4).
[469] ZPO § 411 (3).
[470] ZPO § 410.
[471] ZPO § 412.

issue, the court even may appoint a further expert (*Obergutachter*) of exceptional ability to review the earlier expert testimony.

e) Remuneration of Experts

The remuneration of court-appointed experts is set by the court within the statutory ranges of the German Judicial Remuneration and Compensation Act.[472] In practice, the court, the parties and the expert quite often agree on a negotiated fee more in line with market rates. The party having the burden of proof on the fact to be addressed by the expert has to make a prepayment of the expert fees. Like other fees and costs, the expert fees will ultimately be assessed against the party unsuccessful in the lawsuit.

f) Probative Value of Expert Testimony

The court has discretion to evaluate and determine what weight it shall give to the testimony of the court-appointed expert.[473] In practice, it is very rare that a court departs from the opinion of an expert. Additional experts are even more rarely appointed by the court, and only if there is clear evidence that the initial expert opinion is deficient. Given the importance of technical, scientific or accounting issues in litigation, many cases are in practice ultimately decided by the expert.

g) Expert Witnesses

The position of an expert witness (*sachverständiger Zeuge*) is a mixture between a normal third-party witness giving testimony and an expert rendering a formal expert opinion. For example, a physician who treated a patient and testifies in court will be deemed an expert witness as he combines giving testimony on his work performed on the patient with expert knowledge. In German proceedings, the statement of an expert witness is technically considered third-party witness testimony,[474] although the court may give more weight to such testimony due to the witness's expert knowledge.

5. Proof by Party Testimony

a) Informal Hearing of a Party

As a rule, the parties are requested to appear at the oral hearing.[475] German courts frequently hear the parties informally in the oral hearing to clarify the facts (*Parteianhörung*). Technically, the statements made are not party testimony, but only part of the respective party's pleadings.

In practice, however, the courts quite often tend to give substantial probative value to a party's statements in the oral hearing, as such statements are not "filtered" by the parties' attorneys. In particular in consumer and banking cases, parties being questioned by the court quite frequently deviate from the pleadings made by their attorneys in a way which is detrimental to their case. If a party refuses to participate in an informal hearing, the court may, and often will, draw negative inferences therefrom.

---

[472] ZPO § 413.
[473] ZPO § 286. *Cf. Greger* in: Zöller, Zivilprozessordnung, 30th ed., 2014, § 402 no. 7a.
[474] ZPO § 414.
[475] *Cf.* ZPO §§ 141, 273 (2) No. 3 and see *infra*, at pp. 55, 69 et seq.

b) Formal Party Testimony

A party may be requested by an order to take evidence to serve as a party witness (*Parteivernehmung*).[476]

The court may order the hearing of a party witness on its own initiative.[477] To do so, however, the court must already have concluded that the facts to be proven by means of hearing the party witness are likely to prove true. In addition, all other possible evidentiary means must have been exhausted.[478] Therefore, such orders *ex officio* are rare.

A party may make a motion to hear the opponent as a party witness.[479] A party, however, usually feels uncomfortable with relying on the opponent's testimony regarding a fact for which such party bears the burden of proof. A party may rather prefer to hear itself as a party witness to prove its own allegations of fact. A court order to this effect, however, requires the consent of the opponent,[480] which for obvious reasons is hardly ever granted.

Party testimony is taken by the court in the same manner as testimony from a third-party witness.[481] However, a party cannot be forced to testify. The court may, however, draw negative inferences from a refusal to testify, provided that there are no reasonable grounds for the refusal.[482] Reasonable grounds may include *e.g.* economic or other disadvantages likely or possibly resulting from testifying, the threat of criminal prosecution of the party, or the fear of disclosing trade secrets.[483]

6. Frustration of Taking Evidence

As mentioned above, a German court may draw negative inferences from the fact that a party refuses to produce documents or objects for inspection, to participate in an informal party hearing, or to serve as a party witness.[484] This rule applies to all other aspects of a party's conduct related to the taking of evidence as well.[485] For example, the court may draw negative inferences from a refusal to give a signature to prove the authenticity of documents, a refusal to participate in a reasonable medical examination, or the destruction of objects which should have been inspected by the court.

III. Privileges

Compared with *e.g.* the U.S., the parties to a German litigation as well as third parties are protected by quite extensive privileges.

---

[476] ZPO §450.
[477] ZPO §448.
[478] Federal Court of Justice (BGH), Decision of 8 November 1993 (Docket No. II ZR 26/93), Neue Juristische Wochenschrift, 1994, p. 320.
[479] ZPO §§445, 446.
[480] ZPO §447.
[481] ZPO §451.
[482] ZPO §§453, 454, 446.
[483] *Greger* in: Zöller, Zivilprozessordnung, 30th ed., 2014, §446 no. 1.
[484] See *supra*, at pp. 68 et seq, 79.
[485] *Greger* in: Zöller, Zivilprozessordnung, 30th ed., 2014, §286 no. 14a.

1. Party Privilege

a) Privileges as to Informal Hearings and as to Serving as a Party Witness

A party can neither be forced to participate in an informal hearing before the court (*Parteianhörung*) nor to testify as a party witness.[486]

The court will evaluate the refusal to produce information when deciding whether the respective allegation as to facts should be regarded as true or untrue.[487] There is, however, the risk that the court will draw negative inferences from the refusal.[488]

b) Privilege and Disclosure Orders

As set out above,[489] the court may order a party to produce documents or to grant inspection rights. These orders are not enforceable against a party, but the refusal to comply may be taken into account to the detriment of the party when the court decides whether the allegation of a factual issue should be regarded as true.[490] In practice, the courts will follow the same standards which are applied when a party refuses to provide information in an informal hearing, or to testify as a party witness.

2. Privileges for Third-Party Witnesses

a) Professional Privilege

A person who is by virtue of his office, profession or trade entrusted with information that is to be kept secret due to its nature or pursuant to a law may refuse to testify with regard to facts that fall within the scope of his duty of confidentiality.[491]

aa) (Former) Corporate Officers. Professional privilege applies to current and former members of the management board (*Vorstand*) and of the supervisory board (*Aufsichtsrat*) of a German stock corporation as well as to the managing directors (*Geschäftsführer*) of a limited liability company or of a partnership. The privilege extends to all information which is confidential by its nature, including trade secrets, and is therefore very broad.[492]

bb) Bank Secrecy Rules. Further, bank employees are entitled to withhold testimony relating to matters subject to the obligation of a bank to observe secrecy. Although German law contains no statutory definition of bank secrecy, the concept is acknowledged in German law. The bank secrecy privilege relates to financial institutions of any kind.

Different from *e.g.* the U.S., the scope of the protection is very broad. The privilege extends to everything that the bank has learned by or in connection with the business relationship (including the existence of such relationship). It relates

---

[486] ZPO §454.
[487] ZPO §286.
[488] ZPO §§453, 446; see *supra*, at p. 79.
[489] See *supra*, at pp. 68 et seq.
[490] ZPO §286.
[491] ZPO §383 (1) No. 6.
[492] Higher Regional Court (OLG) Koblenz, Decision of 5 March 1987 (Docket No. 6 W 38/87), Neue Juristische Wochenschrift – Rechtsprechungsreport, 1987, p. 809.

not only to facts regarding the financial or personal situation of the customer, but also to assessments of any kind that the bank is in a position to make only because of information it has received in the course of the banking relationship. The secrecy obligation also extends to information received in the phase of negotiations preceding the signing of a banking contract and survives the termination of the banking relationship. Even third parties other than the customer may be protected by the secrecy obligation in certain circumstances, *e.g.* other members of the customer's business partnership.

cc) Professional Advisors. Professional advisors such as attorneys (*Rechtsanwälte*), certified auditors (*Wirtschaftsprüfer*), certified tax advisors (*Steuerberater*), and notary publics (*Notare*)[493] are bound by professional duties of confidentiality. These duties cover all information concerning the professional relationship between the client and the advisor, including the existence of such relationship, and all information which became known to the professional in his capacity as an advisor. The duty to maintain confidentiality also extends to all members of the staff of the professional advisor.

A professional advisor, as well as every member of his staff, has the duty to exercise his privilege with regard to all matters and all information falling within the scope of the duty of confidentiality. Therefore, a professional advisor or a member of his staff is required by law to refuse to testify in court. Violations are subject to criminal prosecution[494]. If the client, however, releases the advisor from the duty to secrecy, the professional is required to testify like any other third-party witness.[495]

dd) In-house Counsel. Different from other countries, a professional employed as in-house counsel is not necessarily protected by professional privilege.

A notary public may not act in his professional capacity when employed by a company. The same applies to certified auditors and to certified tax advisors, unless employed by a tax or auditing firm. Therefore, these professionals cannot invoke professional privilege if employed as in-house counsel.

As to lawyers, there is a lively discussion on whether or not they may invoke professional privilege. Lawyers not admitted to the bar certainly cannot invoke professional privilege. As to lawyers admitted to the bar, the prevailing view seems to be that if their position and status within the company is comparable to that of an independent outside attorney, such in-house counsel may invoke privilege.[496]

ee) Clergy and Media. Clergymen are entitled to withhold testimony with respect to matters entrusted to them in the exercise of their duties.[497] Press, radio and TV journalists may invoke privilege as regards their sources and their editorial work.[498]

---

[493] The function and status of a German notary public is very different from *e.g.* a U.S. notary public, see the short description in English at http://www.bnotk.de/en/what_for.php.
[494] German Penal Code (*Strafgesetzbuch, StGB*) §203.
[495] ZPO §385 (2).
[496] *Cf.*, with a brief summary of the discussion, Regional Court (LG) Berlin, Decision of 30 November 2005 (Docket No. 505 Qs 185/05) Neue Zeitschrift für Strafrecht 2006, p. 470.
[497] ZPO §383 (1) No. 4.
[498] ZPO §383 (1) No. 5.

b) Personal Privilege

aa) Familial Privilege. German civil procedure law grants familial privileges to a party's present, past or future spouse(s) as well as to persons who are related to the party by blood or marriage up to the third degree of relation by blood and the second degree of relation by marriage.[499] This applies *mutatis mutandis* to the partners and relatives of a registered cohabitation (*eingetragene Lebenspartnerschaft*), i.e. a same-sex marriage.[500]

The privileges do not apply, *inter alia*,[501] to testimony concerning legal transactions for which the witness served as a formal witness[502] or in which the witness has been involved as predecessor in interest or agent of a party.[503]

bb) Privilege to Avoid Financial Harm, Disgrace, or Self-Incrimination. Any witness may withhold testimony for a number of other reasons.[504] A witness may refuse to answer a specific question if the answer would be likely to cause immediate financial harm to him or to any person within the scope of the familial privilege. The same exceptions apply as with the familial privilege. Further, a witness may refuse to answer a question if the answer would disgrace or incriminate him or one of the persons covered by the familial privilege.

cc) Privilege to Protect Trade Secrets Owned by Third Parties. A witness may invoke privilege if his testimony would require him to disclose a trade secret.[505] The trade secret may be the witness's or a trade secret of another who is not a party to the litigation and which was disclosed to the witness under a confidentiality obligation.

The content of a trade secret is very broadly defined under German law. It includes all facts related to a business which are known only to a limited number of people, which according to the intent of the principal of the business shall be confidential, and for which a legitimate business interest regarding confidentiality exists.[506]

It is important to note that trade secrets owned by one of the parties to the litigation are not protected by this privilege. Therefore, if an employee of one of the parties is named and ordered to testify as a witness, the employee needs to testify even if his testimony relates to trade secrets owned by his employer.

c) Public Servants Privilege

Government officials are under a legal duty to refuse to testify on information acquired by them while acting in their official capacity.[507] This privilege may be waived by the respective public authority.[508] If not, a government official is neither allowed nor required to testify in a civil court.

---

[499] ZPO § 383 (1) No. 1 – 3.
[500] ZPO § 383 (1) No. 1, No. 2a.
[501] ZPO § 385.
[502] ZPO § 385 (1) No. 1.
[503] ZPO § 385 (1) No. 4.
[504] ZPO § 384.
[505] ZPO § 384 No. 3.
[506] *Cf. Greger* in: Zöller, Zivilprozessordnung, 30th ed., 2014, § 384 no. 7.
[507] ZPO § 383 (1) No. 6.
[508] ZPO § 385 (2).

For members of the German federal parliament (*Bundestag*), the German constitution contains a special privilege related to their activity as legislators.[509] Similar provisions exist for the members of the federal state parliaments.

Judges are under an obligation to maintain confidentiality with regard to the deliberations and the voting on a court decision.[510]

d) Invoking Privilege

A third-party witness invoking privilege is required to state and to credibly substantiate (*glaubhaft machen*) the basis for the privilege to the court.[511] The court will decide on the legality of the refusal to testify in an interlocutory judgment, which may be challenged by an immediate miscellaneous appeal (*sofortige Beschwerde*).[512]

3. Privilege for Experts

An expert not willing to testify may refuse to accept the appointment by the court. Although this is possible in theory,[513] he will not be forced by the court against his will to accept the appointment.

An expert who has accepted the appointment is entitled to refuse to give an expert opinion for the same reasons as a witness.[514] In practice an expert who may invoke privilege and says so will usually not be appointed by the court.

4. Third-Party Privileges Relating to Orders for Document Production and for Inspection

The court may order a third party to produce documents or to grant inspection rights. These orders may be enforced against a third party by coercive penalty payments and by detention.[515]

The third party may invoke the same privileges as a third-party witness.[516] In addition, a third party is not obliged to produce documents or to grant inspection rights insofar as this is unreasonable (*unzumutbar*). This may be the case if the production of the document or the inspection requires substantial efforts on the part of the third party, or if the business of the third party would be disrupted.[517]

IV. Evidence Located Abroad

1. Statutory Sources

Taking evidence abroad for use in German proceedings is governed by the Brussels Evidence Regulation, the Hague Evidence Convention and several bilateral treaties.[518] The German implementation laws set out additional rules on how the German authorities are to handle foreign requests for judicial assistance under the

---

[509] GG Art. 47.
[510] German Judges Act (*Deutsches Richtergesetz, DRiG*), §43.
[511] ZPO §386.
[512] ZPO §387; see *infra*, at p. 101 et seq.
[513] ZPO §407 (1).
[514] ZPO §408 (1).
[515] See *supra*, at pp. 68 et seq.
[516] ZPO §§142 (2), 144 (2).
[517] *Greger* in: Zöller, Zivilprozessordnung, 30th ed., 2014, §142 no. 12.
[518] Bilateral treaties exist with Greece, Morocco, Tunisia, Turkey, and the United Kingdom.

Brussels Evidence Regulation[519] as well as under the Hague Evidence Convention and the treaties.[520] For matters outside the scope of these legal instruments, ZPO §§ 363, 364 and 369 apply. With regard to the practical aspects of how to deal with questions of legal assistance, the courts are guided by the ZRHO.

2. Procurement of Evidence by the Court

According to a view held among German legal authors, German courts are generally neither prevented by European law nor by international treaties from attempting to procure evidence located abroad, as this will not affect the sovereignty of the respective foreign state.[521]

Therefore, the court may request a party to submit to the court documents or objects for inspection which are located abroad. If the party does not comply, the court may draw negative inferences. The court is further allowed to commission a German or foreign expert to render an opinion on facts in a foreign country.

The court may also ask a third-party witness residing abroad to appear in court in Germany and to testify as a witness. Alternatively, the court may issue a letter rogatory and ask such witness to provide written testimony. It is, however, not permissible for the court to apply coercive measures against such third-party witness but only to ask for his voluntary cooperation.

3. Requests for Legal Assistance

a) Brussels Evidence Regulation

A German court as the "requesting court" may request any court of one of the other Member States of the European Union as the "requested court" to take evidence in aid of a German lawsuit in a civil matter.[522]

The request will follow the standard form attached to the Brussels Evidence Regulation. The request shall be drawn up in the language of the requested foreign court. It shall contain the details of the parties to the lawsuit, the requesting German court, the nature and subject matter of the case, a brief statement of facts, the description of the taking of evidence to be performed, and the details of the specific means of evidence such as the name and address of a witness or the specification of an object for inspection. The request shall be transmitted directly by the German court to the requested foreign court without involving the central authority the Member State has designated under the Brussels Evidence Regulation.[523]

Within seven days after receipt of the request, the requested foreign court shall send out a receipt. If the request is incomplete, it shall notify the requesting German court and ask for the missing information. The foreign court may refuse to execute the request only on very limited grounds. In practice, only the failure by the German court to respond to a notice that the request is incomplete, or to make an advance payment requested by the foreign court in order to commission an expert, may become relevant.

---

[519] ZPO §§ 1072 *et seq.*
[520] See implementation law at Part 2, A. IV.
[521] See *Nagel/Gottwald*, Internationales Zivilprozessrecht, 7th ed., 2013, § 9 no. 137 et seq.
[522] Brussels Evidence Regulation Art. 1 *et seq.*, except Denmark.
[523] Brussels Evidence Regulation Art. 2; *cf.* ZPO § 1072 No. 1.
See supra, at p. 120. The competent foreign court can be determined via the European Judicial Atlas in Civil Matters: htm http://ec.europa.eu/justice_home/judicialatlascivil/html/index_en.htm?countrySession=1&.

R. Evidentiary Proceedings

The request shall be executed without delay according to the law of the requested foreign court. The parties to the German litigation and their attorneys as well as the members of the German court are allowed to be present at the taking of evidence. The procedure for taking evidence is governed by the domestic law of the foreign court. Alternatively, the German court may call for the request to be executed in accordance with the special procedures provided for in German law. The foreign court requested must comply with this request, unless compliance would violate the law to which it is subject or poses significant practical difficulties. The special procedures under German law have to be set out in detail in the request. Therefore, a foreign court may be required to conduct the taking of evidence in accordance with German law.

The German court will receive from the requested foreign court without delay the documents establishing the execution of the request, including a confirmation of execution.

b) Hague Evidence Convention

When applying the Hague Evidence Convention, a German court will issue a formal order to take evidence. The order will specify the disputed facts and the means of evidence such as *e.g.* witness testimony, the inspection of objects located abroad, expert testimony, or the examination of documents.[524] Even if the foreign law allows more extensive taking of evidence, the German courts will adhere to what is permissible under German law. The order to take evidence will include a summary of the relevant facts of the German litigation to ensure its proper execution abroad. The order will be accompanied by a translation into the language of the state to which the request is directed. If the German court and the parties wish to attend the taking of evidence abroad, the request should specify the need to be advised of the date and place of taking evidence.

The request may be addressed to the German consular officials in the respective foreign state, or to the competent foreign central authority designated under the Hague Evidence Convention.

Requests made to the German consular officials are rare because the consular officials may not apply any coercive measures in seeking compliance with a request. Furthermore, most foreign states have made extensive reservations limiting the authority of consular officials to take evidence. Using German consular officials may, however, have advantages. For example, testimony may be taken in the German language without the need for translation, the oath may be administered, and the testimony is governed by German law which might prove useful when the testimony is assessed by the German court.

More commonly, however, requests are addressed to the competent foreign central authority, which examines the permissibility of the request. Execution may only be refused to the extent that the execution does not fall within the functions of the judiciary of the respective foreign state, or the state addressed considers that its sovereignty or security would be prejudiced. If the requesting German court asks that a special procedure be followed by the foreign court in the taking of evidence requested, this may be refused only by the foreign central authority if the execution is incompatible with the foreign law applicable to the taking of evidence, or if the special procedure requested by the German court is impossible to perform.

---

[524] Hague Evidence Convention Art. 3 (1).

The competent court of the foreign state will execute the request in accordance with its domestic procedural law. If the German court requests a special procedure to be followed, the requested court will do so to the extent permissible. Measures to compel compliance, *e.g.* for a witness to testify, will be applied only in accordance with the domestic law of the foreign court.

The documents establishing the execution of the request will be sent back to the German court by the foreign central authority via the same channels used in forwarding the request.

4. Direct Taking of Evidence

Direct taking of evidence is possible under the Brussels Evidence Regulation,[525] but not under the Hague Evidence Regulation.

The Brussels Evidence Regulation allows the German court to take evidence directly in another Member State, provided the taking of evidence can be performed on a voluntary basis, and provided that the central authority of the foreign Member State accepts such direct taking of evidence upon request.[526]

The foreign central authority may only refuse the direct taking of evidence if the request is incomplete, or if the direct taking of evidence is contrary to fundamental principles of law in the foreign Member State. Therefore, such requests are usually granted.

The German court's ability to take evidence directly has the advantage that it honors the principle of immediacy and that the taking of evidence is governed by German procedural law. However, it seems that there is only a quite limited need for the direct taking of evidence abroad. Not only may a German court order the parties to submit documents and objects for inspection even when these are located abroad. As regards witnesses, a witness willing to testify voluntarily before a German court abroad may also be willing to travel to Germany to do so. Finally, the German court may commission a foreign expert directly, and often photos render the inspection of an immovable object abroad unnecessary. Accordingly, German courts apparently very rarely use this method.

5. Foreign Privileges

In practice, foreign privileges only play a role with regard to third-party witnesses residing abroad. Instead of relying on a privilege, foreign experts may simply refuse an appointment as expert by the German court. Different from German residents, third parties domiciled abroad are not subject to coercive measures by the German courts which force them to produce documents or allow the inspection of objects.

Privileges of a person who is requested to serve as a witness are protected both under the Brussels Evidence Regulation and the Hague Evidence Convention. The person concerned may invoke the applicable privileges under German law.[527] In addition, he may rely on the privileges under the law applicable to the foreign court requested to take his testimony.[528] Therefore, a witness is extensively protected. In order to safeguard any existing privileges, the request by the German

---

[525] *Nuyts/Depulchre*, Taking of Evidence in the European Union under EC Regulation 1206/2001, Business Law International, Vol. 5, No. 3, 2004, pp. 305 *et seq.*
[526] Brussels Evidence Regulation Articles 17.
[527] See *supra*, at pp. 79 et seq.
[528] Brussels Evidence Regulation Art. 14 (1); Hague Evidence Convention Art. 11 (1).

court for legal assistance must state any applicable privilege under German law. If a person relies on a privilege not stipulated in the request, the competent foreign court will request a confirmation of this privilege from the respective German central authority.

Under both the Brussels Evidence Regulation and the Hague Evidence Convention, coercive measures may not be used to compel a person residing abroad to appear in a German court to testify. Likewise, testimony before a German consular official or before a German court directly taking evidence abroad may only take place on a voluntary basis. Therefore, there is usually no need for a person to rely on his privileges. The Brussels Evidence Regulation further provides that a court which directly takes evidence abroad needs to explicitly notify a potential witness that his testimony is voluntary.[529]

V. Evaluation of Evidence and Standard of Proof

The court is required to evaluate the evidence taken and then to make a factual determination based on that evidence. By doing so, the court may evaluate most forms of evidence according to its sound judgment and common sense without being bound by rules on how to assess evidence (principle of free evaluation of proof, *freie Beweiswürdigung*).[530] Exceptions apply *e.g.* with respect to documentary evidence such as public documents.[531]

The court is required to comprehensively review all the facts provided by the parties as well as all factual proof when reaching a decision. It will consider furthermore not only the formal taking of evidence but everything which was subject to the oral hearing,[532] which also includes the written statements and *e.g.* the behavior of the parties during the proceedings.[533]

The standard of proof in civil cases is that the court must be "fully convinced" that a particular contested fact is true in order to base the judgment on that fact. This neither requires certainty nor a degree of probability close to certitude, but the court must be sure to a practically viable degree of certainty that puts doubts to silence without eliminating them entirely. Therefore, the standard of proof is stricter than *e.g.* in the U.S. where a plaintiff prevails if only "the preponderance of the evidence" speaks in his favor. A lower standard of proof may apply to damages and the causation of damages.[534]

S. Establishing the Law

I. German Law and German Private International Law

A German court will apply German civil procedure law, including the relevant legislation of the European Union, and the applicable international conventions and treaties.

---

[529] Brussels Evidence Regulation Art. 17 (2).
[530] ZPO § 286.
[531] See *supra*, at pp. 73 et seq.
[532] ZPO § 286 (1).
[533] *Cf. Greger* in: Zöller, Zivilprozessordnung, 30th ed., 2014, § 286 no. 2 and 14 *et seq.*
[534] *Cf.* ZPO § 287.

The court will apply German substantive law in purely domestic cases. If the case has an international dimension, the court is bound to determine the applicable substantive law according to German private international law.

By applying German private international law, the court may conclude that foreign substantive law is applicable to the case. Nevertheless, if German private international law allows the parties to choose the applicable law, and if both parties plead under German law, the courts will generally take this as a tacit choice of German law by the parties. This might even be done if the parties were seemingly unaware of the possibility that foreign law might apply to their case.[535] The parties to a German litigation are, therefore, well advised to review the applicable substantive law properly to ascertain that the most advantageous substantive law is applied to the matter.

Since the court is deemed to know all German procedural and substantive law (*iura novit curia*), it is not necessary for the parties to plead the applicable law. In practice, the parties usually outline at least briefly the applicable legal doctrines.[536]

II. Establishing Foreign Law[537]

Procedurally, the applicable foreign law is treated as law, not as a fact. Although German courts are not required to have knowledge of foreign law, they are under a duty to determine the relevant provisions of the respective foreign law and how these provisions are interpreted in practice. In so doing, the courts may use any appropriate means.

Very often, foreign law is pleaded by the parties. Usually, opinions by foreign lawyers are submitted setting out the relevant legal rules and their application in practice. If both parties agree on foreign law to take a certain position, courts may take this into account when establishing the foreign law. However, the contents of foreign law cannot be "admitted", and the parties, therefore, cannot bind the court in its reading of foreign law.

In commercial litigation, the courts usually request an expert opinion of a lawyer trained in the relevant jurisdiction. There is a tendency not to commission practitioners, but German university professors teaching comparative law. The court will send the entire court file to the expert, together with an order which lists questions that the expert is required to answer. The rules regarding proof by expert testimony apply.[538] Although the expert is usually given a time limit for answering the questions, such time limits are very often not kept. Requesting an expert opinion on foreign law frequently results in a substantial delay of the proceedings.

In addition or alternatively, a court may educate itself on the foreign law by consulting relevant foreign statutes and textbooks. However, the court is under an obligation to determine the foreign law as it is practiced, not as it is in the books. Therefore, possibly with the exception of Austrian or Swiss law which is available in the German language and in which the basic concepts are quite close to the German system, courts are hesitant to rely on these sources only.

---

[535] Federal Court of Justice (BGH), Decision of 18 January 1988 (Docket No. II ZR 42/87), Neue Juristische Wochenschrift, 1988, p. 1592.

[536] See *supra*, at p. 25.

[537] See *Dannemann*, Access to Justice – an Anglo-German Comparison, available at http://www.iuscomp.org/gla/ for a detailed description in English.

[538] See *supra*, at pp. 76 et seq.

A court may also choose to determine the foreign law by making a request under the European Convention on Information on Foreign Law.[539] However, these requests have proven to be slow and inefficient.

There is no presumption under German law about the content of foreign law. If there is no way of establishing the position of foreign law on a certain issue, the court may apply the relevant rules of another foreign legal system which is accessible and related to the inaccessible foreign law. If everything else fails, the court has to apply substantive German law. It is not permissible, however, to dismiss an action on the grounds that foreign law could not be ascertained.

T. Judgments

I. Uncontested Judgments

German civil procedure law puts an emphasis on amicably settling a dispute in or out of court. Therefore, a large number of civil actions are settled.

Of the remainder, quite a number of proceedings are terminated by uncontested judgments. The most common form is the default judgment (*Versäumnisurteil*)[540] when a party fails or declines to defend the claim asserted against it. Judgments by consent (*Anerkenntnisurteile*)[541] or by waiver (*Verzichtsurteile*)[542] are other forms of uncontested judgments, but are quite rare in practice.

An uncontested judgment constitutes an execution title (*Vollstreckungstitel*) and thus may serve as the basis for execution proceedings.

II. Contested Judgments

Only about 25% of all civil actions commenced in German courts are decided by contested judgment (*streitiges Urteil*).[543]

1. Types of Judgments

Corresponding to the three different categories of relief,[544] there are three categories of judgments: judgments for affirmative relief (*Leistungsurteile*), declaratory judgments (*Feststellungsurteile*) and judgments for altering a legal relationship (*Gestaltungsurteile*). The court is bound by the motions of the parties when rendering a judgment.[545] No relief may be different or go beyond these motions. However, within the motions of the party, the court is free to grant only a part thereof. The motions as pleaded in the last oral hearing are determinative.[546]

---

[539] The European Convention on Information on Foreign Law of 7 June 1968 can be found at http://conventions.coe.int.

[540] ZPO § 330.

[541] ZPO § 307.

[542] ZPO § 306.

[543] *Cf.* the detailed statistics for 2013 provided by the Federal Statistical Office at https://www.destatis.de (https://www.destatis.de/DE/Publikationen/Thematisch/Rechtspflege/GerichtePersonal/Zivilgerichte2100210137004.pdf?__blob=publicationFile).

[544] See *supra*, at p. 52.

[545] ZPO § 308.

[546] For amendments and extensions of claims see supra pp. 63 et seq.

The court at its discretion may render a judgment on only a part of the claims, leaving the other claims or the remaining parts of the claim still pending (partial judgment, *Teilurteil*)[547].

In civil actions, *e.g.* for damages, if a court is convinced that there is liability and at least some damages suffered, an interlocutory judgment on the basis of the claim (*Grundurteil*)[548] may be rendered, leaving the amount of damages open. Such judgments quite often result in the parties settling as regards the amount of damages, making a contested judgment on the damages unnecessary.

The court may also render an interlocutory judgment (*Zwischenurteil*)[549] on certain issues relevant to the subject matter of the case. Common examples are interlocutory judgments regarding the jurisdiction of the court, interlocutory judgments regarding procedural steps taken by one party and disputed by the other, such as the extension or change of the claim, or an interlocutory judgment as to whether the intervention of a third party is admissible or not.

2. Form and Contents of a Judgment

Any judgment starts with the head (*Rubrum*) which sets out the court, the judges, the date of the last oral hearing, the parties and their attorneys. Then the operative provisions of the judgment (*Tenor*) follow, including the decision on the allocation of costs. Thereafter, the uncontested and the contested facts are restated briefly, followed by the court's opinion. The judgment ends with the signature(s) of the judge(s).[550]

Contested judgments are rendered orally by reading the operative provisions of the judgment in open court. Sometimes, the rendition of the judgment follows after the end of the last oral hearing (*Stuhlurteil*). More commonly, the court sets a special date (*Verkündungstermin*) when the judgment is to be rendered.[551]

The parties and their attorneys may attend the session where the judgment is rendered. This is, however, not necessary as long as the date for rendering the judgment has been properly called.[552] Usually no one except the judges is present. In practice the attorneys simply call the court and ask for the contents of the operative provisions of the judgment.

3. Corrections of Judgments

a) Apparent Mistakes

Apparent mistakes of a judgment, such as typographical errors, errors in arithmetic, or apparent errors of expression, may be corrected by the court at any time. The corrections are made by order of the court.[553]

---

[547] ZPO §301; see *infra*, at pp. 91 et seq.
[548] ZPO §304.
[549] ZPO §303.
[550] ZPO §313.
[551] ZPO §§310 *et seq.*
[552] ZPO §§311 (2), 312.
[553] ZPO §319.

b) Amendments and Supplements

In all other cases, a judgment once rendered may only be amended or supplemented in very limited circumstances. The motion by a party to this end has to be made within two weeks of service of judgment on such party.

Mistakes, omissions and ambiguities regarding the facts stated in the judgment may be corrected upon written motion by one of the parties. The court will then schedule an oral hearing and will determine the issue based on the record of the case and its own memory. Any such amendment (*Tatbestandsberichtigung*) is made by order which is annexed to the judgment.[554]

In very rare cases, a party may make a motion to the court for supplementing the judgment if there are apparent oversights such as not including a decision on the costs etc. The court will then schedule an oral hearing upon which a supplementary judgment (*Ergänzungsurteil*) may be rendered.[555]

c) Practical Relevance

It is important for the attorneys of the parties to review a judgment thoroughly and to make such motions. The factual findings in the judgment are not only relevant to this decision, but also form the basis on which the appellate court decides in a first appeal.[556] As the pleading of new facts on first appeal is limited,[557] an amendment of incomplete factual findings should be requested.[558] Further, there is no opportunity for re-examination of facts in a second appeal.[559] Therefore, it has to be ascertained that the judgment fully reflects the facts as pleaded.

4. Service of Judgment

A judgment will be served on the parties by the court *ex officio*.[560]

III. Effects of a Judgment

1. Binding Effect on the Court

A German court is bound by its own judgments in the sense that the court has to adhere to any partial or preliminary judgment in its later final judgment. Further, the court may neither change nor revoke its judgment, even if it discovers later that the judgment might be erroneous (*innerprozessuale Bindungswirkung*).[561]

2. Binding Effect on the Parties

A judgment which is not subject to any further appeal becomes final and binding on the courts and on the parties (*Rechtskraft*).[562] Once the judgment is non-appealable (*formelle Rechtskraft*), the litigation on the subject matter of the judgment (*Streitgegenstand*) is terminated once and for all. As of this time, the judgment is

---

[554] ZPO § 320.
[555] ZPO § 321.
[556] *Cf.* ZPO § 314.
[557] *Cf.* ZPO § 529.
[558] See *Heßler* in: Zöller, Zivilprozessordnung, 30th ed., 2014, § 529 no. 2.
[559] ZPO § 513 (1).
[560] ZPO § 317.
[561] ZPO § 318.
[562] ZPO §§ 322, 325.

of final force and effect (*materielle Rechtskraft*). If one of the parties commences a lawsuit thereafter with the same subject matter, such action will be dismissed by the German courts (*Einwand der Rechtskraft*).

However, the binding effect of the judgment is limited in three ways: First, only the judgment on the subject matter of the lawsuit, as determined by the motions by the parties and the facts stated supporting these motions, becomes final and binding.[563] Second, the judgment generally is only binding on the parties to the litigation, including their legal successors, but not on third parties.[564] The most important exception insofar is judgments for altering a legal relationship (*Gestaltungsurteile*), which are also binding on third parties. Third, the binding force of the judgment only relates to the state of the facts as they appeared at the time of the final oral hearing. Facts appearing after the end of the oral hearing are, therefore, not affected by the final and binding force of the judgment and may form the basis for fresh proceedings between the parties.[565]

3. Procedures for Setting Aside a Final and Binding Judgment

In case of very severe violations of procedural rights or serious tampering with the factual basis of a judgment, a final and binding judgment may be set aside upon motion of a party. However, these motions do not play a major role in German litigation because the prerequisites for eliminating a judgment are extremely strict.

a) Motion for a New Trial

The aggrieved party may move for resumption of the proceedings (*Wiederaufnahmeklage*).[566] The motion may be directed at having the final judgment set aside (*Nichtigkeitsklage*) because of severe procedural irregularities such as *e.g.* incorrect composition of the court or lack of impartiality of the judge.[567] The motion may alternatively seek a retrial of the case (*Restitutionsklage*) on the grounds that the prior court proceedings or the final and binding judgment had serious defects such as being based on false material statements under oath by the opposing party, forgery of documents, criminal conduct by a party or a judge in connection with the judgment or if the judgment is based on a violation of the European Convention on Human Rights which is recognized by the European Court of Human Rights.[568] Other grounds for a motion for retrial are that the aggrieved party finds a prior judgment on the same subject matter, or that the party is now in a position to use a newly discovered document that would have led to a more favorable judgment.

b) Action for Damages

In very limited circumstances, an aggrieved party may seek a reversal of a final and binding judgment by bringing an action for damages. The action would be based on tort law on the grounds that such judgment was obtained by the opponent to intentionally injure in bad faith (*vorsätzlich-sittenwidrige Schädigung*, *BGB* § 826). The claim would be directed at either forbidding the opponent to enforce

---

[563] ZPO § 322 (1).
[564] ZPO § 325 (1).
[565] ZPO § 322 (1).
[566] ZPO §§ 578 *et seq.*
[567] ZPO § 579.
[568] ZPO §§ 580 *et seq.*

U. Appellate Remedies

I. General

1. Overview: Appellate Remedies

Generally, all acts by the court and the various court officers may be appealed by the aggrieved party. The proper appellate remedy depends on the kind of act – judgments, other court decisions, acts in the course of executing an execution title – and the court officer – judge, judicial officer (*Rechtspfleger*), bailiff (*Gerichtsvollzieher*) – who rendered or performed the act.

The proper appellate remedies against judgments are generally the first appeal (*Berufung*)[570] and the second appeal (*Revision*).[571] Interlocutory court orders and other relatively minor decisions by the courts are usually appealed by lodging a miscellaneous appeal (*Beschwerde*).[572] These appeals in general suspend the effect of the judgment, court order or decision, respectively (suspensory effect, *Suspensiveffekt*), and the appellate court will be seized of the matter (*Devolutiveffekt*). The miscellaneous appeal, however, has automatic suspensory effect only if directed against coercive measures, but the court or the presiding judge who issued the contested decision or the appellate court may suspend the enforcement of the decision in other cases.[573]

A number of other decisions or acts by the court or by court officers may be challenged by various appellate remedies such as the protest (*Widerspruch* or *Einspruch*) or the objection (*Erinnerung*).

In addition to these regular appellate remedies, there is the special one under ZPO §321a because of the violation of the party's right to be heard.[574] Special appeals may be brought in to the Federal Constitutional Court, to the European Court of Justice, or to the European Court of Human Rights on the grounds that fundamental guarantees on civil procedure of the German constitution,[575] European Union law, or human rights guaranteed by the European Convention on Human Rights, respectively,[576] have been violated. These remedies are rare in practice.

The following will only deal with the most frequent appellate remedies, *i.e.* first and second appeals, and miscellaneous appeals *(Beschwerde)*.

---

[569] See for this remedy *Vollkommer* in: Zöller, Zivilprozessordnung, 30th ed., 2014, before §322 no. 72 *et seq.*
[570] ZPO §§511 *et seq.*
[571] ZPO §§542 *et seq.*
[572] ZPO §§567 *et seq.*
[573] ZPO §570.
[574] See *supra*, at p. 3.
[575] See *supra*, at pp. 3, 14.
[576] See *supra*, at p. 14.

2. General Features of Appellate Remedies

An appellate remedy must be admissible (*Zulässigkeit*). Therefore, the decision must be appealable and the appellant must be a person entitled to appeal (*Statthaftigkeit*). The appellant must show an aggrievement (*Beschwer*) by the decision of the lower court subject to appeal, and the appellate remedy must be filed in due form within the applicable time limits. The appellate court will only review the merits of the case (*Begründetheitsprüfung*) if the appeal is admissible.

The appellate court is bound by the motions of the appellant.[577] The decision of the lower court subject to appeal may only be modified to the extent the appellant moved for. Further, a party may only be granted new benefits at the appellate level if such party lodged an appeal. If *e.g.* a plaintiff has received a smaller award by the lower court than originally sought, and only the defendant appeals, the plaintiff will in the appellate proceedings not be in a position to receive the full amount originally sought, unless he lodges an appeal himself.

A party may be aggrieved by a decision, but may be willing to accept it if the opponent does so as well. To accommodate for this situation, German law allows a party to wait until the opponent appeals, and only then to lodge a cross-appeal (*Anschlussrechtsmittel*)[578] without being bound by the time restrictions for a regular appeal.

The appellant cannot be made worse off by his own appeal than he was according to the decision appealed (*Verbot der reformatio in peius*).[579] However, if the opponent appeals as well, *e.g.* by way of a cross-appeal, the appellate decision may give the appellant less than the appealed decision did.

II. First Appeals

1. Competent Appellate Court

Judgments of the local courts in civil and commercial matters may be appealed to the respective regional court (*Landgericht*),[580] whereas judgments of the regional courts are to be appealed to the higher regional courts (*Oberlandesgerichte*).[581]

2. Admissibility of Appeal

a) Decisions Subject to Appeal

Final judgments (*Endurteile*),[582] default judgments against which no objection (*Einspruch*) can be lodged,[583] intermediate judgments on jurisdiction,[584] judgments on the basis of a claim (*Grundurteile*),[585] and judgments on summary proceedings based on documentary evidence or a bill of exchange (*Urkunds-, Wechsel- und Scheckurteile*)[586] may be subject to a first appeal.

---

[577] ZPO § 528.
[578] ZPO §§ 524, 554, 574 (4).
[579] ZPO §§ 528, 557.
[580] GVG § 72.
[581] GVG § 119 (1) No. 2.
[582] ZPO § 511 (1).
[583] ZPO § 238 (2) – (5).
[584] ZPO § 280 (2).
[585] ZPO § 304.
[586] ZPO § 599.

b) Aggrievement of Appellant

The appellant must show that he is aggrieved by the judgment subject to appeal. The aggrievement is determined by a comparison between the formal motions of the parties in the lower proceedings and the operative provisions of the judgment.

A first appeal is only admissible if the value of the aggrievement of the appellant exceeds EUR 600.00. If not, the entry-level court may allow an appeal by certifying its judgment for appeal (*Zulassungsberufung*).[587]

3. Waiver of Appeal

A party to a civil litigation may waive its right to appeal.[588] A waiver may be made unilaterally after the lower-court judgment is rendered, or by agreement between the parties prior to this date. If the right to appeal is waived by a party, an appeal is inadmissible, and the judgment of the lower court is final.

4. Appellate Written Pleadings

a) Statement of Appeal

A first appeal is lodged with the appellate court by submitting a statement of appeal (*Berufungsschrift*)[589] within one month from service of the full version of the judgment on the appellant.[590]

The statement of appeal is usually very brief. It only needs to contain the docket number of the judgment being appealed, a statement that the judgment shall be appealed, and the names of the parties. An attorney must sign the statement of appeal.

b) Statement of Grounds for Appeal

Unless the grounds for the appeal are already set out in the statement of appeal, they are to be stated by the appellant in a subsequent written pleading. This statement of the grounds for appeal (*Berufungsbegründung*) must be filed with the appellate court no later than two months after service of the full version of the judgment on the appellant.[591] This time limit may be extended by the court only once and only up to one more month[592] Any further extension of this time limit require the consent of the appellee.

The statement of grounds for appeal must contain a motion stating the precise changes in the judgment sought (*Berufungsantrag*). The submission must also describe the reasons why the judgment is erroneous and the significance of the error for the judgment under appeal.[593]

c) Statement of Defense

The appellee will submit a written pleading defending the judgment appealed (*Berufungserwiderung*).[594]

---

[587] ZPO § 512 (1).
[588] ZPO § 515.
[589] ZPO § 519.
[590] ZPO § 517.
[591] ZPO § 520.
[592] *Cf. Heßler* in: Zöller, Zivilprozessordnung, 30th ed., 2014, § 520 no. 19.
[593] ZPO § 520 (3) and (4).
[594] See ZPO § 521 (2).

d) Withdrawal of Appeal

The appellant may withdraw his appeal at any time in the appellate proceedings and as late as immediately prior to the rendition of the appellate judgment.[595] A withdrawal does not require the consent of the appellee. If an appeal is withdrawn, the court will *ex officio* declare the loss of the right to appeal and will allocate the costs of the appellate proceedings to the appellant.[596]

5. Court Orders

a) Procedural Orders by the Court

The appellate court will serve the written pleadings by the parties on the respective opponent.[597] The court will usually set a time limit for the appellee to submit the statement of defense and time limits for further submissions if appropriate.[598] The court also will make a decision as to whether the matter will be transferred to one single judge or is to be heard by the chamber or panel, respectively. Finally, the court will set a date for the oral hearing.[599]

b) Dismissal of Appeal by Court Order

The appellate court will decide on whether the appeal is admissible or not. If not, the appeal may be dismissed by court order without an oral hearing. This decision may be appealed with a miscellaneous appeal on points of law.[600]

Further, even if an appeal is otherwise admissible, it may be dismissed by court order without an oral hearing if the chamber or panel of the appellate court, respectively, finds that the appeal has no prospect of success on the merits, and that an appellate judgment has neither relevance for similar cases nor for developing the law in a certain area.[601] This decision may also be appealed.[602]

If the court is considering an order to dismiss the appeal, it will indicate this in writing to the parties and will give them the opportunity to comment and to withdraw the appeal.[603]

6. Scope of Appellate Review

The appellate court will decide on the merits if it finds the appeal admissible. The first appeal is designed to review the judgment and to correct any errors of law and fact made by the lower court. As a general principle, the appellate court is bound by the factual findings of the lower court, unless these are erroneous.[604]

Firstly, an appellant may base his appeal on a violation of law (*Rechtsverletzung*).[605] The appellant may claim that procedural law was not observed properly by the lower court. In practice, appeals are quite often based on alleged violations

---

[595] ZPO § 516.
[596] ZPO § 516 (3).
[597] *Cf.* ZPO § 521 (1).
[598] ZPO § 521 (2).
[599] ZPO § 523 (1).
[600] ZPO § 522 (1).
[601] ZPO § 522 (2).
[602] See ZPO § 522 (3).
[603] ZPO § 522 (2).
[604] ZPO § 529 (1).
[605] ZPO §§ 513 (1), 546.

of the duty of the judge to give indications and feedback.[606] The appellant may alternatively, or in addition, claim that the substantive law applicable to the case was either not applied, or applied erroneously by the lower court. In any case, the appellant needs to show that the alleged violation of law influenced the operative provisions of the lower-court judgment subject to appeal.

Secondly, the appellant may base his appeal on stating concrete indications which justify doubt as to the correctness or completeness of the fact-findings in the judgment of the lower court and which, therefore, indicate the need for a renewed fact-finding.[607] Here as well, the incorrect or incomplete fact-findings need to be relevant for the operative provisions of the lower-court judgment.

Thirdly, an appeal may be based on new evidence.[608] Evidence is considered "new" if it is neither stated in the part of the lower-court judgment relating to the facts, nor contained in the record of the oral hearing. New evidence, however, may only be admitted by the appellate court in very limited circumstances. It may only be considered if it relates to a point which the lower court clearly overlooked or regarded as irrelevant, if it was not considered due to a defect in the proceedings before the lower court, or if it was not asserted in the first instance without this being due to negligence on the part of the appellant.[609]

The appellee will usually defend the lower-court judgment by using the same defenses against the claim as in the entry-level proceedings. However, if a defense by set-off is made or a counteraction is brought for the first time in the appellate proceedings, such acts are only admissible if either the opponent consents or the court deems them appropriate (*sachdienlich*).[610]

7. Judgment

The appellate court will render a judgment either at the end of the oral hearing or at a later date set for this purpose.

If the appeal is granted, the court will usually replace the lower-court judgment by its own judgment.[611] However, upon motion by one of the parties, the court may in very limited circumstances remit the case to the entry-level court for further proceedings.[612] The underlying rationale is that it may be more efficient to remit the matter if the entry-level court has not had a chance to consider relevant facts relating to the case.

III. Second Appeal

1. Competent Appellate Court

The court competent to hear a second appeal (*Revision*) is the Federal Court of Justice.[613]

---

[606] See *supra*, at p. 54.
[607] ZPO §§ 513 (1), 529 (1) No. 1.
[608] ZPO §§ 513 (1), 529 (1) No. 2, 531 (2).
[609] ZPO § 531 (2).
[610] ZPO § 533.
[611] ZPO § 538 (1).
[612] ZPO § 538 (2), no motion of a party is required in case of ZPO § 538 (1) No 7.
[613] Until 31 December 2004, second appeals against judgments rendered by courts located in Bavaria were to be directed to the Bavarian Highest Regional Court (*Bayerisches Oberstes Landesgericht*). The Bavarian Highest Regional Court has been dissolved by the federal state legislature.

2. Admissibility of Appeal

a) General

Appellate judgments by the regional courts and by the higher regional courts are subject to a second appeal.[614] Second appeals are, however, not admissible against appellate judgments in provisional proceedings for provisional relief.[615] The parties to an entry-level judgment may consent to not lodging a first appeal, but to directly filing a leap-frog second appeal (*Sprungrevision*), which the Federal Court of Justice may admit.[616]

A party filing a second appeal must be aggrieved by the first appellate judgment. A minimum monetary value of the aggrievement is not required.

b) Admission of Appeal and Miscellaneous Appeal against Refusal to Grant Leave to Second Appeal *(Nichtzulassungsbeschwerde)*

A second appeal is, however, only admissible if the lower appellate court explicitly admits a second appeal in the judgment subject to that appeal. If not, the appellant may file a miscellaneous appeal against refusal to grant leave to second appeal (*Nichtzulassungsbeschwerde*).[617]

This miscellaneous appeal must be lodged within one month and grounds must be provided within two months from the service of the lower appellate judgment on the appellant. The appellee will have the opportunity to comment.[618]

The Federal Court of Justice will grant permission for the second appeal if the case is either of fundamental significance (*grundsätzliche Bedeutung*) for the further development of the law, or if the maintenance of consistency in court rulings requires a decision by the Federal Court of Justice.[619] If the Federal Court of Justice grants permission for a second appeal upon a miscellaneous appeal, it will render a court order to this effect.[620] If it does not, the lower appellate judgment becomes final. If the lower appellate court has violated the appellant's right to be heard, the Federal Court of Justice may remit the case to the lower appellate court on these grounds alone.[621] Empirical data indicates that miscellaneous appeals against refusal to grant leave to second appeal *(Nichtzulassungsbeschwerde)* are mostly not successful.[622] However, if the Federal Court of Justice grants permission for a second appeal, chances are rather high that the Federal Court of Justice will find errors in law in the appellate judgment appealed to the Federal Court of Justice.

c) Waiver

Under the same prerequisites as for a first appeal, each of the parties may waive the right to the second appeal.[623]

---

[614] ZPO §542 (1).
[615] See *infra*, at pp. 115, 117.
[616] ZPO §566.
[617] ZPO §§543 (1), 544 (1). Until 31 December 2014, a miscellaneous appeal from denial of permission is only admissible if the amount of the aggrievement exceeds EUR 20,000.00; Introductory Law of the Code of Civil Procedure (*Einführungsgesetz zur Zivilprozeßordnung, EGZPO*) §26 No. 8.
[618] ZPO §544 (1) – (3).
[619] ZPO §543 (2).
[620] ZPO §544 (4).
[621] ZPO §544 (7).
[622] *Cf.* the statistics of the Federal Court of Justice for 2013, available at http://www.bundesgerichtshof.de/DE/BGH/Statistik/Taetigkeitsberichte/Taetigkeit2013/taetigkeit2013_node.html.
[623] ZPO §565 in conjunction with ZPO §515.

3. Submissions

a) Statement of Second Appeal

The statement of second appeal (*Revisionsschrift*)[624] must be filed within one month from the service of the lower appellate judgment on the appellant.[625] In case a miscellaneous appeal against refusal to grant leave to second appeal *(Nichtzulassungsbeschwerde)* is successful, the time limit runs from the service of the order by the Federal Court of Justice granting the appeal.[626]

The content requirements of the statement of second appeal[627] are similar to those for a statement of first appeal. The statement of second appeal, as well as all other written pleadings, must be signed by an attorney admitted to practice before the Federal Court of Justice.

b) Statement of Grounds for Second Appeal

The statement of grounds for second appeal (*Revisionsbegründung*)[628] must be filed within two months from service of the lower appellate judgment or from service of the order by the Federal Court of Justice granting leave to second appeal,[629] respectively. The time limit may be extended by the Federal Court of Justice by up to two months. Any further extensions are only possible with the consent of the appellee.[630]

The statement of grounds for second appeal must contain a motion stating the extent to which the lower judgment is challenged as well as the grounds for such challenge. In case the second appeal was granted pursuant to a miscellaneous appeal against refusal to grant leave to second appeal *(Nichtzulassungsbeschwerde)*, the appellant may refer to his written pleadings in the proceedings for miscellaneous appeal.[631] Nevertheless, it is necessary that the statement of grounds for second appeal sets out in detail the grounds for the alleged violation of law.

c) Statement of Defense

The appellee will submit a statement of defense (*Revisionserwiderung*) supporting and defending the judgment.

4. Court Orders

a) General

The statement of second appeal and the statement of grounds for second appeal will be served *ex officio* by the Federal Court of Justice upon the appellee.[632] The Federal Court of Justice will direct the proceedings by court orders setting time limits for the submission of written pleadings.

---

[624] ZPO § 549.
[625] ZPO § 548.
[626] ZPO § 544 (6).
[627] See ZPO § 549 (1).
[628] ZPO § 551.
[629] ZPO § 544 (6).
[630] ZPO § 551 (2).
[631] ZPO § 551 (3).
[632] ZPO §§ 550, 551 (4).

b) Court Order for Dismissal

The court will dismiss a second appeal by court order if it is not admissible. The court order will usually be rendered without a prior oral hearing.[633] There is no remedy against this decision.

5. Scope of Appellate Review

The second appeal is a review on issues of law only.[634] It is designed primarily not to obtain correct judgments in the individual case, but to render decisions on issues of law which are important to the German system of justice as a whole. Only federal law and state law applicable in more than one higher regional court district are, therefore, subject to review at a second appeal.[635]

The Federal Court of Justice will review whether the judgment under appeal rests on a violation of law. This includes the review whether the lower appellate court observed the relevant procedural law and whether it applied the relevant substantive law properly.[636] With regard to a number of violations of procedural law such as improper composition of the lower court or violations of the principle of publicity, there is a presumption that the judgment appealed rests on these violations.[637]

The Federal Court of Justice generally has to accept the factual findings of the lower courts as correct.[638] As to the scope of these facts, the Federal Court of Justice is bound by the factual findings stated in the appellate judgment, supplemented by the facts contained in the record of the proceedings before the lower appellate court. Only when the lower appellate court has committed a procedural error in not considering facts contained in the record of the case may the Federal Court of Justice base its decision on such facts omitted by the lower appellate court.

6. Judgment

The Federal Court of Justice decides by judgment.[639] If no additional fact-finding is necessary or appropriate to reach a decision based on the correct legal rules, the Federal Court of Justice may decide the case itself. However, this will be the exception.

In many cases, the proper application of the law will require further factual findings to be made by the lower courts. The Federal Court of Justice will, therefore, remit the case back to the lower court.[640] The lower court is bound by the legal analysis of the Federal Court of Justice as regards the issue of law which has been the subject of the second appeal.[641]

---

[633] ZPO § 552.
[634] ZPO §§ 545 *et seq.*
[635] ZPO § 545 (1).
[636] Except the rules on jurisdiction of the court, ZPO § 545 (2).
[637] ZPO § 547.
[638] See ZPO § 559.
[639] ZPO §§ 562 *et seq.*
[640] ZPO § 563.
ZPO § 567. In general, this is the court of first appeal, ZPO § 563 (1). In case of a leap-frog appeal to the Federal Court of Justice, the case will be remitted to the court of first instance, ZPO § 566 (8).
[641] ZPO § 563.

IV. Miscellaneous Appeals *(Beschwerde)*

1. General

The miscellaneous appeal *(Beschwerde)* is an appellate remedy against decisions by a court other than a judgment. The procedure is generally less complex. In particular, the appellate decision may be made without the need for an oral hearing.

The general appellate relief is the immediate miscellaneous appeal *(sofortige Beschwerde)*.[642] The decision of the competent appellate court on an immediate miscellaneous appeal may, in limited circumstances, be further appealed by a miscellaneous appeal on points of law *(Rechtsbeschwerde)*.[643]

Given the active role of a German court in the proceedings and the variety of court orders and other court dispositions, miscellaneous appeals are very frequent in practice.

2. Immediate Miscellaneous Appeal

a) Competent Court

The appellate court competent to decide on immediate miscellaneous appeals *(sofortige Beschwerde)* against the decisions by the local courts is the regional court in whose district the respective local court is located.[644] Immediate miscellaneous appeals against decisions by the regional court are to be heard by the locally competent higher regional court.[645]

b) Admissibility of Appeal

An immediate miscellaneous appeal is admissible against decisions by the local court or by the regional court in entry-level proceedings.[646] The appellant must be aggrieved by the decision.

German procedural law explicitly provides for an immediate miscellaneous appeal against a number of specific decisions. In addition, immediate miscellaneous appeals are admissible against decisions on procedural issues by these courts, if a miscellaneous appeal is not explicitly precluded by law and where an oral hearing for such decision is not required.[647] The right to appeal may be waived by either party.[648]

c) Submissions

The appellant must file a statement of immediate miscellaneous appeal *(Beschwerdeschrift)* either with the court which has rendered the decision appealed *(iudex ad quo)*, or with the appellate court competent to hear the appeal *(iudex ad quem)*.[649] The statement of immediate miscellaneous appeal needs to be filed with the court within two weeks from service of the decision appealed on the appellant.[650]

---

[642] ZPO § 567.
[643] ZPO §§ 574 *et seq.*
[644] GVG § 72.
[645] GVG § 119 (1).
[646] ZPO § 567 (1).
[647] ZPO § 567 (1) No. 2.
[648] See § 567 (3).
[649] ZPO § 569 (1).
[650] ZPO § 569 (1).

The statement of immediate miscellaneous appeal must indicate the relief sought. However, compared with first or second appeals, the requirements as to the contents of the statement are not as strict. Neither is a specific motion necessary, nor is it required to include specific grounds in the statement of immediate miscellaneous appeal. Of course, it is advisable to set out in detail why the relief is sought. The appellee will be given an opportunity by the court to comment on the statement of immediate miscellaneous appeal.

A cross-appeal (*Anschlussbeschwerde*), as well as a withdrawal of appeal, is permissible.[651]

d) Court Decision

Regardless of where the appeal has been filed, the court which rendered the decision appealed will have the opportunity to review its former findings and to grant the appeal. If not, the appellate court will decide on the matter.[652]

The appellate court will review the decision appealed with regard to both the facts and the legal findings. If the appellate court grants the appeal, it may change the decision appealed or may direct the lower court to change the decision.[653]

The appellate decision may be made without an oral hearing and will be rendered in the form of a court order and not a judgment.[654]

3. Miscellaneous Appeal on Points of Law *(Rechtsbeschwerde)*

a) Competent Appellate Court

A miscellaneous appeal on points of law (*Rechtsbeschwerde*) may be brought to the Federal Court of Justice under certain limited circumstances.[655]

b) Admissibility

A miscellaneous appeal on points of law (*Rechtsbeschwerde*) is admissible if it is explicitly provided for in the applicable procedural law. Further, it is admissible against appellate decisions on immediate miscellaneous appeals (*sofortige Beschwerde*), if the lower appellate court explicitly grants permission for a further appeal. In all cases, the issue raised by the appeal must be one that requires a decision by the Federal Court of Justice because it is of fundamental significance for the further development of the law or for securing the maintenance of consistency in court rulings.[656] Further, the appellant must be aggrieved by the lower appellate decision.

c) Submissions

The statement of miscellaneous appeal on points of law (*Rechtsbeschwerdeschrift*) must be filed with the Federal Court of Justice within one month from service of the decision of the lower appellate court appealed.[657]

---

[651] ZPO § 567 (3).
[652] ZPO § 572 (1).
[653] ZPO § 572 (2), (3).
[654] ZPO § 572 (4).
[655] ZPO § 574 (1), (2); GVG § 133.
[656] ZPO § 574 (2).
[657] ZPO § 575 (1).

The contents of the statement of miscellaneous appeal on points of law are basically similar to those required for a statement of second appeal and a statement of grounds for a second appeal. A cross-appeal, as well as a withdrawal of appeal, is permissible. The opponent will have the opportunity to comment on the appeal.

d) Court Decision

When reviewing a miscellaneous appeal on points of law, the Federal Court of Justice will apply a standard similar to the second appeal. The court will determine whether the appeal is admissible and whether the decision of the lower court violates the law.[658]

The Federal Court of Justice may decide with or without an oral hearing. The court will decide by court order and may either dismiss the miscellaneous appeal on points of law, may remit the matter to the lower court for further proceedings or, when there is no need for additional fact-finding, may render a new decision of its own.[659]

V. Enforcement and Execution of German Judgments

I. Enforcement and Execution in Germany

The German courts do not enforce or execute their judgments *ex officio* if the defendant does not voluntarily comply. According to the principle of party autonomy, the party seeking execution of a judgment needs to apply to the court for assistance. The legal rules that apply to the execution of judgments and other enforceable instruments are rather complex. The following will provide a brief outline only.[660]

1. General

A party intending to execute a judgment (judgment creditor, *Vollstreckungsgläubiger*) must file a request for execution, in most cases with the competent local court (*Vollstreckungsgericht*) or with the bailiff (*Gerichtsvollzieher*) at the local court in whose district the enforcement shall take place.

The creditor must show an execution title (*Vollstreckungstitel*). In addition to judgments, execution titles include court settlements (*Prozessvergleiche*), enforceable payment orders (*Vollstreckungsbescheide*), court cost orders *(Kostenfestsetzungsbeschlüsse)*, and enforceable documents (*vollstreckbare Urkunden*). A judgment not being final and binding may nevertheless be provisionally enforceable.

The copy of the execution title generally must bear an enforcement clause (*Vollstreckungsklausel*) issued by the court. Upon request of the creditor, that enforcement clause is appended by the court clerk on a copy of the execution title then called the "enforceable execution copy" (*"vollstreckbare Ausfertigung"*).[661]

---

[658] ZPO §§ 576, 577.
[659] ZPO § 577.
[660] *Cf.* for a more detailed introduction *Rützel/Krapfl* in: Böckstiegel/Kröll/Nacimiento (eds.), Arbitration in Germany, 2nd ed., 2015, pp. 1061 *et seq.*
[661] ZPO § 724.

Finally, the execution title must be formally served on the opponent in the litigation as the judgment debtor (*Vollstreckungsschuldner*). Service may be effected by the creditor directly.

The debtor may have the right to avoid execution of a judgment by providing security to the opponent pending appeal. Further, there are a number of provisions limiting or precluding execution of execution titles based on social policy reasons.

2. Execution of Monetary Claims

The creditor may execute a judgment or other execution title for monetary claims by various means:

a) Execution by Garnishment of Monetary Claims and Other Proprietary Interests

The most common form in practice for a creditor to execute a money-related judgment or other execution title is to initiate garnishment measures (*Pfändungsmassnahmen*) against monetary claims or other proprietary interests of the debtor, such as deposits in bank accounts, uncertificated securities, or claims against third parties.

The creditor will make an application to the local court for the district of the debtor's domicile. If the debtor is not domiciled in Germany, the local court for the district where property of the debtor is located is competent. This is, for example, the court at the garnishee's domicile.

The application must identify the claims or interests to be garnished. The court will neither review whether these claims or interests exist nor whether they are owned by the debtor, but only whether such claims or interests might exist. If there are no claims or interests owned by the debtor, the garnishment will simply have no legal effect. Certain claims or interests such as a minimum amount of wage income are exempt from garnishment. In practice, the application for a garnishment order (*Pfändungsbeschluss*) will be combined with an application for a court order to transfer the claim or interest garnished to the creditor (transfer order, *Überweisungsbeschluss*).

The court will issue the order as requested. The garnishment order will identify the claim or interest garnished, will prohibit the garnishee (*Drittschuldner*) from making payments on the claim to the debtor, and will prohibit the debtor from requesting or receiving such payments.

The transfer order transfers the garnished claim to the creditor for collection.[662] The creditor is then entitled to request payment from the garnishee, although the debtor continues to be the legal owner of the claim. If the garnishee refuses to make payment to the creditor, the creditor may commence litigation against the garnishee for payment.

The garnishment and transfer order takes effect when served on the garnishee. The garnishee is required by law to give a declaration as to the existence and the amount of the garnished claim or interest (*Drittschuldnererklärung*).[663]

---

[662] *Cf.* ZPO § 835 (1), in theory, there is also the possibility that the transfer is in lieu of payment which has no relevance in practice.
[663] ZPO § 840.

b) Execution against Tangible Personal Property

In addition or alternatively, the creditor may make an application to the bailiff (*Gerichtsvollzieher*) to execute the execution title against movable property of the debtor.

The bailiff is expected to search the premises of the debtor for any property to be used to satisfy the judgment, such as cash amounts, merchandise or other movables. If the debtor refuses access to his premises, the bailiff may obtain an order granting access from the local court of the district where the premises are located. The bailiff may then (if necessary, assisted by the police) enforce access to the debtor's premises.

The bailiff will attach (*beschlagnahmen*) all movables subject to execution. The bailiff will take money, negotiable instruments and other valuable objects with him and will hold them in custody for the creditor. All other property is left in the debtor's custody, the attachment being marked by the bailiff's seal. This attachment deprives the debtor of his power of disposition; violations are a criminal offense. The bailiff will usually take possession of any movables which he finds in the debtor's custody, without regard to who may be the owner. If a third party is the owner of property attached on the debtor's premises, the attachment nevertheless is valid. The third party must file a third-party complaint (*Drittwiderspruchsklage*) to assert its ownership rights in the property.

Money will be handed over by the bailiff to the creditor. The bailiff will sell all other property in a public auction. The cost of the execution proceedings will be deducted from the proceeds of the auction, and the remainder will be handed over to the creditor in order to discharge the debt. Any surplus will be remitted to the debtor.

c) Execution against Real Property

A creditor may also decide to execute the enforceable instrument against the debtor's real property. Not only land and all buildings located on it, but also condominiums are treated as real property under German law. All real property in Germany, including condominiums, is registered in the land register (*Grundbuch*).

aa) Options for a Creditor. Execution against real estate is governed by the Law on Involuntary Sale and Administration (*Gesetz über der Zwangsversteigerung und die Zwangsverwaltung, ZVG*). The law gives a creditor several options on how to proceed, which he may pursue simultaneously:

The creditor may opt for only an involuntary lien procedure (*Zwangshypothek*). The lien gives the creditor a priority interest in the property, but does not immediately lead to a liquidation of the real estate.

The creditor also may choose to apply for an involuntary sale procedure (*Zwangsversteigerung*). The real property will then be sold at a public auction, and the proceeds will be applied to all liens on the property in order of their priority.

Finally, if the real estate generates income such as rent, a creditor may choose to initiate involuntary administration proceedings (*Zwangsverwaltung*).

bb) Procedure. An involuntary lien is obtained by filing an application with the office of the land register (*Grundbuchamt*) at the local court where the real property is located. The lien protects the creditor's interest insofar as the registration of the lien gives him priority over all voluntary or involuntary liens which are registered subsequently.

The local court where the real property is located is also competent to initiate, upon application by the creditor, proceedings for an involuntary auction. The auction will be held under the auspices of the local court. Proceeds will be paid out to the owners of liens or other interests in land according to their priority in the land register.

An application for involuntary administration of the real estate is made to the local court where the real property is located. The court will render an order which removes the debtor from possession, installs a court-appointed administrator (*Zwangsverwalter*), and attaches all present and future income, rents or fruits of the real property. The real property will be administered under the direction of the court. The administrator will make payments to the creditors from the income and the profits of the real property.

d) Forced Disclosure Proceedings

The creditor may make a request to the bailiff for forced disclosure proceedings.[664] Under a major reform that went into effect in January 2013,[665] the debtor is now obliged to provide information on his assets (*Vermögensauskunft*) even prior to any other enforcement measure.[666] If, upon notice by the bailiff, the debtor fails to pay his debt within two weeks, he is then required at a date set by the bailiff to provide the information on his assets.[667] The bailiff may require the information immediately if the debtor denied the bailiff access to his premises or if the outcome of an undertaken measure of execution into movables will predictably not result in full satisfaction of the creditor.[668]

The debtor has to specify all of his property as well as all claims against third parties he has or may have. In regard to claims, he also has to indicate the reason for the claim and means of evidence. The debtor is also required to disclose any transfers of property to a relative or to a close associate within the last two years and to disclose all transfers of property to any person for which he did not receive full consideration within the last four years. This information is recorded by the bailiff in an electronic document.[669] The debtor is required by the bailiff to give a formal declaration in lieu of an oath that the information he provided is correct according to his knowledge.[670] Giving a false formal declaration in lieu of an oath is a criminal offence.[671] If the debtor refuses to provide the information or does not respond to the notice by the bailiff, the competent local court may on application of the creditor issue a warrant (*Haftbefehl*) ordering the debtor to be taken into custody until he has provided the information.[672] The information on his assets provided by the debtor is recorded for two years in a central electronic register for every federal state.[673] Within this period of two years after providing information on his assets, the debtor is obliged to provide such information anew only if the creditor substantiates that a relevant change in the debtor's assets oc-

---

[664] ZPO § 802a (2) No. 2.
[665] See *supra*, at p. 4.
[666] ZPO § 802c.
[667] ZPO § 802f.
[668] ZPO § 807.
[669] ZPO § 802f (5).
[670] ZPO § 802c (3).
[671] German Penal Code (*Strafgesetzbuch*, StGB) § 156.
[672] ZPO § 802g.
[673] ZPO §§ 802f (6), 802k.

curred.[674] Otherwise, the bailiff will require the existing information contained in the central register and procure it to the creditor.

The name of a debtor who has been requested to make forced disclosure or who has been subject to a warrant will be entered into the debtors list (*Schuldnerverzeichnis*).[675]

3. Execution of Non-Monetary Claims

a) Delivery or Recovery of Movables

If the creditor has a claim for delivery or recovery of movables, the bailiff will take such movables away from the debtor, if necessary by force. If the movables are in the custody of a third party, however, the claims of the debtor against such third party for delivery to the debtor need to be garnished by the creditor.

b) Surrendering Possession of Real Property

Execution titles which require the debtor to surrender possession of real property are executed by the bailiff. The bailiff will remove the debtor from possession and will place the creditor in possession instead. The bailiff will hand over any personal property of the debtor located at the real property to the debtor or to one of his representatives. Eviction from residential real property is, however, subject to various tenant protection rules.

c) Performance of an Act

If the creditor has an execution title for performance of a specific act by the debtor which does not require the personal performance by the debtor (*vertretbare Handlung*), the creditor will apply for a court order allowing him to have the act performed by somebody else at the cost of the debtor.[676]

If the act must be performed personally by the debtor (*unvertretbare Handlung*), the court will enforce compliance by coercive penalty payments and, if that fails, by detention of the debtor.[677]

The competent court for these measures is the court of first instance.

d) Refraining from or Acquiescence to an Act

Execution titles ordering the debtor to refrain from a specific act (*Unterlassungstitel*) or to acquiesce to a specific act by the creditor or by third parties (*Duldungsanspruch*) by their very nature do not require execution. Non-compliance with such execution title, however, does. Compliance will be enforced by coercive penalty payments or by detention of the debtor, which will be ordered by the court of first instance upon application by the creditor.[678] This, however, requires that the debtor was formally notified by the court that such measures may be executed against him.[679] This notification may be contained in the original judgment, and therefore a creditor should already apply for it in the original proceedings.

---

[674] ZPO §802d.
[675] See *supra*, at pp. 28 et seq.
[676] ZPO §887.
[677] ZPO §888.
[678] ZPO §890 (1).
[679] ZPO §890 (2).

e) Declarations of Intent

A debtor may be required by an execution title to give a certain declaration of intent (*Willenserklärung*), *e.g.* the assent to an offer for a contract or to conveyance of real or personal property. An execution title to this effect also does not require execution. The execution title itself substitutes the respective declaration of intent.[680]

4. Remedies in Execution Proceedings

Most orders and actions by the courts or by the bailiff in the execution proceedings are subject to remedies by the debtor. There are various remedies available to the creditor if the court or the bailiff refuses to take action or to issue an order the creditor applied for.

A debtor may file an action to challenge the execution of a judgment (*Vollstreckungsgegenklage*) with the court that rendered such judgment.[681] This action must be based on facts which have arisen after the last oral hearing in the proceedings in which the execution title was rendered. These new facts must lead the court to the conclusion that the execution title may, in whole or in part, not be executed (any longer). Examples are payments made by the debtor on the claim or a waiver of the claim by the creditor after close of the oral hearing. If an action to challenge the execution of a judgment is successful, the court will render a judgment declaring the execution inadmissible. When this judgment itself is enforceable, even if preliminarily, and if it is presented to the bailiff or any other executing authority the execution has to be stopped.[682]

As mentioned above, the bailiff may validly attach property found on the premises of the debtor which might not be owned by the debtor. A third party being the owner of such property may file an action with the local or regional court in which district the execution took place in order to declare the execution into the property unlawful (*Drittwiderspruchsklage*).[683] If the court grants relief, it will render a judgment declaring the execution inadmissible which has to be presented to the bailiff as mentioned before to suspend the execution into the property.

II. Enforcement Abroad

Enforcement of German judgments abroad is most notably governed by the Brussels Regulation 2012 within the European Union, the Lugano Convention 2007 in regard to Switzerland, Iceland and Norway, the Convention on Choice of Court Agreements with regard to judgments based on agreements on exclusive jurisdiction in relation to other EU member states and to Mexico, several international bilateral treaties,[684] and the law of the foreign country in which enforcement is sought.

---

[680] ZPO §894, *cf.* ZPO §895.
[681] ZPO §767.
[682] ZPO §§775 No.1, 776.
[683] ZPO §771.
[684] These are the treaties for the mutual recognition and enforcement of judgments in civil and commercial matters with Israel (Federal Law Gazette [*Bundesgesetzblatt, BGBl.*] 1980 II, p. 925) and Tunisia (Federal Law Gazette [*Bundesgesetzblatt, BGBl.*] 1994 II, p. 518).

V. Enforcement and Execution of German Judgments

1. Enforcement within the European Union

a) Brussels Regulation 2012

Under the Brussels Regulation 2012,[685] judgments which are enforceable in the Member State where they were rendered are enforceable in all other Member States without any further declaration of enforceability by the authorities in that Member State.[686]

In order to enforce the judgment, the creditor has to present to the competent executing authority a certificate of enforceability issued by the authorities of the Member State where the judgment was rendered.[687] In Germany, this certificate is provided by the authorities competent to issue the enforceable copy of the title (*vollstreckbare Ausfertigung*),[688] usually the court of first instance, without hearing of the defendant.[689] A copy of the judgment which satisfies the conditions necessary to establish its authenticity is also needed. Normally, the copy that has been served on the parties by the German court[690] meets this requirement.

On application of the debtor, the enforcement may be refused by the competent court of a Member State if it is manifestly contrary to public policy in the Member State where enforcement is sought, if a default judgment was rendered without giving the defendant the opportunity to defend himself properly, if the judgment is irreconcilable with a judgment between the parties on the same subject matter in the Member State where enforcement is sought or with an earlier judgment between the parties on the same subject matter in another state recognized in the Member State where enforcement is sought, or if the judgment conflicts with certain provisions on jurisdiction.[691] The application has to be lodged with the court in the Member State where the judgment is supposed to be executed according to a notification on the competent court by the respective Member State.[692] The decision on the application is subject to an appeal which has to be lodged with the competent court according to the notification by the relevant Member State.[693] The appellate decision may furthermore be challenged by a second appeal if the relevant Member State has communicated which court it has to be lodged with.[694]

b) Other European Enforcement Regimes

European enforcement orders pursuant to Regulation (EC) No. 805/2004 of the European Parliament and of the Council of 21 April 2004 creating a European Enforcement Order for uncontested claims[695] can be enforced in all other Member

---

[685] The Regulation also indirectly applies to Denmark.
[686] Brussels Regulation 2012 Art. 39.
[687] Brussels Regulation 2012 Art. 42 (1), Art. 53.
[688] See *supra*, at p. 104.
[689] ZPO §§ 1110, 1111.
[690] See *supra*, at p. 91.
[691] Brussels Regulation 2012 Art. 46 in conjunction with Art. 45.
[692] Brussels Regulation 2012 Artt. 47, 75; the notifications for the different member states can be found at the European e-justice Portal: https://e-justice.europa.eu/content_recast-350-en.do; in Germany, the regional court would be the competent court.
[693] Brussels Regulation 2012, Artt. 49, 75; the notifications for the different member states can be found at the European e-justice Portal: https://e-justice.europa.eu/content_recast-350-en.do; in Germany, the higher regional court would be the competent court.
[694] Brussels Regulation 2012, Artt. 50, 75; the notifications for the different member states can be found at the European e-justice Portal: https://e-justice.europa.eu/content_recast-350-en.do; in Germany, the Federal Court of Justice (BGH) would be the competent court.
[695] The Regulation does not apply to Denmark.

States without any recognition or declaration of enforceability.[696] The proceedings under this Regulation may be chosen alternatively to those of the Brussels Regulation 2012[697] but should be less attractive in practice.

The Regulation (EC) No. 1896/2006 of the European Parliament and of the Council of 12 December 2006 creating a European order for payment procedure and the Regulation (EC) No. 861/2007 of the European Parliament and of the Council of 11 July 2007 establishing a European Small Claims Procedure also contain provisions for the enforcement of titles created under these Regulations in other Member States.[698]

2. Lugano Convention 2007

The procedure under the Lugano Convention 2007 is different from that under the Brussels Regulation 2012 but similar to the procedure under the old Brussels Regulation 2001.[699]

In order to enforce a German judgment under the Lugano Convention 2007, the judgment creditor must request a German court (not necessarily the court which rendered the judgment) to issue a certificate using the standard form in Annex 5 to the Lugano Convention 2007.[700] A copy of the judgment which satisfies the conditions necessary to establish its authenticity is also needed.[701]

Enclosing these documents, the judgment creditor then may apply for declaration of enforceability of the German judgment in the foreign Member State with the respective designated court or competent authority, as listed in Annex 2 to the Lugano Convention 2007.[702] Local jurisdiction is given at the domicile of the party against whom enforcement is sought or at the place of enforcement.

The foreign court or competent authority simply checks the documents accompanying the application in terms of form. It will not review the judgment for potential grounds for refusal of enforcement. Under the Lugano Convention 2007, these grounds will only be investigated upon an appeal by the debtor against whom the declaration of enforceability is being sought.[703] Annex 3 to the Lugano Convention 2007 contains a list of the competent court in the different member states. The decision by this court is again subject to a second appeal.[704]

The grounds for refusal of enforcement of a judgment are essentially similar to those under the Brussels Regulation 2012.[705]

3. Others

The Hague Convention on Choice of Court Agreements stipulates that a judgment rendered by the court agreed upon in an agreement on exclusive jurisdiction shall be recognized and enforced in all other contracting states, subject to a narrow list of exceptions. At this time, only the member states of the European Union

---

[696] Art. 1.5.
[697] Art. 27.
[698] See *supra*, at pp. 46 et seq.
[699] *Cf.* the first edition of this book, pp. 99 *et seq.*
[700] *Cf.* Lugano Convention 2007, Art. 53 (2), 54.
[701] Lugano Convention 2007, Art. 53 (1).
[702] *Cf.* Lugano Convention 2007, Art. 39.
[703] *Cf.* Lugano Convention 2007, Art. 45 (1) in conjunction with Art. 34, 35.
[704] Lugano Convention 2007, Art. 44 in conjunction with Annex IV.
[705] Lugano Convention 2007, Art. 45 (1) in conjunction with Art. 34, 35; *cf.* Brussels Regulation 2012, Art. 46 in conjunction with Art. 45

(except Denmark) and Mexico are bound by the Convention, with Singapore soon to follow. However, since the USA is a signatory as well, which may ratify the Convention at any time, the support from the likes of the European Union and the USA may create a bandwagon effect, prompting a wave of new signings and ratifications throughout the world. Therefore, the Convention may very well have the potential to achieve for cross-border litigation what the New York Convention achieved for international arbitration.

As to Israel and Tunisia, bilateral treaties with Germany govern the recognition and enforcement of German judgments in these countries.

If a party seeks enforcement of a German judgment in a state outside Europe which is also not a signatory to a bilateral international treaty, the applicable standards will be those in place in the foreign country. Each country sets some limits on the recognition and enforcement of foreign judgments. Nevertheless, German judgments are generally broadly recognized abroad. As German procedural law is quite moderate, German judgments normally do not run into difficulties, for instance on grounds of service of process, personal jurisdiction or an extra-territorial application of German law.[706]

W. Provisional Relief

I. General

1. Provisional Remedies Available

German law provides for two categories of provisional relief, *i.e.* attachment (*Arrest*) and preliminary injunction (*einstweilige Verfügung*). These remedies are designed to secure a potential future judgment or to temporarily regulate a legal relationship. They are aimed at safeguarding claims of any kind of the plaintiff, but do not lead to a final resolution of a dispute.

The question of which remedy is available depends on the nature of the claim to be secured. An attachment is the proper remedy to secure monetary claims or claims which may become a monetary claim, whereas a preliminary injunction secures all other claims.

2. Practical Aspects

Applying to a German court for provisional relief is, for a number of reasons, quite effective:

First of all, proceedings for provisional remedies are very fast. These proceedings are handled by the German courts with absolute priority. Normally, it does not take more than two days, sometimes even only a few hours, from filing the application to obtaining the court order.

Secondly, orders for preliminary relief can be, and normally are, issued *ex parte*, *i.e.* without hearing the defendant first. This allows the plaintiff to obtain

---

[706] A description of the prerequisites and procedures for recognition and enforcement of German judgments in various countries can be found at *Nagel/Gottwald*, Internationales Zivilprozessrecht, 7th ed., 2013, § 16.

a court order securing his claims without giving the defendant time to thwart such security.

Finally, the standard of proof is relaxed compared to main proceedings. The plaintiff only has to show *prima facie* evidence.[707] As to burden of proof, it is sufficient that the judge holds the correctness of the alleged facts to be more likely than not. In addition, evidence by formal declaration in lieu of an oath of the plaintiff himself is admissible in proceedings for provisional relief.[708] This possibility not only saves time, but also allows submitting evidence which would not be admissible in main proceedings.

Applying for provisional relief is, therefore, very popular not only with domestic litigants, but also with foreign entities trying to secure their claims against German defendants or against assets located in Germany.

II. Attachments

1. Application for an Attachment

An attachment order (*Arrestbeschluss*) or judgment (*Arresturteil*) is rendered by a German court upon an application by the plaintiff (*Arrestkläger*). The application must contain facts establishing jurisdiction of the court seized, an attachment claim (*Arrestanspruch*) and an attachment reason (*Arrestgrund*). These facts must be supported by *prima facie* evidence:

a) Jurisdiction

International, local and subject matter jurisdiction for attachment proceedings is either with the local court in which district assets of the defendant (*Arrestbeklagter*) are located. Alternatively, a court having jurisdiction regarding the underlying main action is competent to hear the case.[709] Insofar, the general principles on jurisdiction apply.

Domestic plaintiffs may, therefore, often have the choice between different forums. Foreign plaintiffs, however, will regularly have to bring attachment proceedings to the local courts if the only connection of the dispute to Germany is that the defendant has assets located in Germany.

b) Motions

The application must contain a motion specifying the amount of the monetary claim to be secured and that an attachment of assets of the defendant is requested (*dinglicher Arrest*).[710]

The attachment order or judgment rendered will be executed against the defendant's assets. As regards execution by way of garnishment of the defendant's monetary claims and proprietary interests, the court competent to decide on the

---

[707] ZPO §920 (2).
[708] ZPO §920 (2) in conjunction with ZPO §294 (1).
[709] ZPO §919.
[710] ZPO §920. Alternatively, the claimant may seek "personal attachment" (*persönlicher Arrest*) of the debtor by way of detention to prevent the debtor from frustrating the execution against his assets (ZPO §918). This kind of attachment is usually never applied for due to its extremely strict prerequisites.

attachment is also competent for the execution.[711] Therefore, the application for attachment is usually combined with the application for a garnishment order (*Pfändungsantrag*).

c) Attachment Claim

An attachment secures the plaintiff's claim against the defendant (attachment claim, *Arrestanspruch*).[712] This must be either a claim for money or a claim that can give way to a claim for money in the future. Claims that accrue in the future, conditional claims or claims with a fixed future maturity date may all be safeguarded by an attachment. An exception applies only to conditional claims that have no current asset value because of the remote possibility of occurrence of the condition.

d) Grounds for Attachment

In addition to the attachment claim, a plaintiff must show a ground for attachment (*Arrestgrund*).[713]

An attachment will take place if it is feared that the enforcement of a subsequently rendered judgment would otherwise be frustrated or made substantially difficult[714] due to actions or the financial situation of the defendant. The attachment of the defendant's assets must, therefore, be necessary to preliminarily protect the plaintiff's prospects of executing a judgment rendered in the future. This may not only be a German judgment, but also a foreign judgment.[715]

Reasons for an attachment order may include the reasonable suspicion that the defendant attempts by dishonest means to put his assets out of the plaintiff's reach, if the defendant makes or plans dispositions concerning his assets which are objectively prone to make the execution into these assets more difficult, or if there are reasons to believe that the defendant's conduct qualifies as fraud or embezzlement of funds.[716] However, mere financial difficulties of a debtor do not as such constitute an attachment reason.[717]

A special attachment reason exists if the execution of a subsequent judgment would have to take place in a foreign country which does not guarantee reciprocity with regard to recognition and enforcement of German judgments.[718] This applies only to a very limited number of foreign countries. The claimant will have to provide *prima facie* evidence on this prerequisite. Due to possible changes in the foreign legislation and political developments in foreign countries, this might prove difficult in the limited time available to prepare attachment proceedings.

---

[711] ZPO §930 (1) sentence 3.
[712] ZPO §916.
[713] ZPO §917.
[714] ZPO §917 (1).
[715] *Vollkommer* in: Zöller, Zivilprozessordnung, 30th ed., 2014, §917 no. 4.
[716] *Cf. Vollkommer* in: Zöller, Zivilprozessordnung, 30th ed., 2014, §917 no. 5 *et seq.*
[717] Federal Court of Justice (BGH), Decision of 19 October 1995 (Docket-No. IX ZR 82/94), Neue Juristische Wochenschrift, 1996, pp. 321, 324.
[718] ZPO §917 (2); arguably ZPO §917 (2) also applies to judgments given in Member States of the Brussels Regulation 2017 and the Lugano Convention 2007, *cf. Vollkommer* in: Zöller, Zivilprozessordnung, 30th ed., 2014, §917 no. 16.

2. Protective Writ

Attachments are usually granted by the courts by way of an *ex parte* order. Therefore, if a party expects an attachment, it is common to submit a protective writ (*Schutzschrift*) to all courts where the opponent might apply for an attachment order. In essence, a protective writ is in form and contents similar to a statement of defense.

At present, there is a central electronic register for protective writs (*Schutzschriftenregister*) in place where such writs can be registered and accessed by those courts which have agreed to check the register for writs before issuing an *ex parte* attachment order.[719] As of 1 January 2016, all civil and commercial courts in all federal states will be obliged to do so.[720]

3. Attachment Judgment or Order

Depending on the circumstances, the court may notify the defendant of the application, set a time for a written response, and schedule an oral hearing. The court will then render an attachment judgment (*Arresturteil*). However, in most cases, the court will not schedule an oral hearing, but render an attachment order (*Arrestbeschluss*) *ex parte*.[721]

The court may make the order or the judgment, or the execution of them, conditional upon the plaintiff posting a security for potential damages resulting from execution of the attachment.[722]

4. Execution

The plaintiff will have to execute the attachment judgment or the attachment order within one month from service of the attachment order on the plaintiff or from the rendition of the judgment.[723] The plaintiff is also responsible for the service of an attachment order on the defendant,[724] which requires an application by him to the bailiff.[725] An attachment judgment is served *ex officio* by the court on both parties.[726] Execution of an attachment order or judgment is, however, admissible before the service to the defendant is completed if the order is served within one week afterwards and within the period of one month from the rendition of the order.[727]

Attachment orders and judgments may be enforced by garnishing claims and other proprietary interests, by attachment of movable property, or in case of real property, by an involuntary lien procedure.[728] As regards garnishments, it may be noted that the jurisdiction of either the local court or the regional court granting the attachment and the garnishing order is not limited to garnishing assets located within their own judicial district. As soon as a court is competent, it may garnish all assets within other (German) judicial districts.

---

[719] The register is available at www.schutzschriftenregister.de.
[720] ZPO §945a as of 01 January 2016.
[721] ZPO §922.
[722] ZPO §921.
[723] ZPO §929 (2).
[724] ZPO §922 (2).
[725] ZPO §§191 *et seq.*
[726] *Vollkommer* in: Zöller, Zivilprozessordnung, 30th ed., 2014, §922 no. 16.
[727] ZPO §929 (3).
[728] ZPO §§928 *et seq.*

W. Provisional Relief

The general principles on execution apply.[729] However, the enforcement of an attachment order or judgment is restricted to measures that only safeguard the plaintiff but do not fully satisfy his claim. As regards the garnishment of claims and interests, the court will, therefore, not render a transfer order (*Überweisungsbeschluss*).

5. Remedies

An attachment order, but not an attachment judgment, is subject to a protest (*Widerspruch*) by the defendant.[730] The protest does not prevent the plaintiff from further executing the attachment order; it has no suspending effect. However, the court may on motion of the debtor preliminarily suspend or restrict the execution and make special arrangements with regard to sureties.[731] If the defendant has filed a protest, the court will schedule an oral hearing and will render a judgment either confirming or setting aside the previous attachment order.

The unsuccessful party may appeal within one month both against the attachment judgment or against the judgment after a protest filed by the defendant. The provisions on first appeals apply.[732] A second appeal is not admissible.[733]

There are some other options available to a defendant in attachment proceedings. The defendant may also request the court to set a time limit within which the plaintiff must file the main action. If the plaintiff does not comply with this, the court will, on request by the defendant, revoke the attachment decision and lift all enforcement measures without further proceedings.[734] The defendant may also make a motion at any time in the proceedings that the relevant circumstances have changed and that the prerequisites for the attachment are, therefore, no longer given.[735] This not only relates to a change in factual circumstances but also to changes in relevant legislation or jurisdiction and even where it is decided in the main proceedings that the plaintiff's alleged claim does not exist, since the attachment does not automatically lose force.[736] Finally, a defendant may deposit a monetary amount sufficient to satisfy the attachment claim and make a motion to the court to lift the attachment.[737]

III. Preliminary Injunction

1. Application for a Preliminary Injunction

The rules governing an application by a plaintiff for a preliminary injunction (*Verfügungskläger*) against a defendant (*Verfügungsbeklagter*) are largely identical with those for an attachment.[738]

---

[729] See *supra*, at pp. 103 et seq.
[730] ZPO §§ 924 *et seq.*
[731] ZPO § 924 (3) sentence 2 in conjunction with ZPO § 707.
[732] See *supra*, at pp. 94 et seq.
[733] ZPO § 542 (2) sentence 1.
[734] ZPO § 926.
[735] ZPO § 927.
[736] See *Vollkommer* in: Zöller, Zivilprozessordnung, 30th ed., 2014, 927 no. 4 *et seq.*
[737] ZPO § 934.
[738] ZPO § 936.

a) Jurisdiction

The court where the main action on the claim to be secured is pending or, if no main action has been filed yet, the court competent to hear such main action has international, local and subject matter jurisdiction for injunction proceedings.[739]

If the matter is extremely urgent, the application for injunction proceedings may be filed with the local court where the subject matter of the dispute is located.[740] However, the court must set the plaintiff a time limit to file a petition with the competent regional court to have the court initiate protest proceedings. Since this is not advantageous to a plaintiff and since it is difficult to show that the matter is even more urgent than regular injunction proceedings, applications to the local courts are rare. Since these restrictions do not apply if the application for an injunction is aimed at registering a lien in the land register (*Grundbuch*) or in the register of ships (*Schiffsregister*) or the register of ships under construction (*Schiffsbauregister*), the local courts are frequently seized with such matters.

b) Motions

The application must contain a motion specifying the contents of the injunction sought. The plaintiff may seek to secure a claim such as *e.g.* a claim for recovery of movable property (*Sicherungsverfügung*).[741] The plaintiff's aim may be to have a legal relationship temporarily regulated by the court (*Regelungsverfügung*) in order to avoid potential injury or disadvantage.[742] Where mere security would not suffice, the plaintiff may seek performance of a claim by way of injunction (*Leistungsverfügung*). The most frequent examples are injunctions to have the defendant cease and desist from certain acts (*Unterlassungsverfügung*), in particular in unfair competition law.

Injunctions to cease and desist from certain acts, or to order the defendant to perform a certain act personally, are executed by coercive penalty payments and by detention. The execution of these measures requires that the defendant has formally been made aware of these potential consequences by the court (*Zwangsmittelandrohung*). The plaintiff must request this in his application.

Finally, the plaintiff may make a motion that the presiding judge alone and not the chamber shall decide on the application for urgency reasons.[743]

c) Injunction Claim

The plaintiff must show *prima facie* evidence of the claim to be secured by the injunction, or of the legal relationship the court is requested to regulate by injunction (injunction claim, *Verfügungsanspruch*).[744]

d) Grounds for Injunction

The plaintiff further has to state the grounds for why an injunction is necessary to safeguard his rights or to avoid potential injury or disadvantage in case a legal

---

[739] ZPO §937 (1).
[740] ZPO §942.
[741] ZPO §935.
[742] ZPO §940.
[743] ZPO §§944, 937 (2).
[744] ZPO §936 in conjunction with ZPO §920 (2).

relationship is not regulated by injunction (ground for injunction, *Verfügungsgrund*).[745] In certain circumstances, a ground for injunction is legally presumed.[746]

2. Protective Writs

The use of and the requirements for protective writs are identical to the one in attachment proceedings.

3. Injunction Judgment or Order

The prerequisites for rendering an injunction order or an injunction judgment are largely identical to those in attachment proceedings. However, a decision without an oral hearing is only permissible in extremely urgent cases.[747] In such cases the presiding judge may, as mentioned before, upon motion by the claimant, decide instead of the chamber.[748] Within the limits of the motion, the content of the injunction is in the court's discretion.[749]

4. Execution

The injunction order or injunction judgment must be executed by the plaintiff. The plaintiff has to serve an injunction order to the defendant.[750] Compliance with injunctions to cease and desist or to personally perform an act is enforced by penalty payments or detention of the debtor.[751] In all other cases, execution generally follows the same rules as attachments.

5. Remedies

The rules on remedies are largely identical to those applicable to an attachment. The option to provide security in order to have an attachment set aside, however, is only available in very limited circumstances.[752]

IV. No-Fault Liability

A plaintiff applying for provisional remedies in Germany faces the risk of extensive no-fault liability.[753] In case a provisional court order or judgment has initially been rendered and executed by the plaintiff and thereafter is set aside upon a protest by the defendant or upon appeal, the plaintiff is liable on a no-fault basis for all damages which the defendant has suffered from the execution. The claim for damages has to be pursued by the defendant in regular court proceedings.

---

[745] ZPO § 936 in conjunction with ZPO § 917.
[746] See, *e.g.*, BGB § 885 (1); UWG § 12 (2).
[747] ZPO § 937 (2).
[748] ZPO § 944.
[749] ZPO § 938.
[750] ZPO § 936 in conjunction with ZPO § 922 (2).
[751] ZPO § 936 in conjunction with ZPO §§ 928, 888, 890; see *supra*, at p. 108.
[752] ZPO § 939.
[753] ZPO § 945.

V. Enforcement of German Provisional Decisions Abroad[754]

In general, attachment and preliminary injunction orders or judgments by the German courts may be executed abroad. In particular, provisional remedies rendered by German courts are generally recognized and enforced in all states to which either the Brussels Regulation 2012 or the Lugano Convention 2007 apply.[755]

However, recognition and enforcement of provisional remedies under the Lugano Convention 2007 and under many foreign laws require that the defendant had received proper service and had an opportunity to be heard in court.[756] Therefore, only German provisional judgments, but not German *ex parte* court orders, will be recognized and enforced under the Lugano Convention 2007 and in many other parts of the world. This considerably thwarts the purpose of obtaining provisional court orders by divesting them of their swiftness and surprise element.

The Brussels Regulation 2012 explicitly allows for execution of provisional and protective measures in other Member States. However, *ex parte* measures are excluded unless they are served on the defendant prior to enforcement.[757] In order to execute the provisional measure, the plaintiff has to show to the competent executing authority a copy of the decision containing the provisional measure which satisfies the conditions necessary to establish its authenticity, a certificate which *inter alia* states that the court has jurisdiction as to the substance of the matter and that the decision is enforceable in the member state of origin, and in cases of *ex parte* measures additionally proof of service on the defendant.[758]

Therefore, it is, even under the Brussels Regulation 2012, often advisable not to apply for provisional remedies in Germany if they are to be enforced abroad, but rather to apply for provisional measures directly in the respective foreign country.

X. Legal Assistance in Aid of Foreign Proceedings

I. Service of Process

As is the case with service of process by the German courts abroad, service of foreign documents in Germany is governed by the Brussels Service Regulation 2007, the Hague Civil Procedure Convention, the Hague Service Convention, bilateral treaties, or the international principles of reciprocity in granting judicial assistance.[759]

1. Brussels Service Regulation 2007

Germany has generally designated the local courts in the district in which service is to be made as the "receiving agencies" for requests for service of foreign documents under the Brussels Service Regulation 2007.[760] The governments of

---

[754] For enforcement of foreign provisional measures in Germany see *infra*, at pp. 123 et seq.
[755] The same is true under the treaty between Germany and Tunisia.
[756] See against this approach, *Geimer* in: Zöller, Zivilprozessordnung, 30th ed., 2014, Annex I EuGVVO Art. 31, no. 8.
[757] Brussels Regulation 2012, Art. 2 a.
[758] Brussels Regulation 2012 Art. 42 No. 2.
[759] See *supra*, at pp. 56 et seq.
[760] ZPO § 1069 (2).

the federal states may designate one local court for the districts of several other local courts.[761]

Under the Brussels Service Regulation 2007 direct service in Germany through German judicial officers, officials or other competent persons is admissible where such service is admissible under German domestic law,[762] *e.g.* attachment orders.[763] Service by certified mail, return receipt requested, is also allowed.[764] Finally, direct service through diplomatic or consular agents of the state where the document originates under the Brussels Regulation 2007 in Germany is admissible only on citizens of the respective state.[765]

A translation of the document is not necessary. However, the addressee may refuse to accept the document if it is drawn up in a language other than German or in a language which he does not understand.[766] This applies to all above-mentioned kinds of service.[767]

2. Hague Service Convention

In case the Hague Service Convention applies, the party in a foreign state must forward the request for service of documents to the competent German central authority. This is often, but not in every federal state, the Ministry of Justice of the German federal state in which service is to be made.[768] A translation of the document is necessary if formal service is requested.[769] If informal delivery is sufficient for the party, no translation is required, but the addressee may decide whether to refuse or accept such informal delivery.[770]

Normally, service of process under the Hague Service Convention will be handled quite liberally by the German authorities. However, the Federal Constitutional Court held that in cases where the aims of a foreign court action are obviously in conflict with core principles of the German constitution, the German authorities may not be allowed to grant legal assistance in service of process, but the Court left open what exactly such aims could be. The Court did confirm, however, that certain elements of U.S. civil procedure such as punitive damages, high attorney costs not recoverable even in case of success in the proceedings, the possibility to litigate simultaneously in different courts or class actions do not as such constitute a conflict.[771]

---

[761] For the relevant receiving agencies see http://ec.europa.eu/justice_home/judicialatlascivil/html/ds_information_de.htm?countrySession=1&.

[762] Brussels Service Regulation 2007 Art. 15; under the old Brussels Service Regulation 2000 Art. 15 (2) Germany had made a reservation, *cf.* the first edition of this book, p. 106.

[763] *Cf. supra*, at pp. 114 et seq.

[764] Brussels Service Regulation 2007 Art. 14.

[765] Brussels Service Regulation 2007 Art. 13, ZPO § 1067.

[766] Brussels Service Regulation 2007 Art. 8.

[767] See Brussels Regulation 2007 Art. 8 (4).

[768] For the central authorities in the different German States see http://www.hcch.net/upload/auth20de.pdf.

[769] HaagÜbkAG §3, Hague Service Convention Art. 5 (3).

[770] Hague Service Convention Art. 5 (2).

[771] Federal Constitutional Court (BVerfG), Decision of 25 July 2003 (Docket No. 2 BvR 1198/03), Neue Juristische Wochenschrift, 2003, p. 2598 – Bertelsmann vs. Napster. *Cf. Friedrich*, Federal Constitutional Court Grants Interim Legal Protection Against Service of a Writ of Punitive Damages Suit, German Law Journal, Vol. 4, No. 12, 2003, available at https://www.germanlawjournal.com/pdfs/Vol04No12/PDF_Vol_04_No_12_1233-1240_Public_Friedrich.pdf.

Federal Constitutional Court (BVerfG), decision of 9 January 2013 (Docket-No. 2 BvR 2805/12), Neue Juristische Wochenschrift 2013, p. 990 et seq.

3. Other Requests

A request for service of process of documents from countries to which neither the Brussels Service Regulation 2007 nor the Hague Service Convention applies must generally be sent to the president of the German regional court in which judicial district the service is to be made.[772] Service will then be effected by the competent local court.[773] In most cases, such requests for legal assistance are granted by the German authorities.

II. Taking of Evidence in Germany in Aid of Foreign Proceedings

1. Brussels Evidence Regulation

A court in a Member State of the European Union[774] may request from a German court to take evidence in Germany. The procedure will be the same as for requests of German courts for legal assistance under the Brussels Evidence Regulation.[775]

The requesting foreign court will transmit its request directly to the competent German local court without having first to go through the respective German central authority.[776]

The direct taking of evidence by the foreign court is also possible upon request to the respective German central authority and may only be refused on limited grounds.[777]

2. Hague Evidence Convention

Under the Hague Evidence Convention, the foreign court as the requesting authority will normally send a letter of request to the designated German central authority, *i.e.* often the Ministry of Justice of the respective German federal state.[778] However, the German central authorities also accept letters of request that are duly issued by the requesting foreign court but transmitted by one of the parties, which is normally the case with requests from the USA.

According to the Hague Evidence Convention and the applicable German implementation provisions, the letter of request must meet certain requirements as to its contents and, in particular, must be accompanied by a certified translation into German. The German central authority examines the permissibility of the letter of request and may refuse execution only on limited grounds. In particular, execution of letters of request will not be denied on the ground that the claim is for punitive or treble damages. Requests for the taking of extensive witness testimony and for the production of specified documents will also be granted. A request

---

See also Federal Constitutional Court (BVerfG), decision of 14 June 2007 (Docket-No. 2 BvR 2247/06), Neue Juristische Wochenschrift 2007, p. 3709.

Federal Constitutional Court (BVerfG), Decision of 14 June 2007 (Docket-No. 2 BvR 2247/06), Neue Juristische Wochenschrift 2007, p. 3709 et seq; Federal Constitutional Court (BVerfG), Decision of 9 January 2013 (Docket-No. BvR 2805/12), Neue Juristische Wochenschrift 2013, p. 990.

[772] ZRHO §82 (1) lit. d in conjunction with §9 (2).
[773] ZHRO §110 (1).
[774] Except Denmark.
[775] See *supra*, at pp. 84 et seq.
[776] Brussels Evidence Regulation Art. 2, ZPO §1074, see for the competent local courts the European Judicial Atlas in Civil Matters at http://ec.europa.eu/justice_home/judicialatlascivil/html/te_searchmunicipality_en.jsp?countrySession=1&#statePage1.
[777] Brussels Evidence Regulation Art. 17.
[778] ZHRO §82 (1) No. 2, §9 (4).

for pre-trial discovery of documents of U.S. courts, however, will not be executed because Germany has made a reservation to the Hague Evidence Convention.[779]

3. Other International Instruments

The German authorities will also execute requests for the taking of evidence in accordance with the Hague Civil Procedure Convention, the provisions of the respective bilateral international treaties,[780] and based on the international principles of judicial assistance.[781]

III. Information on German Law

If German law is applicable in foreign proceedings, the foreign court may make a request under the European Convention on Information on Foreign Law[782] to the Federal Ministry of Justice (*Bundesjustizministerium*) in Berlin. Requests may only contain abstract legal questions. The reply will be in German without exception. The Federal Ministry of Justice will also provide information in German to the authorities of Morocco based on the respective bilateral treaty.[783] There is no obligation by the German authorities to respond to requests from other countries.[784]

A foreign court of a member state of the European Union[785] may also obtain information on German domestic law via the European Judicial Network in civil and commercial matters. Useful information on German law in general may also be found at the European e-justice portal.[786]

IV. Enforcement of Foreign Judgments

1. Judgments of Courts in the European Union

Enforcement of judgments rendered by the courts of other Member States of the European Union in Germany is governed by the Brussels Regulation 2012 and in regard to Switzerland, Iceland and Norway by the Lugano Convention 2007. The proceedings are the same as with the enforcement of German judgments abroad.

Foreign judgments of courts in the European Union that are enforceable under the domestic law of the respective Member State constitute enforcement titles under German law and do not require a German enforcement clause.[787] Applications for refusal of enforcement are to be lodged with the regional court in the district of the debtor's place of residence or, if he is not resident in Germany, with the regional court in the district where enforcement is to take place.[788]

---

[779] Hague Evidence Convention Art. 23, HaagÜbkAG § 14 (1).
[780] Treaties exist with Turkey (Reich Law Gazette [*Reichsgesetzblatt*] 1930 II, p. 6), Tunisia (Federal Law Gazette [*Bundesgesetzblatt*] 1969 II, p. 889), Morocco (Federal Law Gazette [*Bundesgesetzblatt*] 1988 II, p. 1055; 1994 II, p. 1192) and the United Kingdom (Reich Law Gazette [*Reichsgesetzblatt*] 1928 II, p. 823).
[781] ZRHO §§ 82 *et seq.*
[782] See *supra*, at p. 89.
[783] Federal Law Gazette (*Bundesgesetzblatt*) 1988 II, p. 1054.
[784] *Cf.* ZRHO § 142.
[785] Except Denmark.
[786] Available at https://e-justice.europa.eu/content_ejn_in_civil_and_commercial_matters-21-en.
[787] ZPO § 1112.
[788] ZPO § 1115.

With the same courts, applications for a declaration of enforceability are to be lodged under the Lugano Convention 2007.[789] Several specific formal requirements have to be met.[790] The application has to be accompanied by two duplicates of the judgment for which enforcement is sought and of its translation, if any. Furthermore, if the application is not in German, the court may order the applicant to provide a translation thereof.

2. Other Foreign Judgments

If neither European law nor a treaty[791] governs, German statutory law applies. Rules regulating the procedure for obtaining enforcement of foreign judgments in Germany can be found in ZPO §§ 722 *et seq*.

A judgment creditor who wishes to enforce a foreign judgment in Germany must file a request for execution either with the German local court or with the regional court of the district in which the judgment debtor is domiciled or in which the debtor owns property.[792] It depends on the subject matter jurisdiction whether the local court or the regional court is competent.

A debtor in an action for execution based on a foreign judgment may invoke all grounds for non-recognition or non-enforcement of the foreign judgment as well as grounds in defense of execution such as subsequent payment or satisfaction of the judgment.[793] If none of these grounds exist, the court will render a judgment of enforceability. The judgment of enforceability puts the foreign judgment in the same position as a final and binding German judgment.

The German court will deny enforceability if the judgment cannot be recognized. There are five grounds under German law according to which German courts would not recognize foreign judgments: jurisdiction, service of process, priority of other proceedings, public policy, and reciprocity.[794]

In particular, German courts will recognize the foreign judgment only if the foreign court had international jurisdiction over the subject matter and the parties of the dispute. The German courts apply the so-called "mirror-image test". The foreign court must have had international jurisdiction according to the German rules and standards. This principle does not apply to local or subject matter jurisdiction of the foreign court. The only question is, therefore, whether a court (not necessarily the court that rendered the judgment) in the foreign country had international jurisdiction assuming that German law on jurisdiction would apply in the foreign country. Judgments based on transient or long-arm statutes could face difficulties under this test.

Furthermore, judgments of U.S. courts for punitive damages may not be enforceable in Germany on the ground of a violation of German public policy. In a 1992 decision, the Federal Court of Justice held that German civil law only focuses on the compensation of the plaintiff and has abolished damages that would lead to an enrichment of the victim and a punishment of the defendant. Further, German law makes a clear distinction between the law of damages and public prosecution and criminal law. Although under German law damages for pain and suffering are available, they have no penal character and are connected with the compensa-

---

[789] AVAG § 3; reprinted at Part 2. A. III.
[790] AVAG § 4; reprinted at Part 2. A. III.
[791] Treaties exist with Israel and Tunisia, see *supra*, at p. 109.
[792] ZPO § 722 (2).
[793] *Cf. Geimer* in: Zöller, Zivilprozessordnung, 30th ed., 2014, § 722 no. 79.
[794] ZPO § 723 (2) sentence 2 in conjunction with ZPO § 328 (1).

tory function of damages. On these grounds, the Federal Court of Justice denied the enforcement of a U.S. judgment for punitive damages. The court, however, has left open the possibility of enforcement under special circumstances if the foreign judgment states sufficient grounds that the damages awarded do not have a penal character but are intended to be a compensation for economic loss.[795]

V. Provisional Remedies in Aid of Foreign Proceedings

1. European Union

The Brussels Regulation 2012 and the Lugano Convention 2007 only contain provisions on jurisdiction. The question of what provisional remedies apply is a question of domestic law.

Therefore, a court of a Member State which according to the applicable domestic law is competent to grant preliminary relief may do so even if the courts of another Member State have jurisdiction for the main proceedings on the case.[796] However, there must be a connecting link between the subject matter of the preliminary relief sought and the territorial jurisdiction of the respective court.[797] Therefore, a plaintiff may often have the choice between the courts of several Member States of the European Union to apply for provisional remedies.

A claimant may apply for preliminary relief in Germany, in particular, if the execution shall take place in Germany. However, the courts of some Member States are entitled to grant provisional remedies which significantly exceed the scope of the provisional remedies available in a German court. For example, the prerequisites for obtaining provisional remedies in the Netherlands or in the United Kingdom are generally more relaxed, and French and Dutch courts often issue preliminary decisions concerning the substance of the case which would not be possible in Germany. Therefore, it may be worth considering whether to apply for provisional remedies in other countries and to subsequently enforce them in Germany despite the fact that the surprise element may be lost.[798]

2. Decisions by Courts Outside the European Union

Provisional decisions by courts outside the European Union are generally not recognized in Germany. In principle, German law only recognizes and enforces final and conclusive foreign judgments.[799]

---

[795] Federal Court of Justice (BGH), Decision of 4 June 1992 (Docket No. IX ZR 149/91), Bundesgerichtshofentscheidungen, Vol. 118, p. 312.
[796] Brussels Regulation 2012 Art. 35; Lugano Convention 2007 Art. 31.
[797] Van Uden Maritime BV v. Kommanditgesellschaft in Firma Deco-Line et. al., Decision of 17 November 1998, (Docket No. C-391/95) in regard to the corresponding Article 24 in the Brussels Convention; the decision can be found at http://curia.europa.eu/.
[798] See *supra*, at p. 118.
[799] ZPO §§ 723 (2), 328. *Cf. Geimer* in: Zöller, Zivilprozessordnung, 30th ed., 2014, § 328 no. 68 *et seq.*, also stating the exceptions.

Chapter 2: Arbitration

A. Introduction

I. Brief History

1. German Arbitration Law

The revised German arbitration law which came into force on 1 January 1998 was adopted to better facilitate domestic and international arbitral proceedings in Germany. The law, codified in the German Code of Civil Procedure (*Zivilprozessordnung*, ZPO), §§ 1025 to 1066, was a complete overhaul of the then existing legal arbitration regime which was widely recognized as anachronistic. The new law applies to all agreements to arbitrate concluded on or after 1 January 1998. Furthermore, the arbitral proceedings that are commenced after 1 January 1998 based upon an arbitration agreement pre-dating the coming into effect of the revised law are governed by the new law, but the validity of the underlying arbitration agreement is determined according to the law previously in force.[1] Parties may agree to apply the new law to arbitral proceedings that were pending at the time of the new law coming into force, but to protect the expectations of parties, the new law is not automatically applicable to arbitral proceedings that were pending when the new law came into effect.[2]

2. Legislative Intent behind New German Arbitration Law

Often referred to as the "modernization" of arbitration law in Germany, the revised German arbitration law was modeled after the UNCITRAL Model Law.[3] With the goal of creating an arbitration-friendly jurisdiction that would be attractive to foreign practitioners, the German legislature favored a legal structure that would be familiar to the arbitration community as an accepted international standard. The hope was that even those who were unfamiliar with German language or German law would be able to rely on the fact that an arbitration in Germany, although it would be different from an arbitration in a practitioner's home jurisdiction with maybe a few Germanic idiosyncrasies, would not deviate substantially from familiar and accepted international standards. One of the

---

[1] Article 4 § 1 (1) of the Act on the Reform of the Law relating to Arbitral Proceedings of 22 December 1997, Federal Law Gazette (*Bundesgesetzblatt*) 1997 I, pp. 3224, 3240-3241 as amended by the Bill of the Judicial Communication Act, 22 March 2005, Federal Law Gazette (*Bundesgesetzblatt*) 2005 I, pp. 837-858.

[2] Berger, Das neue Recht der Schiedsgerichtsbarkeit: The New German Arbitration Law, 1998, pp. 44-45; Berger, The German Arbitration Law of 1998 – First Experiences 2001, in: Briner/Fortier/Berger/Bredow (eds.), Law of International Business and Dispute Settlement in the 21st Century: Liber Amicorum Karl-Heinz Böckstiegel, p. 33.

[3] UNCITRAL Model Law on International Commercial Arbitration, United Nations document A/40/17, available under http://documents-dds-ny.un.org/doc/UNDOC/GEN/N85/325/11/pdf/N8532511.pdf?OpenElement.

guiding principles in drafting the revised law, was indeed to keep at a minimum any changes to the UNCITRAL Model Law that would inevitably be necessary to accommodate existing national laws.[4] The lawmakers were diligent in adhering to this principle so that German law does not bear unwelcome surprises for the unwary arbitral party.[5]

3. Arbitration in Germany Today

Equipped with the new legal regime for arbitration, Germany has become in recent years fertile ground for domestic and international arbitration.[6] With an extensive infrastructure, a large and well-qualified bar, a population for the most part proficient in English and, as of late, an arbitration-friendly legal environment, Germany offers today all the necessary prerequisites of a favorable place of arbitration in Europe. Additionally, the German Institution of Arbitration (DIS) has been gaining increased recognition in international arbitration[7] with as much as 121 newly filed cases in 2012 as well as in 2013 and an increase of the number of newly filed cases by almost 10 percent (132 cases) in 2014 (total value in 2014: > EUR 4 billion).[8]

II. Statutory Landscape of German Law on Arbitration

1. International Treaties

Germany is a signatory to a number of international agreements pertaining to arbitration including: the United Nations Convention on the Recognition and Enforcement of Foreign Arbitral Awards of 10 June 1958[9] ("New York Convention"), the European Convention on International Commercial Arbitration of 21 April 1961,[10] the Protocol on Arbitration Clauses of 24 September 1923 ("Geneva Protocol")[11] and the Convention on the Settlement of Investment Disputes between States and Nationals of Other States of 18 March 1965 ("ICSID Convention").[12]

---

[4] *Berger* in: Berger (ed.), Das neue Recht der Schiedsgerichtsbarkeit: The New German Arbitration Law, 1998, pp. 44-45; *Berger* in: Briner/Fortier/Berger/Bredow (eds.), Law of International Business and Dispute Settlement in the 21st Century: The German Arbitration Law of 1998 – First Experiences 2001, p. 33.

[5] *Wilske/Chen*, International Arbitration Practice in Germany, Comparative Law Yearbook of International Business, Vol. 26, 2004, pp. 641, 643.

[6] *Wilske/Chen*, International Arbitration Practice in Germany, Comparative Law Yearbook of International Business, Vol. 26, 2004, pp. 642-43, 656; *Hunter*, Arbitration in Germany – A Common Law Perspective, SchiedsVZ (German Arbitration Journal) 2003, pp. 155-56.

[7] For a List of Arbitration Institutions in Germany see Part 2, D. I.

[8] For statistics see http://www.dis-arb.de/en/39/content/statistik-id54. See also *Wilske/Markert/Bräuninger*, Entwicklungen in der internationalen Schiedsgerichtsbarkeit im Jahr 2013 und Ausblick auf 2014, SchiedsVZ (German Arbitration Journal) 2014, pp. 49, 50 and Entwicklungen in der internationalen Schiedsgerichtsbarkeit im Jahr 2014 und Ausblick auf 2015, SchiedsVZ (German Arbitration Journal) 2015, p. 49, 53.

[9] Federal Law Gazette (*Bundesgesetzblatt*) 1961 II, p. 122; entry into force in Germany on 28 September 1961.

[10] Federal Law Gazette (*Bundesgesetzblatt*) 1964 II, p. 425; entry into force in Germany on 27 October 1964.

[11] Reich Law Gazette (*Reichsgesetzblatt*) 1925 II, p. 47; entry into force in Germany on 5 November 1924.

[12] Federal Law Gazette (*Bundesgesetzblatt*) 1969 II, p. 371; entry into force in Germany on 18 May 1969.

2. Scope of New Legal Regime

a) Place of Arbitration in Germany

German law on arbitration is applicable pursuant to ZPO § 1025 (1) to all arbitral proceedings if the place of arbitration is within Germany. Previously, German arbitration law applied to arbitral proceedings where the place of arbitration was outside Germany, if the award was rendered pursuant to German arbitration law. This "extra-territorial" application of German arbitration law with its seat elsewhere was problematic in that it had the potential of leading to dual competing claims to jurisdiction. For instance, an arbitral award issued pursuant to German arbitration law in an arbitration proceeding with its seat in France would arguably have been subject to both French and German laws on arbitration and courts in the case of appeals for judicial intervention. In a minor deviation from the UNCITRAL Model Law, the German arbitration law leaves still a door open for application of German arbitration law even when the seat of arbitration is outside Germany, by excluding the term *"only"* in its adoption of UNCITRAL Model Law Article 1 (2). Just how wide this largely theoretical door will open, remains a matter of speculation. Undisputed is that German procedural law on arbitration applies to all arbitral proceedings seated in Germany.

Under German law the "seat"[13] or "place" of an arbitration is understood, as it is also in international arbitration, as a legal rather than a geographic concept. It is a legal fiction that forges a theoretical link to a particular country useful for purposes of determining an eventual award's nationality (which is relevant for enforcement and other judicial support) and the relevant judicial system for judicial support. "Place" has little to do with the physical location at which hearings or taking of evidence occur.[14] Often the "seat" or "place" coincidentally or for matters of convenience is also in the country in which the hearings or gathering of evidence takes place, but this is not required under German law to establish Germany as the seat of an arbitration.[15] Therefore, the German law on arbitration will apply theoretically to any arbitration that has established Germany as its seat, independent of the applicable substantive law or physical location of the proceedings.[16]

b) Applicability to Arbitral Proceedings without German Seat

In limited situations, certain provisions of German law on arbitration can be applied to arbitral proceedings in which no "seat" or "place" has been determined.[17] The provisions regarding court determination of whether claims are subject to an arbitration agreement,[18] court orders on interim measures[19] and court taking

---

[13] The unofficial English translation of the German arbitration law by the German Institution of Arbitration (*Deutsche Institution für Schiedsgerichtsbarkeit, DIS*) refers to "place" whereas the same concept is also often discussed in legal literature as "seat". These terms are used herein interchangeably.

[14] *Berger* in: Berger (ed.), Das neue Recht der Schiedsgerichtsbarkeit: The New German Arbitration Law, 1998, p. 45.

[15] ZPO § 1043 (2).

[16] ZPO §§ 1025 (1), 1043 (1).

[17] ZPO § 1025 (2)-(3).

[18] ZPO § 1032.

[19] ZPO § 1033.

of evidence[20] are applicable even if Germany is not the seat of the arbitral proceedings.[21]

Furthermore, certain additional provisions of the German arbitration law regarding the appointment, challenge and removal of arbitrators apply in the absence of a German seat when either the claimant or respondent has its place of business or his habitual residence in Germany.[22] This jurisdiction based upon domicile is meant to address the situation in which a party seeking to apply to the courts for support in an arbitration is unable to do so because the seat of arbitration has not yet been set.[23] Without a German seat of arbitration, the German courts lack authority under ZPO § 1025 (1) to intervene were a party to engage in dilatory tactics. ZPO § 1025 (3) vests the German court with authority to intervene upon a party's request in such a circumstance to appoint arbitrator(s) if the process is stalled. For example, the Bavarian Highest Regional Court held in a decision dated 5 October 2004, that German courts have international jurisdiction to decide on the appointment of an arbitrator if the place of arbitration is abroad, but a particular town or municipality has not been designated by the parties, provided that one party has its place of business or habitual residence in Germany.[24] The court opted for a broad interpretation of ZPO § 1025 (3) based on the rule's objective to prevent stagnation of international arbitral proceedings. The Higher Regional Court Munich in a more recent case did not explicitly reject the earlier decision of 2004 but held that German courts have no international jurisdiction as long as it is certain that the arbitral proceedings will take place abroad and thus German arbitration law is not applicable, and the place of arbitration abroad is ascertainable.[25]

B. The Arbitration Agreement

I. Arbitrability

1. Subjective Arbitrability

In principle, German law does not regulate whether disputes are subjectively arbitrable. Persons who are competent to enter into a contract can equally agree to arbitration.[26] This applies *e.g.* to consumers, who are protected by special form requirements,[27] as well as to states or state agencies. When state parties resort to arbitration, an agreement is generally considered to be a waiver of the defense of sovereign immunity from adjudication.[28]

---

[20] ZPO § 1050.
[21] ZPO § 1025 (2).
[22] ZPO § 1025 (3).
[23] *Berger* in: Berger (ed.) Das neue Recht der Schiedsgerichtsbarkeit: The New German Arbitration Law, 1998, p. 50.
[24] Bavarian Highest Regional Court (BayObLG), Decision of 5 October 2004 (Docket No. 4Z SchH 09/04), SchiedsVZ (German Arbitration Journal) 2004, p. 316 with note by *Wagner*.
[25] Higher Regional Court (OLG) München, Decision of 9 October 2013 (Docket No. 34 SchH 6/13), no. 31.
[26] *Lachmann*, Handbuch für die Schiedsgerichtspraxis, 3rd ed., 2008, no. 286.
[27] See ZPO § 1031 (5).
[28] *Escher/Nacimiento/Weissenborn/Lange*, Investment Arbitration, in: Böckstiegel/Kröll/Nacimiento (eds.), Arbitration in Germany – The Model Law in Practice, 2nd ed., 2015, no. 92; *Geimer* in: Zöller, Zivilprozessordnung, 30th ed., 2014, § 1061, no. 57. For a narrower approach see Federal

Under some circumstances, however, subjective arbitrability can be restricted and problems may arise. For instance, restrictions are contained in § 37h of the German Securities Trading Act (*Wertpapierhandelsgesetz, WpHG*) for non-merchants in specific financial service transactions,[29] in § 160 (2) German Insolvency Act (*Insolvenzordnung, InsO*) for parties subject to insolvency proceedings, and in § 1822 No. 12 German Civil Code (*Bürgerliches Gesetzbuch, BGB*) for legal guardians.

2. Objective Arbitrability

a) Disputes Involving an Economic Interest

A broad range of disputes are arbitrable[30] under German arbitration law. With a view to providing a viable alternative to court proceedings in many areas, German law on arbitration imposes no requirement that arbitrable disputes be of a "commercial nature".[31] Generally any claims involving an economic interest (*vermögensrechtlicher Anspruch*) are arbitrable,[32] whereby an economic interest can be direct or indirect. Furthermore, the economic interest need not be expressed in monetary terms.[33] The German arbitration law adopted a liberal and expansive view of arbitrable disputes.

Even certain claims not involving an economic interest can be subject to arbitration in Germany, so long as they have an economic character.[34] In the case of disputes not involving an economic interest, the German arbitration law requires that the parties are entitled to conclude a settlement on the disputed issue for the dispute to be arbitrable.[35]

b) Disputes Not Subject to Arbitration

As is common in other jurisdictions, certain types of disputes may not be arbitrated. No exhaustive lists are provided in the law, but examples of disputes not subject to arbitration in Germany include questions involving criminal law,[36] family law,[37] and landlord-tenant law.[38] Generally, only those issues for which the

---

Court of Justice (BGH), Decision of 30 January 2013 (Docket No. III ZB 40/12), SchiedsVZ (German Arbitration Journal) 2013, p. 110.

[29] See also *Hanefeld*, Country Report on Germany, in: Weigand (ed.), Practitioner's Handbook on International Arbitration, 2nd ed., 2009, no. 7.29. Whether a party is to be classified as a merchant or not has to be decided according to conflict of law rules and is controversial under German law, see *Kindler* in: Ebenroth/Boujong/Joost/Strohn (eds.), Handelsgesetzbuch 2014 Vol. I, Vor § 1, nos. 74 et seq.

[30] Contrary to its usage in the United States, the term "arbitrable" as understood in German legal literature is meant to address the question of whether a particular type of dispute may be subject to arbitration pursuant to law/public policy and does not include the more case specific question as to whether a particular dispute is subject to arbitration pursuant to a specific agreement to arbitrate.

[31] This is in contrast to the UNCITRAL Model Law which limited its scope of application in Article 1 (1) to "international commercial arbitration".

[32] ZPO § 1030 (1).

[33] *Berger* in: Berger (ed.), Das neue Recht der Schiedsgerichtsbarkeit: The New German Arbitration Law, 1998, p. 49.

[34] ZPO § 1030 (1).

[35] *Id.*

[36] *Cf.* ZPO § 1030 (1).

[37] Examples of family law matters not subject to arbitration would be marital status and child custody issues. *Schwab/Walter*, Schiedsgerichtsbarkeit, 7th ed., 2005, ch. 4, no. 2; *Geimer* in: Zöller, Zivilprozessordnung, 30th ed., 2014, § 1030, no. 6.

[38] ZPO §§ 1030 (2) *et seq.*

state has reserved exclusive rights to adjudication are not arbitrable.[39] Whether actions for declaration of nullity of shareholders' resolutions are arbitrable was controversial for a long time but has since been approved by the Federal Court of Justice in 2009, which held that arbitral proceedings grant the same legal protection as state court proceedings provided that procedural safeguards for all shareholders are met.[40] Also, as a matter of principle, antitrust and patent disputes are considered to be arbitrable.[41]

II. Content Requirement of an Arbitration Agreement

The content requirements of a valid arbitration agreement are set forth in the definition of an arbitration agreement: *"an agreement by the parties to submit to arbitration all or certain disputes which have arisen or which may arise between them in respect of a defined legal relationship, whether contractual or not"*.[42]

In other words, to be valid under German law an arbitration agreement must be clearly linked to a particular legal relationship, such as an underlying contractual relationship, or to a specific existing dispute. Arbitration agreements that refer only generally to future disputes between entities or individuals are invalid.[43] However, to the extent that an agreement to arbitrate is linked to a definite legal relationship, the arbitration agreement may refer to any future disputes that arise from the linked legal relationship in the future.

Further, the agreement to arbitrate must clearly state that the dispute will be subject exclusively to arbitration in place of ordinary court proceedings.[44] However, if there is an arbitration clause and a jurisdiction clause in two separate sets of general terms and conditions the arbitration clause will prevail as long as the jurisdiction clause does not clearly state that court proceedings shall trump the jurisdiction of an arbitral tribunal and thus only concerns the venue of the state

---

[39] *Berger* in: Berger (ed.), Das neue Recht der Schiedsgerichtsbarkeit: The New German Arbitration Law, 1998, p. 49.

[40] Federal Court of Justice (BGH), Decision of 6 April 2009 (Docket No. II ZR 255/08) [*Arbitrability II*], Zeitschrift für Wirtschaftsrecht, 2009, p. 1003; in continuation of Federal Court of Justice (BGH), Decision of 29 March 1996 (Docket No. II ZR 124/95) [*Arbitrability I*], BGHZ Volume 132, p. 278. In both cases the respondents challenged the state court's jurisdiction by reference to an arbitration clause in the articles of incorporation of the company. In *Arbitrability I*, the Court declared the arbitration clause invalid, arguing that §§ 248, 249 of the German Stock Companies Act, which regulate the *inter omnes* effect of a state court's judgment on the nullity or challenge of a shareholders' resolution, may not be applied on decisions by private arbitral tribunals. In deviation of this earlier ruling, in 2009 (*Arbitrability II*) the Court decided that §§ 248, 249 Stock Companies Act may be applied on arbitral decisions by way of analogy, as long as the arbitral proceedings provide for minimum standards of the rule of law comparable to State court proceedings, see *Wilske/Riegger*, Auf dem Weg zu einer allgemeinen Schiedsfähigkeit von Beschlussmängelstreitigkeiten?, Zeitschrift für Unternehmens- und Gesellschaftsrecht, 2010, p. 733; *Markert*, Arbitrating Corporate Disputes – German approaches and international solutions to reconcile conflicting principles, Contemporary Asia Arbitration Journal, Vol. 8 (2015), p. 29. See also the 2009 DIS Supplementary Rules for Corporate Law Disputes (SRCoLD), available at http://www.dis-arb.de/de/16/regeln/dis-supplementary-rules-for-corporate-law-disputes-09-srcold-id15.

[41] *Geimer* in: Zöller, Zivilprozessordnung, 30th ed., 2014, § 1030, nos. 12, 14.

[42] ZPO § 1029 (1).

[43] *Zernin/Eichert* in: Campbell (ed.), Business Transactions in Germany, Vol. 1, 2009, Section 6.03[3].

[44] Federal Court of Justice (BGH), Decision of 29 October 2008 (Docket No. XII ZR 165/06), Neue Juristische Wochenschrift – Rechtsprechungsreport, 2009, p. 637; Higher Regional Court (OLG) Naumburg, Decision of 17 April 2000 (Docket No. 10 Sch 01/00), available at www.dis-arb.de.

courts.⁴⁵ It is also no longer absolutely necessary to unambiguously define the institution or arbitral tribunal that is to decide the dispute as long as it is clear from the arbitration agreement, its structure, and the surrounding circumstances that state court proceedings shall be excluded. Such arbitration agreements are not invalid because, for example, ad hoc arbitration is possible where the designation of an arbitration designation is pathological.⁴⁶

Should a party submit a claim to a state court and ignore an arbitration agreement, ZPO § 1032 (1) is applicable and provides that the court shall, if the respondent raises an objection prior to the beginning of the oral hearing on the substance of the dispute, reject the action as inadmissible unless the court finds that that the arbitration agreement is null and void, inoperative or incapable of being performed.⁴⁷ However, if a party raises the arbitration agreement as a defense, in a later arbitration it may not object to the jurisdiction of the arbitral tribunal and request court proceedings. Such behavior would be contradictory and constitute a violation of good faith (*venire contra factum proprium*).⁴⁸

III. Form Requirements

An arbitration agreement can take the form of a separate stand-alone agreement, termed as the "separate arbitration agreement", or the form of a clause in a contract, termed as the "arbitration clause".⁴⁹ Pursuant to ZPO § 1040 (1), the arbitration agreement is severable from its underlying contract. Therefore the validity of any arbitration clause is determined independent of the remaining clauses of a contract.

1. "In Writing" and Signature Requirement under German Arbitration Law

An agreement to arbitrate must meet certain form requirements to be valid under German law. ZPO § 1029 lists the basic requirements for an arbitration agreement in Germany, distinguishing between consumers who require more protection from the law and all other non-consumers. The provisions of the old arbitration law which recognized oral arbitration agreements among "merchants" no longer exist in the present German law on arbitration.

---

⁴⁵ Federal Court of Justice (BGH), Decision of 25 January 2007 (Docket No. VII ZR 105/06), SchiedsVZ (German Arbitration Journal) 2007, p. 274; *Wilske/Krapfl*, Arbitration clause prevails in the event of conflicting jurisdiction and arbitration clauses, IBA Arbitration Committee Newsletter, March 2008, pp. 25-26.

⁴⁶ Federal Court of Justice (BGH), Decision of 14 July 2011 (Docket No. III ZB 70/10), SchiedsVZ (German Arbitration Journal) 2011, p. 284 where the agreement referred to a non-existent institutional arbitral tribunal; see *Wilske/Krapfl*, German Federal Court of Justice decision on inoperativeness of pathological arbitration agreement (BGH, III ZB 70/10, 14.07.2011), Practical Law Arbitration multi-jurisdictional monthly e-mail for September 2011. For an earlier decision, see Federal Court of Justice (BGH), Decision of 2 December 1982 (Docket No. III ZR 85/81), Neue Juristische Wochenschrift, 1983, p. 1267.

⁴⁷ ZPO § 1032 (1).

⁴⁸ Federal Court of Justice (BGH), Decision of 30 April 2009 (Docket No. III ZB 91/07), SchiedsVZ (German Arbitration Journal) 2009, p. 287.

⁴⁹ ZPO § 1029 (2).

a) Non-Consumers

aa) "In Writing" and Signature Requirements for Non-Consumers. For non-consumers the form requirements for a valid arbitration agreement are essentially comprised of the "in writing" and signature requirements. To be valid, an arbitration agreement must be written and signed by the parties to be bound by the arbitration agreement in a manner that accords with ZPO § 1031.[50] In the case of third party beneficiaries, it is sufficient that the parties to the underlying contract signed the arbitration agreement.[51]

ZPO § 1031(1) does not require that the signatures of the parties appear on the same document. Indeed an exchange of letters, faxed correspondence or any other means of data transmission suffices so long as a record of the agreement is available as a matter of proof.[52] An oral arbitration agreement alone is no longer valid under German law as it does not meet the form requirements under ZPO § 1031 (1). The arbitration agreement can take the form of either a separate contract or an arbitration clause within a contract.

bb) Arbitration Agreement by Incorporation. A contract can also become subject to a valid arbitration agreement through incorporation by reference to another document which contains an arbitration agreement, such as general terms and conditions. In such a case it is required that a reference to the general terms and conditions makes the arbitration agreement part of the contract.[53] It can be a general reference as long as the other party has a reasonable chance to take note of the arbitration agreement.[54] If German law is the *lex causae*, the arbitration clause is subject to the statutory validity control of general terms and conditions pursuant to sections 305 *et seq.* of the German Civil Code.[55]

cc) Unilateral Arbitration Agreement. Unilateral arbitration agreements have the potential of being valid under German law, where pursuant to common usage a receiving party's silence upon receipt of an arbitration agreement can be considered an acceptance. According to ZPO § 1031 (2), the "in writing" and signature requirements can be deemed to have been met if a non-consumer fails to raise an objection within a reasonable time after receiving from either another

---

[50] *Wegen/Wilske*, The "In-Writing-Requirement" for Arbitration Agreements: An Anachronism?, A Comment on OLG (Higher Regional Court) Celle, Decision of September 4, 2003 – 8 Sch 11/02, Journal of International Dispute Resolution, Vol. 2, 2004, p. 77.

[51] Bavarian Highest Regional Court (BayObLG), Decision of 9 September 1999 (Docket No. 4 Z SchH 3/99), Betriebsberater 2000, Suppl. No. 8, pp. 16, 19. In this case, the court determined that an arbitration agreement entered into by the great grandfather of two siblings, claimant and respondent in a dispute over hereditary succession was valid and binding on the parties, as third party beneficiaries. Even though neither sibling had been born in 1934 when the great grandfather entered the arbitration agreement, the great grandfather had declared the agreement to be for the benefit of his heirs and descendants. See also Federal Court of Justice (BGH), Decision of 22 May 1967 (Docket No. VII ZR 188/64), Bundesgerichtshofentscheidungen, Vol. 48, pp. 35, 45. For the signature requirement, see *Wilske/Gack*, Commencement of Arbitral Proceedings and Unsigned Requests for Arbitration, Journal of International Arbitration, Vol. 24, Issue 3, p. 319.

[52] ZPO § 1031 (1).

[53] ZPO § 1031 (3).

[54] Such a reasonable chance is assumed, if the other party is in possession of the general terms and conditions, Bavarian Highest Regional Court (BayObLG), Decision of 17 September 1998 (Docket No. 4Z Sch 1/98), Neue Juristische Wochenschrift – Rechtsprechungsreport, 1999, p. 644.

[55] For a detailed description, see *Hanefeld/Wittighofer*, Schiedsklauseln in Allgemeinen Geschäftsbedingungen, SchiedsVZ (German Arbitration Journal) 2005, p. 217.

party or a third party a document containing the arbitration agreement. If the failure to object timely to the arbitration agreement would lead under common usage to the inclusion of the arbitration agreement in the contract, that arbitration agreement so communicated is valid.[56] In practice, ZPO § 1031 (2) is relevant in case of failure to object to a commercial letter of confirmation (*Kaufmännisches Bestätigungsschreiben*).[57]

b) Consumers

A "consumer" is defined in Civil Code (*BGB*) § 13 as *"any natural person who concludes a transaction for non-commercial purposes, that is, outside of his trade or self-employed profession"*. The German law on arbitration contains provisions to protect consumers from inadvertently forfeiting their right to seek recourse in courts of law. Accordingly, agreements to arbitrate must meet additional form requirements.

For consumers, the arbitration agreement must be in a document separate from the contract to which it applies and personally signed by both parties on the same document to be valid.[58] The lack of a separate document can be invoked by either party, not only the consumer.[59] However, if the agreement is notarized by a German notary public,[60] it may contain clauses in addition to the arbitration agreement and need not be separate from the contract to which it applies.[61]

c) Remedying Form Defects in Arbitration Agreement

Furthermore, any failure to meet the "in writing" or signature requirements, or any of the form requirements under ZPO § 1031 can be remedied if the parties involved subsequently participate in the arbitral proceedings without raising an objection as to the arbitration agreement's validity.[62] Conversely, an otherwise valid arbitration agreement may be waived if a party initiates or makes a general appearance before a German court without raising an objection based upon the arbitration agreement.

Consumers, however, are offered special protection by the European Council Directive on unfair terms in consumer contracts:[63] The European Court of Justice held that national courts should examine the validity of the arbitration agreement *ex officio* in proceedings to set aside arbitral awards even if the consumer had not raised an objection with the arbitral tribunal.[64]

---

[56] ZPO § 1031 (2).
[57] *Wilske/Markert* in: Vorwerk/Wolf (eds.), Beck'scher Online-Kommentar ZPO, ZPO § 1031, No. 13.
[58] ZPO § 1031 (5).
[59] Higher Regional Court (OLG) Hamm, Decision of 28 March 2006 (Docket No. 21 U 134/04), OLG Report Hamm, 2006, p. 527.
[60] See *supra*, at p. 73.
[61] ZPO § 1031 (5).
[62] ZPO § 1031 (6).
[63] Council Directive 93/13/EEC of 5 April 1993 on unfair terms in consumer contracts, OJ 1993 L 095, pp. 29-34.
[64] European Court of Justice, *Elisa María Mostaza Claro v. Centro Móvil Milenium SL*, Decision of 26 October 2006 (Docket No. C-168/05), ECR 2006 I-10421; with critical comment *Wagner*, SchiedsVZ (German Arbitration Journal) 2007, p. 49. See also *Asturcom Telecomunicaciones SL v. Cristina Rodríguez Nogueira*, Decision of 6 October 2009 (Docket No. C-40/08), , ECR 2009 I-09579.

2. "In Writing" and Signature Requirement of the New York Convention

For arbitral proceedings involving international parties, however, the form requirements of Article II of the New York Convention play a role to the extent parties intend to enforce an eventual award in foreign jurisdictions that are signatories to the New York Convention. In contrast to the form requirements under German law, those of the New York Convention do not differentiate between consumers and non-consumers and define the "in writing" requirement more stringently without providing for the possibility of electronic transmission or waiver through subsequent participation in arbitral proceedings.

Since Germany is a signatory to the New York Convention, any party seeking enforcement of an award resulting from arbitral proceedings outside Germany is well-advised to make sure a valid arbitration agreement exists under Article II of the New York Convention before seeking enforcement before a German court.[65]

However, in light of the national treatment principle in Art. VII (1) New York Convention, ZPO § 1031 (2)[66] can again be an advantage, even where foreign arbitration agreements are concerned. In a recent case the Federal Court of Justice (BGH) considered how to interpret Article VII (1) of the New York Convention when the recognition of an award based on an arbitration agreement contained in a confirmation letter between merchants was concerned.[67] The court acknowledged the importance of the rule to not treat foreign arbitral awards less favorably than national ones, the drafting history of the New York Convention, and above all the Convention's objective to encourage international recognition and enforcement of arbitral awards and held that international law suggests a broad interpretation of Art. VII (1) New York Convention and thus declared the award valid, even though it did not conform to Art. II New York Convention.

German case law interprets the New York Convention as placing the burden of production and proof on the party seeking enforcement of a foreign award to show that an arbitral award is based upon a valid written arbitration agreement in compliance with Article II.[68] Moreover, German courts are not bound by the factual or legal findings of an arbitral tribunal and need not show deference to the arbitral tribunal's findings when determining whether an award is based upon a valid written arbitration agreement.[69] This is due to the overriding policy that no party should be bound by an arbitration to which it never agreed.

In one case, a German court refused to declare a foreign award issued pursuant to the China International Economic and Trade Arbitration Commission (CIETAC)

---

[65] Higher Regional Court (OLG) Celle, Decision of 4 September 2003 (Docket No. 8 Sch 11/02), Journal of International Dispute Resolution, 2004, pp. 95, 98 (in English language) with note by *Wegen/Wilske*, p. 77.

[66] See *supra*, at p. 132 et seq.

[67] Federal Court of Justice (BGH), Decision of 30 September 2010 (Docket No. III ZB 69/09), SchiedsVZ (German Arbitration Journal) 2010, p. 332, with note by *Wilske/Krapfl*, The enforcement of a foreign award when the underlying arbitration agreement satisfies German Law, but not the New York Convention, IBA Newsletter Arbitration and ADR, Vol. 16., No.1, 2011, pp. 107-108 Reaffirmed by Federal Court of Justice (BGH), Decision of 8 May 2014 (Docket No. III ZR 371/12), SchiedsVZ (German Arbitration Journal) 2014, pp. 151, 154.

[68] Higher Regional Court (OLG) Celle, Decision of 4 September 2003 (Docket No. 8 Sch 11/02), Journal of International Dispute Resolution, 2004, pp. 95, 97 (in English language) with note by *Wegen/Wilske*, p. 77. See also *Wilske/Markert*, National Reports – Germany, in: Mistelis/Shore (eds.), World Arbitration Reporter, Vol. I, 2nd ed., 2014, p. GER-51.

[69] Higher Regional Court (OLG) Celle, Decision of 4 September 2003 (Docket No. 8 Sch 11/02), Journal of International Dispute Resolution, 2004, pp. 95, 98 (in English language) with note by *Wegen/Wilske*, p. 77.

Arbitration Rules 2002 enforceable because the petitioner had failed to show that a valid written arbitration agreement existed.[70] More specifically, the court held that the arbitration agreement upon which the award was based was invalid, having been signed by a person not authorized to represent one of the parties. Although there was evidence that the arbitral tribunal considered the question during the arbitral proceedings, the German court undertook a *de novo* review of the issue and came to a different conclusion.

IV. Effect on Third Parties

Generally an arbitration agreement only binds the parties to the agreement. It may only be considered binding on third parties if they have specifically contracted with one of the parties in this regard,[71] or if they are the successors to a party by way of, *e.g.* inheritance,[72] assignment,[73] or accession[74] to a contract. The 'group of companies' doctrine is not provided for in German arbitration law, and so far no arbitral tribunals or German courts are known to have decided on the doctrine and its applicability to German arbitration law. However, the German Federal Court of Justice (BGH) in May 2014 dealt with a case concerning Danish and Indian companies and the applicability of an arbitration agreement to a third party. In its decision it considered which law to apply[75] and whether the application of the 'group of companies' doctrine under the respective Indian law violated German public policy and Art. II (1) of the New York Convention.[76] The court referred the case back to the Higher Regional Court for a more detailed analysis of the facts and held that the application of the arbitration agreement to the third party depends on the law applicable to the arbitration agreement. To protect the third party it considered applying the law applicable to the third party, but saw no reason to do so. However, it left the question open for future cases. Finally, the Federal Court of Justice denied a violation of German public policy based on the application of the 'group of companies' doctrine by the arbitral tribunal.

---

[70] Higher Regional Court (OLG) Celle, Decision of 4 September 2003 (Docket No. 8 Sch 11/02), Journal of International Dispute Resolution, 2004, pp. 95, 98 (in English language) with note by *Wegen/Wilske*, p. 77.

[71] Higher Regional Court (OLG) Düsseldorf, Decision of 19 May 2006 (Docket No. 17 U 162/05), SchiedsVZ (German Arbitration Journal) 2006, pp. 331, 333.

[72] Federal Court of Justice (BGH), Decision of 5 May 1977 (Docket No. III ZR 177/74), Neue Juristische Wochenschrift, 1977, pp. 1397, 1398.

[73] Federal Court of Justice (BGH), Decision of 2 March 1977 (Docket No. III ZR 99/76), Neue Juristische Wochenschrift, 1977, p. 1585; Federal Court of Justice (BGH), Decision of 20 March 1980 (Docket No. III ZR 151/79), Neue Juristische Wochenschrift, 1980, pp. 2022, 2023; Federal Court of Justice (BGH), Decision of 2 October 1997 (Docket No. III ZR 2/96), Neue Juristische Wochenschrift, 1998, p. 371.

[74] Federal Court of Justice (BGH), Decision of 3 May 2000 (Docket No. VII ZR 42/98), Neue Juristische Wochenschrift, 2000, p. 2346; Higher Regional Court (OLG) Frankfurt, Decision of 31 July 2006 (Docket No. 26 Sch 8/06), available at www.dis-arb.de.

[75] The court had to decide whether to apply the law applicable to the arbitration agreement (*Schwab/Walter*, Schiedsgerichtsbarkeit, 7th ed., 2005, ch. 44, no. 24; Higher Regional Court (OLG) Düsseldorf, Decision of 17 November 1995 (Docket No. 17 U 103/95), Recht der Internationalen Wirtschaft, 1996, p. 239) or the law supposedly applicable to the legal relationship between the third party and one of the parties to the arbitration agreement (*Hausmann* in: Reithmann/Martiny (eds.), Internationales Vertragsrecht, 7th ed., 2009, no. 6783; *Schlosser* in: Stein/Jonas, Zivilprozessordnung, Vol. 10, 23rd ed., 2014, Anh. zu § 1061, no. 85).

[76] Federal Court of Justice (BGH), Decision of 8 May 2014 (Docket No. III ZR 371/12), SchiedsVZ (German Arbitration Journal) 2014, p. 151.

As to the extension of an arbitration agreement to third parties, the elaborate provisions of the German Code on Civil Procedure on third-party intervention and notices for court proceedings are not directly applicable to arbitral proceedings. Similar rules are not provided for by German arbitration law.

However, parties are free to agree on a third-party intervention in their arbitration agreement or during the course of the proceedings.[77] Also, if the third party submits to the proceedings before or after the dispute has arisen, a third-party notice is considered permissible. For the outcome of the proceedings to be binding on the third party, it is necessary that the third party and the noticing party enter into an agreement to that effect. Concerning such proceedings, the third party is not in a position to challenge the composition of the arbitral tribunal, however, it is preferable to aim for consent of all parties and the arbitrators.[78]

German arbitration law equally does not address the topic of multi-party arbitral proceedings. Nevertheless, joinder of parties is deemed permissible as long as all parties and arbitrators agree. Where the arbitral tribunal has not yet been established, it is important to maintain the equality of all parties in participating in the procedure of the tribunal's formation.[79]

V. Termination and Breach

As any other continuing obligation under German law, an arbitration agreement can be unilaterally terminated by a party for due cause under BGB §314. Such due cause shall only be asserted when one party to the agreement endangers the conduct of the arbitral proceedings by committing significant breaches of important obligations provided for by the arbitration agreement.[80] However, according to the German Federal Court of Justice, termination is not needed where one party's lack of funds ends the arbitration agreement automatically as it renders it "incapable of being performed" (ZPO §1032 (1)).[81]

C. Constitution and Composition of the Arbitral Tribunal

I. Party Autonomy

Party autonomy is the fundamental principle in German arbitral proceedings. Therefore, as a general rule, parties conducting an arbitration to which German arbitration law is applicable are free to agree on many of the parameters of the

---

[77] *Wagner*, Die Beteiligung Dritter am Schiedsverfahren, in: Böckstiegel/Berger/Bredow (eds.), 2005, p. 44.

[78] Controversial, see *Lachmann*, Handbuch für die Schiedsgerichtspraxis, 3rd ed., 2008, no. 2823; *Elsing*, Streitverkündung und Schiedsverfahren, SchiedsVZ (German Arbitration Journal) 2004, pp. 88, 92.

[79] *Wilske*, Ad hoc Arbitration in Germany, in: Böckstiegel/Kröll/Nacimiento (eds.), Arbitration in Germany – The Model Law in Practice, 2nd ed., 2015, no. 15 with reference to the French Cour de Cassation's *Dutco* decision of 7 January 1992.

[80] *E.g.* where a party fails to pay its share of the advance on costs, or persistently obstructs the proceedings, *Lachmann*, Handbuch für die Schiedsgerichtspraxis, 3rd ed., 2008, no. 620.

[81] Federal Court of Justice (BGH), Decision of 14 September 2000 (Docket No. III ZR 33/00), Neue Juristische Wochenschrift, 2000, pp. 3720, 3721; with critical comment by *Wagner* in: German Institution of Arbitration (ed.), Financial Capacity of the Parties – A Condition for the Validity of Arbitration Agreements?, pp. 9 *et seq.*

proceedings, *i.e.* number of arbitrators to decide the dispute, appointment procedures for arbitrators, language of arbitration, arbitral tribunal's jurisdiction over interim measures, necessity of oral hearings, timing of written submissions. Although the German arbitration law provides default rules when the arbitration agreement is silent on certain issues, the German law on arbitration envisions that parties will tailor through mutual agreement arbitral proceedings that meet their individual needs and circumstances. Accordingly, the default rules set forth in the German law do not possess normative character, so much as they are meant to supplement choices made by parties. Parties may determine whether they prefer to individually tailor various aspects of proceedings (*e.g.*, ad hoc arbitration) or may choose to have proceedings governed by institutional rules (*e.g.*, the DIS Rules,[82] or ICC Rules[83]).

II. Number of Arbitrators

The German arbitration law sets the default number of arbitrators at three when parties fail to agree otherwise.[84] Whereas other jurisdictions set the default number of arbitrators at one based on economic considerations, the lawmakers in Germany favored a default of three, which is viewed as being more conducive to fair proceedings as it provides each party an opportunity to appoint an arbitrator.

III. Appointment of Arbitrators and Chairperson

1. Qualifications of Arbitrators

Arbitrators in Germany are not required to be members of the German bar or have a legal background, nor do they need to be resident in or a citizen of Germany. In theory, any person who has the capacity to enter into a contract may act as arbitrator according to German law. If for some reason, a legal entity is named as arbitrator, any person legally entitled to represent the legal entity may be named as arbitrator.[85]

As a practical matter, parties to an arbitration typically prefer arbitrators with some form of legal education. When considering candidates who are judges[86] or in the civil service[87] in Germany, parties should be aware that these candidates will require approval from their respective supervisory authorities before they can accept an appointment as an arbitrator. Such approval is regularly subject to certain conditions and can take a substantial amount of time, thereby delaying the arbitral proceedings. Any appointment undertaken without the prescribed authorization would void the contractual relationship between the arbitrator and the parties, thereby jeopardizing the proceedings. Additionally, the supervisory authority will only provide the necessary approval if the acting judge is appoint-

---

[82] Arbitration Rules of the German Institution of Arbitration (*Deutsche Institution für Schiedsgerichtsbarkeit, DIS*) reprinted at Part 2 D. II.
[83] Rules of Arbitration of the International Chamber of Commerce administered by the International Court of Arbitration available at http://www.iccwbo.org/products-and-services/arbitration-and-adr/arbitration/icc-rules-of-arbitration/.
[84] ZPO § 1034 (1).
[85] *Schwab/Walter*, Schiedsgerichtsbarkeit, 7th ed., 2005, ch. 9, no. 1.
[86] Judiciary Employment Act (*Deutsches Richtergesetz, DRiG*) § 40 (1).
[87] Federal Civil Service Act (*Bundesbeamtengesetz, BBG*) § 99.

ed by both sides or by a neutral institution as chairperson or sole arbitrator. It is not sufficient if only one side appoints the judge as party-appointed arbitrator.[88]

2. Party Autonomy in Appointment of Arbitrators

German procedural law on arbitration envisions that parties will agree on an appropriate procedure for appointment of arbitrators. No specific form is required for such a procedural agreement, but it can only be made after the arbitration agreement has been concluded.[89] Nevertheless, it provides a default mechanism for the appointment of arbitrators, in the event parties are unable or forget to agree on a nomination procedure. In accordance with the focus on party autonomy, this default procedure only applies in the absence of parties' own agreed upon procedure, or parties' agreement to apply procedures of institutional arbitration rules.

In extreme cases, when the parties have agreed upon a procedure for nomination of arbitrators that provides one party preponderant rights over another, a German court can intervene upon request of a party to appoint the arbitrators in a fairer manner.[90] For instance, an arbitration agreement that foresees the appointment of all arbitrators by only one party to the dispute would not survive the scrutiny of German courts. If a party does not raise an objection against the unequal composition, however, it is precluded from raising such an objection in setting-aside proceedings.[91] Also, ZPO § 1035 provides for intervention by courts upon request of a party should a party fail to act in accordance with an agreed upon appointment procedure.[92] For instance, if a party contrary to its previous agreement indulges in dilatory behavior in appointing an arbitrator, a court may be called upon to appoint an arbitrator for that dilatory party.

Barring any agreement to the contrary, a nomination is binding on a party upon receipt of the notice of appointment by the other party/parties to an arbitration.[93]

3. Default Rules for Appointing Arbitrators

a) Default Rule for Proceedings with Sole Arbitrator

When the arbitral tribunal is to be composed of a sole arbitrator, the parties shall try to agree on the appointment of a sole arbitrator.[94] If the parties are unable to reach an agreement on a sole arbitrator, the court will appoint a sole arbitrator upon request of a party.[95]

---

[88] Higher Regional Court Berlin (KG), Decision of 6 May 2002 (Docket No. 23 Sch 01/02), SchiedsVZ (German Arbitration Journal) 2003, p. 185 with note by *Mecklenbrauck*.
[89] *Nacimiento/Abt* in: Böckstiegel/Kröll/Nacimiento (eds.), Arbitration in Germany – The Model Law in Practice, 2nd ed., 2015, ZPO § 1035, no. 5.
[90] ZPO § 1034 (2).
[91] Higher Regional Court (OLG) Frankfurt, Decision of 24 November 2005 (Docket No. 26 Sch 13/05), SchiedsVZ (German Arbitration Journal) 2006, p. 219.
[92] ZPO § 1035 (4).
[93] ZPO § 1035 (2).
[94] ZPO § 1035 (3).
[95] ZPO § 1035 (3) sentence 1.

C. Constitution and Composition of the Arbitral Tribunal

b) Default Rule for Proceedings with Three Arbitrators

Each party shall appoint one arbitrator.[96] The party-nominated arbitrators in turn jointly appoint the third arbitrator.[97] The thus appointed third arbitrator will serve as chairperson of the arbitral tribunal.[98]

ZPO § 1035 (3) further provides that a party will appoint its arbitrator within one month[99] of being requested to do so by the other party. Meeting the statutory time limit in this context requires that a party's written appointment of an arbitrator must reach the other party within one month after having received the request to make the appointment. Similarly, the two party-appointed arbitrators are allotted one month to agree upon the appointment of a third arbitrator.[100] An untimely appointment of an arbitrator requires the consent of the other party to be effective.[101] If parties or arbitrators are unable or unwilling to agree within these statutory time limits, either party has the option of seeking state court assistance to appoint an arbitrator.

4. Court Intervention in Appointment of Arbitrators

Upon a party's petition, the court can under certain circumstances take measures necessary to secure the appointment of an arbitrator.[102]

a) Court Appointment of Arbitrators When Nomination Procedures Fail

Recourse to the state courts is available when parties are unable to reach an agreement under the default statutory procedure.[103] Recourse to the state courts is also available when the appointment procedure agreed upon between the parties fails, to the extent the agreed upon procedures do not provide alternative means of securing an appointment.[104] That is, if, *e.g.*, an agreement calls for appointment by a third party if parties are unable to agree on an arbitrator, that alternative must be exhausted before a court will intervene to appoint an arbitrator. To the extent a third party, such as an institution, fails to fulfill its task of appointing an arbitrator, either party is entitled to petition the court for an appointment.

b) Court Appointment of Arbitrators when Nomination Procedures are Unconscionable

Finally, a court can appoint or replace[105] arbitrator(s) in disregard of parties' nomination procedures, to the extent it finds upon request of a party that the procedures in question place a party at such an unfair disadvantage that allowing such a procedure would be contrary to public policy.[106] A court also has discretion

---

[96] *Id.*
[97] *Id.*
[98] *Id.*
[99] The one month time period begins on the date of receipt and its computation includes all intervening weekends and official holidays. If, however, the one month time period ends on a weekend or official holiday, the period will extend until the next day which is not a weekend or official holiday (Civil Code [*BGB*] §§ 187, 188 and 193).
[100] ZPO § 1035 (3).
[101] *Schwab/Walter*, Schiedsgerichtsbarkeit, 7th ed., 2005, ch. 10, no. 21.
[102] ZPO §§ 1034 and 1035.
[103] *Id.*
[104] ZPO § 1035 (4).
[105] For a more detailed discussion of replacement of arbitrators see *supra*, at pp. 142 et seq.
[106] ZPO § 1034 (2).

to modify an unfair nomination procedure into a workable one.[107] In the case of unconscionable nomination procedures, a party must petition the court within two weeks after becoming aware of an arbitral tribunal's formation.[108]

c) Petition to the Court

The petition for state court intervention must be filed at the Higher Regional Court (*Oberlandesgericht*) that is designated in the arbitration agreement.[109] In the absence of a designation, the petition is to be directed to the Higher Regional Court within the district in which the arbitration is seated.[110] Upon making the requisite findings, the relevant court will issue an order (*Beschluss*). Because oral hearings are generally not mandatory for orders that do not constitute judgments, the relevant court may decide the issue based entirely on the papers submitted without an oral hearing.[111] In fulfilling a party's request to take necessary measures for appointment of an arbitrator, a court shall consider all factors that are likely to lead to the appointment of an independent and impartial arbitrator and shall give due regard to qualifications that parties request the arbitrator possess.[112] One factor that the law mandates consideration by the court is the nationality of an arbitrator.[113] German procedural law on arbitration favors the appointment of persons who are of different nationalities than any of the parties for the position of sole arbitrator or chairperson of an arbitral tribunal.[114]

IV. Multi-Party Arbitration

In order to avoid controversy regarding multi-party arbitration, the German arbitration law does not address the issue of multi-party arbitration directly,[115] deferring to parties' autonomy to come to an agreement by which all parties have a say in the appointment of arbitrators. ZPO § 1034 (2) allows for any solution to the problem of composing an arbitral tribunal in multi-party arbitration so long as the ensuing procedure does not grant "preponderant rights" to any party.

DIS Rules Section 13.2 and ICC Rules Article 12 provide for joint nominations by co-parties and failing joint nomination some form of appointment by either the DIS Appointing Committee or ICC Court, respectively. However, such a joint nomination by co-parties, *i.e.* parties on one side of the dispute, may already constitute a difference in the parties' influence on the appointment procedure, if the respective parties have not impliedly agreed on a multi-party proceeding in the arbitration agreement.[116] Some authors propose increasing the number of

---

[107] *Id.*
[108] *Id.*
[109] ZPO § 1062 (1).
[110] *Id.*
[111] ZPO § 1063(1) and (2).
[112] ZPO § 1035 (5).
[113] *Id.*
[114] *Id.*
[115] Bill of the New Arbitration Act, BT-Drucksache 13/5274, p. 26.
[116] Federal Court of Justice (BGH), Decision of 29 March 1996 (Docket No. II ZR 124/95), Neue Juristische Wochenschrift, 1996, p. 1753; Higher Regional Court (OLG) Frankfurt, Decision of 24 November 2005 (Docket No. 26 Sch 13/05), SchiedsVZ (German Arbitration Journal) 2006, p. 219; Higher Regional Court (KG) Berlin, Decision of 21 April 2008 (Docket No. 20 SchH 4/07), Neue Juristische Wochenschrift, 2008, p. 2719.

arbitrators as a solution.[117] But such an increase might also amount to a granting of "preponderant rights".[118] Thus, by looking at other arbitration rules and keeping in mind that German arbitration law does not provide a default mechanism, an appointment by a neutral outsider may seem favorable.[119]

V. Challenge, Removal and Replacement of Arbitrators

1. Challenge of an Arbitrator

a) Grounds upon which Arbitrators can be Challenged

ZPO § 1036 sets forth the circumstances under which an arbitrator can be challenged. Parties may challenge an arbitrator based on only two grounds: either (i) circumstances exist that could give rise to *"justifiable* doubts *as* to *his impartiality or independence"*; or (ii) the arbitrator lacks the qualifications that the parties agreed upon.[120] Of these two grounds, the trait of impartiality or independence is often the more common point of contention. Partially, this is because there is no clear definition of what qualifies as a circumstance that gives rise to justifiable doubts.

Every potential arbitrator has an obligation to disclose *"any circumstances likely to give rise to justifiable doubts as to his impartiality or independence"* as soon as he is approached regarding a possible appointment.[121] Based upon the potential arbitrator's disclosure duty, ZPO § 1036 (2) limits a party's ability to challenge an arbitrator in whose appointment a party has participated, by requiring that a party base its challenge only on information that has come to light after the appointment. Thus, a party who nominates an arbitrator despite knowledge of circumstances that might bring into question the contemplated arbitrator's independence (*e.g.,* arbitrator's family relationship to a party) cannot later challenge the arbitrator based on that relationship of which it was aware when it nominated the arbitrator.[122] In such a case, the party has assumed a certain risk by nominating (or agreeing to the nomination) of an arbitrator despite the potentially problematic circumstances. However, if after a nomination, a party discovers circumstances that bring the arbitrator's independence into doubt, that discovering party is entitled to request the arbitrator's removal based upon the information that came to light after the fact.[123]

The standards for impartiality are the same for all arbitrators, including the chairperson of an arbitral tribunal.[124] Examples of circumstances that could raise concerns regarding impartiality or independence include, *e.g.,* family relationship to one of the parties, former attorney-client relationship with a party, or former dealings with the dispute at hand as witness or arbitrator. On questions of impar-

---

[117] See *e.g. Lionnet/Lionnet,* Handbuch der internationalen und nationalen Schiedsgerichtsbarkeit, 3rd ed., 2005, p. 432.
[118] *Nacimiento/Abt/Stein* in: Böckstiegel/Kröll/Nacimiento (eds.), Arbitration in Germany – The Model Law in Practice, 2nd ed., 2015, ZPO § 1035, no. 40.
[119] For arbitration rules other than DIS and ICC *cf.* Art. 8 LCIA Rules 2014, Art. 12 (5) ICDR Rules 2014, Art. 8 (3)-(5) Swiss Rules 2012, Art. 13 (4) SCC Rules 2010, Art. 18 WIPO Rules 2014.
[120] ZPO § 1036 (2).
[121] ZPO § 1036 (1).
[122] ZPO § 1036 (2).
[123] ZPO § 1036 (2).
[124] *Geimer* in: Zöller, Zivilprozessordnung, 30th ed., 2014, § 1036, no. 2.

tiality or independence, German courts will seek guidance from the provisions ZPO §§ 41 *et seq.* applicable to German judges.[125]

The revised IBA Guidelines on Conflicts of Interest in International Arbitration, approved on 23 October 2014 by the Council of the International Bar Association, may offer further guidelines on indications of potential bias. Although these guidelines have not been incorporated into the German Code of Civil Procedure, the trend in Germany amongst the bar is to accord such internationally agreed upon standards some persuasive value.

b) Procedure for Challenging an Arbitrator

In accordance with the *leitmotiv* of party autonomy, parties are free to agree upon a procedure for challenging an arbitrator.[126] In the absence of an agreement on procedure, ZPO § 1037 (2) sets a time limit of two weeks from becoming aware of either (i) the appointment of the arbitrator, or (ii) circumstances that give rise to justifiable doubts as to an arbitrator's impartiality or independence to challenge an arbitrator. Within this two week period, the challenging party must send a written statement, communicating its reasons for challenging the composition of the arbitral tribunal. Any circumstance that has been known for more than two weeks cannot be a basis for challenging an arbitrator. Similarly, a nominating party is precluded from challenging an arbitrator it nominated or agreed to nominate, based upon information of which it was aware prior to the nomination.[127]

The arbitral tribunal shall decide on the challenge of one of its arbitrators, to the extent the other party does not agree to the challenge and the challenged arbitrator does not resign. If the challenge is rejected by the arbitral tribunal, the challenging party has one month[128] to seek judicial review of its challenge by a German court. When a sole arbitrator is challenged, the challenge is determined by the German court, as it would not be feasible for an arbitrator to decide his own challenge. The court's decision on a challenge is final and binding.

The court review on composition of the arbitral tribunal can be conducted in parallel with the arbitral proceedings. The arbitral tribunal has discretion to either stay the arbitral proceedings pending resolution of the challenge or continue with the proceedings.[129] However, the award will be subject to resolution of the challenge and any proceedings to enforce an award in Germany are stayed pending resolution of the challenge.[130]

2. Removal of an Arbitrator

When an arbitrator becomes, for any reason, unable to perform his duties as arbitrator he can withdraw from the proceedings or the parties can agree to terminate the appointment.[131] If the parties are unable to agree or the arbitrator does not withdraw, any party can request the competent German court for removal of an

---

[125] See, for example, Higher Regional Court (OLG) Hamburg, Decision of 11 March 2003 (Docket No. 6 SchH 03/02), SchiedsVZ (German Arbitration Journal) 2003, p. 191.
[126] ZPO § 1037 (1).
[127] ZPO § 1036 (2).
[128] This time limit may be shortened or lengthened by parties' agreement pursuant to ZPO § 1037 (3).
[129] ZPO § 1037 (3).
[130] *Schwab/Walter*, Schiedsgerichtsbarkeit, 7th ed., 2005, ch. 14, no. 26.
[131] ZPO § 1038 (1).

arbitrator from office.¹³² The act of withdrawal does not imply that any grounds upon which an arbitrator withdrew or may have been challenged pursuant to ZPO §§ 1037 or 1038 were valid or accepted.¹³³ No inferences are to be drawn from the mere act of withdrawal.

3. Replacement of an Arbitrator

The procedures for appointing a substitute arbitrator are the same as those for the original appointment of arbitrators unless the parties have agreed upon a different procedure for appointing replacement arbitrators.¹³⁴ If a court appoints an arbitrator after a party has failed to nominate one, that party has lost its right not only to appoint that arbitrator but also to appoint a replacement arbitrator, if the court-appointed arbitrator is unable to fulfill his duties. Therefore, in the case of replacing a court-appointed arbitrator, the court will appoint a substitute arbitrator, regardless of the agreed upon procedure.¹³⁵

D. The Arbitrator's Contract

The legal relationship between the parties and the arbitrator(s) is a contractual one. Even when a court or a third party appoints an arbitrator, it does so as an agent of the parties.¹³⁶

The contract that is concluded between an arbitrator and the parties upon notice of appointment is not necessarily governed by the same law as that of the arbitration agreement or arbitral proceedings. The governing law is determined by an express or implied choice of law. If neither can be ascertained, the arbitrator's place of business determines the applicable law.¹³⁷ If the arbitrators are from different countries, the law of the place with the "closest connection" to the arbitrators' agreement applies.¹³⁸ The prevailing view among legal commentators is that in the context of arbitration the law that governs the arbitral proceedings has the closest connection to the arbitrators' agreement.¹³⁹

I. Arbitrator Contract under German Law

The arbitrator's contract is viewed under German law as a service contract (*Dienstvertrag*) and subject to the substantive law applicable thereto. The contract between a party and the arbitrator it appointed is formed upon the arbitrator's acceptance of the appointment. The contract between a nominated arbitrator and

---

¹³² *Id.*
¹³³ ZPO § 1038 (2).
¹³⁴ ZPO § 1039 (1) and (2).
¹³⁵ *Schwab/Walter*, Schiedsgerichtsbarkeit, 7th ed., 2005, ch. 10, no. 27.
¹³⁶ *Schwab/Walter*, Schiedsgerichtsbarkeit, 7th ed., 2005, ch. 11, no. 1.
¹³⁷ Regulation (EC) No 593/2008 of the European Parliament and of the Council of 17 June 2008 on the law applicable to contractual obligations ("Rome I Regulation"), Art. 4. The arbitrator's contract as a contract of services is not excluded from the scope of the regulation by Art. 1 (2) e Rome I Regulation.
¹³⁸ *Id.*
¹³⁹ *Geimer in:* Zöller, Zivilprozessordnung, 30th ed., 2014, § 1035, no. 23; *Schwab/Walter*, Schiedsgerichtsbarkeit, 7th ed., 2005, ch. 48, no. 3; *Schlosser in:* Stein/Jonas, Zivilprozessordnung Vol. 10, 23rd ed., 2014, Vor § 1025, no. 33.

the parties of the arbitration comes into being upon notification of the acceptance of the nomination to the non-appointing party.[140]

Under an arbitrators' agreement, the arbitrator is obligated to administer to the best of his abilities an orderly and expeditious proceeding in accordance with the rule of law and the arbitration agreement.[141] To that end, an arbitrator is authorized by virtue of the arbitrators' agreement: (i) to undertake investigations as he deems necessary, and (ii) to enter into contracts with experts as agent of the parties.[142] The parties' complementary duty is to compensate the arbitrator for this service.[143]

An arbitrator may not assign the service contract to another person without the consent of the parties.[144] The contract can be terminated jointly at any time by the parties.[145] The arbitrator, in contrast, can only terminate the service contract either with the consent of all parties or for an important reason.[146] An important reason could be, for example, non-payment of advance fees, serious illness, move to another country or irreconcilable differences between the parties and the arbitral tribunal on how to conduct the proceedings,[147] but not allegedly irreconcilable differences amongst the arbitrators.[148]

II. Remuneration of Arbitrator

1. Duty to Compensate Arbitrator

The presumption is that arbitrators shall be compensated for their services, even if this is not expressly stated in the arbitrators' agreement.[149] It is the obligation of the parties under an arbitrators' contract to compensate the arbitrator(s) for services performed under the arbitrator agreement. Both parties are jointly and severally liable for the remuneration.[150] Generally, unless the award foresees otherwise, each party is to contribute equally to the compensation.[151]

---

[140] *Schwab/Walter*, Schiedsgerichtsbarkeit, 7th ed., 2005, ch. 11, no. 2.

[141] Federal Court of Justice (BGH), Decision of 5 May 1986 (Docket No. III ZR 233/84), Neue Juristische Wochenschrift, 1986, p. 3077.

[142] *Id*.

[143] There is no requirement for consideration of compensation for the formation of an arbitration agreement under German law, but an agreement on remuneration is typical and advisable, see *Albers* in: Baumbach/Lauterbach/Albers/Hartmann, Zivilprozessordnung, 73rd ed., 2005, Supp. § 1035, no. 1; *Nacimiento/Abt/Stein*, Introduction to §§ 1034-1039, in: Böckstiegel/Kröll/Nacimiento (eds.), Arbitration in Germany – The Model Law in Practice, 2nd ed., 2015, no. 27.

[144] *Schwab/Walter*, Schiedsgerichtsbarkeit, 7th ed., 2005, ch. 12, no. 6.

[145] *Schwab/Walter*, Schiedsgerichtsbarkeit, 7th ed., 2005, ch. 13, no. 8.

[146] *Albers* in: Baumbach/Lauterbach/Albers/Hartmann, Zivilprozessordnung, 73rd ed., 2015, Supp. § 1035, no. 15.

[147] *Albers* in: Baumbach/Lauterbach/Albers/Hartmann, Zivilprozessordnung, 73rd ed., 2015, Supp. § 1035, no. 15. However, a party bias of one of the arbitrators alone does not qualify as an important reason.

[148] See Regional Court (LG) Köln, Decision of 15 January 2013 (Docket No. 29 O 159/12), Neue Juristische Wochenschrift – Rechtsprechungsreport, 2013, p. 1273.

[149] *Schwab/Walter*, Schiedsgerichtsbarkeit, 7th ed., 2005, ch. 12, no. 10.

[150] Federal Court of Justice (BGH), Decision of 22 February 1971 (Docket No. VII ZR 110/69), Neue Juristische Wochenschrift, 1971, p. 888; *Hanefeld*, Country Report on Germany in: Weigand (ed.), Practitioner's Handbook on International Arbitration, 2nd ed., 2009, no. 7.208; *Schwab/Walter*, Schiedsgerichtsbarkeit, 7th ed., 2005, ch. 12, no. 10.

[151] *Hanefeld*, Country Report on Germany in: Weigand (ed.), Practitioner's Handbook on International Arbitration, 2nd ed., 2009, no. 7.208.

Typically, arbitrators will request prepayments of the remuneration. This practice has become so common that there is also a presumption, even if not expressly provided for in the arbitrators' agreement, that the arbitrator may request prepayments during the course of the arbitral proceedings.[152] As with the remuneration in whole, the parties are jointly and severally liable for the prepayments.[153] If the parties fail to make the requested prepayments, the arbitrator can refuse to perform services until payment.[154] If one party fails to remit prepayment fees, the arbitrator may not sue the party. However, the other party has several options: it may make the payment for the non-paying party; it may rescind the arbitration agreement; or it may commence an action in the German courts against the non-paying party for failing to perform under the arbitration agreement.[155] The arbitral tribunal may declare the arbitral proceedings suspended during such court action.

Although the arbitrator may stop performing altogether, the arbitrator may not in his decision-making process decline to hear or disregard relevant evidence from a party on the basis of that party's non-payment of fees.[156] Such a practice could potentially place a party in the position of having to submit prepayment fees it may find objectionable in order to avoid exclusion of its evidence from the arbitral proceedings.

If a party is insolvent, an arbitration agreement is incapable of being performed because that party will not be able to carry its part of the costs. Either party may then initiate court proceedings without having to first rescind the arbitration agreement and the respondent is barred from relying on the arbitration agreement.[157]

2. Amount of Fees

The amount of fees is usually set either in the arbitrators' agreement or in the institutional rules. In the absence of an agreement regarding the amount of fees, the compensation reflects the fee schedule that is customary at the place where the service is provided. If the place of arbitration is situated in Germany, it is still not conclusively settled how to determine these customary fees for arbitrator services.[158]

If the arbitrator is admitted to the German bar, until July 2004, his fees generally followed those set by the statute regulating attorney fees (*Bundesrechtsan-*

---

[152] *Albers* in: Baumbach/Lauterbach/Albers/Hartmann, Zivilprozessordnung, 73rd ed., 2015, Supp. § 1035, no. 12; *Schwab/Walter*, Schiedsgerichtsbarkeit, 7th ed., 2005, ch. 12, no. 16.
[153] *Albers* in: Baumbach/Lauterbach/Albers/Hartmann, Zivilprozessordnung, 73rd ed., 2015, Supp. § 1035, no. 12.
[154] *Von Schlabrendorff/Sessler* in: Böckstiegel/Kröll/Nacimiento (eds.), Arbitration in Germany – The Model Law in Practice, 2nd ed., 2015, ZPO § 1057, no. 11; *Albers* in: Baumbach/Lauterbach/Albers/Hartmann, Zivilprozessordnung, 73rd ed., 2015, Supp. § 1035, no. 13.
[155] Federal Court of Justice (BGH), Decision of 7 March 1985 (Docket No. III ZR 169/83), Neue Juristische Wochenschrift, 1985, pp. 1903, 1904.
[156] Federal Court of Justice (BGH), Decision of 7 March 1985 (Docket No. III ZR 169/83), Neue Juristische Wochenschrift, 1985, pp. 1903, 1904-1905.
[157] Federal Court of Justice (BGH), Decision of 14 September 2000 (Docket No. III ZR 33/00) Neue Juristische Wochenschrift, 2000, pp. 3720, 3721.
[158] *Cf.* DIS Conference on costs in arbitral proceedings (Kosten im Schiedsverfahren) on 29 April 2004 in Düsseldorf, DIS-MAT X, 2005, in particular *Elsing*, Bemessungsgrundlagen für Honorare und Auslagen der Schiedsrichter, DIS-MAT X, 2005, pp. 5 *et seq.*

waltsgebührenordnung, BRAGO) for appellate level services.[159] Technically, these provisions determine fees of attorneys who represent clients, and, therefore, not arbitrators' services. However, it had become customary that arbitrators set their fee schedules in accordance with the BRAGO.[160] The BRAGO had a sliding scale fee schedule that was calculated based upon the value in dispute, with special fees for participation in oral and evidentiary hearings.[161] It was the general custom for the chairperson to receive 45/10 of the fee based upon the value in dispute and for the party-appointed arbitrators to receive 39/10.

A new statute (*Rechtsanwaltsvergütungsgesetz, RVG*) was adopted in July 2004, which completely reorganized the fee schedules for attorneys.[162] A strict calculation of the fees according to the RVG would reduce arbitrators' fees, although this was certainly not the intent of the new law.[163] Nevertheless, a few commentators – mostly commentators of the RVG – maintain that fees should be calculated by applying the RVG without any alteration.[164] However, such an approach should not be taken, since RVG §1 (2) itself states that the statute does not apply to arbitrators. If arbitrators nevertheless wish to base their fee arrangements on the RVG, they should make this clear in their arbitrators' agreement. Otherwise, it has become common practice to apply the fee schedule of the DIS Rules by analogy.[165]

If the customary fees are not ascertainable, the arbitrator can determine an amount of compensation, the appropriateness of which can be reviewed by a German court.[166] The final decision on compensation cannot be made by the arbitral tribunal, directly or indirectly. For instance, the arbitral tribunal cannot ultimately determine the value of the dispute, as that indirectly affects the amount of compensation under certain institutional rules and the BRAGO/RVG.[167]

3. Accrual and Expiration of Claim for Compensation

Unless otherwise provided for, the arbitrator's claim for compensation arises upon the termination of the arbitral proceedings.[168] The arbitrator's claim to compensation is not dependent on the validity of the award.[169] The corresponding

---

[159] The same applied for non-lawyers acting as arbitrators to avoid unequal payment, *Wilske*, Ad hoc Arbitration in Germany, in: Böckstiegel/Kröll/Nacimiento (eds.), Arbitration in Germany – The Model Law in Practice, 2nd ed., 2015, no. 47.

[160] *Wagner*, Country Report on Germany in: Weigand (ed.), Practitioner's Handbook on International Arbitration, 2002, Part 4.D., no. 139.

[161] See *supra*, at pp. 69 et seq.

[162] See *supra*, at pp. 4, 10.

[163] *Lachmann*, Handbuch für die Schiedsgerichtspraxis, 3rd ed., 2008, nos. 4205 *et seq.*

[164] *Mayer* in: Mayer/Kroiß (eds.), Rechtsanwaltsvergütungsgesetz (, 6th ed., 2013, §1, no. 200; *Madert* in: Gerold/Schmidt (eds.), Rechtsanwaltsvergütungsgesetz, 17th ed., 2006, §1, no. 194 (but see *Müller-Rabe* in: Gerold/Schmidt (eds.), Rechtsanwaltsvergütungsgesetz, 20th ed., 2012, §1, nos. 744-746); *Schwab/Walter*, Schiedsgerichtsbarkeit, 7th ed., 2005, ch. 12, no. 12; *Kreindler/Schäfer/Wolff*, Schiedsgerichtsbarkeit – Kompendium für die Praxis, 2006, nos. 587, 1213, 1214.

[165] *Wilske*, Ad hoc Arbitration in Germany, in: Böckstiegel/Kröll/Nacimiento (eds.), Arbitration in Germany – The Model Law in Practice, 2nd ed., 2015, no. 50.

[166] An appropriate compensation might be an amount equal to the earnings of a court judge, see *Nacimiento/Abt/Stein*, Introduction to §§1034-139, in: Böckstiegel/Kröll/Nacimiento (eds.), Arbitration in Germany – The Model Law in Practice, 2nd ed., 2015, no. 27.

[167] *Albers* in: Baumbach/Lauterbach/Albers/Hartmann, Zivilprozessordnung, 73rd ed., 2015, Supp. §1035, no. 10.

[168] *Schwab/Walter*, Schiedsgerichtsbarkeit, 7th ed., 2005, ch. 12, no. 14.

[169] *Schwab/Walter*, Schiedsgerichtsbarkeit, 7th ed., 2005, ch. 12, no. 15.

limitation period is three years and commences at the end of the year in which the claim accrued.[170]

III. Liability of Arbitrator – Duties of the Arbitrator(s)

In institutional arbitration, liability of arbitrators for anything but an intentional breach of duty is excluded.[171] In *ad hoc* arbitrations, arbitrators will also generally include an exclusion of liability for negligence in their arbitrators' agreement. If there is no such agreement, arbitrators may be liable.

1. Liability for Negligence

Generally, arbitrators are liable for negligence. Thus, an arbitrator can be liable for damages if he delays proceedings without a justifiable reason or if he refuses to perform his duties as arbitrator. For instance, an arbitrator will be liable for damages that arise from termination of the arbitrators' agreement without party consent or good cause.

2. Liability for Specific Performance

Liability for negligence, however, does not extend to remedies such as specific performance. An arbitrator is generally not subject to claims for specific performance under the arbitrators' contract. Therefore, refusal to perform will typically expose an arbitrator to damages but not require any performance of duties that has been refused. Some legal commentators believe that parties should be able to sue for specific performance to sign an award, when an arbitrator who has participated in arbitral proceedings later refuses to sign the resulting award.[172] Others argue that the arbitrator, by signing the award, not only verifies that the award correctly reflects the result of the final session, but also identifies with its content.[173] This may speak against the option of being able to sue for specific performance within the meaning of ZPO § 888.[174]

3. No Liability for Decision in Award

Finally, arbitrators are not liable for a "wrong" decision in their award, unless the wrong decision is a result of intentional wrongdoing.[175] The liability of arbitrators for their decisions is similar to those of German judges for their decisions.[176] A negligent misapplication of law or finding of fact in error in an award will not typically expose the arbitrators who authored the award to damages from the aggrieved party to the arbitral proceedings.

---

[170] Civil Code (BGB) §§ 195 and 199 (1).
[171] See for example DIS Rules Section 44.
[172] *Voit* in: Musielak/Voit, Zivilprozessordnung, 12th ed., 2015, § 1054, no. 6.
[173] *Wilske/Markert* in: Vorwerk/Wolf (eds.), Beck'scher Online-Kommentar ZPO, ZPO § 1054, no. 9; *Münch* in: Münchener Kommentar zur Zivilprozessordnung, 4th ed., 2013, § 1054, no. 7.
[174] *Wilske/Markert* in: Vorwerk/Wolf (eds.), Beck'scher Online-Kommentar ZPO, ZPO § 1054, no. 9. An exception can be made if the arbitrator's omission prevents the arbitral tribunal from reaching a majority according to § 1054 (1) Sentence 2, see. *Saenger*, Zivilprozessordnung, 6th ed., 2015, § 1054, no. 4.
[175] *Schwab/Walter*, Schiedsgerichtsbarkeit, 7th ed., 2005, ch. 12, no. 9.
[176] *Id.*

E. Jurisdiction of Arbitral Tribunal

I. Competence of Arbitral Tribunal to Rule on its Jurisdiction

Generally, the arbitral tribunal has jurisdiction to determine whether it has the requisite jurisdiction to determine the dispute put before it (*Kompetenz-Kompetenz*).[177]

Challenges to an arbitral tribunal's jurisdiction can be brought any time prior to the submission of the statement of defense.[178] Once challenged, the arbitral tribunal must review and rule on its jurisdiction over a dispute pursuant to the relevant arbitration agreement. To the extent it determines that it is competent to hear and decide the matters in dispute, the arbitral tribunal will generally issue an interim award, from which the parties may seek relief in a court of law.[179]

In contrast to the situation under the superseded German law on arbitration, it is no longer the case that parties may authorize an arbitral tribunal to be the final arbiter of its own powers.[180] An arbitral tribunal's ruling on jurisdiction is subject to judicial review to the extent a party seeks to review a determination on jurisdiction by a court of law.[181] Thus, the final decision over the tribunal's jurisdiction will not lie with the arbitral tribunal itself.[182] A request challenging the arbitral tribunal's assessment of jurisdiction must be made within one month of having received written notice of the ruling on jurisdiction.[183] The arbitral tribunal may continue arbitral proceedings and even render an award while a challenge to its assessment of jurisdiction is pending before a court of law.[184] The court's decision on jurisdiction is binding on the arbitral tribunal, and a negative decision will render a potential arbitral award on the merits void *ipso jure*. Nevertheless, to avoid legal uncertainty a challenge of the arbitral award on the merits remains admissible.[185]

II. Interim Measures of Protection

The German arbitration law provides for a dual system for parties to an arbitration to seek interim measures of protection.[186] That is, both the local courts as well as the arbitral tribunal are vested with the power to order interim measures, unless otherwise agreed by the parties.[187] A party has the choice between a court and the arbitral tribunal at all stages of the arbitral proceedings. In some cases, the court proceedings might be advantageous as the court proceedings, unlike in arbitral

---

[177] ZPO § 1040 (1).
[178] ZPO § 1040 (2).
[179] ZPO § 1040 (3).
[180] *Cf.* Federal Court of Justice (BGH), Decision of 5 May 1977 (Docket No. III ZR 177/74), Neue Juristische Wochenschrift, 1977, p. 1397.
[181] ZPO § 1040 (3).
[182] Federal Court of Justice (BGH), Decision of 13 January 2005 (Docket No. III ZR 265/03), SchiedsVZ (German Arbitration Journal) 2005, p. 95; *Wilske/Krapfl*, A Final Farewell to the German Concept of Kompetenz-Kompetenz, International Journal of Dispute Resolution, 2/2005, p. 93.
[183] *Id.*
[184] ZPO §§ 1040(3).
[185] *Wilske/Markert*, National Reports – Germany, in: Mistelis/Shore (eds.), World Arbitration Reporter, Vol. I, 2nd ed., 2014, p. GER-10.
[186] ZPO §§ 1033 and 1041.
[187] ZPO § 1041.

proceedings, do not necessarily require that the opposing party be heard before issuing an order for interim measures.[188]

The arbitral tribunal has discretion to order interim measures it considers necessary given the subject matter in dispute and may require a requesting party to provide appropriate security in connection with the interim measure.[189] Interim measures that would preempt the resolution of the dispute, whether granted by the arbitral tribunal or the court, are admissible only if the applying party would suffer irreparable harm without their issuance.[190] "Anti-suit injunctions" may not be ordered, as they mostly protect the arbitral process and not the "subject matter in dispute".[191]

Arbitral tribunals may not enforce their own orders for interim measures. Instead, interim measures ordered by an arbitral tribunal can only be enforced by a court of law. To the extent a party has not petitioned for the same measures in a court, a court can declare an order for interim measures enforceable and even alter the arbitral tribunal's order for interim measures to make the order enforceable.[192] Furthermore, the court can later amend, or repeal its order of enforcement upon party request.[193]

If it is later determined that an interim measure ordered by an arbitral tribunal was unjustified from the outset, the party who sought the interim measure is obligated to compensate the other party for any damage suffered by the harmed party as a result of enforcement of the arbitral tribunal's interim measure or caused by the harmed party's provision of any security in avoiding enforcement.[194] These claims for compensation are to be made in the arbitral proceedings and decided in the ensuing award.[195]

F. The Arbitral Proceedings

I. General Rules of Procedure

ZPO § 1042 defines the procedural rules in the same general terms as Articles 18 and 19 of the UNCITRAL Model Law. The parties must be treated equally and given a full opportunity to present their case.[196] In addition, the parties must be able to use counsel to represent them in the proceedings.[197] Subject to these mandatory rules, the parties are free to determine the procedure themselves by

---

[188] *Ex parte* measures, see *supra*, at p. 60.
[189] ZPO § 1041(1).
[190] Higher Regional Court (OLG) Frankfurt, Decision of 5 April 2001 (Docket No. 24 Sch 1/01), Neue Juristische Wochenschrift Rechtsprechungsreport, 2001, p. 1078; *Schroth*, Einstweiliger Rechtsschutz im deutschen Schiedsverfahren, SchiedsVZ (German Arbitration Journal) 2003, pp. 102, 103.
[191] *Wilske/Markert*, National Reports – Germany, in: Mistelis/Shore (eds.), World Arbitration Reporter, Vol. I, 2nd ed., 2014, p. GER-28; but see *Schlosser*, Anti-suit Injunctions zur Unterstützung von internationalen Schiedsverfahren, Recht der Internationalen Wirtschaft, 2006, pp. 486, 491.
[192] ZPO § 1041(2).
[193] ZPO § 1041(3).
[194] ZPO § 1041(4).
[195] ZPO § 1041(4).
[196] ZPO § 1042 (1).
[197] ZPO § 1042 (2).

individual agreement or by referring to a set of arbitration rules.[198] If the parties have not agreed on a specific procedure, which is usually the case, it is up to the discretion of the arbitral tribunal to determine the procedure within the framework of the mandatory rules.[199] However, the arbitral tribunal should be cautious when formally agreeing with the parties on the content of procedural orders. If a procedural order records the parties' agreement on certain issues, the tribunal may later be kept from deviating from the procedural order without the parties' consent to avoid any risk of evoking setting-aside procedures.[200] As to the arbitral tribunal's discretion, ZPO § 1042 (4) Sentence 2 provides that the arbitral tribunal has the power to determine the admissibility, relevance, materiality and weight of any evidence. The arbitral tribunal is also empowered to conduct the taking of evidence. For a German lawyer, these rights of a court or arbitral tribunal are self-evident. They were included in ZPO § 1042 to accentuate for common law participants that the arbitral tribunal is to be in charge of the taking of evidence and is to actively manage the case.

The chairperson of the arbitral tribunal may be authorized either by the parties or the party-appointed arbitrators to decide on individual questions of procedure alone, particularly on questions encompassing the formal structuring of the proceedings.[201] In general, the drafts of procedural orders will be prepared by the chairman, who is in charge of coordinating the conduct of the proceedings.[202] The chairman's authority encompasses – even without explicit authorization – certain housekeeping issues as well as formal questions such as the determination of the order of witness testimonies.[203] Failing an authorization by the chairman of the arbitral tribunal, decisions regarding the proceedings' conduct must be decided by the majority of the members of the arbitral tribunal.[204]

II. Place of Arbitration

Pursuant to ZPO § 1043, the parties are free to agree on the place of arbitration. They may agree on the place of arbitration in their arbitration agreement or after the dispute has arisen. If the parties do not or cannot reach an agreement, the place of arbitration shall be determined by the arbitral tribunal.[205] When choosing

---

[198] ZPO § 1042 (3).
[199] ZPO § 1042 (4).
[200] Higher Regional Court (OLG) Frankfurt, Decision of 6 June 2011 (Docket No. 26 Sch 13/10), SchiedsVZ (German Arbitration Journal) 2013, p. 49; for a critical view see *Wagner/Bülau*, Procedural Orders by Arbitral Tribunals: In the Stays of Party Agreements?, SchiedsVZ (German Arbitration Journal) 2013, p. 6. *Wilske/Heuser*, Higher Court in Germany finds procedural order is an instrument of partes' agreement, IBA Newsletter Arbitration and ADR, Vol.17, No. 2, 2012, pp. 71-73.
[201] ZPO § 1042 (3); these questions include time limits and extensions, the language of the proceedings, orders for interim measures, or the appointment of experts, Bill of the Arbitration Law Reform Act, BT-Drucksache 13/5274, p. 54.
[202] *Sachs/Lörcher* in: Böckstiegel/Kröll/Nacimiento (eds.), Arbitration in Germany – The Model Law in Practice, 2nd ed., 2015, ZPO § 1042, no. 29.
[203] *Wilske/Markert* in: Vorwerk/Wolf (eds.), Beck'scher Online-Kommentar ZPO, ZPO § 1052, no. 36, noting however that also decisions on the formal structuring such as the determination of the language of the proceedings may have far-reaching consequences (no. 37). Some authors even doubt whether the authorization in ZPO § 1052 (3) covers decisions on the language of the proceedings, see *Von Schlabrendorff/Sessler* in: Böckstiegel/Kröll/Nacimiento (eds.), Arbitration in Germany – The Model Law in Practice, 2nd ed., 2015, ZPO § 1052, no. 15.
[204] ZPO § 1052 (1).
[205] ZPO § 1043 (1) Sentence 2.

a place of arbitration, the arbitral tribunal shall take into account the circumstances of the case and the convenience of the parties.[206] According to ZPO § 1025 (1), once a German city has been chosen as the place of arbitration, either by the parties or by the arbitral tribunal, the German arbitration law will necessarily apply to the proceedings.[207] This does not mean that the arbitral tribunal will always have to convene at the place of arbitration. According to ZPO § 1043 (2), the arbitral tribunal may meet at any place it considers appropriate for an oral hearing, for hearing witnesses, experts or the parties, or for the inspection of goods or documents. However, this right of the arbitral tribunal, can be excluded by agreement of the parties.

III. Language of Arbitral Proceedings

The parties may agree on the language of the proceedings in the same manner as on the place of arbitration.[208] If they do not agree on a language or languages in the arbitration clause or after their dispute has arisen, the arbitral tribunal shall determine the language or the languages to be used in the proceedings. The language agreed or decided upon shall apply to any written statements by a party, any hearing and any award, decision or other communication by the arbitral tribunal.[209] In addition, the arbitral tribunal may order that any documentary evidence be translated into the language of the proceedings.[210] If documents need to be translated, the arbitral tribunal should make sure that it is clear from the beginning which party will bear the costs of translation.

Overall it will be practical to choose a language all participants are proficient in and which was used in the pre-dispute correspondence of the parties. Although unusual and not advisable, it is possible to choose or determine more than one language for the proceedings.[211] If such an approach is used, it will be necessary for the main participants to be proficient in all chosen languages.

Parties should in general be careful when omitting to decide on a language before the dispute has arisen, as they may choose one (unknowingly) in an implicit way. This can be the case by agreeing on certain institutional arbitration rules or by appointing arbitrators with a rather narrow linguistic knowledge.[212] Thus, to avoid any uncertainty it is advisable to expressly agree on the language of the proceedings.

---

[206] ZPO § 1043 (1) Sentence 3.
[207] For details regarding the so-called principle of territoriality see *Wagner* in: Böckstiegel/Kröll/Nacimiento (eds.), Arbitration in Germany – The Model Law in Practice, 2nd ed., 2015, ZPO § 1025, nos. 23 et seq. Only a few provisions of the German arbitration law apply when the place of arbitration is not yet agreed in or outside Germany (ZPO § 1025 (2)).
[208] ZPO § 1045.
[209] ZPO § 1045 (1) Sentence 3.
[210] ZPO § 1045 (2).
[211] Critical *Geimer* in: Zöller, Zivilprozessordnung, 30th ed., 2014, § 1045, no. 1.
[212] See *e.g.* Art. 81 (1) CIETAC Rules 2015: "In the absence of such agreement, the language of arbitration to be used in the proceedings shall be Chinese."; *Wilske/Markert* in: Vorwerk/Wolf (eds.), Beck'scher Online-Kommentar ZPO, ZPO § 1045 No. 2.

If the parties do not respect the choice of language, their submissions may be excluded.[213] The non-observance of the choice of language by the arbitral tribunal on the other hand may constitute a ground for annulment.[214]

IV. Exchange of Submissions and Notifications

1. Initiation of Proceedings

A claimant can initiate arbitral proceedings by sending a notice of arbitration to the respondent. According to ZPO § 1044, the arbitral proceedings in respect of that particular dispute commence on the date on which the notice of arbitration is received by the respondent.[215] The notice of arbitration must include an indication of the relevant parties, a short description of the issues in dispute and a reference to the arbitration agreement.[216] The parties may agree on a different procedure for initiating the proceedings. If the parties have agreed on institutional arbitration rules, such rules will usually include details on initiating the proceedings.

2. Statements of Claim and Defense

Once arbitral proceedings have been properly initiated, it is necessary for the claimant to substantiate his claim and for respondent to reply. According to ZPO § 1046 (1), the claimant shall present his claim and state the facts supporting his claim and the relief or remedy sought, and the respondent shall state his defense in respect of these particulars, within the time period agreed on by the parties or determined by the arbitral tribunal. In contrast to Article 23 (1) of the UNCITRAL Model Law, the parties may not deviate from the required elements of such statements. The first exchange of statement of claim and statement of defense is meant to clarify the issues of the case at an early stage. When deciding on time limits for written submissions, it must be ensured that each party has enough time to prepare its submission. Otherwise, this could deprive a party of a fair and equal opportunity to present its case. The parties are free to submit with their statements all documents they consider to be relevant or may add a reference to any other evidence they will submit, but there is no obligation to do so.[217] This stands in contrast to German court proceedings, where the claimant is obligated to present any relevant evidence with his statement of claim.[218] These provisions for presentation of evidence in arbitration allow for a more flexible approach to accommodate common law procedures.

Once statements of claim and defense have been submitted, the parties may generally amend or supplement their claims or defenses during the course of the arbitral proceedings, unless the arbitral tribunal considers it inappropriate because a party has not properly excused the delay.[219] Pursuant to ZPO § 1046 (3), the

---

[213] *Wilske/Markert* in: Vorwerk/Wolf (eds.), Beck'scher Online-Kommentar ZPO, ZPO § 1045 No. 6.
[214] *Wilske/Markert* in: Vorwerk/Wolf (eds.), Beck'scher Online-Kommentar ZPO, ZPO § 1045 No. 7.
[215] It is received when it reaches the other party, Civil Code (BGB) § 130 *mutatis mutandis*.
[216] ZPO § 1044 Sentence 2.
[217] ZPO § 1046 (1) Sentence 2.
[218] See *supra*, at pp. 24 et seq.
[219] ZPO § 1046 (2).

provisions of ZPO § 1046 (1) and (2) also apply to counterclaims. A counterclaim is admissible if it is covered by the arbitration agreement.

3. Notification for Insolvency

Unless the parties have agreed otherwise, insolvency of one party does not terminate or interrupt arbitral proceedings. Rather, the insolvency administrator is from that point onwards bound by the arbitration clause.[220] To allow a fair treatment, the arbitral tribunal should grant the insolvency administrator sufficient time to prepare for the proceedings.[221]

V. Oral Hearings and Written Proceedings

According to ZPO § 1047 (1), the parties may choose whether they want the proceedings to include an oral hearing or not. Failing a party agreement, it is up to the arbitral tribunal to decide whether to hold oral hearings or to conduct the proceedings on the basis of documents and other materials only. However, if a party requests a hearing, it will usually be appropriate for the arbitral tribunal to follow this request. Even if the parties have agreed that no hearings shall be held, it may be necessary for the arbitral tribunal to hold a hearing in order to protect the right of due process or to simply get a better understanding of the issues in dispute. The arbitral tribunal may hold hearings that concern only part of the proceedings. Even though an oral hearing is not obligatory, it is the understanding in German arbitration practice, that it should be the rule rather than the exception.[222] The arbitral tribunal may not choose written proceedings solely as a matter of convenience. There must be a factual reason beyond convenience that justifies written proceedings.[223]

ZPO § 1047 (2) and (3) concern the right of due process. The arbitral tribunal must notify the parties in a timely fashion of any oral hearing or any taking of evidence. All statements, documents or other information supplied to the arbitral tribunal by one party shall be communicated to the other party. Any written material provided by the arbitral tribunal, such as expert reports, must be communicated to both parties if the arbitral tribunal wishes to base its decision on them.

VI. Default of a Party

If a claimant has initiated arbitral proceedings with a notice of arbitration, but fails to present its statement of claim in a timely fashion, the arbitral tribunal shall terminate the proceedings.[224] On the other hand, if a respondent fails to submit its statement of defense within the relevant time limits,[225] the arbitral tribunal shall

---

[220] Federal Court of Justice (BGH), Decision of 28 February 1957 (Docket No. VII ZR 204/56, Neue Juristische Wochenschrift, 1957, p. 791; Decision of 20 November 2003 (Docket No. III ZB 24/03), Zeitschrift für das gesamte Insolvenzrecht, 2004, p. 88; Decision of 19 July 2004 (Docket No. II ZR 65/03), SchiedsVZ (German Arbitration Journal) 2004, p. 259.

[221] *Flöther*, Auswirkungen des inländischen Insolvenzverfahrens auf Schiedsverfahren und Schiedsabrede, 2001, p. 44. *Böckstiegel/Kröll/Nacimiento* in: Böckstiegel/Kröll/Nacimiento (eds.), Arbitration in Germany – The Model Law in Practice, 2nd ed., 2015, Part. I, General Overview, No. 162.

[222] Written proceedings are also the exception in German litigation.

[223] *Schwab/Walter*, Schiedsgerichtsbarkeit, 7th ed., 2005, ch. 16, no. 32.

[224] ZPO § 1048 (1).

[225] ZPO § 1048 (2).

continue the proceedings without treating such failure in itself as an admission of the claimant's allegations. If in the course of the proceedings any party fails to appear at a hearing or to produce documentary evidence, the arbitral tribunal may continue the proceedings and make the award on the evidence before it.[226] This includes the right of the arbitral tribunal to draw negative inferences, even though the provision does not explicitly say so. The right to draw negative inferences if a party is in default is an accepted principle under German procedural law.[227] All possible consequences of default may be avoided if a party can show sufficient cause for the delay.[228] In addition, the rules on default of a party are not binding.[229] The parties may agree on other consequences.

VII. Establishing the Facts of the Case

1. General Approach to Fact Finding and Gathering Evidence

The German arbitration law leaves it to the arbitral tribunal to decide on how it approaches fact-finding and the gathering of evidence if there is no specific agreement by the parties.[230]

The previous German arbitration law stated that the arbitral tribunal was to establish the facts of the case by all appropriate means (*beschränkter Untersuchungsgrundsatz*). The same principle applies in arbitrations under the Rules of Arbitration of the International Chamber of Commerce ("ICC Rules") and the DIS Rules.[231] Although the German arbitration law no longer states this principle explicitly, it is generally accepted that it continues to apply.[232]

If the arbitral tribunal is allowed to establish the facts of the case by all appropriate means, it is not limited by the submissions and offers to produce evidence by the parties. Such a limitation exists in German court proceedings (*Beibringungsgrundsatz*).[233] This principle of German civil procedure is similar to the adversarial system under common law. Whereas under both systems it is up to the parties to define the scope of their dispute, a German court participates more actively in shaping the proceedings than a common law court. It decides which offers of evidence to pursue and when to take evidence. This allows the parties to present evidence throughout the proceedings and not just up to the oral hearing.

In common law proceedings, the parties spend the pre-trial phase collecting evidence without much participation of the court, unless there are disputes on the

---

[226] ZPO § 1048 (3).
[227] See *supra*, pp. 60 et seq, 79.
[228] ZPO § 1048 (4) Sentence 1.
[229] ZPO § 1048 (4) Sentence 2.
[230] ZPO § 1042 (4) Sentence 2. For details on fact finding and gathering of evidence see *Eberl* (ed.), Beweis im Schiedsverfahren, 2015.
[231] See ICC Rules 2012 Article 25 (1): *"The arbitral tribunal shall proceed within as short a time as possible to establish the facts of the case by all appropriate means."* and DIS Rules Section 27.1: *" The arbitral tribunal shall establish the facts underlying the dispute. To this end it has the discretion to give directions and, in particular, to hear witnesses and experts and order the production of documents. The arbitral tribunal is not bound by the parties' applications for the admission of evidence."*
[232] *Wilske/Markert*, National Reports – Germany, in: World Arbitration Reporter (Mistelis/Shore (eds.)), Vol. I, 2nd ed., 2014, p. GER-20. For an opposing view see *Lionnet/Lionnet*, Handbuch der internationalen und nationalen Schiedsgerichtsbarkeit, 3rd ed., 2005, pp. 307, 308, p. 359, see fn. 172 with further references.
[233] See *supra*, at pp. 6, 24.

exchange of information which the parties cannot solve themselves. The parties then decide which evidence to present in the oral hearing.

In German arbitral proceedings, both alternatives are possible. Since the arbitral tribunal can establish the facts of the case by all appropriate means, it has the necessary flexibility to adapt to the wishes and needs of the parties. It can either leave it up to the parties to collect the necessary evidence and present it to the arbitral tribunal or it can actively manage the proceedings by deciding on issues of evidence from the beginning and only ordering the taking of relevant and material evidence. In arbitral proceedings with mainly German participants, the second procedure will usually prevail, as the expectations of the parties concerning the procedure need to be respected by the arbitral tribunal.[234]

2. Documents

a) Production of Documents in the Possession of a Party

The statutory provisions in German civil procedure allow only a limited production of documents.[235] These rules are not applicable in arbitral proceedings in Germany. However, a right of an arbitral tribunal to order production of documents must nevertheless be seen against this backdrop. The German arbitration law does not specifically state that the arbitral tribunal may order the parties to produce documents. It merely mentions in ZPO § 1049 (1) Sentence 2 that the arbitral tribunal can order the parties to produce documents to an expert. In addition, ZPO § 1048 (3) states that the arbitral tribunal may continue the proceedings if a party fails to produce documentary evidence. This provision only makes sense if the arbitral tribunal has the right to order a party to produce documents.[236]

Thus, it follows from ZPO §§ 1049 (1) and 1048 (3) and from the principle that the arbitral tribunal may establish the facts of the case by all appropriate means that it may order the parties to produce documents. The right of the arbitral tribunal is nevertheless limited to cases where a document has been described with reasonable particularity and the arbitral tribunal considers it to be relevant and material to the dispute.[237] These limitations follow from the traditions of German civil procedure law and from the aim to avoid "fishing expeditions" in German arbitral proceedings.[238] Such limitations are also in line with internationally accepted principles on document production such as the IBA Rules on the Taking of Evidence in International Arbitration ("IBA Rules on Evidence"). Further, the courts may not compel a party to produce documents.[239] In case of failure of a party to produce documents the arbitral tribunal may continue the proceedings

---

[234] *Wilske/Markert* in: Vorwerk/Wolf (eds.), Beck'scher Online-Kommentar ZPO, ZPO § 1042, no. 24.

[235] See *supra*, at pp. 68–69, 83. ZPO §§ 420-444 and 142; see also *Wilske/Mack*, Production of documents under the revised German Code of Civil Procedure, IBA Newsletter Arbitration and ADR, Vol. 8, No. 1, 2003, p. 43.

[236] A general overview is provided by *Krapfl*, Die Dokumentenvorlage im Schiedsverfahren, 2007, pp. 141 *et seq*. *Wilske* in: Böckstiegel/Kröll/Nacimiento (eds.), Arbitration in Germany – The Model Law in Practice, 2nd ed., 2015.

[237] In detail *Sachs/Lörcher* in: Böckstiegel/Kröll/Nacimiento (eds.), Arbitration in Germany – The Model Law in Practice, 2nd ed., 2015, ZPO § 1047, nos. 20 *et seq*.

[238] See *Sachs*, Use of documents and document discovery: "Fishing expeditions" versus transparency and burden of proof, SchiedsVZ (German Arbitration Journal) 2003, pp. 193 *et seq*.

[239] *Wilske/Markert*, National Reports – Germany, in: Mistelis/Shore (eds.), World Arbitration Reporter, Vol. I, 2nd ed., 2014, p. GER-23; *Sachs/Lörcher* in: Böckstiegel/Kröll/Nacimiento (eds.), Arbitration in Germany – The Model Law in Practice, 2nd ed., 2015, ZPO § 1047, no. 26.

and make the award on the evidence before it according to ZPO § 1048 (3). Due to the broad evidentiary discretion contained in section ZPO § 1042 (4), it may draw negative inferences from that failure.[240]

b) Production of Documents in the Possession of Third Parties

An arbitral tribunal does not have any rights with regard to third parties since its rights follow solely from the parties' agreement to arbitrate. For the arbitral tribunal to be able to order a third party to produce documents, there must be a statutory provision to that effect. There is no such explicit provision in the German arbitration law. Nevertheless, since the arbitral tribunal may establish the facts of the case by all appropriate means, the right to request third parties to voluntarily produce documents if they are relevant and material to the dispute is included as well. If a third party refuses to comply voluntarily, the arbitral tribunal may request the assistance of the court according to ZPO § 1050 if it feels that the document is absolutely necessary for the resolution of the dispute.

c) Confidentiality of Documents and Privilege

There are no provisions in German arbitration law dealing with the confidentiality of documents or privilege. As disclosure obligations are rather rare in German arbitration law,[241] this is not surprising. Yet, some of the substantive German law provisions can be useful to determine issues of confidentiality or privilege, for example professional privileges, privilege against self-incrimination, or confidentiality of trade secrets.[242]

3. Witnesses

a) Written Statements and Testimony

There are no specific provisions concerning witnesses in the German arbitration law. Nevertheless, it is generally accepted that an arbitral tribunal may hear witnesses in an oral hearing or accept written witness statements as evidence. This can occur upon request of a party or upon the initiative of the arbitral tribunal. The decision as to whether a written witness statement is sufficient or whether an oral examination of the witness is necessary is left up to the arbitral tribunal.[243] It should hear the parties on the issue. Since the parties must bear the costs incurred by the oral examination of a witness, they may generally be more inclined to save costs by relying on written testimony. Even though this approach is possible, it is generally agreed that written statements do not have the same probative value as oral testimony. A written statement does not give the arbitral tribunal a personal impression of the witness and does not allow an evaluation of his personal credibility.[244] Indeed, if a party requests an oral hearing of a witness presented

---

[240] *Sachs/Lörcher* in: Böckstiegel/Kröll/Nacimiento (eds.), Arbitration in Germany – The Model Law in Practice, 2nd ed., 2015, ZPO § 1047, no. 26.
[241] See for example ZPO § 1049 (1) Sentence 2.
[242] For example professional privilege between a lawyer and his client, see *Wilske/Markert*, National Reports – Germany , in: Mistelis/Shore (eds.), World Arbitration Reporter, Vol. I, 2nd ed., 2014 p. GER-23.
[243] *Münch* in: Münchener Kommentar zur Zivilprozessordnung, 4th ed., 2013, § 1042 no. 118, § 1049, no. 61; *Schwab/Walter*, Schiedsgerichtsbarkeit, 7th ed., 2005, ch. 15, no. 14.
[244] Concerning the probative value of a witness's testimony overall, the arbitral tribunal shall also take the personal interest of the witness and the respective party in the outcome of the case

by the other party, the arbitral tribunal will usually hear the witness to ensure fair proceedings and prevent a violation of the right to be heard as a ground to challenge the award later. If a party wishes to present a witness at an oral hearing of its own accord, it will usually be necessary to inform the arbitral tribunal and the other party of the identity of the witness and the issues the witness will testify to in a timely manner before the hearing.

An arbitral tribunal may question a witness itself and/or allow party counsel to examine the witness.[245] In German court proceedings, a witness is generally questioned by the judge. There is no cross-examination in a common law sense, although it is possible for counsel to put direct questions to a witness with approval of the court.[246] Since arbitral proceedings are more flexible than court proceedings, cross-examinations are not categorically excluded in German arbitration practice.[247] The concrete course of the proceedings will usually depend on the origin and expectations of the parties and their counsel as well as of the arbitrators. If counsel is accustomed to personally questioning witnesses, even arbitrators with a civil law background will generally not stand in the way of such a procedure, although they may add questions of their own.[248]

An arbitral tribunal has no means of compelling a witness to attend an oral hearing, nor can it administer oaths.[249] If a witness refuses to cooperate or if the arbitral tribunal wishes to verify the truthfulness of testimony, it must apply to a court for assistance.[250] Also, it is important to note that false testimony given in front of an arbitral tribunal does not entail criminal liability per se, even though witnesses are admonished to make truthful statements.[251] The witness, however, can make himself liable to prosecution for (attempting or aiding) fraud.[252]

b) Preparation of Witnesses

There are no provisions in German arbitration law making it *per se* unethical for counsel to contact a witness out of court or prepare a witness for his testimony. Thus, arbitral tribunals should be aware that written witness statements are frequently drafted with the help of counsel. In particular, it is not uncommon to prepare witnesses for cross-examination.[253] Thus far no strict limitations on witness preparations are apparent in German law or jurisprudence, as long as counsel do not influence the content of a witness's testimony.[254] However, counsel should refrain from testing these limits and diligently avoid unduly influencing witnesses.

---

into account, *Sachs/Lörcher* in: Böckstiegel/Kröll/Nacimiento (eds.), Arbitration in Germany – The Model Law in Practice, 2nd ed., 2015, ZPO § 1047, no. 11.

[245] *Hanefeld*, Country Report on Germany in: Weigand (ed.), Practitioner's Handbook on International Arbitration, 2nd ed., 2009, no. 7.110.

[246] See *supra*, at p. 75.

[247] *Münch* in: Münchener Kommentar zur Zivilprozessordnung, 4th ed., 2013, § 1049 no. 63.

[248] *Sachs/Lörcher* in: Böckstiegel/Kröll/Nacimiento (eds.), Arbitration in Germany – The Model Law in Practice, 2nd ed., 2015, ZPO § 1047, no. 16; Markus Wirth, Ihr Zeuge, Herr Rechtsanwalt!, SchiedsVZ (German Arbitration Journal) 2003, p. 9, 14.

[249] *Münch* in: Münchener Kommentar zur Zivilprozessordnung, 4th ed., 2013, § 1049, no. 52.

[250] ZPO § 1050.

[251] *Voit* in: Musielak/Voit, Zivilprozessordnung, 12th ed., 2015, § 1042, no. 26.

[252] *Wilske/Markert* in: Vorwerk/Wolf (eds.), Beck'scher Online-Kommentar ZPO, ZPO § 1042, no. 28.

[253] *Schlosser*, Verfahrensrechtliche und berufsrechtliche Zulässigkeit der Zeugenvorbereitung, SchiedsVZ (German Arbitration Journal) 2004, pp. 225, 228 *et seq*.

[254] For an examination of German procedural law, German rules of professional conduct and German criminal law see *Timmerbeil*, Witness Coaching und Adversary System, 2004, pp. 103 *et*

c) Transcript or Summary of Witness Testimony

A question that comes up in practice is what sort of record the arbitral tribunal should prepare when a witness testifies in an oral hearing. In principle, the arbitral tribunal is free to decide whether to summarize the witness testimony in the minutes of the oral hearing or to have a court reporter produce a transcript of the evidentiary hearing.[255] A summary is less expensive, but also less reliable than a transcript. In German court proceedings, the judge will prepare a summary of the witness testimony.[256] An arbitral tribunal may follow this procedure as well, unless the parties request a transcript. If the parties are willing to bear the costs, the arbitral tribunal will usually honor their request. If the proceedings are conducted in the English language, there is usually no difficulty in finding the necessary court reporters. Since there is no need for court reporters in German court practice, it is more difficult to locate a court reporter who can transcribe a hearing in German. However, more and more court reporter services are offered in Germany, predominantly in English, but also in German.

d) Parties as Witnesses

An important difference between German court proceedings and arbitral proceedings is the treatment of parties as witnesses. In court proceedings, testimony of a party – which includes the executive officers of a corporation – is treated differently from testimony of a witness. While a German court may hear the parties in person at any stage of the proceedings, restrictions are placed on a party's testimony for evidentiary purposes.[257] This restriction does not apply in German arbitral proceedings unless the parties have specifically agreed on the application of the ZPO. Therefore, the arbitral tribunal is free to hear the parties on all issues in dispute for evidentiary purposes.[258]

e) Reimbursement of Witnesses

An interested party will usually present a witness at an oral hearing. The interested party will then initially carry the costs of the witness itself – such as travel costs and compensation for loss of earnings. At the end of the proceedings, the arbitral tribunal may allocate costs to the unsuccessful party in an award on costs, including costs incurred by the successful party for witnesses. Even if the arbitral tribunal itself summons a witness to appear voluntarily before it, the costs will eventually have to be borne by the parties. This again can be decided in the award on costs.

---

seq.
  [255] *Hanefeld*, Country Report on Germany in: Weigand (ed.), Practitioner's Handbook on International Arbitration, 2nd ed., 2009, no. 7.111.
  [256] See *supra*, at p. 76.
  [257] See *supra*, at pp. 78 et seq.
  [258] *Hanefeld*, Country Report on Germany in: Weigand (ed.), Practitioner's Handbook on International Arbitration, 2nd ed., 2009, no. 7.103.

4. Experts

a) Party-Appointed Experts in Common Law and Court-Appointed Experts in Civil Law

ZPO § 1049 contains rules regarding tribunal-appointed experts. To understand this provision, one must be aware of the different treatment of experts in common and civil law jurisdictions.

Whereas in civil law jurisdictions court-appointed experts are the rule, in common law proceedings party-appointed experts still seem to predominate. In the civil law tradition, the expert is an assistant of the court. It is his duty to use his expert knowledge on technical or commercial questions to inform the court on such issues. Therefore, the court selects and instructs the expert.[259]

In the common law tradition, the parties choose and instruct their own experts during the pre-trial phase and then present his testimony at trial to the jury and/or the judge.

ZPO § 1049, which corresponds to Article 26 of the UNCITRAL Model Law, compromises between these two extremes. The compromise is based on the premise that arbitral proceedings usually do not resemble the adversarial process of U.S. civil procedure, which requires party-appointed experts. At the same time, the arbitral tribunal should retain the necessary flexibility to accommodate the needs and expectations of the parties. Therefore, the parties may agree to exclude tribunal-appointed experts and to only allow party-appointed experts. If there is no specific party agreement, the arbitral tribunal may admit party-appointed experts, as well as appoint its own experts.

b) Impartiality and Independence of Tribunal-Appointed Expert

Pursuant to ZPO § 1049 (3), an expert appointed by an arbitral tribunal, unlike a party-appointed expert, must fulfill the same impartiality and independence requirements as an arbitrator. This is a German addition to the UNCITRAL Model Law, which does not consider the question. Since ZPO § 1049 (3) refers to ZPO §§ 1036, 1037 (1) and (2), an expert approached by an arbitral tribunal must disclose any circumstances likely to give rise to justifiable doubts as to his impartiality or independence. If an expert fails to disclose any relevant circumstances, a party may challenge him for lack of neutrality. The right to challenge an expert is limited to an application before the arbitral tribunal. An application to a court as provided in ZPO § 1037 (3) for challenging an arbitrator is excluded. If an arbitral tribunal does not release an expert once he has been challenged, this may provide successful grounds for challenging the award.[260]

c) Appointing a Tribunal-Appointed Expert

For due process reasons, the arbitral tribunal should make sure to hear the parties on who is to be appointed as expert and on what specific issues he is to report, even though ZPO § 1049 (1) does not require this. If both parties agree on a specific person as expert, such person will regularly be appointed by the arbitral tribunal

---

[259] See *supra*, at pp. 76 et seq.
[260] *Hanefeld*, Country Report on Germany in: Weigand (ed.), Practitioner's Handbook on International Arbitration, 2nd ed., 2009, no. 7.128.

acting as an agent of the parties to conclude a *Werkvertrag*[261] in their name.[262] The costs incurred by a tribunal-appointed expert must be borne by the parties. Therefore, the arbitral tribunal is well advised to discuss the issue of reimbursement of the expert with the parties before appointing the expert. The arbitral tribunal should carefully and clearly define its questions when drafting the terms of reference for the expert. Since the success of an expert depends largely on the cooperation of the parties, it will usually be helpful to involve the parties in the process of drafting the terms of reference.

To prepare his report, the expert will often need to inspect documents, objects or property of a party. The arbitral tribunal is specifically empowered to require a party to give an expert any relevant information or to produce any relevant documents, objects or other property for his inspection.[263] As with direct evidence requested by the arbitral tribunal, a party cannot be forced to submit the evidence needed by the expert. The arbitral tribunal is limited to drawing negative inferences. In the context of an expert report, this means that the arbitral tribunal may advise the expert to base his report on factual allegations made by the cooperative party if the other party without sufficient cause is unwilling to provide the necessary evidence.[264] In case of trade secrets a submission of sensitive information to the arbitral tribunal may suffice under appropriate circumstances.[265]

d) Duties of a Tribunal-Appointed Expert

A tribunal-appointed expert can be asked to deliver a written and/or oral report. Unless otherwise agreed by the parties, he must appear at a hearing if a party requests his appearance or if the arbitral tribunal considers it necessary.[266] The hearing must give the parties the opportunity to put questions to the expert and to confront him with their own experts. If there is no agreement of the parties on a hearing, it lies in the discretion of the arbitral tribunal to schedule a hearing or not.

Expert liability arises from the contractual relationship with the parties[267] and is generally restricted to intentional or grossly negligent breaches of duties.[268]

---

[261] BGB §631, a contract where the achieved result is decisive, not the service which is rendered.
[262] The arbitral tribunal is generally authorized to do so by the arbitrator's contract, *Wilske/Markert* in: Vorwerk/Wolf (eds.), Beck'scher Online-Kommentar ZPO, ZPO §1049, no. 2.1; different view as to reimbursement *Schlosser* in: Stein/Jonas, Zivilprozessordnung Vol. 10, 23rd ed., 2014, §1049, no. 7 remuneration to be borne by the party bearing the burden of proof; different view *Münch* in: Münchener Kommentar Zivilprozessordnung, 4th ed., 2013, §1049, no. 22, costs remuneration to be borne by the arbitrators.
[263] ZPO §1047 (1) Sentence 2.
[264] *Lachmann*, Handbuch für die Schiedsgerichtspraxis, 3rd ed., 2008, nos. 1535, 1548.
[265] See the IBA Rules on the Taking of Evidence in International Arbitration: Art. 3 (5) on general objections to documents requested; Art. 6 (3) and Art. 9 (2) (e) on the possibility to request exclusion of documents from evidence on grounds of confidentiality, and Art. 52 WIPO Arbitration Rules on the possibility to make an application to have the information classified as confidential.
[266] ZPO §1049 (2).
[267] BGB §§631 *et seq.*
[268] *Voit* in: Musielak/Voit, Zivilprozessordnung, 12th ed., 2015, §1049, no. 10; *Schwab/Walter*, Schiedsgerichtsbarkeit, 7th ed., 2005, ch. 15, no. 18; *Münch* in: Münchener Kommentar Zivilprozessordnung, 4th ed., 2013, §1049, no. 31. For a comparative overview see *Jung*, Die deliktische Haftung des Prozesssachverständigen im deutschen, englischen und französischen Recht, Zeitschrift für Vergleichende Rechtswissenschaft, 2008, pp. 32 *et seq.* and *Freedman/Farrell* (eds.), Kendall on Expert Determination, 5th ed., 2015, pp. 449-482.

e) Party-Appointed Experts

Even if the arbitral tribunal has appointed an expert, the parties are free to additionally appoint their own experts. Party-appointed experts are specifically mentioned in § 1049 (2) Sentence 2. Once a party has appointed its own expert in arbitral proceedings, it may discuss the issues with the expert to make sure he presents them in a favorable light for the party. The parties should be aware that an arbitral tribunal with a German law background will place more emphasis on the tribunal-appointed expert than on a party-appointed expert.[269] Party-appointed experts may not be challenged by the other party as ZPO §§ 1049 (3), 1036, 1037 only apply to tribunal-appointed experts. Also, there is no need to produce any documents according to ZPO § 1049 (1) sentence 2 where party-appointed experts are concerned.[270]

5. Court Assistance in Taking Evidence

a) Possible Assistance Measures

ZPO § 1050 allows the arbitral tribunal or a party with approval of the arbitral tribunal to request the assistance of a court in the taking of evidence. Possible measures include testimony of a witness or an expert, the administration of an oath, or orders for production of documents in the possession of third parties.[271]

If the necessary evidence is located abroad, a request to proceed according to the Hague Evidence Convention or Council Regulation (EC) No 1206/2001 via a court is possible. Pursuant to the prevailing opinion among legal commentators, the arbitral tribunal itself cannot directly request the assistance of a foreign court because it is not considered as a "judicial authority" under Article 1 of the Hague Evidence Convention[272] or a "court of a member state" under Art. 1 (1) of Council Regulation (EC) No 1206/2001.[273] Requests of an arbitral tribunal with its seat in Germany for assistance with taking evidence abroad are very unusual because of the loss of time associated with such a request.[274]

b) International Character of ZPO § 1050

According to ZPO § 1025 (2), the German provision of ZPO § 1050 applies even if the arbitral tribunal has its seat abroad or the seat has not been defined. This is a novelty among arbitration laws, since pursuant to Article 1 (2) of the UNCITRAL Model Law, Article 27 of the UNCITRAL Model Law only provides for court assistance at the seat of the arbitral tribunal. The liberal approach of the German arbitration law has hardly been noticed internationally, which is certainly due to the fact that a German court is very limited in its ability to enforce orders for production of evidence.

---

[269] Bill of the New Arbitration Act, BT-Drucksache 13/5274, pp. 50, 51.
[270] *Sachs/Lörcher* in: Böckstiegel/Kröll/Nacimiento (eds.), Arbitration in Germany – The Model Law in Practice, 2nd ed., 2015, ZPO § 1049, no. 11.
[271] *Schwab/Walter*, Schiedsgerichtsbarkeit, 7th ed., 2005, ch. 17, no. 15.
[272] *Geimer* in: Zöller, Zivilprozessordnung, 30th ed., 2014, § 1050, no. 5 with further references.
[273] *Von Hein* in: Rauscher (ed.), Europäisches Zivilprozess- und Kollisionsrecht EuZPR / EuIPR Kommentar, 3rd ed., 2010, Art. 1 EG-BewVO, no. 9.
[274] But see the possible example described by *Markus Wirth*, Rechtshilfe deutscher Gerichte zugunsten ausländischer Schiedsgerichte bei der Beweisaufnahme – ein Erfahrungsbericht, SchiedsVZ (German Arbitration Journal) 2005, pp. 66 et seq.

c) Sanctions Available to German Courts

The German court executes all requests according to its own rules on the taking of evidence.[275] This means that it does not have any enforcement rights towards parties of the proceedings and only few enforcement rights towards third parties.

The court, however, may order a third party to produce documents and, if the third party refuses to cooperate, may impose sanctions.[276]

d) Competent Court

The competent court for an application under ZPO § 1050 is the lower court of first instance (*Amtsgericht*) at the place where the order is to be executed, usually the place of residence of the witness or third party.[277] When applying to a lower court of first instance (*Amtsgericht*), representation by an attorney is not necessary.[278] Therefore, when requesting assistance in the taking of evidence, an arbitral tribunal or a party can apply directly to the court. This can save costs, especially in international proceedings with foreign counsel.

e) Requirements for the Application

The application to the court is not bound to any specific form, but shall be in writing and because of § 184 German Judicature Act (*Gerichtsverfassungsgesetz, GVG*), which declares German as the language in court, shall be written in German.[279] It will usually be appropriate to provide the court with the arbitration agreement, the statement of claim in the arbitration, the written approval of the arbitral tribunal to request the assistance of the court, a submission by the arbitral tribunal as to why it cannot take the evidence itself and documentation to prove that the requested local court is competent.[280] Of course, the most important piece of information is the order by the arbitral tribunal for the taking of evidence. If documentary evidence is concerned, the application must provide the court with the necessary means to distinguish the specific documents. If testimonial evidence is requested, the court must be informed as to which questions to put to the witness or expert.

According to ZPO § 1050 Sentence 3, the arbitral tribunal may participate in an evidentiary hearing and put questions to the witness or expert itself. The court must therefore inform the arbitral tribunal of the date, time and place of its evidentiary hearing. If it fails to do this in a timely fashion, which allows the arbitral tribunal to attend, the arbitral tribunal may require a second evidentiary hearing.[281]

The court will deny the request if the arbitral tribunal could have completed the taking of evidence itself.[282] This requirement is not treated strictly since the options of the arbitral tribunal are limited or may call for an unreasonable ef-

---

[275] ZPO § 1050.
[276] ZPO §§ 142, 428, 429, see *supra*, at p. 83.
[277] ZPO § 1062 (4).
[278] ZPO §§ 79 (1) Sentence 1, 78 (1).
[279] *Wilske/Markert* in: Vorwerk/Wolf (eds.), Beck'scher Online Kommentar ZPO, ZPO § 1050, no. 11. Note however that GVG § 184 allows the Sorbs to speak Sorbian in the homeland regions of the Sorbian population.
[280] ZPO § 1050.
[281] *Schwab/Walter*, Schiedsgerichtsbarkeit, 7th ed., 2005, ch. 17, no. 17.
[282] *Geimer* in: Zöller, Zivilprozessordnung, 30th ed., 2014, § 1050, no. 6 (principle of subsidiarity).

fort.[283] If the arbitral tribunal has requested a third party to voluntarily provide documentary evidence or testimony, it has no further options to enforce compliance. It has therefore done everything in its power and may request assistance of the court. It is not up to the court to determine whether the requested evidence is necessary, relevant or material to the proceedings. This is left entirely up to the arbitral tribunal. The request will furthermore be denied if the parties by agreement have excluded a particular requested measure.

f) Admissibility of a Request

The main obstacle for any assistance of the court is the fact that ZPO § 1050 provides for the court to only execute requests it considers admissible. It is disputed whether the request must be admissible according to German procedural law applicable in court proceedings or according to the rules of procedure applicable in arbitration. While it might seem logical to apply the more flexible law of arbitral procedure,[284] most commentators refer to German procedural law.[285] Therefore, a request is inadmissible, if it concerns a method of evidence that the ZPO does not provide for. The legislative history on the German arbitration law specifically mentions discovery of documents as an inadmissible method of evidence taking.[286] This is probably meant to correspond to Article 23 of the Hague Evidence Convention and further limits the usefulness of assistance measures by German courts.

To date, there are few relevant court decisions on assistance measures for arbitral tribunals. It remains to be seen whether German courts will follow the restrictive approach of applying their own procedural law or will react more flexibly, allowing for example broadly formulated requests for the production of documents in the possession of third parties.[287]

6. Privileges

In assistance proceedings, a German court will apply the privileges of the ZPO.[288] If no court is involved, it is up to the arbitral tribunal to apply the relevant privileges. For the German law on privileges for parties, an arbitral tribunal would have to refer to the case law on the subject.

---

[283] See *Schlosser* in: Stein/Jonas, Zivilprozessordnung Vol. 10, 23rd ed., 2014, § 1050, no. 12 and *Saenger*, Zivilprozessordnung, 6th ed., 2015, § 1050, no. 4, suggesting that the arbitral tribunal may request the assistance from a court according to ZPO § 1050 not only when the arbitral tribunal is not legally empowered to carry out the performance, but also exceptionally if the performance calls for an unreasonable effort.
[284] In this sense *Schwab/Walter*, Schiedsgerichtsbarkeit, 7th ed., 2005, ch. 17, no. 8; *Hanefeld*, Country Report on Germany in: Weigand (ed.), Practitioner's Handbook on International Arbitration, 2nd ed., 2009, no. 7.142.
[285] See for example *Geimer* in: Zöller, Zivilprozessordnung, 30th ed., 2014, § 1050, no. 6; *Voit* in: Musielak/Voit, Zivilprozessordnung, 12th ed., 2015, § 1050, no. 5; *Albers* in: Baumbach / Lauterbach /Albers / Hartmann, Zivilprozessordnung, 73rd ed., 2015, § 1050, no. 4.
[286] Bill of the New Arbitration Act, BT-Drucksache 13/5274, p. 51; critical *Krapfl*, Die Dokumentenvorlage im Schiedsverfahren, 2007, p. 161.
[287] Reported cases before German courts concerned assistance measures as to the assessment of the amount in dispute (Lower Court of First Instance (AG) Stuttgart, Decision of 8 April 2008 (Docket No. 18 C 7402/07), SchiedsVZ (German Arbitration Journal) 2012, p. 54), and reference of a question to the European Court of Justice (Higher Regional Court (OLG) Frankfurt, Decision of 10 December 2012 (Docket No. 26 SchH 11/10), SchiedsVZ (German Arbitration Journal) 2013, p. 119).
[288] See *supra*, at pp. 79 et seq.

If an arbitral tribunal refused to observe privileges, this might at times result in unfair and unequal treatment of the parties. For this reason, it is necessary to apply the relevant privileges also in arbitral proceedings. Especially in international arbitral proceedings, it may be difficult for an arbitral tribunal to determine which privileges to apply. The parties will usually be from different countries and therefore used to different laws on privilege. In addition, the place of arbitration may provide a third law on privilege. An arbitral tribunal is therefore well advised to consider privileges from all relevant laws on privilege. This follows from the duty of an arbitral tribunal to treat the parties equally.[289] As acknowledged by the IBA Rules on Evidence in Article 9.2 (g), an arbitral tribunal must consider principles of fairness and equality when determining privileges. If a party validly refers to a privilege, the arbitral tribunal is barred from drawing negative inferences from a failure to cooperate.

G. Making of Award and Termination of Proceedings

I. Rules Applicable to Substance of Dispute

1. Determination by the Parties

The decisive principle in ZPO § 1051 regarding rules applicable to the substance of the dispute is party autonomy. The parties are free to choose the applicable rules of law. The term "rules of law" allows the parties to choose the law of a particular country or jurisdiction to govern their entire dispute or to determine the applicability of particular provisions for specific issues. In addition, the parties may refer to the rules of an international convention such as the Vienna Convention for the International Sale of Goods of 11 April 1980 ("CISG") or to international principles such as the UNIDROIT Principles of International Commercial Contracts 2004 ("UNIDROIT Principles"). If the parties have designated the law or legal system of a certain country, this is to be construed as a direct reference to the substantive law of that country and not to its conflict of laws rules unless the parties have agreed otherwise.[290]

The freedom to choose the applicable law is not without limits. If the seat of the arbitration is in Germany, certain mandatory rules of German law which cannot be overridden by private agreement will apply.[291]

2. Determination by the Arbitral Tribunal

If the parties have not determined the applicable law either in their contract or after the dispute has arisen, the arbitral tribunal shall apply the law of the country to which the dispute has the closest or most significant relationship.[292] This deviates from Article 28 (2) of the UNCITRAL Model Law, which refers the arbitral tribunal to the law determined by the conflict of laws rules which it considers applicable.

---

[289] ZPO § 1042 (1) Sentence 1.
[290] ZPO § 1051 (1) sentence 2.
[291] See for example Rome I Regulation, Art. 9; Regulation (EC) No 864/2007 of the European Parliament and of the Council of 11 July 2007 on the law applicable to non-contractual obligations ("Rome II Regulation"), Art. 16.
[292] ZPO § 1051 (2).

G. Making of Award and Termination of Proceedings

Even though the German provision does not refer directly to the conflict of laws rules, it does use the definition for determining the applicable law that follows from German conflict of laws rules. Therefore, arbitral tribunals may follow the Rome I Regulation, especially Art. 4. The closest relationship can be determined by regarding all circumstances of the case, such as the common citizenship of the parties, the place of business, the seat of a company, the place of performance, the location of goods or (im)moveable property, and trade customs.[293] It is disputed, however, whether the arbitral tribunal must strictly follow German choice of law rules regarding criteria on how to assess the closest connection or if it may freely assess the question. The better arguments militate in favor of the latter view.[294]

Even though the arbitral tribunal is limited to applying the law of a specific country whereas the parties may refer to international rules of law, an arbitral tribunal shall in all cases decide in accordance with the terms of the contract and shall take into account trade usages applicable to the transaction.[295] This means that the arbitral tribunal might apply international rules such as the UNIDROIT Principles as trade usages.

Only if there is a specific agreement by the parties, the arbitral tribunal may decide *ex aequo et bono* or as *amiable compositeur*.[296] The arbitral tribunal is then not bound to specific rules of law in reaching a decision, including overriding mandatory provisions, and is only limited according to ZPO § 1051 (4) by the terms of the contract concluded between the parties and the usages of the trade; a further limitation constitutes the *ordre public*.[297] The parties should only empower the arbitral tribunal to decide *ex aequo et bono* if they have full trust in the specific knowledge, judgment and common sense of the arbitral tribunal.

II. Making of the Award

On the making of the award, the German arbitration law contains provisions on majority voting, on a recalcitrant arbitrator and on decisions by the chairperson alone.

1. Majority Voting

According to ZPO § 1052 (1), the parties are free to require an unanimous vote for every decision of the arbitral tribunal or may agree on any type of majority voting. If there is no specific agreement by the parties, in arbitral proceedings with more than one arbitrator, any decision of the arbitral tribunal shall be made by a majority of all its members. If the arbitral tribunal is unable to reach the necessary majority, it has to terminate the proceedings because a continuation has become impossible.[298]

---

[293] *Wilske/Markert* in: Vorwerk/Wolf (eds.), Beck'scher Online-Kommentar ZPO, ZPO § 1051, no. 10.

[294] *Wegen*, Die objektive Anknüpfung von Verträgen in deutschen internationalen Schiedsverfahren nach Inkrafttreten der Rom I-Verordnung, in: Sandrock/Baur/Scholtka/Shapira (eds.), Festschrift Kühne , 2009, pp. 933, 937 *et seq.*; *Schmidt-Ahrendts/Höttler*, Anwendbares Recht bei Schiedsverfahren mit Sitz in Deutschland, SchiedsVZ (German Arbitration Journal) 2011, pp. 267, 271.

[295] ZPO § 1051 (4).

[296] ZPO § 1051 (3).

[297] *Wilske/Markert* in: Vorwerk/Wolf (eds.), Beck'scher Online-Kommentar ZPO, ZPO § 1051, no. 12.

[298] ZPO § 1056 (2) No. 3.

It is up to the arbitral tribunal to decide how it deliberates and votes on issues. It may allow third parties such as an administrative secretary to participate in its deliberations, but a third party may not assume the function of establishing the facts of the case or of evaluating the legal issues for the arbitral tribunal.[299] The deliberations and a vote by the arbitral tribunal are confidential and cannot be examined by a state court in setting aside proceedings.[300]

2. Recalcitrant Arbitrator

If an arbitrator obstructs the proceedings by refusing to take part in a vote, ZPO § 1052 (2) allows the other arbitrators to make a decision without him, subject to any other party agreement on the issue. This is a helpful German addition to the UNCITRAL Model Law. The German wording of ZPO § 1052 (2) reads "one" arbitrator, thus a decision would seem impossible if several arbitrators refused to vote.[301] If, in contrast, two arbitrators bar the third one from consulting and voting, *e.g.* by not giving him an actual chance to influence the content of the award, the arbitral award may be set aside according to ZPO § 1059 (2) No. 1 (d) due to a procedural error.[302]

If the refusal concerns the vote on the arbitral award, the other arbitrators must inform the parties of their intention to vote on the award without the participation of the recalcitrant arbitrator before actually making the decision.[303] This gives the party who appointed the recalcitrant arbitrator a chance to try to convince him to participate or recall him.[304] Regarding other decisions during the proceedings, the arbitrators may make their decision without the recalcitrant arbitrator and may inform the parties of this procedure afterwards, for example in the arbitral award.[305]

To ensure that the award is equally influenced by every member of the tribunal, the chairperson has no tie-breaking vote in case of impasse.[306]

3. Separate, Concurring, and Dissenting Opinions

German arbitration law does not address separate arbitrator opinions, either as dissenting or concurring opinions. This does not concern cases of hidden differing opinions, when decisions are made by a majority vote and the disagreeing arbitrator's opinion is not revealed. A typical dissenting or concurring opinion is a separate document which can be added to the award but is not part of it. The differing opinion, however, can also be integrated into the award.[307]

In international arbitral proceedings, it is important to respect the legal background of the parties, their counsel, and the arbitrators, who might act on the

---

[299] Federal Court of Justice (BGH), Decision of 18 January 1990 (Docket No. III ZR 269/88), Bundesgerichtshofentscheidungen, Vol. 110, pp. 104, 107-8.
[300] *Schwab/Walter*, Schiedsgerichtsbarkeit, 7th ed., 2005, ch. 19, no. 5.
[301] *Münch* in: Münchener Kommentar Zivilprozessordnung, 4th ed., 2013, § 1052, no. 18.
[302] *Wilske/Markert* in: Vorwerk/Wolf (eds.), Beck'scher Online-Kommentar ZPO, ZPO § 1052 no. 23.
[303] ZPO § 1052 (2) Sentence 2.
[304] ZPO §§ 1038, 1039; Bill of the New Arbitration Act, BT-Drucksache 13/5274, p. 54; Higher Regional Court (OLG) Saarbrücken, Decision of 29 October 2002 (Docket No. 4 Sch 2/02), SchiedsVZ (German Arbitration Journal) 2003, p. 92.
[305] ZPO § 1052 (2) Sentence 3; *Schwab/Walter*, Schiedsgerichtsbarkeit, 7th ed., 2005, ch. 19, no. 6.
[306] Bill of the New Arbitration Act, BT-Drucksache 13/5274, p. 54.
[307] For an overview of international practice see *Born*, International Commercial Arbitration, 2nd ed., 2014, pp. 3053 *et seq.*

assumption that dissenting and concurring opinions are allowed and common.[308] Dissenting and concurring opinions are generally allowed if the parties have not expressly excluded them and the confidentiality of deliberations is upheld.[309] In this regard it should be noted that German Judges' Act (*Deutsches Richtergesetz, DRiG*) §43, which prescribes secrecy of deliberations and voting after service has ended, does not directly apply to arbitrators, and it is by all means possible to present a dissenting opinion without violating the confidentiality of deliberations.

At least in extreme cases, where fundamental procedural maxims or the *ordre public* are concerned, arbitrators generally may not be hindered from presenting dissenting opinions, which can help the losing party challenge the award. Also it is a means for the arbitrator to uphold his reputation.[310]

The announcement of a dissenting opinion without an authorization by the parties does not constitute a ground to void the award.[311] Otherwise "guerrilla" arbitrators[312] would only be encouraged to enable their preferred party to override the award.[313] However, a dissenting opinion should not be rendered imprudently, as it may weaken the pacifying effect of an arbitral award.

4. Decisions on Procedure by Chairperson Alone

According to ZPO § 1052 (3), the chairperson of the arbitral tribunal may decide questions of procedure alone if so authorized unanimously by the parties or by all members of the arbitral tribunal. Such an authorization should usually be included in the terms of reference or in an early procedural order. The chairperson is thereby authorized to sign decisions on procedural matters alone after consultation with his co-arbitrators, or to make the decision himself in cases of urgency.

Procedural matters concern questions such as time limits, extension of time limits and arrangements for hearings, but also issues such as determining the language of the proceedings, appointing an expert, issuing an order for interim measures, determining whether to hold an oral hearing or just conducting written proceedings. Each action requires a separate authorization; an "unlimited power of attorney" is not an option.[314] The question of whether an authorization can

---

[308] *Wilske* in: Geimer/Kaissis/Thümmel (eds.), Ars Aequi et Boni in Mundo, Festschrift für Rolf A. Schütze, 2014, pp. 729, 730 *et seq.* with further references to national laws and institutional rules.

[309] *Wilske/Markert* in: Vorwerk/Wolf (eds.), Beck'scher Online-Kommentar ZPO, ZPO § 1052, no. 13; *Böckstiegel/Kröll/Nacimiento* in: Böckstiegel/Kröll/Nacimiento (eds.), Arbitration in Germany – The Model Law in Practice, 2nd ed., 2015, General Overview, no. 109; others demand for an express inclusion, *Schütze*, Das Zustandekommen des Schiedsspruchs, SchiedsVZ (German Arbitration Journal) 2008, pp. 10, 13 *et seq.* with further references, or even the approval of the other arbitrators to protect the confidentiality of deliberations, *Geimer* in: Zöller, Zivilprozessordnung, 30th ed., 2014, § 1052, no. 5.

[310] *Wilske/Markert* in: Vorwerk/Wolf (eds.), Beck'scher Online-Kommentar ZPO, ZPO § 1052, no. 15.

[311] *Wilske/Markert* in: Vorwerk/Wolf (eds.), Beck'scher Online-Kommentar ZPO, ZPO § 1052, no. 16. Different opinion *Schütze*, Das Zustandekommen des Schiedsspruchs, SchiedsVZ (German Arbitration Journal) 2008, pp. 10, 14 with further references.

[312] For the phenomenon of such „guerrilla tactics" see *Horvath/ Wilske* (eds.), Guerrilla Tactics in International Arbitration, 2013, with many references.

[313] *Wilske*, Abweichende Meinung zur *dissenting opinion* in internationalen Schiedsverfahren, in: Geimer/Kaissis/Thümmel (eds.), Ars Aequi et Boni in Mundo, Festschrift für Rolf. A. Schütze, 2014, pp. 729, 734.

[314] *Schwab/Walter*, Schiedsgerichtsbarkeit, 7th ed., 2005, ch. 19, no. 7. For a general authorization, as long as no final facts are evoked, *Münch* in: Münchener Kommentar Zivilprozessordnung, 4th ed., 2013, § 1052, no. 14.

be given in an implied way or even *ex tunc* is not yet settled.[315] The appropriate answer is to first ask for explicit authorization and then allow implicit authorization for subsequent similar procedural issues.[316] An authorization with effect *ex tunc* supports the efficiency of the arbitration where an arbitrator was unable to participate in a vote or was recalcitrant.[317]

III. Form and Contents of Award

1. Required Contents

An arbitral award must be in writing and must state the orders of the arbitral tribunal – the operative part of the award – and the reasons for such orders.

According to ZPO § 1054 (1), an award shall be made in writing and shall be signed personally by the arbitrator or arbitrators.[318] If an arbitrator has refused to participate in deliberating and voting on an award, it is sufficient if the majority of the arbitrators signs the award, as long as the reason for the missing signature is stated.[319] This is in keeping with ZPO § 1052 (2). As long as the award is missing the required number of signatures to express the approval of the final decision, the award is not an arbitral award in the sense of the ZPO.[320] However, a signature can be added to the award later, even during enforcement or setting-aside proceedings.[321]

After the arbitrators sign the award they may only decide unanimously to deliberate again, because they bind themselves to one another upon signing the respective document.[322] After issuing the award, such deliberation is no longer possible.

The arbitral award shall clearly describe the parties and state whether they are claimant or respondent.[323] Additionally, the award should include the names of counsel of the parties. The most important parts of the award are its operative provisions (*Tenor*). The award must show clearly and unambiguously what the arbitral tribunal has decided on.

---

[315] See *Albers* in: Baumbach / Lauterbach /Albers / Hartmann, Zivilprozessordnung, 73rd ed., 2015, § 1052, no. 8; dismissive *Münch* in: Münchener Kommentar Zivilprozessordnung, 4th ed., 2013, § 1052, no. 10; *Saenger*, Zivilprozessordnung, 6th ed., 2015, § 1052, no. 6.

[316] *Wilske/Markert* in: Vorwerk/Wolf (eds.), Beck'scher Online-Kommentar ZPO, ZPO § 1052, no. 32.

[317] *Wilske/Markert* in: Vorwerk/Wolf (eds.), Beck'scher Online-Kommentar ZPO, ZPO § 1052, no. 32.

[318] However, due to the ambiguous wording of ZPO § 1054 (1), it should suffice that each arbitrator signs an identical copy and not all arbitrators have to sign the exact same document, as long as the arbitral award correctly reflects the result of the final session, *Wilske/Markert* in: Vorwerk/Wolf (eds.), Beck'scher Online-Kommentar ZPO, ZPO § 1054, no. 9.

[319] ZPO § 1054 (1) Sentence 2.

[320] Higher Regional Court (OLG) München, Decision of 25 February 2013 (Docket No. 34 Sch 12/12), SchiedsVZ (German Arbitration Journal) 2013, pp. 230, 233; Higher Regional Court (OLG) Düsseldorf, Decision of 14 August 2007 (Docket No. I-4 Sch 2/06), SchiedsVZ (German Arbitration Journal) 2008, pp. 156, 159.

[321] *Von Schlabrendorff/Sessler* in: Böckstiegel/Kröll/Nacimiento (eds.), Arbitration in Germany – The Model Law in Practice, 2nd ed., 2015, ZPO § 1054, no. 18.

[322] *Voit* in: Musielak/Voit, Zivilprozessordnung, 12th ed., 2015, § 1054, no. 10; for a majority vote *Geimer* in: Zöller, Zivilprozessordnung, 30th ed., 2014, § 1052, no. 5.

[323] This is to clarify the identities of the parties, in particular for purposes of enforcement. See Higher Regional Court (OLG) München, Decision of 19 November 2012 (Docket No. 34 Sch 7/11), SchiedsVZ (German Arbitration Journal) 2013, p. 62.

G. Making of Award and Termination of Proceedings

Pursuant to ZPO § 1054 (2), the arbitral award shall state the reasons upon which it is based, unless the parties have agreed that no reasons must be given, or the award is an award on agreed terms under ZPO § 1053. The reasons provided by the arbitral tribunal need not fulfill the same standards that govern judgments of German courts.[324] The arbitral tribunal can therefore freely decide on how to structure its reasons. It must make sure that there are no obvious contradictions in the reasons and that it provides more than just empty phrases to justify its decision.[325] The arbitral tribunal should comment on each claim and each main objection[326], but it is not necessary to discuss the entire pleadings of the parties.[327] If the arbitral tribunal fails to provide reasons or fails to fulfill any of the aforementioned requirements, the award is subject to be set aside according to ZPO § 1059 (2) No. 1(d).

2. Termination of Proceedings by Award

ZPO § 1054 aims to ensure that the termination of the proceedings is evinced by observable events. These observable events are (1) the signatures of the members of the arbitral tribunal under the arbitral award, (2) a statement as to the date of the arbitral award and the place of arbitration in the arbitral award,[328] and (3) the delivery of a signed copy of the award to each party.[329] All three requirements must be fulfilled for the proceedings to be terminated. The arbitral award need not be officially served on the parties. It is sufficient that the award is sent to the parties by post. If the arbitral tribunal wishes to have proof that each party has received the award, it should send the award by certified mail with return receipt (*Einschreiben mit Rückschein*). Since 2005, electronically transmitting the award is also allowed.[330] The arbitral tribunal may send the arbitral award either directly to the parties or to counsel of the parties.[331] If counsel requests the arbitral tribunal to send the award to counsel, the arbitral tribunal should comply.

The date of the award is not of decisive importance but is meant to ease the identification of the award. Since an award is generally circulated for signature by the arbitrators, the relevant date will usually be the day of the last signature by an arbitrator. The relevant place of arbitration is not the place where the award was rendered or deliberated but the official seat of the arbitration according to ZPO § 1043 (1). The determination of the place of arbitration can have important consequences for the applicable law to the proceedings in enforcement or setting aside proceedings and on the place where an arbitral award may be set aside.

---

[324] See *supra*, at p. 90.
[325] Higher Regional Court (OLG) Köln, Decision of 3 June 2003 (Docket No. 9 Sch 23/01), available at www.juris.de.
[326] Since a decision *infra petita* is a reason for setting aside or might call for a supplementary award, *Von Schlabrendorff/Sessler* in: Böckstiegel/Kröll/Nacimiento (eds.), Arbitration in Germany – The Model Law in Practice, 2nd ed., 2015, ZPO § 1054, no. 11.
[327] See for example Federal Court of Justice (BGH), Decision of 26 September 1985 (Docket No. III ZR 16/84), Bundesgerichtshofentscheidungen, Vol., 96, pp. 40, 47; Federal Court of Justice (BGH), Decision of 29 September 1983 (Docket No. III ZR 213/82), Wertpapiermitteilungen 1983, pp. 1207, 1208.
[328] ZPO § 1054 (3).
[329] ZPO § 1054 (4).
[330] Bill of the Judicial Communication Act, BT-Drucksache 15/4067, pp. 8, 36.
[331] *Schwab/Walter*, Schiedsgerichtsbarkeit, 7th ed., 2005, ch. 20, no. 11.

IV. Settlement

1. Types of Settlement

According to ZPO § 1053, the parties may end the proceedings by settling the dispute at any time during the proceedings before the final award is rendered. Although not explicitly stated in the German arbitration law, arbitral tribunals with a German background will likely encourage the parties to settle their dispute as it is the traditional practice of German judges.[332] A settlement by the parties can occur with or without participation of the arbitral tribunal.

If the parties reach a settlement without participation of the arbitral tribunal, they should additionally agree on the termination of the proceedings and inform the arbitral tribunal accordingly.[333] The arbitral tribunal will then issue an order for the termination of the proceedings. German arbitration law does not require a specific form for settlements without participation of the arbitral tribunal. However, for a private settlement to be valid it is necessary that both parties make concessions, if only in minor points.[334]

The other possibility is for both parties to request the arbitral tribunal to record their settlement in the form of an "award on agreed terms" or "award by consent".[335] The main goal of this option is to provide the parties with an enforceable award pursuant to the New York Convention, even if they have settled their dispute. Only if the settlement has been recorded in the form of an award on agreed terms which states that it is an award can it be declared enforceable.[336] In case the parties have not requested an award on agreed terms, the settlement agreement will not be enforceable under ZPO § 1060 or the New York Convention. It may however be converted into an execution title pursuant to the procedure in ZPO § 796a (*Anwaltsvergleich*), provided that it is signed by the attorneys of record for the parties and the respective debtor expressly submits to immediate execution (*Unterwerfung unter die sofortige Zwangsvollstreckung*).[337] .

If the parties do not state their intention as to whether they wish to have an award on agreed terms, it is up to the arbitral tribunal to determine how the parties want to proceed: either by simply terminating the proceedings or by recording the settlement in an award on agreed terms. The arbitral tribunal must ask the parties what their preference is.[338]

---

[332] Also see in this tradition Art. 32 (1) DIS Rules (*"At every stage of the proceedings, the arbitral tribunal should seek to encourage an amicable settlement of the dispute or of individual issues in dispute."*).

[333] ZPO § 1056 (2) No. 2.

[334] Higher Regional Court (OLG) München, Decision of 26 July 2005 (Docket No. 31 Wx 50/50), GmbH Rundschau, 2005, p. 1568; *Wilske/Markert* in: Vorwerk/Wolf (eds.), Beck'scher Online-Kommentar ZPO, ZPO § 1053, no. 4; critical: *Von Schlabrendorff/Sessler* in: Böckstiegel/Kröll/Nacimiento (eds.), Arbitration in Germany – The Model Law in Practice, 2nd ed., 2015, ZPO § 1053, no. 8-9; *Schroeter*, Der Schiedsspruch mit vereinbartem Wortlaut als Formäquivalent zur notariellen Beurkundung, SchiedsVZ (German Arbitration Journal) 2006, pp. 298, 303.

[335] ZPO § 1053 (1).

[336] Higher Regional Court (OLG) Frankfurt, Decision of 14 March 2003 (Docket No. 20 Sch 01/02), SchiedsVZ (German Arbitration Journal) 2003, p. 288.

[337] See Chapter I. N. II. 2. See also *Wilske/Markert* in: Vorwerk/Wolf (eds.), Beck'scher Online-Kommentar ZPO, ZPO § 1053 no.7; *Von Schlabrendorff/Sessler* in: Böckstiegel/Kröll/Nacimiento (eds.), Arbitration in Germany – The Model Law in Practice, 2nd ed., 2015, ZPO § 1053, no. 17, noting however that the enforcement of such a settlement on the international level raises difficult questions.

[338] *Schwab/Walter*, Schiedsgerichtsbarkeit, 7th ed., 2005, ch. 23, no. 3.

2. Form and Contents of Award on Agreed Terms

An award on agreed terms shall fulfill the same requirements as any other arbitral award. Therefore, ZPO § 1053 (2) refers to the formal requirements of ZPO § 1054 and requires that the award on agreed terms state that it is an award. As a consequence, an award on agreed terms has the same effect as any other award on the merits of the case.

Settlement and award on agreed terms can concern the entire dispute or involve separable parts of the dispute, *i.e.* one of several claims. It may also solely cover the costs of the dispute. According to Article 30 (1) of the UNCITRAL Model Law an arbitral tribunal may reject the request for an award on agreed terms if it objects to the content of the settlement. The German legislator has narrowed this language to only allow the arbitral tribunal to reject a request if the content of the settlement agreement is contrary to public policy.[339] Public policy includes the question of arbitrability, as well as a violation of law or morality (*e.g.* money-laundering).[340]

The settlement itself may contain an allocation of costs, which may be included in an award on agreed terms as well. If the parties cannot agree on how to distribute the costs, it will be up to the arbitral tribunal to decide on the costs in a final award. The arbitral tribunal may rely on ZPO § 98, which provides that in the event of a settlement, each party shall bear its own costs and that the costs of the court will be divided equally between the parties.[341]

ZPO § 1053 (3) concerns a German particularity. It states that an award on agreed terms fulfills the requirements of a notarial act, which may be relevant for the effectiveness of a declaration in the settlement agreement. Additionally, ZPO § 1053 (4) provides that an award by consent may be declared enforceable by a public notary in addition to the competent court. The public notary may refuse enforcement of the award only if the award on agreed terms violates public policy and not for reasons listed in ZPO § 1059.[342] An application to a public notary may be less costly than an application to the court, but does not have the preclusive effect on an application for setting aside as stated in ZPO § 1059 (3) Sentence 4.

V. Termination of Proceedings

1. Types of Awards

According to ZPO § 1056 (1), the arbitral proceedings are terminated by a final award. As in the UNCITRAL Model Law and in most other national arbitration laws, the German arbitration law does not define the term award. To distinguish between final awards, interim or interlocutory awards and partial awards, German commentators generally refer to the rules of German civil procedure in ZPO §§ 300 to 305.[343]

---

[339] ZPO § 1053 (1).
[340] Civil Code (BGB) §§ 134 and 138; *Schwab/Walter*, Schiedsgerichtsbarkeit, 7th ed., 2005, ch. 23, no. 10.
[341] *Schwab/Walter*, Schiedsgerichtsbarkeit, 7th ed., 2005, p. ch. 33, no. 19.
[342] ZPO § 1053 (4) Sentence 2.
[343] See *supra*, at p. 90.

a) Final Award

A final award can be a procedural award, which denies the claim as inadmissible, or an award on the merits, which disposes of all of the issues of the case.

b) Partial Award

A partial award, on the other hand, finally disposes of one or more specific issues of the case.[344] Such an award should state that it is a partial award and must fulfill the requirements of ZPO § 1054. It can be challenged under ZPO § 1059, and enforced according to ZPO §§ 1060, 1061.

ZPO § 302 concerns partial awards in cases of set-off. Two cases must be distinguished, concerning whether or not the arbitral tribunal is competent to decide on the claim brought by the respondent for set-off purposes. If the arbitral tribunal is competent, it may first decide on the principal claim, and then move on to the respondent's claim. A decision granting a principal claim, but stating that the respondent's claim is still to be decided upon, is not an enforceable partial award, because the set-off question is still unresolved. If, on the other hand, the arbitral tribunal decides on the principal claim and states that it is not competent to hear the respondent's claim, such an award is final and enforceable. The respondent must then raise his claim and set-off argument in the enforcement proceedings.

c) Interim or Interlocutory Award

While a partial award finally disposes of one or more separable issues of the case, an interim award concerns particular issues, usually procedural ones, which are relevant to the dispute as a whole.[345] The German arbitration law refers to one type of interim award in ZPO § 1040 (3): the arbitral tribunal may rule on its own jurisdiction in an interim award. Even though such a preliminary ruling might be termed interim "award" and might fulfill the formal requirements of ZPO § 1054, it is not a final award since it does not finally dispose of any specific issues of the case and therefore, is not capable of being enforced. Instead, such an interim award simply binds the arbitral tribunal for the remaining proceedings. If a party wishes to challenge such an interim award, it must wait until the final award has been rendered and challenge the entire award. However, if the arbitral tribunal affirms its jurisdiction in an interim award, parties may turn to the state courts with a request to decide on the tribunal's jurisdiction within one month after receiving written notice of the tribunal's jurisdictional ruling.[346]

It is also an interim award if the arbitral tribunal first decides on the issue of liability, and then on the amount of damages in separate awards.[347] In this case which is similar to an interlocutory judgment on the basis of a claim in German state court proceedings,[348] the first award on the issue of liability is not enforceable on its own, but the arbitral tribunal is bound by its decision. Yet, the dispute's outcome is not finally determined, since the arbitral tribunal may still dismiss

---

[344] ZPO § 301 (1).
[345] *Hanefeld*, Country Report on Germany in: Weigand (ed.), Practitioners Handbook on International Arbitration, 2nd ed., 2009, no. 7.151.
[346] ZPO § 1040 (3) Sentence 2.
[347] ZPO § 304.
[348] See *supra*, at p. 90.

the entire claim if it concludes that the claimed amount is not justified because no damage occurred.[349]

2. Order Terminating the Proceedings

The proceedings may either be terminated by a final award or by an order of the arbitral tribunal according to ZPO § 1056 (2). This provision enumerates the cases in which the arbitral tribunal shall order the termination of the proceedings.[350] Any termination will depend on the parties' conduct:

(i) The claimant fails to communicate his statement of claim in accordance with ZPO § 1046 and does not show sufficient cause for the delay according to ZPO § 1048 (4);[351]
(ii) the claimant withdraws his claim, unless the respondent objects and the arbitral tribunal recognize a legitimate interest on his part in obtaining a final award resolving the dispute;[352]
(iii) the parties agree on the termination of the proceedings;[353]
(iv) the parties refuse to continue the proceedings although the arbitral tribunal has so requested; or[354]
(v) the arbitral tribunal finds that the continuation of the proceedings has for any other reason become impossible.[355]

According to ZPO § 1056 (3), the order terminating the proceedings also terminates the mandate of the arbitral tribunal. The arbitral tribunal only remains competent to decide on the costs of the proceedings according to ZPO § 1057 (2), to correct and interpret the award according to ZPO § 1058, and to resume the arbitral proceedings upon remittal of the court according to ZPO § 1059 (4).

VI. Decision on Costs

Although the UNCITRAL Model Law does not address the issue of costs, the German legislator included guidelines on the costs of arbitration in ZPO § 1057. Firstly, the parties are free to agree on the allocation of costs themselves. If there is no agreement of the parties, the arbitral tribunal shall decide in an award on how to allocate the costs between the parties.

1. Discretion of the Arbitral Tribunal

The arbitral tribunal is not bound to specific rules when deciding on how to allocate the costs of the arbitration, but instead has broad discretion. It should take into account the specific circumstances of the case, especially who prevailed

---

[349] Higher Regional Court (OLG) Frankfurt, Decision of 10 May 2007 (Docket No. 26 Sch 20/06), SchiedsVZ (German Arbitration Journal) 2007, p. 278.
[350] It is disputed whether the order terminating the proceedings can be set aside under ZPO § 1059. The prevailing opinion rejects this view on the grounds that termination orders do not constitute arbitral awards, and, even if they are considered as such, their effects are comparable to an interim award and do not settle the legal dispute entirely or partly, see *Haas*, Aufhebungsklage und Beendigungsbeschluss nach § 1056 Abs. 2 ZPO, SchiedsVZ (German Arbitration Journal) 2010, pp. 286 *et seq.*
[351] ZPO § 1056 (2) No. 1(a).
[352] ZPO § 1056 (2) No. 1(b).
[353] ZPO § 1056 (2) No. 2.
[354] ZPO § 1056 (2) No. 3.
[355] ZPO § 1056 (2) No. 3.

on the principal issues.[356] Even though it is a general principle in German civil procedure that the costs will be allowed in proportion to the outcome,[357] this need not necessarily be the only basis for the decision of the arbitral tribunal. It can take other circumstances into account as well. For example, even if a party is successful with all its claims, but delayed the proceedings without sufficient cause, the arbitral tribunal may order it to bear part of the costs.

The arbitral tribunal can only allocate the costs between the parties. This leads to a claim by one party against the other party. An arbitral award cannot establish a claim of a third party against the parties to the arbitral proceedings.

2. Costs of the Arbitration

The costs of the arbitration include (i) costs of the arbitrators, such as fees and administrative costs, (ii) costs of the parties, such as travelling costs to an oral hearing, (iii) costs for the taking of evidence, such as costs for witnesses or experts, and (iv) lawyer's fees or other fees for representation.

The arbitrators may not decide on their fees themselves in the arbitral award, unless they have been authorized to do so by the parties. If the arbitral tribunal were to decide on the amount of fees itself without the consent of the parties, this would violate public policy and make the award unenforceable.[358] The payment of the advance on costs in equal shares can include the implied authorization by the parties for the arbitral tribunal to allocate the advance payment as it sees fit, if the advance constitutes the agreed upon full amount for fees.[359] This procedure does not violate public policy. Usually, the arbitrators will reach an agreement with the parties as to the amount of their fees at the beginning of the proceedings. If the arbitrators' fees depend on the amount in dispute, the arbitral tribunal must refrain from determining the amount in dispute, as that would be considered a conflict of interest and therefore contrary to public policy.[360]

An arbitral tribunal usually requires the parties to pay an advance on costs. If the parties refuse to pay an advance on costs, the only sanction available to the arbitrators is to suspend the proceedings. For example, if the advance was due for the taking of evidence, the arbitral tribunal may not proceed with an award without the taking of evidence.[361] If the arbitrators have rendered an award without an advance on costs, they must apply to the courts to claim their fees against the parties. On the other hand, if the parties have paid too much in advance and the arbitral tribunal refuses to reimburse them, the parties must also claim reimbursement from the arbitrators in court.

---

[356] ZPO § 1057 (1) Sentence 2.
[357] See *supra*, at p. 11.
[358] Federal Court of Justice (BGH), Decision of 7 March 1985 (Docket No. III ZR 169/83) Bundesgerichtshofentscheidungen, Vol. 94, p. 92; Federal Court of Justice, (BGH), Decision of 25 November 1976 (Docket No. III ZR 112/74), Juristenzeitung, 1977, p. 185.
[359] Higher Regional Court (OLG) Dresden, Decision of 28 October 2003 (Docket No. 11 Sch 09/03), SchiedsVZ (German Arbitration Journal) 2004, p. 44.
[360] Federal Court of Justice (BGH), Decision of 28 March 2012 (Docket No. III ZB 63/10 (KG)), Neue Juristische Wochenschrift, 2012, p. 1811; for a critical analysis see *Wolff*, Streitwertfestsetzung bei wertabhängiger Schiedsrichtervergütung – Schiedsrichter in eigener Sache?, SchiedsVZ (German Arbitration Journal) 2006, pp. 131 *et seq.*
[361] Federal Court of Justice (BGH), Decision of 7 March 1985 (Docket No. III ZR 169/83), Neue Juristische Wochenschrift, 1985, pp. 1903, 1904-1905.

Attorney's fees must only be reimbursed if they were necessary for the proper pursuit of the claim or defense.[362] Parties generally cannot be expected to conduct an arbitration without professional legal assistance.[363] If counsel's remuneration is based on hourly charged rates, as is common in international practice, the fees are reimbursable if the parties agreed on a reasonable hourly rate and the effort spent by counsel was necessary.[364] So far it is unclear whether contingency fees may be reimbursed. In its decision on costs the arbitral tribunal should respect such a fee arrangement, as a party should not be able to benefit from the fact that the other party can only pursue its rights because of the fee arrangement. Whether the whole amount of a contingency fee is reimbursable or not depends on the circumstances of the case but should be answered in the positive when the fees are reasonable compared to the fees of the other party's counsel.[365]

The arbitral tribunal must decide on the actual amount of the costs of the arbitration. Anything less is not a final award, but must later be specified as to the amount. Therefore, the arbitral tribunal should require the parties to submit statements of costs, which should include all legal and other costs incurred by the parties. It should inform the parties that any costs not mentioned in the statement of costs will not be considered. Legal costs of parties will as a general rule only include outside counsel, not in-house counsel.[366] This does not exclude that good arguments may be raised in favor of reimbursement of costs for in-house counsel.[367]

While ZPO § 1057 (1) concerns the general ratio of costs between the parties, ZPO § 1057 (2) concerns the actual amount. If the costs of the arbitration have not been fixed as to their actual amount by the time the arbitral tribunal renders its final award, the arbitral tribunal must decide on the amount in a separate award at a later date.[368] A party may request such an additional decision on costs under ZPO § 1058 (1) No. 3.

---

[362] ZPO § 1057 (1).
[363] *Von Schlabrendorff/Sessler* in: Böckstiegel/Kröll/Nacimiento (eds.), Arbitration in Germany – The Model Law in Practice , 2nd ed., 2015, ZPO § 1057, no. 19.
[364] Higher Regional Court (OLG) München, Decision of 11 April 2012 (Docket No. 34 Sch 21/11), SchiedsVZ (German Arbitration Journal) 2012, p. 156 on ICC Rules; Higher Regional Court (OLG) München, Decision of 23 July 2012 (Docket No. 34 Sch 19/11), SchiedsVZ (German Arbitration Journal) 2012, p. 282 on DIS Rules; *Saenger/Uphoff*, Erstattungsfähigkeit anwaltlicher Zeithonorare, Neue Juristische Wochenschrift, 2014, pp. 1412, 1413; *Risse/Altenkirch*, Kostenerstattung im Schiedsverfahren: fünf Probleme aus der Praxis, SchiedsVZ (German Arbitration Journal) 2012, pp. 5, 11; *Von Schlabrendorff/Sessler* in: Böckstiegel/Kröll/Nacimiento (eds.), Arbitration in Germany – The Model Law in Practice (, 2nd ed., 2015, ZPO § 1057, nos. 21 *et seq.*
[365] *Wilske/Markert* in: Vorwerk/Wolf (eds.), Beck'scher Online-Kommentar ZPO, ZPO § 1057, no. 6; see also *Adem Dogan v. Turkmenistan*, ICSID Award of 12 August 2014 (Docket No. ICSID ARB/09/9), no. 307; *Peterson*, In New Ruling – Contingency Fees Can Be Reimbursed, Investment Arbitration Reporter, 19 August 2014, available at www.iareporter.com. Critical *Schlosser* in: Stein/Jonas, Zivilprozessordnung Vol. 10, 23rd ed., 2014, § 1057, no. 12.
[366] *Hanefeld*, Country Report on Germany in: Weigand (ed.), Practitioners Handbook on International Arbitration, 2nd ed., 2009, no. 7.216.
[367] For example in case a party decides to use its in-house counsel as opposed to an external counsel in order to reduce the arbitration costs, see *Risse/Altenkirch*, Kostenerstattung im Schiedsverfahren: fünf Probleme aus der Praxis, SchiedsVZ (German Arbitration Journal) 2012, pp. 5, 12 et seq.
[368] ZPO § 1057 (2) Sentence 2.

3. Costs of a Procedural Award

If the arbitral tribunal declares itself incompetent to decide the dispute in a procedural award, many commentators assume that it does not have the power to decide on the costs. Instead, a national court would have to reach a decision on the costs.[369] Other commentators argue that the German arbitration law does give the arbitral tribunal the right to render an award on costs even if it declares itself incompetent in a procedural award.[370] This follows from the fact that ZPO § 1057 allows the arbitral tribunal to render a separate award on costs. This is a sensible solution, because it makes further court proceedings solely on the issue of costs unnecessary.

To ensure that the arbitral tribunal is competent to decide on the costs even if it declares itself incompetent on the substance, the parties have two options. If a respondent challenges the jurisdiction of the arbitral tribunal, he can state at the same time that he submits to the jurisdiction of the arbitral tribunal on the issue of costs. Alternatively, the parties may agree in a separate arbitration agreement to let the arbitral tribunal decide on the costs, even if it determines that it does not have jurisdiction.

If the proceedings are not terminated by an award but by an order of the arbitral tribunal according to ZPO § 1056 (2) – such as if the claimant withdraws his claim – the other party can request a decision on the costs.

4. Enforceability of Decision on Costs

A decision on costs is enforceable, but can only be enforced in conjunction with a main award. This is so because the decision on costs follows from the decision on the issues in dispute, and therefore depends on whether the main decision is set aside or not.[371] If the arbitral award is limited to a decision on costs – for example, if the parties settled the rest of their dispute – such a decision can be enforceable as well, but only if it fulfills the requirements of ZPO § 1054 regarding signature of all arbitrators and inclusion of reasoning.[372]

An award on costs may be challenged like any other award. If an award includes decisions on substantive issues and on costs, it is possible to challenge only the decision on costs, which is separable from the other parts of the decision.[373] If an award on the substance is set aside, this includes the decision on costs, as it forms part of the arbitral award.[374] If a party still wishes to have costs from the first arbitral proceedings reimbursed, it must claim these costs in the following arbitral proceedings or court proceedings relating to the dispute. If there are no specific circumstances the new court or tribunal can rely on, it should divide the costs in half.[375]

---

[369] *Schwab/Walter*, Schiedsgerichtsbarkeit, 7th ed., 2005, ch. 33, no. 4.
[370] *Raeschke-Kessler/Berger*, Recht und Praxis des Schiedsverfahrens, 3rd ed., 1999, nos. 889-890.
[371] *Schwab/Walter*, Schiedsgerichtsbarkeit, 7th ed., 2005, ch. 33, no. 8.
[372] Higher Regional Court (OLG) Cologne, Decision of 15 January 2004 (Docket No. 9 Sch 17/03), SchiedsVZ (German Arbitration Journal) 2004, p. 269.
[373] *Hanefeld*, Country Report on Germany in: Weigand (ed.), Practitioners Handbook on International Arbitration, 2nd ed., 2009, no. 7.218; *von Schlabrendorff/Sessler* in: Böckstiegel/Kröll/Nacimiento (eds.), Arbitration in Germany – The Model Law in Practice, 2nd ed., 2015, ZPO § 1057, no. 43.
[374] Federal Court of Justice (BGH), Decision of 29 January 2009 (Docket No. III ZB 88/07), SchiedsVZ (German Arbitration Journal) 2009, p. 176.
[375] *Schwab/Walter*, Schiedsgerichtsbarkeit, 7th ed., 2005, ch. 33, no. 12.

If the arbitral tribunal refuses to decide on the costs, this results in the termination of the arbitration agreement and allows a party to refer the decision on costs to a court. The party claiming costs may then do so in separate court proceedings or in the proceedings concerning the enforcement of the award.[376]

VII. Correction and Interpretation of Award; Additional Award

1. Formal Requirements

ZPO § 1058 concerns the correction and interpretation of awards, as well as additional awards. Once an award has been rendered, the parties have one month after receipt of the award to make a request for correction or interpretation of the award.[377] The parties may also agree on other time limits for requests according to ZPO § 1058.

Upon request the arbitral tribunal may:
(i) correct in the award any errors in computation, any clerical or typographical errors or any errors of a similar nature,[378]
(ii) give an interpretation of a specific point or part of the award,[379] or
(iii) make an additional award as to claims presented in the arbitral proceedings but omitted from the award.[380]

The arbitral tribunal has one month to decide on cases of correction and interpretation of an award, and two months to render an additional award.[381] These time limits for the arbitral tribunal are not binding and can be extended by the arbitral tribunal.[382]

If a correction is necessary, the arbitral tribunal may correct the error on its own initiative.[383] In case the correction was requested by one party, the other party has to be heard before the tribunal decides on the request.[384] If the tribunal acts on its own initiative, it may but must not consult with the parties.[385] The interpretation of an award and the additional award are only possible if so requested by a party. The arbitral tribunal cannot act on its own initiative. According to ZPO § 1058 (5) the rules regarding the making of an award under ZPO § 1054 are also applicable to the correction or interpretation of an award or to an additional award. This does not mean that the correction or interpretation of an award is in itself a separate award. Instead, such actions of the arbitral tribunal are part of

---

[376] *Schwab/Walter*, Schiedsgerichtsbarkeit, 7th ed., 2005, ch. 33, nos. 10-11.
[377] ZPO § 1058 (2).
[378] ZPO § 1058 (1) No. 1.
[379] ZPO § 1058 (1) No. 2.
[380] ZPO § 1058 (1) No. 3.
[381] ZPO § 1058 (3).
[382] For the one month time limit as a general *ratio* Münch in: Münchener Kommentar Zivilprozessordnung, 4th ed., 2013, § 1058, no. 6.
[383] ZPO § 1058 (4). However, the tribunal is only entitled to make a correction if the error constitutes a mistake on the content of the declaration as in BGB § 119 (1) case 2 (*Erklärungsirrtum*), see, DIS Case No. SV-B-652/06, SchiedsVZ (German Arbitration Journal) 2008, p. 207, 208.
[384] *Von Schlabrendorff/Sessler* in: Böckstiegel/Kröll/Nacimiento (eds.), Arbitration in Germany – The Model Law in Practice, 2nd ed., 2015, ZPO § 1058, no. 4; Bill of the Arbitration Law Reform Act, BT-Drucksache 13/5274, p. 58.
[385] Higher Regional Court (OLG) Frankfurt, Decision of 17 May 2005 (Docket No. 2 Sch 2/03), SchiedsVZ (German Arbitration Journal) 2005, p. 311, 312; critical: *Von Schlabrendorff/Sessler* in: Böckstiegel/Kröll/Nacimiento (eds.), Arbitration in Germany – The Model Law in Practice, 2nd ed., 2015, ZPO § 1058, no. 5.

the original award.[386] All general procedural rules also apply to the procedure of correcting and interpreting an award, as well as to making an additional award. This means that upon a request according to ZPO § 1058, the other party must be notified and heard on the issue.

2. Correction and Interpretation

A correction of the award according to ZPO § 1058 (1) No. 1 is only possible if the mistake is obvious. Any change to the arbitral award is only a correction if the written part is thereby adapted to the original intention of the arbitral tribunal.[387] Any changes that amount to a change of the intention of the arbitral tribunal are no longer a mere correction of the award. Such a corrected award may be set aside because of an incorrect procedure according to ZPO § 1059 (2) No. 1(d).[388] Evident mistakes in writing may even be corrected by state courts under narrow circumstances in enforcement proceedings.[389]

If the award is uncertain or ambiguous or contains contradictions that cannot be corrected under No. 1, a party may request interpretation of the award under ZPO § 1058 (1) No. 2. The rule regarding interpretation of an award hopes to help avoid proceedings for the setting aside of an award.[390] The arbitral tribunal should handle requests for correction or interpretation of the award carefully, because the parties may abuse this option if they are not satisfied with the result of the arbitral proceedings in the award. Any correction and/or interpretation is typically made by an addendum to the original award.[391]

3. Additional Award

An additional award is necessary if claims presented in the proceedings were not decided on in the award. The award to date is then only a partial and incomplete award and must be supplemented by the additional award. An additional award can, for example, be necessary if the arbitral tribunal did not decide on the costs of the proceedings in the original award.[392] An additional award is also possible as a separate award, for example solely on costs if the arbitral proceedings are terminated by an order under ZPO § 1056 (2). Under no circumstances may the additional award lead to a correction of the content of the award and represent a "mini appeal".[393] The proceedings regarding the additional award must conform fully to the procedural rules for an award.

---

[386] *Schwab/Walter*, Schiedsgerichtsbarkeit, 7th ed., 2005, ch. 21, no. 18.
[387] *Christ*, Berichtigung, Auslegung und Ergänzung des Schiedsspruchs, 2008, pp. 83 *et seq.*
[388] *Schwab/Walter*, Schiedsgerichtsbarkeit, 7th ed., 2005, ch. 21, no. 14.
[389] Higher Regional Court (OLG) München, Decision of 29 October 2009 (Docket No. 34 Sch 15/09), Beck Rechtsprechung, 2009, 86918. see also *Schwab/Walter*, Schiedsgerichtsbarkeit, 7th ed., 2005, ch. 28, no. 7.
[390] Bill of the New Arbitration Act, BT-Drucksache 13/5274, p. 58; *Schütze*, Die gerichtliche Überprüfung von Entscheidungen des Schiedsgerichts, SchiedsVZ (German Arbitration Journal) 2009, pp. 241, 245.
[391] *Christ*, Berichtigung, Auslegung und Ergänzung des Schiedsspruchs, 2008, p. 288.
[392] *Christ*, Berichtigung, Auslegung und Ergänzung des Schiedsspruchs, 2008, pp. 131 *et seq.*
[393] *Wilske/Markert* in: Vorwerk/Wolf (eds.), Beck'scher Online-Kommentar ZPO, ZPO § 1058, no. 10; differently *Schroth*, Die „kleine Berufung" gegen Schiedsurteile im deutschen Recht, SchiedsVZ (German Arbitration Journal) 2007, pp. 291, 293 *et seq.*

H. Recourse against Award

I. Reasons for Setting Aside an Award

According to ZPO § 1055 an arbitral award has the same final effect as a court judgment (*res judicata*). As for final judgments under ZPO §§ 578, 579, the reasons for setting aside an award are – subject to the *ordre public* exception – limited to procedural irregularities and aim to ensure minimum requirements of procedural fairness and due process as constitutionally guaranteed rights of effective legal protection.[394] A court may not review the substantive part of an award in setting aside proceedings.[395]

A party who wishes to have an award set aside may either request the setting aside of an award according to ZPO § 1059 or may wait until the other party requests enforcement of the award under ZPO § 1060 for domestic awards or ZPO § 1061 for foreign awards and then claim grounds for refusing enforcement. The grounds for setting aside an award under ZPO § 1059 closely follow Art. 34 of the UNCITRAL Model Law and mirror those of Article V of the New York Convention. This has a positive effect for international participants, who can rely on the fact that the German grounds for setting aside an award will be the same as those under the internationally accepted New York Convention. The grounds under which an arbitral award can be set aside are limited to those enumerated in ZPO § 1059 (2) and will be interpreted narrowly by German courts to give the award full effect. While a party may request the setting aside of a procedural award denying jurisdiction, just as it may request the setting aside of an award on the merits, it cannot base its request on the ground that the arbitral tribunal erroneously denied its jurisdiction, since this is not a statutory reason for setting aside an award.[396]

1. Invalid Arbitration Agreement

An award can be set aside under ZPO § 1059 (2) No. 1(a) if the arbitration agreement was invalid. One reason for the invalidity of an arbitration agreement is if a party to the arbitration agreement did not have the capacity to conclude the agreement. According to ZPO § 1059 (2) No. 1(a), the capacity of a party is determined by the law applicable to the parties themselves. Under Artt. 7 (1), 12 of the Introductory Law of the Civil Code (*Einführungsgesetz zum Bürgerlichen Gesetzbuch, EGBGB*) this means that the law of their nationality applies. For German nationals, therefore, German domestic law covers the issue of capacity. For legal entities (*juristische Personen*) the rules of capacity at the law of their seat (according to the traditional German theory)[397] or of their place of incorporation (according to the case law of the European Court of Justice)[398] apply. Whether the person who signed the arbitration agreement had power of attorney to do so, is a separate question. This

---

[394] Wilske/Markert,National Reports – Germany , in: Mistelis/Shore (eds.), World Arbitration Reporter , Vol. I, 2nd ed., 2014, p. GER-45.
[395] No *révision au fond*; see *infra*, at p. 181.
[396] Federal Court of Justice (BGH), Decision of 6 June 2002 (Docket No. III ZB 44/01), SchiedsVZ (German Arbitration Journal) 2003, p. 39.
[397] *Schwab/Walter*, Schiedsgerichtsbarkeit, 7th ed., 2005, ch. 44, no. 18.
[398] *Kamer van Koophandel en Fabrieken voor Amsterdam v. Inspire Art Ltd.*, Decision of 30 September 2003 (Docket No. C-167/01), ECR 2003 I-10155; *Überseering BV v. Nordic Construction Company Baumanagement GmbH (NCC)*, Decision of 5 November 2002 (Docket No. C-208/00) ECR

depends on the law applicable according to the conflict of law rules.[399] Whether parties other than the signatories of the arbitration agreement can be bound by the agreement depends on the law applicable to the arbitration agreement.[400]

An arbitration agreement may be invalid for a number of other reasons. It might not have been validly concluded, or it might have been terminated, or it might have been challenged successfully because it was concluded with fraudulent intent (*Arglist*) or under threat (*Bedrohung*).[401]

It is important to note that an arbitration agreement may also be concluded if the parties make submissions to the arbitral tribunal without objecting to its jurisdiction.[402] Also, the invalidity of the arbitration agreement as a ground to set the award aside can be considered waived because of breach of good faith, if the complaining party relied on the validity of the arbitration agreement before the proceedings started, or participated in the arbitral proceedings without reservation.[403]

Even if the arbitral tribunal has explicitly declared the arbitration agreement to be valid, the German court is not bound by this decision. It may still decide to set aside an award based on ZPO § 1059 (2) No. 1(a).[404]

According to ZPO § 1040 (2), a party has to object to the jurisdiction of the arbitral tribunal at the latest in its statement of defense.[405] The Federal Court of Justice has held that the failure of a party to challenge before the courts the positive decision of an arbitral tribunal on its jurisdiction precludes it from relying on the ground of an invalid arbitration agreement in setting aside or enforcement proceedings.[406] Nevertheless, a party only loses its right to object to the validity of the arbitration agreement in setting aside proceedings, if it knew or should have known of the reasons for invalidity at an earlier point in time.

2. Due Process

Further grounds for setting aside are fulfilled if a party was not given proper notice of the appointment of an arbitrator or of the arbitral proceedings or was otherwise unable to present its case.[407] ZPO § 1059 (2) No. 1(b) therefore refers to the important right to be heard or the right of due process. There may be some difficulty in deciding whether ZPO § 1059 (2) No. 1(b) or § 1059 (2) No. 2(b) applies, since the right to be heard is also part of the concept of public policy. A differ-

---

2002 I-09919; *Centros Ltd v. Erhvervs- og Selskabsstyrelsen*, Decision of 9 March 1999 (Docket No. C-212/97) ECR 1999 I-01459; the decisions are available at http://www.curia.eu.int.

[399] *Schwab/Walter*, Schiedsgerichtsbarkeit, 7th ed., 2005ch. 44, no. 19.

[400] *Schwab/Walter*, Schiedsgerichtsbarkeit, 7th ed., 2005, ch. 44, no. 24.

[401] *Schwab/Walter*, Schiedsgerichtsbarkeit, 7th ed., 2005, ch. 44, no. 25.

[402] ZPO § 1031 (6).

[403] *Wilske/Markert* in: Vorwerk/Wolf (eds.), Beck'scher Online-Kommentar ZPO, ZPO § 1059, no. 38.

[404] Higher Regional Court (OLG) Celle, Decision of 4 September 2003 (Docket No. 8 Sch 11/02), Journal of International Dispute Resolution, 2004, pp. 95, 98 (in English language) with note by *Wegen/Wilske*, p. 77.

[405] In certain constellations, however, the objection may still be raised at a later point, *i.e.* immediately after the composition of the arbitral tribunal, cf. *Wilske/Markert* in: Vorwerk/Wolf (eds.), Beck'scher Online-Kommentar ZPO, ZPO § 1040, no. 13; arguing in favor of an even later possibility to object but without convincing justification: *Schwab/Walter*, Schiedsgerichtsbarkeit, 7th ed., 2005, ch. 24, no. 8.

[406] Federal Court of Justice (BGH), Decision of 27 March 2003 (Docket No. III ZB 83/02), Zeitschrift für Wirtschafts- und Bankrecht, 2003, pp. 2433 et seq.

[407] ZPO § 1059 (2) No. 1(b).

H. Recourse against Award

entiation may be necessary because No. 1(b) requires the request of a party and No. 2(b) is to be considered by the court *ex officio*.

German courts are very restrictive in finding that due process has been violated. They leave questions on how to organize the proceedings largely to the discretion of the arbitral tribunal. If the arbitral tribunal has refused to hear certain witnesses or to accept certain evidence, it is usually seen by the court as part of the evaluation of evidence or establishing of the facts of the case, and thereby not subject to an objection under ZPO § 1059.[408]

If a party refuses to participate in the arbitral proceedings even though it is informed of each stage of the proceedings, this also does not violate the right to be heard. Only if a party is not informed of the proceedings at all or is not informed of the names of the arbitrators, is there a valid ground for setting aside the award. However, if a party can not be contacted due to its failure to provide new or updated contact information,[409] it may not plead a violation of due process.[410]

For an objection of violation of due process to be successful, a party must be able to show that a correct procedure by the arbitral tribunal would have led to a different outcome of the proceedings. If, for example, a party claims that refusal to hear a witness amounts to a violation of due process, it must submit in detail what the witness would have testified and how this would have influenced the proceedings. The same is true if a party claims that time limits were too short – it must show what information or evidence it would have submitted if the time limit had been extended and how this would have influenced the proceedings.[411]

3. Excess of Competence or Authority

ZPO § 1059 (2) No. 1(c) specifically addresses cases when an award (i) deals with a dispute not contemplated by or not falling within the terms of the submission to arbitration, or (ii) contains decisions on matters beyond the scope of the submission to arbitration.

If the arbitral award can be separated into decisions on matters submitted to arbitration and on matters not so submitted, only that part of the award which contains decisions on matters not submitted to arbitration may be set aside.[412] The provision not only concerns cases where an arbitral tribunal goes beyond the scope of the arbitration agreement, but also cases where the arbitral tribunal decides on issues not part of the concrete claims of the parties.[413] Should an arbitral tribunal interpret the arbitration agreement broadly, a court may not review the result of such an interpretation, as this would amount to a *révision au fond*.[414] It

---

[408] *Schwab/Walter*, Schiedsgerichtsbarkeit, 7th ed., 2005, ch. 24, nos. 12-14.

[409] It follows from ZPO § 1028, that it is incumbent on parties to notify each other of possible changes of their postal address or other contact information, see *Wilske/Markert* in: Vorwerk/Wolf (eds.), Beck'scher Online-Kommentar ZPO, ZPO § 1059, no. 40.

[410] Higher Regional Court (OLG) Dresden, Decision of 15 March 2005 (Docket No. 11 Sch 19/05), SchiedsVZ (German Arbitration Journal) 2006, p. 166. *Lachmann* on the other hand argues that the arbitral tribunal has to conduct and record intensive research as regards the whereabouts of the party failing to provide current contact information, *Lachmann*, Handbuch für die Schiedsgerichtspraxis, 3rd ed., 2008, no. 2201.

[411] For an extensive list of German court decision see *Wilske/Markert* in: Vorwerk/Wolf (eds.), Beck'scher Online-Kommentar ZPO, ZPO § 1059, no. 42.1.

[412] ZPO § 1059 (2) No. 1(c).

[413] *Schwab/Walter*, Schiedsgerichtsbarkeit, 7th ed., 2005, ch. 24, no. 15.

[414] Higher Regional Court (KG) Berlin, Decision of 27 March 2002 (Docket No. 23/29 Sch 17/01, available at www.dis-arb.de.

may at times be difficult to decide whether an arbitral tribunal has gone beyond the scope of the arbitration agreement or has misapplied substantive law. Again, German courts will generally be quite reluctant to set aside awards and do so only in extreme cases.

4. Improper Composition of the Arbitral Tribunal and Violation of the Procedural Rules Applicable to Arbitration

The first part of ZPO § 1059 (2) No. 1(d) is limited to cases where a party gains knowledge of the fact that the composition of the arbitral tribunal was not in accordance with the agreement of the parties after the award has already been rendered. Any facts that the party is aware of before the award is rendered must be raised without undue delay or within the relevant time limits. Otherwise the party shall be deemed to have waived its right to object.[415] Cases where facts come to light regarding the composition of the arbitral tribunal after the award has been rendered will be rare. Such issues will usually be dealt with during the composition phase or in form of a challenge of an arbitrator according to ZPO §§ 1036 to 1039. Examples of an improper composition of the tribunal include scenarios (i) where an arbitrator, whom a party has objected to on the basis of bias, nonetheless participates in the rendering of the award,[416] (ii) where an arbitrator does not participate in the proceedings,[417] and (iii) where a party was kept from appointing an arbitrator.[418]

While there is often little room for the application of the first part of No. 1(d) concerning the composition of the arbitral tribunal, the second part of No. 1(d) regarding the procedure of the arbitration is all the more important. The procedure must conform to the German arbitration law or any admissible agreement on procedure of the parties. If an agreement of the parties includes reference to institutional arbitration rules, such as the Rules of the International Chamber of Commerce, any violation of such institutional rules may also lead to a ground for setting aside an award.[419] According to a decision of the Higher Regional Court of Frankfurt of 17 February 2011, procedural orders of the arbitral tribunal that have been expressly approved by the parties shall also bind the arbitral tribunal and may, if unilaterally amended by the arbitral tribunal, constitute a ground for setting aside an award.[420] Whether such orders can truly be classified as procedural

---

[415] ZPO § 1027.

[416] Federal Court of Justice (BGH), Decision of 11 Dec 2014 (Docket No. I ZB 23/14), Monatsschrift für Deutsches Recht, 2015, p. 670; see also *Wilske/Krapfl*, German Federal Court of Justice on setting aside an award unanimously made by arbitral tribunal including one arbitrator who was later successfully challenged, Practical Law Arbitration weekly email to 27 May 2015.

[417] Including a sleepy arbitrator, see Higher Regional Court (OLG) Karlsruhe, Decision of 4 January 2012 (Docket No. Sch 2/09), SchiedsVZ (German Arbitration Journal) 2012, p. 101, where, however, a party failed to raise any objection as to the sleepy arbitrator in due time; see also *Wilske/Heuser*, German court puts to bed challenge of arbitral award based on a sleepy arbitrator, IBA Arbitration Committee Newsletter, February 2013, pp. 78-79.

[418] *Lachmann*, Handbuch für die Schiedsgerichtspraxis, 3rd ed., 2008, no.2251; Federal Court of Justice (BGH), Decision of 5 May 1986 (Docket No. III ZR 233/84), Neue Juristische Wochenschrift, 1986, p. 3077.

[419] Federal Court of Justice (BGH), Decision of 26 September 1086 (Docket No. 3 ZR 16/84), Neue Juristische Wochenschrift, 1986, p. 1436.

[420] Higher Regional Court (OLG) Frankfurt, Decision of 17 February 2011 (Docket No. 26 Sch 13/10), SchiedsVZ (German Arbitration Journal) 2013, p. 49.

rules in the sense of ZPO § 1059 (2) No. 1(d) seems questionable.[421] Arbitral tribunals are therefore well advised to be cautious about the wording when drafting such orders. Any fundamental deviation from the agreed upon procedure or from the rules of the German arbitration law will be grounds for setting aside the award if the deviation influenced the award, meaning that the outcome would have been different if the agreed upon rules of procedure had been observed. Again, for a party to be able to rely on No. 1(d), the party must have raised a timely objection to the procedure during the arbitral proceedings.[422] Another ground for setting aside an award may be where the arbitral tribunal omits to include its reasoning in the award.[423]

A court will only set aside an award because of a violation of procedural rules if the violation concerns fundamental rules of procedure. Since due process and the right to be heard are already covered by No. 1(b), there will only be few cases where No. 1(d) will apply. According to most commentators the requirement that the outcome of the case would have been different if the correct procedure had been followed also applies to No. 1(b), although not stated there explicitly.

5. Public Policy

The grounds for setting aside an award according to ZPO § 1059 (2) No. 2 (a) and (b) must be considered by the court *ex officio*. According to No. 2 (a) the court may set aside an award if the subject matter of the dispute is not capable of settlement by arbitration under German law.[424] This applies irrespective of the law chosen by the parties, as arbitrability concerns important public interests.[425] Another important boundary for the enforcement of arbitral awards is a conflict with public policy. It is compulsory that an award complies with public policy. A party cannot waive this requirement by failing to make an objection during the proceedings.[426] A violation of public policy may concern the content of the award as well as the procedure leading up to the award.

A violation of public policy concerning the content of the award is only possible if the arbitral tribunal violated mandatory rules of German law. Such mandatory rules are contained in areas such as fundamental rights,[427] antitrust law, foreign exchange rules, or import/export regulations. It is not sufficient, if an arbitral tribunal did not apply the law agreed upon by the parties on substantive issues or applied that law incorrectly.[428]

Deviations from basic principles of German procedural law only violate public policy if the procedure of the arbitral tribunal is manifestly incompatible with

---

[421] *Wilske*, Higher Court in Germany finds procedural order is an instrument of partes' agreement, IBA Newsletter Arbitration and ADR, Vol. 17, No. 2, 2012, pp. 71-73; *Wagner/Bülau*, Procedural Orders by Arbitral Tribunals: In the Stays of Party Agreements?, SchiedsVZ (German Arbitration Journal) 2013, pp. 6 *et seq.* Approving in case of explicit consent of the parties *Wolf/Hasenstab*, Hybride Verfahrensgestaltung internationaler Schiedsverfahren, Recht der internationalen Wirtschaft, 2011, pp. 612 *et seq.*
[422] ZPO § 1027.
[423] ZPO § 1054 (2); Bill of the New Arbitration Act, BT-Drucksache 13/5274, pp. 59 *et seq.*
[424] See *supra*, at pp. 129 *et seq.*
[425] Bill of the New Arbitration Act, BT-Drucksache 13/5274, p. 59.
[426] Bill of the New Arbitration Act, BT-Drucksache 13/5274, p. 59; Federal Court of Justice (BGH), Decision of 2 November 2000 (Docket No. III ZB 55/99), Neue Juristische Wochenschrift, 2001, p. 373.
[427] *Kröll*, Die Entwicklung des Rechts der Schiedsgerichtsbarkeit 2005/2006, Neue Juristische Wochenschrift, 2007, pp. 743, 748.
[428] *Schwab/Walter*, Schiedsgerichtsbarkeit, 7th ed., 2005, ch. 24, no. 33.

the basic principles of German procedural law in such a manner that the arbitral award cannot be considered to have been rendered in accordance with the rule of law.[429] According to the legislative materials, public policy is violated if for example the award was obtained by means of bribery, fraud, false statements or perjury.[430] Since procedural irregularities are covered by ZPO § 1059 (2) Nos. 1 (b), (c), and (d), few cases will fall under the rubric of procedure in violation of public policy. The main difference is that a violation of public policy must be observed by the court *ex officio* and does not require the request of a party. Specifically, the court may refuse to enforce an award if the right to be heard was violated, since this is a fundamental principle of fair proceedings.[431]

One example of a violation of public policy is if the arbitral tribunal decides on the amount of its fees itself. The amount of fees must be agreed upon in conjunction with the parties.[432]

6. International Public Policy

In German setting aside proceedings concerning an award rendered in arbitral proceedings with foreign participants the concept of public policy is even more narrow than for domestic arbitral proceedings. In such cases the relationship with Germany is often limited to Germany as the use of a neutral forum. German courts will then limit themselves to "international public policy".[433] Since German public policy concepts are already limited to fundamental principles at law, this should not make much difference in application.[434]

There are few examples where German courts have declared an arbitral award non-enforceable due to a violation of international public policy. In one Decision of 20 November 2003, the Bavarian Highest Regional Court refused to enforce a foreign arbitral award because the parties had settled their dispute during the arbitral proceedings.[435] Even though the parties had agreed that the claimant would inform the arbitral tribunal and request the termination of the proceedings, the claimant did not do so. Instead, the claimant requested an award on the merits and then attempted to enforce the favorable award. The German court held that this behavior undermines the trust and principles of fairness essential to the efficient conduct of international commerce. Even taking into account the international nature of the case, the court noted that the claimant's conduct was

---

[429] Federal Court of Justice (BGH), Decision of 28 January 2014 (Docket No. III ZB 40/13), SchiedsVZ (German Arbitration Journal) 2014, p. 98; Federal Court of Justice (BGH), Decision of 30 October 2008 (Docket No. III ZB 17/08), Neue Juristische Wochenschrift, 2009, pp. 1215, 1216; Federal Court of Justice (BGH), Decision of 14 April 1988 (Docket No. III ZR 12/87), Bundesgerichtshofentscheidungen, Vol. 104, pp. 178, 184; Higher Regional Court (OLG) München, Decision of 24 August 2010 (Docket No. 34 Sch 21/10), Neue Juristische Online Zeitschrift, 2011, pp. 413, 420.

[430] Bill of the New Arbitration Act, BT-Drucksache 13/5274, p. 59.

[431] For an extensive list of German court decisions concerning the violation of the German *ordre public* see *Wilske/Markert* in: Vorwerk/Wolf (eds.), Beck'scher Online-Kommentar ZPO, ZPO § 1059, nos. 63.1 *et seq*.

[432] See *supra*, at p. 174.

[433] *Raeschke-Kessler/Berger*, Recht und Praxis des Schiedsverfahrens, 3rd ed., 1999, no. 1002; *Schlosser* in: Stein/Jonas, Zivilprozessordnung Vol. 10, 23rd ed., 2014, Anh. Zu § 1061, no. 317.

[434] *Schwab/Walter*, Schiedsgerichtsbarkeit, 7th ed., 2005, ch. 30, no. 21.

[435] Bavarian Highest Regional Court (BayObLG), Decision of 20 November 2003 (Docket No. 4 Z Sch 17/03), Journal of International Dispute Resolution, 2004, p. 48; see also *Wilske/Chen*, Non-Enforcement of Foreign Arbitral Awards, IBA Newsletter Arbitration and ADR, Vol. 9, No. 2, 2004, p. 57.

so outrageous that enforcement of the arbitral award would violate even the more tolerant standards of international public policy.

In a Decision of 1 February 2001 the German Federal Court of Justice denied a violation of international public policy upon the objection of a party to enforcement of an arbitral award because the arbitrator allegedly had been biased.[436] The court held that the objection of bias could have been put to the court in the country of origin of the arbitral award, in the case England, and would have been decided according to the same principles applicable in German law. Since the party now raising the objection had failed to challenge the arbitrator before English courts, it was estopped from raising the objection of a violation of public policy in enforcement proceedings in Germany.

II. Procedure and Time Limits

1. Relationship between Setting Aside Proceedings and Enforcement Proceedings

Grounds for setting aside an award can be brought forward in separate setting aside proceedings under ZPO § 1059 (1) or in enforcement proceedings under ZPO § 1060 (2). An arbitral award is enforceable until there is a binding decision setting aside the award.[437]

If the beneficiary of an arbitral award has initiated enforcement proceedings, additional recourse to the court to set aside the award is inadmissible. In this case, it is easier and less expensive for the debtor to present his grounds for setting aside in the enforcement proceedings.[438] If the debtor initiated setting aside proceedings before the creditor requested enforcement, the setting aside proceedings may be suspended until a decision is reached on the enforcement of the award. The opposite procedure is also possible, but less common: enforcement proceedings are suspended until a decision is reached on the setting aside of the award. If an arbitral award is set aside either in setting aside proceedings or in enforcement proceedings, this will also resolve the request pending in the parallel proceedings.

A request under ZPO § 1059 (2) No. 1 must detail the reasons for setting aside. If further reasons for setting aside are presented during the proceedings, the court will only consider them if it finds it appropriate to deal with such a new submission in the same proceedings.[439] If a request for setting aside is dismissed, the concrete grounds for setting aside presented in the proceedings are used up. They can no longer serve as an objection in enforcement proceedings.[440] This aspect is not mentioned in the UNCITRAL Model Law. However, ZPO § 1060 (2) Sentence 2 explicitly states that grounds for setting aside are precluded if they have been dismissed at the point in time when a request for enforcement is served on the debtor.

---

[436] Federal Court of Justice (BGH), Decision of 1 February 2001 (Docket No. III ZR 332/99), Neue Juristische Wochenschrift Rechtsprechungsreport, 2001, pp. 1059, 1060.
[437] *Schwab/Walter*, Schiedsgerichtsbarkeit, 7th ed., 2005, ch. 24, no. 1.
[438] See Higher Regional Court (OLG) Frankfurt, Decision of 3 March 2011 (Docket No. 26 Sch 24, 28/10). In this case the claimant sought the enforcement of two arbitral awards, whereas the respondent claimed that enforcement would be in conflict with public policy and sought the setting aside of the awards in the same proceeding.
[439] *Schwab/Walter*, Schiedsgerichtsbarkeit, 7th ed., 2005, ch. 25, no. 10.
[440] ZPO § 1060 (2) Sentence 2.

2. Time Limits and Formal Requirements

An application for setting aside must be made within three months after the date on which the party making the application has received the award.[441] If a request is made according to ZPO § 1058, the time limit may be extended up to one month after receipt of a decision on such a request.[442] In contrast to the UNCITRAL Model Law, the parties may agree on longer or shorter time limits.[443] If a German court has declared an award to be enforceable, a request for setting aside is excluded.[444]

The reasons for setting aside an award are divided into two categories: grounds that will only be considered by the court upon request in ZPO § 1059 (2) No. 1 and grounds to be considered by the court *ex officio* in ZPO § 1059 (2) No. 2. This division is also reflected in time limits for setting aside proceedings. According to ZPO § 1060 (2) Sentence 3, grounds under No. 1 are excluded in enforcement proceedings if the time limit for setting aside proceedings has expired. Grounds under No. 2 must be observed by the court at any time. Therefore, if the beneficiary of an award initiates enforcement proceedings after the time limit for setting aside proceedings has expired, only the grounds under No. 2 remain relevant.

The locally competent court may be agreed upon by the parties in their arbitration agreement. If there is no agreement, the court at the seat of the arbitration is competent.[445] Subject matter jurisdiction always lies with the Higher Regional Court (*Oberlandesgericht*). The application for the setting aside of an award must name the parties and their counsel, provide information on the competence of the Higher Regional Court (*Oberlandesgericht*), that is either a copy of the arbitration agreement naming the competent court or a document showing the seat of the arbitration, and include the arbitral award. Additionally, it must detail the reasons why the award should be set aside.

3. Content of Decision Setting Aside the Award

The court cannot modify the award in its decision. It can either set aside the award or dismiss the request for setting aside. If an arbitral award can be separated into specific parts, it is possible for the court to only set aside part of an award.[446] The decision by the Higher Regional Court (*Oberlandesgericht*) can be appealed to the Federal Court of Justice (*Bundesgerichtshof*),[447] whose decision is final and cannot be appealed any further. As to the scope of review by the Federal Court of Justice, it is governed by the ZPO.[448] The appeal to the Federal Court of Justice is limited to complaints of law and only allows for the introduction of factual submissions if they need to be taken into account *ex officio* or might change the procedural basis of the case in the course of the appeal proceedings.[449] If an application for setting

---

[441] ZPO § 1059 (3).
[442] ZPO § 1059 (3) Sentence 3.
[443] ZPO § 1059 (3).
[444] ZPO § 1059 (3) Sentence 4.
[445] ZPO § 1062.
[446] Federal Court of Justice (BGH), Decision of 26 September 1985 (Docket No. III ZR 16/84), Neue Juristische Wochenschrift, 1986, pp. 1436, 1438.
[447] ZPO § 1065.
[448] See *supra*, at p. 100.
[449] Federal Court of Justice (BGH), Decision of 1 March 2007 (Docket No. III ZB 7/06), SchiedsVZ (German Arbitration Journal) 2007, p. 160. An example of the latter would be the setting aside of the award in the country of origin while the Higher Regional Court's decision is on appeal before the Federal Court of Justice, Federal Court of Justice (BGH), Decision of 22 February 2001, Neue Juristische Wochenschrift, 2001, p. 1730.

aside is dismissed, this only excludes the concrete reasons brought forward in the request. Other reasons for setting aside can still be relied upon by a party.[450]

If an award is set aside, this revives the arbitration agreement under ZPO § 1059 (5), unless the parties' intention contradicts this result. The parties then have the option of constituting a new arbitral tribunal to decide on the issues once again. The UNCITRAL Model Law does not contain such a provision.

Under ZPO § 1059 (4) the court may also in appropriate circumstances set aside an award and remit the case to the same arbitral tribunal for a new decision. This differs from article 34 (4) of the UNCITRAL Model Law, which allows the court to suspend the setting aside proceedings in order to give the arbitral tribunal an opportunity to eliminate the grounds for setting aside. Appropriate circumstances under German law will only arise if the arbitral award is set aside solely on formal grounds, such as if the arbitral tribunal was not constituted properly. It has been held by the Higher Regional Courts of Düsseldorf and Köln that the court is not prevented from referring the case back to the arbitral tribunal simply because one party raises an objection against this procedure.[451] Academic opinions on the issue differ.[452] If the case is referred back to the same arbitral tribunal, it must then make a new decision under avoidance of the same mistake.

German courts will furthermore not render a decision on the validity of an interim award on jurisdiction if the final award on the merits was issued prior to the court's final decision on the jurisdictional matter.[453]

I. Recognition and Enforcement of Arbitral Awards

I. Procedure for Enforcement Proceedings

The request for enforcement of an arbitral award is not bound to any specific time limits. The request must name the parties and their counsel. It must describe the arbitral award and the extent to which enforcement is requested. Additionally, it must furnish information on the competence of the Higher Regional Court.[454] The requesting party must attach the arbitral award to its application. It must either provide the court with the original of the award or with a certified copy. The copy may be certified by counsel of the party.[455]

---

[450] *Schwab/Walter*, Schiedsgerichtsbarkeit, 7th ed., 2005, ch. 25, no. 16.
[451] Higher Regional Court (OLG) Düsseldorf, Decision of 14 August 2007 (Docket No. I-4-Sch-02-06), SchiedsVZ (German Arbitration Journal) 2008, p. 156; Higher Regional Court (OLG) Köln, Decision of 28 June 2011 (Docket No. 19 Sch 11/10), SchiedsVZ (German Arbitration Journal) 2012, p. 161.
[452] In conformity with the above mentioned decisions: *Voit* in: Musielak/Voit, Zivilprozessordnung, 12th ed., 2015, § 1059, no. 41 as well as *Münch* in: Münchener Kommentar zur Zivilprozessordnung, 4th ed., 2013, § 1059, no. 78; for a differing opinion see *Schwab/Walter*, Schiedsgerichtsbarkeit, 7th ed., 2005, ch. 25, no. 19 (regularly no remittance if one party objects).
[453] Federal Court of Justice (BGH), Decision of 19 September 2013 (Docket No. III ZB 37/12), SchiedsVZ (German Arbitration Journal) 2013, p. 333; see also *Wilske/Krapfl*, German Federal Court of Justice Postpones Decision on Intra-EU Jurisdictional Objection, IBA Arbitration Committee Newsletter, vol. 19, no. 1, February 2014, p. 62; see also *Huber/Bach* in: Böckstiegel/Kröll/Nacimiento (eds.), Arbitration in Germany – The Model Law in Practice, 2nd ed., 2015, ZPO § 1040, nos. 40, 41.
[454] ZPO § 1062 (1) No. 4.
[455] ZPO § 1064 (1) Sentence 2.

According to ZPO § 1063 (1), an oral hearing is not compulsory in enforcement proceedings. Nevertheless, under ZPO § 1063 (2), the court must provide for an oral hearing if a party raises grounds for setting aside the award in enforcement proceedings or *ex officio* reasons for setting aside under ZPO § 1059 (2) No. 2 may be applicable.[456] A hearing will therefore always be necessary in setting aside proceedings. If a decision on enforcement can be reached without an oral hearing, the other party must be heard in writing.[457]

The opposing party may either raise grounds for setting aside the award or may under certain circumstances raise objections on the merits of the claim. This is possible if the objection did not come into existence until after it could have been raised with the arbitral tribunal. The relevant point in time will either be the end of the arbitral hearing or the exchange of written post-hearing pleadings. An example for a possible objection on the merits in enforcement proceedings is if a set-off situation arises after the arbitral proceedings have been closed.[458]

For appearances before the Higher Regional Court (*Oberlandesgericht*) for an oral hearing, a party must be represented by an attorney admitted to that Higher Regional Court.[459] According to ZPO § 1063 (4) a party may act through any attorney or even without the representation of an attorney as long as the court has not ordered an oral hearing to take place.

II. Decision on Enforcement

The court can either grant enforcement or reject the application if (i) it is inadmissible, (ii) the defendant has successfully raised material defenses against the application, or (iii) there are grounds for setting aside the award.[460] Unless the latter is the case and the award will be additionally and automatically set aside, the court's decision will only amount to a mere rejection of the application and not withdraw the *res judicata* effect the award has between the parties.[461]

If the court grants the application for enforcement of an award, it must take great care when formulating its decision. The decision of the court has to be made by court order[462] which is the execution title. It must therefore include the actual wording of the operative part of the award. The court order should read: "The award (defined according to date, place of arbitration, and the orders made under the award) is enforceable."[463] The court may not make changes to the ar-

---

[456] Higher Regional Court (OLG) Hamm, Decision of 20 June 2001 (Docket No. 8 Sch 2/00), Neue Juristische Wochenschrift Rechtsprechungsreport, 2001, p. 1362; Higher Regional Court (OLG) Köln, Decision of 11 September 2009 (Docket No. 19 Sch 10/09), Beck Rechtsprechung, 2010, 13627.

[457] ZPO § 1063 (1) Sentence 2.

[458] *Schwab/Walter*, Schiedsgerichtsbarkeit, 7th ed., 2005, ch. 27, no. 16; Federal Court of Justice (BGH), Decision of 12 July 1990 (Docket No. III ZR 174/89), Neue Juristische Wochenschrift, 1990, p. 3210.

[459] ZPO § 78.

[460] ZPO § 1060 (2), ZPO § 1059 (2).

[461] *Kröll* in: Böckstiegel/Kröll/Nacimiento (eds.), Arbitration in Germany – The Model Law in Practice, 2nd ed., 2015, ZPO § 1060, no. 41; *Wilske/Markert,* National Reports – Germany, in: Mistelis/Shore (eds.), World Arbitration Reporter, Vol. I, 2nd ed., 2014 p. GER-49.

[462] Federal Court of Justice (BGH), Decision of 20 September 2001 (Docket No. III ZB 57/00), Neue Juristische Wochenschrift, 2001, p. 3787; Higher Regional Court (OLG) Stuttgart, Decision of 4 October 2000 (Docket No. 1 Sch 13/99), Monatsschrift für Deutsches Recht, 2001, p. 595; for an optional decision however Higher Regional Court (OLG) Hamburg, Decision of 25 January 2008 (Docket No. 6 Sch 07/07), SchiedsVZ (German Arbitration Journal) 2009, pp. 71, 72.

[463] *Schwab/Walter*, Schiedsgerichtsbarkeit, 7th ed., 2005, ch. 28, no. 6.

bitral award's decision and should generally refer the parties back to the arbitral tribunal for any corrections.[464]

The court order on an application for enforcement must be served on the parties. German law does not explicitly provide that the order must contain reasons. If the order grants enforcement and the application has not been contested, this may not seem to be necessary. However, following good practice, courts commonly add, at least, cursory reasons. An order denying enforcement, on the other hand, should always include reasons, if only to allow the losing party to prepare its defense on appeal.[465]

III. Foreign Arbitral Awards

An arbitral award is foreign if the seat of the arbitration is in a country other than Germany.[466] The rules for recognition and enforcement of foreign arbitral awards are contained in ZPO §§ 1061 to 1065.[467] Even though ZPO § 1061 (1) provides that foreign arbitral awards are to be recognized and enforced according to the New York Convention, there are hardly any differences to the enforcement of a domestic award. Indeed, the formal requirements of Art. IV of the New York Convention need not be fulfilled, since under Art. VII of the New York Convention, the less strict provision of the ZPO applies.[468] Specifically, this means that a party need not submit a certified translation of the arbitration agreement or the arbitral award. It is sufficient if the party requesting enforcement supplies certified copies of the arbitration agreement and the arbitral award pursuant to ZPO § 1064 (3). A translation of these documents need not be certified in a specific manner.[469] Nevertheless, it is recommended that parties provide the competent Higher Regional Court with a certified translation, as it facilitates the work of the court and may speed up the proceedings.

A party seeking recognition and enforcement of a foreign arbitral award in Germany pursuant to the New York Convention bears the burden of production and proof as to the existence of a valid arbitration agreement.[470] German courts will rule on the objection that there is no valid arbitration agreement without being bound by the findings of the foreign arbitral tribunal on the existence of an effective arbitration agreement. As long as a party consistently objects to the jurisdiction of the arbitral tribunal, it can bring this objection in enforcement

---

[464] *Schwab/Walter*, Schiedsgerichtsbarkeit, 7th ed., 2005, ch. 28, no. 7; *Wilske/Markert* in: Vorwerk/Wolf (eds.), Beck'scher Online-Kommentar ZPO, ZPO § 1060, no. 24.
[465] *Schwab/Walter*, Schiedsgerichtsbarkeit, 7th ed., 2005, ch. 28, no. 9.
[466] ZPO § 1025 (1).
[467] ZPO § 1025 (4).
[468] Federal Court of Justice (BGH), Decision of 25 September 2003 (Docket No. III ZB 68/02), SchiedsVZ (German Arbitration Journal) 2003, p. 281, with note by *Kröll*; Higher Regional Court (OLG) Schleswig, Decision of 15 July 2003 (Docket No. 16 Sch 01/03), SchiedsVZ (German Arbitration Journal) 2003, p. 237; *Wilske/Chen*, Non-Enforcement of Foreign Arbitral Awards, IBA Newsletter Arbitration and ADR, Vol. 9, No. 2, 2004, p. 57.
[469] Federal Court of Justice (BGH), Decision of 25 September 2003 (Docket No. III ZB 68/02), SchiedsVZ (German Arbitration Journal) 2003, p. 281, with note by *Kröll*; see also *Wilske*, Recourse to Domestic Law to Allow Enforcement, IBA Newsletter Arbitration and ADR, Vol. 9, No. 1, 2004, p. 39.
[470] Higher Regional Court (OLG) München, Decision of 19 January 2009 (Docket No. 34 Sch 4/08), OLG Report München, 2009, p. 263; Higher Regional Court (OLG) Celle, Decision of 4 September 2003 (Docket No. 8 Sch 11/02), Journal of International Dispute Resolution, 2004, pp. 95, 98 (in English language) with note by *Wegen/Wilske*, p. 77; see also *Wilske/Chen*, Non-Enforcement of Foreign Arbitral Awards, IBA Newsletter Arbitration and ADR, Vol. 9, No. 2, 2004, p. 57.

proceedings as well. And again: The court will not be bound by the decision of the arbitral tribunal on the cornerstone of its competence.[471]

If the application for enforcement is denied, the court cannot set aside the award but can only declare that the award cannot be recognized in Germany.[472] If the denial is based on procedural defects which are subsequently remedied, a party may apply again to have the arbitral award recognized and enforced.[473] If a foreign arbitral award is declared enforceable in Germany and is later set aside abroad, the party can request the repeal of the enforcement decision.[474] If the court grants the application for enforcement, it must include a translation of the operative part of the award in its own decision.[475] Otherwise it will not be possible to enforce the decision in Germany.

---

[471] See *supra*, at E.I..
[472] ZPO § 1061 (2).
[473] *Wilske/Markert*, National Reports – Germany, in: Mistelis/Shore (eds.), World Arbitration Reporter, Vol. I, 2nd ed., 2014, p. GER-52.
[474] ZPO § 1061 (3).
[475] *Kröll* in: Böckstiegel/Kröll/Nacimiento (eds.), Arbitration in Germany – The Model Law in Practice, 2nd ed., 2015, ZPO § 1061, no. 167.

Chapter 3: Mediation

A. Introduction to Mediation in German Commercial Disputes

I. Brief History and Development of Mediation in Germany

"Mediation is a confidential and structured procedure in which the parties, voluntarily and on their own initiative, strive to amicably resolve their dispute with the aid of one or more mediators."[1] Even though this legal definition of the term "mediation" was introduced in German law as recently as July 2012, the roots of mediation can be traced back to ancient times.[2] As nation states were formed and more and more sophisticated judicial (court) systems developed, however, the notion of mediation began to fade away. In the 1970s, mediation reappeared in the U.S. legal landscape as one of several mechanisms of alternative dispute resolution. It became more prevalent once arbitration started to exhibit negative features commonly attributed to domestic litigation, and more cost and time efficient methods for resolving disputes were sought.[3]

In Germany, corporations seemed to take note of this international development with a mixture of skepticism and indifference.[4] In the mid-1990s, the notion of mediation eventually arrived in the legal mainstream.[5] The European Institute for Conflict Management (EUCON)[6] was founded in 1998 and is promoted by major corporations such as Siemens.[7] Meanwhile, most arbitral institutions have complemented their set of rules by adopting particular mediation rules. For example, the ICC adopted new mediation rules in 2014 which replaced its ADR rules

---

[1] Mediationsgesetz § 1 (1). The German Mediation Act (*Mediationsgesetz, MedG*) came into force on 26 July 2012 (Federal Law Gazette (*Bundesgesetzblatt*) 2012 I, p. 1577). For in-depth presentations of mediation in Germany cf. *Risse*, Wirtschaftsmediation, 2nd ed., 2015 (forthcoming); *Duve/Eidenmüller/Hacke*, Mediation in der Wirtschaft, 2nd ed., 2011; *Haft/Schlieffen*, Handbuch Mediation, 2nd ed., 2009; also see the author's book reviews regarding the aforementioned: *Wegen*, Mediation? – Eine Besprechung grundlegender Werke, DAJV Newsletter, 2005, pp. 32 *et seq.*

[2] The concept of mediation can be found in tribal communities in Africa as well as amongst Native Americans.

[3] *O'Connor*, Alternative Dispute Resolution: Panacea or Placebo?, Arbitration, 1992, p. 109; *Mukhopadhyay/Karl*, Does Business need Mediation, ICC International Court of Arbitration Bulletin, Vol. 24, Number 2, 2013, p. 27; *Weigand*, Alternative Streiterledigung – "Alternative Dispute Resolution" auch in Deutschland, Betriebs-Berater, 1996, p. 2106.

[4] Some scholars, however, recognized the seminal potential of alternative dispute resolution early on: *e.g.* the Negotiation Workshop of Tuebingen [*Tübinger Verhandlungsseminar*], which focuses on research regarding alternative dispute resolution, was founded at the law school of Tuebingen University in 1982.

[5] The prospects and (dis-)advantages of mediation were widely discussed: *Weigand*, Alternative Streiterledigung – "Alternative Dispute Resolution" auch in Deutschland, Betriebs-Berater, 1996, p. 2108; *Schmidt*, Wirtschaftsmediation – die nicht gesehene Chance, Betriebs-Berater Beilage Nr. 10, Issue 40, 1998.

[6] Formerly Society for Commercial Mediation and Conflict Management (*Gesellschaft für Wirtschaftsmediation und Konfliktmanagement, GWMK*).

[7] Available at http:// www.eucon-institute.com.

from 2001.[8] The leading German arbitral institution, the German Institution of Arbitration (*Deutsche Institution für Schiedsgerichtsbarkeit, DIS*), adopted Conciliation and Mediation Rules that have been in force since January 2002 and were amended in 2010.[9] These and similar organizations provide a service infrastructure for mediation procedures.[10] Universities such as the Ludwig-Maximilians-University Munich have founded and maintain centers focusing on mediation.[11] Further, regional (civil) courts started to launch model mediation projects which incorporate mediation procedures into court proceedings (so-called in-court mediation).[12]

II. Introduction to Mediation in Germany and the European Union Today

Despite increasingly gaining acceptance, mediation still plays a significantly smaller role in German dispute resolution in comparison with the USA. One reason for this may be the fact that US procedural law regarding discovery procedures and allocation of legal costs (American rule[13]) provides strong incentives for alternative dispute resolution mechanisms. In Germany, the court system still seems to provide a relatively cost and time efficient way of resolving disputes, notwithstanding the length of court proceedings and the risk of an unfavorable judgment including the obligation of the losing party to pay the expenses of the other party.[14]

In 2014, the European Parliament's Committee on Legal Affairs published its study *"'Rebooting' the Mediation Directive: Assessing the Limited Impact on its Implementation and Proposing Measures to increase the Number of Mediations in the EU"*. The aim of this study was (i) to provide a detailed overview of the current mediation legislation in 11 EU Member States[15] and (ii) to propose measures to increase the use of mediation in judicial proceedings. This study reveals the disillusioning reality that "mediation in civil and commercial matters is still used in less than 1% of the cases in the EU". Only four Member States – Germany, Italy,[16] the Netherlands and the United Kingdom – reported more than 10,000 mediations per year. In Germany, the number of mediations may be positively affected by the

---

[8] For a detailed discussion of the new ICC Mediation Rules see: The New ICC Mediation Rules, ICC International Court of Arbitration Bulletin, Vol. 24, Number 2, 2013, pp. 5 *et seq.*; *Behme/Probst*, Die neuen Mediationsregeln der ICC – ein Meilenstein für die administrierte Mediation?, Zeitschrift für Konfliktmanagement, 2014, pp. 8 *et seq.*

[9] DIS Mediation Rules, reprinted in Part 2, E. II; see also http://www.dis-arb.de.

[10] See List of Mediation Institutions in Part 2, E. I.

[11] Munich Center for Dispute Resolution, available at http://www.mucdr.org. In addition, several centers have been founded around the world; for example, the World Intellectual Property Organization (WIPO) maintains the WIPO Arbitration and Mediation Center.

[12] For a more detailed introduction of the model court-annexed mediation, see *infra* at pp. 196 et seq. Since 1 July 2003 mediation and dispute resolution is part of the training for German jurists, see Judiciary Employment Act (*Deutsches Richtergesetz*) §5a (3).

[13] For an insightful economic analysis of the American and the Continental rule for allocating legal costs, *cf. van Wijck/van Velthoven*, An economic analysis of the American and continental rule for allocating legal costs, European Journal of Law and Economics, 9:2, 2000, pp. 115-125.

[14] See *supra*, at pp. 9 et seq.

[15] Austria, Bulgaria, France, Germany, Greece, Italy, the Netherlands, Poland, Romania, Slovenia and the United Kingdom.

[16] Italy reported more than 200,000 mediations per year.

fact that more and more insurance companies are including mediation in their legal expenses insurance.[17]

B. International Regulatory Developments

Mediation has been on the agenda of a number of intergovernmental organizations for over two decades now.[18] In particular, the United Nations Commission on International Trade Law (UNCITRAL) has played a pioneering role with regard to harmonizing international commercial conciliation: In 1980, UNCITRAL adopted its Conciliation Rules and subsequently, in 2002, a Model Law on International Commercial Conciliation.[19] Meanwhile, legislation based on this model law has been adopted in 14 states in a total of 26 jurisdictions, including Belgium, Canada (Nova Scotia and Ontario), France, Switzerland, Turkey, and 12 US federal states. Currently, UNCITRAL is considering the issue of enforcement of settlement agreements resulting from international commercial conciliation proceedings.[20]

In 2008 – after years of preparation[21] – the European Parliament and the Council of the European Union adopted their directive 2008/52/EC on certain aspects of mediation in civil and commercial matters.[22] This Directive applies to civil and commercial cross-border disputes in which at least one of the parties is domiciled or habitually resident in a Member State except in Denmark.[23] It is the Directive's objective *"to facilitate access to alternative dispute resolution and to promote the amicable settlement of disputes by encouraging the use of mediation and by ensuring a balanced relationship between mediation and judicial proceedings"*.[24] In order to meet this objective, the Member States (except Denmark) shall, *inter alia*, ensure (i) the quality of mediation and the training of mediators,[25] (ii) that content of a written agreement resulting from mediation be made enforceable,[26] (iii) confidentiality of mediation,[27] and (iv) that mediation hinders the expiry of limitation and prescrip-

---

[17] See *Tochtermann* in: Hopt/Steffek (eds.), Mediation – Principles and Regulation in Comparative Perspective, 2013, p. 575.
[18] See also *Eidenmüller*, A Legal Framework for National and International Mediation Proceedings, Recht der Internationalen Wirtschaft, International Dispute Resolution Supplement, 2002, p. 14.
[19] UNCITRAL Model Law on International Commercial Conciliation, United Nations document A/57/17, available at http://www.uncitral.org/pdf/english/texts/arbitration/ml-conc/03-90953_Ebook.pdf.
[20] At the Commission session in July 2014, the United States submitted a proposal suggesting that UNCITRAL develop a convention on the enforceability of conciliated settlement agreements that resolve international commercial disputes, *cf.* United Nations document A/CN.9/WG.II/WP.199, p. 5.
[21] Already at its meeting in Tampere in 1999, the European Council called for alternative, extra-judicial procedures to be created by the Member States. In 2002, the European Commission issued a Green Paper on Alternative Dispute Resolution in civil and commercial matters (*cf.* EC Directive No. 2008/52 recitals 2 and 4). *White*, Directive 2008/52 on certain aspects of mediation in civil and commercial matters: a new culture of access to justice?, Arbitration 79, 2013, pp. 52, 53, traces the Directive's foundations back to the beginning of the 1980s.
[22] Directive 2008/52/EC of 21 May 2008, OJ 2008 L 136/3.
[23] EC Directive No. 2008/52 Art. 1 (2), (3), 2.
[24] EC Directive No. 2008/52 Art. 1 (1).
[25] EC Directive No 2008/52 Art. 4. In 2004, the EU adopted a code of conduct for mediators.
[26] EC Directive No 2008/52 Art. 6 (1).
[27] EC Directive No 2008/52 Art. 7 (1).

tion periods.²⁸ The Member States (except Denmark) were obligated to bring into force the laws, regulations, and administrative provisions necessary to comply with the Directive before 21 May 2011.²⁹

C. Statutory Framework of Mediation in Germany

For a long time, German law did not contain specific provisions dealing with mediation, as the notion of proceedings being adversarial was predominant. However, several reforms of procedural law[30] introduced incentives for the parties to settle their disputes amicably in order to accelerate dispute resolution, promote peace between parties (*Rechtsfrieden*), and relieve and unburden the courts. In 2007, the Federal Constitutional Court of Germany held that amicable dispute resolution is generally preferable to an imposed resolution by court order.[31]

As a general rule, a court is obligated to act in the interest of arriving at an amicable solution of a legal dispute at all stages of the proceedings.[32] For this purpose, every court hearing is to be preceded by a conciliation hearing (*Güteverhandlung*) unless prior efforts to come to a settlement have been made before an alternative dispute-resolution entity, or unless there do not appear to be any prospects for the parties to reach an agreement.[33] During a conciliation hearing the judge will discuss the facts and the circumstances of the case with the parties and will encourage them to reach an amicable settlement. This general idea of reaching an amicable settlement rather than an imposed court decision is further promoted by German law concerning court costs: If the parties resolve their dispute and end court proceedings by way of a settlement, court costs will be reduced[34] and (statutory) lawyer's fees will increase.[35] This way, the courts' obligation to promote an amicable solution is safeguarded by a (financial) incentive for the parties and their lawyers to act in the interest of a settlement.

In 2006, the Legal Services Act (*Rechtsdienstleistungsgesetz, RDG*) entered into force. RDG §2 (3) no. 4 stipulates that – under certain circumstances – mediation and other similar forms of alternative dispute resolution do not constitute unauthorized practice of law.[36] The latest reform of the German civil procedure law further facilitated the concept of amicable dispute resolution: In order to implement EC Directive No. 2008/52, the German parliament passed the Law on the Advancement of Mediation and Other Proceedings of Extrajudicial Dispute Eesolution (*Gesetz zur Förderung der Mediation und anderer Verfahren der außergerichtlichen Konfliktbeilegung*, Mediation Advancement Act), which came into force

---

[28] EC Directive No 2008/52 Art. 8 (1).
[29] EC Directive No 2008/52 Art. 12 (1).
[30] See *supra*, at p. 4.
[31] Federal Constitutional Court of Germany (BVerfG), Decision of 14 February 2007 (Docket No. 1 BvR 1351/01), Neue Juristische Wochenschrift Rechtsprechungs-Report, 2007, p. 1073.
[32] ZPO §278 (1).
[33] ZPO §278 (2). For the general conduct of the conciliation hearing, see *supra*, at pp. 71 et seq.
[34] Procedural Fee according to Number 1211 (3) of the Schedule of Fees (*Gebührenverzeichnis*) of the Court Fees Law (*Gerichtskostengesetz*).
[35] If the parties reach a settlement after proceedings have been initiated, the settlement fee (*Einigungsgebühr*) is 1.0 fee-units, see *supra*, at p. 10.
[36] See *infra*, at p. 201.

on 26 July 2012.[37] The Mediation Advancement Act is an omnibus law including the Mediation Act (*Mediationsgesetz, MediationsG*) as well as changes to German procedural law which incorporate mediation into general procedural law and implement an in-court amicable dispute resolution model.

I. Brief Legislative History of the Mediation Advancement Act

The Mediation Advancement Law came into force well over a year after the transposition deadline contained in EC Directive No. 2008/52 Art. 12 (1) expired. This delay occurred because the legislator debated at length about the future of the model projects that were introduced by German federal states in order to gain experience with in-court mediation at the Regional Court level at the beginning of this century. In 2002, Lower Saxony became the first state in Germany to start such a model project: Court proceedings were stayed if the parties voluntarily entered into mediation proceedings in which a judge acted as mediator. If the mediation failed, the judge acting as mediator was banned from deciding the case. This model project was acclaimed by the judges and achieved remarkable success.[38] Other states followed this example and also introduced their own model projects.[39]

Due to the mainly positive responses to these model projects,[40] the legislator of the Mediation Advancement Act initially intended to embody the states' practice of in-court mediation in the Code of Civil Procedure. This approach was criticized by the private mediation community, which argued that in-court mediation may endanger fair competition and put private mediators at a disadvantage. After the draft solution went back and forth, the legislator eventually agreed on a compromise: Whilst state judges may no longer call themselves (judicial) mediators,[41] in-court mediation will be replaced by the concept of the *Güterichter* (roughly: conciliation judge).[42] This model resembles the model projects that were initially introduced in the states of Bavaria and Thuringia.[43]

II. In-Court Mediation: *Güterichter* Model

The (obligatory) conciliation hearing (*Güteverhandlung*)[44] is generally held before a trial judge. However, if the trial judge sees fit, he may refer the parties to a conciliation judge (*Güterichter*) who has been delegated for this purpose and before whom the conciliation hearing may be held instead. Such referral may be made

---

[37] Federal Law Gazette (*Bundesgesetzblatt*) 2012 I, pp. 1577 *et seq.*
[38] For the Lower Saxonian Regional Court (LG) Göttingen it is reported that 600 out of 2,000 cases were referred to court-annexed mediation in 2003. In approximately 75 per cent of these cases the parties chose – an often specially trained – state judge as mediator. 90 per cent of these mediation proceedings led to amicable court settlements.
[39] For a detailed description of the different models, see *Fritz/Pielsticker*, Mediationsgesetz, 2013, Einl. no. 38 *et seq.*; see also *Tochtermann* in: Hopt/Steffek (eds.), Mediation – Principles and Regulation in Comparative Perspective, 2013, pp. 530 *et seq.*
[40] *Cf. Wegen/Gack*, Mediation in pending civil proceedings in Germany: practical experiences to strengthen mediatory elements in pending court proceedings, IBA Mediation Newsletter, Vol. 12, 2006, pp. 8 *et seq.*
[41] Under Mediation Act §9 (1) in-court mediation could be conducted by judicial mediators until 1 August 2013.
[42] *Cf. Tochtermann* in: Hopt/Steffek (eds.), Mediation – Principles and Regulation in Comparative Perspective, 2013, pp. 530 *et seq.*
[43] *Fritz/Pielsticker*, Mediationsgesetz, 2013, Introduction, nos. 46, 51.
[44] See *supra* accompanying text to fn. 508.

by the courts of first instance as well as by an appellate judge.[45] However, the trial judge cannot *order* the parties to hold a conciliation hearing before a conciliation judge; the parties' consent is necessary.[46] If the parties do not give their consent, the conciliation hearing will be held before the trial judge.

The conciliation judge is not authorized to make a decision. In order to promote an amicable settlement of the dispute, he may avail himself of all methods of conflict resolution, including mediation. As compared to a mediator, the conciliation judge has broader powers: He may access the files of the case without the parties' consent and may present the parties a (preliminary) legal assessment of the dispute.[47] Further, the conciliation judge may order the parties to appear before him in person and may impose a fine on a party failing to appear.[48] If the parties so wish, the conciliation judge may also record a settlement agreement for the record of the court.[49] Such court-reported settlement agreement may be enforced the same way as a court judgment.[50]

III. Out-of-Court Mediation During Ongoing Proceedings

Instead of referring the parties to a conciliation judge (*Güterichter*), the judge may also suggest that the parties pursue (private out-of-court) mediation or other alternative conflict resolution procedures.[51] If the parties decide to pursue mediation (they are not obliged to do so), the proceedings will be stayed.[52]

IV. Mandatory Court-Annexed Mediation

With regard to certain claims, federal states are authorized to pass laws that oblige a possible claimant to make efforts to resolve the dispute amicably, by way of out-of-court mediation before a state-approved conciliation entity (*anerkannte Gütestelle*[53]), prior to initiating actual court proceedings.[54] However, such a mandatory mediation procedure (*obligatorisches außergerichtliches Güterverfahren*) may only be made a precondition for the admissibility of a lawsuit if (i) the amount in dispute

---

[45] Note that in 2009, the Federal Court of Justice (BGH), Decision of 12 February 2009 (Docket No. VII ZB 76/07), Neue Juristische Wochenschrift, 2009, p. 1149 held that the time limit for filing a notice of appeal will not be automatically suspended by pending mediation proceedings; *cf.* Wegen/Naumann, Mediation in pending civil proceedings in Germany: no automatic suspension of the time limit for filing a notice of appeal, IBA Mediation Newsletter, Vol. 10, 2009, p. 16.

[46] Bundestag Document (*BT-Drucksache*) 17/8058, p. 21.

[47] Bundestag Document (*BT-Drucksache*) 17/8058, p. 17.

[48] ZPO § 278 (3).

[49] ZPO § 278 (6).

[50] ZPO § 794 (1); for an overview of enforcement and execution of German judgments, see *supra*, at pp. 103 et seq.

[51] ZPO § 278a (1); this provision was also newly introduced by way of the Mediation Advancement Law in 2012.

[52] ZPO § 278a (2); also see *supra*, at pp. 67 et seq.

[53] See also *infra*, at p. 208.

[54] EGZPO § 15a (this provision was enacted in 1999); *cf.* Wegen/Wilske, Non-Compliance with Obligatory Mediation Procedure Makes Court Proceedings Inadmissible – No Settled Case Law as to Consequences of Non-Compliance with Obligatory Mediation Procedure, IBA Mediation Committee Newsletter, Vol. 4, 2005, pp. 19 *et seq.*; Wegen/Gack, Obligatory Mediation as a Precondition for Court Proceedings – First Experiences of a new Concept in German Civil Procedural Law, IBA Mediation Newsletter, Vol. 8, 2005, pp. 29 *et seq.*; Wegen/Gack, Obligatory mediation for court proceedings: promotion of alternative dispute resolution and attempts to avoid it, IBA Mediation Committee Newsletter, Vol. 9, 2006, pp. 25 *et seq.*

does not exceed EUR 750, (ii) the dispute involves certain claims under "neighbor law", (iii) the dispute involves claims based on defamations that have not been made in the press or on the radio, or (iv) the dispute involves claims under section 3 of the General Equal Treatment Act (*Allgemeines Gleichbehandlungsgesetz, AGG*). Because of this scope which basically limits a mandatory mediation procedure to disputes in the private, non-commercial area, the mandatory mediation procedure has no practical implications on commercial mediation in Germany.

V. Further Mandatory Mediation

There are further potential situations in which German substantive law might require prior attempts to reach a settlement before a dispute may be brought before a court: With regard to certain claims under the Act Against Unfair Competition (*Unlauterer Wettbewerb-Gesetz, UWG*), where a dispute has been brought before a judge without prior referral to a conciliation board, the judge can – upon request of one party and upon setting a new date for a hearing – order the parties to refer the matter to the conciliation board in order to amicably settle the dispute. Also, with respect to certain building contracts, courts have ruled that the parties are obliged to enter into good faith negotiations and try to reach an amicable settlement. Even though it does not create procedural hurdles for commencing court proceedings, a breach of this duty may result in a loss of certain substantive rights, such as the right to extraordinary termination.[55]

VI. The Mediation Act

Article 1 of the Mediation Advancement Act introduces the Mediation Act (*Mediationsgesetz, MediationsG*). The Mediation Act basically contains all provisions necessary to comply with the EC Directive No. 2008/52. Whilst the scope of the EC Directive No. 2008/52 is limited to cross-border disputes,[56] the Mediation Act does not contain a comparable restriction as to its scope. The Mediation Act is applicable in national as well as in cross-border disputes. It regulates the main features of the mediation process for private, out-of-court mediation such as (i) the general process and the tasks of the mediator,[57] (ii) the mediator's conflicts of interest,[58] (iii) the duty of confidentiality,[59] and (iv) education and training of mediators.[60] The provisions of the Mediation Act will be discussed in further detail in the context of mediation proceedings in Germany below.

---

[55] See Federal Court of Justice (BGH), Decision of 28 October 1999 (Docket No. VII ZR 393/98), Neue Juristische Wochenschrift, 2000, p. 807; see also Federal Court of Justice (BGH), Decision of 23 May 1996 (Docket No. VII ZR 245/94), Neue Juristische Wochenschrift, 1996, p. 2158.
[56] EC Directive No. 2008/52, Art. 1 (2).
[57] Mediation Act § 2.
[58] Mediation Act § 3.
[59] Mediation Act § 4.
[60] Mediation Act § 5.

D. Mediation Clauses and Agreements

Notwithstanding the exceptional cases in which parties are ordered to pursue mediation,[61] mediation proceedings are initiated because the parties agreed on a mediation clause *"on a voluntary basis"*.[62] The parties are free to agree on when and how to initiate mediation proceedings (freedom of contract). Mediation clauses are governed by the German law of contracts.

I. Content of a Mediation Clause

There are no specific content or form requirements for mediation clauses under German law.[63] The mediation clause may form part of the dispute resolution provisions of a separate contract or it may be concluded after a dispute has arisen. The mediation clause may call for the application of institutional mediation rules or merely call for *ad hoc* mediation. In any event, the parties are free to adapt the mediation clause to their special needs. The parties should, however, define the scope of the mediation clause by identifying the issues subject to mediation. The parties should take special care in order to draft clear and unambiguous clauses. The parties may include the place of mediation proceedings and the language.

The parties are free to establish mediation proceedings as a mandatory precondition for commencing court or arbitral proceedings (mandatory mediation). Also, the parties may merely acknowledge that mediation proceedings are always available to them in order to remind themselves of the possibility of amicable dispute resolution without committing either party (optional mediation).

II. General Terms and Conditions

Mediation clauses that form part of the standard business terms of a contract are subject to the provisions of the German Civil Code (*Bürgerliches Gesetzbuch, BGB*) regarding the drafting of contractual obligations by means of standard business terms.[64] These provisions allow the court to scrutinize the standard terms and apply a test of reasonableness of contents: Provisions in standard business terms are ineffective if, contrary to the requirement of good faith, they unreasonably disadvantage the other party to the contract. An unreasonable disadvantage may also arise from the provision not being clear and comprehensible.[65] With respect to mediation clauses, only exceptional circumstances will constitute such an unreasonable disadvantage for a party. Under normal circumstances, a mediation clause included in general terms and conditions will be regarded as having been validly incorporated into the contract.[66]

---

[61] See *supra*, at pp. 196 et seq.
[62] Mediation Act § 1 (1).
[63] In particular, the content and form requirements for arbitration clauses under ZPO § 1029 (1) and ZPO § 1031 do not apply to mediation clauses; *cf. supra*, at pp. 130 et seq.
[64] Civil Code (BGB) § 305 to § 310. These provisions also serve to implement Directive 93/13/EEC of the Council of 5 April 1993 on unfair terms in consumer contracts, OJ 1993 L 95, p. 29.
[65] Civil Code (BGB) § 307 (1).
[66] However, in 2010, the Regional Court (LG) Heilbronn was of the opinion that a mediation clause that does not contain "elementary procedural rules", such as a framework regarding costs, duration and timing of proceedings, etc. may be null and void under BGB § 307 (1), see Regional Court (LG) Heilbronn, Decision of 10 September 2010 (Docket No. 4 O 259/09).

E. Mediation and Court Proceedings

I. Defense of Mediation

Should proceedings be brought before a court regarding a matter that is subject to a valid mandatory mediation clause, the court will generally dismiss the complaint as (currently) inadmissible provided that the respondent has raised the defense of mediation.[67] The claimant will be bound by its contractual obligation stemming from the mediation clause and will be obliged to commence mediation proceedings, *i.e.* appoint a mediator and participate in at least one mediation session. A mediation clause may not bar a party from requesting interim measures by a court.[68]

Whilst a valid mediation clause may obligate a party to commence mediation, a party cannot actually be forced to settle the dispute or negotiate in a certain manner. Furthermore, each party is free to terminate the mediation at any time.[69] Yet, the obligation to commence mediation proceedings should not be regarded as a mere formality.[70] Even if one of the parties has lost its interest in pursuing mediation, one cannot rule out the possibility that the parties may reach an amicable settlement once they have actually participated in a mediation session led by an impartial mediator.[71]

If, upon a failed obligatory mediation attempt, one party initiates court proceedings and subsequently extends or amends its claim, the Federal Court of Justice (*Bundesgerichtshof*) has held that a further mediation attempt regarding the extended or amended claim is not necessary.[72] The court found that the goal of obligatory mediation proceedings to help parties reach an out-of-court settlement can no longer be achieved in such cases.

II. Suspension of the Limitation Period

Under German law, claims are subject to limitation periods.[73] The standard limitation period is three years.[74] EC Directive No 2008/52 obligates the EU Member States to ensure that the limitation period is suspended by mediation.[75] German statutory law stipulates that the limitation period is suspended by, *inter alia*, (i) arranging for notice to be given of an application for conciliation filed with a

---

[67] Federal Court of Justice (BGH), Decision of 23 November 1983 (Docket No. VIII ZR 197/82) Neue Juristische Wochenschrift, 1984, p. 669; Federal Court of Justice (BGH), Decision of 18 November 1998 (Docket No. VIII ZR 344/97), Neue Juristische Wochenschrift, 1999, pp. 647, 648 (also ruling that this defense of mediation will be overruled if the defendant is not acting in good faith, *e.g.* if the defendant has boycotted the claimant's attempt to initiate mediation proceedings).
[68] *Cf.* ZPO § 1033 (*a maiore ad minus*).
[69] Mediation Act § 2 (5).
[70] *Cf.* Regional Court (LG) Heilbronn, Decision of 10 September 2010 (Docket No. 4 O 259/09) (denying the defendant its defense of mediation).
[71] Federal Court of Justice (BGH), Decision of 29 October 2008 (Docket No. VII ZR 165/06), Neue Juristische Wochenschrift Rechtsprechungs-Report, 2009, pp. 637, 639 (regarding conciliation).
[72] Federal Court of Justice (BGH), Decision of 22 October 2004 (Docket No. V ZR 47/04), not published.
[73] BGB § 194 (1).
[74] BGB § 195. This standard limitation period does not apply to certain claims, including claims for defects of sold goods (BGB § 438: 2 years as a rule) or claims for defects of work products such as artwork or buildings (BGB § 634a: 2-5 years).
[75] EC Directive No 2008/52 Art. 8 (1).

conciliation body established or recognized by the federal state's justice administration authority (*anerkannte Gütestelle*),[76] or (ii) if the parties seek conciliation in mutual agreement, with any other conciliation body that settles disputes.[77] In these events, the suspension of the limitation period ends six months after the proceedings are concluded or have come to a standstill because of the parties' inaction.[78]

Under this provision, a unilateral application for mediation may only suspend the limitation period if the application is addressed to a state-approved conciliation entity (*anerkannte Gütestelle*). Commencement of mediation proceedings before a mediator or mediation center that is not an *anerkannte Gütestelle* may suspend the limitation period only if the parties act in mutual agreement.

Further, the limitation period is generally suspended during negotiations between the parties with respect to the claim or the circumstances giving rise to the claim.[79] In this event, the suspension ends, at the earliest, three months after the negotiations have failed. Negotiations are defined as the parties' exchange of opinions regarding the claim or the set of facts giving rise to the claim unless one party immediately refuses to negotiate. Accordingly, commencement of mediation proceedings as well as discussions as to whether the parties should commence mediation proceedings may be considered negotiations. If, for example, one party suggests commencing mediation and the other party indicates that it will consider this suggestion, the limitation period is suspended. In this case suspension would end once one party clearly shows that it is not willing to commence mediation. If the parties stay the mediation proceedings in order to consider the results obtained thus far and to subsequently decide on whether to continue the mediation proceedings, suspension will not end before one party has clearly and unambiguously objected to continuing the mediation proceedings.[80]

However, it is advisable for the parties to clearly determine when the suspension period starts in mediation, *e.g.* the date on which the request is received by the secretariat of a defined mediation institution or the date on which the other party agreed to conduct mediation proceedings.[81] Further, the parties may include a waiver of the limitation defense in the mediation clause or their agreement on mediation procedures.

F. Mediation Procedure

German law does not regulate how to conduct mediation proceedings. Mediation is defined as a *"confidential and structured procedure"*,[82] but the law does not further elaborate on the specific structure of the procedure. The only provision on "mediation process" simply stipulates that the *"mediator shall be selected by the parties"*

---

[76] See also *infra*, at p. 208.
[77] BGB § 204 (1) No. 4.
[78] BGB § 204 (2).
[79] BGB § 203.
[80] See Bundestag Document [*BT-Drucksache*] 17/5335, p. 11.
[81] See *e.g.*, EUCON Mediation Rules 2013, §§ 2, 3, 18.
[82] Mediation Act § 1 (1).

and that he "shall ensure that the parties are integrated into the mediation process in an appropriate and fair manner".[83]

Consequently, upon initiating mediation, the parties need to decide on a mechanism to select and appoint a mediator. The mediator and/or the parties may then generally tailor the procedure to their individual needs. Mediation of family matters or of matters regarding administrative law[84] or employment and labor law[85] may be structured differently and follow a different approach than commercial mediation. The general principles of mediation as laid out by the Mediation Act are: (i) neutrality, (ii) voluntariness, (iii) self-responsibility, (iv) awareness, and (v) confidentiality.[86] These principles of the Mediation Act constitute the basic procedural framework into which each individual mediation may be embedded.

I. Mediator

By legal definition, a mediator is an independent and impartial person without any decision-making power who guides the parties through the mediation.[87] The European Union has published a European Code of Conduct for Mediators[88] setting out principles to which mediators or organizations providing mediation services may commit themselves.

1. Selection of the Mediator

The Mediation Act simply states that the mediator shall be selected by the parties (right to self-determination).[89] It does not provide for any selection process. The parties may either agree on a certain mediator or ask a third party – *e.g.* a court or a mediation institution – to suggest a mediator. If the parties' mediation clause refers to rules of a mediation institution, these rules most likely provide for a mechanism to select the mediator.[90]

When selecting the mediator, the parties should be aware that mediators who are not authorized to practice law are not allowed to intervene in the parties' negotiations by making legal proposals or giving legal advice.[91] The legislator differentiates between *"(mere) mediation"* and *"dispute resolution by way of legal means"*.[92] Accordingly, a mediator who is not authorized to practice law may not draft settlement agreements to conclude the mediation proceedings to the extent that legal aspects are touched upon.[93] Such mediator may, however, simply record the results of mediation (without giving legal advice). This principle seems to be

---

[83] Mediation Act §2 (1), (3).
[84] *Cf. Wegen/Uechtritz/Gack*, Mediation and Administrative Law in Germany, IBA Mediation Newletter, Vo. 12, 2005, pp. 32 *et seq.*
[85] *Cf. Wegen/Gotham/Naumann*, Mediation in employment and labor law in Germany – emerging opportunities?, IBA Mediation Newsletter, Vol. 12, 2007, pp. 24 *et seq.*
[86] See *Fritz/Pielsticker*, Mediationsgesetz, 2013, §2 paras. 22 *et seq.*
[87] Mediation Act §1 (2). For a detailed discussion on the "professional law" of mediators with regard to education, admission, and practice, see *Tochtermann* in: Hopt/Steffek (eds.), Mediation – Principles and Regulation in Comparative Perspective, 2013, pp. 562 *et seq.*
[88] *Cf.* EC Directive No. 2008/52, Recital 17.
[89] Mediation Act §2 (1).
[90] See, for example, EUCON Mediation Rules 2013, §§4 *et seq.*
[91] RDG §2 (3) no. 4; see also *Tochtermann* in: Hopt/Steffek (eds.), Mediation – Principles and Regulation in Comparative Perspective, 2013, p. 552.
[92] Bundestag Document (*BT-Drucksache*) 16/3655, p. 50.
[93] See Bundestag Document (*BT-Drucksache*) 16/3655, p. 50 (pointing out that such a mediator could be a lawyer).

contradicted by the mediator's obligation to ensure that the parties are aware of the underlying circumstances and understand the content of a possible settlement agreement.[94] However, this contradiction is resolved to some extent by the fact that the mediator is also obliged to remind the parties of their right to have such agreement examined by a lawyer (or other specialist).[95]

2. Independence and Impartiality – Disclosure Obligations of the Mediator

Under German law, prior to entering into a mediator agreement with the parties, the mediator selected by the parties is subject to disclosure obligations. He must disclose all circumstances that could impede his independence or impartiality.[96] Such circumstances may include (i) any personal or business relationship (including former mediation) with any of the parties, (ii) former attorney-client relationship of the mediator (or his firm) with one of the parties, or (iii) any form of personal interest in the outcome of the mediation.[97] Despite a potential conflict, the parties may explicitly exempt a mediator from these restrictions.[98] Further, the mediator must provide the parties with information about his professional background, training and experience in the field of mediation if the parties so request.[99]

3. Mediator's Duty to Guarantee each Party's Integration into the Mediation

The mediator shall guarantee that each party is integrated into the mediation process in an appropriate and fair manner.[100] The mediator is required to take all *appropriate* measures in order to facilitate the mediation in the interests of both parties. This aspect refers to the procedural structure of the mediation which, in turn, shall be conducted in a *fair* manner; *i.e.* the mediator shall guarantee equal, decent, and truthful conduct of all participants in the mediation.[101] Thus, the mediator is obliged to implement rules of mediation procedure and to ensure that the parties adhere to these rules.

4. Mediator's Duty of Confidentiality

Effective mediation requires confidentiality. Under the Mediation Act, the mediator and the persons involved in conducting the mediation process (such as office assistants, paralegals or translators, but not the parties!) are subject to a duty of confidentiality.[102] They must treat all information that has been revealed during the course of mediation as confidential. Pursuant to the Mediation Act,[103] the duty of confidentiality shall not apply in cases where (i) disclosure is required by law, (ii) disclosure of the content of the settlement agreement is necessary for it to be

---

[94] Mediation Act § 2 (6) sentence 1.
[95] Mediation Act § 2 (6) sentence 2.
[96] Mediation Act § 3 (1) sentence 1.
[97] Mediation Act § 3 (2), (3).
[98] Mediation Act § 3 (1) sentence 2, (4).
[99] Mediation Act § 3 (5).
[100] Mediation Act § 2 (3) sentence 2.
[101] Cf. *Fritz/Pielsticker*, Mediationsgesetz, 2013, § 2, no. 88.
[102] Mediation Act § 4.
[103] Mediation Act § 4 sentences 1 and 3.

implemented or enforced, (iii) disclosure is necessary for overriding considerations of public policy,[104] or (iv) facts are concerned that are common knowledge.

The duty of confidentiality protects the confidentiality of the proceedings. It allows the creation of a "protected area" in which the conflicting parties may try to form a common understanding to reach a fair settlement. Furthermore, the duty of confidentiality has an impact on possible court proceedings after failed mediation. This duty ensures that offers, concessions, or acknowledgments made will not be brought into court proceedings by way of summoning the mediator as witness. Accordingly, in court proceedings mediators are entitled to refuse to testify with regard to previous mediation proceedings.[105]

The parties and the mediator are free to agree on confidentiality provisions that deviate from the Mediation Act. This way, the parties may choose to extend the duty of confidentiality to each party. In any event, the mediator is obligated to inform the parties about the extent of his legal duty of confidentiality.[106]

5. Mediator Contract

Under German law, the (legal) relationship between the parties and the mediator is based on a (mediator) contract.[107] Such mediator contract is subject to the provisions dealing with service contracts.[108] There are no specific content or form requirements for mediator contracts under German law. Typically, a mediator contract deals with its termination, the mediator's remuneration, the mediator's obligations,[109] his liability, and record retention.[110]

a) Remuneration of Mediator

Mediators' fees are not subject to a statutory regulation in Germany. Therefore, the mediator and the parties will generally agree on the mediator's remuneration in their mediator contract. The fees will either be calculated on the basis of the time spent working on the mediation or on the basis of the amount in dispute. Hourly fees tend to range between EUR 200 and 450.[111] Fee arrangements should also include clauses regulating whether the mediator's preparation and post-processing phase are calculated on the same basis and whether the mediator will earn an additional fee if the parties successfully settle their dispute. A lawyer serving as mediator shall reach an agreement on fees with the parties.[112] Absent a valid fee agreement, general civil law applies so that mediators are entitled to the "usual remuneration".[113] Unless otherwise agreed, the parties will be jointly and severally liable for the mediator's fees.[114]

---

[104] This exception is to be applied, in particular, when disclosure is required to avert a risk posed to a child's well-being or to prevent serious harm to a person's physical or mental integrity.
[105] ZPO §383 (1) no. 6.
[106] Mediation Act §4 sentence 4.
[107] Note that the mediator contract and the agreement on procedure (see *infra* section II.) may be contained in one document.
[108] BGB §§611 *et seq.*, 675 (1).
[109] Generally, a mediator contract will reflect the mediator's obligations under the Mediation Act and (possibly) a certain code of conduct for mediators.
[110] *Fritz/Pielsticker*, Mediationsgesetz, 2013, §2, no. 78.
[111] *Fritz/Pielsticker*, Mediationsgesetz, 2013, §2, no. 54.
[112] Federal Attorney Renumeration Act (*Rechtsanwaltsvergütungsgesetz, RVG*), §34.
[113] BGB §612 (2).
[114] BGB §421.

b) Liability of Mediator

Generally, a mediator may be held liable for damages caused by a negligent or willful breach of his obligations stemming from either the mediator contract or the Mediation Act.[115] While general service contract law does not stipulate particular legal duties, the Mediation Act introduces specific legal obligations for mediators.[116] However, these statutory obligations are worded rather vaguely. In a given situation, it will be difficult to determine whether the parties *have understood the basic principles of mediation* or *understand the content of a settlement agreement*. In order to avoid liability risks, it is advisable to (i) specify the obligations in the mediator contract and (ii) interpret the legal obligations in a rigorous manner. In particular, the mediator should frequently (and possibly repeatedly) offer guidance to the parties, reassure himself regarding their knowledge and understanding as well as invite the parties to ask questions regarding the mediation process. The mediator should document such general advice, information, and reassurance in writing. If the mediator is a lawyer or a notary, the respective codes of professional conduct stipulate further duties, the breach of which could result in additional liability. The burden of proof for showing that (1) the mediator breached a contractual obligation and that (2) this breach caused concrete damage to the party is born by the party asserting the damage claim.

Generally, the mediator contract may limit the mediator's liability. In cases where the mediator is a lawyer, however, there are certain statutory restrictions on the limitation of liability under German law. In particular, the limitation of a lawyer's liability due to negligence (including gross negligence) must be *in writing*.[117] If the mediation contract is a standard contract, liability may only be limited with regard to damage due to ordinary negligence and not gross negligence or willful conduct.[118] In the absence of explicit provisions, claims against the mediator expire after three years. The limitation period commences upon the end of the year in which the claim has arisen and the damaged party becomes aware of the circumstances giving rise to the claim or ought to have become aware of such circumstances.[119]

c) Termination

Under German general service contract law, the mediator may terminate the mediator contract at any time because the mediator's services are rendered on the basis of special trust.[120] This understanding corresponds to the Mediation Act, pursuant to which the mediator may terminate the mediation if he is of the opinion that the mediation will likely not succeed.[121]

---

[115] See Bundestag Document (*BT-Drucksache*) 17/5335, p. 16.

[116] Mediation Act §§ 2-4.

[117] Federal Attorneys' Code (*Bundesrechtsanwaltsordnung, BRAO*) § 52 (1) no. 1, *i.e.* original agreement (not just a copy) must be signed by all parties with their names in their own hand (BGB § 126).

[118] BGB § 309 No. 7(b).

[119] BGB §§ 195, 199 (1).

[120] BGB § 627 (1); *Tochtermann* in: Hopt/Steffek (eds.), Mediation – Principles and Regulation in Comparative Perspective, 2013, p. 551.

[121] Mediation Act § 2 (5) sentence 2.

II. Agreement on Procedures

Upon initiating the actual mediation, the mediator (together with the parties) should lay down the procedural structure according to which the mediation shall be conducted. The mediator is obligated to guarantee that the parties are – at all times – fully informed of the procedure and participate in the mediation voluntarily.[122] Therefore, he should indicate to the parties that they have the possibility of entering into an agreement on procedures which may contain the basic rules of procedure, communication, and general conduct.[123]

Such agreements on procedures may contain manifold provisions dealing with various different topics and issues. In particular, such agreements may contain provisions dealing with:[124]

- personal attendance at mediation sessions;
- virtual mediation;
- attendance of the parties' counselors or lawyers;[125]
- attendance of independent experts;
- place and envisaged duration of the mediation;
- specified procedural timetable;
- general code of conduct during the mediation;
- confidentiality;[126]
- evidentiary rules regarding facts revealed during mediation;
- inspection of mediation documents;
- retention of mediation documents;
- costs of mediation and payment mechanisms;
- remuneration of mediator;[127]
- conduct of separate discussions with each party;[128]
- waiver of the limitation defense;
- contractual penalty with regard to a breach of the agreement on procedrues;
- conclusion of the mediation.

The agreement on procedures should be made in writing and should be signed by the mediator and the parties. The mediator should make sure that the parties fully understand the content of the agreement on procedure.

III. Reference to Rules of a Mediation Institution

Instead of drafting the agreement on procedures from scratch, the parties may refer to the rules of a mediation institution. These rules will provide for a relatively comprehensive framework for the mediation. Generally, the rules will repeat and possibly refine the procedural mediation framework contained in the Mediation Act – in particular with regard to the mediator's and the parties'

---

[122] Mediation Act § 2 (2).
[123] See Bundestag Document (*BT-Drucksache*) 17/5335, p. 15.
[124] See Bundestag Document (*BT-Drucksache*) 17/5335, p. 15; *Fritz/Pielsticker*, Mediationsgesetz, 2013, § 2, no. 79.
[125] Mediation Act § 2 (4): Third parties may be involved in the mediation only with the parties' consent.
[126] Note that the parties themselves are not bound by the duty of confidentiality under Mediation Act § 4.
[127] Note that the mediator agreement and the agreement on procedure may be contained in one document.
[128] Mediation Act § 2 (3) sentence 3.

duties. In addition, institutional mediation rules will usually contain provisions regarding (i) the selection and appointment of the mediator, (ii) commencement and conclusion of the mediation, (iii) the remuneration of the mediator, and (iv) costs of the proceedings. However, such rules will not usually contain provisions regarding the actual structure of the mediation itself. The mediator will still be responsible for structuring the mediation procedures to meet the individual needs of the conflicting parties.[129]

G. Conclusion of Mediation Proceedings

The way in which a mediation is concluded depends on its outcome. Essentially, the parties may either reach an agreement that settles all or at least part of their dispute, or the dispute remains unsettled and the mediation is terminated.

I. Termination of Mediation and its Consequences

The parties are free to terminate the mediation at any time and without cause (right to self-determination).[130] In addition, the mediator may terminate the mediation if he is of the opinion that the mediation will not lead to an amicable settlement.[131]

1. Mediation after Initiation of Court Proceedings

If the mediation proceedings were conducted before a conciliation judge (*Güterichter*), the judge who referred the parties to the conciliation judge[132] will take up the case again and the (still pending) proceedings will simply continue. If the parties pursued the mediation upon suggestion of a judge under ZPO § 278a, the proceedings that were stayed will be resumed.[133]

2. Mediation without Initiation of Court Proceedings

Where the parties conducted mediation without having initiated prior court proceedings, the further proceedings with regard to their dispute are not predetermined. Therefore, it is advisable for the parties to determine in advance how they will proceed if the mediation fails and their dispute remains unsettled. For instance, the parties could agree that court or arbitral proceedings will follow unsuccessful mediation.[134] Such a provision may have the positive effect that it could facilitate the parties' willingness to settle the dispute in the mediation proceedings.

    The parties may choose the mediator to become their arbitrator. German law does not provide an obstacle for doing so based on concerns of the arbitrator's impartiality due to his prior engagement as mediator. Only reasons occurring after the nomination of the arbitrator can be regarded as grounds for a potential

---

[129] See, for example, § 9 of the EUCON Mediation Rules.
[130] Mediation Act § 2 (5) sentence 1.
[131] Mediation Act § 2 (5) sentence 2; Bundestag Document (*BT-Drucksache*) 17/5335, p. 15.
[132] See *supra*, at pp. 195 et seq.
[133] See *supra*, at p. 196.
[134] See for example the ICC model mediation clause D.

rejection, since the parties have already agreed on his nomination as mediator. However, a mediator may not want to become arbitrator for fear of the chilling effect this might have on mediation. The parties might have reservations about discussing the case freely with a mediator who might later be in a position to impose a binding arbitral award.

In any event, the unsuccessful conclusion may have implications with regard to a possible defense of mediation[135] which ceases to exist upon the conclusion of mediation. Further, the end of a suspension of a limitation period may be affected by the date on which mediation has ended.[136] Under BGB §203 sentence 2, the suspension ends, at the earliest, three months after the negotiations have failed, *i.e.* after the mediation has ended.

II. Conclusion of a Settlement Agreement

If mediation is successful and the parties settle their dispute, the mediator shall ensure that the parties settle their dispute in full knowledge of the facts and full understanding of the content.[137] Thus, the mediator is obliged to ensure that the result of the mediation is in accordance with the parties' right to self-determination. In particular, the mediator shall remind the parties of their opportunity to involve a specialist (for instance, a lawyer) in order to review the terms of the settlement.[138] In order to avoid any risk of liability, the mediator should inform the parties of this opportunity in writing. He shall make sure that the parties freely decide whether they wish to involve a specialist or instead assume the risk of waiving this right.

The parties can record the terms of their settlement in a final and binding settlement agreement.[139] Under German law, such settlement agreement is considered a contract by means of which a dispute or uncertainty of the parties with regard to a legal relationship is resolved by way of mutual concession (*Vergleich*).[140] There is no particular form requirement for a settlement agreement. However, the form requirements of general contract law apply to settlement agreements. Thus, if – for example – a settlement agreement stipulates an obligation for the transfer of title in real estate[141] or for the transfer of shares in a limited liability company (*Gesellschaft mit beschränkter Haftung*),[142] the settlement agreement would be void unless it is notarized.[143]

III. Enforcement of the Settlement Agreement

Settlement agreements generally stipulate obligations that have to be fulfilled by one of the parties. Therefore, the respective other party must be provided with effective means of enforcement in case the obligee refuses to perform its obliga-

---

[135] See *supra*, at p. 199.
[136] See *supra*, at pp. 199 et seq.
[137] Mediation Act §2 (6) sentence 1.
[138] Mediation Act §2 (6) sentence 2.
[139] Mediation Act §2 (6) sentence 3.
[140] See BGB §779 (1).
[141] BGB §311b (1).
[142] Law on Limited Liability Companies (*Gesetz betreffend die Gesellschaften mit beschränkter Haftung, GmbHG*) §15 (4).
[143] See BGB §§125, 128.

tions under the settlement agreement.[144] German law provides for the remedies of specific performance or damages.

In order to obtain these remedies by way of compulsory enforcement, the debtor must obtain an enforceable instrument. An enforceable instrument cannot be created in the course of the actual mediation proceedings. However, there are several different ways for the parties to mediation to obtain an enforceable instrument. The following instruments seem most relevant with regard to the enforcement of settlement agreements:
(i) final and binding judgments;
(ii) court settlements;
(iii) settlements made before a state-approved conciliation entity (*Gütestelle*);
(iv) notarial deeds in which the debtor agreed to immediate enforcement; or
(v) lawyers' settlements in which the obligee agreed to immediate enforcement.

A brief outline of the subsequent enforcement and execution of an enforceable instrument in Germany can be found *supra*, at pp. 103 et seq (regarding judgments).

1. Final and Binding Judgments

A party intending to enforce its claims under a settlement agreement may always initiate court proceedings. This option, however, may prove burdensome and protracted. The settlement agreement would simply be treated as any other contract.

2. Court Settlements

Where the mediation proceedings were commenced after court proceedings had already been initiated,[145] the parties may submit to the court a draft settlement agreement in writing. The court can then issue an order in which it establishes the conclusion of a settlement (agreement) and records the content of the settlement (agreement).[146] Such court settlement constitutes an enforceable instrument.[147] The recognition and enforcement of court settlements within the EU is facilitated by Article 59 of EU Regulation No. 1215/2012.[148]

3. Settlements before a State-Approved Conciliatory Entity

The parties may conclude a settlement before a state-approved conciliation entity (*Gütestelle*). Such settlements are equivalent to court settlements. Most federal states have approved such conciliation entities but the situation varies from state to state. For example, in the state of Baden-Württemberg, each local court (*Amtsgericht*) has established conciliation entities which are staffed with lawyers. In Bavaria, all notaries and certain lawyers who are approved by the bar association as conciliators are considered state-approved entities.

---

[144] EC Directive No 2008/52 Art. 6 (1) obliges the Member States to ensure that it is possible for the parties to request that the content of a written agreement resulting from mediation be made enforceable, see *supra*, at pp. 193 et seq.
[145] See *supra*, at pp. 195 et seq.
[146] ZPO § 278 (6).
[147] ZPO § 794 no. 1.
[148] Regulation (EU) No 1215/2012 of the European Parliament and of the Council of 12 December 2012 on jurisdiction and the recognition and enforcement of judgments in civil and commercial matters, OJ 2012 L 351/1.

4. Notarial Deeds

A settlement agreement that is recorded by a notary public may be an enforceable instrument if the debtor has subjected himself to immediate compulsory enforcement of the claim as specified in the agreement.[149] Such deeds are enforceable within the European Union.[150] The parties should be aware of the relatively high costs for notarization that are calculated based on the amount in dispute. A notarial deed may, however, be a convenient option where the notary has been involved in the mediation proceedings anyway.

5. Enforceable Lawyers' Settlements

A settlement agreement (1) that has been concluded by lawyers on behalf and with the authority of the parties they represent and (2) in which the debtor has subjected himself to immediate compulsory enforcement of the claim as specified in the agreement may be declared enforceable in two ways:

First, at the request of a party, a court may declare the settlement agreement enforceable if (i) the settlement has been deposited with a local court (*Amtsgericht*) in the district of which one of the parties had its general venue at the time the settlement was reached and (ii) the settlement agreement specifies the date on which it was reached.[151] Second, with the consent of the parties, a notary public who has his official residence in the district of said local court (*Amtsgericht*) may also declare the settlement enforceable if the settlement agreement remains in his safekeeping.[152]

Since the parties to mediation will often be represented by lawyers, the option of having a lawyers' settlement declared enforceable seems to be a convenient way to obtain an enforceable instrument.

6. Award on Agreed Terms

Once the parties have settled their dispute during mediation proceedings, they may choose to appoint the mediator as arbitrator. The arbitrator may in turn transform the settlement into an award on agreed terms. An award on agreed terms is enforceable virtually worldwide,[153] because most countries regard an award on agreed terms to be within the scope of the New York Convention. Whether this procedure results in a valid award on agreed terms under German law has not yet been decided by a court. However, the parties may not refuse the arbitrator because his previous appointment as mediator may give rise to doubts as to the arbitrator's impartiality. A party may only challenge an arbitrator whom it has appointed for reasons it becomes aware of after the appointment.[154]

---

[149] ZPO §794 no. 5.
[150] Regulation (EU) No 1215/2012, 44/2001 Art. 58.
[151] ZPO §796a (1).
[152] ZPO §796c (1).
[153] See *supra*, at pp. 187 et seq.
[154] ZPO §1136 para. 2 sentence 2. Note that a judge is disqualified by law from exercising judicial office in all matters in which he assisted in mediation proceedings or in any other alternative conflict resolution procedures under ZPO §41 no. 8; also *cf. Wegen/Gack*, Previous Mediator as Later Judge or Arbitrator – Involvement of a judge as mediator does not necessarily prevent him from later deciding the case, IBA Mediation Newsletter, Vol. 7, 2007, p. 37 (regarding the prevailing legal norms before the enforcement of the Mediation Advancement Law).

Part 2
Relevant Statutory and Regulatory Materials

A. German Statutory Instruments

I. Zivilprozessordnung (Auszüge)

I. Code of Civil Procedure (Excerpts)

Buch 10[1]
Schiedsrichterliches Verfahren

Book 10[1, 2]
Arbitration Procedure

Abschnitt 1
Allgemeine Vorschriften

Chapter 1
General provisions

§ 1025
Anwendungsbereich

§ 1025
Scope of application

(1) Die Vorschriften dieses Buches sind anzuwenden, wenn der Ort des schieds-

(1) The provisions of this Book apply if the place of arbitration as referred to in § 1043 (1) is situated in Germany.

---

[1] Zum schiedsrichterlichen Verfahren beachte die in § 33 des Gesetzes betreffend die Einführung der Zivilprozessordnung (EGZPO) erlassenen Überleitungsvorschriften zum Schiedsverfahrens-Neuregelungsgesetz v. 19.4.2006 (BGBl. I S. 866): § 33
(1) Die Wirksamkeit von Schiedsvereinbarungen, die vor dem Inkrafttreten des Schiedsverfahrens-Neuregelungsgesetzes vom 2. Dezember 1997 (BGBl. I S. 3224) am 1. Januar 1998 geschlossen worden sind, beurteilt sich nach dem bis zu diesem Zeitpunkt geltenden Recht.
(2) Für schiedsrichterliche Verfahren, die am 1. Januar 1998 noch nicht beendet waren, ist das bis zu diesem Zeitpunkt geltende Recht mit der Maßgabe anzuwenden, dass an die Stelle des schiedsrichterlichen Vergleichs der Schiedsspruch mit vereinbartem Wortlaut tritt. Die Parteien können jedoch die Anwendung des neuen Rechts vereinbaren
(3) Für gerichtliche Verfahren, die bis zum 1. Januar 1998 anhängig geworden sind, ist das bis zu diesem Zeitpunkt geltende Recht weiter anzuwenden. (4) Aus für vollstreckbar erklärten schiedsrichterlichen Vergleichen, die vor dem 1. Januar 1998 geschlossen worden sind, findet die Zwangsvollstreckung statt, sofern die Entscheidung über die Voll-

[1] *Unofficial translation by the German Institution of Arbitration (DIS) and the German Federal Ministry of Justice, see http://www.trans-lex.org/600550/#head_0.
[2] In regard to arbitral proceedings note the transitional provisions to the Act on the Reform of the Law relating to Arbitral Proceedings in § 33 of the Introductory Act of the Code of Civil Procedure (EGZPO), Federal Law Gazette, 19 April 2006 (BGBl. I S. 866):
§ 33
(1) The effectiveness of arbitration agreements that have been concluded prior to the entry into force of the Act on the Reform of the Law relating to Arbitral Proceedings, Federal Law Gazette, 22 December 1997 (BGBl. I S. 3224) shall be determined according to the law in force at that time.
(2) Arbitral proceedings that were not terminated on 1 January 1998 are governed by the law in force at that time provided that the arbitral settlement („schiedsrichterlicher Vergleich") is substituted by the award on agreed terms. The parties may agree to apply the new law.
(3) Court proceedings pending upon 1 January 1998 remain subject to the law in force at that time.

richterlichen Verfahrens im Sinne des § 1043 Abs. 1 in Deutschland liegt.

(2) Die Bestimmungen der §§ 1032, 1033 und 1050 sind auch dann anzuwenden, wenn der Ort des schiedsrichterlichen Verfahrens im Ausland liegt oder noch nicht bestimmt ist.

(3) Solange der Ort des schiedsrichterlichen Verfahrens noch nicht bestimmt ist, sind die deutschen Gerichte für die Ausübung der in §§ 1034, 1035, 1037 und 1038 bezeichneten gerichtlichen Aufgaben zuständig, wenn der Beklagte oder der Kläger seinen Sitz oder seinen gewöhnlichen Aufenthalt in Deutschland hat.

(4) Für die Anerkennung und Vollstreckung ausländischer Schiedssprüche gelten die §§ 1061 bis 1065.

(2) The provisions of §§ 1032, 1033 and 1050 also apply if the place of arbitration is situated outside Germany or has not yet been determined.

(3) If the place of arbitration has not yet been determined, the German courts are competent to perform the court functions specified in §§ 1034, 1035, 1037 and 1038 if the respondent or the claimant has his place of business or habitual residence in Germany.

(4) §§ 1061 to 1065 apply to the recognition and enforcement of foreign arbitral awards.

§ 1026
Umfang gerichtlicher Tätigkeit

Ein Gericht darf in den in §§ 1025 bis 1061 geregelten Angelegenheiten nur tätig werden, soweit dieses Buch es vorsieht.

§ 1026
Extent of court intervention

In matters governed by §§ 1025 to 1061, no court shall intervene except where so provided in this Book.

§ 1027
Verlust des Rügerechts

Ist einer Bestimmung dieses Buches, von der die Parteien abweichen können, oder einem vereinbarten Erfordernis des schiedsrichterlichen Verfahrens nicht entsprochen worden, so kann eine Partei, die den Mangel nicht unverzüglich oder innerhalb einer dafür vorgesehenen Frist rügt, diesen später nicht mehr geltend machen. Dies gilt nicht, wenn der Partei der Mangel nicht bekannt war.

§ 1027
Loss of right to object

A party who knows that any provision of this Book from which the parties may derogate or any agreed requirement under the arbitral procedure has not been complied with and yet proceeds with the arbitration without stating his objection to such non-compliance without undue delay or, if a time limit is provided therefore, within such period of time, may not raise that objection later.

---

streckbarkeit rechtskräftig oder für vorläufig vollstreckbar erklärt worden ist. Für die Entscheidung über die Vollstreckbarkeit gilt das bis zum Inkrafttreten des Schiedsverfahrens-Neuregelungsgesetzes vom 22. Dezember 1997 (BGBl. I S. 3224) geltende Recht.

(4) Arbitral settlements that have been concluded and declared enforceable prior to 1 January 1998 are subject to enforcement provided that the decision on their enforceability has become final and binding or has been declared provisionally enforceable. The law applicable upon the entry into force of the Act on the Reform of the Law relating to Arbitral Proceedings, Federal Law Gazette, 22 December 1997 (BGBl. I S. 3224) applies to the decision on enforceability.

§ 1028
Empfang schriftlicher Mitteilungen bei unbekanntem Aufenthalt

(1) Ist der Aufenthalt einer Partei oder einer zur Entgegennahme berechtigten Person unbekannt, gelten, sofern die Parteien nichts anderes vereinbart haben, schriftliche Mitteilungen an dem Tag als empfangen, an dem sie bei ordnungsgemäßer Übermittlung durch Einschreiben gegen Rückschein oder auf eine andere Weise, welche den Zugang an der letztbekannten Postanschrift oder Niederlassung oder dem letztbekannten gewöhnlichen Aufenthalt des Adressaten belegt, dort hätten empfangen werden können.

(2) Absatz 1 ist auf Mitteilungen in gerichtlichen Verfahren nicht anzuwenden.

§ 1028
Receipt of written communications in case of unknown whereabouts

(1) Unless otherwise agreed by the parties, if the whereabouts of a party or of a person entitled to receive communications on his behalf are not known, any written communication shall be deemed to have been received on the day on which it could have been received at the addressee's last-known mailing address, place of business or habitual residence after proper transmission by registered mail/return receipt requested or any other means which provides a record of the attempt to deliver it there.

(2) Subsection 1 does not apply to communications in court proceedings.

Abschnitt 2
Schiedsvereinbarung

Chapter 2
Arbitration agreement

§ 1029
Begriffsbestimmung

(1) Schiedsvereinbarung ist eine Vereinbarung der Parteien, alle oder einzelne Streitigkeiten, die zwischen ihnen in Bezug auf ein bestimmtes Rechtsverhältnis vertraglicher oder nichtvertraglicher Art entstanden sind oder künftig entstehen, der Entscheidung durch ein Schiedsgericht zu unterwerfen.

(2) Eine Schiedsvereinbarung kann in Form einer selbständigen Vereinbarung (Schiedsabrede) oder in Form einer Klausel in einem Vertrag (Schiedsklausel) geschlossen werden.

§ 1029
Definition

(1) „Arbitration agreement" is an agreement by the parties to submit to arbitration all or certain disputes which have arisen or which may arise between them in respect of a defined legal relationship, whether contractual or not.

(2) An arbitration agreement may be in the form of a separate agreement („separate arbitration agreement") or in the form of a clause in a contract („arbitration clause").

§ 1030
Schiedsfähigkeit

(1) Jeder vermögensrechtliche Anspruch kann Gegenstand einer Schiedsvereinbarung sein. Eine Schiedsvereinbarung über nichtvermögensrechtliche Ansprüche hat insoweit rechtliche Wirkung, als die Parteien berechtigt sind, über den

§ 1030
Arbitrability

(1) Any claim involving an economic interest („vermögensrechtlicher Anspruch") can be the subject of an arbitration agreement. An arbitration agreement concerning claims not involving an economic interest shall have legal effect to the extent that the parties

Gegenstand des Streites einen Vergleich zu schließen.

(2) Eine Schiedsvereinbarung über Rechtsstreitigkeiten, die den Bestand eines Mietverhältnisses über Wohnraum im Inland betreffen, ist unwirksam. Dies gilt nicht, soweit es sich um Wohnraum der in §549 Abs.2 Nr.1 bis 3 des Bürgerlichen Gesetzbuchs bestimmten Art handelt.

(3) Gesetzliche Vorschriften außerhalb dieses Buches, nach denen Streitigkeiten einem schiedsrichterlichen Verfahren nicht oder nur unter bestimmten Voraussetzungen unterworfen werden dürfen, bleiben unberührt.

§ 1031
Form der Schiedsvereinbarung

(1) Die Schiedsvereinbarung muss entweder in einem von den Parteien unterzeichneten Dokument oder in zwischen ihnen gewechselten Schreiben, Fernkopien, Telegrammen oder anderen Formen der Nachrichtenübermittlung, die einen Nachweis der Vereinbarung sicherstellen, enthalten sein.

(2) Die Form des Absatzes 1 gilt auch dann als erfüllt, wenn die Schiedsvereinbarung in einem von der einen Partei der anderen Partei oder von einem Dritten beiden Parteien übermittelten Dokument enthalten ist und der Inhalt des Dokuments im Fall eines nicht rechtzeitig erfolgten Widerspruchs nach der Verkehrssitte als Vertragsinhalt angesehen wird.

(3) Nimmt ein den Formerfordernissen der Absätze 1 oder 2 entsprechender Vertrag auf ein Dokument Bezug, das eine Schiedsklausel enthält, so begründet dies eine Schiedsvereinbarung, wenn die Bezugnahme dergestalt ist, dass sie diese Klausel zu einem Bestandteil des Vertrages macht.

(4) Eine Schiedsvereinbarung wird auch durch die Begebung eines Konnossements begründet, in dem ausdrücklich

are entitled to conclude a settlement on the issue in dispute.

(2) An arbitration agreement relating to disputes on the existence of a lease of residential accommodation within Germany shall be null and void. This does not apply to residential accommodation as specified in §549 (2) no.1 to 3 of the Civil Code.

(3) Statutory provisions outside this Book by virtue of which certain disputes may not be submitted to arbitration, or may be submitted to arbitration only under certain conditions, remain unaffected.

§ 1031
Form of arbitration agreement

(1) The arbitration agreement shall be contained either in a document signed by the parties or in an exchange of letters, telefaxes, telegrams or other means of telecommunication which provide a record of the agreement.

(2) The form requirement of subsection 1 shall be deemed to have been complied with if the arbitration agreement is contained in a document transmitted from one party to the other party or by a third party to both parties and – if no objection was raised in good time – the contents of such document are considered to be part of the contract in accordance with common usage.

(3) The reference in a contract complying with the form requirements of subsection 1 or 2 to a document containing an arbitration clause constitutes an arbitration agreement provided that the reference is such as to make that clause part of the contract.

(4) An arbitration agreement is also concluded by the issuance of a bill of lading, if the latter contains an express

auf die in einem Chartervertrag enthaltene Schiedsklausel Bezug genommen wird.

(5) Schiedsvereinbarungen, an denen ein Verbraucher[2] beteiligt ist, müssen in einer von den Parteien eigenhändig unterzeichneten Urkunde enthalten sein. Die schriftliche Form nach Satz 1 kann durch die elektronische Form nach § 126a des Bürgerlichen Gesetzbuches[3] ersetzt werden. Andere Vereinbarungen als solche, die sich auf das schiedsrichterliche Verfahren beziehen, darf die

reference to an arbitration clause in a charter party.

(5) Arbitration agreements to which a consumer[3] is a party must be contained in a document which has been personally signed by the parties. The written form pursuant to subsection 1 may be substituted by electronic form pursuant to § 126a of the Civil Code („Bürgerliches Gesetzbuch – BGB")[4]. No agreements other than those referring to the arbitral proceedings may be contained in such a

---

[2] Verbraucher ist jede natürliche Person, die ein Rechtsgeschäft zu einem Zweck abschließt, der weder ihrer gewerblichen noch ihrer selbständigen beruflichen Tätigkeit zugeordnet werden kann (§ 13 BGB).

[3] § 126a BGB [Elektronische Form]: (1) Soll die gesetzlich vorgeschriebene schriftliche durch die elektronische Form ersetzt werden, so muss der Aussteller der Erklärung dieser seinen Namen hinzufügen und das elektronische Dokument mit einer qualifizierten elektronischen Signatur nach dem Signaturgesetz versehen.
(2) Bei einem Vertrag müssen die Parteien jeweils ein gleichlautendes Dokument in der in Absatz 1 bezeichneten Weise elektronisch signieren.
§ 2 SigG [Qualifizierte elektronische Form]: Im Sinne dieses Gesetzes sind

1. „elektronische Signaturen" Daten in elektronischer Form, die anderen elektronischen Daten beigefügt oder logisch mit ihnen verknüpft sind und die zur Authentifizierung dienen,
2. „fortgeschrittene elektronische Signaturen" elektronische Signaturen nach Nummer 1, die a) ausschließlich dem Signaturschlüssel-Inhaber zugeordnet sind, b) die Identifizierung des Signaturschlüssel-Inhabers ermöglichen, c) mit Mitteln erzeugt werden, die der Signaturschlüssel-Inhaber unter seiner alleinigen Kontrolle halten kann, und d) mit den Daten, auf die sie sich beziehen, so verknüpft sind, dass eine nachträgliche Veränderung der Daten erkannt werden kann,
3. „qualifizierte elektronische Signaturen" elektronische Signaturen nach Nummer 2, die a) auf einem zum Zeitpunkt ihrer Erzeugung gültigen qualifizierten Zertifikat beruhen und b) mit einer sicheren Signaturerstellungseinheit erzeugt werden, [...]
4.–15. [...]

[3] A consumer is any natural person who concludes a transaction for a purpose which can be regarded as being outside his trade or self-employed profession („gewerbliche oder selbständige berufliche Tätigkeit") – § 13 Civil Code.

[4] § 126a Civil Code („BGB") [Electronic form]: (1) If the statutory written form is to be substituted by electronic form, the author of the statement must add his name to the statement and append a qualified electronic signature pursuant to the Signature Act.
(2) In the case of a contract, the parties must each electronically sign a document identical in wording in the manner prescribed in subsection 1.
§ 2 Signature Act („Signaturgesetz – SigG") [Qualified electronic form]: For the purpose of this Act,

1. „electronic signature" means data in electronic form which are attached to or logically associated with other electronic data and which serve as a method of authentication;
2. „advanced electronic signature" means an electronic signature pursuant to No. 1 which a) is uniquely linked to the signatory, b) is capable of identifying the signatory, c) is created using means that the signatory can maintain under his sole control, and d) is linked to the data to which it relates in such a manner that any subsequent change of the data is detectable;
3. „qualified electronic signature" means an electronic signature pursuant to No. 2 which a) is based on a qualified certificate valid at the time of the signature's creation, and b) is created with a secure signature-creation device; [...]
4.–15. [...]

Urkunde oder das elektronische Dokument nicht enthalten; dies gilt nicht bei notarieller Beurkundung.	document or electronic document; this shall not apply in the case of a notarial certification.
(6) Der Mangel der Form wird durch die Einlassung auf die schiedsgerichtliche Verhandlung zur Hauptsache geheilt.	(6) Any non-compliance with the form requirements is cured by entering into argument on the substance of the dispute in the arbitral proceedings.

§ 1032	§ 1032
Schiedsvereinbarung und Klage vor Gericht	**Arbitration agreement and substantive claim before court**
(1) Wird vor einem Gericht Klage in einer Angelegenheit erhoben, die Gegenstand einer Schiedsvereinbarung ist, so hat das Gericht die Klage als unzulässig abzuweisen, sofern der Beklagte dies vor Beginn der mündlichen Verhandlung zur Hauptsache rügt, es sei denn, das Gericht stellt fest, dass die Schiedsvereinbarung nichtig, unwirksam oder undurchführbar ist.	(1) A court before which an action is brought in a matter which is the subject of an arbitration agreement shall, if the respondent raises an objection prior to the beginning of the oral hearing on the substance of the dispute, reject the action as inadmissible unless the court finds that the arbitration agreement is null and void, inoperative or incapable of being performed.
(2) Bei Gericht kann bis zur Bildung des Schiedsgerichts Antrag auf Feststellung der Zulässigkeit oder Unzulässigkeit eines schiedsrichterlichen Verfahrens gestellt werden.	(2) Prior to the constitution of the arbitral tribunal, an application may be made to the court to determine whether or not arbitration is admissible.
(3) Ist ein Verfahren im Sinne des Absatzes 1 oder 2 anhängig, kann ein schiedsrichterliches Verfahren gleichwohl eingeleitet oder fortgesetzt werden und ein Schiedsspruch ergehen.	(3) Where an action or application referred to in subsection 1 or 2 has been brought, arbitral proceedings may nevertheless be commenced or continued, and an arbitral award may be made, while the issue is pending before the court.

§ 1033	§ 1033
Schiedsvereinbarung und einstweilige gerichtliche Maßnahmen	**Arbitration agreement and interim measures by court**
Eine Schiedsvereinbarung schließt nicht aus, dass ein Gericht vor oder nach Beginn des schiedsrichterlichen Verfahrens auf Antrag einer Partei eine vorläufige oder sichernde Maßnahme in Bezug auf den Streitgegenstand des schiedsrichterlichen Verfahrens anordnet.	It is not incompatible with an arbitration agreement for a court to grant, before or during arbitral proceedings, an interim measure of protection relating to the subject-matter of the arbitration upon request of a party.

Abschnitt 3
Bildung des Schiedsgerichts

§ 1034
Zusammensetzung des Schiedsgerichts

(1) Die Parteien können die Anzahl der Schiedsrichter vereinbaren. Fehlt eine solche Vereinbarung, so ist die Zahl der Schiedsrichter drei.

(2) Gibt die Schiedsvereinbarung einer Partei bei der Zusammensetzung des Schiedsgerichts ein Übergewicht, das die andere Partei benachteiligt, so kann diese Partei bei Gericht beantragen, den oder die Schiedsrichter abweichend von der erfolgten Ernennung oder der vereinbarten Ernennungsregelung zu bestellen. Der Antrag ist spätestens bis zum Ablauf von zwei Wochen, nachdem der Partei die Zusammensetzung des Schiedsgerichts bekannt geworden ist, zu stellen. § 1032 Abs. 3 gilt entsprechend.

§ 1035
Bestellung der Schiedsrichter

(1) Die Parteien können das Verfahren zur Bestellung des Schiedsrichters oder der Schiedsrichter vereinbaren.

(2) Sofern die Parteien nichts anderes vereinbart haben, ist eine Partei an die durch sie erfolgte Bestellung eines Schiedsrichters gebunden, sobald die andere Partei die Mitteilung über die Bestellung empfangen hat.

(3) Fehlt eine Vereinbarung der Parteien über die Bestellung der Schiedsrichter, wird ein Einzelschiedsrichter, wenn die Parteien sich über seine Bestellung nicht einigen können, auf Antrag einer Partei durch das Gericht bestellt. In schiedsrichterlichen Verfahren mit drei Schiedsrichtern bestellt jede Partei einen Schiedsrichter; diese beiden Schiedsrichter bestellen den dritten Schiedsrichter, der als Vorsitzender des Schiedsgerichts tätig wird. Hat eine Partei den Schiedsrichter nicht innerhalb

Chapter 3
Constitution of arbitral tribunal

§ 1034
Composition of arbitral tribunal

(1) The parties are free to determine the number of arbitrators. Failing such determination, the number of arbitrators shall be three.

(2) If the arbitration agreement grants preponderant rights to one party with regard to the composition of the arbitral tribunal which place the other party at a disadvantage, that other party may request the court to appoint the arbitrator or arbitrators in deviation from the nomination made, or from the agreed nomination procedure. The request must be submitted at the latest within two weeks of the party becoming aware of the constitution of the arbitral tribunal. § 1032 (3) applies *mutatis mutandis*.

§ 1035
Appointment of arbitrators

(1) The parties are free to agree on a procedure of appointing the arbitrator or arbitrators.

(2) Unless otherwise agreed by the parties, a party shall be bound by his appointment of an arbitrator as soon as the other party has received notice of the appointment.

(3) Failing an agreement between the parties on the appointment of the arbitrators, a sole arbitrator shall, if the parties are unable to agree on his appointment, be appointed, upon request of a party, by the court. In an arbitration with three arbitrators, each party shall appoint one arbitrator, and the two arbitrators thus appointed shall appoint the third arbitrator who shall act as chairman of the arbitral tribunal. If a party fails to appoint the arbitrator within one month of receipt of a request to do so

eines Monats nach Empfang einer entsprechenden Aufforderung durch die andere Partei bestellt oder können sich die beiden Schiedsrichter nicht binnen eines Monats nach ihrer Bestellung über den dritten Schiedsrichter einigen, so ist der Schiedsrichter auf Antrag einer Partei durch das Gericht zu bestellen.

(4) Haben die Parteien ein Verfahren für die Bestellung vereinbart und handelt eine Partei nicht entsprechend diesem Verfahren oder können die Parteien oder die beiden Schiedsrichter eine Einigung entsprechend diesem Verfahren nicht erzielen oder erfüllt ein Dritter eine ihm nach diesem Verfahren übertragene Aufgabe nicht, so kann jede Partei bei Gericht die Anordnung der erforderlichen Maßnahmen beantragen, sofern das vereinbarte Bestellungsverfahren zur Sicherung der Bestellung nichts anderes vorsieht.

(5) Das Gericht hat bei der Bestellung eines Schiedsrichters alle nach der Parteivereinbarung für den Schiedsrichter vorgeschriebenen Voraussetzungen zu berücksichtigen und allen Gesichtspunkten Rechnung zu tragen, die die Bestellung eines unabhängigen und unparteiischen Schiedsrichters sicherstellen. Bei der Bestellung eines Einzelschiedsrichters oder eines dritten Schiedsrichters hat das Gericht auch die Zweckmäßigkeit der Bestellung eines Schiedsrichters mit einer anderen Staatsangehörigkeit als derjenigen der Parteien in Erwägung zu ziehen.

from the other party, or if the two arbitrators fail to agree on the third arbitrator within one month of their appointment, the appointment shall be made, upon request of a party, by the court.

(4) Where, under an appointment procedure agreed upon by the parties, a party fails to act as required under such procedure, or if the parties, or two arbitrators, are unable to reach an agreement expected of them under such procedure, or a third party fails to perform any function entrusted to it under such procedure, any party may request the court to take the necessary measure, unless the agreement on the appointment procedure provides other means for securing the appointment.

(5) The court, in appointing an arbitrator, shall have due regard to any qualifications required of the arbitrator by the agreement of the parties and to such considerations as are likely to secure the appointment of an independent and impartial arbitrator. In the case of a sole or third arbitrator, the court shall take into account as well the advisability of appointing an arbitrator of a nationality other than those of the parties.

§ 1036
Ablehnung eines Schiedsrichters

(1) Eine Person, der ein Schiedsrichteramt angetragen wird, hat alle Umstände offen zu legen, die Zweifel an ihrer Unparteilichkeit oder Unabhängigkeit wecken können. Ein Schiedsrichter ist auch nach seiner Bestellung bis zum Ende des schiedsrichterlichen Verfahrens verpflichtet, solche Umstände den Parteien unverzüglich offen zu legen,

§ 1036
Challenge of an arbitrator

(1) When a person is approached in connection with his possible appointment as an arbitrator, he shall disclose any circumstances likely to give rise to justifiable doubts as to his impartiality or independence. An arbitrator, from the time of his appointment and throughout the arbitral proceedings, shall without delay disclose any such circumstances

wenn er sie ihnen nicht schon vorher mitgeteilt hat.	to the parties unless they have already been informed of them by him.
(2) Ein Schiedsrichter kann nur abgelehnt werden, wenn Umstände vorliegen, die berechtigte Zweifel an seiner Unparteilichkeit oder Unabhängigkeit aufkommen lassen, oder wenn er die zwischen den Parteien vereinbarten Voraussetzungen nicht erfüllt. Eine Partei kann einen Schiedsrichter, den sie bestellt oder an dessen Bestellung sie mitgewirkt hat, nur aus Gründen ablehnen, die ihr erst nach der Bestellung bekannt geworden sind.	(2) An arbitrator may be challenged only if circumstances exist that give rise to justifiable doubts as to his impartiality or independence, or if he does not possess qualifications agreed to by the parties. A party may challenge an arbitrator appointed by him, or in whose appointment he has participated, only for reasons of which he becomes aware after the appointment has been made.

§ 1037
Ablehnungsverfahren

§ 1037
Challenge procedure

(1) Die Parteien können vorbehaltlich des Absatzes 3 ein Verfahren für die Ablehnung eines Schiedsrichters vereinbaren.

(1) The parties are free to agree on a procedure for challenging an arbitrator, subject to the provisions of subsection 3 of this section.

(2) Fehlt eine solche Vereinbarung, so hat die Partei, die einen Schiedsrichter ablehnen will, innerhalb von zwei Wochen, nachdem ihr die Zusammensetzung des Schiedsgerichts oder ein Umstand im Sinne des § 1036 Abs. 2 bekannt geworden ist, dem Schiedsgericht schriftlich die Ablehnungsgründe darzulegen. Tritt der abgelehnte Schiedsrichter von seinem Amt nicht zurück oder stimmt die andere Partei der Ablehnung nicht zu, so entscheidet das Schiedsgericht über die Ablehnung.

(2) Failing such agreement, a party who intends to challenge an arbitrator shall, within two weeks after becoming aware of the constitution of the arbitral tribunal or after becoming aware of any circumstance referred to in § 1036 (2), send a written statement of the reasons for the challenge to the arbitral tribunal. Unless the challenged arbitrator withdraws from his office or the other party agrees to the challenge, the arbitral tribunal shall decide on the challenge.

(3) Bleibt die Ablehnung nach dem von den Parteien vereinbarten Verfahren oder nach dem in Absatz 2 vorgesehenen Verfahren erfolglos, so kann die ablehnende Partei innerhalb eines Monats, nachdem sie von der Entscheidung, mit der die Ablehnung verweigert wurde, Kenntnis erlangt hat, bei Gericht eine Entscheidung über die Ablehnung beantragen; die Parteien können eine andere Frist vereinbaren. Während ein solcher Antrag anhängig ist, kann das Schiedsgericht einschließlich des abgelehnten Schiedsrichters das schiedsrich-

(3) If a challenge under any procedure agreed upon by the parties or under the procedure of subsection 2 of this section is not successful, the challenging party may request, within one month after having received notice of the decision rejecting the challenge, the court to decide on the challenge; the parties may agree on a different time-limit. While such a request is pending, the arbitral tribunal, including the challenged arbitrator, may continue the arbitral proceedings and make an award.

terliche Verfahren fortsetzen und einen Schiedsspruch erlassen.

§ 1038
Untätigkeit oder Unmöglichkeit der Aufgabenerfüllung

(1) Ist ein Schiedsrichter rechtlich oder tatsächlich außerstande, seine Aufgaben zu erfüllen, oder kommt er aus anderen Gründen seinen Aufgaben in angemessener Frist nicht nach, so endet sein Amt, wenn er zurücktritt oder wenn die Parteien die Beendigung seines Amtes vereinbaren. Tritt der Schiedsrichter von seinem Amt nicht zurück oder können sich die Parteien über dessen Beendigung nicht einigen, kann jede Partei bei Gericht eine Entscheidung über die Beendigung des Amtes beantragen.

(2) Tritt ein Schiedsrichter in den Fällen des Absatzes 1 oder des § 1037 Abs. 2 zurück oder stimmt eine Partei der Beendigung des Schiedsrichteramtes zu, so bedeutet dies nicht die Anerkennung der in Absatz 1 oder § 1036 Abs. 2 genannten Rücktrittsgründe.

§ 1039
Bestellung eines Ersatzschiedsrichters

(1) Endet das Amt eines Schiedsrichters nach den §§ 1037, 1038 oder wegen seines Rücktritts vom Amt aus einem anderen Grund oder wegen der Aufhebung seines Amtes durch Vereinbarung der Parteien, so ist ein Ersatzschiedsrichter zu bestellen. Die Bestellung erfolgt nach den Regeln, die auf die Bestellung des zu ersetzenden Schiedsrichters anzuwenden waren.

(2) Die Parteien können eine abweichende Vereinbarung treffen.

§ 1038
Failure or impossibility to act

(1) If an arbitrator becomes *de jure* or *de facto* unable to perform his functions or for other reasons fails to act without undue delay, his mandate terminates if he withdraws from his office or if the parties agree on the termination. If the arbitrator does not withdraw from his office or if the parties cannot agree on the termination, any party may request the court to decide on the termination of the mandate.

(2) If, under subsection 1 of this section or § 1037 (2), an arbitrator withdraws from his office or a party agrees to the termination of the mandate of an arbitrator, this does not imply acceptance of the validity of any ground for withdrawal referred to in subsection 1 of this section or § 1036 (2).

§ 1039
Appointment of substitute arbitrator

(1) Where the mandate of an arbitrator terminates under §§ 1037, 1038 or because of his withdrawal from office for any other reason or because of the revocation of his mandate by agreement of the parties, a substitute arbitrator shall be appointed according to the rules that were applicable to the appointment of the arbitrator being replaced.

(2) The parties are free to agree on another procedure.

Abschnitt 4
Zuständigkeit des Schiedsgerichts

§ 1040
Befugnis des Schiedsgerichts zur Entscheidung über die eigene Zuständigkeit

(1) Das Schiedsgericht kann über die eigene Zuständigkeit und im Zusammenhang hiermit über das Bestehen oder die Gültigkeit der Schiedsvereinbarung entscheiden. Hierbei ist eine Schiedsklausel als eine von den übrigen Vertragsbestimmungen unabhängige Vereinbarung zu behandeln.

(2) Die Rüge der Unzuständigkeit des Schiedsgerichts ist spätestens mit der Klagebeantwortung vorzubringen. Von der Erhebung einer solchen Rüge ist eine Partei nicht dadurch ausgeschlossen, dass sie einen Schiedsrichter bestellt oder an der Bestellung eines Schiedsrichters mitgewirkt hat. Die Rüge, das Schiedsgericht überschreite seine Befugnisse, ist zu erheben, sobald die Angelegenheit, von der dies behauptet wird, im schiedsrichterlichen Verfahren zur Erörterung kommt. Das Schiedsgericht kann in beiden Fällen eine spätere Rüge zulassen, wenn die Partei die Verspätung genügend entschuldigt.

(3) Hält das Schiedsgericht sich für zuständig, so entscheidet es über eine Rüge nach Absatz 2 in der Regel durch Zwischenentscheid. In diesem Fall kann jede Partei innerhalb eines Monats nach schriftlicher Mitteilung des Entscheids eine gerichtliche Entscheidung beantragen. Während ein solcher Antrag anhängig ist, kann das Schiedsgericht das schiedsrichterliche Verfahren fortsetzen und einen Schiedsspruch erlassen.

§ 1041
Maßnahmen des einstweiligen Rechtsschutzes

(1) Haben die Parteien nichts anderes vereinbart, so kann das Schiedsgericht auf Antrag einer Partei vorläufige oder sichernde Maßnahmen anordnen, die

Chapter 4
Jurisdiction of arbitral tribunal

§ 1040
Competence of arbitral tribunal to rule on its jurisdiction

(1) The arbitral tribunal may rule on its own jurisdiction and in this connection on the existence or validity of the arbitration agreement. For that purpose, an arbitration clause which forms part of a contract shall be treated as an agreement independent of the other terms of the contract.

(2) A plea that the arbitral tribunal does not have jurisdiction shall be raised not later than the submission of the statement of defense. A party is not precluded from raising such a plea by the fact that he has appointed, or participated in the appointment of, an arbitrator. A plea that the arbitral tribunal is exceeding the scope of its authority shall be raised as soon as the matter alleged to be beyond the scope of its authority is raised during the arbitral proceedings. The arbitral tribunal may, in either case, admit a later plea if it considers that the party has justified the delay.

(3) If the arbitral tribunal considers that it has jurisdiction, it rules on a plea referred to in subsection 2 of this section in general by means of a preliminary ruling. In this case, any party may request, within one month after having received written notice of that ruling, the court to decide the matter. While such a request is pending, the arbitral tribunal may continue the arbitral proceedings and make an award.

§ 1041
Interim measures of protection

(1) Unless otherwise agreed by the parties, the arbitral tribunal may, at the request of a party, order such interim measures of protection as the arbitral

es in Bezug auf den Streitgegenstand für erforderlich hält. Das Schiedsgericht kann von jeder Partei im Zusammenhang mit einer solchen Maßnahme angemessene Sicherheit verlangen.

(2) Das Gericht kann auf Antrag einer Partei die Vollziehung einer Maßnahme nach Absatz 1 zulassen, sofern nicht schon eine entsprechende Maßnahme des einstweiligen Rechtsschutzes bei einem Gericht beantragt worden ist. Es kann die Anordnung abweichend fassen, wenn dies zur Vollziehung der Maßnahme notwendig ist.

(3) Auf Antrag kann das Gericht den Beschluss nach Absatz 2 aufheben oder ändern.

(4) Erweist sich die Anordnung einer Maßnahme nach Absatz 1 als von Anfang an ungerechtfertigt, so ist die Partei, welche ihre Vollziehung erwirkt hat, verpflichtet, dem Gegner den Schaden zu ersetzen, der ihm aus der Vollziehung der Maßnahme oder dadurch entsteht, dass er Sicherheit leistet, um die Vollziehung abzuwenden. Der Anspruch kann im anhängigen schiedsrichterlichen Verfahren geltend gemacht werden.

tribunal may consider necessary in respect of the subject-matter of the dispute. The arbitral tribunal may require any party to provide appropriate security in connection with such measure.

(2) The court may, at the request of a party, permit enforcement of a measure referred to in subsection 1, unless application for a corresponding interim measure has already been made to a court. It may recast such an order if necessary for the purpose of enforcing the measure.

(3) The court may, upon request, repeal or amend the decision referred to in subsection 2.

(4) If a measure ordered under subsection 1 proves to have been unjustified from the outset, the party who obtained its enforcement is obliged to compensate the other party for damage resulting from the enforcement of such measure or from his providing security in order to avoid enforcement. This claim may be put forward in the pending arbitral proceedings.

Abschnitt 5
Durchführung des schiedsrichterlichen Verfahrens

Chapter 5
Conduct of arbitral proceedings

§ 1042
Allgemeine Verfahrensregeln

§ 1042
General rules of procedure

(1) Die Parteien sind gleich zu behandeln. Jeder Partei ist rechtliches Gehör zu gewähren.

(2) Rechtsanwälte dürfen als Bevollmächtigte nicht ausgeschlossen werden.

(3) Im Übrigen können die Parteien vorbehaltlich der zwingenden Vorschriften dieses Buches das Verfahren selbst oder durch Bezugnahme auf eine schiedsrichterliche Verfahrensordnung regeln.

(4) Soweit eine Vereinbarung der Parteien nicht vorliegt und dieses Buch

(1) The parties shall be treated with equality and each party shall be given a full opportunity of presenting his case.

(2) Counsel may not be excluded from acting as authorized representatives.

(3) Otherwise, subject to the mandatory provisions of this Book, the parties are free to determine the procedure themselves or by reference to a set of arbitration rules.

(4) Failing an agreement by the parties, and in the absence of provisions in this

keine Regelung enthält, werden die Verfahrensregeln vom Schiedsgericht nach freiem Ermessen bestimmt. Das Schiedsgericht ist berechtigt, über die Zulässigkeit einer Beweiserhebung zu entscheiden, diese durchzuführen und das Ergebnis frei zu würdigen.

Book, the arbitral tribunal shall conduct the arbitration in such manner as it considers appropriate. The arbitral tribunal is empowered to determine the admissibility of taking evidence, take evidence and assess freely such evidence.

§ 1043
Ort des schiedsrichterlichen Verfahrens

§ 1043
Place of arbitration

(1) Die Parteien können eine Vereinbarung über den Ort des schiedsrichterlichen Verfahrens treffen. Fehlt eine solche Vereinbarung, so wird der Ort des schiedsrichterlichen Verfahrens vom Schiedsgericht bestimmt. Dabei sind die Umstände des Falles einschließlich der Eignung des Ortes für die Parteien zu berücksichtigen.

(1) The parties are free to agree on the place of arbitration. Failing such agreement, the place of arbitration shall be determined by the arbitral tribunal having regard to the circumstances of the case, including the convenience of the parties.

(2) Haben die Parteien nichts anderes vereinbart, so kann das Schiedsgericht ungeachtet des Absatzes 1 an jedem ihm geeignet erscheinenden Ort zu einer mündlichen Verhandlung, zur Vernehmung von Zeugen, Sachverständigen oder der Parteien, zur Beratung zwischen seinen Mitgliedern, zur Besichtigung von Sachen oder zur Einsichtnahme in Dokumente zusammentreten.

(2) Notwithstanding the provisions of subsection 1 of this section, the arbitral tribunal may, unless otherwise agreed by the parties, meet at any place it considers appropriate for an oral hearing, for hearing witnesses, experts or the parties, for consultation among its members or for inspection of property or documents.

§ 1044
Beginn des schiedsrichterlichen Verfahrens[4]

§ 1044
Commencement of arbitral proceedings[5]

Haben die Parteien nichts anderes vereinbart, so beginnt das schiedsrichterliche Verfahren über eine bestimmte Streitigkeit mit dem Tag, an dem der Beklagte den Antrag, die Streitigkeit einem Schiedsgericht vorzulegen, empfangen hat. Der Antrag muss die Bezeichnung der Parteien, die Angabe des Streitgegenstandes und einen Hinweis auf die Schiedsvereinbarung enthalten.

Unless otherwise agreed by the parties, the arbitral proceedings in respect of a particular dispute commence on the date on which a request for that dispute to be referred to arbitration is received by the respondent. The request shall state the names of the parties, the subject-matter of the dispute and contain a reference to the arbitration agreement.

---

[4] Vgl. §204 Abs. 1 Nr. 11 BGB [Hemmung der Verjährung durch Rechtsverfolgung] „(1) Die Verjährung wird gehemmt durch . . . 11. den Beginn des schiedsrichterlichen Verfahrens."

[5] Cf. §204 (1), no. 11 of the Civil Code [Suspension of the limitation period] „(1) The limitation period is suspended by . . . 11. commencement of arbitral proceedings."

§ 1045
Verfahrenssprache

(1) Die Parteien können die Sprache oder die Sprachen, die im schiedsrichterlichen Verfahren zu verwenden sind, vereinbaren. Fehlt eine solche Vereinbarung, so bestimmt hierüber das Schiedsgericht. Die Vereinbarung der Parteien oder die Bestimmung des Schiedsgerichts ist, sofern darin nichts anderes vorgesehen wird, für schriftliche Erklärungen einer Partei, mündliche Verhandlungen, Schiedssprüche, sonstige Entscheidungen und andere Mitteilungen des Schiedsgerichts maßgebend.

(2) Das Schiedsgericht kann anordnen, dass schriftliche Beweismittel mit einer Übersetzung in die Sprache oder die Sprachen versehen sein müssen, die zwischen den Parteien vereinbart oder vom Schiedsgericht bestimmt worden sind.

§ 1046
Klage und Klagebeantwortung

(1) Innerhalb der von den Parteien vereinbarten oder vom Schiedsgericht bestimmten Frist hat der Kläger seinen Anspruch und die Tatsachen, auf die sich dieser Anspruch stützt, darzulegen und der Beklagte hierzu Stellung zu nehmen. Die Parteien können dabei alle ihnen erheblich erscheinenden Dokumente vorlegen oder andere Beweismittel bezeichnen, derer sie sich bedienen wollen.

(2) Haben die Parteien nichts anderes vereinbart, so kann jede Partei im Laufe des schiedsrichterlichen Verfahrens ihre Klage oder die Angriffs- und Verteidigungsmittel ändern oder ergänzen, es sei denn, das Schiedsgericht lässt dies wegen Verspätung, die nicht genügend entschuldigt wird, nicht zu.

(3) Absätze 1 und 2 gelten für die Widerklage entsprechend.

§ 1045
Language of proceedings

(1) The parties are free to agree on the language or languages to be used in the arbitral proceedings. Failing such agreement, the arbitral tribunal shall determine the language or languages to be used in the proceedings. This agreement or determination, unless otherwise specified therein, shall apply to any written statement by a party, any hearing and any award, decision or other communication by the arbitral tribunal.

(2) The arbitral tribunal may order that any documentary evidence shall be accompanied by a translation into the language or languages agreed upon by the parties or determined by the arbitral tribunal.

§ 1046
Statements of claim and defense

(1) Within the period of time agreed by the parties or determined by the arbitral tribunal, the claimant shall state his claim and the facts supporting the claim, and the respondent shall state his defense in respect of these particulars. The parties may submit with their statements all documents they consider to be relevant or may add a reference to other evidence they will submit.

(2) Unless otherwise agreed by the parties, either party may amend or supplement his claim or defense during the course of the arbitral proceedings, unless the arbitral tribunal considers it inappropriate to allow such amendment having regard to the delay in making it without sufficient justification.

(3) Subsections 1 and 2 apply *mutatis mutandis* to counter-claims.

§ 1047
Mündliche Verhandlung und schriftliches Verfahren

(1) Vorbehaltlich einer Vereinbarung der Parteien entscheidet das Schiedsgericht, ob mündlich verhandelt werden soll oder ob das Verfahren auf der Grundlage von Dokumenten und anderen Unterlagen durchzuführen ist. Haben die Parteien die mündliche Verhandlung nicht ausgeschlossen, hat das Schiedsgericht eine solche Verhandlung in einem geeigneten Abschnitt des Verfahrens durchzuführen, wenn eine Partei es beantragt.

(2) Die Parteien sind von jeder Verhandlung und jedem Zusammentreffen des Schiedsgerichts zu Zwecken der Beweisaufnahme rechtzeitig in Kenntnis zu setzen.

(3) Alle Schriftsätze, Dokumente und sonstigen Mitteilungen, die dem Schiedsgericht von einer Partei vorgelegt werden, sind der anderen Partei, Gutachten und andere schriftliche Beweismittel, auf die sich das Schiedsgericht bei seiner Entscheidung stützen kann, sind beiden Parteien zur Kenntnis zu bringen.

§ 1047
Oral hearings and written proceedings

(1) Subject to agreement by the parties, the arbitral tribunal shall decide whether to hold oral hearings or whether the proceedings shall be conducted on the basis of documents and other materials. Unless the parties have agreed that no hearings shall be held, the arbitral tribunal shall hold such hearings at an appropriate stage of the proceedings, if so requested by a party.

(2) The parties shall be given sufficient advance notice of any hearing and of any meeting of the arbitral tribunal for the purpose of taking evidence.

(3) All statements, documents or other information supplied to the arbitral tribunal by one party shall be communicated to the other party. Also, any expert report or evidentiary document on which the arbitral tribunal may rely in making its decision shall be communicated to both parties.

§ 1048
Säumnis einer Partei

(1) Versäumt es der Kläger, seine Klage nach § 1046 Abs. 1 einzureichen, so beendet das Schiedsgericht das Verfahren.

(2) Versäumt es der Beklagte, die Klage nach § 1046 Abs. 1 zu beantworten, so setzt das Schiedsgericht das Verfahren fort, ohne die Säumnis als solche als Zugeständnis der Behauptungen des Klägers zu behandeln.

(3) Versäumt es eine Partei, zu einer mündlichen Verhandlung zu erscheinen oder innerhalb einer festgelegten Frist ein Dokument zum Beweis vorzulegen, so kann das Schiedsgericht das Verfahren fortsetzen und den Schiedsspruch

§ 1048
Default of a party

(1) If the claimant fails to communicate his statement of claim in accordance with § 1046 (1), the arbitral tribunal shall terminate the proceedings.

(2) If the respondent fails to communicate his statement of defense in accordance with § 1046 (1), the arbitral tribunal shall continue the proceedings without treating such failure in itself as an admission of the claimant's allegations.

(3) If any party fails to appear at an oral hearing or to produce documentary evidence within a set time-limit, the arbitral tribunal may continue the proceedings and make the award on the evidence before it.

nach den vorliegenden Erkenntnissen erlassen.

(4) Wird die Säumnis nach Überzeugung des Schiedsgerichts genügend entschuldigt, bleibt sie außer Betracht. Im Übrigen können die Parteien über die Folgen der Säumnis etwas Anderes vereinbaren.

(4) Any default which has been justified to the tribunal's satisfaction will be disregarded. Apart from that, the parties may agree otherwise on the consequences of default.

§ 1049
Vom Schiedsgericht bestellter Sachverständiger

§ 1049
Expert appointed by arbitral tribunal

(1) Haben die Parteien nichts anderes vereinbart, so kann das Schiedsgericht einen oder mehrere Sachverständige zur Erstattung eines Gutachtens über bestimmte vom Schiedsgericht festzulegende Fragen bestellen. Es kann ferner eine Partei auffordern, dem Sachverständigen jede sachdienliche Auskunft zu erteilen oder alle für das Verfahren erheblichen Dokumente oder Sachen zur Besichtigung vorzulegen oder zugänglich zu machen.

(1) Unless otherwise agreed by the parties, the arbitral tribunal may appoint one or more experts to report to it on specific issues to be determined by the arbitral tribunal. It may also require a party to give the expert any relevant information or to produce, or to provide access to, any relevant documents or property for his inspection.

(2) Haben die Parteien nichts anderes vereinbart, so hat der Sachverständige, wenn eine Partei dies beantragt oder das Schiedsgericht es für erforderlich hält, nach Erstattung seines schriftlichen oder mündlichen Gutachtens an einer mündlichen Verhandlung teilzunehmen. Bei der Verhandlung können die Parteien dem Sachverständigen Fragen stellen und eigene Sachverständige zu den streitigen Fragen aussagen lassen.

(2) Unless otherwise agreed by the parties, if a party so requests or if the arbitral tribunal considers it necessary, the expert shall, after delivery of his written or oral report, participate in an oral hearing where the parties have the opportunity to put questions to him and to present expert witnesses in order to testify on the points at issue.

(3) Auf den vom Schiedsgericht bestellten Sachverständigen sind die §§ 1036, 1037 Abs. 1 und 2 entsprechend anzuwenden.

(3) §§ 1036, 1037 (1) and (2) apply *mutatis mutandis* to an expert appointed by the arbitral tribunal.

§ 1050
Gerichtliche Unterstützung bei der Beweisaufnahme und sonstige richterliche Handlungen

§ 1050
Court assistance in taking evidence and other judicial acts

Das Schiedsgericht oder eine Partei mit Zustimmung des Schiedsgerichts kann bei Gericht Unterstützung bei der Beweisaufnahme oder die Vornahme sonstiger richterlicher Handlungen, zu

The arbitral tribunal or a party with the approval of the arbitral tribunal may request from a court assistance in taking evidence or performance of other judicial acts which the arbitral tribunal

denen das Schiedsgericht nicht befugt ist, beantragen. Das Gericht erledigt den Antrag, sofern es ihn nicht für unzulässig hält, nach seinen für die Beweisaufnahme oder die sonstige richterliche Handlung geltenden Verfahrensvorschriften. Die Schiedsrichter sind berechtigt, an einer gerichtlichen Beweisaufnahme teilzunehmen und Fragen zu stellen.

is not empowered to carry out. Unless it regards the application as inadmissible, the court shall execute the request according to its rules on taking evidence or other judicial acts. The arbitrators are entitled to participate in any judicial taking of evidence and to ask questions.

Abschnitt 6
Schiedsspruch und Beendigung des Verfahrens

§ 1051
Anwendbares Recht

Chapter 6
Making of award and termination of proceedings

§ 1051
Rules applicable to substance of dispute

(1) Das Schiedsgericht hat die Streitigkeit in Übereinstimmung mit den Rechtsvorschriften zu entscheiden, die von den Parteien als auf den Inhalt des Rechtsstreits anwendbar bezeichnet worden sind. Die Bezeichnung des Rechts oder der Rechtsordnung eines bestimmten Staates ist, sofern die Parteien nicht ausdrücklich etwas Anderes vereinbart haben, als unmittelbare Verweisung auf die Sachvorschriften dieses Staates und nicht auf sein Kollisionsrecht zu verstehen.

(1) The arbitral tribunal shall decide the dispute in accordance with such rules of law as are chosen by the parties as applicable to the substance of the dispute. Any designation of the law or legal system of a given State shall be construed, unless otherwise expressed, as directly referring to the substantive law of that State and not to its conflict of laws rules.

(2) Haben die Parteien die anzuwendenden Rechtsvorschriften nicht bestimmt, so hat das Schiedsgericht das Recht des Staates anzuwenden, mit dem der Gegenstand des Verfahrens die engsten Verbindungen aufweist.

(2) Failing any designation by the parties, the arbitral tribunal shall apply the law of the State with which the subject-matter of the proceedings is most closely connected.

(3) Das Schiedsgericht hat nur dann nach Billigkeit zu entscheiden, wenn die Parteien es ausdrücklich dazu ermächtigt haben. Die Ermächtigung kann bis zur Entscheidung des Schiedsgerichts erteilt werden.

(3) The arbitral tribunal shall decide *ex aequo et bono* or as amiable *compositeur* only if the parties have expressly authorized it to do so. The parties may so authorize the arbitral tribunal up to the time of its decision.

(4) In allen Fällen hat das Schiedsgericht in Übereinstimmung mit den Bestimmungen des Vertrages zu entscheiden und dabei bestehende Handelsbräuche zu berücksichtigen.

(4) In all cases, the arbitral tribunal shall decide in accordance with the terms of the contract and shall take into account the usages of the trade applicable to the transaction.

§ 1052
Entscheidung durch ein Schiedsrichterkollegium

(1) Haben die Parteien nichts anderes vereinbart, so ist in schiedsrichterlichen Verfahren mit mehr als einem Schiedsrichter jede Entscheidung des Schiedsgerichts mit Mehrheit der Stimmen aller Mitglieder zu treffen.

(2) Verweigert ein Schiedsrichter die Teilnahme an einer Abstimmung, können die übrigen Schiedsrichter ohne ihn entscheiden, sofern die Parteien nichts anderes vereinbart haben. Die Absicht, ohne den verweigernden Schiedsrichter über den Schiedsspruch abzustimmen, ist den Parteien vorher mitzuteilen. Bei anderen Entscheidungen sind die Parteien von der Abstimmungsverweigerung nachträglich in Kenntnis zu setzen.

(3) Über einzelne Verfahrensfragen kann der vorsitzende Schiedsrichter allein entscheiden, wenn die Parteien oder die anderen Mitglieder des Schiedsgerichts ihn dazu ermächtigt haben.

§ 1053
Vergleich

(1) Vergleichen sich die Parteien während des schiedsrichterlichen Verfahrens über die Streitigkeit, so beendet das Schiedsgericht das Verfahren. Auf Antrag der Parteien hält es den Vergleich in der Form eines Schiedsspruchs mit vereinbartem Wortlaut fest, sofern der Inhalt des Vergleichs nicht gegen die öffentliche Ordnung (ordre public) verstößt.

(2) Ein Schiedsspruch mit vereinbartem Wortlaut ist gemäß § 1054 zu erlassen und muss angeben, dass es sich um einen Schiedsspruch handelt. Ein solcher Schiedsspruch hat dieselbe Wirkung wie jeder andere Schiedsspruch zur Sache.

(3) Soweit die Wirksamkeit von Erklärungen eine notarielle Beurkundung erfordert, wird diese bei einem Schieds-

§ 1052
Decision making by panel of arbitrators

(1) In arbitral proceedings with more than one arbitrator, any decision of the arbitral tribunal shall be made, unless otherwise agreed by the parties, by a majority of all its members.

(2) If an arbitrator refuses to take part in the vote on a decision, the other arbitrators may take the decision without him, unless otherwise agreed by the parties. The parties shall be given advance notice of the intention to make an award without the arbitrator refusing to participate in the vote. In the case of other decisions, the parties shall subsequent to the decision be informed of the refusal to participate in the vote.

(3) Individual questions of procedure may be decided by a presiding arbitrator alone if so authorized by the parties or all members of the arbitral tribunal.

§ 1053
Settlement

(1) If, during arbitral proceedings, the parties settle the dispute, the arbitral tribunal shall terminate the proceedings. If requested by the parties, it shall record the settlement in the form of an arbitral award on agreed terms, unless the contents are in violation of public policy (*ordre public*).

(2) An award on agreed terms shall be made in accordance with § 1054 and shall state that it is an award. Such an award has the same effect as any other award on the merits of the case.

(3) If notarial certification is required for a declaration to be effective, it will be substituted, in the case of an arbitral

spruch mit vereinbartem Wortlaut durch die Aufnahme der Erklärungen der Parteien in den Schiedsspruch ersetzt.

(4) Mit Zustimmung der Parteien kann ein Schiedsspruch mit vereinbartem Wortlaut auch von einem Notar, der seinen Amtssitz im Bezirk des nach § 1062 Abs. 1, 2 für die Vollstreckbarerklärung zuständigen Gerichts hat, für vollstreckbar erklärt werden. Der Notar lehnt die Vollstreckbarerklärung ab, wenn die Voraussetzungen des Absatzes 1 Satz 2 nicht vorliegen.

§ 1054
Form und Inhalt des Schiedsspruchs

(1) Der Schiedsspruch ist schriftlich zu erlassen und durch den Schiedsrichter oder die Schiedsrichter zu unterschreiben. In schiedsrichterlichen Verfahren mit mehr als einem Schiedsrichter genügen die Unterschriften der Mehrheit aller Mitglieder des Schiedsgerichts, sofern der Grund für eine fehlende Unterschrift angegeben wird.

(2) Der Schiedsspruch ist zu begründen, es sei denn, die Parteien haben vereinbart, dass keine Begründung gegeben werden muss, oder es handelt sich um einen Schiedsspruch mit vereinbartem Wortlaut im Sinne des § 1053.

(3) Im Schiedsspruch sind der Tag, an dem er erlassen wurde, und der nach § 1043 Abs. 1 bestimmte Ort des schiedsrichterlichen Verfahrens anzugeben. Der Schiedsspruch gilt als an diesem Tag und diesem Ort erlassen.

(4) Jeder Partei ist ein von den Schiedsrichtern unterschriebener Schiedsspruch zu übermitteln.

§ 1055
Wirkungen des Schiedsspruchs

Der Schiedsspruch hat unter den Parteien die Wirkungen eines rechtskräftigen gerichtlichen Urteils.

award on agreed terms, by recording the declaration of the parties in the award.

(4) An award on agreed terms may, upon agreement between the parties, also be declared enforceable by a notary whose notarial office is in the district of the court competent for the declaration of enforceability according to § 1062 (1), no. 2. The notary shall refuse the declaration of enforceability, if the requirements of subsection 1, sentence 2 are not complied with.

§ 1054
Form and contents of award

(1) The award shall be made in writing and shall be signed by the arbitrator or arbitrators. In arbitral proceedings with more than one arbitrator, the signatures of the majority of all members of the arbitral tribunal shall suffice, provided that the reason for any omitted signature is stated.

(2) The award shall state the reasons upon which it is based, unless the parties have agreed that no reasons are to be given or the award is an award on agreed terms under § 1053.

(3) The award shall state its date and the place of arbitration as determined in accordance with § 1043 (1). The award shall be deemed to have been made on that date and at that place.

(4) A copy of the award signed by the arbitrators shall be delivered to each party.

§ 1055
Effect of arbitral award

The arbitral award has the same effect between the parties as a final and binding court judgment.

§ 1056
Beendigung des schiedsrichterlichen Verfahrens

(1) Das schiedsrichterliche Verfahren wird mit dem endgültigen Schiedsspruch oder mit einem Beschluss des Schiedsgerichts nach Absatz 2 beendet.

(2) Das Schiedsgericht stellt durch Beschluss die Beendigung des schiedsrichterlichen Verfahrens fest, wenn

1. der Kläger
   a) es versäumt, seine Klage nach § 1046 Abs. 1 einzureichen und kein Fall des § 1048 Abs. 4 vorliegt, oder
   b) seine Klage zurücknimmt, es sei denn, dass der Beklagte dem widerspricht und das Schiedsgericht ein berechtigtes Interesse des Beklagten an der endgültigen Beilegung der Streitigkeit anerkennt; oder
2. die Parteien die Beendigung des Verfahrens vereinbaren; oder
3. die Parteien das schiedsrichterliche Verfahren trotz Aufforderung des Schiedsgerichts nicht weiter betreiben oder die Fortsetzung des Verfahrens aus einem anderen Grund unmöglich geworden ist.

(3) Vorbehaltlich des § 1057 Abs. 2 und der §§ 1058, 1059 Abs. 4 endet das Amt des Schiedsgerichts mit der Beendigung des schiedsrichterlichen Verfahrens.

§ 1057
Entscheidung über die Kosten

(1) Sofern die Parteien nichts anderes vereinbart haben, hat das Schiedsgericht in einem Schiedsspruch darüber zu entscheiden, zu welchem Anteil die Parteien die Kosten des schiedsrichterlichen Verfahrens einschließlich der den Parteien erwachsenen und zur zweckentsprechenden Rechtsverfolgung notwendigen Kosten zu tragen haben. Hierbei entscheidet das Schiedsgericht nach pflichtgemäßem Ermessen unter Berücksichtigung der Umstände des

§ 1056
Termination of proceedings

(1) The arbitral proceedings are terminated by the final award or by an order of the arbitral tribunal in accordance with subsection 2 of this section.

(2) The arbitral tribunal shall issue an order for the termination of the arbitral proceedings when

1. the claimant:
   a) fails to state his claim according to § 1046 (1) and § 1048 (4) does not apply, or
   b) withdraws his claim, unless the respondent objects thereto and the arbitral tribunal recognizes a legitimate interest on his part in obtaining a final settlement of the dispute, or
2. the parties agree on the termination of the proceedings, or
3. the parties fail to pursue the arbitral proceedings in spite of being so requested by the arbitral tribunal or when the continuation of the proceedings has for any other reason become impossible.

(3) The mandate of the arbitral tribunal terminates with the termination of the arbitral proceedings, subject to the provisions of §§ 1057 (2), 1058 and 1059 (4).

§ 1057
Decision on costs

(1) Unless the parties agree otherwise, the arbitral tribunal shall allocate, by means of an arbitral award, the costs of the arbitration as between the parties, including those incurred by the parties necessary for the proper pursuit of their claim or defense. It shall do so at its discretion and take into consideration the circumstances of the case, in particular the outcome of the proceedings.

Einzelfalles, insbesondere des Ausgangs des Verfahrens.

(2) Soweit die Kosten des schiedsrichterlichen Verfahrens feststehen, hat das Schiedsgericht auch darüber zu entscheiden, in welcher Höhe die Parteien diese zu tragen haben. Ist die Festsetzung der Kosten unterblieben oder erst nach Beendigung des schiedsrichterlichen Verfahrens möglich, wird hierüber in einem gesonderten Schiedsspruch entschieden.

(2) To the extent that the costs of the arbitral proceedings have been fixed, the arbitral tribunal shall also decide on the amount to be borne by each party. If the costs have not been fixed or if they can only be fixed once the arbitral proceedings have been terminated, the decision shall be taken by means of a separate award.

§ 1058
Berichtigung, Auslegung und Ergänzung des Schiedsspruchs

§ 1058
Correction and interpretation of award; additional award

(1) Jede Partei kann beim Schiedsgericht beantragen,

1. Rechen-, Schreib- und Druckfehler oder Fehler ähnlicher Art im Schiedsspruch zu berichtigen;
2. bestimmte Teile des Schiedsspruchs auszulegen;
3. einen ergänzenden Schiedsspruch über solche Ansprüche zu erlassen, die im schiedsrichterlichen Verfahren zwar geltend gemacht, im Schiedsspruch aber nicht behandelt worden sind.

(1) Any party may request the arbitral tribunal

1. to correct in the award any errors in computation, any clerical or typographical errors or any errors of similar nature,
2. to give an interpretation of specific parts of the award,
3. to make an additional award as to claims presented in the arbitral proceedings but omitted from the award.

(2) Sofern die Parteien keine andere Frist vereinbart haben, ist der Antrag innerhalb eines Monats nach Empfang des Schiedsspruchs zu stellen.

(2) Unless otherwise agreed by the parties, the request shall be made within one month of receipt of the award.

(3) Das Schiedsgericht soll über die Berichtigung oder Auslegung des Schiedsspruchs innerhalb eines Monats und über die Ergänzung des Schiedsspruchs innerhalb von zwei Monaten entscheiden.

(3) The arbitral tribunal shall make the correction or give the interpretation within one month and make an additional award within two months.

(4) Eine Berichtigung des Schiedsspruchs kann das Schiedsgericht auch ohne Antrag vornehmen.

(4) The arbitral tribunal may make a correction of the award on its own initiative.

(5) § 1054 ist auf die Berichtigung, Auslegung oder Ergänzung des Schiedsspruchs anzuwenden.

(5) § 1054 shall apply to a correction or interpretation of the award or to an additional award.

Abschnitt 7
Rechtsbehelf gegen den Schiedsspruch

§ 1059
Aufhebungsantrag

(1) Gegen einen Schiedsspruch kann nur der Antrag auf gerichtliche Aufhebung nach den Absätzen 2 und 3 gestellt werden.

(2) Ein Schiedsspruch kann nur aufgehoben werden,

1. wenn der Antragsteller begründet geltend macht, dass
   a) eine der Parteien, die eine Schiedsvereinbarung nach §§ 1029, 1031 geschlossen haben, nach dem Recht, das für sie persönlich maßgebend ist, hierzu nicht fähig war, oder dass die Schiedsvereinbarung nach dem Recht, dem die Parteien sie unterstellt haben oder, falls die Parteien hierüber nichts bestimmt haben, nach deutschem Recht ungültig ist; oder
   b) er von der Bestellung eines Schiedsrichters oder von dem schiedsrichterlichen Verfahren nicht gehörig in Kenntnis gesetzt worden ist oder dass er aus einem anderen Grund seine Angriffs- oder Verteidigungsmittel nicht hat geltend machen können; oder
   c) der Schiedsspruch eine Streitigkeit betrifft, die in der Schiedsabrede nicht erwähnt ist oder nicht unter die Bestimmungen der Schiedsklausel fällt, oder dass er Entscheidungen enthält, welche die Grenzen der Schiedsvereinbarung überschreiten; kann jedoch der Teil des Schiedsspruchs, der sich auf Streitpunkte bezieht, die dem schiedsrichterlichen Verfahren unterworfen waren, von dem Teil, der Streitpunkte betrifft, die ihm nicht unterworfen waren, getrennt werden, so

Chapter 7
Recourse against award

§ 1059
Application for setting aside

(1) Recourse to a court against an arbitral award may be made only by an application for setting aside in accordance with subsections 2 and 3 of this section.

(2) An arbitral award may be set aside only if:

1. the applicant shows sufficient cause that:
   a) a party to the arbitration agreement referred to in §§ 1029, 1031 was under some incapacity pursuant to the law applicable to him; or the said agreement is not valid under the law to which the parties have subjected it or, failing any indication thereon, under German law; or
   b) he was not given proper notice of the appointment of an arbitrator or of the arbitral proceedings or was otherwise unable to present his case; or
   c) the award deals with a dispute not contemplated by or not falling within the terms of the submission to arbitration, or contains decisions on matters beyond the scope of the submission to arbitration; provided that, if the decisions on matters submitted to arbitration can be separated from those not so submitted, only that part of the award which contains decisions on matters not submitted to arbitration may be set aside; or

kann nur der letztgenannte Teil des Schiedsspruchs aufgehoben werden; oder
d) die Bildung des Schiedsgerichts oder das schiedsrichterliche Verfahren einer Bestimmung dieses Buches oder einer zulässigen Vereinbarung der Parteien nicht entsprochen hat und anzunehmen ist, dass sich dies auf den Schiedsspruch ausgewirkt hat; oder
2. wenn das Gericht feststellt, dass
   a) der Gegenstand des Streites nach deutschem Recht nicht schiedsfähig ist; oder
   b) die Anerkennung oder Vollstreckung des Schiedsspruchs zu einem Ergebnis führt, das der öffentlichen Ordnung (ordre public) widerspricht.
	d) the composition of the arbitral tribunal or the arbitral procedure was not in accordance with a provision of this Book or with an admissible agreement of the parties and this presumably affected the award; or
	2. the court finds that
	   a) the subject-matter of the dispute is not capable of settlement by arbitration under German law; or
	   b) recognition or enforcement of the award leads to a result which is in conflict with public policy (ordre public).

(3) Sofern die Parteien nichts anderes vereinbaren, muss der Aufhebungsantrag innerhalb einer Frist von drei Monaten bei Gericht eingereicht werden. Die Frist beginnt mit dem Tag, an dem der Antragsteller den Schiedsspruch empfangen hat. Ist ein Antrag nach § 1058 gestellt worden, verlängert sich die Frist um höchstens einen Monat nach Empfang der Entscheidung über diesen Antrag. Der Antrag auf Aufhebung des Schiedsspruchs kann nicht mehr gestellt werden, wenn der Schiedsspruch von einem deutschen Gericht für vollstreckbar erklärt worden ist.	(3) Unless the parties have agreed otherwise, an application for setting aside to the court may not be made after three months have elapsed. The period of time shall commence on the date on which the party making the application had received the award. If a request had been made under § 1058, the time-limit shall be extended by not more than one month from receipt of the decision on the request. No application for setting aside the award may be made once the award has been declared enforceable by a German court.
(4) Ist die Aufhebung beantragt worden, so kann das Gericht in geeigneten Fällen auf Antrag einer Partei unter Aufhebung des Schiedsspruchs die Sache an das Schiedsgericht zurückverweisen.	(4) The court, when asked to set aside an award, may, where appropriate, set aside the award and remit the case to the arbitral tribunal.
(5) Die Aufhebung des Schiedsspruchs hat im Zweifel zur Folge, dass wegen des Streitgegenstandes die Schiedsvereinbarung wiederauflebt.	(5) Setting aside the arbitral award shall, in the absence of any indication to the contrary, result in the arbitration agreement becoming operative again in respect of the subject-matter of the dispute.

Abschnitt 8
Voraussetzungen der Anerkennung und Vollstreckung von Schiedssprüchen

§ 1060
Inländische Schiedssprüche

(1) Die Zwangsvollstreckung findet statt, wenn der Schiedsspruch für vollstreckbar erklärt ist.

(2) Der Antrag auf Vollstreckbarerklärung ist unter Aufhebung des Schiedsspruchs abzulehnen, wenn einer der in § 1059 Abs. 2 bezeichneten Aufhebungsgründe vorliegt. Aufhebungsgründe sind nicht zu berücksichtigen, soweit im Zeitpunkt der Zustellung des Antrags auf Vollstreckbarerklärung ein auf sie gestützter Aufhebungsantrag rechtskräftig abgewiesen ist. Aufhebungsgründe nach § 1059 Abs. 2 Nr. 1 sind auch dann nicht zu berücksichtigen, wenn die in § 1059 Abs. 3 bestimmten Fristen abgelaufen sind, ohne dass der Antragsgegner einen Antrag auf Aufhebung des Schiedsspruchs gestellt hat.

§ 1061
Ausländische Schiedssprüche

(1) Die Anerkennung und Vollstreckung ausländischer Schiedssprüche richtet sich nach dem Übereinkommen vom 10. Juni 1958 über die Anerkennung und Vollstreckung ausländischer Schiedssprüche (BGBl. 1961 II S. 121). Die Vorschriften in anderen Staatsverträgen über die Anerkennung und Vollstreckung von Schiedssprüchen bleiben unberührt.

(2) Ist die Vollstreckbarerklärung abzulehnen, stellt das Gericht fest, dass der Schiedsspruch im Inland nicht anzuerkennen ist.

(3) Wird der Schiedsspruch, nachdem er für vollstreckbar erklärt worden ist, im Ausland aufgehoben, so kann die Aufhebung der Vollstreckbarerklärung beantragt werden.

Chapter 8
Recognition and enforcement of awards

§ 1060
Domestic awards

(1) Enforcement of the award takes place if it has been declared enforceable.

(2) An application for a declaration of enforceability shall be refused and the award set aside if one of the grounds for setting aside under § 1059 (2) exists. Grounds for setting aside shall not be taken into account, if at the time when the application for a declaration of enforceability is served, an application for setting aside based on such grounds has been finally rejected. Grounds for setting aside under § 1059 (2), no. 1 shall also not be taken into account if the time-limits set by § 1059 (3) have expired without the party opposing the application having made an application for setting aside the award.

§ 1061
Foreign awards

(1) Recognition and enforcement of foreign arbitral awards shall be granted in accordance with the Convention on the Recognition and Enforcement of Foreign Arbitral Awards of 10 June 1958 (Bundesgesetzblatt [BGBl.] 1961 Part II p. 121). The provisions of other treaties on the recognition and enforcement of arbitral awards shall remain unaffected.

(2) If the declaration of enforceability is to be refused, the court shall rule that the arbitral award is not to be recognized in Germany.

(3) If the award is set aside abroad after having been declared enforceable, application for setting aside the declaration of enforceability may be made.

Abschnitt 9 **Gerichtliches Verfahren**	**Chapter 9** **Court proceedings**
§ 1062 **Zuständigkeit**	**§ 1062** **Competence**

(1) Das Oberlandesgericht, das in der Schiedsvereinbarung bezeichnet ist oder, wenn eine solche Bezeichnung fehlt, in dessen Bezirk der Ort des schiedsrichterlichen Verfahrens liegt, ist zuständig für Entscheidungen über Anträge betreffend

1. die Bestellung eines Schiedsrichters (§§ 1034, 1035), die Ablehnung eines Schiedsrichters (§ 1037) oder die Beendigung des Schiedsrichteramtes (§ 1038);
2. die Feststellung der Zulässigkeit oder Unzulässigkeit eines schiedsrichterlichen Verfahrens (§ 1032) oder die Entscheidung eines Schiedsgerichts, in der dieses seine Zuständigkeit in einem Zwischenentscheid bejaht hat (§ 1040);
3. die Vollziehung, Aufhebung oder Änderung der Anordnung vorläufiger oder sichernder Maßnahmen des Schiedsgerichts (§ 1041);
4. die Aufhebung (§ 1059) oder die Vollstreckbarerklärung des Schiedsspruchs (§§ 1060 ff.) oder die Aufhebung der Vollstreckbarerklärung (§ 1061).

(2) Besteht in den Fällen des Absatzes 1 Nr. 2 erste Alternative, Nr. 3 oder 4 kein deutscher Schiedsort, so ist für die Entscheidungen das Oberlandesgericht zuständig, in dessen Bezirk der Antragsgegner seinen Sitz oder gewöhnlichen Aufenthalt hat oder sich Vermögen des Antragsgegners oder der mit der Schiedsklage in Anspruch genommene oder von der Maßnahme betroffene Gegenstand befindet, hilfsweise das Kammergericht.

(3) In den Fällen des § 1025 Abs. 3 ist für die Entscheidung das Oberlandesgericht zuständig, in dessen Bezirk der Kläger

(1) The higher regional court („*Oberlandesgericht*") designated in the arbitration agreement or, failing such designation, the higher regional court in whose district the place of arbitration is situated, is competent for decisions on applications relating to

1. the appointment of an arbitrator (§§ 1034, 1035), the challenge of an arbitrator (§ 1037) or the termination of an arbitrator's mandate (§ 1038);
2. the determination of the admissibility or inadmissibility of arbitration (§ 1032) or the decision of an arbitral tribunal confirming its competence in a preliminary ruling (§ 1040);
3. the enforcement, setting aside or amendment of an order for interim measures of protection by the arbitral tribunal (§ 1041);
4. the setting aside (§ 1059) or the declaration of enforceability of the award (§ 1060 *et seq.*) or the setting aside of the declaration of enforceability (§ 1061).

(2) If the place of arbitration in the cases referred to in subsection 1, no. 2, first alternative, nos. 3 and 4 is not in Germany, competence lies with the higher regional court („*Oberlandesgericht*") where the party opposing the application has his place of business or place of habitual residence, or where assets of that party or the property in dispute or affected by the measure is located, failing which the Berlin Higher Regional Court („*Kammergericht*") shall be competent.

(3) In the cases referred to in § 1025 (3), the higher regional court („*Oberlandesgericht*") in whose district the claimant or the respondent has his place of busi-

oder der Beklagte seinen Sitz oder seinen gewöhnlichen Aufenthalt hat.

(4) Für die Unterstützung bei der Beweisaufnahme und sonstige richterliche Handlungen (§ 1050) ist das Amtsgericht zuständig, in dessen Bezirk die richterliche Handlung vorzunehmen ist.

(5) Sind in einem Land mehrere Oberlandesgerichte errichtet, so kann die Zuständigkeit von der Landesregierung durch Rechtsverordnung einem Oberlandesgericht oder dem obersten Landesgericht[5] übertragen werden; die Landesregierung kann die Ermächtigung durch Rechtsverordnung auf die Landesjustizverwaltung übertragen. Mehrere Länder können die Zuständigkeit eines Oberlandesgerichts über die Ländergrenzen hinaus vereinbaren.

ness or place of habitual residence is competent.

(4) For assistance in the taking of evidence and other judicial acts (§ 1050), the Local Court (*„Amtsgericht"*), in whose district the judicial act is to be carried out, is competent.

(5) Where there are several higher regional courts (*„Oberlandesgerichte"*) in one *Land*, the Government of that *Land* may transfer by ordinance competence to one higher regional court, or, where existent, to the highest regional court (*„oberstes Landesgericht"*)[6]; the *Land* Government may transfer such authority to the Department of Justice of the Land concerned by ordinance. Several Länder may agree on cross-border competence of a single higher regional court.

§ 1063
Allgemeine Vorschriften

(1) Das Gericht entscheidet durch Beschluss.[6] Vor der Entscheidung ist der Gegner zu hören.

(2) Das Gericht hat die mündliche Verhandlung anzuordnen, wenn die Aufhebung des Schiedsspruchs beantragt wird oder wenn bei einem Antrag auf Anerkennung oder Vollstreckbarerklärung des Schiedsspruchs Aufhebungsgründe nach § 1059 Abs. 2 in Betracht kommen.

§ 1063
General provisions

(1) The court shall decide by means of an order.[7] The party opposing the application shall be given an opportunity to comment before a decision is taken.

(2) The court shall order an oral hearing to be held, if the setting aside of the award has been requested or if, in an application for recognition or declaration of enforceability of the award, grounds for setting aside in terms of § 1059 (2) are to be considered.

---

[5] Das einzige Gericht dieser Art, das „Bayerische Oberste Landesgericht,", wird aufgelöst durch das „Gesetz zur Auflösung des Bayerischen Obersten Landesgerichts und der Staatsanwaltschaft bei diesem Gericht (Gerichtsauflösungsgesetz – BayObLGAuflG),", vom 25. Oktober 2004, BayGVBl. 2004, S. 400. Das Gericht nimmt seit 1. Januar 2005 keine neue Sachen an.

[6] Vgl. § 128 ZPO [Grundsatz der Mündlichkeit] (4) Entscheidungen des Gerichts, die nicht Urteile sind, können ohne mündliche Verhandlung ergehen, soweit nichts anderes bestimmt ist.

[6] The only court of this type, the *„Bayerisches Oberstes Landesgericht"* in Bavaria, is being dissolved pursuant to the *„Gesetz zur Auflösung des Bayerischen Obersten Landesgerichts und der Staatsanwaltschaft bei diesem Gericht (Gerichtsauflösungsgesetz – BayObLGAuflG)"* (Act to Dissolve the Bavarian Highest Regional Court and the Prosecutor's Office Located at this Court) of 25 October 2004, published in *Bayerisches Gesetz- und Verordnungsblatt* 2004, p. 400. The Court does not accept any new cases as of 1 January 2005.

[7] *Cf.* ZPO § 128 [Principle of Oral Procedure]: (4) Unless provided otherwise, decisions of the court which do not constitute judgments can be rendered without oral hearing.

(3) Der Vorsitzende des Zivilsenats kann ohne vorherige Anhörung des Gegners anordnen, dass der Antragsteller bis zur Entscheidung über den Antrag die Zwangsvollstreckung aus dem Schiedsspruch betreiben oder die vorläufige oder sichernde Maßnahme des Schiedsgerichts nach §1041 vollziehen darf. Die Zwangsvollstreckung aus dem Schiedsspruch darf nicht über Maßnahmen zur Sicherung hinausgehen. Der Antragsgegner ist befugt, die Zwangsvollstreckung durch Leistung einer Sicherheit in Höhe des Betrages, wegen dessen der Antragsteller vollstrecken kann, abzuwenden.

(4) Solange eine mündliche Verhandlung nicht angeordnet ist, können zu Protokoll der Geschäftsstelle Anträge gestellt und Erklärungen abgegeben werden.

§ 1064
Besonderheiten bei der Vollstreckbarerklärung von Schiedssprüchen

(1) Mit dem Antrag auf Vollstreckbarerklärung eines Schiedsspruchs ist der Schiedsspruch oder eine beglaubigte Abschrift des Schiedsspruchs vorzulegen. Die Beglaubigung kann auch von dem für das gerichtliche Verfahren bevollmächtigten Rechtsanwalt vorgenommen werden.

(2) Der Beschluss, durch den ein Schiedsspruch für vollstreckbar erklärt wird, ist für vorläufig vollstreckbar zu erklären.

(3) Auf ausländische Schiedssprüche sind die Absätze 1 und 2 anzuwenden, soweit Staatsverträge nicht ein anderes bestimmen.

§ 1065
Rechtsmittel

(1) Gegen die in §1062 Abs.1 Nr.2 und 4 genannten Entscheidungen findet die Rechtsbeschwerde statt. Im Übrigen sind die Entscheidungen in den in

(3) The presiding judge of the civil court senate („*Zivilsenat*") may issue, without prior hearing of the party opposing the application, an order to the effect that, until a decision on the request has been reached, the applicant may pursue enforcement of the award or enforce the interim measure of protection of the arbitration court pursuant to §1041. In the case of an award, enforcement of the award may not go beyond measures of protection. The party opposing the application may prevent enforcement by providing as security an amount corresponding to the amount that may be enforced by the applicant.

(4) As long as no oral hearing is ordered, applications and declarations may be put on record at the court registry.

§ 1064
Particularities regarding the enforcement of awards

(1) At the time of the application for a declaration of enforceability of an arbitral award the award or a certified copy of the award shall be supplied. The certification may also be made by counsel authorized to represent the party in the judicial proceedings.

(2) The order declaring the award enforceable shall be declared provisionally enforceable.

(3) Unless otherwise provided in treaties, subsections 1 and 2 shall apply to foreign awards.

§ 1065
Legal remedies

(1) A complaint on a point of law is available against the decisions mentioned under §1062 (1), nos. 2 and 4. No recourse against other decisions in the

§ 1062 Abs. 1 bezeichneten Verfahren unanfechtbar.

(2) Die Rechtsbeschwerde kann auch darauf gestützt werden, dass die Entscheidung auf einer Verletzung eines Staatsvertrages beruht. Die §§ 707, 717 sind entsprechend anzuwenden.

Abschnitt 10
Außervertragliche Schiedsgerichte

§ 1066
Entsprechende Anwendung der Vorschriften des Zehnten Buches

Für Schiedsgerichte, die in gesetzlich statthafter Weise durch letztwillige oder andere nicht auf Vereinbarung beruhende Verfügungen angeordnet werden, gelten die Vorschriften dieses Buches entsprechend.

Buch 11
Justizielle Zusammenarbeit in der Europäischen Union

Abschnitt 1
Zustellung nach der Verordnung (EG) Nr. 1393/2007

§ 1067
Zustellung durch diplomatische oder konsularische Vertretungen

Eine Zustellung nach Artikel 13 Abs. 1 der Verordnung (EG) Nr. 1393/2007, die in der Bundesrepublik Deutschland bewirkt werden soll, ist nur zulässig, wenn der Adressat des zuzustellenden Schriftstücks Staatsangehöriger des Übermittlungsmitgliedstaats ist.

§ 1068
Zustellung durch die Post

(1) Zum Nachweis der Zustellung nach Artikel 14 der Verordnung (EG) Nr. 1393/2007 genügt der Rückschein oder der gleichwertige Beleg.

proceedings specified in § 1062 (1) may be made.

(2) The complaint on a point of law can also be based on the ground that the decision is based on a violation of a treaty. §§ 707 and 717 apply *mutatis mutandis*.

Chapter 10
Arbitral tribunals not established by agreement

§ 1066
Mutatis mutandis application of the provisions of the Tenth Book

The provisions of this Book apply *mutatis mutandis* to arbitral tribunals established lawfully by disposition on death or other dispositions not based on an agreement.

Book 11[8]
Judicial Cooperation in the European Union

Chapter 1
Service in accordance with Council Regulation (EC) No. 1393/2007

§ 1067
Service through diplomatic or consular agents

Service in accordance with Article 13 (1) of the Council Regulation (EC) No. 1393/2007 which shall be effected in the Federal Republic of Germany is only permitted if the addressee of the document to be served is a national of the transmitting Member State.

§ 1068
Service by post

(1) The return receipt or equivalent shall suffice as evidence of service having been effected in accordance with Ar-

---

[8] Translation by Hildegard Rosenzweig.

(2) Ein Schriftstück, dessen Zustellung eine deutsche Empfangsstelle im Rahmen von Artikel 7 Abs. 1 der Verordnung (EG) Nr. 1393/2007 zu bewirken oder zu veranlassen hat, kann ebenfalls durch Einschreiben mit Rückschein zugestellt werden.

(2) A document the service of which must be effected or arranged by a German receiving agency under Article 7 of the Council Regulation (EC) No. 1393/2007 may also be served by registered letter with return receipt.

§ 1069
Zuständigkeiten

§ 1069
Competences

(1) Für Zustellungen im Ausland sind als deutsche Übermittlungsstelle im Sinne von Artikel 2 Abs. 1 der Verordnung (EG) Nr. 1393/2007 zuständig:

(1) With regard to the service of documents abroad, the following courts shall be competent as German transmitting agency within the meaning of Article 2 (1) of Council Regulation (EC) No. 1393/2007:

1. für gerichtliche Schriftstücke das die Zustellung betreibende Gericht und
2. für außergerichtliche Schriftstücke dasjenige Amtsgericht, in dessen Bezirk die Person, welche die Zustellung betreibt, ihren Wohnsitz oder gewöhnlichen Aufenthalt hat; bei notariellen Urkunden auch dasjenige Amtsgericht, in dessen Bezirk der beurkundende Notar seinen Amtssitz hat; bei juristischen Personen tritt an die Stelle des Wohnsitzes oder des gewöhnlichen Aufenthalts der Sitz; die Landesregierungen können die Aufgaben der Übermittlungsstelle einem Amtsgericht für die Bezirke mehrerer Amtsgerichte durch Rechtsverordnung zuweisen.

1. with regard to judicial documents, the court pursuing the service, and
2. with regard to extrajudicial documents, that local court in whose district the person pursuing the service has his place of residence or customary abode; with regard to notarial deeds, also that local court in whose district the recording notary public has his office; in the case of legal persons, the place of residence or customary abode is replaced by the registered office; the Federal State governments may assign the responsibilities of the transmitting agency to one local court for the districts of several local courts by way of an ordinance.

(2) Für Zustellungen in der Bundesrepublik Deutschland ist als deutsche Empfangsstelle im Sinne von Artikel 2 Abs. 2 der Verordnung (EG) Nr. 1393/2007 dasjenige Amtsgericht zuständig, in dessen Bezirk das Schriftstück zugestellt werden soll. Die Landesregierungen können die Aufgaben der Empfangsstelle einem Amtsgericht für die Bezirke mehrerer Amtsgerichte durch Rechtsverordnung zuweisen.

(2) With regard to the service of documents within the Federal Republic of Germany, that local court shall be competent as German receiving agency within the meaning of Article 2 (2) of Council Regulation (EC) No. 1393/2007, in whose district service of the document shall be effected. The Federal State governments may assign the responsibilities of the receiving agency to one local court for the districts of several local courts by way of an ordinance.

(3) Die Landesregierungen bestimmen durch Rechtsverordnung die Stelle, die in dem jeweiligen Land als deutsche Zentralstelle im Sinne von Artikel 3 Satz 1 der Verordnung (EG) Nr. 1393/2007 zuständig ist. Die Aufgaben der Zentralstelle können in jedem Land nur einer Stelle zugewiesen werden.	(3) The Federal State governments shall designate by way of an ordinance the body which is competent in the relevant Federal State as German central body within the meaning of Article 3 first sentence of Council Regulation (EC) No. 1393/2007. The responsibilities of the central body may only be assigned to one body in each Federal State.
(4) Die Landesregierungen können die Befugnis zum Erlass einer Rechtsverordnung nach Absatz 1 Nr. 2, Absatz 2 Satz 2 und Absatz 3 Satz 1 einer obersten Landesbehörde übertragen.	(4) The Federal State governments may transfer the authority to issue an ordinance in accordance with sub-section (1) no. 2, sub-section (2) second sentence and sub-section (3) first sentence to a supreme Federal State authority.

§ 1070
(weggefallen)

§ 1070
(repealed)

§ 1071
(weggefallen)

§ 1071
(repealed)

Abschnitt 2
Beweisaufnahme nach der Verordnung (EG) Nr. 1206/2001

Chapter 2
Taking of evidence in accordance with Council Regulation (EC) No. 1206/2001

§ 1072
Beweisaufnahme in den Mitgliedstaaten der Europäischen Union

§ 1072
Taking of evidence in the Member States of the European Union

Soll die Beweisaufnahme nach der Verordnung (EG) Nr. 1206/2001 erfolgen, so kann das Gericht	If the taking of evidence shall be performed in accordance with Council Regulation (EC) No. 1206/2001, the court may
1. unmittelbar das zuständige Gericht eines anderen Mitgliedstaats um Aufnahme des Beweises ersuchen oder	1. directly request the competent court of another Member State to take the evidence or
2. unter den Voraussetzungen des Artikels 17 der Verordnung (EG) Nr. 1206/2001 eine unmittelbare Beweisaufnahme in einem anderen Mitgliedstaat beantragen.	2. apply for the evidence to be taken directly in another Member State under the conditions of Article 17 of Council Regulation (EC) No. 1206/2001.

§ 1073
Teilnahmerechte

§ 1073
Rights of participation

(1) Das ersuchende deutsche Gericht oder ein von diesem beauftragtes Mitglied darf im Geltungsbereich der Verordnung (EG) Nr. 1206/2001 bei der	(1) Within the scope of Council Regulation (EC) No. 1206/2001, the requesting German court or a member designated by such court may be present and take

part in the execution of the request for the taking of evidence by the requested foreign court. Parties, their representatives as well as experts may in this regard take part to the extent that their participation is possible in the performance of the taking of evidence in their domestic country in the relevant proceedings.

(2) The direct taking of evidence in a foreign country in accordance with Article 17 (3) of Council Regulation (EC) No. 1206/2001 may be performed by members of the court and by experts designated by the court.

§ 1074
Competences in accordance with Council Regulation (EC) No. 1206/2001

(1) With regard to the taking of evidence in the Federal Republic of Germany, that local court shall be competent as requested court within the meaning of Article 2 (1) of Council Regulation (EC) No. 1206/2001, in whose district the procedural act shall be performed.

(2) The Federal State governments may assign the responsibilities of the requested court to one local court for the districts of several local courts by way of an ordinance.

(3) The Federal State governments shall designate by way of an ordinance the body which, in the relevant country,

1. shall be competent as the German central body within the meaning of Article 3 (1) of Council Regulation (EC) No. 1206/2001,
2. shall receive, as the competent body, requests for the direct taking of evidence within the meaning of Article 17 (1) of Council Regulation (EC) No. 1206/2001.

The responsibilities in accordance with nos. 1 and 2 may only be assigned to one body in each Federal State.

(4) Die Landesregierungen können die Befugnis zum Erlass einer Rechtsverordnung nach den Absätzen 2 und 3 Satz 1 einer obersten Landesbehörde übertragen.

(4) The Federal State governments may transfer the authority to issue an ordinance in accordance with sub-sections (2) and (3) first sentence to a supreme Federal State authority.

§ 1075
Sprache eingehender Ersuchen

§ 1075
Language of requests received

Aus dem Ausland eingehende Ersuchen auf Beweisaufnahme sowie Mitteilungen nach der Verordnung (EG) Nr. 1206/2001 müssen in deutscher Sprache abgefasst oder von einer Übersetzung in die deutsche Sprache begleitet sein.

Requests received from foreign countries for the taking of evidence and notifications in accordance with Council Regulation (EC) No. 1206/2001 must be in German or must be accompanied by a translation into German.

Abschnitt 3
Prozesskostenhilfe nach der Richtlinie 2003/8/EG

Chapter 3
Legal Aid in accordance with EC Directive 2003/8/EC

§ 1076
Anwendbare Vorschriften

§ 1076
Applicable regulations

Für die grenzüberschreitende Prozesskostenhilfe innerhalb der Europäischen Union nach der Richtlinie 2003/8/EG des Rates vom 27. Januar 2003 zur Verbesserung des Zugangs zum Recht bei Streitsachen mit grenzüberschreitendem Bezug durch Festlegung gemeinsamer Mindestvorschriften für die Prozesskostenhilfe in derartigen Streitsachen (ABl. EG Nr. L 26 S. 41, ABl. EU Nr. L 32 S. 15) gelten die §§ 114 bis 127a, soweit nachfolgend nichts Abweichendes bestimmt ist.

With regard to cross-border legal aid within the European Union in accordance with EC Directive 2003/8/EC of the European Council of 27 January 2003 to improve access to justice in cross-border disputes by establishing minimum common rules relating to legal aid in such disputes (O. J. EC No. L 26 p. 41, O. J. EU No. L 32 p. 15), §§ 114–127a shall apply, unless otherwise provided hereinafter.

§ 1077
Ausgehende Ersuchen

§ 1077
Outgoing applications

(1) Für die Entgegennahme und Übermittlung von Anträgen natürlicher Personen auf grenzüberschreitende Prozesskostenhilfe ist das Amtsgericht zuständig, in dessen Bezirk der Antragsteller seinen Wohnsitz oder gewöhnlichen Aufenthalt hat (Übermittlungsstelle). Die Landesregierungen können die Aufgaben der Übermittlungsstelle einem Amtsgericht für die Bezirke mehrere Amtsgerichte durch Rechtsverordnung zuweisen. Sie können die Ermäch-

(1) With regard to the acceptance and transmission of applications of natural persons for cross-border legal aid, that local court shall be competent in whose district the applicant has his residence or customary abode (transmitting authority). The Federal State governments may assign the responsibilities of the transmitting authority to one local court for the districts of several local courts by way of an ordinance. They may transfer the authority of the Federal State to

tigung durch Rechtsverordnung auf die Landesjustizverwaltungen übertragen. § 21 Satz 1 des Auslandsunterhaltsgesetzes bleibt unberührt.

(2) Das Bundesministerium der Justiz wird ermächtigt, durch Rechtsverordnung mit Zustimmung des Bundesrates die in Artikel 16 Abs. 1 der Richtlinie 2003/8/EG vorgesehenen Standardformulare für Anträge auf grenzüberschreitende Prozesskostenhilfe und für deren Übermittlung einzuführen. Soweit Standardformulare für Anträge auf grenzüberschreitende Prozesskostenhilfe und für deren Übermittlung eingeführt sind, müssen sich der Antragsteller und die Übermittlungsstelle ihrer bedienen.

(3) Die Übermittlungsstelle kann die Übermittlung durch Beschluss vollständig oder teilweise ablehnen, wenn der Antrag offensichtlich unbegründet ist oder offensichtlich nicht in den Anwendungsbereich der Richtlinie 2003/8/EG fällt. Sie kann von Amts wegen Übersetzungen von dem Antrag beigefügten fremdsprachigen Anlagen fertigen, soweit dies zur Vorbereitung einer Entscheidung nach Satz 1 erforderlich ist. Gegen die ablehnende Entscheidung findet die sofortige Beschwerde nach Maßgabe des § 127 Abs. 2 Satz 2 und 3 statt.

(4) Die Übermittlungsstelle fertigt von Amts wegen Übersetzungen der Eintragungen im Standardformular für Anträge auf Prozesskostenhilfe sowie der beizufügenden Anlagen

a) in eine der Amtssprachen des Mitgliedstaats der zuständigen Empfangsstelle, die zugleich einer der Amtssprachen der Europäischen Union entspricht oder
b) in eine andere von diesem Mitgliedstaat zugelassene Sprache.

Die Übermittlungsstelle prüft die Vollständigkeit des Antrags und wirkt da-

the respective administration of justice by way of an ordinance. Section 21 Sentence 1 of the Foreign Enforcement of Support Act (*Auslandsunterhaltsgesetz-AUG*) remains unaffected.

(2) The Federal Ministry of Justice shall be authorized to introduce, by way of an ordinance, the standard forms for applications for cross-border legal aid and for their transmission, as provided for in Article 16 (1) of EC Directive 2003/8/EC, with the consent of the *Bundesrat* [Upper House of Parliament]. To the extent that standard forms for applications for cross-border legal aid and for their transmission have been introduced, the applicant and the transmitting authority must use such standard forms.

(3) The transmitting authority may decide to refuse to transmit an application either in whole or in part by way of a court order, if the application is manifestly unfounded or is manifestly outside the scope of EC Directive 2003/8/EC. The transmitting authority may provide, *ex officio*, translations of the supporting documents in a foreign language accompanying the application, to the extent this is necessary for the preparation of a decision in accordance with the first sentence. The decision of refusal shall be subject to immediate miscellaneous appeal in accordance with § 127 (2) second and third sentence.

(4) The transmitting authority shall provide, *ex officio*, translations of the entries in the standard form for applications for legal aid and the supporting documents to be attached

a) into one of the official languages of the Member State of the competent receiving authority which is at the same time one of the official languages of the European Union or
b) into another language admitted by such Member State.

The transmitting authority shall review the application for completeness and

rauf hin, dass Anlagen, die nach ihrer Kenntnis zur Entscheidung über den Antrag erforderlich sind, beigefügt werden.

(5) Die Übermittlungsstelle übersendet den Antrag und die beizufügenden Anlagen ohne Legalisation oder gleichwertige Förmlichkeiten an die zuständige Empfangsstelle des Mitgliedstaats des Gerichtsstands oder des Vollstreckungsmitgliedstaats. Die Übermittlung erfolgt innerhalb von 14 Tagen nach Vorliegen der gemäß Absatz 4 zu fertigenden Übersetzungen.

(6) Hat die zuständige Stelle des anderen Mitgliedstaats das Ersuchen um Prozesskostenhilfe aufgrund der persönlichen und wirtschaftlichen Verhältnisse des Antragstellers abgelehnt oder eine Ablehnung angekündigt, so stellt die Übermittlungsstelle auf Antrag eine Bescheinigung der Bedürftigkeit aus, wenn der Antragsteller in einem entsprechenden deutschen Verfahren nach §115 Abs. 1 und 2 als bedürftig anzusehen wäre. Absatz 4 Satz 1 gilt für die Übersetzung der Bescheinigung entsprechend. Die Übermittlungsstelle übersendet der Empfangsstelle des anderen Mitgliedstaats die Bescheinigung der Bedürftigkeit zwecks Ergänzung des ursprünglichen Ersuchens um grenzüberschreitende Prozesskostenhilfe.

shall try to ensure that the application is accompanied by supporting documents which, according to the authority's knowledge, are required for a decision on the application.

(5) The transmitting authority shall forward the application and the supporting documents to be attached to the competent receiving authority of the Member State of the place of jurisdiction or the enforcing Member State exempt from legalization or any equivalent formality. The transmission shall be effected within 14 days after the translations to be provided in accordance with sub-section (4) are available.

(6) If the competent authority of the other Member State has rejected the application for legal aid due to the applicant's personal and financial situation or has announced such rejection, the transmitting authority shall issue a certificate of neediness upon application, if the applicant would have to be considered as needy in accordance with §115 (1) and (2) in corresponding German proceedings. Sub-section (4) first sentence shall apply *mutatis mutandis* to the translation of the certificate. The transmitting authority shall forward the certificate of neediness to the receiving authority of the other Member State for the purpose of supplementing the original application for cross-border legal aid.

§ 1078
Eingehende Ersuchen

(1) Für eingehende Ersuchen um grenzüberschreitende Prozesskostenhilfe ist das Prozessgericht oder das Vollstreckungsgericht zuständig. Die Anträge müssen in deutscher Sprache ausgefüllt und die Anlagen von einer Übersetzung in die deutsche Sprache begleitet sein. Eine Legalisation oder gleichwertige Förmlichkeiten dürfen nicht verlangt werden.

§ 1078
Incoming applications

(1) With regard to incoming applications for cross-border legal aid, the court conducting the legal proceedings or the court of enforcement shall be competent. The applications shall be completed in the German language, and the supporting documents shall be accompanied by a translation into the German language. Legalization or an equivalent formality may not be demanded.

(2) Das Gericht entscheidet über das Ersuchen nach Maßgabe der §§ 114 bis 116. Es übersendet der übermittelnden Stelle eine Abschrift seiner Entscheidung.

(3) Der Antragsteller erhält auch dann grenzüberschreitende Prozesskostenhilfe, wenn er nachweist, dass er wegen unterschiedlich hoher Lebenshaltungskosten im Mitgliedstaat seines Wohnsitzes oder gewöhnlichen Aufenthalts einerseits und im Geltungsbereich dieses Gesetzes andererseits die Kosten der Prozessführung nicht, nur zum Teil oder nur in Raten aufbringen kann.

(4) Wurde grenzüberschreitende Prozesskostenhilfe bewilligt, so gilt für jeden weiteren Rechtszug, der von dem Antragsteller oder dem Gegner eingeleitet wird, ein neuerliches Ersuchen um grenzüberschreitende Prozesskostenhilfe als gestellt. Das Gericht hat dahin zu wirken, dass der Antragsteller die Voraussetzungen für die Bewilligung der grenzüberschreitenden Prozesskostenhilfe für den jeweiligen Rechtszug darlegt.

(2) The court shall decide on the application in accordance with §§ 114 to 116. It shall forward a copy of its decision to the transmitting authority.

(3) The applicant shall be granted cross-border legal aid also, if he provides evidence that, due to different levels of the cost of living in the Member State of his residence or customary abode on the one hand and within the scope of this Code on the other hand, he is not able to pay the costs of conducting the legal proceedings at all or is only able to pay such costs in part or in installments.

(4) If cross-border legal aid was granted, it shall be deemed that a new application for cross-border legal aid has been made for each further instance instituted by the applicant or the opponent. The court shall try to ensure that the applicant presents the conditions required for cross-border legal aid to be granted with regard to the respective instance.

Abschnitt 4
Europäische Vollstreckungstitel nach der Verordnung (EG) Nr. 805/2004

Chapter 4
European Enforcement Orders in accordance with Regulation (EC) No 805/2004

Titel 1
Bestätigung inländischer Titel als Europäische Vollstreckungstitel

Title 1
Certification of German executory titles as European Enforcement Orders

§ 1079
Zuständigkeit

§ 1079
Competence

Für die Ausstellung der Bestätigungen nach

1. Artikel 9 Abs. 1, Artikel 24 Abs. 1, Artikel 25 Abs. 1 und
2. Artikel 6 Abs. 2 und 3

der Verordnung (EG) Nr. 805/2004 sind die Gerichte, Behörden oder Notare zuständig, denen die Erteilung einer

As regards the issuance of certificates pursuant to

1. Article 9 (1), Article 24 (1), Article 25 (1) and
2. Article 6 (2) and (3)

of Regulation (EC) No 805/2004, the courts, authorities or notaries competent to issue an enforceable executed copy of

vollstreckbaren Ausfertigung des Titels obliegt.

the executory title shall be competent to issue such certificates.

§ 1080
Entscheidung

(1) Bestätigungen nach Artikel 9 Abs. 1, Artikel 24 Abs. 1, Artikel 25 Abs. 1 und Artikel 6 Abs. 3 der Verordnung (EG) Nr. 805/2004 sind ohne Anhörung des Schuldners auszustellen. Eine Ausfertigung der Bestätigung ist dem Schuldner von Amts wegen zuzustellen.

(2) Wird der Antrag auf Ausstellung einer Bestätigung zurückgewiesen, so sind die Vorschriften über die Anfechtung der Entscheidung über die Erteilung einer Vollstreckungsklausel entsprechend anzuwenden.

§ 1080
Decision

(1) Certificates pursuant to Article 9 (1), Article 24 (1), Article 25 (1) and Article 6 (3) of Regulation (EC) No. 805/2004 shall be issued without the debtor being heard. An executed copy of the certificate shall be served on the debtor *ex officio*.

(2) If the application for issuance of a certificate is rejected, the regulations regarding the contestation of the decision on the issuance of a court's certificate of enforceability shall be applicable *mutatis mutandis*.

§ 1081
Berichtigung und Widerruf

(1) Ein Antrag nach Artikel 10 Abs. 1 der Verordnung (EG) Nr. 805/2004 auf Berichtigung oder Widerruf einer gerichtlichen Bestätigung ist bei dem Gericht zu stellen, das die Bestätigung ausgestellt hat. Über den Antrag entscheidet dieses Gericht. Ein Antrag auf Berichtigung oder Widerruf einer notariellen oder behördlichen Bestätigung ist an die Stelle zu richten, die die Bestätigung ausgestellt hat. Die Notare oder Behörden leiten den Antrag unverzüglich dem Amtsgericht, in dessen Bezirk sie ihren Sitz haben, zur Entscheidung zu.

(2) Der Antrag auf Widerruf durch den Schuldner ist nur binnen einer Frist von einem Monat zulässig. Ist die Bestätigung im Ausland zuzustellen, beträgt die Frist zwei Monate. Sie ist eine Notfrist und beginnt mit der Zustellung der Bestätigung, jedoch frühestens mit der Zustellung des Titels, auf den sich die Bestätigung bezieht. In dem Antrag auf Widerruf sind die Gründe darzulegen, weshalb die Bestätigung eindeutig zu Unrecht erteilt worden ist.

§ 1081
Rectification and withdrawal

(1) An application pursuant to Article 10 (1) of Regulation (EC) No 805/2004 for rectification or withdrawal of a court certificate shall be filed with the court that issued the certificate. This court shall decide on the application. An application for rectification or withdrawal of a certificate issued by a notary or an authority shall be addressed to the body that issued the certificate. The notaries or authorities shall promptly forward the application to the local court in whose district they are located for the local court ("*Amtsgericht*") to decide thereon.

(2) The debtor's filing of an application for withdrawal of the certificate shall only be admissible within a time limit of one month. If the certificate is to be served abroad, the time limit shall be two months. This time limit is a statutory time limit and shall commence upon the certificate being served, at the earliest, however, upon the enforcement title to which the certificate makes reference being served. The application for withdrawal shall present the grounds why the certificate was evidently issued wrongly.

(3) § 319 Abs. 2 und 3 ist auf die Berichtigung und den Widerruf entsprechend anzuwenden.

Titel 2
Zwangsvollstreckung aus Europäischen Vollstreckungstiteln im Inland

§ 1082
Vollstreckungstitel

Aus einem Titel, der in einem anderen Mitgliedstaat der Europäischen Union nach der Verordnung (EG) Nr. 805/2004 als Europäischer Vollstreckungstitel bestätigt worden ist, findet die Zwangsvollstreckung im Inland statt, ohne dass es einer Vollstreckungsklausel bedarf.

§ 1083
Übersetzung

Hat der Gläubiger nach Artikel 20 Abs. 2 Buchstabe c der Verordnung (EG) Nr. 805/2004 eine Übersetzung vorzulegen, so ist diese in deutscher Sprache zu verfassen und von einer hierzu in einem der Mitgliedstaaten der Europäischen Union befugten Person zu beglaubigen.

§ 1084
Anträge nach den Artikeln 21 und 23 der Verordnung (EG) Nr. 805/2004

(1) Für Anträge auf Verweigerung, Aussetzung oder Beschränkung der Zwangsvollstreckung nach den Artikeln 21 und 23 der Verordnung (EG) Nr. 805/2004 ist das Amtsgericht als Vollstreckungsgericht zuständig. Die Vorschriften des Buches 8 über die örtliche Zuständigkeit des Vollstreckungsgerichts sind entsprechend anzuwenden. Die Zuständigkeit nach den Sätzen 1 und 2 ist ausschließlich.

(2) Die Entscheidung über den Antrag nach Artikel 21 der Verordnung (EG) Nr. 805/2004 ergeht durch Beschluss. Auf die Einstellung der Zwangsvollstre-

(3) § 319 (2) and (3) shall be applicable *mutatis mutandis* to the rectification and the withdrawal.

Title 2
Compulsory enforcement under European enforcement orders in Germany

§ 1082
Enforcement orders

A title of enforcement which has been certified as a European Enforcement Order in another Member State of the European Union in accordance with Regulation (EC) No 805/2004 shall be made subject to compulsory enforcement in Germany without a court's certificate of enforceability being required.

§ 1083
Translation

If the creditor is obliged to submit a translation pursuant to Article 20 (2) lit. c of Regulation (EC) No 805/2004, such translation shall be in German and shall be certified by a person authorised for this purpose in one of the Member States of the European Union.

§ 1084
Applications in accordance with Articles 21 and 23 of Regulation (EC) No 805/2004

(1) The local court as the court having jurisdiction over enforcement shall be competent for applications for the refusal, suspension or limitation of compulsory enforcement in terms of Articles 21 and 23 of Regulation (EC) No 805/2004. The regulations of Book 8 regarding the local jurisdiction of court having jurisdiction over enforcement shall be applicable *mutatis mutandis*. The competence pursuant to sentences 1 and 2 shall be exclusive.

(2) The decision on an application filed in accordance with Article 21 of Regulation (EC) No 805/2004 shall be issued by a court order. § 769 (1) and (3) and § 770

ckung und die Aufhebung der bereits getroffenen Vollstreckungsmaßregeln sind § 769 Abs. 1 und 3 sowie § 770 entsprechend anzuwenden. Die Aufhebung einer Vollstreckungsmaßregel ist auch ohne Sicherheitsleistung zulässig.

(3) Über den Antrag auf Aussetzung oder Beschränkung der Vollstreckung nach Artikel 23 der Verordnung (EG) Nr. 805/2004 wird durch einstweilige Anordnung entschieden. Die Entscheidung ist unanfechtbar.

§ 1085
Einstellung der Zwangsvollstreckung

Die Zwangsvollstreckung ist entsprechend den §§ 775 und 776 auch dann einzustellen oder zu beschränken, wenn die Ausfertigung einer Bestätigung über die Nichtvollstreckbarkeit oder über die Beschränkung der Vollstreckbarkeit nach Artikel 6 Abs. 2 der Verordnung (EG) Nr. 805/2004 vorgelegt wird.

§ 1086
Vollstreckungsabwehrklage

(1) Für Klagen nach § 795 Satz 1 in Verbindung mit § 767 ist das Gericht ausschließlich örtlich zuständig, in dessen Bezirk der Schuldner seinen Wohnsitz hat, oder, wenn er im Inland keinen Wohnsitz hat, das Gericht, in dessen Bezirk die Zwangsvollstreckung stattfinden soll oder stattgefunden hat. Der Sitz von Gesellschaften oder juristischen Personen steht dem Wohnsitz gleich.

(2) § 767 Abs. 2 ist entsprechend auf gerichtliche Vergleiche und öffentliche Urkunden anzuwenden.

shall be applicable *mutatis mutandis* to the termination of compulsory enforcement and to the cancellation of any enforcement measures already taken. The cancellation of an enforcement measure shall also be admissible without security being provided.

(3) The decision on an application for the suspension or limitation of enforcement filed in accordance with Article 23 of Regulation (EC) No 805/2004 shall be issued by an interim order. The decision is incontestable.

§ 1085
Termination of compulsory enforcement

In accordance with §§ 775 and 776, compulsory enforcement shall also be terminated or limited if the executed copy of a certificate indicating the lack or limitation of enforceability in accordance with Article 6 (2) of Regulation (EC) No. 805/2004 is presented.

§ 1086
Action for averting enforcement

(1) As regards actions brought in accordance with § 795 sentence 1 in conjunction with § 767, that court shall have exclusive local jurisdiction in whose district the debtor has his residence or, if the debtor has no residence in Germany, that court in whose district compulsory enforcement shall take place or has taken place. The registered office of companies or legal entities shall be equivalent to the residence.

(2) § 767 (2) shall be applicable *mutatis mutandis* to court settlements and public documents.

Abschnitt 5
Europäisches Mahnverfahren nach der Verordnung (EG) Nr. 1896/2006

Titel 1
Allgemeine Vorschriften

§ 1087
Zuständigkeit

Für die Bearbeitung von Anträgen auf Erlass und Überprüfung sowie die Vollstreckbarerklärung eines Europäischen Zahlungsbefehls nach der Verordnung (EG) Nr. 1896/2006 ist das Amtsgericht Wedding in Berlin ausschließlich zuständig.

§ 1088
Maschinelle Bearbeitung

(1) Der Antrag auf Erlass des Europäischen Zahlungsbefehls und der Einspruch können in einer nur maschinell lesbaren Form bei Gericht eingereicht werden, wenn, diese dem Gericht für seine maschinelle Bearbeitung geeignet erscheint. § 130a Abs. 3 gilt entsprechend.

(2) Der Senat des Landes Berlin bestimmt durch Rechtsverordnung, die nicht der Zustimmung des Bundesrates bedarf, den Zeitpunkt, in dem beim Amtsgericht Wedding die maschinelle Bearbeitung der Mahnverfahren eingeführt wird; er kann die Ermächtigung durch Rechtsverordnung auf die Senatsverwaltung für Justiz des Landes Berlin übertragen.

§ 1089
Zustellung

(1) Ist der Europäische Zahlungsbefehl im Inland zuzustellen, gelten die Vorschriften über das Verfahren bei Zustellungen von Amts wegen entsprechend. Die §§ 185 bis 188 sind nicht anzuwenden.

Chapter 5
European order for payment procedure in accordance with Regulation (EC) No 1896/2006

Title 1
General provisions

§ 1087
Competence

The local court of Wedding in Berlin shall have exclusive jurisdiction for processing applications for the issuance and review, as well as the declaration of enforceability, of a European payment order under Regulation (EC) No 1896/2006.

§ 1088
Automatic processing

(1) The application for issuance of a European payment order and the statement of opposition may be filed with the court in a form that is only machine-readable, if the court deems such form to be suitable for its automatic processing. § 130a (3) shall apply *mutatis mutandis*.

(2) The Senate of the Federal State of Berlin shall determine by ordinance not requiring the approval of the Federal Council (*Bundesrat*) the point in time when automatic processing of the order for payment procedures is to be introduced at the local court ("*Amtsgericht*") of Wedding; it may confer this authorisation by ordinance to the Senate Administration of Justice ("*Senatsverwaltung*") of the Federal State ("*Land*") of Berlin.

§ 1089
Service

(1) If the European payment order is to be served in Germany, the regulations regarding the procedure for service *ex officio* shall be applicable *mutatis mutandis*. §§ 185 to 188 shall not be applicable.

(2) Ist der Europäische Zahlungsbefehl in einem anderen Mitgliedstaat der Europäischen Union zuzustellen, gelten die Vorschriften der Verordnung (EG) Nr. 1393/2007 sowie für die Durchführung § 1068 Abs. 1 und § 1069 Abs. 1 entsprechend.

(2) If the European payment order is to be served in another Member State of the European Union, the stipulations of Regulation (EC) No 1393/2007 shall be applicable *mutatis mutandis*, and § 1068 (1) and § 1069 (1) shall be applicable *mutatis mutandis* to the performance of the service.

Titel 2
Einspruch gegen den Europäischen Zahlungsbefehl

Title 2
Statement of opposition against the European payment order

§ 1090
Verfahren nach Einspruch

§ 1090
Procedure after a statement of opposition has been filed

(1) Im Fall des Artikels 17 Abs. 1 der Verordnung (EG) Nr. 1896/2006 fordert das Gericht den Antragsteller mit der Mitteilung nach Artikel 17 Abs. 3 der Verordnung (EG) Nr. 1896/2006 auf, das Gericht zu bezeichnen, das für die Durchführung des streitigen Verfahrens zuständig ist. Das Gericht setzt dem Antragsteller hierfür eine nach den Umständen angemessene Frist und weist ihn darauf hin, dass dem für die Durchführung des streitigen Verfahrens bezeichneten Gericht die Prüfung seiner Zuständigkeit vorbehalten bleibt. Die Aufforderung ist dem Antragsgegner mitzuteilen.

(1) In the case of Article 17 (1) of Regulation (EC) No. 1896/2006, the court shall request the claimant by the notice pursuant to Article 17 (3) of Regulation (EC) No 1896/2006 to specify the court which has jurisdiction for conducting the legal proceedings for determining whether or not the claim is justified. The court shall set a time limit for the claimant to do so which is reasonable under the circumstances and shall notify him that the court specified as conducting the legal proceedings for determining whether or not the claim is justified remains responsible for reviewing whether it has jurisdiction. The request shall be communicated to the respondent.

(2) Nach Eingang der Mitteilung des Antragstellers nach Absatz 1 Satz 1 gibt das Gericht, das den Europäischen Zahlungsbefehl erlassen hat, das Verfahren von Amts wegen an das vom Antragsteller bezeichnete Gericht ab. § 696 Abs. 1 Satz 3 bis 5, Abs. 2, 4 und 5 sowie § 698 gelten entsprechend.

(2) Upon receipt of the notice by the claimant pursuant to subsection (1) sentence 1, the court that issued the European payment order shall transfer the proceedings *ex officio* to the court specified by the claimant. § 696 (1) sentences 3 to 5, (2), (4) and (5) and § 698 shall apply *mutatis mutandis*.

(3) Die Streitsache gilt als mit Zustellung des Europäischen Zahlungsbefehls rechtshängig geworden, wenn sie nach Übersendung der Aufforderung nach Absatz 1 Satz 1 und unter Berücksichtigung der Frist nach Absatz 1 Satz 2 alsbald abgegeben wird.

(3) The dispute shall be deemed to have become pending upon service of the European payment order, if it is transferred promptly after the request pursuant to subsection (1) sentence 1 having been sent and by taking the time limit pursuant to subsection 1 sentence 2 into account.

§ 1091
Einleitung des Streitverfahrens

§ 697 Abs. 1 bis 3 gilt entsprechend.

§ 1091
Institution of the dispute proceedings

§ 697 (1) to (3) shall apply *mutatis mutandis*.

Titel 3
Überprüfung des Europäischen Zahlungsbefehls in Ausnahmefällen

Title 3
Review of the European payment order in exceptional cases

§ 1092
Verfahren

(1) Die Entscheidung über einen Antrag auf Überprüfung des Europäischen Zahlungsbefehls nach Artikel 20 Abs. 1 oder Abs. 2 der Verordnung (EG) Nr. 1896/2006 ergeht durch Beschluss. Der Beschluss ist unanfechtbar.

(2) Der Antragsgegner hat die Tatsachen, die eine Aufhebung des Europäischen Zahlungsbefehls begründen, glaubhaft zu machen.

(3) Erklärt das Gericht den Europäischen Zahlungsbefehl für nichtig, endet das Verfahren nach der Verordnung (EG) Nr. 1896/2006.

(4) Eine Wiedereinsetzung in die Frist nach Artikel 16 Abs. 2 der Verordnung (EG) Nr. 1896/2006 findet nicht statt.

§ 1092
Procedure

(1) The decision on an application for review of the Europan payment order filed in accordance with Article 20 (1) or (2) of Regulation (EC) No 1896/2006 shall be issued by way of a court order. The court order is incontestable.

(2) The respondent shall present to the satisfaction of the court the facts which constitute grounds for setting aside the European payment order.

(3) If the court declares the European payment order to be void, the proceedings in accordance with Regulation (EC) No 1896/2006 shall be terminated.

(4) The time limit pursuant to Article 16 (2) of Regulation (EC) No 1896/2006 shall not be reinstated.

Titel 4
Zwangsvollstreckung aus dem Europäischen Zahlungsbefehl

Title 4
Compulsory enforcement under the European payment order

§ 1093
Vollstreckungsklausel

Aus einem nach der Verordnung (EG) Nr. 1896/2006 erlassenen und für vollstreckbar erklärten Europäischen Zahlungsbefehl findet die Zwangsvollstreckung im Inland statt, ohne dass es einer Vollstreckungsklausel bedarf.

§ 1093
Court's certificate of enforceability

A European payment order which has been issued and declared to be enforceable in accordance with Regulation (EC) No 1896/2006 shall be made subject to compulsory enforcement in Germany without a court's certificate of enforceability being required.

§ 1094
Übersetzung

Hat der Gläubiger nach Artikel 21 Abs. 2 Buchstabe b der Verordnung (EG)

§ 1094
Translation

If the creditor is obliged to submit a translation pursuant to Article 21 (2)

Nr. 1896/2006 eine Übersetzung vorzulegen, so ist diese in deutscher Sprache zu verfassen und von einer in einem der Mitgliedstaaten der Europäischen Union hierzu befugten Person zu beglaubigen.

lit. b of Regulation (EC) No 1896/2006, such translation shall be in German and shall be certified by a person authorised for this purpose in one of the Member States of the European Union.

§ 1095
Vollstreckungsschutz und Vollstreckungsabwehrklage gegen den im Inland erlassenen Europäischen Zahlungsbefehl

(1) Wird die Überprüfung eines im Inland erlassenen Europäischen Zahlungsbefehls nach Artikel 20 der Verordnung (EG) Nr. 1896/2006 beantragt, gilt § 707 entsprechend. Für die Entscheidung über den Antrag nach § 707 ist das Gericht zuständig, das über den Antrag nach Artikel 20 der Verordnung (EG) Nr. 1896/2006 entscheidet.

(2) Einwendungen, die den Anspruch selbst betreffen, sind nur insoweit zulässig, als die Gründe, auf denen sie beruhen, nach Zustellung des Europäischen Zahlungsbefehls entstanden sind und durch Einspruch nach Artikel 16 der Verordnung (EG) Nr. 1896/2006 nicht mehr geltend gemacht werden können.

§ 1096
Anträge nach den Artikeln 22 und 23 der Verordnung (EG) Nr. 1896/2006; Vollstreckungsabwehrklage

(1) Für Anträge auf Verweigerung der Zwangsvollstreckung nach Artikel 22 Abs. 1 der Verordnung (EG) Nr. 1896/2006 gilt § 1084 Abs. 1 und 2 entsprechend. Für Anträge auf Aussetzung oder Beschränkung der Zwangsvollstreckung nach Artikel 23 der Verordnung (EG) Nr. 1896/2006 ist § 1084 Abs. 1 und 3 entsprechend anzuwenden.

(2) Für Anträge auf Verweigerung der Zwangsvollstreckung nach Artikel 22 Abs. 2 der Verordnung (EG) Nr. 1896/2006 gilt § 1086 Abs. 1 entsprechend. Für Klagen nach § 795 Satz 1 in

§ 1095
Protection against enforcement and action for averting enforcement against the European payment order issued in Germany

(1) If an application is filed for review of a European payment order issued in Germany in accordance with Article 20 of Regulation (EC) No 1896/2006, § 707 shall apply *mutatis mutandis*. The court deciding on the application pursuant to Article 20 of Regulation (EC) No 1896/2006 shall be competent to decide on the application filed in accordance with § 707.

(2) The raising of objections relating to the claim as such shall be admissible only to the extent that the grounds on which such objections are based arose after the European payment order was served and can no longer be asserted by a statement of opposition in terms of Article 16 of Regulation (EC) No 1896/2006.

§ 1096
Applications in accordance with Articles 22 and 23 of Regulation (EC) No 1896/2006; action for averting enforcement

(1) § 1084 (1) and (2) shall apply *mutatis mutandis* to applications for refusal of compulsory enforcement in terms of Article 22 (1) of Regulation (EC) No 1896/2006. § 1084 (1) and (3) shall apply *mutatis mutandis* to applications for the suspension or limitation of compulsory enforcement in terms of Article 23 of Regulation (EC) No 1896/2006.

(2) § 1086 (1) shall apply *mutatis mutandis* to applications for refusal of compulsory enforcement in terms of Article 22 (2) of Regulation (EC) No 1896/2006. § 1086 (1) and § 1095 (2) shall be applicable *mu-*

Verbindung mit § 767 sind § 1086 Abs. 1 und § 1095 Abs. 2 entsprechend anzuwenden.

Abschnitt 6
Europäisches Verfahren für geringfügige Forderungen nach der Verordnung (EG) Nr. 861/2007

Titel 1
Erkenntnisverfahren

§ 1097
Einleitung und Durchführung des Verfahrens

(1) Die Formblätter gemäß der Verordnung (EG) Nr. 861/2007 und andere Anträge oder Erklärungen können als Schriftsatz, als Telekopie oder nach Maßgabe des § 130a als elektronisches Dokument bei Gericht eingereicht werden.

(2) Im Fall des Artikels 4 Abs. 3 der Verordnung (EG) Nr. 861/2007 wird das Verfahren über die Klage ohne Anwendung der Vorschriften der Verordnung (EG) Nr. 861/2007 fortgeführt.

§ 1098
Annahmeverweigerung auf Grund der verwendeten Sprache

Die Frist zur Erklärung der Annahmeverweigerung nach Artikel 6 Abs. 3 der Verordnung (EG) Nr. 861/2007 beträgt eine Woche. Sie ist eine Notfrist und beginnt mit der Zustellung des Schriftstücks. Der Empfänger ist über die Folgen einer Versäumung der Frist zu belehren.

§ 1099
Widerklage

(1) Eine Widerklage, die nicht den Vorschriften der Verordnung (EG) Nr. 861/2007 entspricht, ist außer im Fall des Artikels 5 Abs. 7 Satz 1 der Verord-

tatis mutandis to actions brought pursuant to § 795 sentence 1 in conjunction with § 767.

Chapter 6
European Small Claims Procedure in accordance with Regulation (EC) No 861/2007

Title 1
Proceedings aiming at a decision on the merits of the case ("Erkenntnisverfahren")

§ 1097
Institution and conduct of the proceedings

(1) The standard forms provided pursuant to Regulation (EC) No 861/2007 as well as other applications or declarations may be filed with the court as a written pleading or a telefax copy or, subject to the requirements of § 130a, as an electronic document.

(2) In the case provided for in Article 4 (3) of Regulation (EC) No 861/2007, the court shall continue the proceedings concerning the claim without applying the stipulations of Regulation (EC) No 861/2007.

§ 1098
Refusal to accept a document by reason of its language

The time limit for declaring the refusal to accept a document on the grounds of Article 6 (3) of Regulation (EC) No 861/2007 shall be one week. This time limit is a statutory time limit and shall commence upon the document being served. The recipient shall be instructed about the consequences of a failure to comply with the time limit.

§ 1099
Counteraction

(1) A counteraction not being in accordance with the stipulations of Regulation (EC) No 861/2007 shall be dismissed as being inadmissible, except in the case

nung (EG) Nr. 861/2007 als unzulässig abzuweisen.

(2) Im Fall des Artikels 5 Abs. 7 Satz 1 der Verordnung (EG) Nr. 861/2007 wird das Verfahren über die Klage und die Widerklage ohne Anwendung der Vorschriften der Verordnung (EG) Nr. 861/2007 fortgeführt. Das Verfahren wird in der Lage übernommen, in der es sich zur Zeit der Erhebung der Widerklage befunden hat.

§ 1100
Mündliche Verhandlung

(1) Das Gericht kann den Parteien sowie ihren Bevollmächtigten und Beiständen gestatten, sich während einer Verhandlung an einem anderen Ort aufzuhalten und dort Verfahrenshandlungen vorzunehmen. § 128a Abs. 1 Satz 2 und Abs. 3 bleibt unberührt.

(2) Die Bestimmung eines frühen ersten Termins zur mündlichen Verhandlung (§ 275) ist ausgeschlossen.

§ 1101
Beweisaufnahme

(1) Das Gericht kann die Beweise in der ihm geeignet erscheinenden Art aufnehmen, soweit Artikel 9 Abs. 2 und 3 der Verordnung (EG) Nr. 861/2007 nichts anderes bestimmt.

(2) Das Gericht kann einem Zeugen, Sachverständigen oder einer Partei gestatten, sich während einer Vernehmung an einem anderen Ort aufzuhalten. § 128a Abs. 2 Satz 2, 3 und Abs. 3 bleibt unberührt.

§ 1102
Urteil

Urteile bedürfen keiner Verkündung. Die Verkündung eines Urteils wird durch die Zustellung ersetzt.

of Article 5 (7) sentence 1 of Regulation (EC) No 861/2007.

(2) In the case provided for in Article 5 (7) sentence 1 of Regulation (EC) No 861/2007, the proceedings regarding the action and the counteraction shall be continued without applying the stipulations of Regulation (EC) No 861/2007. The proceedings shall be taken over in the status at the point in time when the counteraction was brought.

§ 1100
Oral hearing

(1) The court may permit the parties and their attorneys-in-fact and counsels to be at a different location during an oral hearing and to perform procedural acts at such location. § 128a (1) sentence 2 and (3) shall remain unaffected.

(2) The determination of an early first oral hearing (§ 275) shall be excluded.

§ 1101
Taking of evidence

(1) The court may take evidence in the manner deemed appropriate by it, unless provided otherwise in Article 9 (2) and (3) of Regulation (EC) No 861/2007.

(2) The court may permit a witness, expert or party to be at a different location during their examination. § 128a (2) sentences 2, 3 and (3) shall remain unaffected.

§ 1102
Judgment

Judgments need not be pronounced. The pronouncement of a judgment shall be replaced by its service.

§ 1103
Säumnis

Äußert sich eine Partei binnen der für sie geltenden Frist nicht oder erscheint sie nicht zur mündlichen Verhandlung, kann das Gericht eine Entscheidung nach Lage der Akten erlassen. § 251a ist nicht anzuwenden.

§ 1104
Abhilfe bei unverschuldeter Säumnis des Beklagten

(1) Liegen die Voraussetzungen des Artikels 18 Abs. 1 der Verordnung (EG) Nr. 861/2007 vor, wird das Verfahren fortgeführt; es wird in die Lage zurückversetzt, in der es sich vor Erlass des Urteils befand. Auf Antrag stellt das Gericht die Nichtigkeit des Urteils durch Beschluss fest.

(2) Der Beklagte hat die tatsächlichen Voraussetzungen des Artikels 18 Abs. 1 der Verordnung (EG) Nr. 861/2007 glaubhaft zu machen.

Titel 2
Zwangsvollstreckung

§ 1105
Zwangsvollstreckung inländischer Titel

(1) Urteile sind für vorläufig vollstreckbar ohne Sicherheitsleistung zu erklären. Die §§ 712 und 719 Abs. 1 Satz 1 in Verbindung mit § 707 sind nicht anzuwenden.

(2) Für Anträge auf Beschränkung der Zwangsvollstreckung nach Artikel 15 Abs. 2 in Verbindung mit Artikel 23 der Verordnung (EG) Nr. 861/2007 ist das Gericht der Hauptsache zuständig. Die Entscheidung ergeht im Wege einstweiliger Anordnung. Sie ist unanfechtbar. Die tatsächlichen Voraussetzungen des Artikels 23 der Verordnung (EG) Nr. 861/2007 sind glaubhaft zu machen.

§ 1103
Default

If a party fails to make a statement within the time limit applicable to it or fails to appear at the oral hearing, the court may issue a decision on the basis of the court files. § 251a shall not be applicable.

§ 1104
Relief granted in case of the defendant being in default without a fault of his own

(1) If the requirements of Article 18 (1) of Regulation (EC) No 861/2007 are met, the proceedings shall be continued; that status of the proceedings shall be reinstated which existed prior to the issuance of the judgment. Upon an application to this effect, the court shall declare by way of a court order that the judgment is void.

(2) The defendant shall be obliged to present to the satisfaction of the court that the factual requirements of Article 18 (1) of Regulation (EC) No 861/2007 are met.

Title 2
Compulsory enforcement

§ 1105
Compulsory enforcement of German legal titles

(1) Judgments shall be declared to be provisionally enforceable without security being provided. §§ 712 and 719 (1) sentence 1 in conjunction with § 707 shall not be applicable.

(2) The court deciding on the main action shall be competent to decide on applications for the limitation of compulsory enforcement pursuant to Article 15 (2) in conjunction with Article 23 of Regulation (EC) No 861/2007. The decision shall be issued by way of an interim order. It is incontestable. It shall be presented to the satisfaction of the court that the factual requirements of Arti-

cle 23 of Regulation (EC) No 861/2007 are met.

§ 1106
Bestätigung inländischer Titel

(1) Für die Ausstellung der Bestätigung nach Artikel 20 Abs. 2 der Verordnung (EG) Nr. 861/2007 ist das Gericht zuständig, dem die Erteilung einer vollstreckbaren Ausfertigung des Titels obliegt.

(2) Vor Ausfertigung der Bestätigung ist der Schuldner anzuhören. Wird der Antrag auf Ausstellung einer Bestätigung zurückgewiesen, so sind die Vorschriften über die Anfechtung der Entscheidung über die Erteilung einer Vollstreckungsklausel entsprechend anzuwenden.

§ 1107
Ausländische Vollstreckungstitel

Aus einem Titel, der in einem Mitgliedstaat der Europäischen Union nach der Verordnung (EG) Nr. 861/2007 ergangen ist, findet die Zwangsvollstreckung im Inland statt, ohne dass es einer Vollstreckungsklausel bedarf.

§ 1108
Übersetzung

Hat der Gläubiger nach Artikel 21 Abs. 2 Buchstabe b der Verordnung (EG) Nr. 861/2007 eine Übersetzung vorzulegen, so ist diese in deutscher Sprache zu verfassen und von einer in einem der Mitgliedstaaten der Europäischen Union hierzu befugten Person zu erstellen.

§ 1109
Anträge nach den Artikeln 22 und 23 der Verordnung (EG) Nr. 861/2007; Vollstreckungsabwehrklage

(1) Auf Anträge nach Artikel 22 der Verordnung (EG) Nr. 861/2007 ist § 1084 Abs. 1 und 2 entsprechend anzuwenden. Auf Anträge nach Artikel 23 der Verord-

§ 1106
Certification of German enforcement titles

(1) As regards the issuance of the certificate pursuant to Article 20 (2) of Regulation (EC) No 861/2007, the court competent to issue an enforceable executed copy of the enforcement title shall be competent to issue such certificate.

(2) The debtor shall be heard prior to the execution of the certificate. If the application for issuance of a certificate is rejected, the regulations regarding the contestation of the decision on the issuance of a court's certificate of enforceability shall be applicable *mutatis mutandis*.

§ 1107
Foreign titles of enforcement

A title of enforcement which has been issued in a Member State of the European Union in accordance with Regulation (EC) No 861/2007 shall be made subject to compulsory enforcement in Germany without a court's certificate of enforceability being required.

§ 1108
Translation

If the creditor is obliged to submit a translation pursuant to Article 21 (2) lit. b of Regulation (EC) No 861/2007, such translation shall be in German and shall beprepared by a person authorised for this purpose in one of the Member States of the European Union.

§ 1109
Applications in accordance with Articles 22 and 23 of Regulation (EC) No 861/2007; action for averting enforcement

(1) § 1084 (1) and (2) shall be applicable *mutatis mutandis* to applications filed in accordance with Article 22 of Regulation (EC) No 861/2007. § 1084 (1) and (3) shall

nung (EG) Nr. 861/2007 ist § 1084 Abs. 1 und 3 entsprechend anzuwenden.

(2) § 1086 gilt entsprechend.

be applicable *mutatis mutandis* to applications filed in accordance with Article 23 of Regulation (EC) No 861/2007.

(2) § 1086 shall apply *mutatis mutandis*.

Abschnitt 7
Anerkennung und Vollstreckung nach der Verordnung (EU) Nr. 1215/2012

Chapter 7
Recognition and enforcement under Regulation (EU) No 1215/2012

Titel 1
Bescheinigung über inländische Titel

Title 1
Issuance of a certificate regarding German titles of enforcement

§ 1110
Zuständigkeit

§ 1110
Competence

Für die Ausstellung der Bescheinigung nach den Artikeln 53 und 60 der Verordnung (EU) Nr. 1215/2012 sind die Gerichte oder Notare zuständig, denen die Erteilung einer vollstreckbaren Ausfertigung des Titels obliegt.

As regards the issuance of the certificate pursuant to Articles 53 and 60 of Regulation (EU) No 1215/2012, the courts or notaries competent to issue an enforceable executed copy of the title of enforcement shall be competent to issue such certificate.

§ 1111
Verfahren

§ 1111
Procedure

(1) Bescheinigungen nach den Artikeln 53 und 60 der Verordnung (EU) Nr. 1215/2012 sind ohne Anhörung des Schuldners auszustellen. In den Fällen des § 726 Absatz 1 und der §§ 727 bis 729 kann der Schuldner vor der Ausstellung der Bescheinigung gehört werden. Eine Ausfertigung der Bescheinigung ist dem Schuldner von Amts wegen zuzustellen.

(1) Certificates pursuant to Articles 53 and 60 of Regulation (EU) No 1215/2012 shall be issued without the debtor being heard. In the cases provided for in § 726 (1) and §§ 727 to 729, the debtor may be heard prior to the issuance of the certificate. An executed copy of the certificate shall be served on the debtor *ex officio*.

(2) Für die Anfechtbarkeit der Entscheidung über die Ausstellung der Bescheinigung nach Absatz 1 gelten die Vorschriften über die Anfechtbarkeit der Entscheidung über die Erteilung der Vollstreckungsklausel entsprechend.

(2) The regulations regarding the contestability of the decision on the issuance of the court's certificate of enforceability shall apply *mutatis mutandis* to the contestability of the decision on the issuance of the certificate pursuant to subsection (1).

Titel 2
Anerkennung und Vollstreckung ausländischer Titel im Inland

§ 1112
Entbehrlichkeit der Vollstreckungsklausel

Aus einem Titel, der in einem anderen Mitgliedstaat der Europäischen Union vollstreckbar ist, findet die Zwangsvollstreckung im Inland statt, ohne dass es einer Vollstreckungsklausel bedarf.

§ 1113
Übersetzung oder Transliteration

Hat eine Partei nach Artikel 57 der Verordnung (EU) Nr. 1215/2012 eine Übersetzung oder eine Transliteration vorzulegen, so ist diese in deutscher Sprache abzufassen und von einer in einem Mitgliedstaat der Europäischen Union hierzu befugten Person zu erstellen.

§ 1114
Anfechtung der Anpassung eines Titels

Für die Anfechtung der Anpassung eines Titels (Artikel 54 der Verordnung (EU) Nr. 215/2012) sind folgende Rechtsgrundlagen entsprechend anzuwenden:

1. im Fall von Maßnahmen des Gerichtsvollziehers oder des Vollstreckungsgerichts § 766,

2. im Fall von Entscheidungen des Vollstreckungsgerichts oder von Vollstreckungsmaßnahmen des Prozessgerichts § 793 und

3. im Fall von Vollstreckungsmaßnahmen des Grundbuchamts § 71 der Grundbuchordnung.

Title 2
Recognition and enforcement of foreign titles of enforcement in Germany

§ 1112
Dispensability of a court's certificate of enforceability

A title of enforcement which is enforceable in another Member State of the European Union shall be made subject to compulsory enforcement in Germany without a court's certificate of enforceability being required.

§ 1113
Translation or transliteration

If a party is obliged to submit a translation or transliteration pursuant to Article 57 of Regulation (EU) No 1215/2012, such translation or transliteration shall be in German and shall be prepared by a person authorised for this purpose in a Member State of the European Union.

§ 1114
Challenge of the adaptation of a title of enforcement

The following legal grounds shall be applicable *mutatis mutandi*s if the adaptation of an enforcement title is challenged (Article 54 of Regulation (EU) No. 1215/2012):

1. § 766 in the case of measures taken by the executory officer or the court having jurisdiction over enforcement,

2. § 793 in the case of decisions issued by the court having jurisdiction over enforcement or of enforcement measures taken by the court hearing the case, and

3. § 71 of the German Land Register Code in the case of enforcement measures taken by the land registry.

§ 1115
Versagung der Anerkennung oder der Vollstreckung

(1) Für Anträge auf Versagung der Anerkennung oder der Vollstreckung (Artikel 45 Absatz 4 und Artikel 47 Absatz 1 der Verordnung (EU) Nr. 1215/2012) ist das Landgericht ausschließlich zuständig.

(2) Örtlich zuständig ist ausschließlich das Landgericht, in dessen Bezirk der Schuldner seinen Wohnsitz hat. Hat der Schuldner im Inland keinen Wohnsitz, ist ausschließlich das Landgericht zuständig, in dessen Bezirk die Zwangsvollstreckung durchgeführt werden soll. Der Sitz von Gesellschaften und juristischen Personen steht dem Wohnsitz gleich.

(3) Der Antrag auf Versagung kann bei dem zuständigen Landgericht schriftlich eingereicht oder mündlich zu Protokoll der Geschäftsstelle erklärt werden.

(4) Über den Antrag auf Versagung entscheidet der Vorsitzende einer Zivilkammer durch Beschluss. Der Beschluss ist zu begründen und kann ohne mündliche Verhandlung ergehen. Der Antragsgegner ist vor der Entscheidung zu hören.

(5) Gegen die Entscheidung findet die sofortige Beschwerde statt. Die Notfrist des § 569 Absatz 1 Satz 1 beträgt einen Monat und beginnt mit der Zustellung der Entscheidung. Gegen den Beschluss des Beschwerdegerichts findet die Rechtsbeschwerde statt.

(6) Über den Antrag auf Aussetzung oder Beschränkung der Vollstreckung und den Antrag, die Vollstreckung von

§ 1115
Refusal of recognition or enforcement

(1) The Regional Court (*"Landgericht"*) shall have exclusive jurisdiction for deciding on applications for refusal of the recognition or enforcement of a judgment (Article 45 (4) and Article 47 (1) of Regulation (EU) No 1215/2012).

(2) The Regional Court (*"Landgericht"*) in whose district the debtor has his residence shall have exclusive local jurisdiction. If the debtor has no residence in Germany, the Regional Court (*"Landgericht"*) in whose district the compulsory enforcement shall be performed shall have exclusive jurisdiction. The registered office of companies and legal entities shall be equivalent to the residence.

(3) The application for refusal of the recognition and enforcement of a judgment may be filed in writing, or declared orally for the record of the court registry, with the Regional Court having jurisdiction.

(4) The presiding judge of a division for civil matters of such Regional Court (*"Zivilkammer"*) shall decide on the application for refusal by way of a court order. The order shall be issued together with a statement of grounds and may be issued without an oral hearing. The respondent shall be heard prior to the issuance of a decision.

(5) The remedy of immediate miscellaneous appeal (*"sofortige Beschwerde"*) shall be available against the decision. The statutory time limit of § 569 (1) sentence 1 shall be one month and shall commence upon service of the decision. The remedy of a miscellaneous appeal on a point of law (*"Rechtsbeschwerde"*) shall be available against the order issued by the court that decided on the immediate miscellaneous appeal.

(6) The decision on the application for the suspension or limitation of enforcement and on the application for making

der Leistung einer Sicherheit abhängig zu machen (Artikel 44 Absatz 1 der Verordnung (EU) Nr. 1215/2012), wird durch einstweilige Anordnung entschieden. Die Entscheidung ist unanfechtbar.

§ 1116
Wegfall oder Beschränkung der Vollstreckbarkeit im Ursprungsmitgliedstaat

Auf Antrag des Schuldners (Artikel 44 Absatz 2 der Verordnung (EU) Nr. 1215/2012) ist die Zwangsvollstreckung entsprechend § 775 Nummer 1 und 2 und § 776 auch dann einzustellen oder zu beschränken, wenn der Schuldner eine Entscheidung eines Gerichts des Ursprungsmitgliedstaats über die Nichtvollstreckbarkeit oder über die Beschränkung der Vollstreckbarkeit vorlegt. Auf Verlangen des Vollstreckungsorgans ist eine Übersetzung der Entscheidung vorzulegen. § 1108 gilt entsprechend.

§ 1117
Vollstreckungsabwehrklage

(1) Für Klagen nach § 795 Satz 1 in Verbindung mit § 767 gilt § 1086 Absatz 1 entsprechend.

(2) Richtet sich die Klage gegen die Vollstreckung aus einem gerichtlichen Vergleich oder einer öffentlichen Urkunde, ist § 767 Absatz 2 nicht anzuwenden.

the enforcement subject to the provision of security (Article 44 (1) of Regulation (EC) No 1215/2012) shall be issued by an interim order. The decision is incontestable.

§ 1116
Cancellation or limitation of enforceability in the Member State where the judgment was delivered

Upon the application of the debtor (Article 44 (2) of Regulation (EU) No 1215/2012), the compulsory enforcement shall also be discontinued or limited in accordance with § 775 no. 1 and 2 and § 776, if the debtor presents a decision issued by a court of the Member State where the judgment was delivered that the judgment is not enforceable or its enforceability is limited. At the request of the body enforcing the judgment, a translation of the decision shall be presented. § 1108 shall apply *mutatis mutandis*.

§ 1117
Action for averting enforcement

(1) § 1086 (1) shall apply *mutatis mutandis* to actions brought pursuant to § 795 sentence 1 in conjunction with § 767.

(2) If the action is directed against enforcement under a court settlement or a public document, § 767 (2) shall not be applicable.

II. German Judicature Act (Excerpts)[1, 2]

First Title
Jurisdiction

§ 1

[. . .]

§§ 2–9

(repealed)

§ 10

[. . .]

§ 11

(repealed)

§ 12
[Ordinary Courts]

The ordinary jurisdiction shall be exercised by local courts, regional courts, higher regional courts and by the Federal Court of Justice (the supreme court of the Federal Republic for the area of ordinary jurisdiction).

§ 13
[Jurisdiction of the ordinary courts]

The ordinary courts shall have jurisdiction for civil legal disputes, family matters and matters of non-contentious jurisdiction (civil matters), and criminal matters for which neither the jurisdiction of administrative authorities or administrative courts is established nor special courts are appointed or admitted on the basis of regulations of the Federal law.

---

[1] Translation by Elaine Ikizer, amended by Hildegard Rosenzweig.
[2] Headings of sections in square brackets in the German text are unofficial (i. e. not published in the Federal Law Gazette).

§ 13a
[Zuweisung durch Landesrecht]

Durch Landesrecht können einem Gericht für die Bezirke mehrerer Gerichte Sachen aller Art ganz oder teilweise zugewiesen sowie auswärtige Spruchkörper von Gerichten eingerichtet werden.

§ 14

[...]

§ 15

(*weggefallen*)

§ 16

[...]

§ 17
[Rechtshängigkeit; Entscheidung des Rechtsstreits]

(1) Die Zulässigkeit des beschrittenen Rechtsweges wird durch eine nach Rechtshängigkeit eintretende Veränderung der sie begründenden Umstände nicht berührt. Während der Rechtshängigkeit kann die Sache von keiner Partei anderweitig anhängig gemacht werden.

(2) Das Gericht des zulässigen Rechtsweges entscheidet den Rechtsstreit unter allen in Betracht kommenden rechtlichen Gesichtspunkten. Artikel 14 Abs. 3 Satz 4 und Artikel 34 Satz 3 des Grundgesetzes bleiben unberührt.

§ 17a
[Rechtsweg]

(1) Hat ein Gericht den zu ihm beschrittenen Rechtsweg rechtskräftig für zulässig erklärt, sind andere Gerichte an diese Entscheidung gebunden.

(2) Ist der beschrittene Rechtsweg unzulässig, spricht das Gericht dies nach Anhörung der Parteien von Amts wegen aus und verweist den Rechtsstreit zugleich an das zuständige Gericht des zulässigen Rechtsweges. Sind mehrere

§ 13a
[Assignation by Federal State Law]

Federal State law may provide that matters of all kinds be assigned in whole or in part to a single court for the districts of several courts and that external adjudicating bodies of courts be established.

§ 14

[...]

§ 15

(*repealed*)

§ 16

[...]

§ 17
[Pendency; decision of the legal dispute]

(1) The admissibility of the legal recourse taken shall not be affected by a change in the circumstances establishing jurisdiction which occurs after the legal dispute has become pending. During pendency, the legal dispute cannot be made pending before another court by either party.

(2) The court having jurisdiction shall decide the legal dispute from all legal aspects to be considered. Article 14 (3) fourth sentence and Article 34 third sentence of the Constitution of the Federal Republic of Germany shall remain unaffected.

§ 17a
[Legal recourse]

(1) If a court has declared with *res judicata* effect that the legal recourse taken to it is admissible, other courts shall be bound by that decision.

(2) If the legal recourse taken is inadmissible, the court shall declare so *ex officio* after hearing the parties and shall at the same time transfer the legal dispute to the competent court of the admissible legal recourse. If several courts have

Gerichte zuständig, wird an das vom Kläger oder Antragsteller auszuwählende Gericht verwiesen oder, wenn die Wahl unterbleibt, an das vom Gericht bestimmte. Der Beschluss ist für das Gericht, an das der Rechtsstreit verwiesen worden ist, hinsichtlich des Rechtsweges bindend.

(3) Ist der beschrittene Rechtsweg zulässig, kann das Gericht dies vorab aussprechen. Es hat vorab zu entscheiden, wenn eine Partei die Zulässigkeit des Rechtsweges rügt.

(4) Der Beschluss nach den Absätzen 2 und 3 kann ohne mündliche Verhandlung ergehen. Er ist zu begründen. Gegen den Beschluss ist die sofortige Beschwerde nach den Vorschriften der jeweils anzuwendenden Verfahrensordnung gegeben. Den Beteiligten steht die Beschwerde gegen einen Beschluss des oberen Landesgerichts an den obersten Gerichtshof des Bundes nur zu, wenn sie in dem Beschluss zugelassen worden ist. Die Beschwerde ist zuzulassen, wenn die Rechtsfrage grundsätzliche Bedeutung hat oder wenn das Gericht von der Entscheidung eines obersten Gerichtshofes des Bundes oder des Gemeinsamen Senats der obersten Gerichtshöfe des Bundes abweicht. Der oberste Gerichtshof des Bundes ist an die Zulassung der Beschwerde gebunden.

(5) Das Gericht, das über ein Rechtsmittel gegen eine Entscheidung in der Hauptsache entscheidet, prüft nicht, ob der beschrittene Rechtsweg zulässig ist.

(6) Die Absätze 1 bis 5 gelten für die in bürgerlichen Rechtsstreitigkeiten, Familiensachen und Angelegenheiten der freiwilligen Gerichtsbarkeit zuständigen Spruchkörper in ihrem Verhältnis zueinander entsprechend.

jurisdiction, the legal dispute shall be transferred to the court to be chosen by the plaintiff or applicant or, if no such choice is made, to the court determined by the original court. That order shall be binding, with regard to the legal recourse, on the court to which the legal dispute has been transferred.

(3) If the legal recourse taken to a certain court is admissible, the court may declare so at the outset. It must take such decision first, if one party objects to the admissibility of the legal recourse taken.

(4) The court order in accordance with sub-sections (2) and (3) may be issued without an oral hearing. The court must provide the grounds for its decision. The order shall be subject to immediate miscellaneous appeal in accordance with the provisions of the applicable procedural rules. The parties shall only be entitled to file a miscellaneous appeal against an order of a higher regional court with a supreme federal court, if leave was granted for such appeal by the order. Leave shall be granted for a miscellaneous appeal if the legal matter is of fundamental significance or if the court deviates from the decision of a supreme federal court or of the Joint Committee of the supreme federal courts. The respective supreme federal court shall be bound by the admission of the miscellaneous appeal.

(5) The court deciding on a means of appeal against a decision concerning the main issue of a legal dispute will not review whether the legal recourse taken is admissible.

(6) Subsections (1) to (5) shall apply *mutatis mutandis* to the adjudicating bodies having jurisdiction over civil legal disputes, family matters and matters of non-contentious jurisdiction in relation to each other.

§ 17b
[Anhängigkeit nach Verweisung; Kosten]

(1) Nach Eintritt der Rechtskraft des Verweisungsbeschlusses wird der Rechtsstreit mit Eingang der Akten bei dem im Beschluss bezeichneten Gericht anhängig. Die Wirkungen der Rechtshängigkeit bleiben bestehen.

(2) Wird ein Rechtsstreit an ein anderes Gericht verwiesen, so werden die Kosten im Verfahren vor dem angegangenen Gericht als Teil der Kosten behandelt, die bei dem Gericht erwachsen, an das der Rechtsstreit verwiesen wurde. Dem Kläger sind die entstandenen Mehrkosten auch dann aufzuerlegen, wenn er in der Hauptsache obsiegt.

(3) Absatz 2 Satz 2 gilt nicht in Familiensachen und in Angelegenheiten der freiwilligen Gerichtsbarkeit.

§ 18
[Exterritorialität von Mitgliedern der diplomatischen Missionen]

Die Mitglieder der im Geltungsbereich dieses Gesetzes errichteten diplomatischen Missionen, ihre Familienmitglieder und ihre privaten Hausangestellten sind nach Maßgabe des Wiener Übereinkommens über diplomatische Beziehungen vom 18. April 1961 (Bundesgesetzbl. 1964 II S. 957ff.) von der deutschen Gerichtsbarkeit befreit. Dies gilt auch, wenn ihr Entsendestaat nicht Vertragspartei dieses Übereinkommens ist; in diesem Falle findet Artikel 2 des Gesetzes vom 6. August 1964 zu dem Wiener Übereinkommen vom 18. April 1961 über diplomatische Beziehungen (Bundesgesetzbl. 1964 II S. 957) entsprechende Anwendung.

§ 17b
[Pendency after transfer; Costs]

(1) After the court order transferring the legal dispute has become *res judicata*, the legal dispute will become pending, upon receipt of the case files, before the court specified in the court order. The effects of the (original) pendency shall continue to exist.

(2) If a legal dispute is transferred to another court, the costs of the proceedings before the court originally applied to shall be treated as part of the costs which are incurred before that court to which the legal dispute was transferred. The additional costs incurred shall also be imposed on the plaintiff, if he prevails with regard to the main issue of the legal dispute.

(3) Subsection (2), second sentence, shall not apply to family matters and matters of non-contentious jurisdiction.

§ 18
[Exterritoriality of member of diplomatic missions]

The members of the diplomatic missions established within the territorial scope of this Act, their family members and their private servants shall be exempted from the German jurisdiction in accordance with the Vienna Convention on Diplomatic Relations of 18 April 1961 (Federal Law Gazette 1964 II p. 957 *et seq.*). This shall also apply if their sending state is not a party to this Convention; in this case, Article 2 of the Act of 6 August 1964 in relation to the Vienna Convention of 18 April 1961 on Diplomatic Relations (Federal Law Gazette 1964 II p. 957) shall apply *mutatis mutandis*.

II. German Judicature Act (Excerpts)

§ 19
[Exterritorialität von Mitgliedern der konsularischen Vertretungen]

(1) Die Mitglieder der im Geltungsbereich dieses Gesetzes errichteten konsularischen Vertretungen einschließlich der Wahlkonsularbeamten sind nach Maßgabe des Wiener Übereinkommens über konsularische Beziehungen vom 24. April 1963 (Bundesgesetzbl. 1969 II S. 1585ff.) von der deutschen Gerichtsbarkeit befreit. Dies gilt auch, wenn ihr Entsendestaat nicht Vertragspartei dieses Übereinkommens ist; in diesem Falle findet Artikel 2 des Gesetzes vom 26. August 1969 zu dem Wiener Übereinkommen vom 24. April 1963 über konsularische Beziehungen (Bundesgesetzbl. 1969 II S. 1585) entsprechende Anwendung.

(2) Besondere völkerrechtliche Vereinbarungen über die Befreiung der in Absatz 1 genannten Personen von der deutschen Gerichtsbarkeit bleiben unberührt.

§ 20
[Weitere Exterritoriale]

(1) Die deutsche Gerichtsbarkeit erstreckt sich auch nicht auf Repräsentanten anderer Staaten und deren Begleitung, die sich auf amtliche Einladung der Bundesrepublik Deutschland im Geltungsbereich dieses Gesetzes aufhalten.

(2) Im Übrigen erstreckt sich die deutsche Gerichtsbarkeit auch nicht auf andere als die in Absatz 1 und in den §§ 18 und 19 genannten Personen, soweit sie nach den allgemeinen Regeln des Völkerrechts, aufgrund völkerrechtlicher Vereinbarungen oder sonstiger Rechtsvorschriften von ihr befreit sind.

§ 21
[. . .]

§ 19
[Exterritoriality of member of consular representations]

(1) The members of the consular representations established within the territorial scope of this Act including the honorary consular officers shall be exempted from the German jurisdiction in accordance with the Vienna Convention on Consular Relations of 24 April 1963 (Federal Law Gazette 1969 II p. 1585 *et seq.*). This shall also apply if their sending state is not a party to this Convention; in this case, Article 2 of the Act of 26 August 1969 concerning the Vienna Convention of 24 April 1963 on Consular Relations (Federal Law Gazette 1969 II p. 1585) shall apply *mutatis mutandis*.

(2) Any special agreements under international law on the exemption of the persons referred to in sub-section (1) from the German jurisdiction shall remain unaffected.

§ 20
[Further exterritorial persons]

(1) Furthermore, the German jurisdiction shall not extend to representatives of other states and the persons accompanying them who are staying within the territorial scope of this Act as a result of an official invitation from the Federal Republic of Germany.

(2) Otherwise, the German jurisdiction shall also not extend to persons other than those referred to in sub-section (1) and in §§ 18 and 19, to the extent that they are exempted from the German jurisdiction in accordance with the general regulations of international law or on the basis of agreements under international law or other legal provisions.

§ 21
[. . .]

Zweiter Titel
Allgemeine Vorschriften über das Präsidium und die Geschäftsverteilung

§ 21a–21j

[...]

Dritter Titel
Amtsgerichte

§§ 22–22d

[...]

§ 23
[Zuständigkeit in Zivilsachen]

Die Zuständigkeit der Amtsgerichte umfasst in bürgerlichen Rechtsstreitigkeiten, soweit sie nicht ohne Rücksicht auf den Wert des Streitgegenstandes den Landgerichten zugewiesen sind:

1. Streitigkeiten über Ansprüche, deren Gegenstand an Geld oder Geldeswert die Summe von fünftausend Euro nicht übersteigt;

2. ohne Rücksicht auf den Wert des Streitgegenstandes:
   a) Streitigkeiten über Ansprüche aus einem Mietverhältnis über Wohnraum oder über den Bestand eines solchen Mietverhältnisses; diese Zuständigkeit ist ausschließlich;
   b) Streitigkeiten zwischen Reisenden und Wirten, Fuhrleuten, Schiffern oder Auswanderungsexpedienten in den Einschiffungshäfen, die über Wirtszechen, Fuhrlohn, Überfahrtsgelder, Beförderung der Reisenden und ihrer Habe und über Verlust und Beschädigung der letzteren, sowie Streitigkeiten zwischen Reisenden und Handwerkern, die aus Anlass der Reise entstanden sind;
   c) Streitigkeiten nach § 43 Nr. 1 bis 4 und 6 des Wohnungseigentums-

Second Title
General Provisions on the Presidency of the Court and Assignment of Business

§§ 21a–21j

[...]

Third Title
Local Courts

§§ 22–22d

[...]

§ 23
[Jurisdiction in civil law matters]

The jurisdiction of the local courts, in relation to civil proceedings, shall comprise the following, unless the matters are assigned to the regional courts irrespective of the value in dispute:

1. disputes concerning claims the subject matter of which does not exceed, in terms of money or monetary value, the amount of Euro five thousand;

2. irrespective of the value in dispute:
   a) disputes concerning claims under a lease relating to housing space or to the existence of such lease; such jurisdiction shall be exclusive;
   b) disputes between travelers and landlords, carriers, skippers or emigration dispatchers in the embarkment ports, which disputes have arisen in relation to landlords' bills, carriers' wage, crossing fares, transportation of travelers and their belongings and in relation to loss of and damage to the latter, and in relation to disputes between travelers and tradesmen which arose in connection with the journey;
   c) disputes pursuant to section 43 no. 1 to 4 and 6 of the German

gesetzes; diese Zuständigkeit ist ausschließlich; d) Streitigkeiten wegen Wildschadens; e), f) *(weggefallen)* g) Ansprüche aus einem mit der Überlassung eines Grundstücks in Verbindung stehenden Leibgedings-, Leibzuchts-, Altenteils- oder Auszugsvertrag;	Condominium Act; this jurisdiction shall be exclusive; d) disputes based on damage caused by game; e), f) *(repealed)* g) claims based on agreements connected with a permission to use real property, which agreements provide for specific recurrent benefits or uses granted to the person permitting the use.

§§ 23a–27

[. . .]

§§ 23a–27

[. . .]

Vierter Titel
Schöffengerichte

Fourth Title
Courts with Lay Judges

§§ 28–58

[. . .]

§§ 28–58

[. . .]

Fünfter Titel
Landgerichte

Fifth Title
Regional Courts

§§ 59–60

[. . .]

§§ 59–60

[. . .]

§§ 61–69

(weggefallen)

§§ 61–69

(repealed)

§ 70

[. . .]

§ 70

[. . .]

§ 71
[Zuständigkeit in Zivilsachen in 1. Instanz]

§ 71
[Jurisdiction in civil law matters in the first instance]

(1) Vor die Zivilkammern, einschließlich der Kammern für Handelssachen, gehören alle bürgerlichen Rechtsstreitigkeiten, die nicht den Amtsgerichten zugewiesen sind.

(1) The chambers for civil law matters, including the chambers for commercial matters, shall have jurisdiction for all civil proceedings which are not assigned to the local courts.

(2) Die Landgerichte sind ohne Rücksicht auf den Wert des Streitgegenstandes ausschließlich zuständig

(2) The regional courts shall have exclusive jurisdiction, irrespective of the value in dispute, for the following matters:

1. für die Ansprüche, die aufgrund der Beamtengesetze gegen den Fiskus erhoben werden;

1. for claims asserted against fiscal authorities on the basis of the civil service laws;

2. für die Ansprüche gegen Richter und Beamte wegen Überschreitung ihrer amtlichen Befugnisse oder wegen pflichtwidriger Unterlassung von Amtshandlungen.
3. für Ansprüche, die auf eine falsche, irreführende oder unterlassene öffentliche Kapitalmarktinformation, auf die Verwendung einer falschen oder irreführenden öffentlichen Kapitalmarktinformation oder auf die Unterlassung der gebotenen Aufklärung darüber, dass eine öffentliche Kapitalmarktinformation falsch oder irreführend ist, gestützt werden;
4. für Verfahren nach
    a) § 324 des Handelsgesetzbuchs,
    b) den §§ 98, 99, 132, 142, 145, 258, 260, 293c und 315 des Aktiengesetzes,
    c) § 26 des SE-Ausführungsgesetzes,
    d) § 10 des Umwandlungsgesetzes,
    e) dem Spruchverfahrensgesetz,
    f) den §§ 39a und 39b des Wertpapiererwerbs- und Übernahmegesetzes.

(3) Der Landesgesetzgebung bleibt überlassen, Ansprüche gegen den Staat oder eine Körperschaft des öffentlichen Rechts wegen Verfügungen der Verwaltungsbehörden sowie Ansprüche wegen öffentlicher Abgaben ohne Rücksicht auf den Wert des Streitgegenstandes den Landgerichten ausschließlich zuzuweisen.

(4) Die Landesregierungen werden ermächtigt, durch Rechtsverordnung die Entscheidungen in Verfahren nach Absatz 2 Nr. 4 Buchstabe a bis e einem Landgericht für die Bezirke mehrerer Landgerichte zu übertragen, wenn dies der Sicherung einer einheitlichen Rechtsprechung dient. Sie können die Ermächtigung auf die Landesjustizverwaltungen übertragen.

2. for claims against judges and civil servants on the basis of such persons having exceeded their official powers or due to a failure to perform official acts in breach of duty:
3. for claims which are based on false, misleading or omitted public capital market information, on the use of false or misleading public capital market information, or on the omission to make the necessary disclosure that public capital market information is false or misleading;
4. for proceedings under
    a) section 324 of the German Commercial Code,
    b) sections 98, 99, 132, 142, 145, 258, 260, 293c and 315 of the German Stock Corporation Act,
    c) section 26 of the German SE Implementation Act,
    d) section 10 of the German Company Transformation Act,
    e) the German Act on Appraisal Proceedings,
    f) sections 39a and 39b of the German Securities Acquisition and Takeover Act.

(3) It shall be left to the discretion of the Federal State legislation whether to assign claims asserted against the State or a public law corporation based on directions given by administrative authorities and claims based on public charges exclusively to the regional courts, irrespective of the value in dispute.

(4) The Federal State governments shall be authorised to issue statutory instruments assigning the decisions in proceedings pursuant to subsection (2), no. 4, lit. a to e, to one regional court for the districts of several regional courts if this serves to ensure uniform administration of justice. The Federal State governments may transfer this author-

§ 72
[Zuständigkeit in Zivilsachen in 2. Instanz]

(1) Die Zivilkammern, einschließlich der Kammern für Handelssachen, sind die Berufungs- und Beschwerdegerichte in den vor den Amtsgerichten verhandelten bürgerlichen Rechtsstreitigkeiten, soweit nicht die Zuständigkeit der Oberlandesgerichte begründet ist. Die Landgerichte sind ferner die Beschwerdegerichte in Freiheitsentziehungssachen und in den von den Betreuungsgerichten entschiedenen Sachen.

(2) In Streitigkeiten nach § 43 Nr. 1 bis 4 und 6 des Wohnungseigentumsgesetzes ist das für den Sitz des Oberlandesgerichts zuständige Landgericht gemeinsames Berufungs- und Beschwerdegericht für den Bezirk des Oberlandesgerichts, in dem das Amtsgericht seinen Sitz hat. Die Landesregierungen werden ermächtigt, durch Rechtsverordnung anstelle dieses Gerichts ein anderes Landgericht im Bezirk des Oberlandesgerichts zu bestimmen. Sie können die Ermächtigung auf die Landesjustizverwaltungen übertragen.

§ 73
[...]

§ 73a
(*weggefallen*)

§§ 74–74f
[...]

§ 72
[Jurisdiction in civil law matters in the second instance]

(1) The chambers for civil law matters, including the chambers for commercial matters, shall be the courts of first appeal and of miscellaneous appeal concerning the civil proceedings heard before the local courts, unless the jurisdiction of the higher regional courts is established. Further, the regional courts shall be the courts of appeal in imprisonment matters and in matters decided by the adult guardianship courts (*Betreuungsgerichte*).

(2) In disputes pursuant to section 43, no. 1 to 4 and 6 of the German Condominium Act, the regional court with jurisdiction for the seat of the higher regional court shall be the joint court of first appeal and of miscellaneous appeal for the district of the higher regional court in which the local court has its seat. The Federal State governments shall be authorised to issue statutory instruments designating a different regional court in the district of the higher regional court instead of this court. The Federal State governments may transfer this authorisation to the Federal State agencies for the administration of justice.

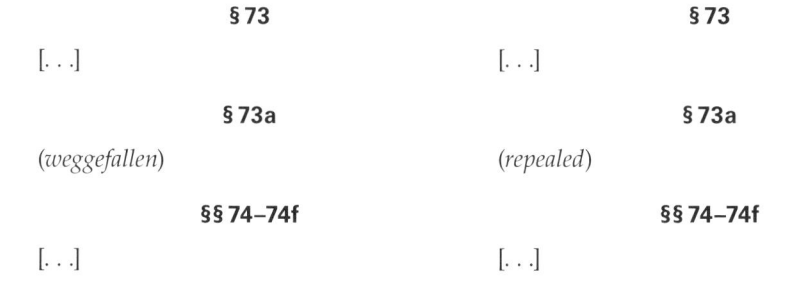

§ 73
[...]

§ 73a
(*repealed*)

§§ 74–74f
[...]

§ 75
[Besetzung der Zivilkammern]

Die Zivilkammern sind, soweit nicht nach den Vorschriften der Prozessgesetze an Stelle der Kammer der Einzelrichter zu entscheiden hat, mit drei Mitgliedern einschließlich des Vorsitzenden besetzt.

§§ 76–78

[. . .]

5a. Titel
Strafvollstreckungskammern

§§ 78a–78b

[. . .]

Sechster Titel
Schwurgerichte

§§ 79–92

(*weggefallen*)

Siebenter Titel
Kammern für Handelssachen

§ 93
[Bildung]

(1) Die Landesregierungen werden ermächtigt, durch Rechtsverordnung bei den Landgerichten für deren Bezirke oder für örtlich abgegrenzte Teile davon Kammern für Handelssachen zu bilden. Solche Kammern können ihren Sitz innerhalb des Landgerichtsbezirks auch an Orten haben, an denen das Landgericht seinen Sitz nicht hat.

(2) Die Landesregierungen können die Ermächtigung nach Absatz 1 auf die Landesjustizverwaltungen übertragen.

§ 94
[Zuständigkeit]

Ist bei einem Landgericht eine Kammer für Handelssachen gebildet, so tritt für

§ 75
[Composition of the chambers for civil law matters]

Unless a single judge shall decide instead of the chamber in accordance with the provisions of procedural law, the chambers for civil law matters shall be composed of three members including the presiding judge.

§§ 76–78

[. . .]

5a Title
Chambers for execution of sentences

§§ 78a–78b

[. . .]

Sixth Title
Court with lay judges

§§ 79–92

(*repealed*)

Seventh Title
Chambers for Commercial Matters

§ 93
[Establishment of chambers]

(1) The Federal State governments shall be authorised to issue statutory instruments to establish chambers for commercial matters within the Regional Courts for their districts or for locally defined parts thereof. Such chambers may also have their seat in places within the district of the regional court where the regional court does not have its seat.

(2) The Federal State governments may transfer the authorisation pursuant to the first sentence to the Federal State administration of justice.

§ 94
[Jurisdiction]

If a chamber for commercial matters has been established within a regional

Handelssachen diese Kammer an die Stelle der Zivilkammern nach Maßgabe der folgenden Vorschriften.

§ 95
[Begriff der Handelssachen]

(1) Handelssachen im Sinne dieses Gesetzes sind die bürgerlichen Rechtsstreitigkeiten, in denen durch die Klage ein Anspruch geltend gemacht wird:

1. gegen einen Kaufmann im Sinne des Handelsgesetzbuches, sofern er in das Handelsregister oder Genossenschaftsregister eingetragen ist oder aufgrund einer gesetzlichen Sonderregelung für juristische Personen des öffentlichen Rechts nicht eingetragen zu werden braucht, aus Geschäften, die für beide Teile Handelsgeschäfte sind;
2. aus einem Wechsel im Sinne des Wechselgesetzes oder aus einer der im § 363 des Handelsgesetzbuchs bezeichneten Urkunden;
3. auf Grund des Scheckgesetzes;
4. aus einem der nachstehend bezeichneten Rechtsverhältnisse:
    a) aus dem Rechtsverhältnis zwischen den Mitgliedern einer Handelsgesellschaft oder Genossenschaft oder zwischen dieser und ihren Mitgliedern oder zwischen dem stillen Gesellschafter und dem Inhaber des Handelsgeschäfts, sowohl während des Bestehens als auch nach Auflösung des Gesellschaftsverhältnisses, und aus dem Rechtsverhältnis zwischen den Vorstehern oder den Liquidatoren einer Handelsgesellschaft oder Genossenschaft und der Gesellschaft oder deren Mitgliedern;
    b) aus dem Rechtsverhältnis, welches das Recht zum Gebrauch der Handelsfirma betrifft;

court, such chamber shall replace the chambers for civil matters in accordance with the following provisions.

§ 95
[Concept of commercial matters]

(1) Commercial matters within the meaning of this Act shall be those civil legal disputes in which a claim is asserted by way of the action:

1. against a merchant within the meaning of the German Commercial Code, if he is registered in the commercial register or the register of cooperatives or such registration is not required on the basis of a statutory special regulation for legal persons under public law, where the claim is based on a transaction which is a commercial transaction for both parties;
2. based on a bill of exchange within the meaning of the German Bills of Exchange Act or on one of the documents specified in § 363 of the German Commercial Code;
3. based on the German Checks Act;
4. based on one of the legal relations set out below:
    a) based on the legal relationship between the partners/shareholders of a business association or cooperative or between that business association or cooperative and its partners/shareholders or between the silent partner and the proprietor of the commercial business, both during the existence and after dissolution of the partnership/shareholders' relationship, and based on the legal relationship between the general partners/directors or liquidators of a business association or cooperative and the business association or its partners/shareholders;
    b) based on the legal relationship which relates to the right to use the trade name;

<table>
<tr><td>

c) aus den Rechtsverhältnissen, die sich auf den Schutz der Marken und sonstigen Kennzeichen sowie der eingetragenen Designs beziehen;

d) aus dem Rechtsverhältnis, das durch den Erwerb eines bestehenden Handelsgeschäfts unter Lebenden zwischen dem bisherigen Inhaber und dem Erwerber entsteht;

e) aus dem Rechtsverhältnis zwischen einem Dritten und dem, der wegen mangelnden Nachweises der Prokura oder Handlungsvollmacht haftet;

f) aus den Rechtsverhältnissen des Seerechts, insbesondere aus denen, die sich auf die Reederei, auf die Rechte und Pflichten des Reeders oder Schiffseigners, des Korrespondentreeders und der Schiffsbesatzung, auf die Haverei, auf den Schadensersatz im Falle des Zusammenstoßes von Schiffen, auf die Bergung und auf die Ansprüche der Schiffsgläubiger beziehen;

5. auf Grund des Gesetzes gegen den unlauteren Wettbewerb;
6. aus den §§ 21, 22 und 24 des Wertpapierprospektgesetzes oder den §§ 20 bis 22 des Vermögensanlagengesetzes.

(2) Handelssachen im Sinne dieses Gesetzes sind ferner

1. die Rechtsstreitigkeiten, in denen sich die Zuständigkeit des Landgerichts nach § 246 Abs. 3 Satz 1, § 396 Abs. 1 Satz 2 des Aktiengesetzes, § 51 Abs. 3 Satz 3 oder nach § 81 Abs. 1 Satz 2 des Genossenschaftsgesetzes, § 87 des Gesetzes gegen Wettbewerbsbeschränkungen, es sei denn, es handelt sich um kartellrechtliche Schadensersatzansprüche, und § 13 Abs. 4 des EG Verbraucherschutzdurchsetzungsgesetzes richtet,

</td><td>

c) based on the legal relations which relate to the protection of the trademarks and other marks and the registered designs;

d) based on the legal relationship created by the acquisition of an existing commercial enterprise among living persons between the former proprietor and the acquirer;

e) based on the legal relationship between a third party and the person who is liable due to a lack of evidence of procuration or a general commercial power of representation;

f) based on the legal relations under maritime law, in particular, based on legal relations relating to the shipping company, to the rights and obligations of the shipowner, the correspondent shipowner and the crew, to the average, to damages in case of a collision between ships, to the salvaging and the claims of the ship's creditors;

5. on the basis of the German Unfair Competition Act;
6. based on §§ 21, 22 and 24 of the German Securities Prospectus Act or §§ 20 to 22 of the German Capital Investment Act.

(2) Commercial matters within the meaning of this Act shall also be

1. the legal disputes in which the jurisdiction of the regional court is determined by § 246 (3) first sentence, § 396 (1), second sentence of the German Stock Corporation Act, § 51 (3) third sentence or § 81 (1), second sentence of the German Cooperatives Act, § 87 of the German Act Against Restraints of Competition, unless the legal disputes concern claims for damages under cartel law, and § 13 (4) of the Act implementing the EC

</td></tr>
</table>

2. die in §71 Abs. 2 Nr. 4 Buchstabe b bis f genannten Verfahren.

§96
[Antrag auf Verhandlung vor der Kammer für Handelssachen]

(1) Der Rechtsstreit wird vor der Kammer für Handelssachen verhandelt, wenn der Kläger dies in der Klageschrift beantragt hat.

(2) Ist ein Rechtsstreit nach den Vorschriften der §§ 281, 506 der Zivilprozessordnung vom Amtsgericht an das Landgericht zu verweisen, so hat der Kläger den Antrag auf Verhandlung vor der Kammer für Handelssachen vor dem Amtsgericht zu stellen.

§97
[Verweisung an Zivilsachen wegen ursprünglicher Unzuständigkeit]

(1) Wird vor der Kammer für Handelssachen eine nicht vor sie gehörige Klage zur Verhandlung gebracht, so ist der Rechtsstreit auf Antrag des Beklagten an die Zivilkammer zu verweisen.

(2) Gehört die Klage oder die im Falle des §506 der Zivilprozessordnung erhobene Widerklage als Klage nicht vor die Kammer für Handelssachen, so ist diese auch von Amts wegen befugt, den Rechtsstreit an die Zivilkammer zu verweisen, solange nicht eine Verhandlung zur Hauptsache erfolgt und darauf ein Beschluss verkündet ist. Die Verweisung von Amts wegen kann nicht aus dem Grund erfolgen, dass der Beklagte nicht Kaufmann ist.

§98
[Verweisung an Kammer für Handelssachen]

(1) Wird vor der Zivilkammer eine vor die Kammer für Handelssachen gehö-

Consumer Protection Cooperation Regulation,

2. the proceedings specified in §71 (2), no. 4, lit. b to f.

§96
[Motion for the legal dispute to be heard before the camber for commercial matters]

(1) The legal dispute shall be heard before the chamber for commercial matters if the plaintiff has filed this motion in the statement of claim.

(2) If a legal dispute must be transferred from the local court to the regional court in accordance with the provisions of §§ 281, 506 of the German Code of Civil Procedure, the plaintiff shall file the motion for hearing before the chamber for commercial matters with the local court.

§97
[Transfer to chamber for civil matters on the basis]

(1) If an action for which the chamber for commercial matters has no jurisdiction is brought before that chamber for hearing, the legal dispute shall be transferred to the chamber for civil matters upon motion of the defendant.

(2) If the chamber for commercial matters has no jurisdiction for the action or the cross-action brought in the case of §506 of the German Code of Civil Procedure as an action, that chamber shall be entitled also *ex officio* to transfer the legal dispute to the chamber for civil matters, as long as no hearing on the main issue has taken place and no court order has been pronounced upon such hearing. The transfer *ex officio* may not be made on the basis that the defendant is not a merchant.

§98
[Transfer to chambers for commercial matters]

(1) If an action for which the chamber for commercial matters has jurisdiction

rige Klage zur Verhandlung gebracht, so ist der Rechtsstreit auf Antrag des Beklagten an die Kammer für Handelssachen zu verweisen. Ein Beklagter, der nicht in das Handelsregister oder Genossenschaftsregister eingetragen ist, kann den Antrag nicht darauf stützen, dass er Kaufmann ist.

(2) Der Antrag ist zurückzuweisen, wenn die im Falle des §506 der Zivilprozessordnung erhobene Widerklage als Klage vor die Kammer für Handelssachen nicht gehören würde.

(3) Zu einer Verweisung von Amts wegen ist die Zivilkammer nicht befugt.

(4) Die Zivilkammer ist zur Verwerfung des Antrags auch dann befugt, wenn der Kläger ihm zugestimmt hat.

is brought before the chamber for civil matters for hearing, the legal dispute shall be transferred to the chamber for commercial matters upon motion of the defendant. A defendant who is not registered in the commercial register or the register of cooperatives may not base his motion on the ground that he is a merchant.

(2) The motion shall be dismissed if the chamber for commercial matters would not have jurisdiction for the counteraction brought in the case of §506 of the German Code of Civil Procedure as an action.

(3) The chamber for civil matters shall not be entitled to transfer the matter *ex officio*.

(4) The chamber for civil matters shall be entitled to dismiss the motion also if the plaintiff consented to such motion.

§99
[Verweisung an Zivilkammer wegen nachträglicher Unzuständigkeit]

(1) Wird in einem bei der Kammer für Handelssachen anhängigen Rechtsstreit die Klage nach §256 Abs. 2 der Zivilprozessordnung durch den Antrag auf Feststellung eines Rechtsverhältnisses erweitert oder eine Widerklage erhoben und gehört die erweiterte Klage oder die Widerklage als Klage nicht vor die Kammer für Handelssachen, so ist der Rechtsstreit auf Antrag des Gegners an die Zivilkammer zu verweisen.

(2) Unter der Beschränkung des §97 Abs. 2 ist die Kammer zu der Verweisung auch von Amts wegen befugt. Diese Befugnis tritt auch dann ein, wenn durch eine Klageänderung ein Anspruch geltend gemacht wird, der nicht vor die Kammer für Handelssachen gehört.

§99
[Transfer to the chambers for civil matters on the basis of subsequent lack of jurisdiction]

(1) If in a legal dispute pending before the chamber for commercial matters the action is extended pursuant to §256 (2) of the German Code of Civil Procedure by the motion for a court declaration that a certain legal relationship exists or a counteraction is filed, and the chamber for commercial matters has no jurisdiction for such extended action or such counteraction as an action, the legal dispute shall be transferred to the chamber for civil matters upon motion of the opposing party.

(2) Under the restriction of §97 (2), the chamber shall also be entitled to transfer the legal dispute *ex officio*. This entitlement shall also arise if a claim is asserted by way of amendment of the action, for which claim the chamber for commercial matters has no jurisdiction.

§ 100
[Zuständigkeit in 2. Instanz]

Die §§ 96 bis 99 sind auf das Verfahren im zweiten Rechtszuge vor den Kammern für Handelssachen entsprechend anzuwenden.

§ 101
[Antrag auf Verweisung]

(1) Der Antrag auf Verweisung des Rechtsstreits an eine andere Kammer ist nur vor der Verhandlung des Antragstellers zur Sache zulässig. Ist dem Antragsteller vor der mündlichen Verhandlung eine Frist zur Klageerwiderung oder Berufungserwiderung gesetzt, so hat er den Antrag innerhalb der Frist zu stellen. § 296 Abs. 3 der Zivilprozessordnung gilt entsprechend; der Entschuldigungsgrund ist auf Verlangen des Gerichts glaubhaft zu machen.

(2) Über den Antrag ist vorab zu entscheiden. Die Entscheidung kann ohne mündliche Verhandlung ergehen.

§ 102
[Unanfechtbarkeit der Verweisung]

Die Entscheidung über Verweisung eines Rechtsstreits an die Zivilkammer oder an die Kammer für Handelssachen ist nicht anfechtbar. Erfolgt die Verweisung an eine andere Kammer, so ist diese Entscheidung für die Kammer, an die der Rechtsstreit verwiesen wird, bindend. Der Termin zur weiteren mündlichen Verhandlung wird von Amts wegen bestimmt und den Parteien bekannt gemacht.

§ 103
[Hauptintervention]

Bei der Kammer für Handelssachen kann ein Anspruch nach § 64 der Zivilprozessordnung nur dann geltend gemacht werden, wenn der Rechtsstreit nach den Vorschriften der §§ 94, 95 vor die Kammer für Handelssachen gehört.

§ 100
[Jurisdiction in the second instance]

§§ 96–99 shall be applied *mutatis mutandis* to the proceedings in the second instance before the chambers for commercial matters.

§ 101
[Motion for transfer of the dispute]

(1) The motion for transfer of the legal dispute to another chamber shall only be admissible prior to the applicant's hearing with regard to the subject matter of the case. If the applicant was set a time limit for making a statement of defense or replying to the statement of first appeal prior to the oral hearing, the applicant shall file the motion within this time limit. § 296 (3) of the German Code of Civil Procedure shall apply *mutatis mutandis*; the ground for the excuse shall be credibly substantiated upon request of the court.

(2) The decision on the motion shall be taken first. The decision may be taken without an oral hearing.

§ 102
[Non-appealability of the transfer]

The decision on the transfer of a legal dispute to the chamber for civil matters or to the chamber for commercial matters shall be non-appealable. If a legal dispute is transferred to another chamber, this decision shall be binding on the chamber to which the legal dispute has been transferred. The time for further oral hearing shall be determined *ex officio* and notified to the parties.

§ 103
[Main hurd-party intervention]

A claim pursuant to § 64 of the German Code of Civil Procedure may only be asserted before the chamber for commercial matters, if the chamber for commercial matters has jurisdiction with regard to the legal dispute in accordance with the provisions of §§ 94, 95.

§ 104
[Verweisung in Beschwerdesachen]

(1) Wird die Kammer für Handelssachen als Beschwerdegericht mit einer vor sie nicht gehörenden Beschwerde befasst, so ist die Beschwerde von Amts wegen an die Zivilkammer zu verweisen. Ebenso hat die Zivilkammer, wenn sie als Beschwerdegericht in einer Handelssache mit einer Beschwerde befasst wird, diese von Amts wegen an die Kammer für Handelssachen zu verweisen. Die Vorschriften des § 102 Satz 1, 2 sind entsprechend anzuwenden.

(2) Eine Beschwerde kann nicht an eine andere Kammer verwiesen werden, wenn bei der Kammer, die mit der Beschwerde befasst wird, die Hauptsache anhängig ist oder diese Kammer bereits eine Entscheidung in der Hauptsache erlassen hat.

§ 104
[Transfer in matter concerning miscellaneous appeals]

(1) If a miscellaneous appeal is referred to the chamber for commercial matters as court of miscellaneous appeal and that chamber has no jurisdiction for such appeal, the miscellaneous appeal shall be transferred *ex officio* to the chamber for civil matters. Likewise, if a miscellaneous appeal is referred to the chamber for civil matters as court of miscellaneous appeal in a commercial matter, it shall transfer this miscellaneous appeal *ex officio* to the chamber for commercial matters. The provisions of § 102 first and second sentence shall be applied *mutatis mutandis*.

(2) A miscellaneous appeal may not be transferred to another chamber, if the main issue is pending before the chamber to which the miscellaneous appeal is referred or if this chamber has already issued a decision on the main issue.

§ 105
[Besetzung]

(1) Die Kammern für Handelssachen entscheiden in der Besetzung mit einem Mitglied des Landgerichts als Vorsitzenden und zwei *ehrenamtlichen Richtern*, soweit nicht nach den Vorschriften der Prozessgesetze an Stelle der Kammer der Vorsitzende zu entscheiden hat.

(2) Sämtliche Mitglieder der Kammer für Handelssachen haben gleiches Stimmrecht.

(3) (*weggefallen*)

§ 105
[Composition of the bench]

(1) The chambers for commercial matters shall decide in the composition of one member of the regional court as presiding judge and two honorary judges, unless the presiding judge shall decide instead of the chamber in accordance with the provisions of the procedural laws.

(2) All members of the chamber for commercial matters shall have equal voting rights.

(3) (*repealed*)

§ 106
[Auswärtige Kammer für Handelssachen]

Im Falle des § 93 Abs. 2 kann ein Richter beim Amtsgericht Vorsitzender der Kammer für Handelssachen sein.

§ 106
[External chamber for Commercial matters]

In the case of § 93 (1) second sentence, a judge at the local court may be the presiding judge of the chamber for commercial matters.

§§ 107–110

[...]

§§ 107–110

[...]

§ 111

(*weggefallen*)

§ 111

(*repealed*)

§§ 112–113

[...]

§§ 112–113

[...]

§ 114
[Entscheidung aufgrund eigener Sachkunde]

Über Gegenstände, zu deren Beurteilung eine kaufmännische Begutachtung genügt, sowie über das Bestehen von Handelsgebräuchen kann die Kammer für Handelssachen aufgrund eigener Sachkunde und Wissenschaft entscheiden.

§ 114
[Decision on the basis of the chamber's own experts knowledge]

In relation to subject matters for the evaluation of which a commercial assessment suffices, and in relation to the existence of trade practices, the chamber for commercial matters may decide on the basis of its own expert knowledge.

Achter Titel
Oberlandesgerichte

Eighth Title
Higher Regional Courts

§ 115

[...]

§ 115

[...]

§ 115a

(*weggefallen*)

§ 115a

(*repealed*)

§§ 116–117

[...]

§§ 116–117

[...]

§ 118
[Zuständigkeit in Musterverfahren]

Die Oberlandesgerichte sind in bürgerlichen Rechtsstreitigkeiten um ersten Rechtszug zuständig für Verhandlung und Entscheidung über Musterverfah-

§ 118
[Jurisdiction in model case proceedings]

The higher regional courts shall have jurisdiction in the first instance for hearing and deciding on model case proceedings proceedings in terms of the

ren nach dem Kapitalanleger-Musterverfahrensgesetz.

German Capital Markets Model Case Act.

§ 119
[Zuständigkeit in Zivilsachen]

(1) Die Oberlandesgerichte sind in Zivilsachen zuständig für die Verhandlung und Entscheidung über die Rechtsmittel:

1. der Beschwerde gegen Entscheidungen der Amtsgerichte
   a) in den von den Familiengerichten entschiedenen Sachen;
   b) in den Angelegenheiten der freiwilligen Gerichtsbarkeit mit Ausnahme der Freiheitsentziehungssachen und der von den Betreuungsgerichten entschiedenen Sachen;
2. der Berufung und der Beschwerde gegen Entscheidungen der Landgerichte.

(2) §23b Abs. 1 und 2 gilt entsprechend.

(3) (weggefallen)

(4) (weggefallen)

(5) (weggefallen)

(6) (weggefallen)

§ 119
[Jurisdiction in civil matters]

(1) The higher regional courts shall have jurisdiction in civil law matters for hearing and deciding on the following means of appeal:

1. miscellaneous appeal against decisions of the local courts
   a) in the matters decided by the family courts;
   b) in matters of non-contentious jurisdiction with the exception of imprisonment matters and matters decided by the adult guardianship courts;
2. first appeal and miscellaneous appeal against decisions of the regional courts.

(2) §23b (1) and (2) shall apply *mutatis mutandis*.

(3) (repealed)

(4) (repealed)

(5) (repealed)

(6) (repealed)

§§ 120–121

[...]

§§ 120–121

[...]

§ 122
[Composition of the court panchs]

(1) Die Senate der Oberlandesgerichte entscheiden, soweit nicht nach den Vorschriften der Prozessgesetze an Stelle des Senats der Einzelrichter zu entscheiden hat, in der Besetzung von drei Mitgliedern mit Einschluss des Vorsitzenden.

(2) [...]

§ 122
[Composition of the court pands]

(1) The panels of the higher regional courts shall decide, unless a single judge shall decide instead of the panel according to the provisions of procedural law, in the composition of three members, including the presiding judge.

(2) [...]

Neunter Titel
Bundesgerichtshof

§ 123
[Sitz]

Sitz des Bundesgerichtshofes ist Karlsruhe.

§ 124
[Besetzung]

Der Bundesgerichtshof wird mit einem Präsidenten sowie mit Vorsitzenden Richtern und weiteren Richtern besetzt.

§ 125

[...]

§§ 126–129

(weggefallen)

§ 130

[...]

§§ 131–131a

(weggefallen)

§ 132

[...]

§ 133
[Zuständigkeit in Zivilsachen]

In Zivilsachen ist der Bundesgerichtshof zuständig für die Verhandlung und Entscheidung über die Rechtsmittel der Revision, der Sprungrevision, der Rechtsbeschwerde und der Sprungrechtsbeschwerde.

§§ 134–134a

(weggefallen)

§ 135

[...]

§§ 136–137

(weggefallen)

Ninth Title
Federal Court of Justice

§ 123
[Seat]

The seat of the Federal Court of Justice shall be Karlsruhe.

§ 124
[Composition]

The Federal Court of Justice shall be composed of a president and presiding judges and further judges.

§ 125

[...]

§§ 126–129

(repealed)

§ 130

[...]

§§ 131–131a

(repealed)

§ 132

[...]

§ 133
[Jurisdiction in civil law matters]

In civil law matters, the Federal Court of Justice shall have jurisdiction concerning the hearing and decision on appellate remedies on the second appellate level, leap-frog appeal, miscellaneous appeal on points of law, and direct appeal on points of law.

§§ 134–134a

(repealed)

§ 135

[...]

§§ 136–137

(repealed)

§ 138
[...]

§ 139
[Besetzung der Senate]

(1) Die Senate des Bundesgerichtshofes entscheiden in der Besetzung von fünf Mitgliedern einschließlich des Vorsitzenden.

(2) [...]

§ 140
[...]

9a. Titel
Zuständigkeit für Wiederaufnahmeverfahren in Strafsachen

§ 140a
[...]

Zehnter Titel
Staatsanwaltschaft

§§ 141–152
[...]

Elfter Titel
Geschäftsstelle

§ 153
[...]

Zwölfter Titel
Zustellungs- und Vollstreckungsbeamte

§§ 154–155
[...]

Dreizehnter Titel
Rechtshilfe

§§ 156–168
[...]

§ 138
[...]

§ 139
[Composition of the pands]

(1) The panels of the Federal Court of Justice shall decide in the composition of five members including the presiding judge.

(2) [...]

§ 140
[...]

9a Title
Jurisdiction for Procedures for Reopeningof the Case in Penal Matters

§ 140a
[...]

Tenth Title
Public Prosecution Service

§§ 141–152
[...]

Eleventh Title
Registry

§ 153
[...]

Twelfth Title
Officers for Service and Enforcement

§§ 154–155
[...]

Thirteenth Title.
Judicial Assistance

§§ 156–168
[...]

Vierzehnter Titel
Öffentlichkeit und Sitzungspolizei

§ 169
[Öffentlichkeit]

Die Verhandlung vor dem erkennenden Gericht einschließlich der Verkündung der Urteile und Beschlüsse ist öffentlich. Ton- und Fernseh-Rundfunkaufnahmen sowie Ton- und Filmaufnahmen zum Zwecke der öffentlichen Vorführung oder Veröffentlichung ihres Inhalts sind unzulässig.

§ 170

[...]

§ 171

(*weggefallen*)

§§ 171a–171b

[...]

§ 172
[Gründe für Ausschluss der Öffentlichkeit]

Das Gericht kann für die Verhandlung oder für einen Teil davon die Öffentlichkeit ausschließen, wenn

1. eine Gefährdung der Staatssicherheit, der öffentlichen Ordnung oder der Sittlichkeit zu besorgen ist,
1a. eine Gefährdung des Lebens, des Leibes oder der Freiheit eines Zeugen oder einer anderen Person zu besorgen ist,
2. ein wichtiges Geschäfts-, Betriebs-, Erfindungs- oder Steuergeheimnis zur Sprache kommt, durch dessen öffentliche Erörterung überwiegende schutzwürdige Interessen verletzt würden,
3. ein privates Geheimnis erörtert wird, dessen unbefugte Offenbarung durch den Zeugen oder Sachverständigen mit Strafe bedroht ist,
4. eine Person unter 18 Jahren vernommen wird.

Fourteenth Title
Public Nature and Court Police

§ 169
[Public nature]

The hearing before the court deciding on the matter including the pronouncement of the judgements and orders shall be public. Sound and television/radio recordings as well as sound and film recordings for the purpose of public showing or the publication of their content are not permitted.

§ 170

[...]

§ 171

(*repealed*)

§§ 171a–171b

[...]

§ 172
[Reasons for exclusion of the general public]

The court may exclude the general public from the hearing or a part thereof, if

1. there is apprehension that the security of the state, the public order or morality is endangered,
1a. there is apprehension that the life, safety or freedom of a witness or other person is in danger,
2. an important business or trade secret, an invention-related or tax secret is brought up, by the public discussion of which prevailing interests warranting protection would be violated,
3. a private secret is discussed, the unauthorized disclosure of which by the witness or the expert is liable to criminal prosecution,
4. a person under the age of 18 is examined.

§§ 173–183

[. . .]

§§ 173–183

[. . .]

**Fünfzehnter Titel
Gerichtssprache**

**Fifteenth Title
Official Language in Court**

**§ 184
[Deutsche Sprache]**

**§ 184
[German language]**

Die Gerichtssprache ist deutsch. Das Recht der Sorben, in den Heimatkreisen der sorbischen Bevölkerung vor Gericht sorbisch zu sprechen, ist gewährleistet.

The language in court shall be German. The right of the Sorbs to speak Sorbian in court in the homeland regions of the Sorbian population has been ensured.

**§ 185
[Dolmetscher]**

**§ 185
[Interpreter]**

(1) Wird unter Beteiligung von Personen verhandelt, die der deutschen Sprache nicht mächtig sind, so ist ein Dolmetscher zuzuziehen. Ein Nebenprotokoll in der fremden Sprache wird nicht geführt; jedoch sollen Aussagen und Erklärungen in fremder Sprache, wenn und soweit der Richter dies mit Rücksicht auf die Wichtigkeit der Sache für erforderlich erachtet, auch in der fremden Sprache in das Protokoll oder in eine Anlage niedergeschrieben werden. In den dazu geeigneten Fällen soll dem Protokoll eine durch den Dolmetscher zu beglaubigende Übersetzung beigefügt werden.

(1) If the hearing is conducted with the participation of persons who do not have a sufficient command of the German language, an interpreter shall be involved. A subsidiary record in the foreign language shall not be recorded; however, statements and declarations in the foreign language shall, if and to the extent that the judge deems this necessary with regard to the importance of the matter, also be placed on the record or recorded as an annex in the foreign language. In the cases suited for this purpose, the record shall be accompanied by a translation to be certified by the interpreter.

(1a) Das Gericht kann gestatten, dass sich der Dolmetscher während der Verhandlung, Anhörung oder Vernehmung an einem anderen Ort aufhält. Die Verhandlung, Anhörung oder Vernehmung wird zeitgleich in Bild und Ton an diesen Ort und in das Sitzungszimmer übertragen.

(1a) The court may permit the interpreter to be at another place during the trial, hearing or examination. Images and sound of the trial, hearing or examination shall be transmitted simultaneously to such place and to the room where the session is held.

(2) Die Zuziehung eines Dolmetschers kann unterbleiben, wenn die beteiligten Personen sämtlich der fremden Sprache mächtig sind.

(2) The judge may refrain from involving an interpreter, if the persons participating in the hearing all have a sufficient command of the foreign language.

(3) In Familiensachen und in Angelegenheiten der freiwilligen Gerichtsbarkeit bedarf es der Zuziehung eines Dolmetschers nicht, wenn der Richter der Sprache, in der sich die beteiligten Personen erklären, mächtig ist.

(3) In family matters and in matters of non-contentious jurisdiction, it shall not be required to involve an interpreter if the judge has sufficient command of the language in which the persons

participating in the hearing make their statements.

§§ 186–187

[...]

**§ 188
[Oaths of persons speaking a foreign language]**

Persons who do not have a sufficient command of the German language shall take oaths in the language familiar to them.

§§ 189–191a

[...]

**Sixteenth Title
Deliberation and Voting**

§§ 192–197

[...]

**Seventeenth Title
Legal Redress in Excessively Long Court Proceedings and in Criminal Investigation Procedures**

§ 198

[...]

§§ 199–201

[...]

III. Gesetz zur Ausführung zwischenstaatlicher Verträge und zur Durchführung von Verordnungen der Europäischen Gemeinschaft auf dem Gebiet der Anerkennung und Vollstreckung in Zivil- und Handelssachen (Anerkennungs- und Vollstreckungsausführungsgesetz – AVAG) (Auszüge)

III. Act for the Implementation of International Treaties and for the Implementation of European Community Regulations in the Area of Recognition and Enforcement in Civil and Commercial Matters (Recognition and Enforcement Implementation Act – AVAG) (Excerpts)[1]

vom 19. Februar 2001[1]

of 19 February 2001[2]

Teil 1
Allgemeines

Part 1
General

Abschnitt 1
Anwendungsbereich; Begriffsbestimmungen

Chapter 1
Scope of application; definitions

§ 1
Anwendungsbereich

§ 1
Scope of application

(1) Diesem Gesetz unterliegen

(1) This Act governs

1. die Ausführung folgender zwischenstaatlicher Verträge (Anerkennungs- und Vollstreckungsverträge):
   a) Übereinkommen vom 27. September 1968 über die gerichtliche Zuständigkeit und die Vollstreckung gerichtlicher Entscheidungen in Zivil- und Handelssachen (BGBl. 1972 II S. 773);
   b) Übereinkommen vom 16. September 1988 über die gerichtliche Zuständigkeit und die Vollstreckung gerichtlicher Entscheidungen in Zivil- und Handelssachen (BGBl. 1994 II S. 2658);
   c) Vertrag vom 17. Juni 1977 zwischen der Bundesrepublik Deutschland und dem Königreich Norwegen über die ge-

1. the implementation of the following international treaties (recognition and enforcement treaties):
   a) Convention of 27 September 1968 on Jurisdiction and the Enforcement of Judgments in Civil and Commercial Matters (Federal Law Gazette 1972 II, p. 773);
   b) Convention of 16 September 1988 on Jurisdiction and the Enforcement of Judgments in Civil and Commercial Matters (Federal Law Gazette 1994 II, p. 2658);
   c) Treaty of 17 June 1977 between the Federal Republic of Germa-

---

[1] BGBl. I S. 288, 436; zuletzt geändert durch Art. 1 Gesetz vom 30. 1. 2002, BGBl. I S. 564.

[1] Translation by Elaine Ikizer, amended by Hildegard Rosenzweig.
[2] Federal Law Gazette I, p. 288, 436; as amended by Art. 1 of the Act of 30 January 2002, Federal Law Gazette I, p. 564.

genseitige Anerkennung und Vollstreckung gerichtlicher Entscheidungen und anderer Schuldtitel in Zivil- und Handelssachen (BGBl. 1981 II S. 341);

d) Vertrag vom 20. Juli 1977 zwischen der Bundesrepublik Deutschland und dem Staat Israel über die gegenseitige Anerkennung und Vollstreckung gerichtlicher Entscheidungen in Zivil- und Handelssachen (BGBl. 1980 II S. 925);

e) Vertrag vom 14. November 1983 zwischen der Bundesrepublik Deutschland und Spanien über die Anerkennung und Vollstreckung von gerichtlichen Entscheidungen und Vergleichen sowie vollstreckbaren öffentlichen Urkunden in Zivil- und Handelssachen (BGBl. 1987 II S. 34);

2. die Durchführung des Übereinkommens vom 30. Oktober 2007 über die gerichtliche Zuständigkeit und die Anerkennung und Vollstreckung von Entscheidungen in Zivil- und Handelssachen.

(2) Abkommen nach Absatz 1 Nummer 2 werden als unmittelbar geltendes Recht der Europäischen Union durch die Durchführungsbestimmungen dieses Gesetzes nicht berührt. Unberührt bleiben auch die Regelungen der Anerkennungs- und Vollstreckungsverträge; dies gilt insbesondere für die Regelungen über

1. den sachlichen Anwendungsbereich,
2. die Art der Entscheidungen und sonstigen Titel, die im Inland anerkannt oder zur Zwangsvollstreckung zugelassen werden können,
3. das Erfordernis der Rechtskraft der Entscheidungen,
4. die Art der Urkunden, die im Verfahren vorzulegen sind, und
5. die Gründe, die zur Versagung der Anerkennung oder Zulassung der Zwangsvollstreckung führen.

ny and the Kingdom of Norway on the Mutual Recognition and Enforcement of Judgments and other Executory Titles in Civil and Commercial Matters (Federal Law Gazette 1981 II, p. 341);

d) Treaty of 20 July 1977 between the Federal Republic of Germany and the State of Israel on the Mutual Recognition and Enforcement of Judgments in Civil and Commercial Matters (Federal Law Gazette 1980 II, p. 925);

e) Treaty of 14 November 1983 between the Federal Republic of Germany and Spain on the Recognition and Enforcement of Judgments and Settlements and of Executable Public Documents in Civil and Commercial Matters (Federal Law Gazette 1987 II, p. 34);

2. the implementation of the Convention of 30 October 2007 on Jurisdiction and the Recognition and Enforcement of Judgments in Civil and Commercial Matters.

(2) Agreements pursuant to subsection (1) no. 2 are not affected by the implementing provisions of this Act because they constitute directly applicable European Union legislation. The provisions of the recognition and enforcement agreements are not affected, either; this applies in particular to the provisions relating to

1. the scope in terms of subject matter,
2. the nature of judgments and other executory titles that can be recognized in Germany or accepted for enforcement,
3. the requirement that the judgments have *res judicata* effect,
4. the nature of the documents to be presented in the proceedings, and
5. the grounds for refusing recognition or authorization of enforcement.

(3) Der Anwendungsbereich des Auslandsunterhaltsgesetzes vom 23. Mai 2011 (BGBl. I S. 898) bleibt unberührt.

§ 2
Begriffsbestimmungen

Im Sinne dieses Gesetzes ist

1. Mitgliedstaat jeder Mitgliedstaat der Europäischen Union,
2. Titel jede Entscheidung, jeder gerichtliche Vergleich und jede öffentliche Urkunde, auf die oder den der jeweils auszuführende Anerkennungs- und Vollstreckungsvertrag nach § 1 Absatz 1 Nummer 1 oder das jeweils durchzuführende Abkommen nach § 1 Absatz 1 Nummer 2 Anwendung findet, und
3. Vertragsstaat jeder Staat, mit dem die Bundesrepublik Deutschland einen Anerkennungs- und Vollstreckungsvertrag nach § 1 Absatz 1 Nummer 1 abgeschlossen hat.

Abschnitt 2
Zulassung der Zwangsvollstreckung aus ausländischen Titeln

§ 3
Zuständigkeit

(1) Für die Vollstreckbarerklärung von Titeln aus einem anderen Staat ist das Landgericht ausschließlich zuständig.

(2) Örtlich zuständig ist ausschließlich das Gericht, in dessen Bezirk der Verpflichtete seinen Wohnsitz hat, oder, wenn er im Inland keinen Wohnsitz hat, das Gericht, in dessen Bezirk die Zwangsvollstreckung durchgeführt werden soll. Der Sitz von Gesellschaften und juristischen Personen steht dem Wohnsitz gleich.

(3) Über den Antrag auf Erteilung der Vollstreckungsklausel entscheidet der Vorsitzende einer Zivilkammer.

(3) The scope of application of the German Foreign Maintenance Act of 23 May 2011 (Federal Law Gazette I p. 898) is not affected.

§ 2
Definitions

For the purposes of this Act

1. Member State shall mean any member state of the European Union,
2. title shall mean any judgment, any judicial settlement and any public deed to which the respective recognition and enforcement treaty pursuant to § 1 subsection (1) no. 1 or the respective agreement to be implemented pursuant to § 1 subsection (1) no. 2 applies, and
3. signatory state shall mean any state with which the Federal Republic of Germany has entered into a recognition and enforcement treaty pursuant to § 1 subsection 1 no. 1.

Chapter 2
Authorization of enforcement of foreign titles

§ 3
Jurisdiction

(1) The regional court shall have exclusive jurisdiction to declare titles from another state enforceable.

(2) The court in whose district the party against whom enforcement is sought has his place of domicile or, if he is not domiciled in Germany, the court in whose district enforcement is to take place shall have exclusive local jurisdiction. The seat of a company or legal entity is equivalent to the place of domicile.

(3) The decision on an application for the issue of an enforcement clause shall be issued by the presiding judge of a chamber for civil matters.

§ 4
Antragstellung

(1) Der in einem anderen Staat vollstreckbare Titel wird dadurch zur Zwangsvollstreckung zugelassen, dass er auf Antrag mit der Vollstreckungsklausel versehen wird.

(2) Der Antrag auf Erteilung der Vollstreckungsklausel kann bei dem zuständigen Gericht schriftlich eingereicht oder mündlich zu Protokoll der Geschäftsstelle erklärt werden.

(3) Ist der Antrag entgegen § 184 des Gerichtsverfassungsgesetzes nicht in deutscher Sprache abgefasst, so kann das Gericht dem Antragsteller aufgeben, eine Übersetzung des Antrags beizubringen, deren Richtigkeit von einer

1. in einem Mitgliedstaat der Europäischen Union oder in einem anderen Vertragsstaat des Abkommens über den Europäischen Wirtschaftsraum oder
2. in einem Vertragsstaat des jeweils auszuführenden Anerkennungs- und Vollstreckungsvertrags

hierzu befugten Person bestätigt worden ist.

(4) Der Ausfertigung des Titels, der mit der Vollstreckungsklausel versehen werden soll, und seiner Übersetzung, soweit eine solche vorgelegt wird, sollen zwei Abschriften beigefügt werden.

§ 5
Erfordernis eines Zustellungsbevollmächtigten

(1) Hat die antragstellende Person in dem Antrag keinen Zustellungsbevollmächtigten benannt, so können bis zur nachträglichen Benennung eines Zustellungsbevollmächtigten alle Zustellungen an sie durch Aufgabe zur Post (§ 184 Absatz 1 Satz 2 und Absatz 2 der Zivilprozessordnung) bewirkt werden.

(2) Absatz 1 gilt nicht, wenn die antragstellende Person einen Verfahrensbe-

§ 4
Application

(1) A title that is executable in another state shall, on application, be authorized for enforcement by adding an enforcement clause.

(2) The application for the grant of an enforcement clause can be lodged in writing with the competent court or made orally for placement on record by the court registry.

(3) If, contrary to § 184 of the German Judicature Act, the application is not in German, the court may order the applicant to provide a translation of the application, the accuracy of which has been confirmed by a person authorized to do so

1. in a Member State of the European Union or in another signatory state to the Agreement on the European Economic Area, or
2. in a signatory state to the respective treaty on recognition and enforcement being implemented.

(4) Two duplicates must be added to the executed copy of the title to which the enforcement clause is to be added and to the translation, if any.

§ 5
Requirement of appointing authorized recipient for service

(1) If the person filing the application has failed to name an authorized recipient for service in the application, all documents may be served on such person by way of mailing until such time as the person subsequently does so (§ 184 (1) sentence 2 and (2) of the German Code of Civil Procedure).

(2) Sub-section (1) shall not apply if the person filing the application has ap-

vollmächtigten für das Verfahren bestellt hat, an den im Inland zugestellt werden kann.

pointed another person to represent them for the purposes of the proceedings, on whom service may be effected in Germany.

§ 6
Verfahren

(1) Das Gericht entscheidet ohne Anhörung des Verpflichteten.

(2) Die Entscheidung ergeht ohne mündliche Verhandlung. Jedoch kann eine mündliche Erörterung mit dem Antragsteller oder seinem Bevollmächtigten stattfinden, wenn der Antragsteller oder der Bevollmächtigte hiermit einverstanden ist und die Erörterung der Beschleunigung dient.

(3) Im ersten Rechtszug ist die Vertretung durch einen Rechtsanwalt nicht erforderlich.

§ 6
Procedure

(1) The court shall decide without hearing the party against whom enforcement is sought.

(2) The decision will be issued without an oral hearing. However, the court may decide to discuss the matter orally with the applicant or his authorized representative, if the applicant, respectively the authorized representative, agrees and such discussion serves to expedite the procedure.

(3) Representation by a lawyer is not required in the first instance.

§ 7
Vollstreckbarkeit ausländischer Titel in Sonderfällen

(1) Hängt die Zwangsvollstreckung nach dem Inhalt des Titels von einer dem Berechtigten obliegenden Sicherheitsleistung, dem Ablauf einer Frist oder dem Eintritt einer anderen Tatsache ab oder wird die Vollstreckungsklausel zugunsten eines anderen als des in dem Titel bezeichneten Berechtigten oder gegen einen anderen als den darin bezeichneten Verpflichteten beantragt, so ist die Frage, inwieweit die Zulassung der Zwangsvollstreckung von dem Nachweis besonderer Voraussetzungen abhängig oder ob der Titel für oder gegen den anderen vollstreckbar ist, nach dem Recht des Staates zu entscheiden, in dem der Titel errichtet ist. Der Nachweis ist durch Urkunden zu führen, es sei denn, dass die Tatsachen bei dem Gericht offenkundig sind.

§ 7
Enforceability of foreign titles in special cases

(1) If, according to the contents of the title, enforcement is dependent on security being provided by the party applying for enforcement, on the expiration of a specific time limit or on the occurrence of some other event, or if the enforcement clause is being applied for in favor of a person other than the party applying for enforcement identified in the title or against a person other than the party against whom enforcement is sought identified therein, the question to what extent the authorization of enforcement is dependent on presentation of evidence to show that certain special requirements are met, or whether the title is enforceable in favor of or against said other person, shall be decided according to the law of that state in which the title was issued. Evidence shall be produced in the form of documents, unless the facts are obvious for the court.

(2) Kann der Nachweis durch Urkunden nicht geführt werden, so ist auf Antrag des Berechtigten der Verpflichtete zu hören. In diesem Falle sind alle Beweismittel zulässig. Das Gericht kann auch die mündliche Verhandlung anordnen.

(2) Where evidence cannot be produced in the form of documents, the party against whom enforcement is sought shall, upon motion by the party applying for enforcement, be heard. In such cases all means of evidence shall be permitted. The court may also order an oral hearing.

§ 8
Entscheidung

(1) Ist die Zwangsvollstreckung aus dem Titel zuzulassen, so beschließt das Gericht, dass der Titel mit der Vollstreckungsklausel zu versehen ist. In dem Beschluss ist die zu vollstreckende Verpflichtung in deutscher Sprache wiederzugeben. Zur Begründung des Beschlusses genügt in der Regel die Bezugnahme auf die durchzuführende Verordnung der Europäischen Union oder den auszuführenden Anerkennungs- und Vollstreckungsvertrag sowie auf von dem Antragsteller vorgelegte Urkunden. Auf die Kosten des Verfahrens ist § 788 der Zivilprozessordnung entsprechend anzuwenden.

(2) Ist der Antrag nicht zulässig oder nicht begründet, so lehnt ihn das Gericht durch mit Gründen versehenen Beschluss ab. Die Kosten sind dem Antragsteller aufzuerlegen.

§ 8
Decision

(1) If the enforcement of the title is to be authorized, the court shall issue an order to the effect that an enforcement clause be added to the title. In such court order, the obligation to be enforced shall be set forth in the German language. As grounds for the court order, it will regularly suffice to refer to the European Union Regulation to be implemented or the treaty on recognition and enforcement to be implemented, and to the documents presented by the applicant. § 788 of the German Code of Civil Procedure shall be applied *mutatis mutandis* to the costs of the proceedings.

(2) Inadmissible or unfounded applications shall be refused by the court by way of a court order providing the grounds. The applicant shall be ordered to pay the costs.

§ 9
Vollstreckungsklausel

(1) Auf Grund des Beschlusses nach § 8 Abs. 1 erteilt der Urkundsbeamte der Geschäftsstelle die Vollstreckungsklausel in folgender Form:

– „Vollstreckungsklausel nach § 4 des Anerkennungs- und Vollstreckungsausführungsgesetzes. Gemäß dem Beschluss des . . . . (Bezeichnung des Gerichts und des Beschlusses) ist die Zwangsvollstreckung aus . . . . (Bezeichnung des Titels) zugunsten . . . . (Bezeichnung des Berechtigten) gegen . . . .

§ 9
Enforcement clause

(1) If a court order is issued in accordance with § 8 (1), the registrar of the court shall issue the enforcement clause in the following form:

– „Enforcement clause in accordance with § 4 of the Recognition and Enforcement Implementation Act. In accordance with the court order of . . . . (details of the court and the order), the enforcement of . . . . (description of title) in favor of . . . . (name of party applying for enforcement) against . . . .

.... (Bezeichnung des Verpflichteten) zulässig.
- Die zu vollstreckende Verpflichtung lautet: ....
.... (Angabe der dem Verpflichteten aus dem ausländischen Titel obliegenden Verpflichtung in deutscher Sprache; aus dem Beschluss nach § 8 Abs. 1 zu übernehmen).

- Die Zwangsvollstreckung darf über Maßregeln zur Sicherung nicht hinausgehen, bis der Gläubiger eine gerichtliche Anordnung oder ein Zeugnis vorlegt, dass die Zwangsvollstreckung unbeschränkt stattfinden darf.,,

Lautet der Titel auf Leistung von Geld, so ist der Vollstreckungsklausel folgender Zusatz anzufügen:

- „Solange die Zwangsvollstreckung über Maßregeln zur Sicherung nicht hinausgehen darf, kann der Schuldner die Zwangsvollstreckung durch Leistung einer Sicherheit in Höhe von ....
. . . (Angabe des Betrages, wegen dessen der Berechtigte vollstrecken darf) abwenden.,,

(2) Wird die Zwangsvollstreckung nur für einen oder mehrere der durch die ausländische Entscheidung zuerkannten oder in einem anderen ausländischen Titel niedergelegten Ansprüche oder nur für einen Teil des Gegenstands der Verpflichtung zugelassen, so ist die Vollstreckungsklausel als „Teil-Vollstreckungsklausel nach § 4 des Anerkennungs- und Vollstreckungsausführungsgesetzes" zu bezeichnen.

(3) Die Vollstreckungsklausel ist von dem Urkundsbeamten der Geschäftsstelle zu unterschreiben und mit dem Gerichtssiegel zu versehen. Sie ist entweder auf die Ausfertigung des Titels oder auf ein damit zu verbindendes Blatt zu setzen. Falls eine Übersetzung des Titels vorliegt, ist sie mit der Ausfertigung zu verbinden.

..... (name of party against whom enforcement is sought) is permitted.
- The obligation to be enforced is as follows: ....
..... (details, in the German language, of the obligation incumbent on the party against whom enforcement is sought under the foreign title; wording to be taken from the court order pursuant to § 8 (1)).

- Until such time as the creditor presents a judicial order or a certificate indicating that enforcement may take place without restriction, enforcement measures shall be restricted to protective measures."

If the title orders payment of money, the following must be added to the enforcement clause:

- „As long as enforcement measures are restricted to protective measures, the debtor may prevent enforcement by providing security in the amount of ....
.... (amount which the party applying for enforcement is allowed to enforce)."

(2) Where enforcement is admitted only for one or several of the claims adjudicated by the foreign judgment or specified in another form of foreign title, or only for a part of the subject matter of the obligation, the enforcement clause shall be designated as a „partial enforcement clause in accordance with § 4 of the Recognition and Enforcement Implementation Act".

(3) The registrar of the court must sign the enforcement clause and affix the court seal. The enforcement clause shall either be added to the executed copy of the title itself or written on a separate page, to be joined to the title. If the title has been translated, the translation must be joined to the executed copy.

III. Recognition and Enforcement Implementation Act (AVAG) (Excerpts)

§ 10
Bekanntgabe der Entscheidung

(1) Im Falle des § 8 Abs. 1 sind dem Verpflichteten eine beglaubigte Abschrift des Beschlusses, eine beglaubigte Abschrift des mit der Vollstreckungsklausel versehenen Titels und gegebenenfalls seiner Übersetzung sowie der gemäß § 8 Abs. 1 Satz 3 in Bezug genommenen Urkunden von Amts wegen zuzustellen.

(2) Muss die Zustellung an den Verpflichteten im Ausland oder durch öffentliche Bekanntmachung erfolgen und hält das Gericht die Beschwerdefrist nach § 11 Abs. 3 Satz 1 nicht für ausreichend, so bestimmt es in dem Beschluss nach § 8 Abs. 1 oder nachträglich durch besonderen Beschluss, der ohne mündliche Verhandlung ergeht, eine längere Beschwerdefrist. Die Bestimmungen über den Beginn der Beschwerdefrist bleiben auch im Falle der nachträglichen Festsetzung unberührt.

(3) Dem Antragsteller sind eine beglaubigte Abschrift des Beschlusses nach § 8, im Falle des § 8 Abs. 1 ferner die mit der Vollstreckungsklausel versehene Ausfertigung des Titels und eine Bescheinigung über die bewirkte Zustellung, zu übersenden. In den Fällen des Absatzes 2 ist die festgesetzte Frist für die Einlegung der Beschwerde auf der Bescheinigung über die bewirkte Zustellung zu vermerken.

Abschnitt 3
Beschwerde, Vollstreckungsabwehrklage

§ 11
Einlegung der Beschwerde; Beschwerdefrist

(1) Die Beschwerde gegen die im ersten Rechtszug ergangene Entscheidung über den Antrag auf Erteilung der Vollstreckungsklausel wird bei dem Beschwerdegericht durch Einreichen einer Beschwerdeschrift oder durch

§ 10
Announcement of decision

(1) In cases covered by § 8 (1), a certified copy of the decision, and a certified copy each of the title bearing the enforcement clause and, where applicable, of the translation of the title, as well as of the documents referred to pursuant to § 8 (1) third sentence, shall be served *ex officio* on the party against whom enforcement is sought.

(2) If the documents have to be served on the party against whom enforcement is sought abroad or by means of a public announcement, and if the court regards the time limit for miscellaneous appeal under § 11(3) first sentence to be insufficient, then it shall determine a longer time limit for miscellaneous appeal in the order pursuant to § 8 (1), or subsequently in a special order which will be issued without an oral hearing. The above is without prejudice to the provisions concerning the commencement of the time limit for miscellaneous appeal.

(3) The applicant shall receive a certified copy of the order pursuant to § 8 and, in cases that come under § 8 (1), also the executed copy of the title with the enforcement clause, and a certificate confirming that service has been effected. In cases that come under § 8 (2), the time limit set for lodging miscellaneous appeal shall be noted on the certificate confirming that service has been effected.

Chapter 3
Miscellaneous appeal, action to avert enforcement

§ 11
Filing of miscellaneous appeal; time limit for miscellaneous appeal

(1) A miscellaneous appeal against the decision issued in the first instance on the application for grant of an enforcement clause must be lodged with the court of miscellaneous appeal either by filing a written statement of miscella-

Erklärung zu Protokoll der Geschäftsstelle eingelegt. Beschwerdegericht ist das Oberlandesgericht. Der Beschwerdeschrift soll die für ihre Zustellung erforderliche Zahl von Abschriften beigefügt werden.

(2) Die Zulässigkeit der Beschwerde wird nicht dadurch berührt, dass sie statt bei dem Beschwerdegericht bei dem Gericht des ersten Rechtszuges eingelegt wird; die Beschwerde ist unverzüglich von Amts wegen an das Beschwerdegericht abzugeben.

(3) Die Beschwerde des Verpflichteten gegen die Zulassung der Zwangsvollstreckung ist innerhalb eines Monats, im Falle des § 10 Abs. 2 Satz 1 innerhalb der nach dieser Vorschrift bestimmten längeren Frist einzulegen. Die Beschwerdefrist beginnt mit der Zustellung nach § 10 Abs. 1. Sie ist eine Notfrist.

(4) Die Beschwerde ist dem Beschwerdegegner von Amts wegen zuzustellen.

§ 12
Einwendungen gegen den zu vollstreckenden Anspruch im Beschwerdeverfahren

(1) Der Verpflichtete kann mit der Beschwerde, die sich gegen die Zulassung der Zwangsvollstreckung aus einer Entscheidung richtet, auch Einwendungen gegen den Anspruch selbst insoweit geltend machen, als die Gründe, auf denen sie beruhen, erst nach dem Erlass der Entscheidung entstanden sind.

(2) Mit der Beschwerde, die sich gegen die Zulassung der Zwangsvollstreckung aus einem gerichtlichen Vergleich oder einer öffentlichen Urkunde richtet, kann der Verpflichtete die Einwendungen gegen den Anspruch selbst ungeachtet der in Absatz 1 enthaltenen Beschränkung geltend machen.

neous appeal or by having an oral statement placed on record by the court registry. The court of miscellaneous appeal is the higher regional court. The number of copies required for service must be attached to the statement of miscellaneous appeal.

(2) If the miscellaneous appeal is filed with the court of first instance instead of the court of miscellaneous appeal, it will still be admissible; the miscellaneous appeal shall be referred to the court of miscellaneous appeal *ex officio* without delay.

(3) The miscellaneous appeal of the party against whom enforcement is sought against the authorization of enforcement shall be filed within one month or, in case of § 10 (2) first sentence, within the longer time limit determined in accordance with that provision. The time limit for miscellaneous appeal commences upon service in accordance with § 10 (1). It is a statutory time limit.

(4) The miscellaneous appeal shall be served on the appellee *ex officio*.

§ 12
Objections against the claim to be enforced in miscellaneous appeal proceedings

(1) In the miscellaneous appeal directed against the authorization of enforcement of a judgment, the party against whom enforcement is sought may also raise objections against the claim itself insofar as the reasons on which they are based came about after the judgment was issued.

(2) In a miscellaneous appeal directed against the authorization of enforcement of a court settlement or a public document, the party against whom enforcement is sought may raise objections against the claim itself regardless of the restriction set forth in sub-section (1) above.

§ 13
Verfahren und Entscheidung über die Beschwerde

(1) Das Beschwerdegericht entscheidet durch Beschluss, der mit Gründen zu versehen ist und ohne mündliche Verhandlung ergehen kann. Der Beschwerdegegner ist vor der Entscheidung zu hören.

(2) Solange eine mündliche Verhandlung nicht angeordnet ist, können zu Protokoll der Geschäftsstelle Anträge gestellt und Erklärungen abgegeben werden. Wird die mündliche Verhandlung angeordnet, so gilt für die Ladung § 215 der Zivilprozessordnung.

(3) Eine vollständige Ausfertigung des Beschlusses ist dem Berechtigten und dem Verpflichteten auch dann von Amts wegen zuzustellen, wenn der Beschluss verkündet worden ist.

(4) Soweit nach dem Beschluss des Beschwerdegerichts die Zwangsvollstreckung aus dem Titel erstmals zuzulassen ist, erteilt der Urkundsbeamte der Geschäftsstelle des Beschwerdegerichts die Vollstreckungsklausel. § 8 Abs. 1 Satz 2 und 4, §§ 9 und 10 Abs. 1 und 3 Satz 1 sind entsprechend anzuwenden. Ein Zusatz, dass die Zwangsvollstreckung über Maßregeln zur Sicherung nicht hinausgehen darf, ist nur aufzunehmen, wenn das Beschwerdegericht eine Anordnung nach diesem Gesetz (§ 22 Abs. 2, § 40 Abs. 1 Nr. 1 oder § 45 Abs. 1 Nr. 1) erlassen hat. Der Inhalt des Zusatzes bestimmt sich nach dem Inhalt der Anordnung.

§ 13
Procedure and decision on the miscellaneous appeal

(1) The court of miscellaneous appeal shall decide by way of court order. Such court order must provide grounds and may be issued without an oral hearing. The appellee shall be heard before the decision is issued.

(2) As long as no oral hearing has been ordered, the parties may lodge applications and statements with the court registry to be placed on record. If an oral hearing is ordered, § 215 of the German Code of Civil Procedure shall apply as regards summons.

(3) A full and complete executed copy of the court order must be served *ex officio* on the party applying for enforcement and the party against whom enforcement is sought also if the court order has been pronounced.

(4) If enforcement of the title is to be authorized for the first time in accordance with the order of the court of miscellaneous appeal, the registrar of the court of miscellaneous appeal shall issue the enforcement clause. § 8 (1) second and fourth sentence, § 9 and § 10 (1) and (3) first sentence shall be applied *mutatis mutandis*. An additional clause to the effect that enforcement measures shall be restricted to protective measures shall only be included if the court of miscellaneous appeal has issued an order in accordance with this Act (§ 22 (2), § 40 (1) no. 1 or § 45 (1) no. 1). How the additional clause is worded depends on how the order is worded.

§ 14
Vollstreckungsabwehrklage

(1) Ist die Zwangsvollstreckung aus einem Titel zugelassen, so kann der Verpflichtete Einwendungen gegen den Anspruch selbst in einem Verfahren nach § 767 der Zivilprozessordnung nur geltend machen, wenn die Gründe, auf

§ 14
Action to avert enforcement

(1) If enforcement of a title is authorized, the party against whom enforcement is sought may raise objections against the claim itself in proceedings under § 767 of the German Code of Civil Procedure, if the reasons on which his objections are based only arose

denen seine Einwendungen beruhen, erst

1. nach Ablauf der Frist, innerhalb deren er die Beschwerde hätte einlegen können, oder
2. falls die Beschwerde eingelegt worden ist, nach Beendigung dieses Verfahrens

entstanden sind.

(2) Die Klage nach § 767 der Zivilprozessordnung ist bei dem Gericht zu erheben, das über den Antrag auf Erteilung der Vollstreckungsklausel entschieden hat. Soweit die Klage einen Unterhaltstitel zum Gegenstand hat, ist das Familiengericht zuständig; für die örtliche Zuständigkeit gelten die Vorschriftendes Gesetzes über das Verfahren in Familiensachen und in den Angelegenheiten der freiwilligen Gerichtsbarkeit für Unterhaltssachen.

1. after expiration of the time limit within which he could have lodged a miscellaneous appeal, or,
2. if the miscellaneous appeal has been lodged, after termination of such proceedings.

(2) Actions under § 767 of the German Code of Civil Procedure must be lodged with the court that ruled on the application for issuance of the enforcement clause. If the action relates to a title concerning an obligation to pay maintenance, the family court shall have competence; local jurisdiction shall be determined by reference to the provisions of the German Act on Proceedings in Family Matters and in Matters of Non-Contentious Jurisdiction on maintenance matters.

Abschnitt 4
Rechtsbeschwerde

§ 15
Statthaftigkeit und Frist

(1) Gegen den Beschluss des Beschwerdegerichts findet die Rechtsbeschwerde nach Maßgabe des § 574 Abs. 1 Nr. 1, Abs. 2 der Zivilprozessordnung statt.

(2) Die Rechtsbeschwerde ist innerhalb eines Monats einzulegen.

(3) Die Rechtsbeschwerdefrist ist eine Notfrist und beginnt mit der Zustellung des Beschlusses (§ 13 Abs. 3).

§ 16
Einlegung und Begründung

(1) Die Rechtsbeschwerde wird durch Einreichen der Beschwerdeschrift bei dem Bundesgerichtshof eingelegt.

Chapter 4
Miscellaneous appeal on points of law

§ 15
Admissibility and time limit

(1) The order of the court of miscellaneous appeal shall be subject to miscellaneous appeal on points of law according to § 574 (1) no. 1, (2) of the Code of Civil Procedure.

(2) The miscellaneous appeal on points of law must be lodged within one month.

(3) The time limit for filing a miscellaneous appeal on points of law is a statutory time limit and commences upon service of the court order (§ 13 (3)).

§ 16
Filing and grounds

(1) The miscellaneous appeal on points of law shall be lodged by filing the written statement of miscellaneous appeal with the Federal Court of Justice.

(2) Die Rechtsbeschwerde ist zu begründen. §575 Abs. 2 bis 4 der Zivilprozessordnung ist entsprechend anzuwenden. Soweit die Rechtsbeschwerde darauf gestützt wird, dass das Beschwerdegericht von einer Entscheidung des Gerichtshofs der Europäischen Union abgewichen sei, muss die Entscheidung, von der der angefochtene Beschluss abweicht, bezeichnet werden.

(3) Mit der Beschwerdeschrift soll eine Ausfertigung oder beglaubigte Abschrift des Beschlusses, gegen den sich die Rechtsbeschwerde richtet, vorgelegt werden.

§ 17
Verfahren und Entscheidung

(1) Der Bundesgerichtshof kann nur überprüfen, ob der Beschluss auf einer Verletzung des Rechts der Europäischen Union, eines Anerkennungs- und Vollstreckungsvertrags, sonstigen Bundesrechts oder einer anderen Vorschrift beruht, deren Geltungsbereich sich über den Bezirk eines Oberlandesgerichts hinaus erstreckt. Es darf nicht prüfen, ob das Gericht seine örtliche Zuständigkeit zu Unrecht angenommen hat.

(2) Der Bundesgerichtshof kann über die Rechtsbeschwerde ohne mündliche Verhandlung entscheiden. Auf das Verfahren über die Rechtsbeschwerde sind §574 Abs. 4, §576 Abs. 3 und §577 der Zivilprozessordnung entsprechend anzuwenden.

(3) Soweit die Zwangsvollstreckung aus dem Titel erstmals durch den Bundesgerichtshof zugelassen wird, erteilt der Urkundsbeamte der Geschäftsstelle dieses Gerichts die Vollstreckungsklausel. §8 Abs. 1 Satz 2 und 4, §§9 und 10 Abs. 1 und 3 Satz 1 gelten entsprechend. Ein Zusatz über die Beschränkung der Zwangsvollstreckung entfällt.

(2) The grounds for the miscellaneous appeal on points of law must be provided. §575 (2) through (4) of the German Code of Civil Procedure shall be applied *mutatis mutandis*. To the extent that the miscellaneous appeal on points of law is based on the fact that the court of miscellaneous appeal deviated from a ruling of the Court of Justice of the European Union, the ruling from which the appealed court order deviates must be identified.

(3) An executed or certified copy of the court order against which the miscellaneous appeal on points of law is directed shall be filed together with the written statement of such miscellaneous appeal.

§ 17
Procedure and decision

(1) The Federal Court of Justice may only review whether the court order is based on a violation of European Union law, of a recognition and enforcement treaty, other Federal law or some other regulation the scope of which extends beyond the district of a higher regional court. The Federal Court of Justice may not review whether the court wrongly assumed that it had local jurisdiction.

(2) The Federal Court of Justice may rule on the miscellaneous appeal on points of law without a hearing. §574 (4), §576 (3) and §577 of the Code of Civil Procedure shall apply *mutatis mutandis* to the proceedings for the miscellaneous appeal on points of law.

(3) Where enforcement of the title is first authorized by the Federal Court of Justice, the registrar of said court shall issue the enforcement clause. §8 (1) second and fourth sentence, §9 and §10 (1) and (3) first sentence shall apply *mutatis mutandis*. An additional clause regarding the restriction on enforcement shall not apply.

Abschnitt 5
Beschränkung der Zwangsvollstreckung auf Sicherungsmaßregeln und unbeschränkte Fortsetzung der Zwangsvollstreckung

§ 18
Beschränkung kraft Gesetzes

Die Zwangsvollstreckung ist auf Sicherungsmaßregeln beschränkt, solange die Frist zur Einlegung der Beschwerde noch läuft und solange über die Beschwerde noch nicht entschieden ist.

§ 19
Prüfung der Beschränkung

Einwendungen des Verpflichteten, dass bei der Zwangsvollstreckung die Beschränkung auf Sicherungsmaßregeln nach § 18 dieses Gesetzes oder auf Grund einer auf diesem Gesetz beruhenden Anordnung (§ 22 Abs. 2, §§ 40, 45) nicht eingehalten werde, oder Einwendungen des Berechtigten, dass eine bestimmte Maßnahme der Zwangsvollstreckung mit dieser Beschränkung vereinbar sei, sind im Wege der Erinnerung nach § 766 der Zivilprozessordnung bei dem Vollstreckungsgericht (§ 764 der Zivilprozessordnung) geltend zu machen.

§ 20
Sicherheitsleistung durch den Verpflichteten

(1) Solange die Zwangsvollstreckung aus einem Titel, der auf Leistung von Geld lautet, nicht über Maßregeln der Sicherung hinausgehen darf, ist der Verpflichtete befugt, die Zwangsvollstreckung durch Leistung einer Sicherheit in Höhe des Betrages abzuwenden, wegen dessen der Berechtigte vollstrecken darf.

(2) Die Zwangsvollstreckung ist einzustellen und bereits getroffene Vollstreckungsmaßregeln sind aufzuheben, wenn der Verpflichtete durch eine öf-

Chapter 5
Restriction of enforcement to protective measures, and unrestricted continuation of enforcement

§ 18
Restriction by law

As long as the time limit for filing a miscellaneous appeal is still running and as long as the miscellaneous appeal has not yet been adjudged, enforcement shall be restricted to protective measures.

§ 19
Verification of restriction

If the party against whom enforcement is sought wishes to object that the requirement under § 18 of this Act or under an order issued on the basis of this Act (§ 22 (2), §§ 40, 45), i. e. that enforcement be restricted to protective measures, is not being complied with, or if the party applying for enforcement wishes to object that a particular enforcement measure is reconcilable with this restriction, such objections shall be asserted by way of a special motion in accordance with § 766 of the German Code of Civil Procedure filed with the court competent for enforcement (§ 764 of the German Code of Civil Procedure).

§ 20
Security to be provided by party against whom enforcement is sought

(1) As long as enforcement of a title ordering payment of money may not go beyond protective measures, the party against whom enforcement is sought is entitled to avert enforcement by providing security in the amount of the sum in relation to which the party applying for enforcement is entitled to enforce the title.

(2) Enforcement shall be ceased and enforcement measures already taken reversed if the party against whom enforcement is sought produces a public

fentliche Urkunde die zur Abwendung der Zwangsvollstreckung erforderliche Sicherheitsleistung nachweist.

document evidencing provision of the security necessary to avert enforcement.

§ 21
Versteigerung beweglicher Sachen

§ 21
Auction of movables

Ist eine bewegliche Sache gepfändet und darf die Zwangsvollstreckung nicht über Maßregeln zur Sicherung hinausgehen, so kann das Vollstreckungsgericht auf Antrag anordnen, dass die Sache versteigert und der Erlös hinterlegt werde, wenn sie der Gefahr einer beträchtlichen Wertminderung ausgesetzt ist oder wenn ihre Aufbewahrung unverhältnismäßige Kosten verursachen würde.

Where a movable object has been garnished and enforcement is restricted to protective measures, the court competent for enforcing the title may order upon application that the object be auctioned and the proceeds deposited, if the object is exposed to the risk of a considerable loss in value or if its safekeeping would incur unreasonable expenses.

§ 22
Unbeschränkte Fortsetzung der Zwangsvollstreckung; besondere gerichtliche Anordnungen

§ 22
Unrestricted continuation of enforcement; special court orders

(1) Weist das Beschwerdegericht die Beschwerde des Verpflichteten gegen die Zulassung der Zwangsvollstreckung zurück oder lässt es auf die Beschwerde des Berechtigten die Zwangsvollstreckung aus dem Titel zu, so kann die Zwangsvollstreckung über Maßregeln zur Sicherung hinaus fortgesetzt werden.

(1) If the court of miscellaneous appeal rejects the miscellaneous appeal of the party against whom enforcement is sought against authorization of enforcement or if it authorizes the enforcement in response to the miscellaneous appeal of the party applying for enforcement, then enforcement is no longer restricted to protective measures.

(2) Auf Antrag des Verpflichteten kann das Beschwerdegericht anordnen, dass bis zum Ablauf der Frist zur Einlegung der Rechtsbeschwerde (§ 15) oder bis zur Entscheidung über diese Beschwerde die Zwangsvollstreckung nicht oder nur gegen Sicherheitsleistung über Maßregeln zur Sicherung hinausgehen darf. Die Anordnung darf nur erlassen werden, wenn glaubhaft gemacht wird, dass die weitergehende Vollstreckung dem Verpflichteten einen nicht zu ersetzenden Nachteil bringen würde. § 713 der Zivilprozessordnung ist entsprechend anzuwenden.

(2) Upon application by the party against whom enforcement is sought, the court of miscellaneous appeal may order that until expiration of the time limit for lodging a miscellaneous appeal on points of law (§ 15) or until a decision has been handed down on said miscellaneous appeal, enforcement may not go beyond protective measures, or – if so – only against provision of security. The order may only be issued if it is credibly substantiated that a more extensive enforcement would cause irreparable detriment to the party against whom enforcement is sought. § 713 of the German Code of Civil Procedure shall be applied *mutatis mutandis*.

(3) Wird Rechtsbeschwerde eingelegt, so kann der Bundesgerichtshof auf An-

(3) If a miscellaneous appeal on points of law is lodged, the Federal Court of

trag des Verpflichteten eine Anordnung nach Absatz 2 erlassen. Der Bundesgerichtshof kann auf Antrag des Berechtigten eine nach Absatz 2 erlassene Anordnung des Beschwerdegerichts abändern oder aufheben.

Justice may issue an order in accordance with sub-section (2) upon application by the party against whom enforcement is sought. Upon application by the party applying for enforcement, the Federal Court of Justice may modify or reverse an order issued by the court of miscellaneous appeal in accordance with sub-section (2).

§ 23
Unbeschränkte Fortsetzung der durch das Gericht des ersten Rechtszuges zugelassenen Zwangsvollstreckung

§ 23
Unrestricted continuation of enforcement authorized by the court of first instance

(1) Die Zwangsvollstreckung aus dem Titel, den der Urkundsbeamte der Geschäftsstelle des Gerichts des ersten Rechtszuges mit der Vollstreckungsklausel versehen hat, ist auf Antrag des Berechtigten über Maßregeln zur Sicherung hinaus fortzusetzen, wenn das Zeugnis des Urkundsbeamten der Geschäftsstelle dieses Gerichts vorgelegt wird, dass die Zwangsvollstreckung unbeschränkt stattfinden darf.

(1) Enforcement of a title to which the registrar of the court of first instance has added an enforcement clause shall be continued beyond protective measures upon application by the party applying for enforcement, if certification by the registrar of said court is presented confirming that enforcement may be effected without restriction.

(2) Das Zeugnis ist dem Berechtigten auf seinen Antrag zu erteilen,

(2) Said certification shall be issued to the party applying for enforcement upon request,

1. wenn der Verpflichtete bis zum Ablauf der Beschwerdefrist keine Beschwerdeschrift eingereicht hat,

1. if the party against whom enforcement is sought has not filed a statement of miscellaneous appeal within the time limit for lodging a miscellaneous appeal,

2. wenn das Beschwerdegericht die Beschwerde des Verpflichteten zurückgewiesen und keine Anordnung nach § 22 Abs. 2 erlassen hat,

2. if the court of miscellaneous appeal has dismissed the miscellaneous appeal of the party against whom enforcement is sought and has not issued an order in accordance with § 22 (2),

3. wenn der Bundesgerichtshof die Anordnung des Beschwerdegerichts nach § 22 Abs. 2 aufgehoben hat (§ 22 Abs. 3 Satz 2) oder

3. if the Federal Court of Justice has reversed the order issued by the court of miscellaneous appeal in accordance with § 22 (2) (§ 22 (3) second sentence), or

4. wenn der Bundesgerichtshof den Titel zur Zwangsvollstreckung zugelassen hat.

4. if the Federal Court of Justice has granted admission for the title to be enforced.

(3) Aus dem Titel darf die Zwangsvollstreckung, selbst wenn sie auf Maßre-

(3) Even if enforcement is restricted to protective measures, the enforcement

geln der Sicherung beschränkt ist, nicht mehr stattfinden, sobald ein Beschluss des Beschwerdegerichts, dass der Titel zur Zwangsvollstreckung nicht zugelassen werde, verkündet oder zugestellt ist.

of a title must cease as soon as an order of the court of miscellaneous appeal stating that admission for the title to be enforced is refused is pronounced or served.

§ 24
Unbeschränkte Fortsetzung der durch das Beschwerdegericht zugelassenen Zwangsvollstreckung

(1) Die Zwangsvollstreckung aus dem Titel, zu dem der Urkundsbeamte der Geschäftsstelle des Beschwerdegerichts die Vollstreckungsklausel mit dem Zusatz erteilt hat, dass die Zwangsvollstreckung auf Grund der Anordnung des Gerichts nicht über Maßregeln zur Sicherung hinausgehen darf (§ 13 Abs. 4 Satz 3), ist auf Antrag des Berechtigten über Maßregeln zur Sicherung hinaus fortzusetzen, wenn das Zeugnis des Urkundsbeamten der Geschäftsstelle dieses Gerichts vorgelegt wird, dass die Zwangsvollstreckung unbeschränkt stattfinden darf.

(2) Das Zeugnis ist dem Berechtigten auf seinen Antrag zu erteilen,

1. wenn der Verpflichtete bis zum Ablauf der Frist zur Einlegung der Rechtsbeschwerde (§ 15 Abs. 2) keine Beschwerdeschrift eingereicht hat,

2. wenn der Bundesgerichtshof die Anordnung des Beschwerdegerichts nach § 22 Abs. 2 aufgehoben hat (§ 22 Abs. 3 Satz 2) oder

3. wenn der Bundesgerichtshof die Rechtsbeschwerde des Verpflichteten zurückgewiesen hat.

§ 24
Unrestricted continuation of enforcement authorized by the court of miscellaneous appeal

(1) Enforcement of a title to which the registrar of the court of miscellaneous appeal has added an enforcement clause with a supplement to the effect that enforcement is restricted to protective measures in accordance with the order issued by the court (§ 13 (4), third sentence) shall be continued beyond protective measures upon application by the party applying for enforcement, if certification by the registrar of said court is presented confirming that enforcement may be made without restriction.

(2) The certification shall be issued to the party applying for enforcement upon his application,

1. if the party against whom enforcement is sought has not lodged a statement of miscellaneous appeal by the expiration of the time limit for filing a miscellaneous appeal on points of law (§ 15 (2)),

2. if the Federal Court of Justice has set aside the order of the court of miscellaneous appeal in accordance with § 22 (2) (§ 22 (3) second sentence), or

3. if the Federal Court of Justice has dismissed the miscellaneous appeal on points of law of a party against whom enforcement is sought.

Abschnitt 6 **Feststellung der Anerkennung einer ausländischen Entscheidung**	**Chapter 6** **Determination of recognition of a decision issued by a foreign court**
§ 25 **Verfahren und Entscheidung in der Hauptsache**	**§ 25** **Procedure and decision on the subject matter of the case**
(1) Auf das Verfahren, das die Feststellung zum Gegenstand hat, ob eine Entscheidung aus einem anderen Staat anzuerkennen ist, sind die §§ 3 bis 6, 8 Abs. 2, die §§ 10 bis 12, § 13 Abs. 1 bis 3, die §§ 15 und 16 sowie § 17 Abs. 1 und 2 entsprechend anzuwenden.	(1) §§ 3–6, 8 (2), §§ 10–12, § 13 (1)–(3), §§ 15 and 16, as well as § 17 (1) and (2) shall be applied *mutatis mutandis* to the procedure for determination of whether a decision issued by a foreign state is to be recognized.
(2) Ist der Antrag auf Feststellung begründet, so beschließt das Gericht, dass die Entscheidung anzuerkennen ist.	(2) If the application for determination is well-founded, the court shall rule that the decision is to be recognized.
§ 26 **Kostenentscheidung**	**§ 26** **Decision on costs**
In den Fällen des § 25 Abs. 2 sind die Kosten dem Antragsgegner aufzuerlegen. Dieser kann die Beschwerde (§ 11) auf die Entscheidung über den Kostenpunkt beschränken. In diesem Falle sind die Kosten dem Antragsteller aufzuerlegen, wenn der Antragsgegner nicht durch sein Verhalten zu dem Antrag auf Feststellung Veranlassung gegeben hat.	In cases covered by § 25 (2), the opponent shall be ordered to pay the costs. The opponent may limit the miscellaneous appeal (§ 11) solely to the decision on the costs. In this case the applicant shall be ordered to pay the costs, provided the opponent did not give cause for the application for determination on account of his conduct.
Abschnitt 7 **Aufhebung oder Änderung der Beschlüsse über die Zulassung der Zwangsvollstreckung oder die Anerkennung**	**Chapter 7** **Setting aside or modification of decisions on authorization of enforcement or recognition**
§ 27 **Verfahren nach Aufhebung oder Änderung des für vollstreckbar erklärten ausländischen Titels im Ursprungsstaat**	**§ 27** **Procedure following the setting aside or modification of the title declared enforceable in the country of origin**
(1) Wird der Titel in dem Staat, in dem er errichtet worden ist, aufgehoben oder geändert und kann der Verpflichtete diese Tatsache in dem Verfahren der Zulassung der Zwangsvollstreckung nicht mehr geltend machen, so kann er die Aufhebung oder Änderung der Zu-	(1) If a title is set aside or modified in the country in which it was made and if the party against whom enforcement is sought can no longer assert this fact in the procedure for authorization of enforcement, it may lodge an application for the setting aside or modification of the admission in a special procedure.

lassung in einem besonderen Verfahren beantragen.

(2) Für die Entscheidung über den Antrag ist das Gericht ausschließlich zuständig, das im ersten Rechtszug über den Antrag auf Erteilung der Vollstreckungsklausel entschieden hat.

(3) Der Antrag kann bei dem Gericht schriftlich oder durch Erklärung zu Protokoll der Geschäftsstelle gestellt werden. Über den Antrag kann ohne mündliche Verhandlung entschieden werden. Vor der Entscheidung, die durch Beschluss ergeht, ist der Berechtigte zu hören. § 13 Abs. 2 und 3 gilt entsprechend.

(4) Der Beschluss unterliegt der Beschwerde nach den §§ 567 bis 577 der Zivilprozessordnung. Die Notfrist für die Einlegung der sofortigen Beschwerde beträgt einen Monat.

(5) Für die Einstellung der Zwangsvollstreckung und die Aufhebung bereits getroffener Vollstreckungsmaßregeln sind die §§ 769 und 770 der Zivilprozessordnung entsprechend anzuwenden. Die Aufhebung einer Vollstreckungsmaßregel ist auch ohne Sicherheitsleistung zulässig.

§ 28
Schadensersatz wegen ungerechtfertigter Vollstreckung

(1) Wird die Zulassung der Zwangsvollstreckung auf die Beschwerde (§ 11) oder die Rechtsbeschwerde (§ 15) aufgehoben oder abgeändert, so ist der Berechtigte zum Ersatz des Schadens verpflichtet, der dem Verpflichteten durch die Vollstreckung des Titels oder durch eine Leistung zur Abwendung der Vollstreckung entstanden ist. Das Gleiche gilt, wenn die Zulassung der Zwangsvollstreckung nach § 27 aufgehoben oder abgeändert wird, sofern die zur Zwangsvollstreckung zugelassene Entscheidung zum Zeitpunkt der Zulassung nach dem Recht des Staats, in

(2) The court that decided on the application for the issuance of an enforcement clause in the first instance shall have exclusive jurisdiction to rule on said application.

(3) The application may be lodged with the court in writing or by placing it on record with the court registry. The court may decide on the application without an oral hearing. The party applying for enforcement shall be heard before a decision is taken in the form of a court order. § 13 (2) and (3) shall apply *mutatis mutandis*.

(4) The court order is subject to miscellaneous appeal in accordance with §§ 567 to 577 of the Code of Civil Procedure. The statutory time limit within which such immediate miscellaneous appeal must be filed is one month

(5) §§ 769 and 770 of the Code of Civil Procedure shall be applied *mutatis mutandis* to cessation of enforcement and cancellation of enforcement measures already taken. An enforcement measure may be cancelled without provision of security.

§ 28
Damages for unwarranted enforcement

(1) If the authorization of enforcement is cancelled or modified in response to the miscellaneous appeal (§ 11) or the miscellaneous appeal on points of law (§ 15), the party applying for enforcement is obliged to compensate the party against whom enforcement is sought for damage the latter incurred as a result of enforcement of the title or of having to pay to avert enforcement. The same shall apply if the authorization of enforcement is cancelled or modified in accordance with § 27 insofar as, at the time when the enforcement was admitted, the decision authorized for enforcement

dem sie ergangen ist, noch mit einem ordentlichen Rechtsmittel angefochten werden konnte.	was still appealable by regular means of appeal under the law of the country in which it was issued.
(2) Für die Geltendmachung des Anspruchs ist das Gericht ausschließlich zuständig, das im ersten Rechtszug über den Antrag, den Titel mit der Vollstreckungsklausel zu versehen, entschieden hat.	(2) The court that decided on the application to add an enforcement clause to the title in the first instance shall have exclusive jurisdiction for claims for damages.

§ 29
Aufhebung oder Änderung ausländischer Entscheidungen, deren Anerkennung festgestellt ist

§ 29
Setting aside or modification of decisions of foreign courts that have been recognized

Wird die Entscheidung in dem Staat, in dem sie ergangen ist, aufgehoben oder abgeändert und kann die davon begünstigte Partei diese Tatsache nicht mehr in dem Verfahren über den Antrag auf Feststellung der Anerkennung (§ 25) geltend machen, so ist § 27 Abs. 1 bis 4 entsprechend anzuwenden.

If the decision is cancelled or modified in the country in which it was issued and if the person benefiting from such setting aside/modification is no longer able to assert this fact in the proceedings concerning the application for determination of recognition (§ 25), § 27 (1)–(4) shall apply *mutatis mutandis*.

Abschnitt 8
Vorschriften für Entscheidungen deutscher Gerichte und für das Mahnverfahren

Chapter 8
Rules governing decisions by German courts and collection proceedings

§ 30
Vervollständigung inländischer Entscheidungen zur Verwendung im Ausland

§ 30
Completion of decisions of domestic courts for use abroad

[nicht abgedruckt]

[not printed]

§ 31
Vollstreckungsklausel zur Verwendung im Ausland

§ 31
Enforcement clause for use abroad

[nicht abgedruckt]

[not printed]

§ 32
Mahnverfahren mit Zustellung im Ausland

§ 32
Collection proceedings involving service abroad

[nicht abgedruckt]

[not printed]

Abschnitt 9 Verhältnis zu besonderen Anerkennungsverfahren; Konzentrationsermächtigung	**Chapter 9** Relationship with special recognition procedures; authorization for concentration
§ 33 (weggefallen)	**§ 33** (repealed)
§ 34 Konzentrationsermächtigung	**§ 34** Authorization for concentration
[nicht abgedruckt]	[not printed]
Teil 2 **Besonderes**	**Part 2** **Special clauses**
Abschnitt 1 Übereinkommen über die gerichtliche Zuständigkeit und die Vollstreckung gerichtlicher Entscheidungen in Zivil- und Handelssachen vom 27. September 1968 und vom 16. September 1988	**Chapter 1** Conventions of 27 September 1968 and 16 September 1988 on Jurisdiction and the Enforcement of Judgments in Civil and Commercial Matters
§ 35 Sonderregelungen über die Beschwerdefrist	**§ 35** Special rules on time limit for filing miscellaneous appeal
[nicht abgedruckt]	[not printed]
§ 36 Aussetzung des Beschwerdeverfahrens	**§ 36** Stay of miscellaneous appeal proceedings
[nicht abgedruckt]	[not printed]
Abschnitt 2 (weggefallen)	**Chapter 2** (repealed)
§ 37 (weggefallen)	**§ 37** (repealed)
§ 38 (weggefallen)	**§ 38** (repealed)
§ 39 (weggefallen)	**§ 39** (repealed)

Abschnitt 3
Vertrag vom 17. Juni 1977 zwischen der Bundesrepublik Deutschland und dem Königreich Norwegen über die gegenseitige Anerkennung und Vollstreckung gerichtlicher Entscheidungen und anderer Schuldtitel in Zivil- und Handelssachen

§ 40
Abweichungen von § 22

[nicht abgedruckt]

§ 41
Abweichungen von § 23

[nicht abgedruckt]

§ 42
Abweichungen von § 24

[nicht abgedruckt]

§ 43
Folgeregelungen für das Rechtsbeschwerdeverfahren

[nicht abgedruckt]

§ 44
Weitere Sonderregelungen

[nicht abgedruckt]

Abschnitt 4
Vertrag vom 20. Juli 1977 zwischen der Bundesrepublik Deutschland und dem Staat Israel über die gegenseitige Anerkennung und Vollstreckung gerichtlicher Entscheidungen in Zivil- und Handelssachen

§ 45
Abweichungen von § 22

[nicht abgedruckt]

§ 46
Abweichungen von § 23

[nicht abgedruckt]

Chapter 3
Treaty of 17 June 1977 between the Federal Republic of Germany and the Kingdom of Norway on the Mutual Recognition and Enforcement of Judgments and other Executory Titles in Civil and Commercial Matters

§ 40
Derogations from § 22

[not printed]

§ 41
Derogations from § 23

[not printed]

§ 42
Derogations from § 24

[not printed]

§ 43
Follow-up rules for proceedings concerning miscellaneous appeal on points of law

[not printed]

§ 44
Further special rules

[not printed]

Chapter 4
Treaty of 20 July 1977 between the Federal Republic of Germany and the State of Israel on the Mutual Recognition and Enforcement of Judgments in Civil and Commercial Matters

§ 45
Derogations from § 22

[not printed]

§ 46
Derogations from § 23

[not printed]

§ 47
Abweichungen von § 24

[nicht abgedruckt]

§ 48
Folgeregelungen für das Rechtsbeschwerdeverfahren

[nicht abgedruckt]

§ 49
Weitere Sonderregelungen

[nicht abgedruckt]

Abschnitt 5
(weggefallen)

§§ 50–54
(weggefallen)

Abschnitt 6
Übereinkommen vom 30. Oktober 2007 über die gerichtliche Zuständigkeit und die Anerkennung und Vollstreckung von Entscheidungen in Zivil- und Handelssachen

§ 55
Abweichungen von Vorschriften des Allgemeinen Teils; ergänzende Regelungen

[nicht abgedruckt]

§ 56
Sonderregelungen für die Vollstreckungsabwehrklage

[nicht abgedruckt]

§ 57
Bescheinigungen zu inländischen Titeln

[nicht abgedruckt]

---

§ 47
Derogations from § 24

[not printed]

§ 48
Follow-up rules for proceedings concerning miscellaneous appeal on points of law

[not printed]

§ 49
Further special rules

[not printed]

Chapter 5
(repealed)

§ 50–54
(repealed)

Chapter 6
Convention of 30 October 2007 on Jurisdiction and the Recognition and Enforcement of Judgments in Civil and Commercial Matters

§ 55
Derogations from provisions in the general section; supplementary provisions

[not printed]

§ 56
Special rules governing the action to avert enforcement

[not printed]

§ 57
Certifications of domestic titles

[not printed]

IV. Act on the Implementation of the Hague Convention of 15 November 1965 on the Service Abroad of Judicial and Extrajudicial Documents in Civil or Commercial Matters and the Hague Convention of 18 March 1970 on the Taking of Evidence Abroad in Civil or Commercial matters

of 22 December 1977[1]

With the consent of the *Bundesrat* (Upper House of Parliament), the *Bundestag* (Lower House of Parliament) has passed the following Act:

First part
Provisions on the implementation of the Hague Convention of 15 November 1965 on the Service Abroad of Judicial and Extrajudicial Documents in Civil or Commercial Matters

§ 1

The tasks of the Central Authority (Articles 2, 18 (3) of the Convention) shall be performed by the agencies designated by the Federal State governments. Each Federal State may only set up one Central Authority. The Federal State governments may delegate the authorisation pursuant to the first sentence to the respective Federal State administration of justice.

§ 2

The Central Authority of the Federal State in which the service is to be effected and the agencies which, pursuant to § 1 of the Act on the Implementation of the Hague Convention of 1 March 1954

---

[1] Translation by Elaine Ikizer.

IV. Act on the Implementation of the Hague Convention

soll, und die Stellen zuständig, die gemäß §1 des Gesetzes zur Ausführung des Haager Übereinkommens vom 1. März 1954 über den Zivilprozess vom 18. Dezember 1958 (BGBl. I S. 939) zur Entgegennahme von Anträgen des Konsuls eines ausländischen Staates zuständig sind.

relating to civil procedure of 18 December 1958 (Federal Law Gazette I p. 939), are competent for the acceptance of requests from a consul of a foreign state, shall be responsible for the acceptance of requests for service forwarded by a foreign consul within the Federal Republic of Germany (Article 9 (1) of the Convention).

§3

Eine förmliche Zustellung (Artikel 5 Abs. 1 des Übereinkommens) ist nur zulässig, wenn das zuzustellende Schriftstück in deutscher Sprache abgefasst oder in diese Sprache übersetzt ist.

§3

A formal service (Article 5 (1) of the Convention) is only permissible if the document to be served is written in German or is translated into this language.

§4

(1) Die Zentrale Behörde ist befugt, Zustellungsanträge unmittelbar durch die Post erledigen zu lassen, wenn die Voraussetzungen für eine Zustellung gemäß Artikel 5 Abs. 1 Buchstabe a des Übereinkommens erfüllt sind. In diesem Fall händigt die Zentrale Behörde das zu übergebende Schriftstück der Post zur Zustellung aus. Die Vorschriften der Zivilprozessordnung über die Zustellung von Amts wegen gelten entsprechend.

(2) Im übrigen ist für die Erledigung von Zustellungsanträgen das Amtsgericht zuständig, in dessen Bezirk die Zustellung vorzunehmen ist. Die Zustellung wird durch die Geschäftsstelle des Amtsgerichts bewirkt.

§4

(1) The Central Authority is empowered to effect requests for service directly by the Postal Service if the prerequisites for service pursuant to Article 5 (1) lit. a of the Convention are fulfilled. In such case, the Central Authority shall hand over the document to be delivered to the Postal Service for service. The provisions of the German Code of Civil Procedure on the service of documents *ex officio* shall apply *mutatis mutandis*.

(2) In all other cases, the local court in whose district the service shall be effected is competent for handling requests for service. The service shall be effected by the registry of the local court.

§5

Das Zustellungszeugnis (Artikel 6 Abs. 1, 2 des Übereinkommens) erteilt im Fall des §4 Abs. 1 die Zentrale Behörde, im übrigen die Geschäftsstelle des Amtsgerichts.

§5

The certificate stating that the document has been served (Article 6 (1), (2) of the Convention) shall be issued by the Central Authority in the case of §4 (1), in all other cases by the registry of the local court.

§6

Eine Zustellung durch diplomatische oder konsularische Vertreter (Artikel 8 des Übereinkommens) ist nur zulässig,

§6

Service of documents by diplomatic or consular agents (Article 8 of the Convention) is only permissible if the doc-

wenn das Schriftstück einem Angehörigen des Absendestaates zuzustellen ist. Eine Zustellung nach Artikel 10 des Übereinkommens findet nicht statt.	ument shall be served upon a national of the sending state. Service pursuant to Article 10 of the Convention shall not be effected.

Zweiter Teil **Vorschriften zur Ausführung des Haager Übereinkommens vom 18. März 1970 über die Beweisaufnahme im Ausland in Zivil- oder Handelssachen**	**Second Part** **Provisions on the implementation of the Hague Convention of 18 March 1970 on the Taking of Evidence Abroad in Civil or Commercial Matters**
§ 7	**§ 7**
Die Aufgaben der Zentralen Behörde (Artikel 2, 24 Abs. 2 des Übereinkommens) nehmen die von den Landesregierungen bestimmten Stellen wahr. Jedes Land kann nur eine Zentrale Behörde einrichten. Die Landesregierungen können die Befugnis nach Satz 1 auf die Landesjustizverwaltungen übertragen.	The tasks of the Central Authority (Articles 2, 24 (2) of the Convention) shall be performed by the agencies designated by the Federal State governments. Each Federal State may set up only one Central Authority. The Federal State governments may delegate the authorisation pursuant to the first sentence to the respective Federal State administration of justice.
§ 8	**§ 8**
Für die Erledigung von Rechtshilfeersuchen ist das Amtsgericht zuständig, in dessen Bezirk die Amtshandlung vorzunehmen ist.	The local court in whose district the official act shall be performed is responsible for the execution of requests for judicial assistance.
§ 9	**§ 9**
Rechtshilfeersuchen, die durch das Amtsgericht zu erledigen sind (Kapitel I des Übereinkommens), müssen in deutscher Sprache abgefasst oder von einer Übersetzung in diese Sprache begleitet sein (Artikel 4 Abs. 1, 5 des Übereinkommens).	Requests for judicial assistance which are to be executed by the local court (Chapter I of the Convention) must be written in German or accompanied by a translation into this language (Article 4 (1), (5) of the Convention).
§ 10	**§ 10**
Mitglieder des ersuchenden ausländischen Gerichts können bei der Erledigung eines Rechtshilfeersuchens durch das Amtsgericht anwesend sein, wenn die Zentrale Behörde dies genehmigt hat.	Members of the requesting foreign court may be present in the execution of a request for judicial assistance by the local court if the Central Authority has given its permission.

§ 11

Eine Beweisaufnahme durch diplomatische oder konsularische Vertreter ist unzulässig, wenn sie deutsche Staatsangehörige betrifft. Betrifft sie Angehörige eines dritten Staates oder Staatenlose, so ist sie nur zulässig, wenn die Zentrale Behörde sie genehmigt hat (Artikel 16 Abs. 1 des Übereinkommens). Eine Genehmigung ist nicht erforderlich, wenn der Angehörige eines dritten Staates zugleich die Staatsangehörigkeit des Staates des ersuchenden Gerichts besitzt.

§ 12

(1) Ein Beauftragter des ersuchenden Gerichts (Artikel 17 des Übereinkommens) darf eine Beweisaufnahme nur durchführen, wenn die Zentrale Behörde sie genehmigt hat. Die Genehmigung kann mit Auflagen verbunden werden.

(2) Das Gericht, das für die Erledigung eines Rechtshilfeersuchens in derselben Angelegenheit nach §8 zuständig wäre, ist befugt, die Vorbereitung und die Durchführung der Beweisaufnahme zu überwachen. Ein Mitglied dieses Gerichts kann an der Beweisaufnahme teilnehmen (Artikel 19 Satz 2 des Übereinkommens).

§ 13

Für die Erteilung der Genehmigung nach den §§ 10, 11 und 12 (Artikel 19 des Übereinkommens) ist die Zentrale Behörde des Landes zuständig, in dem die Beweisaufnahme durchgeführt werden soll.

§ 14

(1) Rechtshilfeersuchen, die ein Verfahren nach Artikel 23 des Übereinkommens zum Gegenstand haben, werden nicht erledigt.

(2) Jedoch können, soweit die tragenden Grundsätze des deutschen Verfahrensrechts nicht entgegenstehen, solche Ersuchen unter Berücksichtigung der schutzwürdigen Interessen der Betrof-

§ 11

The taking of evidence by diplomatic officers or consular agents is not permissible if German nationals are concerned. If nationals of a third state or stateless persons are concerned, such taking of evidence is only permissible if the Central Authority has given its permission (Article 16 (1) of the Convention). Permission is not necessary if the national of a third state is at the same time a national of the state of the requesting court.

§ 12

(1) A commissioner of the requesting court (Article 17 of the Convention) may only take evidence if the Central Authority has given its permission. The permission may be subject to conditions.

(2) The court that would be competent for the execution of a request for judicial assistance in the same matter pursuant to §8 is entitled to monitor the preparation for and the actual taking of evidence. A member of this court may be present at the taking of evidence (Article 19 second sentence of the Convention).

§ 13

The Central Authority of the Federal State in which the evidence is to be taken is competent to give permission pursuant to §§ 10, 11 and 12 (Article 19 of the Convention).

§ 14

(1) Requests for judicial assistance concerning proceedings pursuant to Article 23 of the Convention shall not be executed.

(2) However, to the extent that this is not contrary to the primary principles of German procedural law, such requests may be executed by taking into consideration the interests warranting pro-

fenen erledigt werden, nachdem die Voraussetzungen der Erledigung und das anzuwendende Verfahren durch Rechtsverordnung näher geregelt sind, die der Bundesminister der Justiz mit Zustimmung des Bundesrates erlassen kann.

tection of the persons concerned, once the prerequisites for execution and the applicable procedure have been regulated in more detail by a legal regulation which may be enacted by the Federal Minister of Justice with the approval of the *Bundesrat*.

**Dritter Teil
Sonstige Bestimmungen**

**Third Part
Other Provisions**

§ 15

§ 15

Der Bundesminister der Justiz wird ermächtigt, durch Rechtsverordnung, die der Zustimmung des Bundesrates bedarf, die nach den §§ 1 und 7 dieses Gesetzes errichteten Zentralen Behörden als die Stellen zu bestimmen, die gemäß den §§ 1 und 3 Abs. 2 des Gesetzes vom 5. April 1909 zur Ausführung des Haager Abkommens über den Zivilprozess vom 17. Juli 1905 (RGBl. 1909 S. 430) und gemäß den §§ 1 und 9 des Gesetzes zur Ausführung des Haager Übereinkommens vom 1. März 1954 über den Zivilprozess zur Entgegennahme von Anträgen und Ersuchen des Konsuls eines ausländischen Staates zuständig sind.

The Federal Minister of Justice is empowered to designate, by legal regulation requiring the approval of the *Bundesrat*, the Central Authorities set up pursuant to §§ 1 and 7 of this Act to be the agencies competent to accept applications and requests of the consul of a foreign state pursuant to §§ 1 and 3 (2) of the Act of 5 April 1909 on the Implementation of the Hague Convention on Civil Proceedings of 17 July 1905 (Reich Law Gazette 1909 p. 430) and pursuant to §§ 1 and 9 of the Act on the Implementation of the Hague Convention of 1 March 1954 on Civil Proceedings.

§ 16

§ 16

Dieses Gesetz gilt nach Maßgabe des § 13 Abs. 1 des Dritten Überleitungsgesetzes auch im Land Berlin. Rechtsverordnungen, die aufgrund dieses Gesetzes erlassen werden, gelten im Land Berlin nach § 14 des Dritten Überleitungsgesetzes.

In accordance with § 13 (1) of the Third Transitional Act, this Act shall also apply in the Federal State of Berlin. Legal regulations enacted on the basis of this Act shall apply in the Federal State of Berlin pursuant to § 14 of the Third Transitional Act.

§ 17

§ 17

Dieses Gesetz tritt am Tage nach der Verkündung in Kraft.

This Act shall enter into force one day after its promulgation.

V. Mediationsgesetz

§ 1
Begriffsbestimmungen

(1) Mediation ist ein vertrauliches und strukturiertes Verfahren, bei dem Parteien mithilfe eines oder mehrerer Mediatoren freiwillig und eigenverantwortlich eine einvernehmliche Beilegung ihres Konflikts anstreben.

(2) Ein Mediator ist eine unabhängige und neutrale Person ohne Entscheidungsbefugnis, die die Parteien durch die Mediation führt.

§ 2
Verfahren; Aufgaben des Mediators

(1) Die Parteien wählen den Mediator aus.

(2) Der Mediator vergewissert sich, dass die Parteien die Grundsätze und den Ablauf des Mediationsverfahrens verstanden haben und freiwillig an der Mediation teilnehmen.

(3) Der Mediator ist allen Parteien gleichermaßen verpflichtet. Er fördert die Kommunikation der Parteien und gewährleistet, dass die Parteien in angemessener und fairer Weise in die Mediation eingebunden sind. Er kann im allseitigen Einverständnis getrennte Gespräche mit den Parteien führen.

(4) Dritte können nur mit Zustimmung aller Parteien in die Mediation einbezogen werden.

(5) Die Parteien können die Mediation jederzeit beenden. Der Mediator kann die Mediation beenden, insbesondere wenn er der Auffassung ist, dass eine eigenverantwortliche Kommunikation oder eine Einigung der Parteien nicht zu erwarten ist.

V. German Mediation Act[1]

§ 1
Definitions

(1) "Mediation" means a confidential and structured process whereby two or more parties to a dispute attempt by themselves, on a voluntary basis, to reach an agreement on the settlement of their dispute with the assistance of one or more mediators.

(2) A mediator shall be an independent and impartial person without any decision-making authority who shall guide the parties through the mediation process.

§ 2
Process; tasks of the mediator

(1) The mediator shall be selected by the parties.

(2) The mediator shall satisfy himself that the parties have understood the basic principles of the mediation process and the way in which it is conducted, and that they are participating in mediation on a voluntary basis.

(3) The mediator's obligations shall be equal towards all parties. He shall promote communication between the parties and shall ensure that the parties are involved in the mediation process in an appropriate and fair manner. The mediator may conduct separate discussions with the parties subject to agreement thereto by all parties.

(4) Third parties may only be involved in the mediation process with the consent of all parties.

(5) The parties may terminate the mediation at any time. The mediator may terminate the mediation, in particular

---

[1] Translation by the Federal Ministry of Justice and Consumer Protection, available at http://www.gesetze-im-internet.de/englisch_mediationsg/index.html, amended by Hildegard Rosenzweig.

when he is of the opinion that autonomous communication or an agreement between the parties is not to be expected.

(6) Der Mediator wirkt im Falle einer Einigung darauf hin, dass die Parteien die Vereinbarung in Kenntnis der Sachlage treffen und ihren Inhalt verstehen. Er hat die Parteien, die ohne fachliche Beratung an der Mediation teilnehmen, auf die Möglichkeit hinzuweisen, die Vereinbarung bei Bedarf durch externe Berater überprüfen zu lassen. Mit Zustimmung der Parteien kann die erzielte Einigung in einer Abschlussvereinbarung dokumentiert werden.

(6) In the event that an agreement on the settlement of the dispute is reached by the parties, the mediator shall make efforts to ensure that the parties enter into the agreement in awareness of the facts and that they understand the content of the agreement. He shall inform those parties which participate in the mediation process without availing themselves of expert advice of the possibility of having the agreement reviewed by external advisors, if necessary. Subject to the parties' consent, the agreement that has been reached may be documented in the form of a final agreement.

§ 3
Offenbarungspflichten; Tätigkeitsbeschränkungen

§ 3
Disclosure obligations; restrictions on acting as a mediator

(1) Der Mediator hat den Parteien alle Umstände offenzulegen, die seine Unabhängigkeit und Neutralität beeinträchtigen können. Er darf bei Vorliegen solcher Umstände nur als Mediator tätig werden, wenn die Parteien dem ausdrücklich zustimmen.

(1) The mediator shall disclose all circumstances to the parties which may impede his independence or impartiality. If such circumstances exist, the mediator shall be permitted to act as a mediator only if the parties explicitly agree thereto.

(2) Als Mediator darf nicht tätig werden, wer vor der Mediation in derselben Sache für eine Partei tätig gewesen ist. Der Mediator darf auch nicht während oder nach der Mediation für eine Partei in derselben Sache tätig werden.

(2) A person who has acted in the same matter for one of the parties prior to the mediation shall not be permitted to act as a mediator. The mediator shall also not be permitted to act in the same matter for any of the parties either during or subsequent to the mediation.

(3) Eine Person darf nicht als Mediator tätig werden, wenn eine mit ihr in derselben Berufsausübungs- oder Bürogemeinschaft verbundene andere Person vor der Mediation in derselben Sache für eine Partei tätig gewesen ist. Eine solche andere Person darf auch nicht während oder nach der Mediation für eine Partei in derselben Sache tätig werden.

(3) A person shall not be permitted to act as a mediator if another person who is part of the same professional cooperative or office-sharing arrangement has acted in the same matter for any of the parties prior to the mediation. Such other person shall also not be permitted to act in the same matter for any of the parties either during or subsequent to the mediation.

(4) Die Beschränkungen des Absatzes 3 gelten nicht, wenn sich die betroffenen

(4) The restrictions provided for in subsection (3) shall not apply if the parties

Parteien im Einzelfall nach umfassender Information damit einverstanden erklärt haben und Belange der Rechtspflege dem nicht entgegenstehen.

(5) Der Mediator ist verpflichtet, die Parteien auf deren Verlangen über seinen fachlichen Hintergrund, seine Ausbildung und seine Erfahrung auf dem Gebiet der Mediation zu informieren.

§ 4
Verschwiegenheitspflicht

Der Mediator und die in die Durchführung des Mediationsverfahrens eingebundenen Personen sind zur Verschwiegenheit verpflichtet, soweit gesetzlich nichts anderes geregelt ist. Diese Pflicht bezieht sich auf alles, was ihnen in Ausübung ihrer Tätigkeit bekannt geworden ist. Ungeachtet anderer gesetzlicher Regelungen über die Verschwiegenheitspflicht gilt sie nicht, soweit

1. die Offenlegung des Inhalts der im Mediationsverfahren erzielten Vereinbarung zur Umsetzung oder Vollstreckung dieser Vereinbarung erforderlich ist,
2. die Offenlegung aus vorrangigen Gründen der öffentlichen Ordnung (ordre public) geboten ist, insbesondere um eine Gefährdung des Wohles eines Kindes oder eine schwerwiegende Beeinträchtigung der physischen oder psychischen Integrität einer Person abzuwenden, oder
3. es sich um Tatsachen handelt, die offenkundig sind oder ihrer Bedeutung nach keiner Geheimhaltung bedürfen.

Der Mediator hat die Parteien über den Umfang seiner Verschwiegenheitspflicht zu informieren.

involved, after having been provided with comprehensive information, have declared their agreement thereto in an individual case and if this does not conflict with concerns relating to the administration of justice.

(5) The mediator shall be obliged to provide the parties with information about his professional background, his training and his experience in the field of mediation if they so request.

§ 4
Obligation to maintain confidentiality

The mediator and the persons involved in conducting the mediation process shall be obliged to maintain confidentiality, unless provided otherwise by law. This obligation shall relate to all information of which they have become aware in the course of performing their activities. Notwithstanding other legal provisions regarding the obligation to maintain confidentiality, this obligation shall not apply to the extent that

1. it is required to disclose the content of the agreement reached in the mediation process in order to implement or enforce that agreement,
2. the relevant disclosure is necessary for overriding reasons of public policy (*ordre public*), in particular in order to avert a risk posed to a child's well-being or to prevent serious harm to the physical or mental integrity of a person, or
3. facts are concerned which are obvious or which are not sufficiently significant to warrant confidential treatment.

The mediator shall inform the parties about the extent of his obligation to maintain confidentiality.

§ 5
Aus- und Fortbildung des Mediators; zertifizierter Mediator

(1) Der Mediator stellt in eigener Verantwortung durch eine geeignete Ausbildung und eine regelmäßige Fortbildung sicher, dass er über theoretische Kenntnisse sowie praktische Erfahrungen verfügt, um die Parteien in sachkundiger Weise durch die Mediation führen zu können. Eine geeignete Ausbildung soll insbesondere vermitteln:

1. Kenntnisse über Grundlagen der Mediation sowie deren Ablauf und Rahmenbedingungen,
2. Verhandlungs- und Kommunikationstechniken,
3. Konfliktkompetenz,
4. Kenntnisse über das Recht der Mediation sowie über die Rolle des Rechts in der Mediation sowie
5. praktische Übungen, Rollenspiele und Supervision.

(2) Als zertifizierter Mediator darf sich bezeichnen, wer eine Ausbildung zum Mediator abgeschlossen hat, die den Anforderungen der Rechtsverordnung nach § 6 entspricht.

(3) Der zertifizierte Mediator hat sich entsprechend den Anforderungen der Rechtsverordnung nach § 6 fortzubilden.

§ 6
Verordnungsermächtigung

Das Bundesministerium der Justiz wird ermächtigt, durch Rechtsverordnung ohne Zustimmung des Bundesrates nähere Bestimmungen über die Ausbildung zum zertifizierten Mediator und über die Fortbildung des zertifizierten Mediators sowie Anforderungen an Aus- und Fortbildungseinrichtungen zu erlassen. In der Rechtsverordnung nach Satz 1 können insbesondere festgelegt werden:

§ 5
Initial and further training of the mediator; certified mediator

(1) The mediator himself shall be responsible for ensuring, by way of appropriate initial training and regular further training, that he has the theoretical knowledge and practical experience required to enable him to guide the parties through the mediation process in a competent manner. Such appropriate initial training shall impart the following in particular:

1. knowledge about the basic principles of mediation and the process of and framework therefor,
2. negotiation and communication techniques,
3. competence in conflict management,
4. knowledge about the law governing mediation and the role of the law in mediation, and
5. practical exercises, role playing and supervision.

(2) A person shall be permitted to call himself a certified mediator if he has completed initial training as a mediator which satisfies the requirements of the ordinance pursuant to section 6.

(3) Certified mediators shall undergo further training in accordance with the requirements stipulated in the ordinance pursuant to section 6.

§ 6
Authorisation to issue an ordinance having the force of law

The Federal Ministry of Justice shall be authorised to issue more specific provisions regarding the initial training for certified mediators and further training for certified mediators and regarding the requirements to be satisfied by institutions providing initial and further training by way of an ordinance (*Rechtsverordnung*) not requiring the approval of the Federal Council (*Bundesrat*). The ordinance pursuant to the first

1. nähere Bestimmungen über die Inhalte der Ausbildung, wobei eine Ausbildung zum zertifizierten Mediator die in §5 Absatz 1 Satz 2 aufgeführten Ausbildungsinhalte zu vermitteln hat, und über die erforderliche Praxiserfahrung;	sentence may stipulate the following in particular: 1. more specific provisions regarding the contents of initial training, within the scope of which the initial training as a certified mediator shall impart the elements listed in section 5 subsection (1) second sentence, and regarding the practical experience required;
2. nähere Bestimmungen über die Inhalte der Fortbildung;	2. more specific provisions regarding the contents of further training;
3. Mindeststundenzahlen für die Aus- und Fortbildung;	3. minimum numbers of lessons for initial and further training;
4. zeitliche Abstände, in denen eine Fortbildung zu erfolgen hat;	4. intervals at which further training must be undergone;
5. Anforderungen an die in den Aus- und Fortbildungseinrichtungen eingesetzten Lehrkräfte;	5. requirements to be satisfied by the teaching staff deployed in the institutions providing initial and further training;
6. Bestimmungen darüber, dass und in welcher Weise eine Aus- und Fortbildungseinrichtung die Teilnahme an einer Aus- und Fortbildungsveranstaltung zu zertifizieren hat;	6. provisions stipulating that, and indicating how, an institution providing initial and further training shall certify participation in an initial and further training programme;
7. Regelungen über den Abschluss der Ausbildung;	7. rules regarding the completion of initial training;
8. Übergangsbestimmungen für Personen, die bereits vor Inkrafttreten dieses Gesetzes als Mediatoren tätig sind.	8. transitional provisions for persons who were already working as mediators prior to the entry into force of this Act.

§ 7 Wissenschaftliche Forschungsvorhaben; finanzielle Förderung der Mediation	§ 7 Academic research projects; financial support of mediation
(1) Bund und Länder können wissenschaftliche Forschungsvorhaben vereinbaren, um die Folgen einer finanziellen Förderung der Mediation für die Länder zu ermitteln.	(1) The Federal Government and the Federal State Governments may agree upon academic research projects in order to ascertain the consequences of financial support of mediation schemes for the Federal States.
(2) Die Förderung kann im Rahmen der Forschungsvorhaben auf Antrag einer rechtsuchenden Person bewilligt werden, wenn diese nach ihren persönlichen und wirtschaftlichen Verhältnissen die Kosten einer Mediation nicht, nur zum Teil oder nur in Raten aufbringen kann und die beabsichtigte Rechts-	(2) Support may be granted as part of such research projects upon application by a person seeking legal redress if, due to that person's personal and financial circumstances, the costs of a mediation process cannot or can only partially be paid, or can be paid only in instalments, by that person and the intended pur-

verfolgung oder Rechtsverteidigung nicht mutwillig erscheint. Über den Antrag entscheidet das für das Verfahren zuständige Gericht, sofern an diesem Gericht ein Forschungsvorhaben durchgeführt wird. Die Entscheidung ist unanfechtbar. Die Einzelheiten regeln die nach Absatz 1 zustande gekommenen Vereinbarungen zwischen Bund und Ländern.	suit of legal action or legal defence does not appear to be vexatious. The court having jurisdiction for the proceedings shall decide on the application, subject to the proviso that a research project is being conducted at this court. The decision shall be incontestable. The details shall be governed by the agreements made between the Federal Government and the Federal State Governments pursuant to subsection (1).
(3) Die Bundesregierung unterrichtet den Deutschen Bundestag nach Abschluss der wissenschaftlichen Forschungsvorhaben über die gesammelten Erfahrungen und die gewonnenen Erkenntnisse.	(3) Following completion of the academic research projects, the Federal Government shall inform the Federal Parliament (*Deutscher Bundestag*) of the experience gathered and the findings obtained.

§ 8
Evaluierung

§ 8
Evaluation

(1) Die Bundesregierung berichtet dem Deutschen Bundestag bis zum 26. Juli 2017, auch unter Berücksichtigung der kostenrechtlichen Länderöffnungsklauseln, über die Auswirkungen dieses Gesetzes auf die Entwicklung der Mediation in Deutschland und über die Situation der Aus- und Fortbildung der Mediatoren. In dem Bericht ist insbesondere zu untersuchen und zu bewerten, ob aus Gründen der Qualitätssicherung und des Verbraucherschutzes weitere gesetzgeberische Maßnahmen auf dem Gebiet der Aus- und Fortbildung von Mediatoren notwendig sind.	(1) The Federal Government shall report to the Federal Parliament by 26 July 2017, also taking into account the provisions for the Federal States under the law governing costs, on the effects which this Act has on the development of mediation in Germany and on the situation regarding initial and further training for mediators. In particular, the report shall examine and evaluate whether further legislative measures in the field of initial and further training for mediators are required for reasons of quality assurance and consumer protection.
(2) Sofern sich aus dem Bericht die Notwendigkeit gesetzgeberischer Maßnahmen ergibt, soll die Bundesregierung diese vorschlagen.	(2) If it becomes apparent from the report that legislative measures are required, the Federal Government shall propose such measures.

§ 9
Übergangsbestimmung

§ 9
Transitional provision

(1) Die Mediation in Zivilsachen durch einen nicht entscheidungsbefugten Richter während eines Gerichtsverfahrens, die vor dem 26. Juli 2012 an einem Gericht angeboten wird, kann unter Fortführung der bisher verwendeten Bezeichnung (gerichtlicher Mediator)	(1) Mediation in a civil matter conducted during court proceedings by a judge having no competence to decide on the matter concerned, which is offered at a court prior to 26 July 2012, may continue to be conducted until 1 August 2013 with the designation previously used (court mediator).

bis zum 1. August 2013 weiterhin durchgeführt werden.

(2) Absatz 1 gilt entsprechend für die Mediation in der Verwaltungsgerichtsbarkeit, der Sozialgerichtsbarkeit, der Finanzgerichtsbarkeit und der Arbeitsgerichtsbarkeit.

(2) Subsection (1) shall apply *mutatis mutandis* to mediation conducted within the courts of administrative jurisdiction, of social jurisdiction, of fiscal jurisdiction, and of labour jurisdiction.

B. EC Regulations

I. Regulation (EU) No 1215/2012 of the European Parliament and of the Council of 12 December 2012 on jurisdiction and the recognition and enforcement of judgments in civil and commercial matters (recast)

THE EUROPEAN PARLIAMENT AND THE COUNCIL OF THE EUROPEAN UNION,
Having regard to the Treaty on the Functioning of the European Union, and in particular Article 67(4) and points (a), (c) and (e) of Article 81(2) thereof,
Having regard to the proposal from the European Commission,
After transmission of the draft legislative act to the national parliaments,
Having regard to the opinion of the European Economic and Social Committee[1],
Acting in accordance with the ordinary legislative procedure[2],

Whereas:

(1) On 21 April 2009, the Commission adopted a report on the application of Council Regulation (EC) No 44/2001 of 22 December 2000 on jurisdiction and the recognition and enforcement of judgments in civil and commercial matters[3]. The report concluded that, in general, the operation of that Regulation is satisfactory, but that it is desirable to improve the application of certain of its provisions, to further facilitate the free circulation of judgments and to further enhance access to justice. Since a number of amendments are to be made to that Regulation it should, in the interests of clarity, be recast.

(2) At its meeting in Brussels on 10 and 11 December 2009, the European Council adopted a new multiannual programme entitled 'The Stockholm Programme – an open and secure Europe serving and protecting citizens'[4]. In the Stockholm Programme the European Council considered that the process of abolishing all intermediate measures (the exequatur) should be continued during the period covered by that Programme. At the same time the abolition of the exequatur should also be accompanied by a series of safeguards.

(3) The Union has set itself the objective of maintaining and developing an area of freedom, security and justice, *inter alia*, by facilitating access to justice, in particular through the principle of mutual recognition of judicial and extra-judicial decisions in civil matters. For the gradual establishment of such an area, the Union is to adopt measures relating to judicial cooperation in civil matters having cross-border implications, particularly when necessary for the proper functioning of the internal market.

(4) Certain differences between national rules governing jurisdiction and recognition of judgments hamper the sound operation of the internal market. Provi-

---

[1] OJ C 218, 23.7.2011, p. 78.
[2] Position of the European Parliament of 20 November 2012 (not yet published in the Official Journal) and decision of the Council of 6 December 2012.
[3] OJ L 12, 16.1.2001, p. 1.
[4] OJ C 115, 4.5.2010, p. 1.

sions to unify the rules of conflict of jurisdiction in civil and commercial matters, and to ensure rapid and simple recognition and enforcement of judgments given in a Member State, are essential.

(5) Such provisions fall within the area of judicial cooperation in civil matters within the meaning of Article 81 of the Treaty on the Functioning of the European Union (TFEU).

(6) In order to attain the objective of free circulation of judgments in civil and commercial matters, it is necessary and appropriate that the rules governing jurisdiction and the recognition and enforcement of judgments be governed by a legal instrument of the Union which is binding and directly applicable.

(7) On 27 September 1968, the then Member States of the European Communities, acting under Article 220, fourth indent, of the Treaty establishing the European Economic Community, concluded the Brussels Convention on Jurisdiction and the Enforcement of Judgments in Civil and Commercial Matters, subsequently amended by conventions on the accession to that Convention of new Member States[5] ('the 1968 Brussels Convention'). On 16 September 1988, the then Member States of the European Communities and certain EFTA States concluded the Lugano Convention on Jurisdiction and the Enforcement of Judgments in Civil and Commercial Matters[6] ('the 1988 Lugano Convention'), which is a parallel convention to the 1968 Brussels Convention. The 1988 Lugano Convention became applicable to Poland on 1 February 2000.

(8) On 22 December 2000, the Council adopted Regulation (EC) No 44/2001, which replaces the 1968 Brussels Convention with regard to the territories of the Member States covered by the TFEU, as between the Member States except Denmark. By Council Decision 2006/325/EC[7], the Community concluded an agreement with Denmark ensuring the application of the provisions of Regulation (EC) No 44/2001 in Denmark. The 1988 Lugano Convention was revised by the Convention on Jurisdiction and the Recognition and Enforcement of Judgments in Civil and Commercial Matters[8], signed at Lugano on 30 October 2007 by the Community, Denmark, Iceland, Norway and Switzerland ('the 2007 Lugano Convention').

(9) The 1968 Brussels Convention continues to apply to the territories of the Member States which fall within the territorial scope of that Convention and which are excluded from this Regulation pursuant to Article 355 of the TFEU.

(10) The scope of this Regulation should cover all the main civil and commercial matters apart from certain well-defined matters, in particular maintenance obligations, which should be excluded from the scope of this Regulation following the adoption of Council Regulation (EC) No 4/2009 of 18 December 2008 on jurisdiction, applicable law, recognition and enforcement of decisions and cooperation in matters relating to maintenance obligations[9].

(11) For the purposes of this Regulation, courts or tribunals of the Member States should include courts or tribunals common to several Member States, such as the Benelux Court of Justice when it exercises jurisdiction on matters falling

---

[5] OJ L 299, 31.12.1972, p. 32, OJ L 304, 30.10.1978, p. 1, OJ L 388, 31.12.1982, p. 1, OJ L 285, 3.10.1989, p. 1, OJ C 15, 15.1.1997, p. 1. For a consolidated text, see OJ C 27, 26.1.1998, p. 1.
[6] OJ L 319, 25.11.1988, p. 9.
[7] OJ L 120, 5.5.2006, p. 22.
[8] OJ L 147, 10.6.2009, p. 5.
[9] OJ L 7, 10.1.2009, p. 1.

within the scope of this Regulation. Therefore, judgments given by such courts should be recognised and enforced in accordance with this Regulation.

(12) This Regulation should not apply to arbitration. Nothing in this Regulation should prevent the courts of a Member State, when seised of an action in a matter in respect of which the parties have entered into an arbitration agreement, from referring the parties to arbitration, from staying or dismissing the proceedings, or from examining whether the arbitration agreement is null and void, inoperative or incapable of being performed, in accordance with their national law.

A ruling given by a court of a Member State as to whether or not an arbitration agreement is null and void, inoperative or incapable of being performed should not be subject to the rules of recognition and enforcement laid down in this Regulation, regardless of whether the court decided on this as a principal issue or as an incidental question.

On the other hand, where a court of a Member State, exercising jurisdiction under this Regulation or under national law, has determined that an arbitration agreement is null and void, inoperative or incapable of being performed, this should not preclude that court's judgment on the substance of the matter from being recognised or, as the case may be, enforced in accordance with this Regulation. This should be without prejudice to the competence of the courts of the Member States to decide on the recognition and enforcement of arbitral awards in accordance with the Convention on the Recognition and Enforcement of Foreign Arbitral Awards, done at New York on 10 June 1958 ('the 1958 New York Convention'), which takes precedence over this Regulation.

This Regulation should not apply to any action or ancillary proceedings relating to, in particular, the establishment of an arbitral tribunal, the powers of arbitrators, the conduct of an arbitration procedure or any other aspects of such a procedure, nor to any action or judgment concerning the annulment, review, appeal, recognition or enforcement of an arbitral award.

(13) There must be a connection between proceedings to which this Regulation applies and the territory of the Member States. Accordingly, common rules of jurisdiction should, in principle, apply when the defendant is domiciled in a Member State.

(14) A defendant not domiciled in a Member State should in general be subject to the national rules of jurisdiction applicable in the territory of the Member State of the court seised.

However, in order to ensure the protection of consumers and employees, to safeguard the jurisdiction of the courts of the Member States in situations where they have exclusive jurisdiction and to respect the autonomy of the parties, certain rules of jurisdiction in this Regulation should apply regardless of the defendant's domicile.

(15) The rules of jurisdiction should be highly predictable and founded on the principle that jurisdiction is generally based on the defendant's domicile. Jurisdiction should always be available on this ground save in a few well-defined situations in which the subject-matter of the dispute or the autonomy of the parties warrants a different connecting factor. The domicile of a legal person must be defined autonomously so as to make the common rules more transparent and avoid conflicts of jurisdiction.

(16) In addition to the defendant's domicile, there should be alternative grounds of jurisdiction based on a close connection between the court and the action or in order to facilitate the sound administration of justice. The existence of a close

connection should ensure legal certainty and avoid the possibility of the defendant being sued in a court of a Member State which he could not reasonably have foreseen. This is important, particularly in disputes concerning non-contractual obligations arising out of violations of privacy and rights relating to personality, including defamation.

(17) The owner of a cultural object as defined in Article 1(1) of Council Directive 93/7/EEC of 15 March 1993 on the return of cultural objects unlawfully removed from the territory of a Member State[10] should be able under this Regulation to initiate proceedings as regards a civil claim for the recovery, based on ownership, of such a cultural object in the courts for the place where the cultural object is situated at the time the court is seised. Such proceedings should be without prejudice to proceedings initiated under Directive 93/7/EEC.

(18) In relation to insurance, consumer and employment contracts, the weaker party should be protected by rules of jurisdiction more favourable to his interests than the general rules.

(19) The autonomy of the parties to a contract, other than an insurance, consumer or employment contract, where only limited autonomy to determine the courts having jurisdiction is allowed, should be respected subject to the exclusive grounds of jurisdiction laid down in this Regulation.

(20) Where a question arises as to whether a choice-of-court agreement in favour of a court or the courts of a Member State is null and void as to its substantive validity, that question should be decided in accordance with the law of the Member State of the court or courts designated in the agreement, including the conflict-of-laws rules of that Member State.

(21) In the interests of the harmonious administration of justice it is necessary to minimise the possibility of concurrent proceedings and to ensure that irreconcilable judgments will not be given in different Member States. There should be a clear and effective mechanism for resolving cases of *lis pendens* and related actions, and for obviating problems flowing from national differences as to the determination of the time when a case is regarded as pending. For the purposes of this Regulation, that time should be defined autonomously.

(22) However, in order to enhance the effectiveness of exclusive choice-of-court agreements and to avoid abusive litigation tactics, it is necessary to provide for an exception to the general *lis pendens* rule in order to deal satisfactorily with a particular situation in which concurrent proceedings may arise. This is the situation where a court not designated in an exclusive choice-of-court agreement has been seised of proceedings and the designated court is seised subsequently of proceedings involving the same cause of action and between the same parties. In such a case, the court first seised should be required to stay its proceedings as soon as the designated court has been seised and until such time as the latter court declares that it has no jurisdiction under the exclusive choice-of-court agreement. This is to ensure that, in such a situation, the designated court has priority to decide on the validity of the agreement and on the extent to which the agreement applies to the dispute pending before it. The designated court should be able to proceed irrespective of whether the non-designated court has already decided on the stay of proceedings.

This exception should not cover situations where the parties have entered into conflicting exclusive choice-of-court agreements or where a court designated in

---

[10] OJ L 74, 27.3.1993, p. 74.

an exclusive choice-of-court agreement has been seised first. In such cases, the general *lis pendens* rule of this Regulation should apply.

(23) This Regulation should provide for a flexible mechanism allowing the courts of the Member States to take into account proceedings pending before the courts of third States, considering in particular whether a judgment of a third State will be capable of recognition and enforcement in the Member State concerned under the law of that Member State and the proper administration of justice.

(24) When taking into account the proper administration of justice, the court of the Member State concerned should assess all the circumstances of the case before it. Such circumstances may include connections between the facts of the case and the parties and the third State concerned, the stage to which the proceedings in the third State have progressed by the time proceedings are initiated in the court of the Member State and whether or not the court of the third State can be expected to give a judgment within a reasonable time.

That assessment may also include consideration of the question whether the court of the third State has exclusive jurisdiction in the particular case in circumstances where a court of a Member State would have exclusive jurisdiction.

(25) The notion of provisional, including protective, measures should include, for example, protective orders aimed at obtaining information or preserving evidence as referred to in Articles 6 and 7 of Directive 2004/48/EC of the European Parliament and of the Council of 29 April 2004 on the enforcement of intellectual property rights[11]. It should not include measures which are not of a protective nature, such as measures ordering the hearing of a witness. This should be without prejudice to the application of Council Regulation (EC) No 1206/2001 of 28 May 2001 on cooperation between the courts of the Member States in the taking of evidence in civil or commercial matters[12].

(26) Mutual trust in the administration of justice in the Union justifies the principle that judgments given in a Member State should be recognised in all Member States without the need for any special procedure. In addition, the aim of making cross-border litigation less time-consuming and costly justifies the abolition of the declaration of enforceability prior to enforcement in the Member State addressed. As a result, a judgment given by the courts of a Member State should be treated as if it had been given in the Member State addressed.

(27) For the purposes of the free circulation of judgments, a judgment given in a Member State should be recognised and enforced in another Member State even if it is given against a person not domiciled in a Member State.

(28) Where a judgment contains a measure or order which is not known in the law of the Member State addressed, that measure or order, including any right indicated therein, should, to the extent possible, be adapted to one which, under the law of that Member State, has equivalent effects attached to it and pursues similar aims. How, and by whom, the adaptation is to be carried out should be determined by each Member State.

(29) The direct enforcement in the Member State addressed of a judgment given in another Member State without a declaration of enforceability should not jeopardise respect for the rights of the defence. Therefore, the person against whom enforcement is sought should be able to apply for refusal of the recognition or enforcement of a judgment if he considers one of the grounds for refusal of

---

[11] OJ L 157, 30.4.2004, p. 45.
[12] OJ L 174, 27.6.2001, p. 1.

recognition to be present. This should include the ground that he had not had the opportunity to arrange for his defence where the judgment was given in default of appearance in a civil action linked to criminal proceedings. It should also include the grounds which could be invoked on the basis of an agreement between the Member State addressed and a third State concluded pursuant to Article 59 of the 1968 Brussels Convention.

(30) A party challenging the enforcement of a judgment given in another Member State should, to the extent possible and in accordance with the legal system of the Member State addressed, be able to invoke, in the same procedure, in addition to the grounds for refusal provided for in this Regulation, the grounds for refusal available under national law and within the time-limits laid down in that law.

The recognition of a judgment should, however, be refused only if one or more of the grounds for refusal provided for in this Regulation are present.

(31) Pending a challenge to the enforcement of a judgment, it should be possible for the courts in the Member State addressed, during the entire proceedings relating to such a challenge, including any appeal, to allow the enforcement to proceed subject to a limitation of the enforcement or to the provision of security.

(32) In order to inform the person against whom enforcement is sought of the enforcement of a judgment given in another Member State, the certificate established under this Regulation, if necessary accompanied by the judgment, should be served on that person in reasonable time before the first enforcement measure. In this context, the first enforcement measure should mean the first enforcement measure after such service.

(33) Where provisional, including protective, measures are ordered by a court having jurisdiction as to the substance of the matter, their free circulation should be ensured under this Regulation. However, provisional, including protective, measures which were ordered by such a court without the defendant being summoned to appear should not be recognised and enforced under this Regulation unless the judgment containing the measure is served on the defendant prior to enforcement. This should not preclude the recognition and enforcement of such measures under national law. Where provisional, including protective, measures are ordered by a court of a Member State not having jurisdiction as to the substance of the matter, the effect of such measures should be confined, under this Regulation, to the territory of that Member State.

(34) Continuity between the 1968 Brussels Convention, Regulation (EC) No 44/2001 and this Regulation should be ensured, and transitional provisions should be laid down to that end. The same need for continuity applies as regards the interpretation by the Court of Justice of the European Union of the 1968 Brussels Convention and of the Regulations replacing it.

(35) Respect for international commitments entered into by the Member States means that this Regulation should not affect conventions relating to specific matters to which the Member States are parties.

(36) Without prejudice to the obligations of the Member States under the Treaties, this Regulation should not affect the application of bilateral conventions and agreements between a third State and a Member State concluded before the date of entry into force of Regulation (EC) No 44/2001 which concern matters governed by this Regulation.

(37) In order to ensure that the certificates to be used in connection with the recognition or enforcement of judgments, authentic instruments and court settlements under this Regulation are kept up-to-date, the power to adopt acts in

accordance with Article 290 of the TFEU should be delegated to the Commission in respect of amendments to Annexes I and II to this Regulation. It is of particular importance that the Commission carry out appropriate consultations during its preparatory work, including at expert level. The Commission, when preparing and drawing up delegated acts, should ensure a simultaneous, timely and appropriate transmission of relevant documents to the European Parliament and to the Council.

(38) This Regulation respects fundamental rights and observes the principles recognised in the Charter of Fundamental Rights of the European Union, in particular the right to an effective remedy and to a fair trial guaranteed in Article 47 of the Charter.

(39) Since the objective of this Regulation cannot be sufficiently achieved by the Member States and can be better achieved at Union level, the Union may adopt measures in accordance with the principle of subsidiarity as set out in Article 5 of the Treaty on European Union (TEU). In accordance with the principle of proportionality, as set out in that Article, this Regulation does not go beyond what is necessary in order to achieve that objective.

(40) The United Kingdom and Ireland, in accordance with Article 3 of the Protocol on the position of the United Kingdom and Ireland, annexed to the TEU and to the then Treaty establishing the European Community, took part in the adoption and application of Regulation (EC) No 44/2001. In accordance with Article 3 of Protocol No 21 on the position of the United Kingdom and Ireland in respect of the area of freedom, security and justice, annexed to the TEU and to the TFEU, the United Kingdom and Ireland have notified their wish to take part in the adoption and application of this Regulation.

(41) In accordance with Articles 1 and 2 of Protocol No 22 on the position of Denmark annexed to the TEU and to the TFEU, Denmark is not taking part in the adoption of this Regulation and is not bound by it or subject to its application, without prejudice to the possibility for Denmark of applying the amendments to Regulation (EC) No 44/2001 pursuant to Article 3 of the Agreement of 19 October 2005 between the European Community and the Kingdom of Denmark on jurisdiction and the recognition and enforcement of judgments in civil and commercial matters[13],

HAVE ADOPTED THIS REGULATION:

CHAPTER I
SCOPE AND DEFINITIONS

Article 1

1. This Regulation shall apply in civil and commercial matters whatever the nature of the court or tribunal. It shall not extend, in particular, to revenue, customs or administrative matters or to the liability of the State for acts and omissions in the exercise of State authority (acta iure imperii).

---

[13] OJ L 299, 16.11.2005, p. 62.

2. This Regulation shall not apply to:
(a) the status or legal capacity of natural persons, rights in property arising out of a matrimonial relationship or out of a relationship deemed by the law applicable to such relationship to have comparable effects to marriage;
(b) bankruptcy, proceedings relating to the winding-up of insolvent companies or other legal persons, judicial arrangements, compositions and analogous proceedings;
(c) social security;
(d) arbitration;
(e) maintenance obligations arising from a family relationship, parentage, marriage or affinity;
(f) wills and succession, including maintenance obligations arising by reason of death.

Article 2

For the purposes of this Regulation:
(a) 'judgment' means any judgment given by a court or tribunal of a Member State, whatever the judgment may be called, including a decree, order, decision or writ of execution, as well as a decision on the determination of costs or expenses by an officer of the court.
   For the purposes of Chapter III, 'judgment' includes provisional, including protective, measures ordered by a court or tribunal which by virtue of this Regulation has jurisdiction as to the substance of the matter. It does not include a provisional, including protective, measure which is ordered by such a court or tribunal without the defendant being summoned to appear, unless the judgment containing the measure is served on the defendant prior to enforcement;
(b) 'court settlement' means a settlement which has been approved by a court of a Member State or concluded before a court of a Member State in the course of proceedings;
(c) 'authentic instrument' means a document which has been formally drawn up or registered as an authentic instrument in the Member State of origin and the authenticity of which:
   (i) relates to the signature and the content of the instrument; and
   (ii) has been established by a public authority or other authority empowered for that purpose;
(d) 'Member State of origin' means the Member State in which, as the case may be, the judgment has been given, the court settlement has been approved or concluded, or the authentic instrument has been formally drawn up or registered;
(e) 'Member State addressed' means the Member State in which the recognition of the judgment is invoked or in which the enforcement of the judgment, the court settlement or the authentic instrument is sought;
(f) 'court of origin' means the court which has given the judgment the recognition of which is invoked or the enforcement of which is sought.

Article 3

For the purposes of this Regulation, 'court' includes the following authorities to the extent that they have jurisdiction in matters falling within the scope of this Regulation:
(a) in Hungary, in summary proceedings concerning orders to pay (fizetési meghagyásos eljárás), the notary (közjegyző);
(b) in Sweden, in summary proceedings concerning orders to pay (betalningsföreläggande) and assistance (handräckning), the Enforcement Authority (Kronofogdemyndigheten).

CHAPTER II
JURISDICTION

Section 1
General provisions

Article 4

1. Subject to this Regulation, persons domiciled in a Member State shall, whatever their nationality, be sued in the courts of that Member State.

2. Persons who are not nationals of the Member State in which they are domiciled shall be governed by the rules of jurisdiction applicable to nationals of that Member State.

Article 5

1. Persons domiciled in a Member State may be sued in the courts of another Member State only by virtue of the rules set out in Sections 2 to 7 of this Chapter.

2. In particular, the rules of national jurisdiction of which the Member States are to notify the Commission pursuant to point (a) of Article 76(1) shall not be applicable as against the persons referred to in paragraph 1.

Article 6

1. If the defendant is not domiciled in a Member State, the jurisdiction of the courts of each Member State shall, subject to Article 18(1), Article 21(2) and Articles 24 and 25, be determined by the law of that Member State.

2. As against such a defendant, any person domiciled in a Member State may, whatever his nationality, avail himself in that Member State of the rules of jurisdiction there in force, and in particular those of which the Member States are to notify the Commission pursuant to point (a) of Article 76(1), in the same way as nationals of that Member State.

Section 2
Special jurisdiction

Article 7

A person domiciled in a Member State may be sued in another Member State:
(1)

(a) in matters relating to a contract, in the courts for the place of performance of the obligation in question;
(b) for the purpose of this provision and unless otherwise agreed, the place of performance of the obligation in question shall be:
  – in the case of the sale of goods, the place in a Member State where, under the contract, the goods were delivered or should have been delivered,
  – in the case of the provision of services, the place in a Member State where, under the contract, the services were provided or should have been provided;
(c) if point (b) does not apply then point (a) applies;
(2) in matters relating to tort, delict or quasi-delict, in the courts for the place where the harmful event occurred or may occur;
(3) as regards a civil claim for damages or restitution which is based on an act giving rise to criminal proceedings, in the court seised of those proceedings, to the extent that that court has jurisdiction under its own law to entertain civil proceedings;
(4) as regards a civil claim for the recovery, based on ownership, of a cultural object as defined in point 1 of Article 1 of Directive 93/7/EEC initiated by the person claiming the right to recover such an object, in the courts for the place where the cultural object is situated at the time when the court is seised;
(5) as regards a dispute arising out of the operations of a branch, agency or other establishment, in the courts for the place where the branch, agency or other establishment is situated;
(6) as regards a dispute brought against a settlor, trustee or beneficiary of a trust created by the operation of a statute, or by a written instrument, or created orally and evidenced in writing, in the courts of the Member State in which the trust is domiciled;
(7) as regards a dispute concerning the payment of remuneration claimed in respect of the salvage of a cargo or freight, in the court under the authority of which the cargo or freight in question:
(a) has been arrested to secure such payment; or
(b) could have been so arrested, but bail or other security has been given;
provided that this provision shall apply only if it is claimed that the defendant has an interest in the cargo or freight or had such an interest at the time of salvage.

Article 8

A person domiciled in a Member State may also be sued:
(1) where he is one of a number of defendants, in the courts for the place where any one of them is domiciled, provided the claims are so closely connected that it is expedient to hear and determine them together to avoid the risk of irreconcilable judgments resulting from separate proceedings
(2) as a third party in an action on a warranty or guarantee or in any other third-party proceedings, in the court seised of the original proceedings, unless these were instituted solely with the object of removing him from the jurisdiction of the court which would be competent in his case;
(3) on a counter-claim arising from the same contract or facts on which the original claim was based, in the court in which the original claim is pending;

(4) in matters relating to a contract, if the action may be combined with an action against the same defendant in matters relating to rights in rem in immovable property, in the court of the Member State in which the property is situated.

Article 9

Where by virtue of this Regulation a court of a Member State has jurisdiction in actions relating to liability from the use or operation of a ship, that court, or any other court substituted for this purpose by the internal law of that Member State, shall also have jurisdiction over claims for limitation of such liability.

Section 3
Jurisdiction in matters relating to insurance

Article 10

In matters relating to insurance, jurisdiction shall be determined by this Section, without prejudice to Article 6 and point 5 of Article 7.

Article 11

1. An insurer domiciled in a Member State may be sued:
(a) in the courts of the Member State in which he is domiciled;
(b) in another Member State, in the case of actions brought by the policyholder, the insured or a beneficiary, in the courts for the place where the claimant is domiciled; or
(c) if he is a co-insurer, in the courts of a Member State in which proceedings are brought against the leading insurer.

2. An insurer who is not domiciled in a Member State but has a branch, agency or other establishment in one of the Member States shall, in disputes arising out of the operations of the branch, agency or establishment, be deemed to be domiciled in that Member State.

Article 12

In respect of liability insurance or insurance of immovable property, the insurer may in addition be sued in the courts for the place where the harmful event occurred. The same applies if movable and immovable property are covered by the same insurance policy and both are adversely affected by the same contingency.

Article 13

1. In respect of liability insurance, the insurer may also, if the law of the court permits it, be joined in proceedings which the injured party has brought against the insured.

2. Articles 10, 11 and 12 shall apply to actions brought by the injured party directly against the insurer, where such direct actions are permitted.

(3) If the law governing such direct actions provides that the policyholder or the insured may be joined as a party to the action, the same court shall have jurisdiction over them.

Article 14

1. Without prejudice to Article 13(3), an insurer may bring proceedings only in the courts of the Member State in which the defendant is domiciled, irrespective of whether he is the policyholder, the insured or a beneficiary.

2. The provisions of this Section shall not affect the right to bring a counter-claim in the court in which, in accordance with this Section, the original claim is pending.

Article 15

The provisions of this Section may be departed from only by an agreement:
(1) which is entered into after the dispute has arisen;
(2) which allows the policyholder, the insured or a beneficiary to bring proceedings in courts other than those indicated in this Section;
(3) which is concluded between a policyholder and an insurer, both of whom are at the time of conclusion of the contract domiciled or habitually resident in the same Member State, and which has the effect of conferring jurisdiction on the courts of that Member State even if the harmful event were to occur abroad, provided that such an agreement is not contrary to the law of that Member State;
(4) which is concluded with a policyholder who is not domiciled in a Member State, except in so far as the insurance is compulsory or relates to immovable property in a Member State; or
(5) which relates to a contract of insurance in so far as it covers one or more of the risks set out in Article 16.

Article 16

The following are the risks referred to in point 5 of Article 15:
(1) any loss of or damage to:
   (a) seagoing ships, installations situated offshore or on the high seas, or aircraft, arising from perils which relate to their use for commercial purposes;
   (b) goods in transit other than passengers' baggage where the transit consists of or includes carriage by such ships or aircraft;
(2) any liability, other than for bodily injury to passengers or loss of or damage to their baggage:
   (a) arising out of the use or operation of ships, installations or aircraft as referred to in point 1(a) in so far as, in respect of the latter, the law of the Member State in which such aircraft are registered does not prohibit agreements on jurisdiction regarding insurance of such risks;
   (b) for loss or damage caused by goods in transit as described in point 1(b);
(3) any financial loss connected with the use or operation of ships, installations or aircraft as referred to in point 1(a), in particular loss of freight or charter-hire;
(4) any risk or interest connected with any of those referred to in points 1 to 3;
(5) notwithstanding points 1 to 4, all 'large risks' as defined in Directive 2009/138/EC of the European Parliament and of the Council of 25 November 2009 on the taking-up and pursuit of the business of Insurance and Reinsurance (Solvency II)[14].

---

[14] OJ L 335, 17.12.2009, p. 1.

Section 4
Jurisdiction over consumer contracts

Article 17

1. In matters relating to a contract concluded by a person, the consumer, for a purpose which can be regarded as being outside his trade or profession, jurisdiction shall be determined by this Section, without prejudice to Article 6 and point 5 of Article 7, if:
(a) it is a contract for the sale of goods on instalment credit terms;
(b) it is a contract for a loan repayable by instalments, or for any other form of credit, made to finance the sale of goods; or
(c) in all other cases, the contract has been concluded with a person who pursues commercial or professional activities in the Member State of the consumer's domicile or, by any means, directs such activities to that Member State or to several States including that Member State, and the contract falls within the scope of such activities.

2. Where a consumer enters into a contract with a party who is not domiciled in a Member State but has a branch, agency or other establishment in one of the Member States, that party shall, in disputes arising out of the operations of the branch, agency or establishment, be deemed to be domiciled in that Member State.

3. This Section shall not apply to a contract of transport other than a contract which, for an inclusive price, provides for a combination of travel and accommodation.

Article 18

1. A consumer may bring proceedings against the other party to a contract either in the courts of the Member State in which that party is domiciled or, regardless of the domicile of the other party, in the courts for the place where the consumer is domiciled.

2. Proceedings may be brought against a consumer by the other party to the contract only in the courts of the Member State in which the consumer is domiciled.

3. This Article shall not affect the right to bring a counter-claim in the court in which, in accordance with this Section, the original claim is pending.

Article 19

The provisions of this Section may be departed from only by an agreement:
(1) which is entered into after the dispute has arisen;
(2) which allows the consumer to bring proceedings in courts other than those indicated in this Section; or
(3) which is entered into by the consumer and the other party to the contract, both of whom are at the time of conclusion of the contract domiciled or habitually resident in the same Member State, and which confers jurisdiction on the courts of that Member State, provided that such an agreement is not contrary to the law of that Member State.

Section 5
Jurisdiction over individual contracts of employment

Article 20

1. In matters relating to individual contracts of employment, jurisdiction shall be determined by this Section, without prejudice to Article 6, point 5 of Article 7 and, in the case of proceedings brought against an employer, point 1 of Article 8.

2. Where an employee enters into an individual contract of employment with an employer who is not domiciled in a Member State but has a branch, agency or other establishment in one of the Member States, the employer shall, in disputes arising out of the operations of the branch, agency or establishment, be deemed to be domiciled in that Member State.

Article 21

1. An employer domiciled in a Member State may be sued:
(a) in the courts of the Member State in which he is domiciled; or
(b) in another Member State:
    (i) in the courts for the place where or from where the employee habitually carries out his work or in the courts for the last place where he did so; or
    (ii) if the employee does not or did not habitually carry out his work in any one country, in the courts for the place where the business which engaged the employee is or was situated.

2. An employer not domiciled in a Member State may be sued in a court of a Member State in accordance with point (b) of paragraph 1.

Article 22

1. An employer may bring proceedings only in the courts of the Member State in which the employee is domiciled.

2. The provisions of this Section shall not affect the right to bring a counter-claim in the court in which, in accordance with this Section, the original claim is pending.

Article 23

The provisions of this Section may be departed from only by an agreement:
(1) which is entered into after the dispute has arisen; or
(2) which allows the employee to bring proceedings in courts other than those indicated in this Section.

Section 6
Exclusive jurisdiction

Article 24

The following courts of a Member State shall have exclusive jurisdiction, regardless of the domicile of the parties:
(1) in proceedings which have as their object rights in rem in immovable property or tenancies of immovable property, the courts of the Member State in which the property is situated.

However, in proceedings which have as their object tenancies of immovable property concluded for temporary private use for a maximum period of six consecutive months, the courts of the Member State in which the defendant is domiciled shall also have jurisdiction, provided that the tenant is a natural person and that the landlord and the tenant are domiciled in the same Member State;

(2) in proceedings which have as their object the validity of the constitution, the nullity or the dissolution of companies or other legal persons or associations of natural or legal persons, or the validity of the decisions of their organs, the courts of the Member State in which the company, legal person or association has its seat. In order to determine that seat, the court shall apply its rules of private international law;

(3) in proceedings which have as their object the validity of entries in public registers, the courts of the Member State in which the register is kept;

(4) in proceedings concerned with the registration or validity of patents, trade marks, designs, or other similar rights required to be deposited or registered, irrespective of whether the issue is raised by way of an action or as a defence, the courts of the Member State in which the deposit or registration has been applied for, has taken place or is under the terms of an instrument of the Union or an international convention deemed to have taken place.

Without prejudice to the jurisdiction of the European Patent Office under the Convention on the Grant of European Patents, signed at Munich on 5 October 1973, the courts of each Member State shall have exclusive jurisdiction in proceedings concerned with the registration or validity of any European patent granted for that Member State;

(5) in proceedings concerned with the enforcement of judgments, the courts of the Member State in which the judgment has been or is to be enforced.

Section 7
Prorogation of jurisdiction

Article 25

1. If the parties, regardless of their domicile, have agreed that a court or the courts of a Member State are to have jurisdiction to settle any disputes which have arisen or which may arise in connection with a particular legal relationship, that court or those courts shall have jurisdiction, unless the agreement is null and void as to its substantive validity under the law of that Member State. Such jurisdiction shall be exclusive unless the parties have agreed otherwise. The agreement conferring jurisdiction shall be either:

(a) in writing or evidenced in writing;
(b) in a form which accords with practices which the parties have established between themselves; or
(c) in international trade or commerce, in a form which accords with a usage of which the parties are or ought to have been aware and which in such trade or commerce is widely known to, and regularly observed by, parties to contracts of the type involved in the particular trade or commerce concerned.

2. Any communication by electronic means which provides a durable record of the agreement shall be equivalent to 'writing'.

3. The court or courts of a Member State on which a trust instrument has conferred jurisdiction shall have exclusive jurisdiction in any proceedings brought against a settlor, trustee or beneficiary, if relations between those persons or their rights or obligations under the trust are involved.

4. Agreements or provisions of a trust instrument conferring jurisdiction shall have no legal force if they are contrary to Articles 15, 19 or 23, or if the courts whose jurisdiction they purport to exclude have exclusive jurisdiction by virtue of Article 24.

5. An agreement conferring jurisdiction which forms part of a contract shall be treated as an agreement independent of the other terms of the contract.

The validity of the agreement conferring jurisdiction cannot be contested solely on the ground that the contract is not valid.

Article 26

1. Apart from jurisdiction derived from other provisions of this Regulation, a court of a Member State before which a defendant enters an appearance shall have jurisdiction. This rule shall not apply where appearance was entered to contest the jurisdiction, or where another court has exclusive jurisdiction by virtue of Article 24.

2. In matters referred to in Sections 3, 4 or 5 where the policyholder, the insured, a beneficiary of the insurance contract, the injured party, the consumer or the employee is the defendant, the court shall, before assuming jurisdiction under paragraph 1, ensure that the defendant is informed of his right to contest the jurisdiction of the court and of the consequences of entering or not entering an appearance.

Section 8
Examination as to jurisdiction and admissibility

Article 27

Where a court of a Member State is seised of a claim which is principally concerned with a matter over which the courts of another Member State have exclusive jurisdiction by virtue of Article 24, it shall declare of its own motion that it has no jurisdiction.

Article 28

1. Where a defendant domiciled in one Member State is sued in a court of another Member State and does not enter an appearance, the court shall declare of its own motion that it has no jurisdiction unless its jurisdiction is derived from the provisions of this Regulation.

2. The court shall stay the proceedings so long as it is not shown that the defendant has been able to receive the document instituting the proceedings or an equivalent document in sufficient time to enable him to arrange for his defence, or that all necessary steps have been taken to this end.

3. Article 19 of Regulation (EC) No 1393/2007 of the European Parliament and of the Council of 13 November 2007 on the service in the Member States of judicial and extrajudicial documents in civil or commercial matters (service of

documents)[15] shall apply instead of paragraph 2 of this Article if the document instituting the proceedings or an equivalent document had to be transmitted from one Member State to another pursuant to that Regulation.

4. Where Regulation (EC) No 1393/2007 is not applicable, Article 15 of the Hague Convention of 15 November 1965 on the Service Abroad of Judicial and Extrajudicial Documents in Civil or Commercial Matters shall apply if the document instituting the proceedings or an equivalent document had to be transmitted abroad pursuant to that Convention.

Section 9
Lis pendens — related actions

Article 29

1. Without prejudice to Article 31(2), where proceedings involving the same cause of action and between the same parties are brought in the courts of different Member States, any court other than the court first seised shall of its own motion stay its proceedings until such time as the jurisdiction of the court first seised is established.

2. In cases referred to in paragraph 1, upon request by a court seised of the dispute, any other court seised shall without delay inform the former court of the date when it was seised in accordance with Article 32.

3. Where the jurisdiction of the court first seised is established, any court other than the court first seised shall decline jurisdiction in favour of that court.

Article 30

1. Where related actions are pending in the courts of different Member States, any court other than the court first seised may stay its proceedings.

2. Where the action in the court first seised is pending at first instance, any other court may also, on the application of one of the parties, decline jurisdiction if the court first seised has jurisdiction over the actions in question and its law permits the consolidation thereof.

3. For the purposes of this Article, actions are deemed to be related where they are so closely connected that it is expedient to hear and determine them together to avoid the risk of irreconcilable judgments resulting from separate proceedings.

Article 31

1. Where actions come within the exclusive jurisdiction of several courts, any court other than the court first seised shall decline jurisdiction in favour of that court.

2. Without prejudice to Article 26, where a court of a Member State on which an agreement as referred to in Article 25 confers exclusive jurisdiction is seised, any court of another Member State shall stay the proceedings until such time as the court seised on the basis of the agreement declares that it has no jurisdiction under the agreement.

---

[15] OJ L 324, 10.12.2007, p. 79.

3. Where the court designated in the agreement has established jurisdiction in accordance with the agreement, any court of another Member State shall decline jurisdiction in favour of that court.

4. Paragraphs 2 and 3 shall not apply to matters referred to in Sections 3, 4 or 5 where the policyholder, the insured, a beneficiary of the insurance contract, the injured party, the consumer or the employee is the claimant and the agreement is not valid under a provision contained within those Sections.

Article 32

1. For the purposes of this Section, a court shall be deemed to be seised:
(a) at the time when the document instituting the proceedings or an equivalent document is lodged with the court, provided that the claimant has not subsequently failed to take the steps he was required to take to have service effected on the defendant; or
(b) if the document has to be served before being lodged with the court, at the time when it is received by the authority responsible for service, provided that the claimant has not subsequently failed to take the steps he was required to take to have the document lodged with the court.

The authority responsible for service referred to in point (b) shall be the first authority receiving the documents to be served.

2. The court, or the authority responsible for service, referred to in paragraph 1, shall note, respectively, the date of the lodging of the document instituting the proceedings or the equivalent document, or the date of receipt of the documents to be served.

Article 33

1. Where jurisdiction is based on Article 4 or on Articles 7, 8 or 9 and proceedings are pending before a court of a third State at the time when a court in a Member State is seised of an action involving the same cause of action and between the same parties as the proceedings in the court of the third State, the court of the Member State may stay the proceedings if:
(a) it is expected that the court of the third State will give a judgment capable of recognition and, where applicable, of enforcement in that Member State; and
(b) the court of the Member State is satisfied that a stay is necessary for the proper administration of justice.

2. The court of the Member State may continue the proceedings at any time if:
(a) the proceedings in the court of the third State are themselves stayed or discontinued;
(b) it appears to the court of the Member State that the proceedings in the court of the third State are unlikely to be concluded within a reasonable time; or
(c) the continuation of the proceedings is required for the proper administration of justice.

3. The court of the Member State shall dismiss the proceedings if the proceedings in the court of the third State are concluded and have resulted in a judgment capable of recognition and, where applicable, of enforcement in that Member State.

4. The court of the Member State shall apply this Article on the application of one of the parties or, where possible under national law, of its own motion.

Article 34

1. Where jurisdiction is based on Article 4 or on Articles 7, 8 or 9 and an action is pending before a court of a third State at the time when a court in a Member State is seised of an action which is related to the action in the court of the third State, the court of the Member State may stay the proceedings if:
(a) it is expedient to hear and determine the related actions together to avoid the risk of irreconcilable judgments resulting from separate proceedings;
(b) it is expected that the court of the third State will give a judgment capable of recognition and, where applicable, of enforcement in that Member State; and
(c) the court of the Member State is satisfied that a stay is necessary for the proper administration of justice.

2. The court of the Member State may continue the proceedings at any time if:
(a) it appears to the court of the Member State that there is no longer a risk of irreconcilable judgments;
(b) the proceedings in the court of the third State are themselves stayed or discontinued;
(c) it appears to the court of the Member State that the proceedings in the court of the third State are unlikely to be concluded within a reasonable time; or
(d) the continuation of the proceedings is required for the proper administration of justice.

3. The court of the Member State may dismiss the proceedings if the proceedings in the court of the third State are concluded and have resulted in a judgment capable of recognition and, where applicable, of enforcement in that Member State.

4. The court of the Member State shall apply this Article on the application of one of the parties or, where possible under national law, of its own motion.

Section 10
Provisional, including protective, measures

Article 35

Application may be made to the courts of a Member State for such provisional, including protective, measures as may be available under the law of that Member State, even if the courts of another Member State have jurisdiction as to the substance of the matter.

CHAPTER III
RECOGNITION AND ENFORCEMENT

Section 1
Recognition

Article 36

1. A judgment given in a Member State shall be recognised in the other Member States without any special procedure being required.

2. Any interested party may, in accordance with the procedure provided for in Subsection 2 of Section 3, apply for a decision that there are no grounds for refusal of recognition as referred to in Article 45.

3. If the outcome of proceedings in a court of a Member State depends on the determination of an incidental question of refusal of recognition, that court shall have jurisdiction over that question.

Article 37

1. A party who wishes to invoke in a Member State a judgment given in another Member State shall produce:
(a) a copy of the judgment which satisfies the conditions necessary to establish its authenticity; and
(b) the certificate issued pursuant to Article 53.

2. The court or authority before which a judgment given in another Member State is invoked may, where necessary, require the party invoking it to provide, in accordance with Article 57, a translation or a transliteration of the contents of the certificate referred to in point (b) of paragraph 1. The court or authority may require the party to provide a translation of the judgment instead of a translation of the contents of the certificate if it is unable to proceed without such a translation.

Article 38

The court or authority before which a judgment given in another Member State is invoked may suspend the proceedings, in whole or in part, if:
(a) the judgment is challenged in the Member State of origin; or
(b) an application has been submitted for a decision that there are no grounds for refusal of recognition as referred to in Article 45 or for a decision that the recognition is to be refused on the basis of one of those grounds.

Section 2
Enforcement

Article 39

A judgment given in a Member State which is enforceable in that Member State shall be enforceable in the other Member States without any declaration of enforceability being required.

Article 40

An enforceable judgment shall carry with it by operation of law the power to proceed to any protective measures which exist under the law of the Member State addressed.

Article 41

1. Subject to the provisions of this Section, the procedure for the enforcement of judgments given in another Member State shall be governed by the law of the Member State addressed. A judgment given in a Member State which is enforceable in the Member State addressed shall be enforced there under the same conditions as a judgment given in the Member State addressed.

2. Notwithstanding paragraph 1, the grounds for refusal or of suspension of enforcement under the law of the Member State addressed shall apply in so far as they are not incompatible with the grounds referred to in Article 45.

3. The party seeking the enforcement of a judgment given in another Member State shall not be required to have a postal address in the Member State addressed. Nor shall that party be required to have an authorised representative in the Member State addressed unless such a representative is mandatory irrespective of the nationality or the domicile of the parties.

Article 42

1. For the purposes of enforcement in a Member State of a judgment given in another Member State, the applicant shall provide the competent enforcement authority with:
(a) a copy of the judgment which satisfies the conditions necessary to establish its authenticity; and
(b) the certificate issued pursuant to Article 53, certifying that the judgment is enforceable and containing an extract of the judgment as well as, where appropriate, relevant information on the recoverable costs of the proceedings and the calculation of interest.

2. For the purposes of enforcement in a Member State of a judgment given in another Member State ordering a provisional, including a protective, measure, the applicant shall provide the competent enforcement authority with:
(a) a copy of the judgment which satisfies the conditions necessary to establish its authenticity;
(b) the certificate issued pursuant to Article 53, containing a description of the measure and certifying that:
   (i) the court has jurisdiction as to the substance of the matter;
   (ii) the judgment is enforceable in the Member State of origin; and
(c) where the measure was ordered without the defendant being summoned to appear, proof of service of the judgment.

3. The competent enforcement authority may, where necessary, require the applicant to provide, in accordance with Article 57, a translation or a transliteration of the contents of the certificate.

4. The competent enforcement authority may require the applicant to provide a translation of the judgment only if it is unable to proceed without such a translation.

Article 43

1. Where enforcement is sought of a judgment given in another Member State, the certificate issued pursuant to Article 53 shall be served on the person against whom the enforcement is sought prior to the first enforcement measure. The certificate shall be accompanied by the judgment, if not already served on that person.

2. Where the person against whom enforcement is sought is domiciled in a Member State other than the Member State of origin, he may request a translation of the judgment in order to contest the enforcement if the judgment is not written in or accompanied by a translation into either of the following languages:
(a) a language which he understands; or
(b) the official language of the Member State in which he is domiciled or, where there are several official languages in that Member State, the official language or one of the official languages of the place where he is domiciled.

Where a translation of the judgment is requested under the first subparagraph, no measures of enforcement may be taken other than protective measures until that translation has been provided to the person against whom enforcement is sought.

This paragraph shall not apply if the judgment has already been served on the person against whom enforcement is sought in one of the languages referred to in the first subparagraph or is accompanied by a translation into one of those languages.

3. This Article shall not apply to the enforcement of a protective measure in a judgment or where the person seeking enforcement proceeds to protective measures in accordance with Article 40.

Article 44

1. In the event of an application for refusal of enforcement of a judgment pursuant to Subsection 2 of Section 3, the court in the Member State addressed may, on the application of the person against whom enforcement is sought:
(a) limit the enforcement proceedings to protective measures;
(b) make enforcement conditional on the provision of such security as it shall determine; or
(c) suspend, either wholly or in part, the enforcement proceedings.

2. The competent authority in the Member State addressed shall, on the application of the person against whom enforcement is sought, suspend the enforcement proceedings where the enforceability of the judgment is suspended in the Member State of origin.

Section 3
Refusal of recognition and enforcement

Subsection 1
Refusal of recognition

Article 45

1. On the application of any interested party, the recognition of a judgment shall be refused:
(a) if such recognition is manifestly contrary to public policy (ordre public) in the Member State addressed;
(b) where the judgment was given in default of appearance, if the defendant was not served with the document which instituted the proceedings or with an equivalent document in sufficient time and in such a way as to enable him to arrange for his defence, unless the defendant failed to commence proceedings to challenge the judgment when it was possible for him to do so;
(c) if the judgment is irreconcilable with a judgment given between the same parties in the Member State addressed;
(d) if the judgment is irreconcilable with an earlier judgment given in another Member State or in a third State involving the same cause of action and between the same parties, provided that the earlier judgment fulfils the conditions necessary for its recognition in the Member State addressed; or
(e) if the judgment conflicts with:

(i) Sections 3, 4 or 5 of Chapter II where the policyholder, the insured, a beneficiary of the insurance contract, the injured party, the consumer or the employee was the defendant; or

(ii) Section 6 of Chapter II.

2. In its examination of the grounds of jurisdiction referred to in point (e) of paragraph 1, the court to which the application was submitted shall be bound by the findings of fact on which the court of origin based its jurisdiction.

3. Without prejudice to point (e) of paragraph 1, the jurisdiction of the court of origin may not be reviewed. The test of public policy referred to in point (a) of paragraph 1 may not be applied to the rules relating to jurisdiction.

4. The application for refusal of recognition shall be made in accordance with the procedures provided for in Subsection 2 and, where appropriate, Section 4.

Subsection. 2
Refusal of enforcement

Article 46

On the application of the person against whom enforcement is sought, the enforcement of a judgment shall be refused where one of the grounds referred to in Article 45 is found to exist.

Article 47

1. The application for refusal of enforcement shall be submitted to the court which the Member State concerned has communicated to the Commission pursuant to point (a) of Article 75 as the court to which the application is to be submitted.

2. The procedure for refusal of enforcement shall, in so far as it is not covered by this Regulation, be governed by the law of the Member State addressed.

3. The applicant shall provide the court with a copy of the judgment and, where necessary, a translation or transliteration of it.

The court may dispense with the production of the documents referred to in the first subparagraph if it already possesses them or if it considers it unreasonable to require the applicant to provide them. In the latter case, the court may require the other party to provide those documents.

4. The party seeking the refusal of enforcement of a judgment given in another Member State shall not be required to have a postal address in the Member State addressed. Nor shall that party be required to have an authorised representative in the Member State addressed unless such a representative is mandatory irrespective of the nationality or the domicile of the parties.

Article 48

The court shall decide on the application for refusal of enforcement without delay.

Article 49

1. The decision on the application for refusal of enforcement may be appealed against by either party.

2. The appeal is to be lodged with the court which the Member State concerned has communicated to the Commission pursuant to point (b) of Article 75 as the court with which such an appeal is to be lodged.

Article 50

The decision given on the appeal may only be contested by an appeal where the courts with which any further appeal is to be lodged have been communicated by the Member State concerned to the Commission pursuant to point (c) of Article 75.

Article 51

1. The court to which an application for refusal of enforcement is submitted or the court which hears an appeal lodged under Article 49 or Article 50 may stay the proceedings if an ordinary appeal has been lodged against the judgment in the Member State of origin or if the time for such an appeal has not yet expired. In the latter case, the court may specify the time within which such an appeal is to be lodged.

2. Where the judgment was given in Ireland, Cyprus or the United Kingdom, any form of appeal available in the Member State of origin shall be treated as an ordinary appeal for the purposes of paragraph 1.

Section 4
Common provisions

Article 52

Under no circumstances may a judgment given in a Member State be reviewed as to its substance in the Member State addressed.

Article 53

The court of origin shall, at the request of any interested party, issue the certificate using the form set out in Annex I.

Article 54

1. If a judgment contains a measure or an order which is not known in the law of the Member State addressed, that measure or order shall, to the extent possible, be adapted to a measure or an order known in the law of that Member State which has equivalent effects attached to it and which pursues similar aims and interests.

Such adaptation shall not result in effects going beyond those provided for in the law of the Member State of origin.

2. Any party may challenge the adaptation of the measure or order before a court.

3. If necessary, the party invoking the judgment or seeking its enforcement may be required to provide a translation or a transliteration of the judgment.

Article 55

A judgment given in a Member State which orders a payment by way of a penalty shall be enforceable in the Member State addressed only if the amount of the payment has been finally determined by the court of origin.

Article 56

No security, bond or deposit, however described, shall be required of a party who in one Member State applies for the enforcement of a judgment given in another Member State on the ground that he is a foreign national or that he is not domiciled or resident in the Member State addressed.

Article 57

1. When a translation or a transliteration is required under this Regulation, such translation or transliteration shall be into the official language of the Member State concerned or, where there are several official languages in that Member State, into the official language or one of the official languages of court proceedings of the place where a judgment given in another Member State is invoked or an application is made, in accordance with the law of that Member State.

2. For the purposes of the forms referred to in Articles 53 and 60, translations or transliterations may also be into any other official language or languages of the institutions of the Union that the Member State concerned has indicated it can accept.

3. Any translation made under this Regulation shall be done by a person qualified to do translations in one of the Member States.

CHAPTER IV
AUTHENTIC INSTRUMENTS AND COURT SETTLEMENTS

Article 58

1. An authentic instrument which is enforceable in the Member State of origin shall be enforceable in the other Member States without any declaration of enforceability being required. Enforcement of the authentic instrument may be refused only if such enforcement is manifestly contrary to public policy (ordre public) in the Member State addressed.

The provisions of Section 2, Subsection 2 of Section 3, and Section 4 of Chapter III shall apply as appropriate to authentic instruments.

2. The authentic instrument produced must satisfy the conditions necessary to establish its authenticity in the Member State of origin.

Article 59

A court settlement which is enforceable in the Member State of origin shall be enforced in the other Member States under the same conditions as authentic instruments.

Article 60

The competent authority or court of the Member State of origin shall, at the request of any interested party, issue the certificate using the form set out in Annex II containing a summary of the enforceable obligation recorded in the authentic instrument or of the agreement between the parties recorded in the court settlement.

CHAPTER V
GENERAL PROVISIONS

Article 61

No legalisation or other similar formality shall be required for documents issued in a Member State in the context of this Regulation.

Article 62

1. In order to determine whether a party is domiciled in the Member State whose courts are seised of a matter, the court shall apply its internal law.

2. If a party is not domiciled in the Member State whose courts are seised of the matter, then, in order to determine whether the party is domiciled in another Member State, the court shall apply the law of that Member State.

Article 63

1. For the purposes of this Regulation, a company or other legal person or association of natural or legal persons is domiciled at the place where it has its:
(a) statutory seat;
(b) central administration; or
(c) principal place of business.

2. For the purposes of Ireland, Cyprus and the United Kingdom, 'statutory seat' means the registered office or, where there is no such office anywhere, the place of incorporation or, where there is no such place anywhere, the place under the law of which the formation took place.

3. In order to determine whether a trust is domiciled in the Member State whose courts are seised of the matter, the court shall apply its rules of private international law.

Article 64

Without prejudice to any more favourable provisions of national laws, persons domiciled in a Member State who are being prosecuted in the criminal courts of another Mernber State of which they are not nationals for an offence which was not intentionally committed may be defended by persons qualified to do so, even if they do not appear in person. However, the court seised of the matter may order appearance in person; in the case of failure to appear, a judgment given in the civil action without the person concerned having had the opportunity to arrange for his defence need not be recognised or enforced in the other Member States.

Article 65

1. The jurisdiction specified in point 2 of Article 8 and Article 13 in actions on a warranty or guarantee or in any other third-party proceedings may be resorted to in the Member States included in the list established by the Commission pursuant to point (b) of Article 76(1) and Article 76(2) only in so far as permitted under national law. A person domiciled in another Member State may be invited to join the proceedings before the courts of those Member States pursuant to the rules on third-party notice referred to in that list.

2. Judgments given in a Member State by virtue of point 2 of Article 8 or Article 13 shall be recognised and enforced in accordance with Chapter III in any other Member State. Any effects which judgments given in the Member States included in the list referred to in paragraph 1 may have, in accordance with the law of those Member States, on third parties by application of paragraph 1 shall be recognised in all Member States.

3. The Member States included in the list referred to in paragraph 1 shall, within the framework of the European Judicial Network in civil and commercial matters established by Council Decision 2001/470/EC[16] ('the European Judicial Network') provide information on how to determine, in accordance with their national law, the effects of the judgments referred to in the second sentence of paragraph 2.

CHAPTER VI
TRANSITIONAL PROVISIONS

Article 66

1. This Regulation shall apply only to legal proceedings instituted, to authentic instruments formally drawn up or registered and to court settlements approved or concluded on or after 10 January 2015.

2. Notwithstanding Article 80, Regulation (EC) No 44/2001 shall continue to apply to judgments given in legal proceedings instituted, to authentic instruments formally drawn up or registered and to court settlements approved or concluded before 10 January 2015 which fall within the scope of that Regulation.

CHAPTER VII
RELATIONSHIP WITH OTHER INSTRUMENTS

Article 67

This Regulation shall not prejudice the application of provisions governing jurisdiction and the recognition and enforcement of judgments in specific matters which are contained in instruments of the Union or in national legislation harmonised pursuant to such instruments.

Article 68

1. This Regulation shall, as between the Member States, supersede the 1968 Brussels Convention, except as regards the territories of the Member States which

---

[16] OJ L 174, 27.6.2001, p. 25.

fall within the territorial scope of that Convention and which are excluded from this Regulation pursuant to Article 355 of the TFEU.

2. In so far as this Regulation replaces the provisions of the 1968 Brussels Convention between the Member States, any reference to that Convention shall be understood as a reference to this Regulation.

Article 69

Subject to Articles 70 and 71, this Regulation shall, as between the Member States, supersede the conventions that cover the same matters as those to which this Regulation applies. In particular, the conventions included in the list established by the Commission pursuant to point (c) of Article 76(1) and Article 76(2) shall be superseded.

Article 70

1. The conventions referred to in Article 69 shall continue to have effect in relation to matters to which this Regulation does not apply.

2. They shall continue to have effect in respect of judgments given, authentic instruments formally drawn up or registered and court settlements approved or concluded before the date of entry into force of Regulation (EC) No 44/2001.

Article 71

1. This Regulation shall not affect any conventions to which the Member States are parties and which, in relation to particular matters, govern jurisdiction or the recognition or enforcement of judgments.

2. With a view to its uniform interpretation, paragraph 1 shall be applied in the following manner:
(a) this Regulation shall not prevent a court of a Member State which is party to a convention on a particular matter from assuming jurisdiction in accordance with that convention, even where the defendant is domiciled in another Member State which is not party to that convention. The court hearing the action shall, in any event, apply Article 28 of this Regulation;
(b) judgments given in a Member State by a court in the exercise of jurisdiction provided for in a convention on a particular matter shall be recognised and enforced in the other Member States in accordance with this Regulation.

Where a convention on a particular matter to which both the Member State of origin and the Member State addressed are parties lays down conditions for the recognition or enforcement of judgments, those conditions shall apply. In any event, the provisions of this Regulation on recognition and enforcement of judgments may be applied.

Article 72

This Regulation shall not affect agreements by which Member States, prior to the entry into force of Regulation (EC) No 44/2001, undertook pursuant to Article 59 of the 1968 Brussels Convention not to recognise judgments given, in particular in other Contracting States to that Convention, against defendants domiciled or habitually resident in a third State where, in cases provided for in Article 4 of that Convention, the judgment could only be founded on a ground of jurisdiction specified in the second paragraph of Article 3 of that Convention.

Article 73

1. This Regulation shall not affect the application of the 2007 Lugano Convention.

2. This Regulation shall not affect the application of the 1958 New York Convention.

3. This Regulation shall not affect the application of bilateral conventions and agreements between a third State and a Member State concluded before the date of entry into force of Regulation (EC) No 44/2001 which concern matters governed by this Regulation.

CHAPTER VIII
FINAL PROVISIONS

Article 74

The Member States shall provide, within the framework of the European Judicial Network and with a view to making the information available to the public, a description of national rules and procedures concerning enforcement, including authorities competent for enforcement, and information on any limitations on enforcement, in particular debtor protection rules and limitation or prescription periods.

The Member States shall keep this information permanently updated.

Article 75

By 10 January 2014, the Member States shall communicate to the Commission:
(a) the courts to which the application for refusal of enforcement is to be submitted pursuant to Article 47(1);
(b) the courts with which an appeal against the decision on the application for refusal of enforcement is to be lodged pursuant to Article 49(2);
(c) the courts with which any further appeal is to be lodged pursuant to Article 50; and
(d) the languages accepted for translations of the forms as referred to in Article 57(2).

The Commission shall make the information publicly available through any appropriate means, in particular through the European Judicial Network.

Article 76

1. The Member States shall notify the Commission of:
(a) the rules of jurisdiction referred to in Articles 5(2) and 6(2);
(b) the rules on third-party notice referred to in Article 65; and
(c) the conventions referred to in Article 69.

2. The Commission shall, on the basis of the notifications by the Member States referred to in paragraph 1, establish the corresponding lists.

3. The Member States shall notify the Commission of any subsequent amendments required to be made to those lists. The Commission shall amend those lists accordingly.

4. The Commission shall publish the lists and any subsequent amendments made to them in the Official Journal of the European Union.

5. The Commission shall make all information notified pursuant to paragraphs 1 and 3 publicly available through any other appropriate means, in particular through the European Judicial Network.

Article 77

The Commission shall be empowered to adopt delegated acts in accordance with Article 78 concerning the amendment of Annexes I and II.

Article 78

1. The power to adopt delegated acts is conferred on the Commission subject to the conditions laid down in this Article.

2. The power to adopt delegated acts referred to in Article 77 shall be conferred on the Commission for an indeterminate period of time from 9 January 2013.

3. The delegation of power referred to in Article 77 may be revoked at any time by the European Parliament or by the Council. A decision to revoke shall put an end to the delegation of the power specified in that decision. It shall take effect the day following the publication of the decision in the Official Journal of the European Union or at a later date specified therein. It shall not affect the validity of any delegated acts already in force.

4. As soon as it adopts a delegated act, the Commission shall notify it simultaneously to the European Parliament and to the Council.

5. A delegated act adopted pursuant to Article 77 shall enter into force only if no objection has been expressed either by the European Parliament or the Council within a period of two months of notification of that act to the European Parliament and the Council or if, before the expiry of that period, the European Parliament and the Council have both informed the Commission that they will not object. That period shall be extended by two months at the initiative of the European Parliament or of the Council.

Article 79

By 11 January 2022 the Commission shall present a report to the European Parliament, to the Council and to the European Economic and Social Committee on the application of this Regulation. That report shall include an evaluation of the possible need for a further extension of the rules on jurisdiction to defendants not domiciled in a Member State, taking into account the operation of this Regulation and possible developments at international level. Where appropriate, the report shall be accompanied by a proposal for amendment of this Regulation.

Article 80

This Regulation shall repeal Regulation (EC) No 44/2001. References to the repealed Regulation shall be construed as references to this Regulation and shall be read in accordance with the correlation table set out in Annex III.

Article 81

This Regulation shall enter into force on the twentieth day following that of its publication in the Official Journal of the European Union.

It shall apply from 10 January 2015, with the exception of Articles 75 and 76, which shall apply from 10 January 2014.

II. Regulation (EC) No 1393/2007 of the European Parliament and of the Council of 13 November 2007 on the service in the Member States of judicial and extrajudicial documents in civil or commercial matters (service of documents), and repealing Council Regulation (EC) No 1348/2000

THE EUROPEAN PARLIAMENT AND THE COUNCIL OF THE EUROPEAN UNION,

Having regard to the Treaty establishing the European Community, and in particular Article 61(c) and Article 67(5), second indent, thereof,

Having regard to the proposal from the Commission,

Having regard to the opinion of the European Economic and Social Committee,

Acting in accordance with the procedure laid down in Article 251 of the Treaty,

Whereas:

(1) The Union has set itself the objective of maintaining and developing the Union as an area of freedom, security and justice, in which the free movement of persons is assured. To establish such an area, the Community is to adopt, among others, the measures relating to judicial cooperation in civil matters needed for the proper functioning of the internal market.

(2) The proper functioning of the internal market entails the need to improve and expedite the transmission of judicial and extrajudicial documents in civil or commercial matters for service between the Member States.

(3) The Council, by an Act dated 26 May 1997, drew up a Convention on the service in the Member States of the European Union of judicial and extrajudicial documents in civil or commercial matters and recommended it for adoption by the Member States in accordance with their respective constitutional rules. That Convention has not entered into force. Continuity in the results of the negotiations for conclusion of the Convention should be ensured.

(4) On 29 May 2000 the Council adopted Regulation (EC) No 1348/2000 on the service in the Member States of judicial and extrajudicial documents in civil or commercial matters. The main content of that Regulation is based on the Convention.

(5) On 1 October 2004 the Commission adopted a report on the application of Regulation (EC) No 1348/2000. The report concludes that the application of Regulation (EC) No 1348/2000 has generally improved and expedited the transmission and the service of documents between Member States since its entry into force in 2001, but that nevertheless the application of certain provisions is not fully satisfactory.

(6) Efficiency and speed in judicial procedures in civil matters require that judicial and extrajudicial documents be transmitted directly and by rapid means between local bodies designated by the Member States. Member States may indicate their intention to designate only one transmitting or receiving agency or one agency to perform both functions, for a period of five years. This designation may, however, be renewed every five years.

(7) Speed in transmission warrants the use of all appropriate means, provided that certain conditions as to the legibility and reliability of the document received are observed.

Security in transmission requires that the document to be transmitted be accompanied by a standard form, to be completed in the official language or one of the official languages of the place where service is to be effected, or in another language accepted by the Member State in question.

(8) This Regulation should not apply to service of a document on the party's authorized representative in the Member State where the proceedings are taking place regardless of the place of residence of that party.

(9) The service of a document should be effected as soon as possible, and in any event within one month of receipt by the receiving agency.

(10) To secure the effectiveness of this Regulation, the possibility of refusing service of documents should be confined to exceptional situations.

(11) In order to facilitate the transmission and service of documents between Member States, the standard forms set out in the Annexes to this Regulation should be used.

(12) The receiving agency should inform the addressee in writing using the standard form that he may refuse to accept the document to be served at the time of service or by returning the document to the receiving agency within one week if it is not either in a language which he understands or in the official language or one of the official languages of the place of service. This rule should also apply to the subsequent service once the addressee has exercised his right of refusal. These rules on refusal should also apply to service by diplomatic or consular agents, service by postal services and direct service. It should be established that the service of the refused document can be remedied through the service on the addressee of a translation of the document.

(13) Speed in transmission warrants documents being served within days of receipt of the document. However, if service has not been effected after one month has elapsed, the receiving agency should inform the transmitting agency. The expiry of this period should not imply that the request be returned to the transmitting agency where it is clear that service is feasible within a reasonable period.

(14) The receiving agency should continue to take all necessary steps to effect the service of the document also in cases where it has not been possible to effect service within the month, for example, because the defendant has been away from his home on holiday or away from his office on business. However, in order to avoid an open-ended obligation for the receiving agency to take steps to effect the service of a document, the transmitting agency should be able to specify a time limit in the standard form after which service is no longer required.

(15) Given the differences between the Member States as regards their rules of procedure, the material date for the purposes of service varies from one Member State to another. Having regard to such situations and the possible difficulties that may arise, this Regulation should provide for a system where it is the law of the Member State addressed which determines the date of service. However, where according to the law of a Member State a document has to be served within a particular period, the date to be taken into account with respect to the applicant should be that determined by the law of that Member State. This double date system exists only in a limited number of Member States. Those Member States which apply this system should communicate this to the Commission, which should publish the information in the *Official Journal of the European Union* and make it available through the European Judicial Network in Civil and Commercial Matters established by Council Decision 2001/470/EC (1).

(16) In order to facilitate access to justice, costs occasioned by recourse to a judicial officer or a person competent under the law of the Member State addressed should correspond to a single fixed fee laid down by that Member State in advance

which respects the principles of proportionality and non-discrimination. The requirement of a single fixed fee should not preclude the possibility for Member States to set different fees for different types of service as long as they respect these principles.

(17) Each Member State should be free to effect service of documents directly by postal services on persons residing in another Member State by registered letter with acknowledgement of receipt or equivalent.

(18) It should be possible for any person interested in a judicial proceeding to effect service of documents directly through the judicial officers, officials or other competent persons of the Member State addressed, where such direct service is permitted under the law of that Member State.

(19) The Commission should draw up a manual containing information relevant for the proper application of this Regulation, which should be made available through the European Judicial Network in Civil and Commercial Matters. The Commission and the Member States should do their utmost to ensure that this information is up to date and complete especially as regards contact details of receiving and transmitting agencies.

(20) In calculating the periods and time limits provided for in this Regulation, Regulation (EEC, Euratom) No 1182/71 of the Council of 3 June 1971 determining the rules applicable

to periods, dates and time limits should apply.

(21) The measures necessary for the implementation of this Regulation should be adopted in accordance with Council Decision 1999/468/EC of 28 June 1999 laying down the procedures for the exercise of implementing powers conferred on the Commission.

(22) In particular, power should be conferred on the Commission to update or make technical amendments to the standard forms set out in the Annexes. Since those measures are of general scope and are designed to amend/delete nonessential elements of this Regulation, they must be adopted in accordance with the regulatory procedure with scrutiny provided for in Article 5a of Decision 1999/468/EC.

(23) This Regulation prevails over the provisions contained in bilateral or multilateral agreements or arrangements having the same scope, concluded by the Member States, and in particular the Protocol annexed to the Brussels Convention of 27 September 1968 and the Hague Convention of 15 November 1965 in relations between the Member States party thereto. This Regulation does not preclude Member States from maintaining or concluding agreements or arrangements to expedite or simplify the transmission of documents, provided that they are compatible with this Regulation.

(24) The information transmitted pursuant to this Regulation should enjoy suitable protection. This matter falls within the scope of Directive 95/46/EC of the European Parliament and of the Council of 24 October 1995 on the protection of individuals with regard to the processing of personal data and on the free movement of such data, and of Directive 2002/58/EC of the European Parliament and of the Council of 12 July 2002 concerning the processing of personal data and the protection of privacy in the electronic communications sector (Directive on privacy and electronic communications).

(25) No later than 1 June 2011 and every five years thereafter, the Commission should review the application of this Regulation and propose such amendments as may appear necessary.

(26) Since the objectives of this Regulation cannot be sufficiently achieved by the Member States and can therefore, by reason of the scale or effects of the action, be better achieved at Community level, the Community may adopt measures, in accordance with the principle of subsidiarity as set out in Article 5 of the Treaty. In accordance with the principle of proportionality, as set out in that Article, this Regulation does not go beyond what is necessary in order to achieve those objectives.

(27) In order to make the provisions more easily accessible and readable, Regulation (EC) No 1348/2000 should be repealed and replaced by this Regulation.

(28) In accordance with Article 3 of the Protocol on the position of the United Kingdom and Ireland, annexed to the Treaty on European Union and to the Treaty establishing the European Community, the United Kingdom and Ireland are taking part in the adoption and application of this Regulation.

(29) In accordance with Articles 1 and 2 of the Protocol on the position of Denmark, annexed to the Treaty on European Union and to the Treaty establishing the European Community, Denmark does not take part in the adoption of this Regulation and is not bound by it or subject to its application,

HAVE ADOPTED THIS REGULATION:

CHAPTER I
GENERAL PROVISIONS

Article 1. Scope

(1) This Regulation shall apply in civil and commercial matters where a judicial or extrajudicial document has to be transmitted from one Member State to another for service there. It shall not extend in particular to revenue, customs or administrative matters or to liability of the State for actions or omissions in the exercise of state authority (*acta iure imperii*).

(2) This Regulation shall not apply where the address of the person to be served with the document is not known.

(3) In this Regulation, the term 'Member State' shall mean the Member States with the exception of Denmark.

Article 2. Transmitting and receiving agencies

(1) Each Member State shall designate the public officers, authorities or other persons, hereinafter referred to as 'transmitting agencies', competent for the transmission of judicial or extrajudicial documents to be served in another Member State.

(2) Each Member State shall designate the public officers, authorities or other persons, hereinafter referred to as 'receiving agencies', competent for the receipt of judicial or extrajudicial documents from another Member State.

(3) A Member State may designate one transmitting agency and one receiving agency, or one agency to perform both functions. A federal State, a State in which several legal systems apply or a State with autonomous territorial units shall be free to designate more than one such agency. The designation shall have effect for a period of five years and may be renewed at five-year intervals.

(4) Each Member State shall provide the Commission with the following information:

(a) the names and addresses of the receiving agencies referred to in paragraphs 2 and 3; (b) the geographical areas in which they have jurisdiction; (c) the means of receipt of documents available to them; and (d) the languages that may be used for the completion of the standard form set out in Annex I.

Member States shall notify the Commission of any subsequent modification of such information.

Article 3. Central body

Each Member State shall designate a central body responsible for:

(a) supplying information to the transmitting agencies; (b) seeking solutions to any difficulties which may arise during transmission of documents for service; (c) forwarding, in exceptional cases, at the request of a transmitting agency, a request for service to the competent receiving agency.

A federal State, a State in which several legal systems apply or a State with autonomous territorial units shall be free to designate more than one central body.

CHAPTER II
JUDICIAL DOCUMENTS

Section 1
Transmission and service of judicial documents

Article 4. Transmission of documents

(1) Judicial documents shall be transmitted directly and as soon as possible between the agencies designated pursuant to Article 2.

(2) The transmission of documents, requests, confirmations, receipts, certificates and any other papers between transmitting agencies and receiving agencies may be carried out by any appropriate means, provided that the content of the document received is true and faithful to that of the document forwarded and that all information in it is easily legible.

(3) The document to be transmitted shall be accompanied by a request drawn up using the standard form set out in Annex I. The form shall be completed in the official language of the Member State addressed or, if there are several official languages in that Member State, the official language or one of the official languages of the place where service is to be effected, or in another language which that Member State has indicated it can accept. Each Member State shall indicate the official language or languages of the institutions of the European Union other than its own which is or are acceptable to it for completion of the form.

(4) The documents and all papers that are transmitted shall be exempted from legalisation or any equivalent formality.

(5) When the transmitting agency wishes a copy of the document to be returned together with the certificate referred to in Article 10, it shall send the document in duplicate.

Article 5. Translation of documents

(1) The applicant shall be advised by the transmitting agency to which he forwards the document for transmission that the addressee may refuse to accept it if it is not in one of the languages provided for in Article 8.

(2) The applicant shall bear any costs of translation prior to the transmission of the document, without prejudice to any possible subsequent decision by the court or competent authority on liability for such costs.

Article 6. Receipt of documents by receiving agency

(1) On receipt of a document, a receiving agency shall, as soon as possible and in any event within seven days of receipt, send a receipt to the transmitting agency by the swiftest possible means of transmission using the standard form set out in Annex I.

(2) Where the request for service cannot be fulfilled on the basis of the information or documents transmitted, the receiving agency shall contact the transmitting agency by the swiftest possible means in order to secure the missing information or documents.

(3) If the request for service is manifestly outside the scope of this Regulation or if non-compliance with the formal conditions required makes service impossible, the request and the documents transmitted shall be returned, on receipt, to the transmitting agency, together with the notice of return using the standard form set out in Annex I.

(4) A receiving agency receiving a document for service but not having territorial jurisdiction to serve it shall forward it, as well as the request, to the receiving agency having territorial jurisdiction in the same Member State if the request complies with the conditions laid down in Article 4(3) and shall inform the transmitting agency accordingly using the standard form set out in Annex I. That receiving agency shall inform the transmitting agency when it receives the document, in the manner provided for in paragraph 1.

Article 7. Service of documents

(1) The receiving agency shall itself serve the document or have it served, either in accordance with the law of the Member State addressed or by a particular method requested by the transmitting agency, unless that method is incompatible with the law of that Member State.

(2) The receiving agency shall take all necessary steps to effect the service of the document as soon as possible, and in any event within one month of receipt. If it has not been possible to effect service within one month of receipt, the receiving agency shall:

(a) immediately inform the transmitting agency by means of the certificate in the standard form set out in Annex I, which shall be drawn up under the conditions referred to in Article 10(2); and (b) continue to take all necessary steps to effect the service of the document, unless indicated otherwise by the transmitting agency, where service seems to be possible within a reasonable period of time.

Article 8. Refusal to accept a document

(1) The receiving agency shall inform the addressee, using the standard form set out in Annex II, that he may refuse to accept the document to be served at

the time of service or by returning the document to the receiving agency within one week if it is not written in, or accompanied by a translation into, either of the following languages:

(a) a language which the addressee understands; or (b) the official language of the Member State addressed or, if there are several official languages in that Member State, the official language or one of the official languages of the place where service is to be effected.

(2) Where the receiving agency is informed that the addressee refuses to accept the document in accordance with paragraph 1, it shall immediately inform the transmitting agency by means of the certificate provided for in Article 10 and return the request and the documents of which a translation is requested.

(3) If the addressee has refused to accept the document pursuant to paragraph 1, the service of the document can be remedied through the service on the addressee in accordance with the provisions of this Regulation of the document accompanied by a translation into a language provided for in paragraph 1. In that case, the date of service of the document shall be the date on which the document accompanied by the translation is served in accordance with the law of the Member State addressed. However, where according to the law of a Member State, a document has to be served within a particular period, the date to be taken into account with respect to the applicant shall be the date of the service of the initial document determined pursuant to Article 9(2).

(4) Paragraphs 1, 2 and 3 shall also apply to the means of transmission and service of judicial documents provided for in Section 2.

(5) For the purposes of paragraph 1, the diplomatic or consular agents, where service is effected in accordance with Article 13, or the authority or person, where service is effected in accordance with Article 14, shall inform the addressee that he may refuse to accept the document and that any document refused must be sent to those agents or to that authority or person respectively.

Article 9. Date of service

(1) Without prejudice to Article 8, the date of service of a document pursuant to Article 7 shall be the date on which it is served in accordance with the law of the Member State addressed.

(2) However, where according to the law of a Member State a document has to be served within a particular period, the date to be taken into account with respect to the applicant shall be that determined by the law of that Member State.

(3) Paragraphs 1 and 2 shall also apply to the means of transmission and service of judicial documents provided for in Section 2.

Article 10. Certificate of service and copy of the document served

(1) When the formalities concerning the service of the document have been completed, a certificate of completion of those formalities shall be drawn up in the standard form set out in Annex I and addressed to the transmitting agency, together with, where Article 4(5) applies, a copy of the document served.

(2) The certificate shall be completed in the official language or one of the official languages of the Member State of origin or in another language which the Member State of origin has indicated that it can accept. Each Member State shall indicate the official language or languages of the institutions of the European Union other than its own which is or are acceptable to it for completion of the form.

Article 11. Costs of service

(1) The service of judicial documents coming from a Member State shall not give rise to any payment or reimbursement of taxes or costs for services rendered by the Member State addressed.

(2) However, the applicant shall pay or reimburse the costs occasioned by:

(a) recourse to a judicial officer or to a person competent under the law of the Member State addressed; (b) the use of a particular method of service.

Costs occasioned by recourse to a judicial officer or to a person competent under the law of the Member State addressed shall correspond to a single fixed fee laid down by that Member State in advance which respects the principles of proportionality and non-discrimination. Member States shall communicate such fixed fees to the Commission.

Section 2
Other means of transmission and service of judicial documents

Article 12. Transmission by consular or diplomatic channels

Each Member State shall be free, in exceptional circumstances, to use consular or diplomatic channels to forward judicial documents, for the purpose of service, to those agencies of another Member State which are designated pursuant to Articles 2 or 3.

Article 13. Service by diplomatic or consular agents

(1) Each Member State shall be free to effect service of judicial documents on persons residing in another Member State, without application of any compulsion, directly through its diplomatic or consular agents.

(2) Any Member State may make it known, in accordance with Article 23(1), that it is opposed to such service within its territory, unless the documents are to be served on nationals of the Member State in which the documents originate.

Article 14. Service by postal services

Each Member State shall be free to effect service of judicial documents directly by postal services on persons residing in another Member State by registered letter with acknowledgement of receipt or equivalent.

Article 15. Direct service

Any person interested in a judicial proceeding may effect service of judicial documents directly through the judicial officers, officials or other competent persons of the Member State addressed, where such direct service is permitted under the law of that Member State.

CHAPTER III
EXTRAJUDICIAL DOCUMENTS

Article 16. Transmission

Extrajudicial documents may be transmitted for service in another Member State in accordance with the provisions of this Regulation.

CHAPTER IV
FINAL PROVISIONS

Article 17. Implementing rules

Measures designed to amend non-essential elements of this Regulation relating to the updating or to the making of technical amendments to the standard forms set out in Annexes I and II shall be adopted in accordance with the regulatory procedure with scrutiny referred to in Article 18(2).

Article 18. Committee

(1) The Commission shall be assisted by a committee.

(2) Where reference is made to this paragraph, Article 5a(1) to (4), and Article 7 of Decision 1999/468/EC shall apply, having regard to the provisions of Article 8 thereof.

Article 19. Defendant not entering an appearance

(1) Where a writ of summons or an equivalent document has had to be transmitted to another Member State for the purpose of service under the provisions of this Regulation and the defendant has not appeared, judgment shall not be given until it is established that:

(a) the document was served by a method prescribed by the internal law of the Member State addressed for the service of documents in domestic actions upon persons who are within its territory; or (b) the document was actually delivered to the defendant or to his residence by another method provided for by this Regulation;

and that in either of these cases the service or the delivery was effected in sufficient time to enable the defendant to defend.

(2) Each Member State may make it known, in accordance with Article 23(1), that the judge, notwithstanding the provisions of paragraph 1, may give judgment even if no certificate of service or delivery has been received, if all the following conditions are fulfilled:

(a) the document was transmitted by one of the methods provided for in this Regulation; (b) a period of time of not less than six months, considered adequate by the judge in the particular case, has elapsed since the date of the transmission of the document; (c) no certificate of any kind has been received, even though every reasonable effort has been made to obtain it through the competent authorities or bodies of the Member State addressed.

(3) Notwithstanding paragraphs 1 and 2, the judge may order, in case of urgency, any provisional or protective measures.

(4) When a writ of summons or an equivalent document has had to be transmitted to another Member State for the purpose of service under the provisions of this Regulation and a judgment has been entered against a defendant who has not appeared, the judge shall have the power to relieve the defendant from the effects of the expiry of the time for appeal from the judgment if the following conditions are fulfilled:

(a) the defendant, without any fault on his part, did not have knowledge of the document in sufficient time to defend, or knowledge of the judgment in sufficient time to appeal; and (b) the defendant has disclosed a *prima facie* defence to the action on the merits.

An application for relief may be filed only within a reasonable time after the defendant has knowledge of the judgment.

Each Member State may make it known, in accordance with Article 23(1), that such application will not be entertained if it is filed after the expiry of a time to be stated by it in that communication, but which shall in no case be less than one year following the date of the judgment.

(5) Paragraph 4 shall not apply to judgments concerning the status or capacity of persons.

Article 20. Relationship with agreements or arrangements to which Member States are party

(1) This Regulation shall, in relation to matters to which it applies, prevail over other provisions contained in bilateral or multilateral agreements or arrangements concluded by the Member States, and in particular Article IV of the Protocol to the Brussels Convention of 1968 and the Hague Convention of 15 November 1965.

(2) This Regulation shall not preclude individual Member States from maintaining or concluding agreements or arrangements to expedite further or simplify the transmission of documents, provided that they are compatible with this Regulation.

(3) Member States shall send to the Commission:

a) a copy of the agreements or arrangements referred to in paragraph 2 concluded between the Member States as well as drafts of such agreements or arrangements which they intend to adopt; and
b) any denunciation of, or amendments to, these agreements or arrangements.

Article 21. Legal aid

This Regulation shall not affect the application of Article 23 of the Convention on civil procedure of 17 July 1905, Article 24 of the Convention on civil procedure of 1 March 1954 or Article 13 of the Convention on international access to justice of 25 October 1980 between the Member States party to those Conventions.

Article 22. Protection of information transmitted

(1) Information, including in particular personal data, transmitted under this Regulation shall be used by the receiving agency only for the purpose for which it was transmitted.

(2) Receiving agencies shall ensure the confidentiality of such information, in accordance with their national law.

(3) Paragraphs 1 and 2 shall not affect national laws enabling data subjects to be informed of the use made of information transmitted under this Regulation.

(4) This Regulation shall be without prejudice to Directives 95/46/EC and 2002/58/EC.

Article 23. Communication and publication

(1) Member States shall communicate to the Commission the information referred to in Articles 2, 3, 4, 10, 11, 13, 15 and 19. Member States shall communicate to the Commission if, according to their law, a document has to be served within a particular period as referred to in Articles 8(3) and 9(2).

(2) The Commission shall publish the information communicated in accordance with paragraph 1 in the *Official Journal of the European Union* with the exception of the addresses and other contact details of the agencies and of the central bodies and the geographical areas in which they have jurisdiction.

(3) The Commission shall draw up and update regularly a manual containing the information referred to in paragraph 1, which shall be available electronically, in particular through the European Judicial Network in Civil and Commercial Matters.

Article 24. Review

No later than 1 June 2011, and every five years thereafter, the Commission shall present to the European Parliament, the Council and the European Economic and Social Committee a report on the application of this Regulation, paying special attention to the effectiveness of the agencies designated pursuant to Article 2 and to the practical application of Article 3(c) and Article 9. The report shall be accompanied if need be by proposals for adaptations of this Regulation in line with the evolution of notification systems.

Article 25. Repeal

(1) Regulation (EC) No 1348/2000 shall be repealed as from the date of application of this Regulation.

(2) References made to the repealed Regulation shall be construed as being made to this Regulation and should be read in accordance with the correlation table in Annex III.

Article 26. Entry into force

This Regulation shall enter into force on the 20th day following its publication in the *Official Journal of the European Union*.

It shall apply from 13 November 2008 with the exception of Article 23 which shall apply from 13 August 2008.

III. Council regulation (EC) No. 1206/2001 of 28 May 2001 on Cooperation between the Courts of the Member States in the Taking of Evidence in Civil or Commercial Matters

THE COUNCIL OF THE EUROPEAN UNION,
Having regard to the Treaty establishing the European Community, and in particular Article 61(c) and Article 67(1) thereof,
Having regard to the initiative of the Federal Republic of Germany,
Having regard to the opinion of the European Parliament,
Having regard to the opinion of the Economic and Social Committee,

Whereas:
(1) The European Union has set itself the objective of maintaining and developing the European Union as an area of freedom, security and justice in which the free movement of persons is ensured. For the gradual establishment of such an area, the Community is to adopt, among others, the measures relating to judicial cooperation in civil matters needed for the proper functioning of the internal market.
(2) For the purpose of the proper functioning of the internal market, cooperation between courts in the taking of evidence should be improved, and in particular simplified and accelerated.
(3) At its meeting in Tampere on 15 and 16 October 1999, the European Council recalled that new procedural legislation in cross-border cases, in particular on the taking of evidence, should be prepared.
(4) This area falls within the scope of Article 65 of the Treaty.
(5) The objectives of the proposed action, namely the improvement of cooperation between the courts on the taking of evidence in civil or commercial matters, cannot be sufficiently achieved by the Member States and can therefore be better achieved at Community level. The Community may adopt measures in accordance with the principle of subsidiarity as set out in Article 5 of the Treaty. In accordance with the principle of proportionality, as set out in that Article, this Regulation does not go beyond what is necessary to achieve those objectives.
(6) To date, there is no binding instrument between all the Member States concerning the taking of evidence. The Hague Convention of 18 March 1970 on the taking of evidence abroad in civil or commercial matters applies between only 11 Member States of the European Union.
(7) As it is often essential for a decision in a civil or commercial matter pending before a court in a Member State to take evidence in another Member State, the Community's activity cannot be limited to the field of transmission of judicial and extrajudicial documents in civil or commercial matters which falls within the scope of Council Regulation (EC) No 1348/2000 of 29 May 2000 on the serving in the Member States of judicial and extrajudicial documents in civil or commercial matters. It is therefore necessary to continue the improvement of cooperation between courts of Member States in the field of taking of evidence.
(8) The efficiency of judicial procedures in civil or commercial matters requires that the transmission and execution of requests for the performance of taking of evidence is to be made directly and by the most rapid means possible between Member States' courts.
(9) Speed in transmission of requests for the performance of taking of evidence warrants the use of all appropriate means, provided that certain conditions as

to the legibility and reliability of the document received are observed. So as to ensure the utmost clarity and legal certainty the request for the performance of taking of evidence must be transmitted on a form to be completed in the language of the Member State of the requested court or in another language accepted by that State. For the same reasons, forms should also be used as far as possible for further communication between the relevant courts.

(10) A request for the performance of the taking of evidence should be executed expeditiously. If it is not possible for the request to be executed within 90 days of receipt by the requested court, the latter should inform the requesting court accordingly, stating the reasons which prevent the request from being executed swiftly.

(11) To secure the effectiveness of this Regulation, the possibility of refusing to execute the request for the performance of taking of evidence should be confined to strictly limited exceptional situations.

(12) The requested court should execute the request in accordance with the law of its Member State.

(13) The parties and, if any, their representatives, should be able to be present at the performance of the taking of evidence, if that is provided for by the law of the Member State of the requesting court, in order to be able to follow the proceedings in a comparable way as if evidence were taken in the Member State of the requesting court. They should also have the right to request to participate in order to have a more active role in the performance of the taking of evidence. However, the conditions under which they may participate should be determined by the requested court in accordance with the law of its Member State.

(14) The representatives of the requesting court should be able to be present at the performance of the taking of evidence, if that is compatible with the law of the Member State of the requesting court, in order to have an improved possibility of evaluation of evidence. They should also have the right to request to participate, under the conditions laid down by the requested court in accordance with the law of its Member State, in order to have a more active role in the performance of the taking of evidence.

(15) In order to facilitate the taking of evidence it should be possible for a court in a Member State, in accordance with the law of its Member State, to take evidence directly in another Member State, if accepted by the latter, and under the conditions determined by the central body or competent authority of the requested Member State.

(16) The execution of the request, according to Article 10, should not give rise to a claim for any reimbursement of taxes or costs. Nevertheless, if the requested court requires reimbursement, the fees paid to experts and interpreters, as well as the costs occasioned by the application of Article 10 (3) and (4), should not be borne by that court. In such a case, the requesting court is to take the necessary measures to ensure reimbursement without delay. Where the opinion of an expert is required, the requested court may, before executing the request, ask the requesting court for an adequate deposit or advance towards the costs.

(17) This Regulation should prevail over the provisions applying to its field of application, contained in international conventions concluded by the Member States. Member States should be free to adopt agreements or arrangements to further facilitate cooperation in the taking of evidence.

(18) The information transmitted pursuant to this Regulation should enjoy protection. Since Directive 95/46/EC of the European Parliament and of the Council

of 24 October 1995 on the protection of individuals with regard to the processing of personal data and on the free movement of such data, and Directive 97/66/EC of the European Parliament and of the Council of 15 December 1997 concerning the processing of personal data and the protection of privacy in the telecommunications sector, are applicable, there is no need for specific provisions on data protection in this Regulation.

(19) The measures necessary for the implementation of this Regulation should be adopted in accordance with Council Decision 1999/468/EC of 28 June 1999 laying down the procedures for the exercise of implementing powers conferred on the Commission.

(20) For the proper functioning of this Regulation, the Commission should review its application and propose such amendments as may appear necessary.

(21) The United Kingdom and Ireland, in accordance with Article 3 of the Protocol on the position of the United Kingdom and Ireland annexed to the Treaty on the European Union and to the Treaty establishing the European Community, have given notice of their wish to take part in the adoption and application of this Regulation.

(22) Denmark, in accordance with Articles 1 and 2 of the Protocol on the position of Denmark annexed to the Treaty on European Union and to the Treaty establishing the European Community, is not participating in the adoption of this Regulation, and is therefore not bound by it nor subject to its application,

HAS ADOPTED THIS REGULATION:

CHAPTER I
GENERAL PROVISIONS

Article 1. Scope

(1) This Regulation shall apply in civil or commercial matters where the court of a Member State, in accordance with the provisions of the law of that State, requests: (a) the competent court of another Member State to take evidence; or (b) to take evidence directly in another Member State.

(2) A request shall not be made to obtain evidence which is not intended for use in judicial proceedings, commenced or contemplated.

(3) In this Regulation, the term 'Member State' shall mean Member States with the exception of Denmark.

Article 2. Direct transmission between the courts

(1) Requests pursuant to Article 1(1) (a), hereinafter referred to as 'requests', shall be transmitted by the court before which the proceedings are commenced or contemplated, hereinafter referred to as the 'requesting court', directly to the competent court of another Member State, hereinafter referred to as the 'requested court', for the performance of the taking of evidence.

(2) Each Member State shall draw up a list of the courts competent for the performance of taking of evidence according to this Regulation. The list shall also indicate the territorial and, where appropriate, the special jurisdiction of those courts.

Article 3. Central body

(1) Each Member State shall designate a central body responsible for: (a) supplying information to the courts; (b) seeking solutions to any difficulties which may arise in respect of a request; (c) forwarding, in exceptional cases, at the request of a requesting court, a request to the competent court.

(2) A federal State, a State in which several legal systems apply or a State with autonomous territorial entities shall be free to designate more than one central body.

(3) Each Member State shall also designate the central body referred to in paragraph 1 or one or several competent authority(ies) to be responsible for taking decisions on requests pursuant to Article 17.

CHAPTER II
TRANSMISSION AND EXECUTION OF REQUESTS

Section 1
Transmission of the request

Article 4. Form and content of the request

(1) The request shall be made using form A or, where appropriate, form I in the Annex. It shall contain the following details:
a) the requesting and, where appropriate, the requested court;
b) the names and addresses of the parties to the proceedings and their representatives, if any;
c) the nature and subject matter of the case and a brief statement of the facts;
d) a description of the taking of evidence to be performed;
e) where the request is for the examination of a person:
   – the name(s) and address(es) of the person(s) to be examined,
   – the questions to be put to the person(s) to be examined or a statement of the facts about which he is (they are) to be examined,
   – where appropriate, a reference to a right to refuse to testify under the law of the Member State of the requesting court,
   – any requirement that the examination is to be carried out under oath or affirmation in lieu thereof, and any special form to be used,
   – where appropriate, any other information that the requesting court deems necessary;
f) where the request is for any other form of taking of evidence, the documents or other objects to be inspected;
g) where appropriate, any request pursuant to Article 10 (3) and (4), and Articles 11 and 12 and any information necessary for the application thereof.

(2) The request and all documents accompanying the request shall be exempted from authentication or any equivalent formality.

(3) Documents which the requesting court deems it necessary to enclose for the execution of the request shall be accompanied by a translation into the language in which the request was written.

Article 5. Language

The request and communications pursuant to this Regulation shall be drawn up in the official language of the requested Member State or, if there are several official languages in that Member State, in the official language or one of the official languages of the place where the requested taking of evidence is to be performed, or in another language which the requested Member State has indicated it can accept. Each Member State shall indicate the official language or languages of the institutions of the European Community other than its own which is or are acceptable to it for completion of the forms.

Article 6. Transmission of requests and other communications

Requests and communications pursuant to this Regulation shall be transmitted by the swiftest possible means, which the requested Member State has indicated it can accept. The transmission may be carried out by any appropriate means, provided that the document received accurately reflects the content of the document forwarded and that all information in it is legible.

Section 2
Receipt of request

Article 7. Receipt of request

(1) Within seven days of receipt of the request, the requested competent court shall send an acknowledgement of receipt to the requesting court using form B in the Annex. Where the request does not comply with the conditions laid down in Articles 5 and 6, the requested court shall enter a note to that effect in the acknowledgement of receipt.

(2) Where the execution of a request made using form A in the Annex, which complies with the conditions laid down in Article 5, does not fall within the jurisdiction of the court to which it was transmitted, the latter shall forward the request to the competent court of its Member State and shall inform the requesting court thereof using form A in the Annex.

Article 8. Incomplete request

(1) If a request cannot be executed because it does not contain all of the necessary information pursuant to Article 4, the requested court shall inform the requesting court thereof without delay and, at the latest, within 30 days of receipt of the request using form C in the Annex, and shall request it to send the missing information, which should be indicated as precisely as possible.

(2) If a request cannot be executed because a deposit or advance is necessary in accordance with Article 18 (3), the requested court shall inform the requesting court thereof without delay and, at the latest, within 30 days of receipt of the request using form C in the Annex and inform the requesting court how the deposit or advance should be made. The requested Court shall acknowledge receipt of the deposit or advance without delay, at the latest within 10 days of receipt of the deposit or the advance using form D.

Article 9. Completion of the request

(1) If the requested court has noted on the acknowledgement of receipt pursuant to Article 7 (1) that the request does not comply with the conditions laid down in Articles 5 and 6 or has informed the requesting court pursuant to Article 8 that the request cannot be executed because it does not contain all of the necessary information pursuant to Article 4, the time limit pursuant to Article 10 shall begin to run when the requested court received the request duly completed.

(2) Where the requested court has asked for a deposit or advance in accordance with Article 18 (3), this time limit shall begin to run when the deposit or the advance is made.

Section 3
Taking of evidence by the requested court

Article 10. General provisions on the execution of the request

(1) The requested court shall execute the request without delay and, at the latest, within 90 days of receipt of the request.

(2) The requested court shall execute the request in accordance with the law of its Member State.

(3) The requesting court may call for the request to be executed in accordance with a special procedure provided for by the law of its Member State, using form A in the Annex. The requested court shall comply with such a requirement unless this procedure is incompatible with the law of the Member State of the requested court or by reason of major practical difficulties. If the requested court does not comply with the requirement for one of these reasons it shall inform the requesting court using form E in the Annex.

(4) The requesting court may ask the requested court to use communications technology at the performance of the taking of evidence, in particular by using videoconference and teleconference. The requested court shall comply with such a requirement unless this is incompatible with the law of the Member State of the requested court or by reason of major practical difficulties. If the requested court does not comply with the requirement for one of these reasons, it shall inform the requesting court, using form E in the Annex. If there is no access to the technical means referred to above in the requesting or in the requested court, such means may be made available by the courts by mutual agreement.

Article 11. Performance with the presence and participation of the parties

(1) If it is provided for by the law of the Member State of the requesting court, the parties and, if any, their representatives, have the right to be present at the performance of the taking of evidence by the requested court.

(2) The requesting court shall, in its request, inform the requested court that the parties and, if any, their representatives, will be present and, where appropriate, that their participation is requested, using form A in the Annex. This information may also be given at any other appropriate time.

(3) If the participation of the parties and, if any, their representatives, is requested at the performance of the taking of evidence, the requested court shall

determine, in accordance with Article 10, the conditions under which they may participate.

(4) The requested court shall notify the parties and, if any, their representatives, of the time when, the place where, the proceedings will take place, and, where appropriate, the conditions under which they may participate, using form F in the Annex.

(5) Paragraphs 1 to 4 shall not affect the possibility for the requested court of asking the parties and, if any their representatives, to be present at or to participate in the performance of the taking of evidence if that possibility is provided for by the law of its Member State.

Article 12. Performance with the presence and participation of representatives of the requesting court

(1) If it is compatible with the law of the Member State of the requesting court, representatives of the requesting court have the right to be present in the performance of the taking of evidence by the requested court.

(2) For the purpose of this Article, the term 'representative' shall include members of the judicial personnel designated by the requesting court, in accordance with the law of its Member State. The requesting court may also designate, in accordance with the law of its Member State, any other person, such as an expert.

(3) The requesting court shall, in its request, inform the requested court that its representatives will be present and, where appropriate, that their participation is requested, using form A in the Annex. This information may also be given at any other appropriate time.

(4) If the participation of the representatives of the requesting court is requested in the performance of the taking of evidence, the requested court shall determine, in accordance with Article 10, the conditions under which they may participate.

(5) The requested court shall notify the requesting court, of the time when, and the place where, the proceedings will take place, and, where appropriate, the conditions under which the representatives may participate, using form F in the Annex.

Article 13. Coercive measures

Where necessary, in executing a request the requested court shall apply the appropriate coercive measures in the instances and to the extent as are provided for by the law of the Member State of the requested court for the execution of a request made for the same purpose by its national authorities or one of the parties concerned.

Article 14. Refusal to execute

(1) A request for the hearing of a person shall not be executed when the person concerned claims the right to refuse to give evidence or to be prohibited from giving evidence, (a) under the law of the Member State of the requested court; or (b) under the law of the Member State of the requesting court, and such right has been specified in the request, or, if need be, at the instance of the requested court, has been confirmed by the requesting court.

(2) In addition to the grounds referred to in paragraph 1, the execution of a request may be refused only if: (a) the request does not fall within the scope of this Regulation as set out in Article 1; or (b) the execution of the request under the

law of the Member State of the requested court does not fall within the functions of the judiciary; or (c) the requesting court does not comply with the request of the requested court to complete the request pursuant to Article 8 within 30 days after the requested court asked it to do so; or (d) a deposit or advance asked for in accordance with Article 18 (3) is not made within 60 days after the requested court asked for such a deposit or advance.

(3) Execution may not be refused by the requested court solely on the ground that under the law of its Member State a court of that Member State has exclusive jurisdiction over the subject matter of the action or that the law of that Member State would not admit the right of action on it.

(4) If execution of the request is refused on one of the grounds referred to in paragraph 2, the requested court shall notify the requesting court thereof within 60 days of receipt of the request by the requested court using form H in the Annex.

Article 15. Notification of delay

If the requested court is not in a position to execute the request within 90 days of receipt, it shall inform the requesting court thereof, using form G in the Annex. When it does so, the grounds for the delay shall be given as well as the estimated time that the requested court expects it will need to execute the request.

Article 16. Procedure after execution of the request

The requested court shall send without delay to the requesting court the documents establishing the execution of the request and, where appropriate, return the documents received from the requesting court. The documents shall be accompanied by a confirmation of execution using form H in the Annex.

Section 4
Direct taking of evidence by the requesting court

Article 17.

(1) Where a court requests to take evidence directly in another Member State, it shall submit a request to the central body or the competent authority referred to in Article 3(3) in that State, using form I in the Annex.

(2) Direct taking of evidence may only take place if it can be performed on a voluntary basis without the need for coercive measures. Where the direct taking of evidence implies that a person shall be heard, the requesting court shall inform that person that the performance shall take place on a voluntary basis.

(3) The taking of evidence shall be performed by a member of the judicial personnel or by any other person such as an expert, who will be designated, in accordance with the law of the Member State of the requesting court.

(4) Within 30 days of receiving the request, the central body or the competent authority of the requested Member State shall inform the requesting court if the request is accepted and, if necessary, under what conditions according to the law of its Member State such performance is to be carried out, using form J. In particular, the central body or the competent authority may assign a court of its Member State to take part in the performance of the taking of evidence in order to ensure the proper application of this Article and the conditions that have been

set out. The central body or the competent authority shall encourage the use of communications technology, such as videoconferences and teleconferences.

(5) The central body or the competent authority may refuse direct taking of evidence only if: (a) the request does not fall within the scope of this Regulation as set out in Article 1; (b) the request does not contain all of the necessary information pursuant to Article 4; or (c) the direct taking of evidence requested is contrary to fundamental principles of law in its Member State.

(6) Without prejudice to the conditions laid down in accordance with paragraph 4, the requesting court shall execute the request in accordance with the law of its Member State.

Section 5
Costs

Article 18.

(1) The execution of the request, in accordance with Article 10, shall not give rise to a claim for any reimbursement of taxes or costs.

(2) Nevertheless, if the requested court so requires, the requesting court shall ensure the reimbursement, without delay, of:
– the fees paid to experts and interpreters, and
– the costs occasioned by the application of Article 10 (3) and (4).

The duty for the parties to bear these fees or costs shall be governed by the law of the Member State of the requesting court.

(3) Where the opinion of an expert is required, the requested court may, before executing the request, ask the requesting court for an adequate deposit or advance towards the requested costs. In all other cases, a deposit or advance shall not be a condition for the execution of a request.

The deposit or advance shall be made by the parties if that is provided for by the law of the Member State of the requesting court.

CHAPTER III
FINAL PROVISIONS

Article 19. Implementing rules

(1) The Commission shall draw up and regularly update a manual, which shall also be available electronically, containing the information provided by the Member States in accordance with Article 22 and the agreements or arrangements in force, according to Article 21.

(2) The updating or making of technical amendments to the standard forms set out in the Annex shall be carried out in accordance with the advisory procedure set out in Article 20(2).

Article 20. Committee

(1) The Commission shall be assisted by a Committee.

(2) Where reference is made to this paragraph, Articles 3 and 7 of Decision 1999/468/EC shall apply.

(3) The Committee shall adopt its Rules of Procedure.

Article 21. Relationship with existing or future agreements or arrangements between Member States

(1) This Regulation shall, in relation to matters to which it applies, prevail over other provisions contained in bilateral or multilateral agreements or arrangements concluded by the Member States and in particular the Hague Convention of 1 March 1954 on Civil Procedure and the Hague Convention of 18 March 1970 on the Taking of Evidence Abroad in Civil or Commercial Matters, in relations between the Member States party thereto.

(2) This Regulation shall not preclude Member States from maintaining or concluding agreements or arrangements between two or more of them to further facilitate the taking of evidence, provided that they are compatible with this Regulation.

(3) Member States shall send to the Commission: (a) by 1 July 2003, a copy of the agreements or arrangements maintained between the Member States referred to in paragraph 2; (b) a copy of the agreements or arrangements concluded between the Member States referred to in paragraph 2 as well as drafts of such agreements or arrangements which they intend to adopt; and (c) any denunciation of, or amendments to, these agreements or arrangements.

Article 22. Communication

By 1 July 2003 each Member State shall communicate to the Commission the following: (a) the list pursuant to Article 2 (2) indicating the territorial and, where appropriate, the special jurisdiction of the courts; (b) the names and addresses of the central bodies and competent authorities pursuant to Article 3, indicating their territorial jurisdiction; (c) the technical means for the receipt of requests available to the courts on the list pursuant to Article 2 (2); (d) the languages accepted for the requests as referred to in Article 5.

Member States shall inform the Commission of any subsequent changes to this information.

Article 23. Review

No later than 1 January 2007, and every five years thereafter, the Commission shall present to the European Parliament, the Council and the Economic and Social Committee a report on the application of this Regulation, paying special attention to the practical application of Article 3(1)(c) and 3, and Articles 17 and 18.

Article 24. Entry into force

(1) This Regulation shall enter into force on 1 July 2001.

(2) This Regulation shall apply from 1 January 2004, except for Articles 19, 21 and 22, which shall apply from 1 July 2001. This Regulation shall be binding in its entirety and directly applicable in the Member States in accordance with the Treaty establishing the European Community.

IV. Regulation (EC) No 1896/2006 of the European Parliament and of the Council of 12 December 2006 creating a European order for payment procedure

THE EUROPEAN PARLIAMENT AND THE COUNCIL OF THE EUROPEAN UNION,
Having regard to the Treaty establishing the European Community, and in particular Article 61(c) thereof,
Having regard to the proposal from the Commission,
Having regard to the Opinion of the European Economic and Social Committee,
Acting in accordance with the procedure laid down in Article 251 of the Treaty,

Whereas:

(1) The Community has set itself the objective of maintaining and developing an area of freedom, security and justice in which the free movement of persons is ensured. For the gradual establishment of such an area, the Community is to adopt, *inter alia*, measures in the field of judicial cooperation in civil matters having cross-border implications and needed for the proper functioning of the internal market.

(2) According to Article 65(c) of the Treaty, these measures are to include measures eliminating obstacles to the good functioning of civil proceedings, if necessary by promoting the compatibility of the rules on civil procedure applicable in the Member States.

(3) The European Council meeting in Tampere on 15 and 16 October 1999 invited the Council and the Commission to prepare new legislation on issues that are instrumental to smooth judicial cooperation and to enhanced access to law and specifically made reference, in that context,to orders for money payment.

(4) On 30 November 2000, the Council adopted a joint Commission and Council programme of measures for implementation of the principle of mutual recognition of decisions in civil and commercial matters. The programme envisages the possibility of a specific, uniform or harmonised procedure laid down within the Community to obtain a judicial decision in specific areas including that of uncontested claims. This was taken forward by the Hague Programme, adopted by the European Council on 5 November 2004, which called for work to be actively pursued on the European order for payment.

(5) The Commission adopted a Green Paper on a European order for payment procedure and on measures to simplify and speed up small claims litigation on 20 December 2002. The Green Paper launched consultations on the possible objectives and features of a uniform or harmonized European procedure for the recovery of uncontested claims.

(6) The swift and efficient recovery of outstanding debts over which no legal controversy exists is of paramount importance for economic operators in the European Union, as late payments constitute a major reason for insolvency threatening the survival of businesses, particularly small and medium-sized enterprises, and resulting in numerous job losses.

(7) All Member States are trying to tackle the issue of mass recovery of uncontested claims, in the majority of States by means of a simplified order for payment procedure, but both the content of national legislation and the performance of domestic procedures vary substantially. Furthermore, the procedures currently in existence are frequently either inadmissible or impracticable in crossborder cases.

(8) The resulting impediments to access to efficient justice in cross-border cases and the distortion of competition within the internal market due to imbalances in the functioning of procedural means afforded to creditors in different Member States necessitate Community legislation guaranteeing a level playing field for creditors and debtors throughout the European Union.

(9) The purpose of this Regulation is to simplify, speed up and reduce the costs of litigation in cross-border cases concerning uncontested pecuniary claims by creating a European order for payment procedure, and to permit the free circulation of European orders for payment throughout the Member States by laying down minimum standards, compliance with which renders unnecessary any intermediate proceedings in the Member State of enforcement prior to recognition and enforcement.

(10) The procedure established by this Regulation should serve as an additional and optional means for the claimant, who remains free to resort to a procedure provided for by national law. Accordingly, this Regulation neither replaces nor harmonises the existing mechanisms for the recovery of uncontested claims under national law.

(11) The procedure should be based, to the largest extent possible, on the use of standard forms in any communication between the court and the parties in order to facilitate its administration and enable the use of automatic data processing.

(12) When deciding which courts are to have jurisdiction to issue a European order for payment, Member States should take due account of the need to ensure access to justice.

(13) In the application for a European order for payment, the claimant should be obliged to provide information that is sufficient to clearly identify and support the claim in order to place the defendant in a position to make a wellinformed choice either to oppose the claim or to leave it uncontested.

(14) In that context, it should be compulsory for the claimant to include a description of evidence supporting the claim. For that purpose the application form should include as exhaustive a list as possible of types of evidence that are usually produced in support of pecuniary claims.

(15) The lodging of an application for a European order for payment should entail the payment of any applicable court fees.

(16) The court should examine the application, including the issue of jurisdiction and the description of evidence, on the basis of the information provided in the application form. This would allow the court to examine *prima facie* the merits of the claim and *inter alia* to exclude clearly unfounded claims or inadmissible applications. The examination should not need to be carried out by a judge.

(17) There is to be no right of appeal against the rejection of the application. This does not preclude, however, a possible review of the decision rejecting the application at the same level of jurisdiction in accordance with national law.

(18) The European order for payment should apprise the defendant of his options to pay the amount awarded to the claimant or to send a statement of opposition within a time limit of 30 days if he wishes to contest the claim. In addition to being provided with full information concerning the claim as supplied by the claimant, the defendant should be advised of the legal significance of the European order for payment and in particular of the consequences of leaving the claim uncontested.

(19) Due to differences between Member States' rules of civil procedure and especially those governing the service of documents, it is necessary to lay down

a specific and detailed definition of minimum standards that should apply in the context of the European order for payment procedure. In particular, as regards the fulfilment of those standards, any method based on legal fiction should not be considered sufficient for the service of the European order for payment.

(20) All the methods of service listed in Articles 13 and 14 are characterised by either complete certainty (Article 13) or a very high degree of likelihood (Article 14) that the document served has reached its addressee.

(21) Personal service on certain persons other than the defendant himself pursuant to Article 14(1)(a) and (b) should be deemed to meet the requirements of those provisions only if those persons actually accepted/received the European order for payment.

(22) Article 15 should apply to situations where the defendant cannot represent himself in court, as in the case of a legal person, and where a person authorised to represent him is determined by law, as well as to situations where the defendant has authorised another person, in particular a lawyer, to represent him in the specific court proceedings at issue.

(23) The defendant may submit his statement of opposition using the standard form set out in this Regulation. However, the courts should take into account any other written form of opposition if it is expressed in a clear manner.

(24) A statement of opposition filed within the time limit should terminate the European order for payment procedure and should lead to an automatic transfer of the case to ordinary civil proceedings unless the claimant has explicitly requested that the proceedings be terminated in that event. For the purposes of this Regulation the concept of ordinary civil proceedings should not necessarily be interpreted within the meaning of national law.

(25) After the expiry of the time limit for submitting the statement of opposition, in certain exceptional cases the defendant should be entitled to apply for a review of the European order for payment. Review in exceptional cases should not mean that the defendant is given a second opportunity to oppose the claim. During the review procedure the merits of the claim should not be evaluated beyond the grounds resulting from the exceptional circumstances invoked by the defendant. The other exceptional circumstances could include a situation where the European order for payment was based on false information provided in the application form.

(26) Court fees covered by Article 25 should not include for example lawyers' fees or costs of service of documents by an entity other than a court.

(27) A European order for payment issued in one Member State which has become enforceable should be regarded for the purposes of enforcement as if it had been issued in the Member State in which enforcement is sought. Mutual trust in the administration of justice in the Member States justifies the assessment by the court of one Member State that all conditions for issuing a European order for payment are fulfilled to enable the order to be enforced in all other Member States without judicial review of the proper application of minimum procedural standards in the Member State where the order is to be enforced. Without prejudice to the provisions of this Regulation, in particular the minimum standards laid down in Article 22(1) and (2) and Article 23, the procedures for the enforcement of the European order for payment should continue to be governed by national law.

(28) For the purposes of calculating time limits, Regulation (EEC, Euratom) No 1182/71 of the Council of 3 June 1971 determining the rules applicable to periods, dates and time limits (1) should apply. The defendant should be advised

of this and should be informed that account will be taken of the public holidays of the Member State in which the court issuing the European order for payment is situated.

(29) Since the objective of this Regulation, namely to establish a uniform rapid and efficient mechanism for the recovery of uncontested pecuniary claims throughout the European Union, cannot be sufficiently achieved by the Member States and can therefore, by reason of the scale and effects of the Regulation, be better achieved at Community level, the Community may adopt measures in accordance with the principle of subsidiarity as set out in Article 5 of the Treaty. In accordance with the principle of proportionality as set out in that Article, this Regulation does not go beyond what is necessary in order to achieve that objective.

(30) The measures necessary for the implementation of this Regulation should be adopted in accordance with Council Decision 1999/468/EC of 28 June 1999 laying down the procedures for the exercise of implementing powers conferred on the Commission.

(31) The United Kingdom and Ireland, in accordance with Article 3 of the Protocol on the position of the United Kingdom and Ireland annexed to the Treaty on European Union and the Treaty establishing the European Community, have given notice of their wish to take part in the adoption and application of this Regulation.

(32) In accordance with Articles 1 and 2 of the Protocol on the position of Denmark annexed to the Treaty on European Union and the Treaty establishing the European Community, Denmark does not take part in the adoption of this Regulation, and is not bound by it or subject to its application,

HAVE ADOPTED THIS REGULATION:

Article 1. Subject matter

(1) The purpose of this Regulation is:
(a) to simplify, speed up and reduce the costs of litigation in cross-border cases concerning uncontested pecuniary claims by creating a European order for payment procedure; and (b) to permit the free circulation of European orders for payment throughout the Member States by laying down minimum standards, compliance with which renders unnecessary any intermediate proceedings in the Member State of enforcement prior to recognition and enforcement.

(2) This Regulation shall not prevent a claimant from pursuing a claim within the meaning of Article 4 by making use of another procedure available under the law of a Member State or under Community law.

Article 2. Scope

(1) This Regulation shall apply to civil and commercial matters in cross-border cases, whatever the nature of the court or tribunal. It shall not extend, in particular, to revenue, customs or administrative matters or the liability of the State for acts and omissions in the exercise of State authority ('acta iure imperii').

(2) This Regulation shall not apply to:
(a) rights in property arising out of a matrimonial relationship, wills and succession; (b) bankruptcy, proceedings relating to the winding-up of insolvent companies or other legal persons, judicial arrangements, compositions and analogous proceedings; (c) social security; (d) claims arising from non-contractual

obligations, unless: (i) they have been the subject of an agreement between the parties or there has been an admission of debt, or (ii) they relate to liquidated debts arising from joint ownership of property.

(3) In this Regulation, the term 'Member State' shall mean Member States with the exception of Denmark.

Article 3. Cross-border cases

(1) For the purposes of this Regulation, a cross-border case is one in which at least one of the parties is domiciled or habitually resident in a Member State other than the Member State of the court seised.

(2) Domicile shall be determined in accordance with Articles 59 and 60 of Council Regulation (EC) No 44/2001 of 22 December 2000 on jurisdiction and the recognition and enforcement of judgments in civil and commercial matters.

(3) The relevant moment for determining whether there is a cross-border case shall be the time when the application for a European order for payment is submitted in accordance with this Regulation.

Article 4. European order for payment procedure

The European order for payment procedure shall be established for the collection of pecuniary claims for a specific amount that have fallen due at the time when the application for a European order for payment is submitted.

Article 5. Definitions

For the purposes of this Regulation, the following definitions shall apply:
1) 'Member State of origin' means the Member State in which a European order for payment is issued;
2) 'Member State of enforcement' means the Member State in which enforcement of a European order for payment is sought;
3) 'court' means any authority in a Member State with competence regarding European orders for payment or any other related matters;
4) 'court of origin' means the court which issues a European order for payment.

Article 6. Jurisdiction

(1) For the purposes of applying this Regulation, jurisdiction shall be determined in accordance with the relevant rules of Community law, in particular Regulation (EC) No 44/2001.

(2) However, if the claim relates to a contract concluded by a person, the consumer, for a purpose which can be regarded as being outside his trade or profession, and if the defendant is the consumer, only the courts in the Member State in which the defendant is domiciled, within the meaning of Article 59 of Regulation (EC) No 44/2001, shall have jurisdiction.

Article 7. Application for a European order for payment

(1) An application for a European order for payment shall be made using standard form A as set out in Annex I.

(2) The application shall state:
a) the names and addresses of the parties, and, where applicable, their representatives, and of the court to which the application is made;

b) the amount of the claim, including the principal and, where applicable, interest, contractual penalties and costs; (c) if interest on the claim is demanded, the interest rate and the period of time for which that interest is demanded unless statutory interest is automatically added to the principal under the law of the Member State of origin;

d) the cause of the action, including a description of the circumstances invoked as the basis of the claim and, where applicable, of the interest demanded;

e) a description of evidence supporting the claim;

f) the grounds for jurisdiction; and

g) the cross-border nature of the case within the meaning of Article 3.

(3) In the application, the claimant shall declare that the information provided is true to the best of his knowledge and belief and shall acknowledge that any deliberate false statement could lead to appropriate penalties under the law of the Member State of origin.

(4) In an Appendix to the application the claimant may indicate to the court that he opposes a transfer to ordinary civil proceedings within the meaning of Article 17 in the event of opposition by the defendant. This does not prevent the claimant from informing the court thereof subsequently, but in any event before the order is issued.

(5) The application shall be submitted in paper form or by any other means of communication, including electronic, accepted by the Member State of origin and available to the court of origin.

(6) The application shall be signed by the claimant or, where applicable, by his representative. Where the application is submitted in electronic form in accordance with paragraph 5, it shall be signed in accordance with Article 2(2) of Directive 1999/93/EC of the European Parliament and of the Council of 13 December 1999 on a Community framework for electronic signatures. The signature shall be recognized in the Member State of origin and may not be made subject to additional requirements.

However, such electronic signature shall not be required if and to the extent that an alternative electronic communications system exists in the courts of the Member State of origin which is available to a certain group of pre-registered authenticated users and which permits the identification of those users in a secure manner. Member States shall inform the Commission of such communications systems.

Article 8. Examination of the application

The court seized of an application for a European order for payment shall examine, as soon as possible and on the basis of the application form, whether the requirements set out in Articles 2, 3, 4, 6 and 7 are met and whether the claim appears to be founded. This examination may take the form of an automated procedure.

Article 9. Completion and rectification

(1) If the requirements set out in Article 7 are not met and unless the claim is clearly unfounded or the application is inadmissible, the court shall give the claimant the opportunity to complete or rectify the application. The court shall use standard form B as set out in Annex II.

(2) Where the court requests the claimant to complete or rectify the application, it shall specify a time limit it deems appropriate in the circumstances. The court may at its discretion extend that time limit.

Article 10. Modification of the application

(1) If the requirements referred to in Article 8 are met for only part of the claim, the court shall inform the claimant to that effect, using standard form C as set out in Annex III. The claimant shall be invited to accept or refuse a proposal for a European order for payment for the amount specified by the court and shall be informed of the consequences of his decision. The claimant shall reply by returning standard form C sent by the court within a time limit specified by the court in accordance with Article 9(2).

(2) If the claimant accepts the court's proposal, the court shall issue a European order for payment, in accordance with Article 12, for that part of the claim accepted by the claimant. The consequences with respect to the remaining part of the initial claim shall be governed by national law.

(3) If the claimant fails to send his reply within the time limit specified by the court or refuses the court's proposal, the court shall reject the application for a European order for payment in its entirety.

Article 11. Rejection of the application

(1) The court shall reject the application if:
(a) the requirements set out in Articles 2, 3, 4, 6 and 7 are not met; or (b) the claim is clearly unfounded; or (c) the claimant fails to send his reply within the time limit specified by the court under Article 9(2); or (d) the claimant fails to send his reply within the time limit specified by the court or refuses the court's proposal, in accordance with Article 10.

The claimant shall be informed of the grounds for the rejection by means of standard form D as set out in Annex IV.

(2) There shall be no right of appeal against the rejection of the application.

(3) The rejection of the application shall not prevent the claimant from pursuing the claim by means of a new application for a European order for payment or of any other procedure available under the law of a Member State.

Article 12. Issue of a European order for payment

(1) If the requirements referred to in Article 8 are met, the court shall issue, as soon as possible and normally within 30 days of the lodging of the application, a European order for payment using standard form E as set out in Annex V.

The 30-day period shall not include the time taken by the claimant to complete, rectify or modify the application.

(2) The European order for payment shall be issued together with a copy of the application form. It shall not comprise the information provided by the claimant in Appendices 1 and 2 to form A.

(3) In the European order for payment, the defendant shall be advised of his options to:
(a) pay the amount indicated in the order to the claimant; or (b) oppose the order by lodging with the court of origin a statement of opposition, to be sent within 30 days of service of the order on him.

(4) In the European order for payment, the defendant shall be informed that:

(a) the order was issued solely on the basis of the information which was provided by the claimant and was not verified by the court; (b) the order will become enforceable unless a statement of opposition has been lodged with the court in accordance with Article 16; (c) where a statement of opposition is lodged, the proceedings shall continue before the competent courts of the Member State of origin in accordance with the rules of ordinary civil procedure unless the claimant has explicitly requested that the proceedings be terminated in that event.

(5) The court shall ensure that the order is served on the defendant in accordance with national law by a method that shall meet the minimum standards laid down in Articles 13, 14 and 15.

Article 13. Service with proof of receipt by the defendant

The European order for payment may be served on the defendant in accordance with the national law of the State in which the service is to be effected, by one of the following methods:

a) personal service attested by an acknowledgement of receipt, including the date of receipt, which is signed by the defendant;

b) personal service attested by a document signed by the competent person who effected the service stating that the defendant has received the document or refused to receive it without any legal justification, and the date of service;

c) postal service attested by an acknowledgement of receipt, including the date of receipt, which is signed and returned by the defendant;

d) service by electronic means such as fax or e-mail, attested by an acknowledgement of receipt, including the date of receipt, which is signed and returned by the defendant.

Article 14. Service without proof of receipt by the defendant

(1) The European order for payment may also be served on the defendant in accordance with the national law of the State in which service is to be effected, by one of the following methods:

a) personal service at the defendant's personal address on persons who are living in the same household as the defendant or are employed there;

b) in the case of a self-employed defendant or a legal person, personal service at the defendant's business premises on persons who are employed by the defendant;

c) deposit of the order in the defendant's mailbox;

d) deposit of the order at a post office or with competent public authorities and the placing in the defendant's mailbox of written notification of that deposit, provided that the written notification clearly states the character of the document as a court document or the legal effect of the notification as effecting service and setting in motion the running of time for the purposes of time limits;

e) postal service without proof pursuant to paragraph 3 where the defendant has his address in the Member State of origin;

f) electronic means attested by an automatic confirmation of delivery, provided that the defendant has expressly accepted this method of service in advance.

(2) For the purposes of this Regulation, service under paragraph 1 is not admissible if the defendant's address is not known with certainty.

(3) Service pursuant to paragraph 1(a), (b), (c) and (d) shall be attested by:

(a) a document signed by the competent person who effected the service, indicating: (i) the method of service used; and (ii) the date of service; and (iii) where the order has been served on a person other than the defendant, the name of that person and his relation to the defendant; or (b) an acknowledgement of receipt by the person served, for the purposes of paragraphs (1)(a) and (b).

Article 15. Service on a representative

Service pursuant to Articles 13 or 14 may also be effected on a defendant's representative.

Article 16. Opposition to the European order for payment

(1) The defendant may lodge a statement of opposition to the European order for payment with the court of origin using standard form F as set out in Annex VI, which shall be supplied to him together with the European order for payment.

(2) The statement of opposition shall be sent within 30 days of service of the order on the defendant.

(3) The defendant shall indicate in the statement of opposition that he contests the claim, without having to specify the reasons for this.

(4) The statement of opposition shall be submitted in paper form or by any other means of communication, including electronic, accepted by the Member State of origin and available to the court of origin.

(5) The statement of opposition shall be signed by the defendant or, where applicable, by his representative. Where the statement of opposition is submitted in electronic form in accordance with paragraph 4, it shall be signed in accordance with Article 2(2) of Directive 1999/93/EC. The signature shall be recognised in the Member State of origin and may not be made subject to additional requirements.

However, such electronic signature shall not be required if and to the extent that an alternative electronic communications system exists in the courts of the Member State of origin which is available to a certain group of pre-registered authenticated users and which permits the identification of those users in a secure manner. Member States shall inform the Commission of such communications systems.

Article 17. Effects of the lodging of a statement of opposition

(1) If a statement of opposition is entered within the time limit laid down in Article 16(2), the proceedings shall continue before the competent courts of the Member State of origin in accordance with the rules of ordinary civil procedure unless the claimant has explicitly requested that the proceedings be terminated in that event.

Where the claimant has pursued his claim through the European order for payment procedure, nothing under national law shall prejudice his position in subsequent ordinary civil proceedings.

(2) The transfer to ordinary civil proceedings within the meaning of paragraph 1 shall be governed by the law of the Member State of origin.

(3) The claimant shall be informed whether the defendant has lodged a statement of opposition and of any transfer to ordinary civil proceedings.

Article 18. Enforceability

(1) If within the time limit laid down in Article 16(2), taking into account an appropriate period of time to allow a statement to arrive, no statement of opposition has been lodged with the court of origin, the court of origin shall without delay declare the European order for payment enforceable using standard form G as set out in Annex VII. The court shall verify the date of service.

(2) Without prejudice to paragraph 1, the formal requirements for enforceability shall be governed by the law of the Member State of origin.

(3) The court shall send the enforceable European order for payment to the claimant.

Article 19. Abolition of exequatur

A European order for payment which has become enforceable in the Member State of origin shall be recognised and enforced in the other Member States without the need for a declaration of enforceability and without any possibility of opposing its recognition.

Article 20. Review in exceptional cases

(1) After the expiry of the time limit laid down in Article 16(2) the defendant shall be entitled to apply for a review of the European order for payment before the competent court in the Member State of origin where:

a) (i) the order for payment was served by one of the methods provided for in Article 14, or (ii) service was not effected in sufficient time to enable him to arrange for his defence, without any fault on his part, or

b) the defendant was prevented from objecting to the claim by reason of force majeure or due to extraordinary circumstances without any fault on his part,

provided in either case that he acts promptly.

(2) After expiry of the time limit laid down in Article 16(2) the defendant shall also be entitled to apply for a review of the European order for payment before the competent court in the Member State of origin where the order for payment was clearly wrongly issued, having regard to the requirements laid down in this Regulation, or due to other exceptional circumstances.

(3) If the court rejects the defendant's application on the basis that none of the grounds for review referred to in paragraphs 1 and 2 apply, the European order for payment shall remain in force.

If the court decides that the review is justified for one of the reasons laid down in paragraphs 1 and 2, the European order for payment shall be null and void.

Article 21. Enforcement

(1) Without prejudice to the provisions of this Regulation, enforcement procedures shall be governed by the law of the Member State of enforcement.

A European order for payment which has become enforceable shall be enforced under the same conditions as an enforceable decision issued in the Member State of enforcement.

(2) For enforcement in another Member State, the claimant shall provide the competent enforcement authorities of that Member State with:

(a) a copy of the European order for payment, as declared enforceable by the court of origin, which satisfies the conditions necessary to establish its authenticity; and (b) where necessary, a translation of the European order for payment into the official language of the Member State of enforcement or, if there are several official languages in that Member State, the official language or one of the official languages of court proceedings of the place where enforcement is sought, in conformity with the law of that Member State, or into another language that the Member State of enforcement has indicated it can accept. Each Member State may indicate the official language or languages of the institutions of the European Union other than its own which it can accept for the European order for payment. The translation shall be certified by a person qualified to do so in one of the Member States.

(3) No security, bond or deposit, however described, shall be required of a claimant who in one Member State applies for enforcement of a European order for payment issued in another Member State on the ground that he is a foreign national or that he is not domiciled or resident in the Member State of enforcement.

Article 22. Refusal of enforcement

(1) Enforcement shall, upon application by the defendant, be refused by the competent court in the Member State of enforcement if the European order for payment is irreconcilable with an earlier decision or order previously given in any Member State or in a third country, provided that:

(a) the earlier decision or order involved the same cause of action between the same parties; and (b) the earlier decision or order fulfils the conditions necessary for its recognition in the Member State of enforcement; and (c) the irreconcilability could not have been raised as an objection in the court proceedings in the Member State of origin.

(2) Enforcement shall, upon application, also be refused if and to the extent that the defendant has paid the claimant the amount awarded in the European order for payment.

(3) Under no circumstances may the European order for payment be reviewed as to its substance in the Member State of enforcement.

Article 23. Stay or limitation of enforcement

Where the defendant has applied for a review in accordance with Article 20, the competent court in the Member State of enforcement may, upon application by the defendant:

(a) limit the enforcement proceedings to protective measures; or (b) make enforcement conditional on the provision of such security as it shall determine; or (c) under exceptional circumstances, stay the enforcement proceedings.

Article 24. Legal representation

Representation by a lawyer or another legal professional shall not be mandatory:

(a) for the claimant in respect of the application for a European order for payment; (b) for the defendant in respect of the statement of opposition to a European order for payment.

Article 25. Court fees

(1) The combined court fees of a European order for payment procedure and of the ordinary civil proceedings that ensue in the event of a statement of opposition to a European order for payment in a Member State shall not exceed the court fees of ordinary civil proceedings without a preceding European order for payment procedure in that Member State.

(2) For the purposes of this Regulation, court fees shall comprise fees and charges to be paid to the court, the amount of which is fixed in accordance with national law.

Article 26. Relationship with national procedural law

All procedural issues not specifically dealt with in this Regulation shall be governed by national law.

Article 27. Relationship with Regulation (EC) No 1348/2000

This Regulation shall not affect the application of Council Regulation (EC) No 1348/2000 of 29 May 2000 on the service in the Member States of judicial and extrajudicial documents in civil and commercial matters.

Article 28. Information relating to service costs and enforcement

Member States shall cooperate to provide the general public and professional circles with information on:

(a) costs of service of documents; and (b) which authorities have competence with respect to enforcement for the purposes of applying Articles 21, 22 and 23,

in particular via the European Judicial Network in civil and commercial matters established in accordance with Council Decision 2001/470/EC.

Article 29. Information relating to jurisdiction, review procedures, means of communication and languages

(1) By 12 June 2008, Member States shall communicate to the Commission:

a) which courts have jurisdiction to issue a European order for payment;

b) the review procedure and the competent courts for the purposes of the application of Article 20;

c) the means of communication accepted for the purposes of the European order for payment procedure and available to the courts;

d) languages accepted pursuant to Article 21(2)(b).

Member States shall apprise the Commission of any subsequent changes to this information.

(2) The Commission shall make the information notified in accordance with paragraph 1 publicly available through publication in the *Official Journal of the European Union* and through any other appropriate means.

Article 30. Amendments to the Annexes

The standard forms set out in the Annexes shall be updated or technically adjusted, ensuring full conformity with the provisions of this Regulation, in accordance with the procedure referred to in Article 31(2).

Article 31. Committee

(1) The Commission shall be assisted by the committee established by Article 75 of Regulation (EC) No 44/2001.

(2) Where reference is made to this paragraph, Article 5a(1)-(4) and Article 7 of Decision 1999/468/EC shall apply, having regard to the provisions of Article 8 thereof.

(3) The Committee shall adopt its Rules of Procedure.

Article 32. Review

By 12 December 2013, the Commission shall present to the European Parliament, the Council and the European Economic and Social Committee a detailed report reviewing the operation of the European order for payment procedure. That report shall contain an assessment of the procedure as it has operated and an extended impact assessment for each Member State.

To that end, and in order to ensure that best practice in the European Union is duly taken into account and reflects the principles of better legislation, Member States shall provide the Commission with information relating to the cross-border operation of the European order for payment. This information shall cover court fees, speed of the procedure, efficiency, ease of use and the internal payment order procedures of the Member States.

The Commission's report shall be accompanied, if appropriate, by proposals for adaptation.

Article 33. Entry into force

This Regulation shall enter into force on the day following the date of its publication in the *Official Journal of the European Union*.

It shall apply from 12 December 2008, with the exception of Articles 28, 29, 30 and 31 which shall apply from 12 June 2008.

This Regulation shall be binding in its entirety and directly applicable in the Member States in accordance with the Treaty establishing the European Community.

V. Regulation (EC) No 805/2004 of the European Parliament and of the Council of 21 April 2004 creating a European Enforcement Order for uncontested claims

THE EUROPEAN PARLIAMENT AND THE COUNCIL OF THE EUROPEAN UNION,

Having regard to the Treaty establishing the European Community, and in particular Articles 61(c) and the second indent of Article 67(5) thereof,

Having regard to the proposal from the Commission[17],

Having regard to the Opinion of the European Economic and Social Committee[18],

Acting in accordance with the procedure laid down in Article 251 of the Treaty[19],

Whereas:

(1) The Community has set itself the objective of maintaining and developing an area of freedom, security and justice, in which the free movement of persons is ensured. To this end, the Community is to adopt, *inter alia*, measures in the field of judicial cooperation in civil matters that are necessary for the proper functioning of the internal market.

(2) On 3 December 1998, the Council adopted an Action Plan of the Council and the Commission on how best to implement the provisions of the Treaty of Amsterdam on an area of freedom, security and justice[20] (the Vienna Action Plan).

(3) The European Council meeting in Tampere on 15 and 16 October 1999 endorsed the principle of mutual recognition of judicial decisions as the cornerstone for the creation of a genuine judicial area.

(4) On 30 November 2000, the Council adopted a programme of measures for implementation of the principle of mutual recognition of decisions in civil and commercial matters[21]. This programme includes in its first stage the abolition of exequatur, that is to say, the creation of a European Enforcement Order for uncontested claims.

(5) The concept of "uncontested claims" should cover all situations in which a creditor, given the verified absence of any dispute by the debtor as to the nature or extent of a pecuniary claim, has obtained either a court decision against that debtor or an enforceable document that requires the debtor's express consent, be it a court settlement or an authentic instrument.

(6) The absence of objections from the debtor as stipulated in Article 3(1)(b) can take the shape of default of appearance at a court hearing or of failure to comply with an invitation by the court to give written notice of an intention to defend the case.

(7) This Regulation should apply to judgments, court settlements and authentic instruments on uncontested claims and to decisions delivered following challenges to judgments, court settlements and authentic instruments certified as European Enforcement Orders.

(8) In its Tampere conclusions, the European Council considered that access to enforcement in a Member State other than that in which the judgment has been

---

[17] OJ C 203 E, 27.8.2002, p. 86.
[18] OJ C 85, 8.4.2003, p. 1.
[19] Opinion of the European Parliament of 8 April 2003 (OJ C 64 E, 12.3.2004, p. 79), Council Common Position of 6.2.2004 (not yet published in the Official Journal) and Position of the European Parliament of 30.3.2004 (not yet published in the Official Journal).
[20] OJ C 19, 23.1.1999, p. 1.
[21] OJ C 12, 15.1.2001, p. 1.

given should be accelerated and simplified by dispensing with any intermediate measures to be taken prior to enforcement in the Member State in which enforcement is sought. A judgment that has been certified as a European Enforcement Order by the court of origin should, for enforcement purposes, be treated as if it had been delivered in the Member State in which enforcement is sought. In the United Kingdom, for example, the registration of a certified foreign judgment will therefore follow the same rules as the registration of a judgment from another part of the United Kingdom and is not to imply a review as to the substance of the foreign judgment. Arrangements for the enforcement of judgments should continue to be governed by national law.

(9) Such a procedure should offer significant advantages as compared with the exequatur procedure provided for in Council Regulation (EC) No 44/2001 of 22 December 2000 on jurisdiction and the recognition and enforcement of judgments in civil and commercial matters[22], in that there is no need for approval by the judiciary in a second Member State with the delays and expenses that this entails.

(10) Where a court in a Member State has given judgment on an uncontested claim in the absence of participation of the debtor in the proceedings, the abolition of any checks in the Member State of enforcement is inextricably linked to and dependent upon the existence of a sufficient guarantee of observance of the rights of the defence.

(11) This Regulation seeks to promote the fundamental rights and takes into account the principles recognised in particular by the Charter of Fundamental Rights of the European Union. In particular, it seeks to ensure full respect for the right to a fair trial as recognised in Article 47 of the Charter.

(12) Minimum standards should be established for the proceedings leading to the judgment in order to ensure that the debtor is informed about the court action against him, the requirements for his active participation in the proceedings to contest the claim and the consequences of his non-participation in sufficient time and in such a way as to enable him to arrange for his defence.

(13) Due to differences between the Member States as regards the rules of civil procedure and especially those governing the service of documents, it is necessary to lay down a specific and detailed definition of those minimum standards. In particular, any method of service that is based on a legal fiction as regards the fulfilment of those minimum standards cannot be considered sufficient for the certification of a judgment as a European Enforcement Order.

(14) All the methods of service listed in Articles 13 and 14 are characterised by either full certainty (Article 13) or a very high degree of likelihood (Article 14) that the document served has reached its addressee. In the second category, a judgment should only be certified as a European Enforcement Order if the Member State of origin has an appropriate mechanism in place enabling the debtor to apply for a full review of the judgment under the conditions set out in Article 19 in those exceptional cases where, in spite of compliance with Article 14, the document has not reached the addressee.

(15) Personal service on certain persons other than the debtor himself pursuant to Article 14(1)(a) and (b) should be understood to meet the requirements of those provisions only if those persons actually accepted/received the document in question.

---

[22] OJ L 12, 16.1.2001, p. 1. Regulation as last amended by Commission Regulation (EC) No 1496/2002 (OJ L 225, 22.8.2002, p. 13).

(16) Article 15 should apply to situations where the debtor cannot represent himself in court, as in the case of a legal person, and where a person to represent him is determined by law as well as situations where the debtor has authorised another person, in particular a lawyer, to represent him in the specific court proceedings at issue.

(17) The courts competent for scrutinising full compliance with the minimum procedural standards should, if satisfied, issue a standardised European Enforcement Order certificate that makes that scrutiny and its result transparent.

(18) Mutual trust in the administration of justice in the Member States justifies the assessment by the court of one Member State that all conditions for certification as a European Enforcement Order are fulfilled to enable a judgment to be enforced in all other Member States without judicial review of the proper application of the minimum procedural standards in the Member State where the judgment is to be enforced.

(19) This Regulation does not imply an obligation for the Member States to adapt their national legislation to the minimum procedural standards set out herein. It provides an incentive to that end by making available a more efficient and rapid enforceability of judgments in other Member States only if those minimum standards are met.

(20) Application for certification as a European Enforcement Order for uncontested claims should be optional for the creditor, who may instead choose the system of recognition and enforcement under Regulation (EC) No 44/2001 or other Community instruments.

(21) When a document has to be sent from one Member State to another for service there, this Regulation and in particular the rules on service set out herein should apply together with Council Regulation (EC) No 1348/2000 of 29 May 2000 on the service in the Member States of judicial and extrajudicial documents in civil or commercial matters[23], and in particular Article 14 thereof in conjunction with Member States declarations made under Article 23 thereof.

(22) Since the objectives of the proposed action cannot be sufficiently achieved by the Member States and can therefore, by reason of the scale or effects of the action, be better achieved at Community level, the Community may adopt measures, in accordance with the principle of subsidiarity as set out in Article 5 of the Treaty. In accordance with the principle of proportionality, as set out in that Article, this Regulation does not go beyond what is necessary in order to achieve those objectives.

(23) The measures necessary for the implementation of this Regulation should be adopted in accordance with Council Decision 1999/468/EC of 28 June 1999 laying down the procedures for the exercise of implementing powers conferred on the Commission[24].

(24) In accordance with Article 3 of the Protocol on the position of the United Kingdom and Ireland annexed to the Treaty on European Union and the Treaty establishing the European Community, the United Kingdom and Ireland have notified their wish to take part in the adoption and application of this Regulation.

(25) In accordance with Articles 1 and 2 of the Protocol on the position of Denmark annexed to the Treaty on European Union and the Treaty establishing

---

[23] OJ L 160, 30.6.2000, p. 37.
[24] OJ L 184, 17.7.1999, p. 23.

the European Community, Denmark does not take part in the adoption of this Regulation, and is therefore not bound by it or subject to its application.

(26) Pursuant to the second indent of Article 67(5) of the Treaty, the codecision procedure is applicable from 1 February 2003 for the measures laid down in this Regulation,

HAVE ADOPTED THIS REGULATION:

CHAPTER I
SUBJECT MATTER, SCOPE AND DEFINITIONS

Article 1. Subject matter

The purpose of this Regulation is to create a European Enforcement Order for uncontested claims to permit, by laying down minimum standards, the free circulation of judgments, court settlements and authentic instruments throughout all Member States without any intermediate proceedings needing to be brought in the Member State of enforcement prior to recognition and enforcement.

Article 2. Scope

1. This Regulation shall apply in civil and commercial matters, whatever the nature of the court or tribunal. It shall not extend, in particular, to revenue, customs or administrative matters or the liability of the State for acts and omissions in the exercise of State authority ("acta iure imperii").
2. This Regulation shall not apply to:
(a) the status or legal capacity of natural persons, rights in property arising out of a matrimonial relationship, wills and succession;
(b) bankruptcy, proceedings relating to the winding-up of insolvent companies or other legal persons, judicial arrangements, compositions and analogous proceedings;
(c) social security;
(d) arbitration.
3. In this Regulation, the term "Member State" shall mean Member States with the exception of Denmark.

Article 3. Enforcement titles to be certified as a European Enforcement Order

1. This Regulation shall apply to judgments, court settlements and authentic instruments on uncontested claims.
  A claim shall be regarded as uncontested if:
(a) the debtor has expressly agreed to it by admission or by means of a settlement which has been approved by a court or concluded before a court in the course of proceedings; or
(b) the debtor has never objected to it, in compliance with the relevant procedural requirements under the law of the Member State of origin, in the course of the court proceedings; or
(c) the debtor has not appeared or been represented at a court hearing regarding that claim after having initially objected to the claim in the course of the court proceedings, provided that such conduct amounts to a tacit admission of the

claim or of the facts alleged by the creditor under the law of the Member State of origin; or

(d) the debtor has expressly agreed to it in an authentic instrument.

2. This Regulation shall also apply to decisions delivered following challenges to judgments, court settlements or authentic instruments certified as European Enforcement Orders.

Article 4. Definitions

For the purposes of this Regulation, the following definitions shall apply:

1. "judgment": any judgment given by a court or tribunal of a Member State, whatever the judgment may be called, including a decree, order, decision or writ of execution, as well as the determination of costs or expenses by an officer of the court;

2. "claim": a claim for payment of a specific sum of money that has fallen due or for which the due date is indicated in the judgment, court settlement or authentic instrument;

3. "authentic instrument":

(a) a document which has been formally drawn up or registered as an authentic instrument, and the authenticity of which:
   (i) relates to the signature and the content of the instrument; and
   (ii) has been established by a public authority or other authority empowered for that purpose by the Member State in which it originates;

or

b) an arrangement relating to maintenance obligations concluded with administrative authorities or authenticated by them;

4. "Member State of origin": the Member State in which the judgment has been given, the court settlement has been approved or concluded or the authentic instrument has been drawn up or registered, and is to be certified as a European Enforcement Order;

5. "Member State of enforcement": the Member State in which enforcement of the judgment, court settlement or authentic instrument certified as a European Enforcement Order is sought;

6. "court of origin": the court or tribunal seised of the proceedings at the time of fulfilment of the conditions set out in Article 3(1)(a), (b) or (c);

7. in Sweden, in summary proceedings concerning orders to pay (betalningsföreläggande), the expression "court" includes the Swedish enforcement service (kronofogdemyndighet).

CHAPTER II
EUROPEAN ENFORCEMENT ORDER

Article 5. Abolition of exequatur

A judgment which has been certified as a European Enforcement Order in the Member State of origin shall be recognised and enforced in the other Member States without the need for a declaration of enforceability and without any possibility of opposing its recognition.

Article 6. Requirements for certification as a European Enforcement Order

1. A judgment on an uncontested claim delivered in a Member State shall, upon application at any time to the court of origin, be certified as a European Enforcement Order if:
(a) the judgment is enforceable in the Member State of origin; and
(b) the judgment does not conflict with the rules on jurisdiction as laid down in sections 3 and 6 of Chapter II of Regulation (EC) No 44/2001; and
(c) the court proceedings in the Member State of origin met the requirements as set out in Chapter III where a claim is uncontested within the meaning of Article 3(1)(b) or (c); and
(d) the judgment was given in the Member State of the debtor's domicile within the meaning of Article 59 of Regulation (EC) No 44/2001, in cases where
    – a claim is uncontested within the meaning of Article 3(1)(b) or (c); and
    – it relates to a contract concluded by a person, the consumer, for a purpose which can be regarded as being outside his trade or profession; and
    – the debtor is the consumer.

2. Where a judgment certified as a European Enforcement Order has ceased to be enforceable or its enforceability has been suspended or limited, a certificate indicating the lack or limitation of enforceability shall, upon application at any time to the court of origin, be issued, using the standard form in Annex IV.

3. Without prejudice to Article 12(2), where a decision has been delivered following a challenge to a judgment certified as a European Enforcement Order in accordance with paragraph 1 of this Article, a replacement certificate shall, upon application at any time, be issued, using the standard form in Annex V, if that decision on the challenge is enforceable in the Member State of origin.

Article 7. Costs related to court proceedings

Where a judgment includes an enforceable decision on the amount of costs related to the court proceedings, including the interest rates, it shall be certified as a European Enforcement Order also with regard to the costs unless the debtor has specifically objected to his obligation to bear such costs in the course of the court proceedings, in accordance with the law of the Member State of origin.

Article 8. Partial European Enforcement Order certificate

If only parts of the judgment meet the requirements of this Regulation, a partial European Enforcement Order certificate shall be issued for those parts.

Article 9. Issue of the European Enforcement Order certificate

1. The European Enforcement Order certificate shall be issued using the standard form in Annex I.
2. The European Enforcement Order certificate shall be issued in the language of the judgment.

Article 10. Rectification or withdrawal of the European Enforcement Order certificate

1. The European Enforcement Order certificate shall, upon application to the court of origin, be

(a) rectified where, due to a material error, there is a discrepancy between the judgment and the certificate;
(b) withdrawn where it was clearly wrongly granted, having regard to the requirements laid down in this Regulation.

2. The law of the Member State of origin shall apply to the rectification or withdrawal of the European Enforcement Order certificate.

3. An application for the rectification or withdrawal of a European Enforcement Order certificate may be made using the standard form in Annex VI.

4. No appeal shall lie against the issuing of a European Enforcement Order certificate.

Article 11. Effect of the European Enforcement Order certificate

The European Enforcement Order certificate shall take effect only within the limits of the enforceability of the judgment.

CHAPTER III
MINIMUM STANDARDS FOR UNCONTESTED CLAIMS PROCEDURES

Article 12. Scope of application of minimum standards

1. A judgment on a claim that is uncontested within the meaning of Article 3(1)(b) or (c) can be certified as a European Enforcement Order only if the court proceedings in the Member State of origin met the procedural requirements as set out in this Chapter.

2. The same requirements shall apply to the issuing of a European Enforcement Order certificate or a replacement certificate within the meaning of Article 6(3) for a decision following a challenge to a judgment where, at the time of that decision, the conditions of Article 3(1)(b) or (c) are fulfilled.

Article 13. Service with proof of receipt by the debtor

1. The document instituting the proceedings or an equivalent document may have been served on the debtor by one of the following methods:
(a) personal service attested by an acknowledgement of receipt, including the date of receipt, which is signed by the debtor;
(b) personal service attested by a document signed by the competent person who effected the service stating that the debtor has received the document or refused to receive it without any legal justification, and the date of the service;
(c) postal service attested by an acknowledgement of receipt including the date of receipt, which is signed and returned by the debtor;
(d) service by electronic means such as fax or e-mail, attested by an acknowledgement of receipt including the date of receipt, which is signed and returned by the debtor.

2. Any summons to a court hearing may have been served on the debtor in compliance with paragraph 1 or orally in a previous court hearing on the same claim and stated in the minutes of that previous court hearing.

Article 14. Service without proof of receipt by the debtor

1. Service of the document instituting the proceedings or an equivalent document and any summons to a court hearing on the debtor may also have been effected by one of the following methods:
(a) personal service at the debtor's personal address on persons who are living in the same household as the debtor or are employed there;
(b) in the case of a self-employed debtor or a legal person, personal service at the debtor's business premises on persons who are employed by the debtor;
(c) deposit of the document in the debtor's mailbox;
(d) deposit of the document at a post office or with competent public authorities and the placing in the debtor's mailbox of written notification of that deposit, provided that the written notification clearly states the character of the document as a court document or the legal effect of the notification as effecting service and setting in motion the running of time for the purposes of time limits;
(e) postal service without proof pursuant to paragraph 3 where the debtor has his address in the Member State of origin;
(f) electronic means attested by an automatic confirmation of delivery, provided that the debtor has expressly accepted this method of service in advance.

2. For the purposes of this Regulation, service under paragraph 1 is not admissible if the debtor's address is not known with certainty.

3. Service pursuant to paragraph 1, (a) to (d), shall be attested by:
(a) a document signed by the competent person who effected the service, indicating:
   (i) the method of service used; and
   (ii) the date of service; and
   (iii) where the document has been served on a person other than the debtor, the name of that person and his relation to the debtor,
   or
b) an acknowledgement of receipt by the person served, for the purposes of paragraphs 1(a) and (b).

Article 15. Service on the debtor's representatives

Service pursuant to Articles 13 or 14 may also have been effected on a debtor's representative.

Article 16

Provision to the debtor of due information about the claim
In order to ensure that the debtor was provided with due information about the claim, the document instituting the proceedings or the equivalent document must have contained the following:
(a) the names and the addresses of the parties;
(b) the amount of the claim;
(c) if interest on the claim is sought, the interest rate and the period for which interest is sought unless statutory interest is automatically added to the principal under the law of the Member State of origin;
(d) a statement of the reason for the claim.

Article 17

Provision to the debtor of due information about the procedural steps necessary to contest the claim

The following must have been clearly stated in or together with the document instituting the proceedings, the equivalent document or any summons to a court hearing:

(a) the procedural requirements for contesting the claim, including the time limit for contesting the claim in writing or the time for the court hearing, as applicable, the name and the address of the institution to which to respond or before which to appear, as applicable, and whether it is mandatory to be represented by a lawyer;

(b) the consequences of an absence of objection or default of appearance, in particular, where applicable, the possibility that a judgment may be given or enforced against the debtor and the liability for costs related to the court proceedings.

Article 18. Cure of non-compliance with minimum standards

1. If the proceedings in the Member State of origin did not meet the procedural requirements as set out in Articles 13 to 17, such non-compliance shall be cured and a judgment may be certified as a European Enforcement Order if:

(a) the judgment has been served on the debtor in compliance with the requirements pursuant to Article 13 or Article 14; and

(b) it was possible for the debtor to challenge the judgment by means of a full review and the debtor has been duly informed in or together with the judgment about the procedural requirements for such a challenge, including the name and address of the institution with which it must be lodged and, where applicable, the time limit for so doing; and

(c) the debtor has failed to challenge the judgment in compliance with the relevant procedural requirements.

2. If the proceedings in the Member State of origin did not comply with the procedural requirements as set out in Article 13 or Article 14, such non-compliance shall be cured if it is proved by the conduct of the debtor in the court proceedings that he has personally received the document to be served in sufficient time to arrange for his defence.

Article 19. Minimum standards for review in exceptional cases

1. Further to Articles 13 to 18, a judgment can only be certified as a European Enforcement Order if the debtor is entitled, under the law of the Member State of origin, to apply for a review of the judgment where:

(a) (i) the document instituting the proceedings or an equivalent document or, where applicable, the summons to a court hearing, was served by one of the methods provided for in Article 14; and

 (ii) service was not effected in sufficient time to enable him to arrange for his defence, without any fault on his part;

 or

(b) the debtor was prevented from objecting to the claim by reason of force majeure, or due to extraordinary circumstances without any fault on his part, provided in either case that he acts promptly.

2. This Article is without prejudice to the possibility for Member States to grant access to a review of the judgment under more generous conditions than those mentioned in paragraph 1.

CHAPTER IV
ENFORCEMENT

Article 20. Enforcement procedure

1. Without prejudice to the provisions of this Chapter, the enforcement procedures shall be governed by the law of the Member State of enforcement.

A judgment certified as a European Enforcement Order shall be enforced under the same conditions as a judgment handed down in the Member State of enforcement.

2. The creditor shall be required to provide the competent enforcement authorities of the Member State of enforcement with:
(a) a copy of the judgment which satisfies the conditions necessary to establish its authenticity; and
(b) a copy of the European Enforcement Order certificate which satisfies the conditions necessary to establish its authenticity; and
(c) where necessary, a transcription of the European Enforcement Order certificate or a translation thereof into the official language of the Member State of enforcement or, if there are several official languages in that Member State, the official language or one of the official languages of court proceedings of the place where enforcement is sought, in conformity with the law of that Member State, or into another language that the Member State of enforcement has indicated it can accept. Each Member State may indicate the official language or languages of the institutions of the European Community other than its own which it can accept for the completion of the certificate. The translation shall be certified by a person qualified to do so in one of the Member States.

3. No security, bond or deposit, however described, shall be required of a party who in one Member State applies for enforcement of a judgment certified as a European Enforcement Order in another Member State on the ground that he is a foreign national or that he is not domiciled or resident in the Member State of enforcement.

Article 21. Refusal of enforcement

1. Enforcement shall, upon application by the debtor, be refused by the competent court in the Member State of enforcement if the judgment certified as a European Enforcement Order is irreconcilable with an earlier judgment given in any Member State or in a third country, provided that:
(a) the earlier judgment involved the same cause of action and was between the same parties; and
(b) the earlier judgment was given in the Member State of enforcement or fulfils the conditions necessary for its recognition in the Member State of enforcement; and
(c) the irreconcilability was not and could not have been raised as an objection in the court proceedings in the Member State of origin.

2. Under no circumstances may the judgment or its certification as a European Enforcement Order be reviewed as to their substance in the Member State of enforcement.

Article 22. Agreements with third countries

This Regulation shall not affect agreements by which Member States undertook, prior to the entry into force of Regulation (EC) No 44/2001, pursuant to Article 59 of the Brussels Convention on jurisdiction and the enforcement of judgments in civil and commercial matters, not to recognise judgments given, in particular in other Contracting States to that Convention, against defendants domiciled or habitually resident in a third country where, in cases provided for in Article 4 of that Convention, the judgment could only be founded on a ground of jurisdiction specified in the second paragraph of Article 3 of that Convention.

Article 23. Stay or limitation of enforcement

Where the debtor has
- challenged a judgment certified as a European Enforcement Order, including an application for review within the meaning of Article 19, or
- applied for the rectification or withdrawal of a European Enforcement Order certificate in accordance with Article 10,

the competent court or authority in the Member State of enforcement may, upon application by the debtor:
(a) limit the enforcement proceedings to protective measures; or
(b) make enforcement conditional on the provision of such security as it shall determine; or
(c) under exceptional circumstances, stay the enforcement proceedings.

CHAPTER V
COURT SETTLEMENTS AND AUTHENTIC INSTRUMENTS

Article 24. Court settlements

1. A settlement concerning a claim within the meaning of Article 4(2) which has been approved by a court or concluded before a court in the course of proceedings and is enforceable in the Member State in which it was approved or concluded shall, upon application to the court that approved it or before which it was concluded, be certified as a European Enforcement Order using the standard form in Annex II.

2. A settlement which has been certified as a European Enforcement Order in the Member State of origin shall be enforced in the other Member States without the need for a declaration of enforceability and without any possibility of opposing its enforceability.

3. The provisions of Chapter II, with the exception of Articles 5, 6(1) and 9(1), and of Chapter IV, with the exception of Articles 21(1) and 22, shall apply as appropriate.

Article 25. Authentic instruments

1. An authentic instrument concerning a claim within the meaning of Article 4(2) which is enforceable in one Member State shall, upon application to the authority designated by the Member State of origin, be certified as a European Enforcement Order, using the standard form in Annex III.

2. An authentic instrument which has been certified as a European Enforcement Order in the Member State of origin shall be enforced in the other Member States without the need for a declaration of enforceability and without any possibility of opposing its enforceability.

3. The provisions of Chapter II, with the exception of Articles 5, 6(1) and 9(1), and of Chapter IV, with the exception of Articles 21(1) and 22, shall apply as appropriate.

CHAPTER VI
TRANSITIONAL PROVISION

Article 26. Transitional provision

This Regulation shall apply only to judgments given, to court settlements approved or concluded and to documents formally drawn up or registered as authentic instruments after the entry into force of this Regulation.

CHAPTER VII
RELATIONSHIP WITH OTHER COMMUNITY INSTRUMENTS

Article 27. Relationship with Regulation (EC) No 44/2001

This Regulation shall not affect the possibility of seeking recognition and enforcement, in accordance with Regulation (EC) No 44/2001, of a judgment, a court settlement or an authentic instrument on an uncontested claim.

Article 28. Relationship with Regulation (EC) No 1348/2000

This Regulation shall not affect the application of Regulation (EC) No 1348/2000.

CHAPTER VIII
GENERAL AND FINAL PROVISIONS

Article 29. Information on enforcement procedures and authorities

The Member States shall cooperate to provide the general public and professional circles with information on:
(a) the methods and procedures of enforcement in the Member States; and
(b) the competent authorities for enforcement in the Member States,
in particular via the European Judicial Network in civil and commercial matters established in accordance with Decision 2001/470/EC[25].

---

[25] OJ L 174, 27.6.2001, p. 25.

Article 30. Information relating to redress procedures, languages and authorities

1. The Member States shall notify the Commission of:
(a) the procedures for rectification and withdrawal referred to in Article 10(2) and for review referred to in Article 19(1);
(b) the languages accepted pursuant to Article 20(2)(c);
(c) the lists of the authorities referred to in Article 25;
and any subsequent changes thereof.

2. The Commission shall make the information notified in accordance with paragraph 1 publicly available through publication in the Official Journal of the European Union and through any other appropriate means.

Article 31. Amendments to the Annexes

Any amendment to the standard forms in the Annexes shall be adopted in accordance with the advisory procedure referred to in Article 32(2).

Article 32. Committee

1. The Commission shall be assisted by the committee provided for by Article 75 of Regulation (EC) No 44/2001.

2. Where reference is made to this paragraph, Articles 3 and 7 of Decision 1999/468/EC shall apply, having regard to the provisions of Article 8 thereof.

3. The Committee shall adopt its Rules of Procedure.

Article 33. Entry into force

This Regulation shall enter into force on 21 January 2004.

It shall apply from 21 October 2005, with the exception of Articles 30, 31 and 32, which shall apply from 21 January 2005.

This Regulation shall be binding in its entirety and directly applicable in the Member States in accordance with the Treaty establishing the European Community.

C. Bilateral and Multilateral Treaties

I. List of Treaties Relevant to International Procedural and Arbitration Law in Germany

1. **Legal Aid, Service Abroad and Taking of Evidence**

1.1 Multilateral Treaties
a) Hague Convention of 17 July 1905 relating to Civil Procedure
b) Hague Convention of 1 March 1954 relating to Civil Procedure
c) Hague Convention of 5 October 1961 Abolishing the Requirement of Legalisation for Foreign Public Documents
d) Hague Convention of 15 November 1965 on the Service Abroad of Judicial and Extrajudicial Documents in Civil or Commercial Matters
e) Hague Convention of 18 March 1970 on the Taking of Evidence Abroad in Civil or Commercial Matters

1.2 Bilateral Treaties
a) German-Luxembourg Agreement of 1 August 1909 on Further Simplification of Mutual Judicial Assistance
b) German-Swedish Agreement of 1 February 1910 on Further Simplification of Mutual Judicial Assistance
c) German-Swiss Agreement of 30 April 1910 on Further Simplification of Mutual Judicial Assistance
d) German-Danish Agreement of 1 June 1910 on Further Simplification of Mutual Judicial Assistance
e) German-British Convention of 20 March 1928 on Legal Relations[1]
f) German-Turkish Convention of 28 May 1929 on Legal Relations in Civil and Commercial Matters
g) German-Swiss Convention of 24 December 1929 on Procedure for Applications for Enforcement of Decisions on Costs designated in Article 18 of the Convention of 17 July 1905 relating to Civil Procedure in Relations between the German Empire and Switzerland
h) German-Greek Convention of 11 May 1938 on Reciprocal Mutual Judicial Assistance in Matters of Civil and Commercial Law
i) German-Liechtenstein Agreement of 17 February/29 May 1958 on Direct Business Relations in Civil and Penal Matters between Legal Authorities in the Federal Republic of Germany and the Principality of Liechtenstein

---

[1] Extended/further application in relation to Australia (18 July 1967), Bahamas (15 June 1978), Barbados (14 Mai 1971), Dominica (13 January 1986), Fiji (7 August 1972), Gambia (27 October 1969), Grenada (19 August 1974), Jamaica (18 August 1966), Canada (14 December 1953), Lesotho (26 June 1974), Malawi (18 May 1967), Malaysia (29 April 1976), Malta (6 February 1968), Mauritius (15 June 1972), Nauru (22 July 1982), New Zealand (13 March 1953), Nigeria (30 January 1967), Solomon Islands (23 September 1980), Seychelles (5 December 1977), Sierra Leone (23 September 1967), Singapore (29 April 1976), St. Lucia (1 December 1983), St. Vincent and the Grenadines (18 August 1987), Swaziland (30 March 1971), Trinidad and Tobago (25 November 1966), and Cyprus (23 April 1975).

j) German-Belgian Agreement of 25 April 1959 on Further Simplification of Mutual Judicial Assistance
k) German-Austrian Agreement of 6 June 1959 on Further Simplification of Legal Relations pursuant to the Hague Convention of 1 March 1954 relating to Civil Procedure
l) German-French Agreement of 6 May 1961 on Further Simplification of Mutual Judicial Assistance pursuant to the Hague Convention of 1 March 1954 relating to Civil Procedure
m) German-Dutch Convention of 30 August 1962 on Further Simplification of Mutual Judicial Assistance pursuant to the Hague Convention of 1 March 1954 relating to Civil Procedure
n) German-Tunisian Convention of 19 July 1966 on Legal Protection and Judicial Assistance, Recognition and Enforcement of Judgments in Civil and Commercial Matters as well as on Commercial Arbitration
o) German-Norwegian Agreement of 17 June 1977 on Further Simplification of Mutual Judicial Assistance pursuant to the Convention of 1 March 1954 relating to Civil Procedure
p) German-Moroccan Convention of 29 October 1985 on Mutual Judicial Assistance and Legal Advice in Civil and Commercial Matters
q) German-Polish Agreement of 14 December 1992 on Further Simplification of Legal Relations pursuant to the Hague Convention of 1 March 1954 relating to Civil Procedure
r) German-Czech Convention of 2 February 2000 on Further Simplification of Mutual Judicial Assistance pursuant to the Hague Convention of 1 March 1954 relating to Civil Procedure, of 15 November 1965 on the Service Abroad of Judicial and Extrajudicial Documents in Civil or Commercial Matters and of 18 March 1970 on the Taking of Evidence Abroad in Civil or Commercial Matters

2. Recognition and Enforcement

2.1 Multilateral Treaties

a) Brussels Convention of 27 September 1968 on Jurisdiction and the Enforcement of Judgments in Civil and Commercial Matters
b) Lugano Convention of 30 October 2007 on Jurisdiction and the Enforcement of Judgments in Civil and Commercial Matters

2.2 Bilateral Treaties

a) German-Swiss Convention of 2 November 1929 on Reciprocal Recognition and Enforcement of Judgments and Arbitral Awards
b) German-Italian Convention of 9 March 1936 on Recognition and Enforcement of Judgments in Civil and Commercial Matters
c) German-Belgian Convention of 30 June 1958 on Reciprocal Recognition and Enforcement of Judgments, Arbitral Awards and Official Documents in Civil and Commercial Matters
d) German-Austrian Convention of 6 June 1959 on Reciprocal Recognition and Enforcement of Judgments, Settlements and Official Documents in Civil and Commercial Matters
e) German-British Convention of 14 July 1960 on the Reciprocal Recognition and Enforcement of Judgments in Civil and Commercial Matters

f) German-Greek Convention of 4 November 1961 on Reciprocal Recognition and Enforcement of Judgments, Settlements and Official Documents in Civil and Commercial Matters
g) German-Dutch Convention of 30 August 1962 on Reciprocal Recognition and Enforcement of Judgments and other Enforceable Legal Documents in Civil and Commercial Matters
h) German-Tunisian Convention of 19 July 1966 on Legal Protection and Mutual Judicial Assistance, Recognition and Enforcement of Judgments in Civil and Commercial Matters as well as on Commercial Arbitration
i) German-Norwegian Convention of 17 June 1977 on Reciprocal Recognition and Enforcement of Judgments and other Enforceable Legal Documents in Civil and Commercial Matters
j) German-Israeli Convention of 20 July 1977 on Reciprocal Recognition and Enforcement of Judgments in Civil and Commercial Matters
k) German-Spanish Convention of 14 November 1983 on Recognition and Enforcement of Judgments and Settlements as well as Executable Official Documents in Civil and Commercial Matters

3. **Arbitration**

3.1 **Multilateral Treaties**
a) Geneva Protocol on Arbitration Clauses of 24 September 1923
b) Geneva Convention on the Execution of Foreign Arbitral Awards of 26 September 1927
c) United Nations Convention on the Recognition and Enforcement of Foreign Arbitral Awards of 10 June 1958 (New York Convention)
d) European Convention on International Commercial Arbitration of 21 April 1961
e) Paris Agreement Relating to Application of the European Convention on International Commercial Arbitration of 17 December 1962
f) Washington Convention on the Settlement of Investment Disputes between States and Nationals of Other States of 18 March 1965

3.2 **Bilateral Treaties**
See II.2.c) and h)

4. **Miscellaneous**
a) International Convention on Certain Rules Concerning Civil Jurisdiction in Matters of Collision of 10 May 1952
b) International Convention of 10 May 1952 relating to the Arrest of Seagoing
c) Convention of 19 May 1956 on the Contract for the International Carriage of Goods by Road (CMR)
d) European Convention on Information on Foreign Law of 7 June 1968 and Additional Protocol to the European Convention on Information on Foreign Law of 15 March 1978

This list is current as of June 2015.

II. Hague Convention on the Service Abroad of Judicial and Extrajudicial Documents in Civil or Commercial Matters[1]

(15 November 1965)

The States signatory to the present Convention,

Desiring to create appropriate means to ensure that judicial and extrajudicial documents to be served abroad shall be brought to the notice of the addressee in sufficient time,

Desiring to improve the organization of mutual judicial assistance for that purpose by simplifying and expediting the procedure,

Have resolved to conclude a Convention to this effect and have agreed upon the following provisions:

Article 1

The present Convention shall apply in all cases, in civil or commercial matters, where there is occasion to transmit a judicial or extrajudicial document for service abroad.

The Convention shall not apply where the address of the person to be served with the document is not known.

CHAPTER I
JUDICIAL DOCUMENTS

Article 2

Each contracting State shall designate a Central Authority which will undertake to receive requests for service coming from other contracting States and to proceed in conformity with the provisions of articles 3 to 6.

Each State shall organize the Central Authority in conformity with its own law.

Article 3

The authority or judicial officer competent under the law of the State in which the documents originate shall forward to the Central Authority of the State addressed a request conforming to the model annexed to the present Convention without any requirement of legalization or other equivalent formality.

The document to be served or a copy thereof shall be annexed to the request. The request and the document shall both be furnished in duplicate.

Article 4

If the Central Authority considers that the request does not comply with the provisions of the present Convention it shall promptly inform the applicant and specify its objections to the request.

---

[1] The Convention came into force in Germany on 26 June 1979. As of August 2015, 68 States are contracting parties.

Article 5

The Central Authority of the State addressed shall itself serve the document or shall arrange to have it served by an appropriate agency, either -
a) by a method prescribed by its internal law for the service of documents in domestic actions upon persons who are within its territory, or
b) by a particular method requested by the applicant, unless such a method is incompatible with the law of the State addressed.

Subject to sub-paragraph b) of the first paragraph of this article, the document may always be served by delivery to an addressee who accepts it voluntarily.

If the document is to be served under the first paragraph above, the Central Authority may require the document to be written in, or translated into, the official language or one of the official languages of the State addressed.

That part of the request, in the form attached to the present Convention, which contains a summary of the document to be served, shall be served with the document.

Article 6

The Central Authority of the State addressed or any authority which it may have designated for that purpose, shall complete a certificate in the form of the model annexed to the present Convention.

The certificate shall state that the document has been served and shall include the method, the place and the date of service and the person to whom the document was delivered. If the document has not been served, the certificate shall set out the reasons which have prevented service.

The applicant may require that a certificate not completed by a Central Authority or by a judicial authority shall be countersigned by one of these authorities.

The certificate shall be forwarded directly to the applicant.

Article 7

The standard terms in the model annexed to the present Convention shall in all cases be written either in French or in English. They may also be written in the official language, or in one of the official languages, of the State in which the documents originate.

The corresponding blanks shall be completed either in the language of the State addressed or in French or in English.

Article 8

Each contracting State shall be free to effect service of judicial documents upon persons abroad, without application of any compulsion, directly through its diplomatic or consular agents.

Any State may declare that it is opposed to such service within its territory, unless the document is to be served upon a national of the State in which the documents originate.

Article 9

Each contracting State shall be free, in addition, to use consular channels to forward documents, for the purpose of service, to those authorities of another contracting State which are designated by the latter for this purpose.

Each contracting State may, if exceptional circumstances so require, use diplomatic channels for the same purpose.

Article 10

Provided the State of destination does not object, the present Convention shall not interfere with –
a) the freedom to send judicial documents, by postal channels, directly to persons abroad,
b) the freedom of judicial officers, officials or other competent persons of the State of origin to effect service of judicial documents directly through the judicial officers, officials or other competent persons of the State of destination,
c) the freedom of any person interested in a judicial proceeding to effect service of judicial documents directly through the judicial officers, officials or other competent persons of the State of destination.

Article 11

The present Convention shall not prevent two or more contracting States from agreeing to permit, for the purpose of service of judicial documents, channels of transmission other than those provided for in the preceding articles and, in particular, direct communication between their respective authorities.

Article 12

The service of judicial documents coming from a contracting State shall not give rise to any payment or reimbursement of taxes or costs for the services rendered by the State addressed.

The applicant shall pay or reimburse the costs occasioned by –
a) the employment of a judicial officer or of a person competent under the law of the State of destination,
b) the use of a particular method of service.

Article 13

Where a request for service complies with the terms of the present Convention, the State addressed may refuse to comply therewith only if it deems that compliance would infringe its sovereignty or security.

It may not refuse to comply solely on the ground that, under its internal law, it claims exclusive jurisdiction over the subject-matter of the action or that its internal law would not permit the action upon which the application is based.

The Central Authority shall, in case of refusal, promptly inform the applicant and state the reasons for the refusal.

Article 14

Difficulties which may arise in connection with the transmission of judicial documents for service shall be settled through diplomatic channels.

Article 15

Where a writ of summons or an equivalent document had to be transmitted abroad for the purpose of service, under the provisions of the present Conven-

tion, and the defendant has not appeared, judgment shall not be given until it is established that –
a) the document was served by a method prescribed by the internal law of the State addressed for the service of documents in domestic actions upon persons who are within its territory, or
b) the document was actually delivered to the defendant or to his residence by another method provided for by this Convention,
and that that in either of these cases the service or the delivery was effected in sufficient time to enable the defendant to defend.

4. Each contracting State shall be free to declare that the judge, notwithstanding the provisions of the first paragraph of this article, may give judgment even if no certificate of service or delivery has been received, if all the following conditions are fulfilled –
a) the document was transmitted by one of the methods provided for in this Convention,
b) a period of time of not less than six months, considered adequate by the judge in the particular case, has elapsed since the date of the transmission of the document,
c) no certificate of any kind has been received, even though every reasonable effort has been made to obtain it through the competent authorities of the State addressed.

5. Notwithstanding the provisions of the preceding paragraphs the judge may order, in case of urgency, any provisional or protective measures.

Article 16

When a writ of summons or an equivalent document had to be transmitted abroad for the purpose of service, under the provision of the present Convention, and a judgment has been entered against a defendant who has not appeared, the judge shall have the power of relieve the defendant from the effects of the expiration of the time for appeal from the judgment if the following conditions are fulfilled –
a) the defendant, without any fault on his part, did not have knowledge of the document in sufficient time to defend, or knowledge of the judgment in sufficient time to appeal, and
b) the defendant has disclosed a *prima facie* defense to the action on the merits.

An application for relief may be filed only within a reasonable time after the defendant has knowledge of the judgment.

Each contracting State may declare that the application will not be entertained, if it is filed after the expiration of time to be stated in the declaration but which shall in no case be less than one year following the date of the judgment.

The article shall not apply to judgments concerning status or capacity of persons.

CHAPTER II
EXTRAJUDICIAL DOCUMENTS

Article 17

Extrajudicial documents emanating from authorities and judicial officers of a contracting State may be transmitted for the purpose of service in another contracting State by the methods and under the provisions of the present Convention.

CHAPTER III
GENERAL CLAUSES

Article 18

Each contracting State may designate other authorities in addition to the Central Authority and shall determine the extent of their competence.

The applicant shall, however, in all cases, have the right to address a request directly to the Central Authority.

Federal States shall be free to designate more than one Central Authority.

Article 19

To the extent that the internal law of a contracting State permits methods of transmission, other than those provided for in the preceding articles, of documents coming from abroad, for service within its territory, the present Convention shall not affect such provisions.

Article 20

The present Convention shall not prevent an agreement between any two or more contracting States to dispense with –
a) the necessity for duplicate copies of transmitted documents as required by the second paragraph of article 3,
b) the language requirements of the third paragraph of article 5 and article 7,
c) the provisions of the fourth paragraph of article 5,
d) the provisions of the second paragraph of article 12.

Article 21

Each contracting State shall, at the time of the deposit of its instrument of ratification or accession, or at a later date, inform the Ministry of Foreign Affairs of the Netherlands of the following –
a) the designation of authorities, pursuant to articles 2 and 18,
b) the designation of the authority competent to complete the certification pursuant to article 6,
c) the designation of the authority competent to receive documents transmitted by consular channels, pursuant to article 9.

Each contracting State shall similarly inform the Ministry, where appropriate, of –
a) opposition to the use of methods of transmission pursuant to articles 8 and 10,

b) declarations pursuant to the second paragraph of article 15 and the third paragraph of article 16,
c) all modifications of the above designations, oppositions and declarations.

Article 22

Where Parties to the present Convention are also Parties to one or both of the Conventions on civil procedure signed at The Hague on 17 July 1905, and on 1 March 1954, this Convention shall replace as between them articles 1 to 7 of the earlier Convention.

Article 23

The present Convention shall not affect the application of article 23 of the Convention on civil procedure signed at The Hague on 17 July 1905, or of article 24 of the Convention on civil procedure signed at The Hague on 1 March 1954.

These articles shall, however, apply only if methods of communication, identical to those provided for in these Conventions, are used.

Article 24

Supplementary agreements between Parties to the Conventions of 1905 and 1954 shall be considered as equally applicable to the present Convention, unless the Parties have otherwise agreed.

Article 25

Without prejudice to the provisions of articles 22 and 24, the present Convention shall not derogate from Conventions containing provisions on the matters governed by this Convention to which the contracting States are, or shall become Parties.

Article 26

The present Convention shall be open for signature by the states represented at the Tenth Session of the Hague Conference on Private International Law.

It shall be ratified, and the instruments of ratification shall be deposited with the Ministry of Foreign Affairs of the Netherlands.

Article 27

The present Convention shall enter into force on the sixtieth day after deposit of the third instrument of ratification referred to in the second paragraph of article 26.

The Convention shall enter into force for each signatory State which ratifies subsequently on the sixtieth day after the deposit of its instrument of ratification.

Article 28

Any State not represented at the Tenth Session of the Hague Conference on Private International Law may accede to the present Convention after it has entered into force in accordance with the first paragraph of article 27. The instrument of accession shall be deposited with the Ministry of Foreign Affairs of the Netherlands.

The Convention shall enter into force for such a State in the absence of any objection from a State, which has ratified the Convention before such deposit, notified to the Ministry of Foreign Affairs of the Netherlands within a period of six months after the date on which the said Ministry has notified it of such accession.

In the absence of any such objection, the Convention shall enter into force for the acceding State on the first day of the month following the expiration of the last of the periods referred to in the preceding paragraph.

Article 29

Any State may, at the time of signature, ratification or accession, declare that the present Convention shall extend to all the territories for the international relations of which it is responsible, or to one or more of them. Such a declaration shall take effect on the date of entry into force of the Convention for the State concerned.

At any time thereafter, such extensions shall be notified to the Ministry of Foreign Affairs of the Netherlands.

The Convention shall enter into force for the territories mentioned in such an extension on the sixtieth day after the notification referred to in the preceding paragraph.

Article 30

The present Convention shall remain in force for five years from the date of its entry into force in accordance with the first paragraph of Article 27, even for States which have ratified it or acceded to it subsequently.

If there has been no denunciation, it shall be renewed tacitly every five years.

Any denunciation shall be notified to the Ministry of Foreign Affairs of the Netherlands at least six months before the end of the five year period.

It may be limited to certain of the territories to which the Convention applies.

The denunciation shall have effect only as regards the State which has notified it. The Convention shall remain in force for the other Contracting States.

Article 31

The Ministry of Foreign Affairs of the Netherlands shall give notice to the States referred to in Article 26, and to the States which have acceded in accordance with Article 28, of the following –
a) the signatures and ratifications referred to in Article 26;
b) the date on which the present Convention enters into force in accordance with the first paragraph of Article 27;
c) the accessions referred to in Article 28 and the dates on which they take effect
d) the extensions referred to in Article 29 and the dates on which they take effect;
e) the designations, oppositions and declarations referred to in Article 21;
f) the denunciations referred to in the third paragraph of Article 30.

In witness whereof the undersigned, being duly authorized thereto, have signed the present Convention.

Done at The Hague, on the 15th day of November, 1965, in the English and French languages, both texts being equally authentic, in a single copy which shall be deposited in the archives of the Government of the Netherlands, and of which a certified copy shall be sent, through the diplomatic channel, to each of the States represented at the Tenth Session of the Hague Conference on Private International Law.

III. Hague Convention on the Taking of Evidence Abroad in Civil or Commercial Matters[1]

(18 March 1970)

The States signatory to the present Convention,

Desiring to facilitate the transmission and execution of Letters of Request and to further the accommodation of the different methods which they use for this purpose,

Desiring to improve mutual judicial co-operation in civil or commercial matters,

Have resolved to conclude a Convention to this effect and have agreed upon the following provisions –

CHAPTER I
LETTERS OF REQUEST

Article 1

In civil or commercial matters a judicial authority of a Contracting State may, in accordance with the provisions of the law of that State request the competent authority of another Contracting State, by means of a Letter of Request, to obtain evidence, or to perform some other judicial art.

A Letter shall not be used to obtain evidence which is not intended for use in judicial proceedings, commenced or contemplated.

The expression „other judicial art" does not cover the service of judicial documents or the issuance of any process by which judgments or orders are executed or enforced, or orders for provisional or protective measures.

Article 2

A Contracting State shall designate a Central Authority which will undertake to receive Letters of Request coming from a judicial authority of another Contracting State and to transmit them to the authority competent to execute them. Each State shall organize the Central Authority in accordance with its own law.

Letters shall be sent to the Central Authority of the State of execution without being transmitted through any other authority of that State.

Article 3

A Letter of Request shall specify –
a) the authority requesting its execution and the authority requested to execute it, if known to the requesting authority;
b) the names and addresses of the parties to the proceedings and their representatives, if any;
c) the nature of the proceedings for which the evidence is required, giving all necessary information in regard thereto;
d) the evidence to be obtained or other judicial act to be performed.

Where appropriate, the Letter shall specify, *inter alia* –

---

[1] The Convention came into force in Germany on 26 June 1979. As of August 2015, 58 States are contracting parties.

e) the names and addresses of the persons to be examined;
f) the questions to be put to the persons to be examined or a statement of the subject-matter about which they are to be examined;
g) the documents or other property, real or personal, to be inspected;
h) any requirement that the evidence is to be given on oath or affirmation, and any special form to be used;
i) any special method or procedure to be followed under Article 9.

A Letter may also mention any information necessary for the application of Article 11.

No legalization or other like formality may be required.

Article 4

A Letter of Request shall be in the language of the authority requested to execute it or be accompanied by a translation into that language.

Nevertheless, a Contracting State shall accept a Letter in either English or French, or a translation into one of these languages, unless it has made the reservation authorized by Article 33.

A Contracting State which has more than one official language and cannot, for reasons of internal law, accept Letters in one of these languages for the whole of its territory, shall by declaration, specify the language in which the Letter of translation thereof shall be expressed for execution in the specified parts of its territory. In case of failure to comply with this, declaration, without justifiable excuse, the costs of translation into the required language shall be borne by the State of origin.

A Contracting State may, by declaration, specify the language or languages other than those referred to in the preceding paragraphs, in which a Letter may be sent to its Central Authority.

Any translation accompanying a Letter shall be certified as correct, either by a diplomatic officer or consular agent or by a sworn translator or by any other person so authorized in either State.

Article 5

If the Central Authority considers that the request does not comply with the provisions of the present Convention, it shall promptly inform the authority of the State of origin which transmitted the Letter of Request, specifying the objections of the Letter.

Article 6

If the authority to whom a Letter of Request has been transmitted is not competent to execute it, the Letter shall be sent forthwith to the authority in the same State which is competent to execute it in accordance with the provisions of its own law.

Article 7

The requesting authority shall, if it so desires, be informed of the time when, and the place where, the proceedings will take place, in order that the parties concerned, and their representatives, if any, may be present. This information shall be sent directly to the parties or their representatives when the authority of the State of origin so requests.

Article 8

A Contracting State may declare that members of the judicial personnel of the requesting authority of another Contracting State may be present at the execution of a Letter of Request. Prior authorization by the competent authority designated by the declaring State may be required.

Article 9

The judicial authority which executes a Letter of Request shall apply its own law as to the methods and procedures to be followed.

However, it will follow a request of the requesting authority that a special method or procedure be followed, unless this is incompatible with the internal law of the State of execution or is impossible of performance by reason of its internal practice and procedure or by reason of practical difficulties.

A Letter of Request shall be executed expeditiously.

Article 10

In executing a Letter of Request the requested authority shall apply the appropriate measures of compulsion in the instances and to the same extent as are provided by its internal law for the execution of orders issued by the authorities of its own country or of requests made by parties in internal proceedings.

Article 11

In the execution of a Letter of Request the person concerned may refuse to give evidence in so far as he has a privilege or duty to refuse to give the evidence -
a) under the law of the State of execution; or
b) under the law of the State of origin, and the privilege or duty has been specified in the Letter or, at the instance of the requested authority, has been otherwise confirmed to that authority by the requesting authority.

A Contracting State may declare that, in addition, it will respect privileges and duties existing under the law of States other than the State of origin and the State of execution, to the extent specified in that declaration

Article 12

The execution of a Letter of Request may be refused only to the extent that –
a) in the State of execution the execution of the Letter does not fall within the functions of the judiciary; or
b) the State addressed considers that its sovereignty or security would be prejudiced thereby.

Execution may not be refused solely on the ground that under its internal law the State of execution claims exclusive jurisdiction over the subject matter of the action or that its internal law would not admit a right of action on it.

Article 13

The documents establishing the execution of the Letter of Request shall be sent by the requested authority to the requesting authority by the same channel which was used by the latter.

In every instance where the Letter is not executed in whole or in part, the requesting authority shall be informed immediately through the same channel and advised of the reasons.

Article 14

The execution of the Letter of Request shall not give rise to any reimbursement of taxes or costs of any nature.

Nevertheless, the State of execution has the right to require the State of origin to reimburse the fees paid to experts and interpreters and the costs occasioned by the use of a special procedure requested by the State of origin under Article 9, paragraph 2.

The requested authority whose law obliges the parties themselves to secure evidence, and which is not able itself to execute the Letter, may, after having obtained the consent of the requesting authority, appoint a suitable person to do so. When seeking this consent the requested authority shall indicate the approximate costs which would result from this procedure. If the requesting authority gives its consent it shall reimburse any costs incurred; without such consent the requesting authority shall not be liable for the costs.

CHAPTER II
TAKING OF EVIDENCE BY DIPLOMATIC OFFICERS, CONSULAR AGENTS AND COMMISSIONERS

Article 15

In civil or commercial matters, a diplomatic officer or consular agent of a Contracting State may, in the territory of another Contracting State and within the area where he exercises his functions, take the evidence without compulsion of nationals of a State which he represents in aid of proceedings commenced in the courts of a State which he represents.

A Contracting State may declare that evidence may be taken by a diplomatic officer or consular agent only if permission to that effect is given upon application made by him or on his behalf to the appropriate authority designated by the declaring State.

Article 16

A diplomatic offer or consular agent of a Contracting State may, in the territory of another Contracting State and within the area where he exercises his functions, also take the evidence, without compulsion, of nationals of the State in which he exercises his functions or of a third State, in aid of proceedings commenced in the courts of a State which he represents, if –
a) a competent authority designated by the State in which he exercises his functions has given its permission either generally or in the particular case, and
b) he complies with the conditions which the competent authority has specified in the permission.

A Contracting State may declare that evidence may be taken under this Article without its prior permission.

Article 17

In civil or commercial matters, a person duly appointed as a commissioner for the purpose may, without compulsion, take evidence in the territory of a Contracting State is aid of proceedings commenced in the courts of another Contracting State, if –
a) a competent authority designated by the State where the evidence is to be taken has given its permission either generally or in the particular case; and
b) he complies with the conditions which the competent authority has specified in the permission.

A Contracting State may declare that evidence may be taken under this Article without its prior permission.

Article 18

A Contracting State may declare that a diplomatic officer, consular agent or commissioner authorized to take evidence under Article 15, 16 or 17, may apply to the competent authority designated by the declaring State for appropriate assistance to obtain the evidence by compulsion. The declaration may contain such conditions as the declaring State may see fit to impose.

In the authority grants the application it shall apply any measures of compulsion which are appropriate and are prescribed by its law for use in internal proceedings.

Article 19

The competent authority, in giving the permission referred to in Articles 15, 16 or 17, or in granting the application referred to in Article 18, may lay down such conditions as it deems fit, *inter alia*, as to the time and place of the taking of the evidence. Similarly it may require that it be given reasonable advance notice of the time, date and place of the taking of the evidence; in such a case a representative of the authority shall be entitled to be present at the taking of the evidence.

Article 20

In the taking of evidence under any Article of this Chapter persons concerned may be legally represented.

Article 21

Where a diplomatic officer, consular agent or commissioner is authorized under Articles 15, 16 or 17 to take evidence –
a) he may take all kinds of evidence which are not incompatible with the law of the State where the evidence is taken or contrary to any permission granted pursuant to the above Articles, and shall have power within such limits to administer an oath or take an affirmation.
b) a request to a person to appear or to give evidence shall, unless the recipient is a national of the State where the action is pending, be drawn up in the language of the place where the evidence is taken or be accompanied by a translation into such language;
c) the request shall inform the person that he may be legally represented and, in any State that has not filed a declaration under Article 18, shall also inform him that he is not compelled to appear or to give evidence;

d) the evidence may be taken in the manner provided by the law applicable to the court in which the action is pending provided that such manner is not forbidden by the law of the State where the evidence is taken;
e) a person requested to give evidence may invoke the privileges and duties to refuse to give the evidence contained in Article 11.

Article 22

The fact that an attempt to take evidence under the procedure laid down in this Chapter has failed, owing to the refusal of a person to give evidence, shall not prevent an application being subsequently made to take the evidence in accordance with Chapter I.

CHAPTER III
GENERAL CLAUSES

Article 23

A Contracting State may at the time of signature, ratification or accession declare that it will not execute Letters of Request issued for the purpose of obtaining pre-trial discovery of documents as known in Common Law countries.

Article 24

A Contracting State may designate other authorities in addition to the Central Authority and shall determine the extent of their competence. However, Letters of Request may in all cases be sent to the Central Authority.

Federal States shall be free to designate more than one Central Authority.

Article 25

A Contracting State which has more than one legal system may designate the authorities of one of such systems, which shall have exclusive competence to execute Letters of Request pursuant to this Convention.

Article 26

A Contracting State, if required to do so because of constitutional limitations, may request the reimbursement by the State of origin of fees and costs, in connection with the execution of Letters of Request, for the service of process necessary to compel the appearance of a person to give evidence, the costs of attendance of such persons, and the cost of any transcript of the evidence.

Where a State has made a request pursuant to the above paragraph, any other Contracting State may request from the State the reimbursement of similar fees and costs.

Article 27

The provisions of the present Convention shall not prevent a Contracting State from –
a) declaring that Letters of Request may be transmitted to its judicial authorities through channels other than those provided for in Article 2;

b) permitting, by internal law or practice, any act provided for in this Convention to be performed upon less restrictive conditions;
c) permitting, by internal law or practice, methods of taking evidence other than those provided for in this Convention

Article 28

The present Convention shall not prevent an agreement between any two or more Contracting States to derogate from –
a) the provisions of Article 2 with respect to methods of transmitting Letters of Request;
b) the provisions of Article 4 with respect to the languages which may be used;
c) the provisions of Article 8 with respect to the presence of judicial personnel at the execution of Letters;
d) the provisions of Article 11 with respect to the privileges and duties of witnesses to refuse to give evidence;
e) the provisions of Article 13 with respect to the methods of returning executed Letters to the requesting authority;
f) the provisions of Article 14 with respect to fees and costs;
g) the provisions of Chapter II.

Article 29

Between Parties to the present Convention who are also Parties to one or both of the Conventions on Civil Procedure signed at The Hague on the 17 July 1905 and the 1st of March 1954, this Convention shall replace Articles 8–16 of the earlier Conventions.

Article 30

The present Convention shall not affect the application of Article 23 of the Convention of 1905, or of Article 24 of the Convention of 1975.

Article 31

Supplementary Agreements between Parties to the Convention of 1905 and 1954 shall be considered as equally applicable to the present Convention unless the Parties have otherwise agreed.

Article 32

Without prejudice to the provisions of Article 29 and 31, the present Convention shall not derogate from conventions containing provisions on the matters covered by this Convention to which the Contracting States are, or shall become Parties.

Article 33

A State may, at the time of signature, ratification or accession exclude, in whole or in part, the application of the provisions of paragraph 2 of Article 4 and of Chapter II. No other reservation shall be permitted.

Each Contracting State may at any time withdraw a reservation it has made; the reservation shall cease to have effect on the sixtieth day after notification of the withdrawal.

When a State has made a reservation, any other State affected thereby may apply the same rule against the reserving State.

Article 34

A State may at any time withdraw or modify a declaration.

Article 35

A Contracting State shall, at the time of the deposit of its instrument of ratification or accession, or at a later date, inform the Ministry of Foreign Affairs of the Netherlands of the designation of authorities, pursuant to Articles 2, 8, 24 and 25.

A Contracting State shall likewise inform the Ministry, where appropriate, of the following –

a) the designation of the authorities to whom notice must be given, whose permission may be required, and whose assistance may be invoked in the taking of evidence by diplomatic officers and consular agents, pursuant to Articles 15, 16 and 18 respectively;
b) the designation of the authorities whose permission may be required in the taking of evidence by commissions pursuant to Article 17 and of those who may grant the assistance provided for in Article 18;
c) declarations pursuant to Articles 4, 8, 11, 15, 16, 17, 18, 23 and 27;
d) any withdrawal or modification of the above designations and declarations;
e) the withdrawal of any reservation.

Article 36

Any difficulties which may arise between Contracting States in connection with the operation of this Convention shall be settled through diplomatic channels.

Article 37

The present Convention shall be open for signature by the States represented at the Eleventh Session of the Hague Convention on Private International Law.

It shall be ratified, and the instruments of ratification shall be deposited with the Ministry of Foreign Affairs of the Netherlands.

Article 38

The present Convention shall enter into force on the sixtieth day after the deposit of the third instrument of ratification referred to in the second paragraph of Article 37.

The Convention shall enter into force for each signatory State which ratifies subsequently on the sixtieth day after the deposit of its instrument of ratification.

Article 39

Any State not represented at the Eleventh Session of the Hague Conference on Private International Law which is a Member of this Conference or of the United Nations or of a specialized agency of that Organization, or a Party to the Statute of the International Court of Justice may accede to the present Convention after it has entered into force in accordance with the fist paragraph of Article. 38.

The instrument of accession shall be desposited with the Ministry of Foreign Affairs of the Netherlands.

The Convention shall enter into force for a State acceding to it on the sixtieth day after the deposit of its instrument of accession.

The accession will have effect only as regards the relations between the acceding State and such Contracting States as will have declared their acceptance of the accession. Such declaration shall be deposited at the Ministry of Foreign Affairs of the Netherlands; this Ministry shall forward, through diplomatic channels, a certified copy to each of the Contracting States.

The Convention will enter into force as between the acceding State and the State that has declared its acceptance of the accession on the sixtieth day after the deposit of the declaration of acceptance.

Article 40

Any State may, at the time of signature, ratification or accession, declare that the present Convention shall extend to all the territories for the international relations of which it is responsible, or to one or more of them. Such a declaration shall take effect on the date of entry into force of the Convention for the State concerned.

At any time thereafter, such extension shall be notified to the Ministry of Foreign Affairs of the Netherlands.

The Convention shall enter into force for the territories mentioned in such an extension on the sixtieths day after the notification indicated in the preceding paragraph.

Article 41

The present Convention shall remain in force for five years from the date of its entry into force in accordance with the first paragraph of Article 38, even for States which have ratified it or acceded to it subsequently.

If there has been no denunciation, if shall be renewed tacitly every five years.

Any denunciation shall be notified to the Ministry of Foreign Affairs of the Netherlands at least six months before the end of the five year period.

It may be limited to certain of the territories to which the Convention applies.

The denunciation shall have effect only as regards the State which has notified it. The Convention shall remain in force for the other Contracting States.

Article 42

The Ministry of Foreign Affairs of the Netherlands shall give notice to the States referred to in Article 37, and to the States which have acceded in accordance with Article 39, of the following –
a) the signatures and ratifications referred to in Article 37;
b) the date on which the present Convention enters into force in accordance with the first paragraph of Article 38;
c) the accessions referred to in Article 39 and the dates on which they take effect;
d) the extensions referred to in Article 40 and the dates on which they take effect;
e) the designations, reservations and declarations referred to in Articles 33 and 35;
f) the denunciations referred to in the third paragraph of Article 41.

IN WITNESS WHEREOF the undersigned being duly authorized thereto, have signed the present Convention.

DONE at The Hague, on the 18 March 1970, in the English and French languages, both texts being equally authentic, in a single copy which shall deposited in the archives of the Government of the Netherlands, and of which a certified copy shall be sent, through the diplomatic channel, to each of the States represented at the Eleventh Session of the Hague Conference on Private International Law.

IV. CONVENTION ON CHOICE OF COURT AGREEMENTS[2]
(Concluded 30 June 2005)

The States Parties to the present Convention,

Desiring to promote international trade and investment through enhanced judicial co-operation,

Believing that such co-operation can be enhanced by uniform rules on jurisdiction and on recognition and enforcement of foreign judgments in civil or commercial matters,

Believing that such enhanced co-operation requires in particular an international legal regime that provides certainty and ensures the effectiveness of exclusive choice of court agreements between parties to commercial transactions and that governs the recognition and enforcement of judgments resulting from proceedings based on such agreements,

Have resolved to conclude this Convention and have agreed upon the following provisions –

CHAPTER I
SCOPE AND DEFINITIONS

Article 1. Scope

(1) This Convention shall apply in international cases to exclusive choice of court agreements concluded in civil or commercial matters.

(2) For the purposes of Chapter II, a case is international unless the parties are resident in the same Contracting State and the relationship of the parties and all other elements relevant to the dispute, regardless of the location of the chosen court, are connected only with that State.

(3) For the purposes of Chapter III, a case is international where recognition or enforcement of a foreign judgment is sought.

Article 2. Exclusions from scope

(1) This Convention shall not apply to exclusive choice of court agreements –
a) to which a natural person acting primarily for personal, family or household purposes (a consumer) is a party;
b) relating to contracts of employment, including collective agreements.

---

[2] The European Union has ratified the Hague Convention on Choice of Court Agreements on 11 June 2015. The Convention will enter into force on 1 October 2015, and will apply to all member states of the European Union (except Denmark) and Mexico. Other signatories are Singapore and notably the United States, which however both have not ratified the Convention yet.

(2) This Convention shall not apply to the following matters –
a) the status and legal capacity of natural persons;
b) maintenance obligations;
c) other family law matters, including matrimonial property regimes and other rights or obligations arising out of marriage or similar relationships;
d) wills and succession;
e) insolvency, composition and analogous matters;
f) the carriage of passengers and goods;
g) marine pollution, limitation of liability for maritime claims, general average, and emergency towage and salvage;
h) anti-trust (competition) matters;
i) liability for nuclear damage;
j) claims for personal injury brought by or on behalf of natural persons;
k) tort or delict claims for damage to tangible property that do not arise from a contractual relationship;
l) rights in rem in immovable property, and tenancies of immovable property;
m) the validity, nullity, or dissolution of legal persons, and the validity of decisions of their organs;
n) the validity of intellectual property rights other than copyright and related rights;
o) infringement of intellectual property rights other than copyright and related rights, except where infringement proceedings are brought for breach of a contract between the parties relating to such rights, or could have been brought for breach of that contract;
p) the validity of entries in public registers.

(3) Notwithstanding paragraph 2, proceedings are not excluded from the scope of this Convention where a matter excluded under that paragraph arises merely as a preliminary question and not as an object of the proceedings. In particular, the mere fact that a matter excluded under paragraph 2 arises by way of defence does not exclude proceedings from the Convention, if that matter is not an object of the proceedings.

(4) This Convention shall not apply to arbitration and related proceedings.

(5) Proceedings are not excluded from the scope of this Convention by the mere fact that a State, including a government, a governmental agency or any person acting for a State, is a party thereto.

(6) Nothing in this Convention shall affect privileges and immunities of States or of international organisations, in respect of themselves and of their property.

Article 3. Exclusive choice of court agreements

For the purposes of this Convention -
a) "exclusive choice of court agreement" means an agreement concluded by two or more parties that meets the requirements of paragraph c) and designates, for the purpose of deciding disputes which have arisen or may arise in connection with a particular legal relationship, the courts of one Contracting State or one or more specific courts of one Contracting State to the exclusion of the jurisdiction of any other courts;
b) a choice of court agreement which designates the courts of one Contracting State or one or more specific courts of one Contracting State shall be deemed to be exclusive unless the parties have expressly provided otherwise;

c) an exclusive choice of court agreement must be concluded or documented –
   i) in writing; or
   ii) by any other means of communication which renders information accessible so as to be usable for subsequent reference;
d) an exclusive choice of court agreement that forms part of a contract shall be treated as an agreement independent of the other terms of the contract. The validity of the exclusive choice of court agreement cannot be contested solely on the ground that the contract is not valid.

Article 4. Other definitions

(1) In this Convention, "judgment" means any decision on the merits given by a court, whatever it may be called, including a decree or order, and a determination of costs or expenses by the court (including an officer of the court), provided that the determination relates to a decision on the merits which may be recognised or enforced under this Convention. An interim measure of protection is not a judgment.

(2) For the purposes of this Convention, an entity or person other than a natural person shall be considered to be resident in the State –
a) where it has its statutory seat;
b) under whose law it was incorporated or formed;
c) where it has its central administration; or
d) where it has its principal place of business.

CHAPTER II
JURISDICTION

Article 5. Jurisdiction of the chosen court

(1) The court or courts of a Contracting State designated in an exclusive choice of court agreement shall have jurisdiction to decide a dispute to which the agreement applies, unless the agreement is null and void under the law of that State.

(2) A court that has jurisdiction under paragraph 1 shall not decline to exercise jurisdiction on the ground that the dispute should be decided in a court of another State.

(3) The preceding paragraphs shall not affect rules -
a) on jurisdiction related to subject matter or to the value of the claim;
b) on the internal allocation of jurisdiction among the courts of a Contracting State. However, where the chosen court has discretion as to whether to transfer a case, due consideration should be given to the choice of the parties.

Article 6. Obligations of a court not chosen

A court of a Contracting State other than that of the chosen court shall suspend or dismiss proceedings to which an exclusive choice of court agreement applies unless –
a) the agreement is null and void under the law of the State of the chosen court;
b) a party lacked the capacity to conclude the agreement under the law of the State of the court seised;
c) giving effect to the agreement would lead to a manifest injustice or would be manifestly contrary to the public policy of the State of the court seised;

d) for exceptional reasons beyond the control of the parties, the agreement cannot reasonably be performed; or
e) the chosen court has decided not to hear the case.

Article 7. Interim measures of protection

Interim measures of protection are not governed by this Convention. This Convention neither requires nor precludes the grant, refusal or termination of interim measures of protection by a court of a Contracting State and does not affect whether or not a party may request or a court should grant, refuse or terminate such measures.

CHAPTER III
RECOGNITION AND ENFORCEMENT

Article 8. Recognition and enforcement

(1) A judgment given by a court of a Contracting State designated in an exclusive choice of court agreement shall be recognised and enforced in other Contracting States in accordance with this Chapter. Recognition or enforcement may be refused only on the grounds specified in this Convention.

(2) Without prejudice to such review as is necessary for the application of the provisions of this Chapter, there shall be no review of the merits of the judgment given by the court of origin. The court addressed shall be bound by the findings of fact on which the court of origin based its jurisdiction, unless the judgment was given by default.

(3) A judgment shall be recognised only if it has effect in the State of origin, and shall be enforced only if it is enforceable in the State of origin.

(4) Recognition or enforcement may be postponed or refused if the judgment is the subject of review in the State of origin or if the time limit for seeking ordinary review has not expired. A refusal does not prevent a subsequent application for recognition or enforcement of the judgment.

(5) This Article shall also apply to a judgment given by a court of a Contracting State pursuant to a transfer of the case from the chosen court in that Contracting State as permitted by Article 5, paragraph 3. However, where the chosen court had discretion as to whether to transfer the case to another court, recognition or enforcement of the judgment may be refused against a party who objected to the transfer in a timely manner in the State of origin.

Article 9. Refusal of recognition or enforcement

Recognition or enforcement may be refused if -
a) the agreement was null and void under the law of the State of the chosen court, unless the chosen court has determined that the agreement is valid;
b) a party lacked the capacity to conclude the agreement under the law of the requested State;
c) the document which instituted the proceedings or an equivalent document, including the essential elements of the claim,
   i) was not notified to the defendant in sufficient time and in such a way as to enable him to arrange for his defence, unless the defendant entered an appearance and presented his case without contesting notification in

the court of origin, provided that the law of the State of origin permitted notification to be contested; or

ii) was notified to the defendant in the requested State in a manner that is incompatible with fundamental principles of the requested State concerning service of documents;

d) the judgment was obtained by fraud in connection with a matter of procedure;
e) recognition or enforcement would be manifestly incompatible with the public policy of the requested State, including situations where the specific proceedings leading to the judgment were incompatible with fundamental principles of procedural fairness of that State;
f) the judgment is inconsistent with a judgment given in the requested State in a dispute between the same parties; or
g) the judgment is inconsistent with an earlier judgment given in another State between the same parties on the same cause of action, provided that the earlier judgment fulfils the conditions necessary for its recognition in the requested State.

Article 10. Preliminary questions

(1) Where a matter excluded under Article 2, paragraph 2, or under Article 21, arose as a preliminary question, the ruling on that question shall not be recognised or enforced under this Convention.

(2) Recognition or enforcement of a judgment may be refused if, and to the extent that, the judgment was based on a ruling on a matter excluded under Article 2, paragraph 2.

(3) However, in the case of a ruling on the validity of an intellectual property right other than copyright or a related right, recognition or enforcement of a judgment may be refused or postponed under the preceding paragraph only where -
a) that ruling is inconsistent with a judgment or a decision of a competent authority on that matter given in the State under the law of which the intellectual property right arose; or
b) proceedings concerning the validity of the intellectual property right are pending in that State.

(4) Recognition or enforcement of a judgment may be refused if, and to the extent that, the judgment was based on a ruling on a matter excluded pursuant to a declaration made by the requested State under Article 21.

Article 11. Damages

(1) Recognition or enforcement of a judgment may be refused if, and to the extent that, the judgment awards damages, including exemplary or punitive damages, that do not compensate a party for actual loss or harm suffered.

(2) The court addressed shall take into account whether and to what extent the damages awarded by the court of origin serve to cover costs and expenses relating to the proceedings.

Article 12. Judicial settlements (transactions judiciaires)

Judicial settlements (transactions judiciaires) which a court of a Contracting State designated in an exclusive choice of court agreement has approved, or which have been concluded before that court in the course of proceedings, and which are enforceable in the same manner as a judgment in the State of origin, shall be enforced under this Convention in the same manner as a judgment.

Article 13. Documents to be produced

(1) The party seeking recognition or applying for enforcement shall produce –
a) a complete and certified copy of the judgment;
b) the exclusive choice of court agreement, a certified copy thereof, or other evidence of its existence;
c) if the judgment was given by default, the original or a certified copy of a document establishing that the document which instituted the proceedings or an equivalent document was notified to the defaulting party;
d) any documents necessary to establish that the judgment has effect or, where applicable, is enforceable in the State of origin;
e) in the case referred to in Article 12, a certificate of a court of the State of origin that the judicial settlement or a part of it is enforceable in the same manner as a judgment in the State of origin.

(2) If the terms of the judgment do not permit the court addressed to verify whether the conditions of this Chapter have been complied with, that court may require any necessary documents.

(3) An application for recognition or enforcement may be accompanied by a document, issued by a court (including an officer of the court) of the State of origin, in the form recommended and published by the Hague Conference on Private International Law.

(4) If the documents referred to in this Article are not in an official language of the requested State, they shall be accompanied by a certified translation into an official language, unless the law of the requested State provides otherwise.

Article 14. Procedure

The procedure for recognition, declaration of enforceability or registration for enforcement, and the enforcement of the judgment, are governed by the law of the requested State unless this Convention provides otherwise. The court addressed shall act expeditiously.

Article 15. Severability

Recognition or enforcement of a severable part of a judgment shall be granted where recognition or enforcement of that part is applied for, or only part of the judgment is capable of being recognised or enforced under this Convention.

CHAPTER IV
GENERAL CLAUSES

Article 16. Transitional provisions

(1) This Convention shall apply to exclusive choice of court agreements concluded after its entry into force for the State of the chosen court.

(2) This Convention shall not apply to proceedings instituted before its entry into force for the State of the court seised.

Article 17. Contracts of insurance and reinsurance

(1) Proceedings under a contract of insurance or reinsurance are not excluded from the scope of this Convention on the ground that the contract of insurance or reinsurance relates to a matter to which this Convention does not apply.

(2) Recognition and enforcement of a judgment in respect of liability under the terms of a contract of insurance or reinsurance may not be limited or refused on the ground that the liability under that contract includes liability to indemnify the insured or reinsured in respect of -
a) a matter to which this Convention does not apply; or
b) an award of damages to which Article 11 might apply.

Article 18. No legalisation

All documents forwarded or delivered under this Convention shall be exempt from legalisation or any analogous formality, including an Apostille.

Article 19. Declarations limiting jurisdiction

A State may declare that its courts may refuse to determine disputes to which an exclusive choice of court agreement applies if, except for the location of the chosen court, there is no connection between that State and the parties or the dispute.

Article 20. Declarations limiting recognition and enforcement

A State may declare that its courts may refuse to recognise or enforce a judgment given by a court of another Contracting State if the parties were resident in the requested State, and the relationship of the parties and all other elements relevant to the dispute, other than the location of the chosen court, were connected only with the requested State.

Article 21. Declarations with respect to specific matters

(1) Where a State has a strong interest in not applying this Convention to a specific matter, that State may declare that it will not apply the Convention to that matter. The State making such a declaration shall ensure that the declaration is no broader than necessary and that the specific matter excluded is clearly and precisely defined.

(2) With regard to that matter, the Convention shall not apply -
a) in the Contracting State that made the declaration;
b) in other Contracting States, where an exclusive choice of court agreement designates the courts, or one or more specific courts, of the State that made the declaration.

Article 22. Reciprocal declaratons on non-exclusive choice of court agreements

(1) A Contracting State may declare that its courts will recognise and enforce judgments given by courts of other Contracting States designated in a choice of court agreement concluded by two or more parties that meets the requirements of Article 3, paragraph c), and designates, for the purpose of deciding disputes which have arisen or may arise in connection with a particular legal relationship,

a court or courts of one or more Contracting States (a non-exclusive choice of court agreement).

(2) Where recognition or enforcement of a judgment given in a Contracting State that has made such a declaration is sought in another Contracting State that has made such a declaration, the judgment shall be recognised and enforced under this Convention, if –
a) the court of origin was designated in a non-exclusive choice of court agreement;
b) there exists neither a judgment given by any other court before which proceedings could be brought in accordance with the non-exclusive choice of court agreement, nor a proceeding pending between the same parties in any other such court on the same cause of action; and
c) the court of origin was the court first seised.

Article 23. Uniform interpretation

In the interpretation of this Convention, regard shall be had to its international character and to the need to promote uniformity in its application.

Article 24. Review of operation of the Convention

The Secretary General of the Hague Conference on Private International Law shall at regular intervals make arrangements for -
a) review of the operation of this Convention, including any declarations; and
b) consideration of whether any amendments to this Convention are desirable.

Article 25. Non-unified legal systems

(1) In relation to a Contracting State in which two or more systems of law apply in different territorial units with regard to any matter dealt with in this Convention -
a) any reference to the law or procedure of a State shall be construed as referring, where appropriate, to the law or procedure in force in the relevant territorial unit;
b) any reference to residence in a State shall be construed as referring, where appropriate, to residence in the relevant territorial unit;
c) any reference to the court or courts of a State shall be construed as referring, where appropriate, to the court or courts in the relevant territorial unit;
d) any reference to a connection with a State shall be construed as referring, where appropriate, to a connection with the relevant territorial unit.

(2) Notwithstanding the preceding paragraph, a Contracting State with two or more territorial units in which different systems of law apply shall not be bound to apply this Convention to situations which involve solely such different territorial units.

(3) A court in a territorial unit of a Contracting State with two or more territorial units in which different systems of law apply shall not be bound to recognise or enforce a judgment from another Contracting State solely because the judgment has been recognised or enforced in another territorial unit of the same Contracting State under this Convention.

(4) This Article shall not apply to a Regional Economic Integration Organisation.

Article 26. Relationship with other international instruments

(1) This Convention shall be interpreted so far as possible to be compatible with other treaties in force for Contracting States, whether concluded before or after this Convention.

(2) This Convention shall not affect the application by a Contracting State of a treaty, whether concluded before or after this Convention, in cases where none of the parties is resident in a Contracting State that is not a Party to the treaty.

(3) This Convention shall not affect the application by a Contracting State of a treaty that was concluded before this Convention entered into force for that Contracting State, if applying this Convention would be inconsistent with the obligations of that Contracting State to any non-Contracting State. This paragraph shall also apply to treaties that revise or replace a treaty concluded before this Convention entered into force for that Contracting State, except to the extent that the revision or replacement creates new inconsistencies with this Convention.

(4) This Convention shall not affect the application by a Contracting State of a treaty, whether concluded before or after this Convention, for the purposes of obtaining recognition or enforcement of a judgment given by a court of a Contracting State that is also a Party to that treaty. However, the judgment shall not be recognised or enforced to a lesser extent than under this Convention.

(5) This Convention shall not affect the application by a Contracting State of a treaty which, in relation to a specific matter, governs jurisdiction or the recognition or enforcement of judgments, even if concluded after this Convention and even if all States concerned are Parties to this Convention. This paragraph shall apply only if the Contracting State has made a declaration in respect of the treaty under this paragraph. In the case of such a declaration, other Contracting States shall not be obliged to apply this Convention to that specific matter to the extent of any inconsistency, where an exclusive choice of court agreement designates the courts, or one or more specific courts, of the Contracting State that made the declaration.

(6) This Convention shall not affect the application of the rules of a Regional Economic Integration Organisation that is a Party to this Convention, whether adopted before or after this Convention -
a) where none of the parties is resident in a Contracting State that is not a Member State of the Regional Economic Integration Organisation;
b) as concerns the recognition or enforcement of judgments as between Member States of the Regional Economic Integration Organisation.

CHAPTER V
FINAL CLAUSES

Article 27. Signature, ratification, acceptance, approval or accession

(1) This Convention is open for signature by all States.

(2) This Convention is subject to ratification, acceptance or approval by the signatory States.

(3) This Convention is open for accession by all States.

(4) Instruments of ratification, acceptance, approval or accession shall be deposited with the Ministry of Foreign Affairs of the Kingdom of the Netherlands, depositary of the Convention.

Article 28. Declarations with respect to non-unified legal systems

(1) If a State has two or more territorial units in which different systems of law apply in relation to matters dealt with in this Convention, it may at the time of signature, ratification, acceptance, approval or accession declare that the Convention shall extend to all its territorial units or only to one or more of them and may modify this declaration by submitting another declaration at any time.

(2) A declaration shall be notified to the depositary and shall state expressly the territorial units to which the Convention applies.

(3) If a State makes no declaration under this Article, the Convention shall extend to all territorial units of that State.

(4) This Article shall not apply to a Regional Economic Integration Organisation.

Article 29. Regional Economic Integration Organisations

(1) A Regional Economic Integration Organisation which is constituted solely by sovereign States and has competence over some or all of the matters governed by this Convention may similarly sign, accept, approve or accede to this Convention. The Regional Economic Integration Organisation shall in that case have the rights and obligations of a Contracting State, to the extent that the Organisation has competence over matters governed by this Convention.

(2) The Regional Economic Integration Organisation shall, at the time of signature, acceptance, approval or accession, notify the depositary in writing of the matters governed by this Convention in respect of which competence has been transferred to that Organisation by its Member States. The Organisation shall promptly notify the depositary in writing of any changes to its competence as specified in the most recent notice given under this paragraph.

(3) For the purposes of the entry into force of this Convention, any instrument deposited by a Regional Economic Integration Organisation shall not be counted unless the Regional Economic Integration Organisation declares in accordance with Article 30 that its Member States will not be Parties to this Convention.

(4) Any reference to a "Contracting State" or "State" in this Convention shall apply equally, where appropriate, to a Regional Economic Integration Organisation that is a Party to it.

Article 30. Accession by a Regional Economic Integration Organisation without its Member States

(1) At the time of signature, acceptance, approval or accession, a Regional Economic Integration Organisation may declare that it exercises competence over all the matters governed by this Convention and that its Member States will not be Parties to this Convention but shall be bound by virtue of the signature, acceptance, approval or accession of the Organisation.

(2) In the event that a declaration is made by a Regional Economic Integration Organisation in accordance with paragraph 1, any reference to a "Contracting State" or "State" in this Convention shall apply equally, where appropriate, to the Member States of the Organisation.

Article 31. Entry into force

(1) This Convention shall enter into force on the first day of the month following the expiration of three months after the deposit of the second instrument of ratification, acceptance, approval or accession referred to in Article 27.

(2) Thereafter this Convention shall enter into force –
a) for each State or Regional Economic Integration Organisation subsequently ratifying, accepting, approving or acceding to it, on the first day of the month following the expiration of three months after the deposit of its instrument of ratification, acceptance, approval or accession;
b) for a territorial unit to which this Convention has been extended in accordance with Article 28, paragraph 1, on the first day of the month following the expiration of three months after the notification of the declaration referred to in that Article.

Article 32. Declarations

(1) Declarations referred to in Articles 19, 20, 21, 22 and 26 may be made upon signature, ratification, acceptance, approval or accession or at any time thereafter, and may be modified or withdrawn at any time.

(2) Declarations, modifications and withdrawals shall be notified to the depositary.

(3) A declaration made at the time of signature, ratification, acceptance, approval or accession shall take effect simultaneously with the entry into force of this Convention for the State concerned.

(4) A declaration made at a subsequent time, and any modification or withdrawal of a declaration, shall take effect on the first day of the month following the expiration of three months after the date on which the notification is received by the depositary.

(5) A declaration under Articles 19, 20, 21 and 26 shall not apply to exclusive choice of court agreements concluded before it takes effect.

Article 33. Denunciation

(1) This Convention may be denounced by notification in writing to the depositary. The denunciation may be limited to certain territorial units of a non-unified legal system to which this Convention applies.

(2) The denunciation shall take effect on the first day of the month following the expiration of twelve months after the date on which the notification is received by the depositary. Where a longer period for the denunciation to take effect is specified in the notification, the denunciation shall take effect upon the expiration of such longer period after the date on which the notification is received by the depositary.

Article 34. Notifications by the depositary

The depositary shall notify the Members of the Hague Conference on Private International Law, and other States and Regional Economic Integration Organisations which have signed, ratified, accepted, approved or acceded in accordance with Articles 27, 29 and 30 of the following -
a) the signatures, ratifications, acceptances, approvals and accessions referred to in Articles 27, 29 and 30;

b) the date on which this Convention enters into force in accordance with Article 31;
c) the notifications, declarations, modifications and withdrawals of declarations referred to in Articles 19, 20, 21, 22, 26, 28, 29 and 30;
d) the denunciations referred to in Article 33.

D. German Institutions and Rules for Arbitration

I. List of Arbitration Institutions in Germany

Name of Institution	Contact	Service	Description	Homepage
Verein der Getreidehändler der Hamburger Börse e.V.	Adolphsplatz 1 (Börse) Kontor 24 D-20457 Hamburg Tel.: +49 (0)40 / 36 98 79-0 Fax: +49 (0)40 / 36 98 79-20 E-Mail: info@vdg-ev.de	Schiedsgerichtsordnung für das Schiedsgericht des Vereins der Getreidehändler der Hamburger Börse e.V.	Arbitral Tribunal specialises in disputes relating to trade in grains, animal feed, oilseeds, fish-meal and pulses (quality and other disputes).	http://www.vdg-ev.de
Waren-Verein der Hamburger Börse e.V.	Große Bäckerstraße 4 D-20095 Hamburg Tel.: +49 (0)40 / 37 47 19-0 Fax: +49 (0)40 / 37 47 19-19 E-Mail: info@waren-verein.de	Schiedsgerichtsordnung / Arbitration Rules	Arbitral Tribunal of the Commodities Association at the Hamburg Stock Exchange; specialises in national and international disputes about quality of goods and other trade-related disputes; selected awards are published as headnotes.	http://www.waren-verein.de/schiedsgericht
Handelskammer Hamburg	Adolphsplatz 1 D-20457 Hamburg Tel.: +49 (0)40 / 36 13 8-138 Fax: +49 (0)40 / 36 13 8-401 E-Mail: service@hk24.de	Regulativ des Schiedsgerichts der Handelskammer Hamburg / Rules of the Court of Arbitration of the Hamburg Chamber of Commerce	Court of Arbitration of the Hamburg Chamber of Commerce; deals with general commercial arbitration on national and international level; also offers „Hamburg Friendly Arbitration" as an alternative procedure.	http://www.hk24.de

D. German Institutions and Rules for Arbitration 427

Name of Institution	Contact	Service	Description	Homepage
Frankfurt International Arbitration Center	IHK Frankfurt am Main Börsenplatz 4 D-60313 Frankfurt am Main Tel.: +49 (0)69 / 2197-13 14 Fax: +49 (0)69 / 2197-15 75 E-Mail: fiac@frankfurt-main.ihk.de	DIS Schiedsgerichtsordnung DIS Arbitration Rules	Frankfurt Chamber of Commerce in cooperation with German Institution of Arbitration (DIS), administers general commercial arbitrations and ICSID arbitrations.	http://www.fiac-arbitration.de
German Maritime Arbitration Association	Willy-Brandt-Straße 57 D-20457 Hamburg Tel.: +49 (0)40 / 5 700 70 0 Fax: +49 (0) 40 / 5 700 70 200 E-Mail: info@gmaa.de	Schiedsgerichtsordnung der German Maritime Arbitration Association / Arbitration Rules of the German Maritime Arbitration Association	Administers *ad hoc* arbitration according to pre-existing rules; specialises in maritime disputes; publishes selected awards.	http://www.gmaa.de
Chinese European Arbitration Centre (CEAC)	c/o Handelskammer Hamburg Adolphsplatz 1 D-20457 Hamburg Tel.: +49 (0)40 / 66 86 40 – 85 Fax: +49 (0)40 / 66 86 40 – 699 E-Mail: contact@ceac-arbitration.com	CEAC Schiedsordnung / CEAC Hamburg Arbitration Rules	Located at the Hamburg Chamber of Commerce, offers services of an institutional arbitration centre tailor-made to the needs of trade with China.	http://www.ceac-arbitration.com/
Deutscher Kaffee-Verband e.V.	Steinhöft 5-7 D-20459 Hamburg Tel.: +49 (0)40 / 374 23 61-0 E-Mail: info@kaffeeverband.de	Schiedsgerichtsordnung / Arbitration Rules	Arbitration Board of the German Coffee Federation, specialises in disputes related to coffee trade.	http://www.kaffeeverband.de

Name of Institution	Contact	Service	Description	Homepage
Schiedsgericht für privates Baurecht	Wilhelmstraße 11 D-53604 Bad Honnef Tel.: +49 (0)2224 / 79 39 1 Fax: +49 (0)2224 / 70 73 0 E-Mail: info@schiedsgericht.org	Schiedsgerichtsordnung / Arbitration Rules	The court administers arbitrations in the area of private construction law in Germany and is also active within the European Union.	http://www.schieds-gericht.org
Schlichtungs- und Schiedsgerichtshof deutscher Notare (SGH)	DNotV GmbH Kronenstraße 73 D-10117 Berlin Tel.: +49 (0)30 / 20 61 57 40 Fax: +49 (0)30 / 20 61 57 50 E-Mail: kontakt@dnotv.de	Statut des SGH / SGH Statute	Court of Arbitration of the Association of German Notaries Public; deals with general arbitration, also for small claims; procedure incorporates reconciliation/mediation.	http://www.dnotv.de
Deutsche Börse Group/ Frankfurter Wertpapierbörse	Deutsche Börse AG D-60485 Frankfurt am Main Deutschland Tel.: +49 (0) 69 / 2 11-0 Fax: +49 (0) 69 / 2 11-1 20 05 E-Mail: info@deutsche-boerse.com	Börsenordnung mit Börsenschiedsgericht / Stock Exchange Rules with	German Stock Exchange (Frankfurt); Stock exchange rules refer to German Arbitration Act (§§ 1025–1066 of the German Code of Civil Procedure).	http://deutsche-boerse.com
Baden-Württembergische Wertpapierbörse	Börsenstraße 4 D-70174 Stuttgart Postal Address: Postfach 10 0643 D-70005 Stuttgart Tel.: +49 (0)711 / 22 29 85 0 Fax: +49 (0) 711 / 222985545 E-Mail: anfrage@boerse-stuttgart.de	Schiedsgerichtsordnung / Arbitration Rules	Stock Exchange Stuttgart; Arbitration Rules refer to German Arbitration Act (§§ 1025–1066 of the German Code of Civil Procedure).	http://www.boerse-stuttgart.de

D. German Institutions and Rules for Arbitration

Name of Institution	Contact	Service	Description	Homepage
BÖAG Börsen AG (Börsen Hamburg – Hannover)	Börse Hamburg: Kleine Johannisstraße 4 D-20457 Hamburg Tel.: +49 (0)40 / 36 13 02 – 0 Fax: +49 (0)40 / 36 13 02 -23 E-Mail: k.homann@boerse-nag.de mailto: Börse Hannover: An der Börse 2 D-30159 Hannover Tel.: +49 (0)511 / 32 76 61 Fax: +49 (0)511 / 32 49 – 15 E-Mail: h.janssen@boerse-nag.de	Schiedsgerichtsordnung / Arbitration Rules	Stock Exchange Hamburg and Hannover.	http://www.boerse-hannover.de
Börse Berlin	Fasanenstraße 85 D-10623 Berlin Tel.: +49 (0)30 / 31 10 91 0 Fax: +49 (0)30 / 31 10 91 79 E-Mail: info@boerse-berlin.de	Börsenschiedsgerichtsordnung / Stock Exchange Arbitration Rules	Stock Exchange Berlin.	http://www.berlinerboerse.de
Börse Düsseldorf	Ernst-Schneider-Platz 1 D-40212 Düsseldorf Tel.: +49 (0)211 / 1389-0 Fax: +49 (0)211 / 133287 E-Mail: kontakt@boerse-duesseldorf.de	Schiedsgerichtsordnung / Arbitration Rules	Stock Exchange Düsseldorf; Arbitration Rules refer to German Arbitration Act (§§ 1025–1066 of the German Code of Civil Procedure).	http://www.bo-erse-duesseldorf.de/
Börse München	Karolinenplatz 6 D-80333 München Tel.: +49 (0)89 / 54 90 45-0 Fax: +49 (0)89 / 54 90 45-31 E-Mail: info@bo-erse-muenchen.de	Schiedsgerichtsordnung / Arbitration Rules	Stock Exchange Munich; Arbitration Rules refer to German Arbitration Act (§§ 1025–1066 of the German Code of Civil Procedure).	http://www.bo-erse-muenchen.de

This list is non-exhaustive. The information is current as of June 2015.

II. Arbitration Rules of the German Institution of Arbitration (Deutsche Institution für Schiedsgerichtsbarkeit e.V. (DIS))[1] in force as of 1 July 1998[2] (Schedule of Costs in force as of 1 April 2014)

Section 1
Scope of application

1.1 The Arbitration Rules set forth herein apply to disputes which, pursuant to an agreement concluded between the parties, are to be decided by an arbitral tribunal in accordance with the Arbitration Rules of the German Institution of Arbitration (DIS).

1.2 Unless otherwise agreed by the parties, the Arbitration Rules in effect on the date of commencement of the arbitral proceedings apply to the dispute.

Section 2
Selection of arbitrators

2.1 The parties are free in their selection and nomination of arbitrators.

2.2 Unless otherwise agreed by the parties, the chairman of the arbitral tribunal or the sole arbitrator, as the case may be, shall be a lawyer.

2.3 Upon request, the DIS will make suggestions for the selection of arbitrators.

Section 3
Number of arbitrators

Unless otherwise agreed by the parties, the arbitral tribunal consists of three arbitrators.

Section 4
Requisite copies of written pleadings and attachments

All written pleadings and attachments shall be submitted in a number of copies at least sufficient to provide one copy for each arbitrator, for each party and, in case the pleadings are filed with the DIS, one copy for the latter.

---

[1] Translation from German by German Institution of Arbitration. Only the German text is authoritative.

[2] The German Institution of Arbitration advises all parties wishing to make reference to DIS Arbitration in their contracts to use the following arbitration clause:

„All disputes arising in connection with this contract or its validity shall be finally settled in accordance with the Arbitration Rules of the German Institution of Arbitration (DIS) without recourse to the ordinary courts of law."

It is recommended that the following provisions be added to the arbitration clause:
- The place of arbitration is . . .;
- The number of arbitrators is …;
- The language of the arbitral proceedings is . . . ;
- The applicable substantive law is …

Section 5
Delivery of written communications

5.1 The statement of claim and written pleadings, containing pleas as to the merits of the claim or a withdrawal of the claim, shall be delivered by registered mail/return receipt requested or by courier, telefax or other means of delivery inasmuch as they provide a record of receipt. All other written communications may be delivered by any other means of delivery. All written communications and information submitted to the arbitral tribunal shall likewise be conveyed to the other party at the same time.
5.2 Delivery of all written communications by the parties, the arbitral tribunal or the DIS Secretariat shall be made to the last-known address, as provided by the addressee or, as the case may be, by the other party.
5.3 If the whereabouts of a party or a person entitled to receive communications on his behalf are not known, any written communication shall be deemed to have been received on the day on which it could have been received at the last-known address upon proper delivery by registered mail/return receipt requested, or by courier, telefax or other means of delivery inasmuch as they provide a record of receipt.
5.4: If a written communication delivered in accordance with subsection 1 of this section is received by any other means, delivery is deemed to have been effected not later than at the time of actual receipt.
5.5: Where a party has retained legal representation, delivery should be made to the latter.

Section 6
Commencement of arbitral proceedings

6.1 The claimant shall file the statement of claim with a DIS Secretariat. Arbitral proceedings commence upon receipt of the statement of claim by a DIS Secretariat.
6.2 The statement of claim shall contain:
   (1) identification of the parties,
   (2) specification of the relief sought,
   (3) particulars regarding the facts and circumstances which give rise to the claim(s),
   (4) reproduction of the arbitration agreement,
   (5) nomination of an arbitrator, unless the parties have agreed on a decision by sole arbitrator.
6.3 In addition, the statement of claim should contain:
   (1) particulars regarding the amount in dispute,
   (2) proposals for the nomination of an arbitrator, where the parties have agreed on a decision by sole arbitrator,
   (3) particulars regarding the place of arbitration, the language of the proceedings and the rules applicable to the substance of the dispute.
6.4 If the statement of claim is incomplete or if the copies or attachments are not submitted in the requisite number, the DIS Secretariat requests the claimant to make a corresponding supplementation and sets a time-limit for compliance.

Commencement of the arbitral proceedings pursuant to subsection 1, sentence 2 of this section is not affected as long as supplementation is made within the set time-limit; otherwise, the proceedings are terminated without prejudice to the claimant's right to reintroduce the same claim.

Section 7
Costs upon commencement of proceedings

7.1 Upon filing the statement of claim, the claimant shall pay to the DIS the administrative fee as well as a provisional advance on the arbitrators' costs in accordance with the schedule of costs (appendix to section 40 sub. 5) in force on the date of receipt of the statement of claim by the DIS Secretariat.

7.2 The DIS Secretariat invoices the claimant for the DIS administrative fee and the provisional advance and, if payment has not already been made, sets a time-limit for payment. If payment is not effected within the time-limit, which may be subject to reasonable extension, the proceedings are terminated without prejudice to the claimant's right to reintroduce the same claim.

Section 8
Delivery of statement of claim to respondent

The DIS Secretariat delivers the statement of claim to the respondent without undue delay. The DIS Secretariat may make delivery of the statement of claim contingent on having received the number of copies of the statement of claim and attachments required pursuant to section 4 as well as payment required pursuant to section 7.

Section 9
Statement of defense

After constitution of the arbitral tribunal pursuant to section 17, the arbitral tribunal sets a time-limit for the respondent to file the statement of defense. When setting the time-limit, appropriate consideration shall be given to the date the respondent received the statement of claim.

Section 10
Counterclaim

10.1 Any counterclaim shall be filed with a DIS Secretariat. Section 6 subs. 1–4 apply mutatis mutandis.

10.2 The arbitral tribunal decides on the admissibility of the counterclaim.

Section 11
Costs of filing counterclaim

11.1 Upon filing a counterclaim, the respondent shall pay to the DIS the administrative fee in accordance with the schedule of costs in force on the date of commencement of the proceedings (appendix to section 40 sub. 5).

11.2 The DIS Secretariat invoices the respondent for the DIS administrative fee and, if payment has not already been made, sets a time-limit for payment. If payment is not effected within the time-limit, which may be subject to reasonable extension, the counterclaim is deemed not to have been filed.

11.3 The DIS Secretariat delivers the counterclaim to the claimant and the arbitral tribunal without undue delay. The DIS Secretariat may make delivery of the counterclaim contingent on having received the number of copies of the counterclaim and attachments required pursuant to section 4 as well as payment required pursuant to subsection 1 of this section.

Section 12
Arbitral tribunal with three arbitrators

12.1 Upon delivery of the statement of claim, the DIS Secretariat calls upon the respondent to nominate an arbitrator. If the DIS Secretariat does not receive a nomination from the respondent within 30 days after receipt of the statement of claim by the respondent, the claimant may request nomination by the DIS Appointing Committee. The DIS Secretariat may extend the 30 day time-limit upon application. A nomination is still timely after expiry of the period of 30 days as long as the DIS Secretariat receives such nomination prior to a request by the claimant for nomination by the DIS Appointing Committee.

A party is bound by his nomination of an arbitrator once the DIS Secretariat has received the nomination.

12.2 The two arbitrators nominate the chairman of the arbitral tribunal and notify the DIS Secretariat thereof without undue delay. When making such nomination, the arbitrators should take into account concurring proposals by the parties. If the DIS Secretariat does not receive a nomination of the chairman of the arbitral tribunal from the two arbitrators within 30 days after calling upon them to do so, each party may request nomination of the chairman by the DIS Appointing Committee. A nomination is still timely after expiry of the period of 30 days as long as the DIS Secretariat receives such nomination prior to a request by one of the parties for nomination by the DIS Appointing Committee.

Section 13
Multiple parties on claimant or respondent side

13.1 Unless otherwise agreed by the parties, multiple claimants shall jointly nominate one arbitrator in their statement of claim.

13.2 If two or more respondents are named in the statement of claim, unless otherwise agreed by the parties, the respondents shall jointly nominate one arbitrator within 30 days after their receipt of the statement of claim. If the respondents have received the statement of claim at different times, the time-limit shall be calculated by reference to the time of receipt by the respondent who last received the statement of claim. The DIS Secretariat may extend the time-limit. If the respondents fail to agree on a joint nomination within the time-limit, the DIS Appointing Committee, after having consulted the parties, nominates two arbitrators, unless the parties agree otherwise.

A nomination made by the claimant side is set aside by the DIS Appointing Committee's nomination.

The two arbitrators nominated by the parties or the DIS Appointing Committee nominate the chairman of the tribunal. Section 12 sub. 2 applies mutatis mutandis, in which case the request of one party is sufficient.

13.3 The arbitral tribunal decides on the admissibility of the multi-party proceedings.

Section 14
Sole arbitrator

Where the arbitral tribunal is to consist of a sole arbitrator and the parties do not reach agreement on a sole arbitrator within 30 days after receipt of the statement of claim by the respondent, each party may request nomination of a sole arbitrator by the DIS Appointing Committee.

Section 15
Impartiality and independence

Each arbitrator must be impartial and independent. He shall exercise his office to the best of his knowledge and abilities, and in doing so is not bound by any directions.

Section 16
Acceptance of mandate as arbitrator

16.1 Each person who is nominated as arbitrator shall without undue delay notify the DIS Secretariat of his acceptance of the office as arbitrator and declare whether he fulfills the qualifications agreed upon by the parties. Such person shall disclose all circumstances which are likely to give rise to doubts as to his impartiality or independence. The DIS Secretariat informs the parties accordingly.

16.2 If circumstances are apparent from an arbitrator's declaration, which are likely to give rise to doubts as to his impartiality or independence or his fulfillment of agreed qualifications, the DIS Secretariat grants the parties an opportunity to comment within an appropriate time-limit.

16.3 An arbitrator shall disclose to the parties and the DIS Secretariat circumstances likely to give rise to doubts as to his impartiality or independence also throughout the arbitral proceedings.

Section 17
Confirmation of arbitrators

17.1 The DIS Secretary General may confirm the nominated arbitrator as soon as the DIS Secretariat receives the arbitrator's declaration of acceptance, and no circumstances likely to give rise to doubts regarding the impartiality or independence of an arbitrator or his fulfillment of agreed qualifications are apparent from the declaration or if within the time-limit set by section 16 sub. 2 no party objects to the confirmation of that arbitrator.

17.2 In all other cases the DIS Appointing Committee decides on the confirmation of the nominated arbitrator.
17.3 Upon confirmation of all arbitrators, the arbitral tribunal is constituted. The DIS Secretariat informs the parties of the constitution of the arbitral tribunal.

Section 18
Challenge of arbitrator

18.1 An arbitrator may be challenged only if circumstances exist that give rise to justifiable doubts as to his impartiality or independence, or if he does not possess qualifications agreed to by the parties. A party may challenge an arbitrator nominated by him, or in whose nomination he has participated, only for reasons of which he becomes aware after the nomination has been made.
18.2 The challenge shall be notified and substantiated to the DIS Secretariat within two weeks of being advised of the constitution of the arbitral tribunal pursuant to section 17 sub. 3 or of the time at which the party learns of the reason for challenge. The DIS Secretariat informs the arbitrators and the other party of the challenge and sets a reasonable time-limit for comments from the challenged arbitrator and the other party. If the challenged arbitrator does not withdraw from his office or the other party does not agree to the challenge within the time-limit fixed, the challenging party may within two weeks request the arbitral tribunal to decide on the challenge unless otherwise agreed by the parties.
18.3: If the other party agrees to the challenge, or if the arbitrator withdraws from his office after being challenged, or if the application of challenge has been granted, a substitute arbitrator shall be nominated. Sections 12 to 17 apply mutatis mutandis to the nomination and confirmation of the substitute arbitrator.

Section 19
Default of an arbitrator

19.1 If an arbitrator becomes de jure or de facto unable to perform his functions or for other reasons fails to act, his mandate terminates if he withdraws from his office or if the parties agree on the termination. If the arbitrator does not withdraw from his office, or if the parties cannot reach agreement on the termination of his mandate, any party may request the competent court to decide on the termination of the mandate.
19.2 If the mandate of an arbitrator is terminated, a substitute arbitrator shall be nominated. Sections 12 to 17 apply mutatis mutandis to the nomination and confirmation of the substitute arbitrator.
19.3 If, pursuant to subsection 1 of this section or of section 18 sub. 2, an arbitrator withdraws from his office or a party agrees to the termination of the mandate of an arbitrator, this does not imply acceptance of the validity of any ground referred to in subsection 1 of this section or section 18 sub. 2.

Section 20
Interim measures of protection

20.1 Unless otherwise agreed by the parties, the arbitral tribunal may, at the request of a party, order any interim measure of protection as the arbitral tribunal may consider necessary in respect of the subject-matter of the dispute. The arbitral tribunal may require any party to provide appropriate security in connection with such measure.

20.2 It is not incompatible with an arbitration agreement for a party to request an interim measure of protection in respect of the subject-matter of the dispute from a court before or during arbitral proceedings.

Section 21
Place of arbitration

21.1 Failing an agreement by the parties on the place of arbitration, this shall be determined by the arbitral tribunal.

21.2 Notwithstanding subsection 1 of this section, the arbitral tribunal may, unless otherwise agreed by the parties, meet at any place it considers appropriate for an oral hearing, for hearing witnesses, experts or the parties, for consultation among its members or for inspection of property or documents.

Section 22
Language of proceedings

22.1 The parties are free to agree on the language or languages to be used in the arbitral proceedings. Failing such agreement, the arbitral tribunal shall determine the language or languages to be used in the proceedings. This agreement or determination, unless otherwise specified therein, shall apply to any written statement by a party, any hearing and any award, decision or other communication by the arbitral tribunal.

22.2 The arbitral tribunal may order that expert reports and other documentary evidence shall be accompanied by a translation into the language or languages agreed upon by the parties or determined by the arbitral tribunal.

Section 23
Applicable law

23.1 The arbitral tribunal shall decide the dispute in accordance with such rules of law as are chosen by the parties as applicable to the substance of the dispute. Any designation of the law or legal system of a given State shall be construed, unless otherwise expressed, as directly referring to the substantive law of that State and not to its conflict of laws rules.

23.2 Failing any designation by the parties, the arbitral tribunal shall apply the law of the State with which the subject-matter of the proceedings is most closely connected.

23.3 The arbitral tribunal shall decide ex aequo et bono or as amiable compositeur only if the parties have expressly authorized it to do so. The parties may so authorize the arbitral tribunal up to the time of its decision.

23.4 In all cases the arbitral tribunal shall decide in accordance with the terms of the contract and shall take into account the usages of trade applicable to the transaction.

Section 24
Rules of procedure

24.1 Statutory provisons of arbitral procedure in force at the place of arbitration from which the parties may not derogate, the Arbitration Rules set forth herein, and, if any, additional rules agreed upon by the parties shall apply to the arbitral proceedings. Otherwise, the arbitral tribunal shall have complete discretion to determine the procedure.
24.2 The arbitral tribunal shall undertake to obtain from the parties comprehensive statements regarding all relevant facts and the proper applications for relief.
24.3 The chairman of the arbitral tribunal presides over the proceedings.
24.4 Individual questions of procedure may be decided by the chairman of the arbitral tribunal alone if so authorized by the other members of the arbitral tribunal.

Section 25
Advance on costs of arbitral tribunal

The arbitral tribunal may make continuation of the arbitral proceedings contingent on payment of advances on the anticipated costs of the arbitral tribunal. It should request each party to pay one half of the advance. In fixing the advance, the arbitrators' total fees and the anticipated reimbursements as well as any applicable value added tax may be taken into consideration. The provisional advance paid by the claimant to the DIS pursuant to section 7 sub. 1 shall be credited to the claimant's share of the advance on costs.

Section 26
Due process

26.1 The parties shall be treated with equality. Each party shall be given a full opportunity to present his case at all stages of the proceedings. The parties shall be given sufficient advance notice of any hearing and of any meeting of the arbitral tribunal for the purpose of taking evidence. The parties are entitled to be legally represented.
26.2 All written pleadings, documents or other communications supplied to the arbitral tribunal by one party shall be communicated to the other party. Likewise, expert reports and other evidentiary documents on which the arbitral tribunal may rely in making its decision are to be communicated to both parties.

Section 27
Establishing the facts

27.1 The arbitral tribunal shall establish the facts underlying the dispute. To this end it has the discretion to give directions and, in particular, to hear witnesses and experts and order the production of documents. The arbitral tribunal is not bound by the parties' applications for the admission of evidence.

27.2 Unless otherwise agreed by the parties, the arbitral tribunal may appoint one or more experts to report to it on specific issues to be determined by the arbitral tribunal. It may also require a party to give the expert any relevant information or to produce, or to provide access to, any relevant documents or property for his inspection.

27.3 Unless otherwise agreed by the parties, if a party so requests or if the arbitral tribunal considers it necessary, the expert shall, after delivery of his written or oral report, participate in an oral hearing where the parties have the opportunity to put questions to him and to present expert witnesses in order to testify on the points at issue.

Section 28
Oral hearing

Subject to agreement by the parties, the arbitral tribunal shall decide whether to hold oral hearings or whether the proceedings shall be conducted on the basis of documents and other materials. Unless the parties have agreed that no hearings shall be held, the arbitral tribunal shall hold such hearings at an appropriate stage of the proceedings, if so requested by a party.

Section 29
Records of oral proceedings

A record shall be made of all oral hearings. The record shall be signed by the chairman. The parties shall each receive a copy of the record.

Section 30
Default of a party

30.1 If the respondent fails to communicate his statement of defense within the time-limit set in accordance with section 9, the arbitral tribunal may continue the proceedings without treating such failure in itself as an admission of the claimant's allegations.

30.2 If any party fails to appear at an oral hearing after having been duly summoned, or to produce documentary evidence within a set time-limit, the arbitral tribunal may continue the proceedings and make the award on the evidence before it.

30.3 Any default which has been justified to the tribunal's satisfaction will be disregarded. Apart from that, the parties may agree otherwise on the consequences of default.

Section 31
Closing of proceedings

The arbitral tribunal may, when satisfied that the parties have had sufficient opportunity to present their case, set a time-limit. Upon the expiry of the time-limit, the arbitral tribunal may reject further pleadings by the parties as to the facts of the case.

Section 32
Settlement

32.1 At every stage of the proceedings, the arbitral tribunal should seek to encourage an amicable settlement of the dispute or of individual issues in dispute.

32.2 If, during arbitral proceedings, the parties settle the dispute, the arbitral tribunal shall terminate the proceedings. If requested by the parties, the arbitral tribunal shall record the settlement in the form of an arbitral award on agreed terms, unless the contents of the settlement are in violation of public policy (ordre public).

32.3 An award on agreed terms shall be made in accordance with section 34 and shall state that it is an award. Such an award has the same effect as any other award on the merits of the case.

Section 33
Rendering of the arbitral award

33.1 The arbitral tribunal shall conduct the proceedings expeditiously and shall render an award within a reasonable period of time.

33.2 In rendering the award, the arbitral tribunal is bound by the requests for relief made by the parties.

33.3 In arbitral proceedings with more than one arbitrator, any decision of the arbitral tribunal shall be made, unless otherwise agreed by the parties, by a majority of all its members.

33.4 If an arbitrator refuses to take part in the vote on a decision, the remaining arbitrators may take the decision without him, unless otherwise agreed by the parties. The remaining arbitrators shall decide by majority vote. The parties shall be given advance notice of the intention to make an award without the arbitrator who refuses to participate in the vote. In the case of other decisions, the parties shall be informed subsequent to the decision of the refusal to participate in the vote.

Section 34
Arbitral award

34.1 The award shall be made in writing and shall be signed by the arbitrator or arbitrators. In arbitral proceedings with more than one arbitrator, the signatures of the majority of all members of the arbitral tribunal shall suffice, provided that the reason for any omitted signature is stated.

34.2 The award shall contain full identification of the parties to the arbitral proceedings and their legal representatives and the names of the arbitrators who have rendered the award.
34.3 The award shall state the reasons upon which it is based, unless the parties have agreed that no reasons are to be given or the award is an award on agreed terms under section 32 sub. 2.
34.4 The award shall state the date on which it was rendered and the place of arbitration as determined in accordance with section 21. The award shall be deemed to have been made on that date and at that place.

Section 35
Decision on costs

35.1 Unless otherwise agreed by the parties, the arbitral tribunal shall also decide in the arbitral award which party is to bear the costs of the arbitral proceedings, including those costs incurred by the parties and which were necessary for the proper pursuit of their claim or defense.
35.2 In principle, the unsuccessful party shall bear the costs of the arbitral proceedings. The arbitral tribunal may, taking into consideration the circumstances of the case, and in particular where each party is partly successful and partly unsuccessful, order each party to bear his own costs or apportion the costs between the parties.
35.3 To the extent that the costs of the arbitral proceedings have been fixed, the arbitral tribunal shall also decide on the amount to be borne by each party. If the costs have not been fixed or if they can be fixed only once the arbitral proceedings are terminated, the decision shall be taken by means of a separate award.
35.4 Subsections 1, 2 and 3 of this section apply mutatis mutandis where the proceedings have been terminated without an arbitral award, provided the parties have not reached an agreement on the costs.

Section 36
Delivery of the arbitral award

36.1 The arbitral tribunal shall provide a sufficient number of originals of the arbitral award. Without undue delay, the DIS Secretariat shall be supplied with one original of the award to keep on file as well as a sufficient number for delivery to the parties.
36.2 The DIS Secretariat delivers one original of the award to each party.
36.3 Delivery of the award to the parties may be withheld until the costs of the arbitral proceedings have been paid in full to the arbitral tribunal and to the DIS.

Section 37
Interpretation and correction of arbitral award

37.1 Any party may request the arbitral tribunal
   – to correct in the award any errors in computation, any clerical or typographical errors or any errors of similar nature,

- to give an interpretation of specific parts of the award,
- to make an additional award as to claims presented in the arbitral proceedings but omitted from the award.

37.2 Unless otherwise agreed by the parties, the request shall be made within 30 days after receipt of the award. A copy of the request shall be delivered to the DIS Secretariat.

37.3 The arbitral tribunal should make the correction or give the interpretation within 30 days and make an additional award within 60 days.

37.4 The arbitral tribunal may also make a correction to the award on its own initiative.

37.5 Sections 33, 34 and 36 apply to correction or interpretation of the award or to an additional award.

Section 38
Effect of arbitral award

The award is final and has the same effect between the parties as a final and binding court judgment.

Section 39
Termination of arbitral proceedings

39.1 The arbitral proceedings are terminated by the final award, by an order of the arbitral tribunal pursuant to subsection 2 of this section or by the DIS Secretariat pursuant to subsection 3 of this section.

39.2 The arbitral tribunal shall issue an order for the termination of the arbitral proceedings when
   (1) the claimant withdraws his claim, unless the respondent objects thereto and the arbitral tribunal recognizes a legitimate interest on his part in obtaining a final settlement of the dispute; or
   (2) the parties agree on the termination of the arbitral proceedings; or
   (3) the parties fail to pursue the arbitral proceedings in spite of being so requested by the arbitral tribunal or when the continuation of the proceedings has for any other reason become impossible.

39.3 If nomination of an arbitrator or substitute arbitrator does not occur within the set time-limit and nomination by the DIS Appointing Committee is not requested by a party, the DIS Secretariat may terminate the proceedings after having consulted the parties.

Section 40
Costs of arbitral proceedings

40.1 The arbitrators are entitled to fees and reimbursement of expenses as well as to value added tax levied on the fees or expenses. The parties are jointly and severally liable to the arbitral tribunal for payment of the administrative fee, notwithstanding any claim for reimbursement by one party against the other.

40.2 The fees shall be fixed by reference to the amount in dispute, which is to be assessed by the arbitral tribunal at its due discretion.

40.3 If proceedings are terminated prematurely, the arbitral tribunal may at its equitable discretion reduce the fees in accordance with the progress of the proceedings.

40.4 The DIS is entitled to an administrative fee as well as to any value added tax levied thereon. The parties are jointly and severally liable to the DIS for payment of the administrative fee, notwithstanding any claim for reimbursement by one party against the other.

40.5 The amount of fees and expenses shall be calculated in accordance with the schedule which forms part of the present Arbitration Rules.

40.6 If the amount in dispute is not specified in a statement of claim or counterclaim, the DIS or the arbitral tribunal, as the case may be, may assess the provisional administrative fees and advances at its due discretion.

Section 41
Loss of right to object

A party who knows that any provision of these Arbitration Rules or any other agreed requirement under the arbitral procedure has not been complied with and yet proceeds with the arbitration without stating his objection to such non-compliance without undue delay, may not raise that objection later.

Section 42
Publication of the arbitral award

The arbitral award may be published only with written permission of the parties and the DIS. Under no circumstances may the publication include the names of the parties, their legal representatives or the arbitrators or any other information specific to the arbitral proceedings.

Section 43
Confidentiality

43.1 The parties, the arbitrators and the persons at the DIS Secretariat involved in the administration of the arbitral proceedings shall maintain confidentiality towards all persons regarding the conduct of arbitral proceedings, and in particular regarding the parties involved, the witnesses, the experts and other evidentiary materials. Persons acting on behalf of any person involved in the arbitral proceedings shall be obligated to maintain confidentiality.

43.2 The DIS may publish information on arbitral proceedings in compilations of statistical data, provided such information excludes identification of the persons involved.

Section 44
Exclusion of liability

44.1 All liability of an arbitrator for any act in connection with deciding a legal matter is excluded, provided such act does not constitute an intentional breach of duty.

44.2 All liability of the arbitrators, the DIS, its officers and its employees for any other act or omission in connection with arbitral proceedings is excluded, provided such acts do not constitute an intentional or grossly negligent breach of duty.

Schedule of Costs

Appendix to Section 40 sub. 5
Revised Schedule of Cost effective as of 1 April 2014!

1) **Amount in dispute up to 5,000.00 €**
   The fee for the chairman of the arbitral tribunal or for a sole arbitrator shall amount to 1,365.00 € and for each co-arbitrator 1,050.00 €.

2) **Amounts in dispute from 5,000.00 € to 50 000,00 €**

Amount	Fee for chairman of arbitral tribunal/sole arbitrator	Fee for each co-arbitrator
up to 6,000.00 EUR	1,560.00 EUR	1,200.00 EUR
up to 7,000.00 EUR	1,755.00 EUR	1,350.00 EUR
up to 8,000.00 EUR	1,950.00 EUR	1,500.00 EUR
up to 9,000.00 EUR	2,145.00 EUR	1,650.00 EUR
up to 10,000.00 EUR	2,340.00 EUR	1,800.00 EUR
up to 12,500.00 EUR	2,535.00 EUR	1,950.00 EUR
up to 15,000.00 EUR	2,730.00 EUR	2,100,00 EUR
up to 17,500.00 EUR	2,925.00 EUR	2,250.00 EUR
up to 20,000.00 EUR	3,120.00 EUR	2,400.00 EUR
up to 22,500.00 EUR	3,315.00 EUR	2,550.00 EUR
up to 25,000.00 EUR	3,510,00 EUR	2,700.00 EUR
up to 30,000.00 EUR	3,705.00 EUR	2,850.00 EUR
up to 35,000.00 EUR	3,900.00 EUR	3,000.00 EUR
up to 40,000.00 EUR	4,095.00 EUR	3,150.00 EUR
up to 45,000.00 EUR	4,290.00 EUR	3,300.00 EUR
up to 50,000.00 EUR	4,485.00 EUR	3,450.00 EUR

   In the case of amounts in dispute exceeding 50 000,00 €, the fee for each co-arbitrator is calculated as follows:

3) For amounts more than 50 000,00 € up to 500,000.00 €
   a fee of 3,450.00 € plus 2% of the amount exceeding 50 000,00 €;
4) For amounts more than 500,000.00 € up to 1,000,000.00 €
   a fee of 12,450.00 € plus 1.4% of the amount exceeding 500,000.00 €;
5) For amounts more than 1,000,000.00 € up to 2,000,000.00 €
   a fee of 19,450.00 € plus 1% of the amount exceeding 1,000,000.00 €;
6) For amounts more than 2,000,000.00 € up to 5,000,000.00 €
   a fee of 29,450.00 € plus 0.5% of the amount exceeding 2,000,000.00 €;
7) For amounts more than 5,000,000.00 € up to 10,000,000.00 €
   a fee of 44,450.00 € plus 0.3% of the amount exceeding 5,000,000.00 €;

8) For amounts more than 10,000,000.00 € up to 50,000,000.00 €
a fee of 59,450.00 € plus 0.1% of the amount exceeding 10,000,000.00 €;
9) For amounts more than 50,000,000.00 € up to 100,000,000.00 €
a fee of 99,450.00 € plus 0.06% of the amount exceeding 50,000,000.00 €;
10) For amounts more than 100,000,000.00 €
a fee of 129,450.00 € plus 0.05% of the amount exceeding 100,000,000.00 € up to an amount of 650,000,000.00 €; any amount exceeding the additional 650,000,000.00 € shall not affect the calculation of the fee.
11) If more than two parties are involved in the arbitral proceedings, the amounts of the arbitrators' fees pursuant to this schedule are increased by 20% for each additional party. The arbitrator's fees are increased by no more than 50% in total;
12) Upon filing of a counterclaim, the Appointing Committee of the DIS, if so requested by the arbitral tribunal and after having consulted the parties, may determine that the the arbitrator's fees pursuant to Nos. 1) – 11) shall be calculated separately on the basis of the value of the claim and counterclaim.
13) In cases of high legal and/or factual complexity and in particular with regard to the time spent, the Appointing Committee of the DIS, if so requested by the arbitral tribunal and after having consulted the parties, may determine an appropriate increase of the arbitrator's fees of up to 50% of the fee pursuant to Nos. 1) – 12);
14) If a request for an interim measure of protection has been made to the arbitral tribunal pursuant to section 20, the arbitrator's fee shall be increased by 30% of the fee at the time of the request;
15) For the chairman of the tribunal and the sole arbitrator, fees are calculated by adding 30% to the fees pursuant to 3) to 14);
16) Reimbursement of expenses pursuant to Sec. 40 sub. 1 is calculated on the basis of such guidelines as are issued by the DIS in force at the time of commencement of the arbitral proceedings;
17) The amount of the provisional advance for the arbitral tribunal levied by the DIS Secretariat upon filing of the statement of claim pursuant to section 7 sub. 1 corresponds to the fees for a co-arbitrator pursuant to this schedule;
18) a) In the case of an amount in dispute up to 50,000.00 € the DIS administrative fee amounts to 2% of the amount in dispute; in case of an amount in dispute more than 50,000.00 € and up to 1,000,000.00 € the DIS administrative fee amounts to 1,000.00 € plus 1% of the amount exceeding 50,000.00 € in the case of the amount in dispute exceeding 1,000,000.00 €, the administrative fee amounts to 10,500.00 € plus 0,5% of the amount exceeding 1,000,000.00 €. The minimum DIS administrative fee is 350.00 €; the maximum fee is 25,000.00 €;
b) Upon filing a counterclaim, the amounts in dispute of claim and counterclaim are added for the purpose of assessing the DIS administrative fee. The DIS administrative fee for a counterclaim is calculated by deducting the DIS administrative fee from the administrative assessed according to the increased overall amount in dispute;
c) The minimum administrative fee for a counterclaim is 350.00 €, the maximum fee for claim and counterclaim is 45,000.00 €;
d) If more than two parties are involved in the arbitral proceedings, the DIS administrative fee set forth in Nos. 18 a) – c) is increased by 20% for each additional party. The additional fee shall not exceed 15,000.00 €. The

D. German Institutions and Rules for Arbitration

sum of the administrative fee calculated pursuant to Nos. 18 a) – c) and the additional fee to this No. 18 d) shall be the DIS administrative fee.

  e) Where the arbitral proceedings are terminated prior to the constitution of the arbitral tribunal, the DIS may, at its own discretion, decrease the DIS administrative fee calculated pursuant to Nos. 18 a) – d) by a maximum of 50% of such fee.

19) If a statement of claim, a counterclaim or any other written pleadings is submitted to the DIS in any language other than German, English or French, the DIS may arrange for a translation. The costs for such translation may be added to the DIS administrative fee levied by the DIS pursuant to 15).

Annotation by the authors:

Parties may also refer to the **DIS Conflict Management Rules** (in force as from May 1, 2010; available at www.dis-arb.de). They regulate a conflict clarification procedure, helping parties to find the suitable (alternative) dispute resolution procedure.

E. German Institutions and Rules for Mediation

I. List of Mediation Institutions in Germany

Name of Institution	Contact	Service	Description	Homepage
Beijing-Hamburg Conciliation Centre	c/o Handelskammer Hamburg Adolphsplatz 1 D-20457 Hamburg Tel.: +49 (0)40 / 36138-343 Fax: +49 (0)40 / 36138-533 E-Mail: petra.sandvoss@hk24.de	Beijing-Hamburg Schlichtungsordnung / Beijing-Hamburg Conciliation Rules	Located at the Hamburg Chamber of Commerce, offers services of an institutional arbitration centre tailor-made to the needs of trade with China.	http://www.ceac-arbitration.com/
Bundesverband Mediation e.V.	Wittestraße 30 K 13509 Berlin Tel.: +49 (0)30 43 57 25 30 Fax: +49 (0)30 43 57 25 31 E-Mail: info@bmev.de	Network for mediators	Organization supporting mediators.	http://www.bmev.de
Bundesverband für Mediation in Wirtschaft und Arbeitswelt e.V.	Prinzregentenstr. 1 86150 Augsburg Tel.: ++49 (0)8 21-58 86 43 66 Fax: ++49 (0)8 21-589 12 98 E-Mail: info@bmwa.de	Mediation Rules Mediation Center	Coalition of mediators acting in commercial disputes in German speaking countries.	http://www.bmwa.de/
Centrale für Mediation (CfM)	Verlag Dr. Otto Schmidt KG Gustav-Heinemann-Ufer 58 50968 Köln Tel.: ++49 (0)2 21/ 937 38-821 Fax: ++49 (0)2 21/ 937 38-926 E-Mail: cfm@mediate.de	Network for mediators and parties Search service for finding mediators	Organization supporting mediators.	http://www.centrale-fuer-mediation.de/

E. German Institutions and Rules for Mediation

Name of Institution	Contact	Service	Description	Homepage
Deutsche Gesellschaft für Mediation in der Wirtschaft e.V.	Grünstraße 1 75172 Pforzheim Telefon +49 711 51866956 Fax +49 7231 1541414 E-Mail: info@dgmw.de	Providing addresses of mediators Network for mediators	Association of independent mediators.	http://www.dgmw.de
Deutsche Institution für Schiedsgerichtsbarkeit e.V.	Beethovenstrasse 5–13 D-50674 Köln (Cologne)Tel.: ++49 (0)221/28 55 2-0 Fax: ++49 (0)221/28 55 2-222 E-Mail: dis@dis-arb.de	DIS Mediation Rules Mediation Center	Approximately 1150 members from Germany and abroad, with the aim of promoting national and international dispute resolution.	http://www.dis-arb.de/
Europäisches Institut für Conflict Management e.V.	Brienner Straße 9 80333 München (Munich) Tel.: ++49 (0)89-57 95 18 34Fax: ++49 (0)89 – 57 86 95 38 E-Mail: info @ eucon-institut. de	Mediation Center Eucon Mediation Rules	Association for commercial mediation in Germany including cross-border mediation.	http://www.eucon-institut.de/
Öffentliche Rechtsauskunft- und Vergleichsstelle	ÖRA-Haus, Dammtorstraße 14, 20354 Hambur Tel.: ++49 (0)40/428 43-3071/307 Fax: ++49 (0)40/42731-1190	Mediation Center	Organization providing in-house mediation services on labor, business, and family issues.	http://fhh.hamburg.de/stadt/ http://www.hamburg.de/oera/
Tenos	Neuer Wall 10D-20354 Hamburg Tel.: +49 (0)40 / 4130 73 0 E-Mail: mail@tenos.de	Mediationsordnung der Tenos Akademie / Tenos Academy Mediation Rules	Independent for-profit organisation, administers business mediation according to its own rules.	

This list is non-exhaustive. The information is current as of June 2015.

II. Mediation Rules
of the
German Institution of Arbitration
(Deutsche Institution für Schiedsgerichtsbarkeit (DIS))[1]
in force as of 1 January 2002, amended in 2010[2]
(Schedule of Costs in force as of 1 October 2004)

Section 1
Scope of application

1.1 The Mediation Rules set forth herein apply where the parties have agreed to conduct mediation proceedings pursuant to these Rules with respect to particular disputes.

1.2 Unless otherwise agreed by the parties, the Mediation Rules in effect of the date of commencement of the mediation proceedings shall apply.

Section 2
Initiation and commencement

2.1 The party wishing to initiate the mediation proceedings (applicant) shall send a written request to the other party (opponent). The request shall contain the names and contact details of the parties and their counsel, if available. It shall further contain a short summary of the conflict, the facts and circumstances which gave rise to the conflict, the asserted claims and, if possible, the amount in dispute. Multiple applicants within the meaning of sentences 1 and 2 shall jointly send the request.

2.2 If the request for initiation of the mediation proceedings provides that more than one other party shall be involved in the proceedings, the request shall be sent to each of these parties.

2.3 The request shall be submitted in a number of copies at least sufficient to provide one copy for each mediator and the DIS. If the copies are not submitted in the requisite number, the DIS Main Secretariat requests the applicant to make a corresponding supplementation and sets a time-limit for compliance. Upon filing the request the applicant shall pay to the DIS the procedural fee in accordance with the schedule of costs (appendix to section 11 subsection 5) in force on the date of receipt of the request by the DIS Main Secretariat. The DIS Main Secretariat invoices the applicant for the DIS procedural fee and, if payment has not already been made, sets a time-limit for payment.

---

[1] Translation from German by German Institution of Arbitration.

[2] The German Institution of Arbitration advises all parties wishing to make reference to the DIS Mediation Rules already at the conclusion of the contract to use the following Mediation clause in the event of a conflict:

„With respect to all disputes arising out of or in connection with the contract (... description of the contract...) mediation proceedings shall be conducted pursuant to the Mediation Rules of the German Institution of Arbitration (DIS)."

Additional provisions concerning the number of mediators, the language and/or the place of mediation should be considered.

It should be noted that mediation agreement pursuant to the DIS Mediation Rules may be concluded any time, also with regard to already existing disputes.

2.4 Mediation proceedings commence upon receipt of the copy of the request by the DIS Main Secretariat (section 2 subsection 3), provided that within the time-limit set by the DIS, which may be subject to reasonable extension, the DIS has received the number of required copies of the request pursuant to subsection 3 and the DIS procedural fee pursuant to subsection 3 has been paid. The DIS informs the parties about commencement of the proceedings without undue delay.

Section 3
Role of the mediator

3.1 The mediator shall organize the mediation proceedings pursuant to the provisions of these rules and apart from that at his discretion. The parties may agree to deviate from the rules.
3.2 The mediator shall be impartial and independent. In particular he may not legally or otherwise represent or consult the parties or third persons on legal issues, which are or have been the subject-matter of the mediation proceedings. The mediator shall disclose to the parties and the DIS all circumstances likely to give rise to doubts as to his independence and impartiality without undue delay.
3.3 A person who consults or represents or who consulted or represented one of the parties on the same issues before the commencement of the mediation proceedings may not act as mediator.
3.4 The mediator shall encourage the settlement of the conflict between the parties in an orderly and efficient manner. He may make proposals for the resolution of the dispute upon consensual wishes of all parties.

Section 4
Nomination of the mediator

4.1 The parties may freely chose and nominate a mediator. Unless otherwise agreed by the parties, the mediation shall be conducted by one mediator.
4.2 Where the parties have agreed on mediation proceedings with one mediator, they shall jointly nominate him to the DIS within one month after commencement of the mediation proceedings, unless they have agreed on the nomination by the DIS. Upon request, the DIS Main Secretariat will make suggestions for the nomination of a mediator.
4.3 Where the parties have agreed on mediation proceedings with two mediators, the mediator nominated pursuant to section 4 subsection 2 shall nominate the co-mediator upon consent of the parties to the DIS without undue delay.
4.4 If a mediator becomes de jure or de facto unable to perform his functions or for other reasons fails to act, subsections 2 and 3 apply mutatis mutandis to the nomination of a substitute mediator as soon as the default of the initially nominated mediator is established.
4.5 Where the parties fail to nominate a mediator within one month, the mediator shall be nominated by the DIS Appointing Committee upon request of at least one party. The request shall be filed within two weeks after the expiry

of the one–month period. After the expiry of the two-weeks time-limit the proceedings are deemed terminated.

4.6 If a party requests the nomination of a mediator by the DIS Appointing Committee, it shall pay the fee for nomination of a mediator in accordance with no. 1.2 of the schedule of costs (appendix to section 11 subsection 5) with the request. The DIS may make the nomination of the mediator contingent on the receipt of payment of the fee.

Section 5
Confirmation of the mediator

The mediator is deemed confirmed upon receipt of his written declaration of acceptance of office by the DIS.

Section 6
Course of mediation

6.1 The mediator and the parties shall jointly agree on a meeting agenda and a time schedule. To prepare for the meeting, the mediator may gather information about the cause and subject-matter of the conflict in written form or in a preparatory meeting. The mediator shall prepare the meeting. He may make preparative remarks or suggestions to the parties.

6.2 The mediation meetings shall be conducted in the presence of the parties. Communications between the mediator and one party on the subject-matter are admissible only with the express consent of the other party. In the case of a one-to-one communication between the mediator and one of the parties, the mediator shall keep the information thus disclosed in confidence, unless the respective party expressly authorizes him to make certain information available to the other parties.

6.3 As a rule, the parties shall personally participate in the meetings. Legal persons as well as associations and organizations shall be represented by their organs or representatives, who are familiar with the dispute and authorized to settle the dispute amicably. Attorneys and other counsel may be involved.

6.4 The mediator is not obliged to take meeting minutes.

6.5 The mediation proceedings are confidential.

Section 7
Place of mediation

The parties shall agree on the place of the mediation meeting. Failing an agreement of the parties, the mediation meeting shall take place in the premises of the DIS Main Secretariat.

Section 8
Termination of proceedings

8.1 The mediation proceedings are terminated:
  (1) if the parties have settled the dispute. In the case of partial settlement, the mediation proceedings are terminated only if at least one party declares that in its opinion the disputed issues may not be settled;
  (2) by declaration of one party, provided that at least one mediation meeting or no mediation meeting within two month after confirmation of the mediator took place. The written declaration is addressed to the other party and the mediator. Specification of reasons is not necessary;
  (3) if nomination of a mediator or mediators does not occur within the set time-limit and a substitute nomination of a mediator by the DIS not requested by a party pursuant to section 4 subsection 5;
  (4) by written declaration of the mediator addressed to both parties that the mediation proceedings are terminated;
  (5) if the mediation proceedings have not been pursued within three months after their commencement. The mediation proceedings have not been pursued, if no written or oral preliminary examination nor a mediation meeting took place
8.2 The mediator declares the termination of the proceedings in writing. Upon request of a party he shall issue a written confirmation that a settlement could not be reached in the mediation proceedings. The DIS declares the termination of the proceedings in writing under section 8 subsection 1 no. (3).

Section 9
Statute of limitations; temporary waiver of action

9.1 The period of limitation is suspended for such claims that are subject to mediation proceedings from the commencement of the mediation proceedings (section 2 subsection 4).
9.2 The suspension ceases at the earliest three month after the termination of the mediation proceedings pursuant to section 8.
9.3 The parties undertake not to bring an (arbitration) action for such claims that are still subject to pending mediation proceedings. The parties are not precluded from applying to a court for interim measures of protection.

Section 10
Confidentiality

10.1 The parties, the mediator and the persons at the DIS Main Secretariat involved in the administration of mediation proceedings shall maintain confidentiality regarding the proceedings, and in particular regarding the parties involved and the documents exchanged.
10.2 This does not apply to information or documents which were known before the mediation proceedings or which demonstrably would otherwise have become known.
10.3 Contractual confidentiality and non-disclosure obligations remain unaffected.

10.4 The DIS may publish information on mediation proceedings in a compilation of statistical data, provided such information excludes identification of the persons involved.

Section 11
Costs

11.1 Each party shall pay half of the costs of the mediation proceedings. Each party shall bear its own costs, including legal fees, if any.
11.2 The mediator is entitled to a fee and reimbursement of expenses as well as to VAT levied on the fee or expenses, if applicable. The parties are jointly and severally liable to the mediator for payment of the costs of the proceedings.
11.3 The mediator's fee is measured by the time spent by him. Travel and accommodation costs shall be reimbursed separately against submission of receipts for the expenses. The mediator is entitled to reasonable advance payments, which shall be paid by the parties in equal shares.
11.4 The DIS is entitled to a registration fee and a fee (fees) for nomination of the mediator, as the case may be, as well as to VAT levied on both fees, if applicable. The parties are jointly and severally liable to the DIS for payment of the fees.
11.5 The amount of fees and expenses ensues from the appendix which is part of these Mediation Rules.

Section 12
Liability

The mediator, the DIS, its organs and employees are only liable for intentional misconduct.

Appendix to Section 11 Subsection 5 DIS Mediation Rules

Schedule of Costs for DIS Mediation Proceedings

1. DIS fees

1.1 The procedural fee (section 2 subsection 4) amounts to € 250.00.
1.2 The fee for nomination of a mediator by the DIS amounts to € 250.00 (section 4 subsection 6).

2. Mediator's fee

The fees of a mediator amount to € 300.00 per hour, unless agreed otherwise.

3. VAT

The fees specified in nos. 1 and 2 are subject to VAT.

Appendix 1
Selected Sample Calculations of Fees in German Proceedings

1. Sample calculation for an amount in dispute of EUR 100.000

Amount in dispute: EUR 100.000

Extrajudicial

General Fee for Out-of Court Work*	1,3	EUR	1.953,90
Expenses		EUR	20,00
Sum		EUR	1.973,90

*Note: The general fee for out-of-court work is usually 1.3; in case of judicial proceedings, however, an offset is made of 50 %.

							EUR	1.973,90

Judicial

Own Attorney Fees

		Entry Level Courts			First Appellate Level			Second Appellate Level
Proceedings	1,3	EUR	1.953,90	1,6 EUR	2.404,80	2,3 EUR	3.456,90
./. Reduction 0,65 General Fee For Out-of-Court Work	0,65	EUR	-976,95		EUR		EUR	
Oral hearing	1,2	EUR	1.803,60	1,2 EUR	1.803,60	1,5 EUR	2.254,50
Expenses		EUR	20,00	EUR	20,00	EUR	20,00
Copies		EUR	0,00	EUR	0,00	EUR	0,00
Sum		EUR	2.800,55	EUR	4.228,40	EUR	5.731,40

| | | | | | | | | EUR | 12.760,35 |

Opponent's Attorney Fees

		Entry Level Courts			First Appellate Level			Second Appellate Level
Proceedings	1,3	EUR	1.953,90	1,6 EUR	2.404,80	2,3 EUR	3.456,90
Date of hearing	1,2	EUR	1.803,60	1,2 EUR	1.803,60	1,5 EUR	2.254,50
Expenses		EUR	20,00	EUR	20,00	EUR	20,00
Copies		EUR	0,00	EUR	0,00	EUR	0,00
Sum		EUR	3.777,50	EUR	4.228,40	EUR	5.731,40

| | | | | | | | | EUR | 13.737,30 |

| Sum | | EUR | 8.551,95 | EUR | 8.456,80 | EUR | 11.462,80 | EUR | 28.471,55 |
| V.A.T., 19 % (if applicable) | | | | | | | | EUR | 5.409,59 |

Court Fees

| Proceedings | 3 | EUR | 3.078,00 | EUR | 4.104,00 | EUR | 5.130,00 | EUR | 12.312,00 |

Total

| | | | | | | | | EUR | 46.193,14 |

454 Appendix 1. Selected Sample Calculations of Fees in German Proceedings

2. Sample calculation for an amount in dispute of EUR 500.000

Extrajudicial

Amount in dispute: EUR 500.000

General Fee for Out-of Court Work*	1,3	EUR	4.176,90		
Expenses		EUR	20,00		
Sum		EUR	4.196,90	EUR	4.196,90

*Note: The general fee for out-of-court work is usually 1.3; in case of judicial proceedings, however, an offset is made of 50 %.

Judicial

Own Attorney Fees			Entry Level Courts			First Appellate Level			Second Appellate Level	
Proceedings	1,3	EUR	4.176,90	1,6	EUR	5.140,80	2,3	EUR	7.389,90	
./. Reduction 0,65 General Fee For Out-of-Court Work	0,65	EUR	-2.088,45		EUR			EUR		
Oral hearing	1,2	EUR	3.855,60	1,2	EUR	3.855,60	1,5	EUR	4.819,50	
Espenses		EUR	20,00		EUR	20,00		EUR	20,00	
Copies		EUR	0,00		EUR	0,00		EUR	0,00	
Sum		EUR	5.964,05		EUR	9.016,40		EUR	12.229,40	EUR 27.209,85

Opponent's Attorney Fees		EUR	Entry Level Courts		EUR	First Appellate Level		EUR	Second Appellate Level	
Proceedings	1,3	EUR	4.176,90	1,6	EUR	5.140,80	2,3	EUR	7.389,90	
Date of hearing	1,2	EUR	3.855,60	1,2	EUR	3.855,60	1,5	EUR	4.819,50	
Expenses		EUR	20,00		EUR	20,00		EUR	20,00	
Copies		EUR	0,00		EUR	0,00		EUR	0,00	
Sum		EUR	8.052,50		EUR	9.016,40		EUR	12.229,40	EUR 29.298,30

Sum				EUR	18.213,45		EUR	18.032,80		EUR	24.458,80	EUR	60.705,05
V.A.T., 19 % (if applicable)												EUR	11.533,96

Court Fees

Proceedings	3	EUR	10.608,00		EUR	14.144,00		EUR	17.680,00	EUR	42.432,00

Total | | | | | | | | | | | EUR | 114.671,01

Appendix 1. Selected Sample Calculations of Fees in German Proceedings 455

3. Sample calculation for an amount in dispute of EUR 1.000.000

Amount in dispute: EUR 1.000.000

Extrajudicial

General Fee for Out-of Court Work*	1,3	EUR	6.126,90
Expenses		EUR	20,00
Sum		EUR	6.146,90
		EUR	**6.146,90**

*Note: The general fee for out-of-court work is usually 1.3; in case of judicial proceedings, however, an offset is made of 50 %.

Judicial

Own Attorney Fees

		Entry Level Courts			First Appellate Level			Second Appellate Level
Proceedings	1,3	EUR	6.126,90	1,6 EUR	7.540,80	2,3 EUR	10.839,90
./. Reduction 0,65 General Fee For Out-of-Court Work	0,65	EUR	-3.063,45		EUR		EUR	
Oral hearing	1,2	EUR	5.655,60	1,2 EUR	5.655,60	1,5 EUR	7.069,50
Expenses		EUR	20,00	EUR	20,00	EUR	20,00
Copies		EUR	0,00	EUR	0,00	EUR	0,00
Sum		EUR	8.739,05	EUR	13.216,40	EUR	17.929,40
							EUR	**39.884,85**

Opponent's Attorney Fees

		Entry Level Courts			First Appellate Level			Second Appellate Level
Proceedings	1,3	EUR	6.126,90	1,6 EUR	7.540,80	2,3 EUR	10.839,90
Date of hearing	1,2	EUR	5.655,60	1,2 EUR	5.655,60	1,5 EUR	7.069,50
Expenses		EUR	20,00	EUR	20,00	EUR	20,00
Copies		EUR	0,00	EUR	0,00	EUR	0,00
Sum		EUR	11.802,50	EUR	13.216,40	EUR	17.929,40
							EUR	**42.948,30**

Sum		EUR	26.688,45	EUR	26.432,80	EUR	35.858,80	EUR	88.980,05
V.A.T., 19 % (if applicable)								EUR	16.906,21

Court Fees

		Entry Level Courts		First Appellate Level		Second Appellate Level	
Proceedings	3	EUR	16.008,00	EUR	21.344,00	EUR	26.680,00	EUR	64.032,00

Total								**EUR**	**169.918,26**

456 Appendix 1. Selected Sample Calculations of Fees in German Proceedings

4. Sample calculation for an amount in dispute of EUR 5.000.000

Amount in dispute: EUR 5.000.000

Extrajudicial

General Fee for Out-of Court Work*	1,3	EUR	21.726,90
Expenses		EUR	20,00
Sum		EUR	21.746,90
		EUR	**21.746,90**

*Note: The general fee for out-of-court work is usually 1,3; in case of judicial proceedings, however, an offset is made of 50 %.

Judicial

Own Attorney Fees

		Entry Level Courts			First Appellate Level			Second Appellate Level		
Proceedings	1,3	EUR	21.726,90	1,6	EUR	26.740,80	2,3	EUR	38.439,90	
./. Reduction 0,65 General Fee For Out-of-Court Work	0,65	EUR	-10.863,45		EUR			EUR		
Oral hearing	1,2	EUR	20.055,60	1,2	EUR	20.055,60	1,5	EUR	25.069,50	
Expenses		EUR	20,00		EUR	20,00		EUR	20,00	
Copies		EUR	0,00		EUR	0,00		EUR	0,00	
Sum		EUR	30.939,05		EUR	46.816,40		EUR	63.529,40	**EUR** **141.284,85**

Opponent's Attorney Fees

		Entry Level Courts			First Appellate Level			Second Appellate Level		
Proceedings	1,3	EUR	21.726,90	1,6	EUR	26.740,80	2,3	EUR	38.439,90	
Date of hearing	1,2	EUR	20.055,60	1,2	EUR	20.055,60	1,5	EUR	25.069,50	
Expenses		EUR	20,00		EUR	20,00		EUR	20,00	
Copies		EUR	0,00		EUR	0,00		EUR	0,00	
Sum		EUR	41.802,50		EUR	46.816,40		EUR	63.529,40	**EUR** **152.148,30**

Sum	EUR	94.488,45	EUR 93.632,80	EUR 127.058,80	**EUR** **315.180,05**
V.A.T., 19 % (if applicable)			**EUR** **59.884,21**

Court Fees

Proceedings	3	EUR	59.208,00	EUR 78.944,00	EUR 98.680,00	**EUR** **236.832,00**

Total   **EUR** **611.896,26**

Appendix 1. Selected Sample Calculations of Fees in German Proceedings 457

5. Sample calculation for an amount in dispute of EUR 10.000.000

Amount in dispute: EUR 10.000.000

Extrajudicial

General Fee for Out-of Court Work*	1,3	EUR	41.226,90
Expenses		EUR	20,00
Sum		EUR	41.246,90

*Note: The general fee for out-of-court work is usually 1.3; in case of judicial proceedings, however, an offset is made of 50 %.

					EUR	41.246,90

Judicial

Own Attorney Fees

		Entry Level Courts			First Appellate Level			Second Appellate Level	
Proceedings	1,3	EUR	41.226,90	1,6	EUR	50.740,80	2,3	EUR	72.939,90
./. Reduction 0,65 General Fee For Out-of Court Work	0,65	EUR	-20.613,45		EUR			EUR	
Oral hearing	1,2	EUR	38.055,60	1,2	EUR	38.055,60	1,5	EUR	47.569,50
Expenses		EUR	20,00		EUR	20,00		EUR	20,00
Copies		EUR	0,00		EUR	0,00		EUR	0,00
Sum		EUR	58.689,05		EUR	88.816,40		EUR	120.529,40	EUR	268.034,85

Opponent's Attorney Fees

		Entry Level Courts			First Appellate Level			Second Appellate Level	
Proceedings	1,3	EUR	41.226,90	1,6	EUR	50.740,80	2,3	EUR	72.939,90
Date of hearing	1,2	EUR	38.055,60	1,2	EUR	38.055,60	1,5	EUR	47.569,50
Expenses		EUR	20,00		EUR	20,00		EUR	20,00
Copies		EUR	0,00		EUR	0,00		EUR	0,00
Sum		EUR	79.302,50		EUR	88.816,40		EUR	120.529,40	EUR	288.648,30

| Sum | | EUR | 179.238,45 | | EUR | 177.632,80 | | EUR | 241.058,80 | EUR | 597.930,05 |
| V.A.T., 19 % (if applicable) | | | | | | | | | | EUR | 113.606,71 |

Court Fees

| Proceedings | 3 | EUR | 113.208,00 | | EUR | 150.944,00 | | EUR | 188.680,00 | EUR | 452.832,00 |

Total

| | | | | | | | | | | EUR | 1.164.368,76 |

458 Appendix 1. Selected Sample Calculations of Fees in German Proceedings

6. Sample calculation for an amount in dispute of EUR 20.000.000

Amount in dispute: EUR 20.000.000

Extrajudicial

General Fee for Out-of Court Work*	1,3	EUR	80.226,90
Expenses		EUR	20,00
Sum		EUR	80.246,90

*Note: The general fee for out-of-court work is usually 1.3; in case of judicial proceedings, however, an offset is made of 50 %.

		EUR							EUR 80.246,90

Judicial

Own Attorney Fees

		Entry Level Courts			First Appellate Level			Second Appellate Level	
Proceedings	1,3	EUR	80.226,90	1,6 EUR	98.740,80	2,3 EUR	141.939,90		
./. Reduction 0,65 General Fee For Out-of-Court Work	0,65	EUR	-40.113,45	EUR		EUR			
Oral hearing	1,2	EUR	74.055,60	1,2 EUR	74.055,60	1,5 EUR	92.569,50		
Expenses		EUR	20,00	EUR	20,00	EUR	20,00		
Copies		EUR	0,00	EUR	0,00	EUR	0,00		
Sum		EUR	114.189,05	EUR	172.816,40	EUR	234.529,40	EUR	521.534,85

Opponent's Attorney Fees

		Entry Level Courts			First Appellate Level			Second Appellate Level	
Proceedings	1,3	EUR	80.226,90	1,6 EUR	98.740,80	2,3 EUR	141.939,90		
Date of hearing	1,2	EUR	74.055,60	1,2 EUR	74.055,60	1,5 EUR	92.569,50		
Expenses		EUR	20,00	EUR	20,00	EUR	20,00		
Copies		EUR	0,00	EUR	0,00	EUR	0,00		
Sum		EUR	154.302,50	EUR	172.816,40	EUR	234.529,40	EUR	561.648,30

Sum		EUR	348.738,45	EUR	345.632,80	EUR	469.058,80	EUR 1.163.430,05
V.A.T., 19 % (if applicable)								EUR 221.051,71

Court Fees

Proceedings	3	EUR	221.208,00	EUR	294.944,00	EUR	368.680,00	EUR 884.832,00

Total — EUR 2.269.313,76

Appendix 1. Selected Sample Calculations of Fees in German Proceedings 459

7. Sample calculation for an amount in dispute of EUR 30.000.000

Amount in dispute: EUR 30.000.000

Extrajudicial

General Fee for Out-of Court Work*	1,3	EUR	119.226,90	
Expenses		EUR	20,00	
Sum		EUR	119.246,90	
				EUR 119.246,90

*Note: The general fee for out-of-court work is usually 1.3; in case of judicial proceedings, however, an offset is made of 50 %.

Judicial

Own Attorney Fees

			Entry Level Courts			First Appellate Level			Second Appellate Level	
Proceedings	1,3	EUR	119.226,90	1,6	EUR	146.740,80	2,3	EUR	210.939,90	
/. Reduction 0,65 General Fee For Out-of-Court Work	0,65	EUR	-59.613,45		EUR			EUR		
Oral hearing	1,2	EUR	110.055,60	1,2	EUR	110.055,60	1,5	EUR	137.569,50	
Expenses		EUR	20,00		EUR	20,00		EUR	20,00	
Copies		EUR	0,00		EUR	0,00		EUR	0,00	
Sum		EUR	169.689,05		EUR	256.816,40		EUR	348.529,40	EUR 775.034,85

Opponent's Attorney Fees

		EUR	Entry Level Courts			First Appellate Level			Second Appellate Level	
Proceedings	1,3	EUR	119.226,90	1,6	EUR	146.740,80	2,3	EUR	210.939,90	
Date of hearing	1,2	EUR	110.055,60	1,2	EUR	110.055,60	1,5	EUR	137.569,50	
Expenses		EUR	20,00		EUR	20,00		EUR	20,00	
Copies		EUR	0,00		EUR	0,00		EUR	0,00	
Sum		EUR	229.302,50		EUR	256.816,40		EUR	348.529,40	EUR 834.648,30

Sum		EUR	518.238,45		EUR	513.632,80		EUR	697.058,80	EUR 1.728.930,05
V.A.T., 19 % (if applicable)										EUR 328.496,71

Court Fees

Proceedings	3	EUR	329.208,00		EUR	438.944,00		EUR	548.680,00	EUR 1.316.832,00

Total

										EUR 3.374.258,76

Appendix 2
Bibliography

I. Commentaries and Books in the German Language

Baumbach/Lauterbach/Albers/Hartmann: Zivilprozessordnung, 73th ed., 2015.
Berger, K. P.: Das neue Recht der Schiedsgerichtsbarkeit, 1998.
Bülow/Böckstiegel/Geimer/Schütze: Internationaler Rechtsverkehr in Zivil- und Handelssachen, Quellensammlung mit Erläuterungen, loose-leaf series, regularly updated (Vol. 4 2014: Editors Geimer/Schütze).
Christ, M.: Berichtigung, Auslegung und Ergänzung des Schiedsspruchs, 2008.
Duve/Eidenmüller/Hacke: Mediation in der Wirtschaft, 2nd ed., 2011.
Fritz/Pielsticker : Mediationsgesetz, 2013.
Gebauer/Wiedmann (eds.): Zivilrecht unter europäischem Einfluss, Die richtlinienkonforme Auslegung des BGB und anderer Gesetze – Kommentierung der wichtigsten EU-Verordnungen, 2nd ed. 2010
Geimer, R.: Internationales Zivilprozessrecht, 7th ed., 2015.
Geimer/Schütze: Europäisches Zivilverfahrensrecht, 3rd ed., 2010.
Gerold/Schmidt: Rechtsanwaltsvergütungsgesetz, 20th ed., 2012.
Haft/Schlieffen: Handbuch Mediation, 2nd ed., 2009.
Kissel/Mayer: Gerichtsverfassungsgesetz, 8th ed., 2015.
Kreindler/Schäfer/Wolff: Schiedsgerichtsbarkeit – Kompendium für die Praxis, 2006.
Kropholler/von Hein: Europäisches Zivilprozessrecht, 9th ed., 2011.
Lachmann, J.-P.: Handbuch für die Schiedsgerichtspraxis, 3rd ed., 2008.
Lionnet/Lionnet: Handbuch der internationalen und nationalen Schiedsgerichtsbarkeit, 3rd ed., 2005.
Mayer/Kroiß: Rechtsanwaltsvergütungsgesetz, 6th ed., 2013.
Münchener Kommentar: Zivilprozessordnung, 4th ed., 2012-2013.
Musielak/Voit (eds.): Kommentar zur Zivilprozessordnung, 12th ed., 2015.
Nagel/Gottwald: Internationales Zivilprozessrecht, 7th ed., 2013.
Palandt (ed.): Bürgerliches Gesetzbuch, 74th ed., 2015.
Prütting/Gehrlein (eds.): ZPO Kommentar, 6th ed. 2014.
Raeschke-Kessler/Berger: Recht und Praxis des Schiedsverfahrens, 3rd ed., 1999.
Rauscher/Gruber/Heiderhoff (eds.): Europäisches Zivilprozess- und Kollisionsrecht EuZPR / EuIPR Kommentar, Vol. 4, 3rd ed., 2010.
Risse, J.: Wirtschaftsmediation, 2nd ed., 2015 (forthcoming).
Saenger, I.: Zivilprozessordnung, 6th ed., 2015.
Schrader/Steinert/Theede: Zivilprozess, 9th ed., 2011.
Schuschke/Walker: Vollstreckung und vorläufiger Rechtsschutz, 5th ed., 2011.
Schütze, R. A.: Das internationale Zivilprozessrecht in der ZPO, Kommentar, 2nd ed. 2011.
Schütze, R. A.: Schiedsgericht und Schiedsverfahren, 5th ed., 2012.
Schwab/Walter: Schiedsgerichtsbarkeit, 7th ed., 2005.
Stein/Jonas (eds.): Zivilprozessordnung Kommentar, Vol. 10, 23rd ed., 2014.
Thomas/Putzo (eds.): Zivilprozessordnung Kommentar, 36th ed., 2015.

Vorwerk/Wolf (eds.): Beck'scher Onlinekommentar ZPO, 18th ed., 2015.
Wieczorek/Schütze (eds.): Zivilprozessordnung und Nebengesetze, 4th ed., 2013-2015.
Zöller, R. (ed.): Zivilprozessordnung Kommentar, 30th ed., 2014.

II. Commentaries, Books, and Articles in the English Language

Allen/Köck/Riechenberg/Rosen: The German Advantage in Civil Procedure: A Plea for More Details and Fewer Generalities, Comparative Scholarship, Northwestern University Law Review, Vol. 82, 1988, p. 705.

Berger, K. P.: The New German Arbitration Law, 1998.

Berger, K. P.: The German Arbitration Law of 1998 – First Experiences, in: Briner/Fortier/Berger/Bredow (eds.), Law of International Business and Dispute Settlement in the 21st Century. Liber Amicorum Karl-Heinz Böckstiegel, 2001, p. 33.

Böckstiegel/Kröll/Nacimiento (eds.): Arbitration in Germany – The Model Law in Practice, 2nd ed., 2015.

Born, G: International Commercial Arbitration, 2nd ed., 2014.

Dietrich/Wittuhn: International Litigation, in: Campbell (ed.), Business Transactions in Germany, Ch. 5A, loose-leaf series, December 2002.

von Dryander, C.: Jurisdiction in Civil and Commercial Matters under the German Code of Civil Procedure, International Lawyer, Vol. 16, 1982, p. 671.

Eidenmüller: A Legal Framework for National and International Mediation Proceedings, Recht der Internationalen Wirtschaft, International Dispute Resolution Supplement, 2002, p. 14.

Fischer-Zernin/Eichert: Arbitration, in: Campbell (ed.), Business Transactions in Germany, Ch. 6, loose-leaf series, November 2009.

Freedman/Farrell (eds.): Kendall on Expert Determination, 5th ed., 2015.

Friedrich, F.: Federal Constitutional Court Grants Interim Legal Protection Against Service of a Writ of Punitive Damages Suit, German Law Journal, Vol. 4, No. 12, 2003.

Gottwald, P.: Civil Justice Reform: Access, Cost, and Expedition. The German Perspective, in: Zuckermann (ed.), Civil Justice in Crisis, 1999, p. 207.

Gottwald, P.: Simplified Civil Procedure in West Germany, The American Journal of Comparative Law, Vol. 31, 1983, p. 687.

Habscheid, W.: Germany, in Fazzalari (ed.), Civil Justice in the Countries of the European Union, 1998, p. 155.

Hauschka, C. E.: Central Issues Of Business Litigation In West German Civil Courts, California Western International Law Journal, Vol. 19, 1988/1989, p. 47.

Hibbert/Hardy: Jurisdiction: the ECJ Tightens the Grip, International Litigation News, 2004, p. 51.

Holdsworth/Kamper/Nacimiento: Germany, in: Kreindler (ed.), Transnational Litigation: A Practitioner's Guide, 1997.

Hopt/Steffek: Mediation – Principles and Regulation in Comparative Perspective, 2013.

Horvath/Wilske (eds.): Guerrilla Tactics in International Arbitration, 2013.

Hunter, R.: Arbitration in Germany – A Common Law Perspective, SchiedsVZ (German Arbitration Journal) 2003, p. 155.

Kaplan/Taylor von Mehren/Schäfer: Phases of German Civil Procedure, Harvard Law Review, Vol. 71, 1958, p. 1193.

Schima/Hoyer: Ordinary Proceedings in First Instance. Central European Countries, in: David (ed.) International Encyclopedia of Comparative Law, Chapter 6: Civil Procedure, Vol. 16, 1984.

Koch/Dietrich: Civil Procedure in Germany, 1998.

Koetz, H.: Civil Litigation and the Public Interest, Civil Justice Quarterly, Vol. 1, 1992, p. 237.

Kreindler/Mahlich: Plumbing the Depths of Germany's Jurisdictional Rules, International Commercial Litigation, Supplement, April 1997, p. 10.

Kröll, S.: Germany, International Handbook on Commercial Arbitration, Vol. II (Suppl. 48, February 2007)

Langbein, J.: The German Advantage in Civil Procedure, Chicago Law Review, Vol. 52, 1985, p. 823.

Markert, L.: Arbitrating Corporate Disputes – German Approaches and International Solutions to Reconcile Conflicting Principles, Contemporary Asia Arbitration Journal, Vol. 8, Issue 1, 2015, p. 29.

Martiny, D.: Recognition and Enforcement of Foreign Money Judgments in the Federal Republic of Germany, The American Journal of Comparative Law, Vol. 35, 1987, p. 721.

Mukhopadhyay/Karl: Does Business Need Mediation, in: ICC International Court of Arbitration Bulletin, Vol. 24, Number 2, 2013, p. 27.

Murray/Stürner: German Civil Justice, 2004.

O'Connor, P.: Alternative Dispute Resolution: Panacea or Placebo?, Arbitration, 1992, p. 109.

Nuyts/Depulchre: Taking of Evidence in the European Union under EC Regulation 1206/2001, Business Law International, Vol. 5, No. 3, 2004, p. 305.

O'Malley/Layton: Federal Republic of Germany, in: O'Malley/Layton (eds.), European Civil Practice, 2nd ed., 2003.

Park, W: Arbitrator Integrity, in: Waibel/Kaushal/Chung/Balchin (eds.), The Backlash against Investment Arbitration, 2010.

Robbers, G.: An Introduction to German Law, 1998.

Rützel/Christ: Chapter on Germany in: Greenwald/Russenberger, Privilege and Confidentiality: An International Handbook, 2nd ed. 2012.

Rützel/Leufgen in: Madden (ed.), Litigation & Dispute Resolution Guide, 3nd ed. 2014.*Sachs, K.:* Use of Documents and Document Discovery: 'Fishing Expeditions' versus Transparency and Burden of Proof, SchiedsVZ (German Arbitration Journal) 2003, p. 193.

Schaner/Scarbbrough: Obtaining Discovery in the USA for Use in German Legal Proceedings – A Powerful Tool, 28 U.S.C. §1782, Anwaltsblatt 2012, p. 325.

Schäfer: Litigation, Arbitration and Bankruptcy, German Tax & Business Law Guide, loose-leaf series, regularly updated.

Shäffer: Strike like Lightning: How to Make Smart Use of German Preliminary Remedies, International Commercial Litigation, May 1998, p. 26.

Shemanski: Obtaining Evidence in the Federal Republic of Germany: The Impact of The Hague Evidence Convention on German-American Judicial Cooperation, International Lawyer, Vol. 17, 1983, p. 465.

Shore/Smith: The U.S. Supreme Court Broadens Evidence-Gathering Assistance to Foreign Tribunals, DAJV-Newsletter, 2004, p. 117.

Spehl/Mark: Litigation in Civil Courts, in: Campbell (ed.), Business Transactions in Germany, loose-leaf series, Chapter 5, January 1995.

Stadler, A.: Introduction to German Civil Procedural Law, in: Ebke/Finkin (eds.), Introduction to German Law, 2nd ed., 2006.
Stürner, R.: Procedural Law and Legal Cultures, in: Gilles/Pfeiffer (eds.), Prozessrecht und Rechtskulturen. XII World Conference of Procedural Law, Mexico City 2003, 2004, p. 9.
Stürner, R.: Suing the Sovereign in Europe and Germany, George Washington International Law Review, Vol. 35, 2003, p. 663.
Stürner, R.: Transnational Civil Procedure: Discovery and Sanctions against Non-Compliance, Uniform Law Review, 2001, p. 871.
Taylor von Mehren, A.: Some Comparative Reflections on First Instance Civil Procedure: Recent Reforms in German Civil Procedure and the Federal Rules, Notre Dame Law Review, Vol. 63, 1988, p. 609.
Timmerbeil, S.: Witness Coaching und Adversary System, 2004.
van Wijck/van Velthoven: An Economic Analysis of the American and the Continental Rule for Allocating Legal Costs, European Journal of Law and Economics, 9:2, p.115 (2000).
Wagner, G: Poor Parties and German Forum: Placing Arbitration under the Sword of Damocles, in: German Institution of Arbitration (ed.), Financial Capacity of the Parties – A Condition for the Validity of Arbitration Agreements?, 2004.
Wagner/Bülau: Procedural Orders by Arbitral Tribunals: In the Stays of Party Agreements?, SchiedsVZ (German Arbitration Journal) 2013, p. 6.
Watt: Avoiding an Unfavorable Forum: A Civilian Perspective, International Litigation News, 2004, p. 10.
Wegen/Gack: Mediation in Pending Civil Proceedings in Germany: Practical Experiences to Strengthen Mediatory Elements in Pending Court Proceedings, IBA Mediation Newsletter, Vol. 12, 2006, p. 8.
Wegen/Gack: Obligatory Mediation as a Precondition for Court Proceedings – First Experiences of a new Concept in German Civil Procedural Law, IBA Mediation Newsletter, Vol. 8, 2005, p. 29.
Wegen/Gack: Previous Mediator as Later Judge or Arbitrator – Involvement of a Judge as Mediator does not Necessarily Prevent him from Later Deciding the Case, IBA Mediation Newsletter, Vol. 7, 2007, p. 37.
Wegen/Gotham/Naumann: Mediation in Employment and Labor Law in Germany – Emerging Opportunities?, IBA Mediation Newsletter, Vol. 12, 2007, p. 24.
Wegen/Naumann: Mediation in Pending Civil Proceedings in Germany – No Automatic Suspension of the Time Limit for Filing a Notice of Appeal, IBA Mediation Newsletter, Vol. 10, 2009, p. 16.
Wegen/Uechtritz/Gack: Mediation and Administrative Law in Germany, IBA Mediation Newletter, Vo. 12, 2005, p. 32.
Wegen/Wilske: Non-Compliance with Obligatory Mediation Procedure Makes Court Proceedings Inadmissible – No Settled Case Law as to Consequences of Non-Compliance with Obligatory Mediation Procedure, IBA Mediation Committee Newsletter, Vol. 4, 2005, p. 19.
Wegen/Wilske: The 'In-Writing-Requirement' for Arbitration Agreements – An Anachronism?, A Comment on OLG (Higher Regional Court) Celle, Decision of September 4, 2003 – 8 Sch 11/02, Journal of International Dispute Resolution (IDR), Vol. 2, 2004, p. 77.
Weigand, F.-B. (ed.): Practitioner's Handbook on International Arbitration, 2nd ed., 2009.

White, S.: Directive 2008/52 on Certain Aspects of Mediation in Civil and Commercial Matters: A new Culture of Access to Justice?, Arbitration 79, 2013, p. 52.

Wilske, S.: Recourse to Domestic Law to Allow Enforcement, IBA Newsletter Arbitration and ADR, Vol. 9, No. 1, 2004, p. 39.

Wilske/Chen: Non-Enforcement of Foreign Arbitral Awards, IBA Newsletter Arbitration and ADR, Vol. 9, No. 2, 2004, p. 57.

Wilske/Chen: International Arbitration Practice in Germany, Comparative Law Yearbook of International Business, Vol. 26, 2004, p. 641.

Wilske/Gack: Commencement of Arbitral Proceedings and Unsigned Requests for Arbitration, Journal of International Arbitration, Vol. 24, Issue 3, p. 319.

Wilske/Heuser: Higher Court in Germany Finds Procedural Order is an Instrument of Parties' Agreement, IBA Newsletter Arbitration and ADR, Vol. 17, No. 2, 2012, p. 71.

Wilske/Krapfl: A Final Farewell to the German Concept of Kompetenz-Kompetenz, International Journal of Dispute Resolution (IDR) 2/2005, p. 93.

Wilske/Krapfl: German Federal Court of Justice Postpones Decision on Intra-EU Jurisdictional Objection, IBA Arbitration Committee Newsletter, Vol. 19, No. 1, February 2014, p. 62.

Wilske/Krapfl: The Enforcement of a Foreign Award when the Underlying Arbitration Agreement Satisfies German Law, but not the New York Convention, IBA Newsletter Arbitration and ADR, Vol. 16, No. 1, 2011, p. 107.

Wilske/Mack: Production of Documents under the Revised German Code of Civil Procedure, IBA Newsletter Arbitration and ADR, Vol. 8, No. 1, 2003, p. 43.

Wilske/Markert: National Reports – Germany, in: Mistelis/Shore (eds.), World Arbitration Reporter, Vol. I, 2nd ed., 2014.

Wilske/Wegen: Enforcement of Foreign Judgments: European Union, in: Garb/Lew (eds.), Enforcement of Foreign Judgments (Suppl. 32, December 2014)

Wilske/Wegen: Enforcement of Foreign Judgments: Germany, in: Garb/Lew (eds.), Enforcement of Foreign Judgments (Suppl. 32, December 2014)

Wittuhn/Stucken/Turowski: Civil Procedure, in: Campbell (ed.), Business Transactions in Germany, Ch. 5, loose-leaf series, June 2006.

Regular articles on arbitration can be found in SchiedsVZ (German Arbitration Journal).

Appendix 3
German-English Glossary

A

Ablehnung eines Richters — challenge of a judge
– Ablehnungsgrund — – reason for challenge
– einen Ablehnungsantrag stellen — – to move to challenge
– sich für befangen erklären — – to recuse/withdraw oneself based on conflict of interest/bias

Akteneinsicht gewähren — to allow inspection of files/records
Aktenübersendung — transfer of documents
Aktenzeichen — docket/file number
Amtsgericht — local court (of first instance)
Anerkenntnis — admission, making admissions, confession

Anhörung der Parteien — hearing the parties
Anspruch auf rechtliches Gehör — right to be heard by the court
Antrag — application/motion
Antrag auf Klageabweisung — motion to dismiss
Anwaltskosten — attorney fees
Arrest — attachment, anticipatory seizure, pre-judgment seizure

Aufhebungsantrag — petition to set aside an award
Ausführungsgesetz — implementation statute
Aussetzung — stay of the proceedings

B

Befangenheit — prejudice or conflict of interest
Befangenheitsantrag — challenge on grounds of prejudice or conflict of interest

Beklagte(r), beklagte Partei — defendant/respondent
Berufsrichter — professional judge/career judge
Berufung — appeal (on questions of fact and law)/first appellate level, see also *Revision*

– Anschlussberufung — – cross appeal
Beschluss — order/decision
Beschwerde — miscellaneous appeal
Bestreiten — denial
Beweis des ersten Anscheins — *prima facie* evidence

Beweis durch Augenschein	evidence through inspection by the court
Beweis durch Parteivernehmung	evidence through party testimony
Beweis(-mittel)	evidence, proof
– gesetzliche Vermutung	– presumption of law
– (un)widerlegbare Vermutung	– (ir)rebuttable presumption
Beweisangebot	offer of proof
Beweisantrag	motion to take specific evidence
Beweisaufnahme	taking of evidence
Beweisbeschluss	order to take evidence
Beweiskraft	evidentiary/probative value
beweiskräftig	having probative value
Beweislast	burden of proof
– Umkehr der Beweislast	– shift in burden of proof
Beweismaß	standard of proof
Beweismittel	forms of evidence
Beweisrecht	law of evidence
Beweissicherung	preservation/conservation of evidence
Beweissicherungsverfahren	proceedings for the preservation of evidence
Beweistermin, Beweisverhandlung	hearing for the taking of evidence
Beweiswürdigung	evaluation/consideration of evidence
Bundesgesetzblatt	Federal Law Gazette
Bundesgerichtshof	Federal Court of Justice (highest court for civil and criminal matters)

D

Darlegungslast	burden of submitting the facts
dieselbe Sache	same claim/same cause of action
Duplik/Gegenerwiderung	rejoinder

E

eidesstattliche Versicherung	sworn affidavit
ein Urteil aufheben	to vacate/reverse a judgment
einen Schiedsspruch aufheben	to set aside an award
einfache Streitgenossenschaft	voluntary joinder of parties
Einrede	defense
Einrede der Unzuständigkeit	plea challenging jurisdiction
Einspruch, Rüge	objection, protest
einstweilige Verfügung	preliminary injunction
– den Erlass einer einstweiligen Verfügung beantragen	– to apply for a preliminary injunction

Endurteil, rechtskräftiges Urteil	final judgment
Erfolgshonorar	contingency fee
Ergänzungsurteil	supplementary judgment

F

Feststellungsurteil	declaratory judgment
Frist	time limit
– Nachfrist	– additional period/extension of time
– Ausschlussfrist	– term of preclusion/preclusion period
– Einlassungsfrist	– time for appearance
– Einspruchsfrist	– time limit for appeal/objection
– Notfrist	– statutory time limit

G

Gericht	court (of justice)
– untergeordnetes Gericht	– lower/inferior court
– übergeordnetes Gericht	– higher/superior court
– jemanden/etwas vor Gericht bringen	– to take somebody to court, to bring something before the court
– gegen jemanden gerichtlich vorgehen	– to proceed against somebody, to take legal action against somebody, to bring a claim against somebody
gerichtlich	judicial, by order of the court
(Gerichts-) Akte	(court) record, file
Gerichtsstand	jurisdiction, venue, forum
– Gerichtsstand vereinbaren	– to stipulate jurisdiction
Gerichtsstandsvereinbarung/Prorogation des Gerichtsstandes	agreement on jurisdiction, choice of forum agreement
Gerichtsverfahren	court/legal proceedings
Gerichtsverhandlung	trial
Gerichtsvollzieher	bailiff
Gläubiger	creditor
gleicher Streitgegenstand	identical subject matter
Grundbuch	land register
Gütestelle	registered conciliation institution
Güteverhandlung	conciliation hearing

H

Handelsregister	commercial register
Hauptintervention	main third party intervention

I

Industrie- und Handelskammer	Chamber of Commerce

internationale Handelsschiedsgerichtsbarkeit	international commercial arbitration
internationale Zuständigkeit	international jurisdiction

J

jemanden gerichtlich vertreten	to represent somebody in court

K

Klage	legal action, lawsuit
– Erfüllungsklage	– action for specific performance
– Feststellungsklage	– action for a declaratory judgment
– Gestaltungsklage	– action for the alteration of a legal relationship
– Leistungsklage	– action for performance (for payment or damages)
– Räumungsklage	– action for possession, action for eviction
– Schadensersatzklage	– action for damages
– Unterlassungsklage	– action for an injunction
– Stufenklage	– action by stages
– Teilklage	– action for a partial claim
– auf Erfüllung klagen	– to sue for specific performance
Klageänderung	amendment of the statement of claim
Klageandrohung	threat of legal action
Klageantrag	prayer for relief
Klagebegehren	plaintiff's claim
Klageerhebung	commencement/ bringing of an action
Klageerweiterung	extension of claim
Klageerwiderung	statement of defense
Klagehäufung/Klageverbindung	joinder of claims
Kläger(in), klagende Partei	plaintiff, claimant
Klagerücknahme	withdrawal of action/claim before oral hearing
Klageschrift/Klagebegründung	statement of claim/complaint
Klageverzicht	withdrawal of claim in oral hearing
Klagezustellung	service of the legal action
Kosten	costs
– Honorar (des Anwalts)	– fees (of attorney)
– Gebührenrechnung	– invoice of fees, bill
– Prozesskosten, Gerichtskosten	– legal costs, court costs
– Honorarabrechnung	– note of fees
– Honorarvorschuss eines Anwalts	– retainer
– Kostenentscheidung	– order for payment of costs, costs award/order
Kostenerstattung	reimbursement of costs

Kostenfestsetzungsbeschluss	court cost order

L
laden	to summon to appear
Ladung	summons (to appear)
– ordnungsgemäß geladen	– duly summoned
– Klageschrift mit Prozessladung	– complaint with writ of summons
Laienrichter	lay-judge

M
Mahnbescheid	collection order
Mahnverfahren	summary proceedings for order to pay debts
Mandant	client
Mandat	client's authorization
Mediation	Mediation

N
Nebenintervention	intervention by a third party in support of a claimant/respondent

O
Oberlandesgericht	higher regional court
öffentliche Zustellung	service by public notice
örtliche Zuständigkeit	venue

P
Parteivereinbarung	party stipulation
Parteivernehmung	questioning/hearing of a party
Parteivorbringen, Schriftsatz	pleadings, written pleading
Pfändung	attachment
– Forderungspfändung	– attachment of a debt
– Pfändungs- und Überweisungsbeschluss	– attachment order and transfer of garnished claim
– Pfändungs-, Vollstreckungsschutz	– protection from execution
Protokoll	record
– zu Protokoll geben	– to place on record
– ein Protokoll verlesen	– to read the record
– vorgelesen und genehmigt	– read and approved
prozessieren	to litigate
Prozesskostenhilfe	legal aid
Prozesspartei	party to an action

– säumige Partei	– defaulting party, party failing to appear
– unterlegene Partei	– unsuccessful party
– erschienene Partei	– party who made appearance
– vorgeladene Partei	– party summoned
– obsiegende Partei	– successful party
Prüfung für die Anwaltszulassung	bar examination

R

Rechtsanwalt	attorney admitted to practice in Germany
Rechtsanwaltskammer	bar association
Rechtsbeschwerde	miscellaneous appeal on points of law
rechtshängig	legally pending
Rechtshängigkeit	pendency, pending suit
– Eintritt der Rechtshängigkeit	– commencement of pendency
Rechtskraft	*res judicata*
Rechtskraft erlangen	to become final
Rechtsmittel	appeal, remedy
– ein Rechtsmittel einlegen	– to file an appeal
– ein Rechtsmittel zurücknehmen	– to withdraw an appeal
Rechtspfleger	judicial officer
Rechtsweg	legal recourse
Replik/Erwiderung	reply, answer
Revision	appeal (on questions of law)/second appellate level, see also Berufung
– Sprungrevision	– leap-frog procedure, leap-frogging appeal (that skips the first level of review)
Richter	judge
Richterschaft, Justiz	judiciary
rügelose Einlassung	general appearance
Rügeverzicht	waiver
ruhendes Verfahren	suspended proceedings

S

sachliche Zuständigkeit	subject matter jurisdiction
Sachverständigenbeweis	expert evidence
Sachverständigengutachten	expert opinion
Sachverständiger	expert
sachverständiger Zeuge	expert witness
Schadensminderungspflicht	duty to mitigate damages
Schiedsgericht	arbitral tribunal

Schiedsgerichtsklausel	arbitration clause
Schiedsmann, Schiedsrichter	arbitrator
Schiedsspruch	(arbitral) award
Schiedsvereinbarung	arbitration agreement
Schiedsverfahren	arbitral proceedings
Schlüssigkeit	conclusiveness
Schuldner	debtor
Schuldnerverzeichnis	register of debtors
selbständiges Beweisverfahren	independent procedure for taking of evidence
Sicherheitsleistung	security
sofortige Beschwerde	immediate miscellaneous appeal
Staatsanwaltschaft	public prosecutor's office
Strafverfahren	criminal procedure
Streitgegenstand	subject matter of a lawsuit/dispute
Streitgenossenschaft	joinder of parties
Streitverkündung	third party notice
Streitwert	value of the matter in dispute

T

Tenor	operative provisions of the judgment
Termin	hearing

U

Unterbrechung	interruption of the proceedings
Urkundenbeweis	documentary evidence
– Urkunde	– document, deed
– öffentliche Urkunde	– public document
– Privaturkunde	– private document
Urkundenprozess	summary procedure, where plaintiff relies entirely on documentary evidence
Urteil/Entscheidung	judgment, decision, decree
– abweisendes Urteil	– adverse judgment
– berufungsfähiges Urteil	– appealable judgment
– Feststellungsurteil	– declaratory judgment
– rechtskräftiges Urteil	– final judgment
– Teilurteil	– partial judgment
– Zwischenurteil	– interlocutory judgment
– Anerkenntnisurteil	– judgment by consent
– Versäumnisurteil	– judgment by default
– Gestaltungsurteil	– judgment for altering a legal relationship
– Zahlungsurteil	– judgment for payment of a sum

– Urteil auf Erfüllung	– judgment for specific performance
– für vollstreckbar erklärtes Urteil	– judgment that has been declared enforceable
– Grundurteil	– judgment on the basis of the claim
– Sachurteil	– judgment on the merits
– Vorbehaltsurteil	– judgment subject to a reservation
– Urteil zustellen	– to serve a judgment
Urteilsgläubiger	judgment creditor
Urteilsschuldner	judgment debtor
Urteilsverkündung	pronouncement of judgment

V

Verband	registered interest group
Vergleich	settlement, agreement, compromise
– außergerichtlicher Vergleich	– out of court settlement
– gerichtlicher Vergleich/Prozessvergleich	– in-court settlement
– einen Vergleich abschließen	– to reach/to conclude a settlement agreement
Verhandlung	court hearing, trial
– mündliche Verhandlung	– hearing
– in nichtöffentlicher Verhandlung	– hearing *in camera*
– in öffentlicher Verhandlung	– in open court
Verjährung	limitation period
Versäumnisurteil	default judgment
Verweisung an das zuständige Gericht	transfer/removal of an action to the competent court
– Verweisungsbeschluss	– order transferring an action
– an ein anderes Gericht verweisen	– to transfer to another court
Verweisung von einem Gericht zum anderen	removal
vollstreckbare Urkunde	enforceable document
Vollstreckungsbefehl	writ of execution
Vollstreckungsbescheid	enforceable collection order
Vollstreckungstitel	execution title

W

Wahrheitspflicht	obligation for truthful and complete pleading
Weigerungsrecht	privilege
Widerklage	counteraction, counterclaim, cross-complaint
Wiederaufnahmeantrag	application for a new trial
(Wohn-)Sitz	domicile/residence

Z

Zeuge	witness
– glaubwürdiger Zeuge	– credible witness
Zeugenaussage	testimony
– als Zeuge aussagen	– to give evidence, to testify
Zeugenbeweis	witness testimony
Zeugeneid	oath taken by a witness
– Eidesformel	– form of oath
– schwören	– to swear
Zeugnisverweigerungsrecht	privilege of a witness
(Zivil-)Gerichtsbarkeit	civil jurisdiction, jurisdiction
Zivilverfahren	civil procedure
Zuständigkeit	competence, jurisdiction
Zustellung auf Betreiben einer Partei	service at the instigation of a party
Zustellung eines Urteils	service of a judgment
– ein Urteil zustellen	– to serve notice of judgment
Zustellung im/ins Ausland	service in a foreign country, service abroad
Zustellung von Amts wegen	official service, service *ex officio*
Zustellungsurkunde	certificate of service
Zwangsvollstreckung	enforcement/execution
– für vollstreckbar erklären	– to declare as enforceable
– ein Urteil für vorläufig vollstreckbar erklären	– to declare a judgment to be provisionally enforceable
– ein Urteil vollstrecken	– to execute/enforce a judgment
– Immobiliarzwangsvollstreckung	– execution of real property
– Mobiliarzwangsvollstreckung	– execution levied upon movable property